T0189054

Xingming Sun · Jinwei Wang ·
Elisa Bertino (Eds.)

Artificial Intelligence and Security

6th International Conference, ICAIS 2020
Hohhot, China, July 17–20, 2020
Proceedings, Part II

Springer

Editors
Xingming Sun ⓘ
Nanjing University of Information Science
and Technology
Nanjing, China

Jinwei Wang ⓘ
Nanjing University of Information Science
and Technology
Nanjing, China

Elisa Bertino ⓘ
Purdue University
West Lafayette, IN, USA

ISSN 1865-0929   ISSN 1865-0937 (electronic)
Communications in Computer and Information Science
ISBN 978-981-15-8085-7   ISBN 978-981-15-8086-4 (eBook)
https://doi.org/10.1007/978-981-15-8086-4

This Springer imprint is published by the registered company Springer Nature Singapore Pte Ltd.
The registered company address is: 152 Beach Road, #21-01/04 Gateway East, Singapore 189721, Singapore

Preface

The 6th International Conference on Artificial Intelligence and Security (ICAIS 2020), formerly called the International Conference on Cloud Computing and Security (ICCCS), was held during July 17–20, 2020, in Hohhot, China. Over the past five years, ICAIS has become a leading conference for researchers and engineers to share their latest results of research, development, and applications in the fields of artificial intelligence and information security.

We used the Microsoft Conference Management Toolkits (CMT) system to manage the submission and review processes of ICAIS 2020. We received 1,064 submissions from 20 countries and regions, including Canada, Italy, Ireland, Japan, Russia, France, Australia, South Korea, South Africa, Iraq, Kazakhstan, Indonesia, Vietnam, Ghana, China, Taiwan, Macao, the USA, and the UK. The submissions cover the areas of artificial intelligence, big data, cloud computing and security, information hiding, IoT security, multimedia forensics, encryption, cybersecurity, and so on. We thank our Technical Program Committee (PC) members and external reviewers for their efforts in reviewing papers and providing valuable comments to the authors. From the total of 1,064 submissions, and based on at least three reviews per submission, the program chairs decided to accept 186 papers, yielding an acceptance rate of 17%. The volume of the conference proceedings contains all the regular, poster, and workshop papers.

The conference program was enriched by a series of keynote presentations, and the keynote speakers included: Xiang-Yang Li, University of Science and Technology of China, China; Hai Jin, Huazhong University of Science and Technology (HUST), China; and Jie Tang, Tsinghua University, China. We look forward to their wonderful speeches.

There were 56 workshops organized in ICAIS 2020 which covered all hot topics in artificial intelligence and security. We would like to take this moment to express our sincere appreciation for the contribution of all the workshop chairs and their participants. We would like to extend our sincere thanks to all authors who submitted papers to ICAIS 2020 and to all PC members. It was a truly great experience to work with such talented and hard-working researchers. We also appreciate the external reviewers for assisting the PC members in their particular areas of expertise. Moreover, we want to thank our sponsors: Nanjing University of Information Science and Technology, New York University, ACM China, Michigan State University, University of Central Arkansas, Université Bretagne Sud, National Natural Science Foundation of China, Tech Science Press, Nanjing Normal University, Inner Mongolia University, and Northeastern State University.

May 2020

Xingming Sun
Jinwei Wang
Elisa Bertino

Organization

General Chairs

Yun Q. Shi   New Jersey Institute of Technology, USA
Mauro Barni   University of Siena, Italy
Elisa Bertino   Purdue University, USA
Guanglai Gao   Inner Mongolia University, China
Xingming Sun   Nanjing University of Information Science
                          and Technology, China

Technical Program Chairs

Aniello Castiglione   University of Salerno, Italy
Yunbiao Guo   China Information Technology Security Evaluation
                          Center, China
Suzanne K. McIntosh   New York University, USA
Jinwei Wang   Nanjing University of Information Science
                          and Technology, China
Q. M. Jonathan Wu   University of Windsor, Canada

Publication Chair

Zhaoqing Pan   Nanjing University of Information Science
                          and Technology, China

Workshop Chair

Baowei Wang   Nanjing University of Information Science
                          and Technology, China

Organization Chairs

Zhangjie Fu   Nanjing University of Information Science
                          and Technology, China
Xiaorui Zhang   Nanjing University of Information Science
                          and Technology, China
Wuyungerile Li   Inner Mongolia University, China

Technical Program Committee Members

Saeed Arif   University of Algeria, Algeria
Anthony Ayodele   University of Maryland, USA

Zhifeng Bao	Royal Melbourne Institute of Technology University, Australia
Zhiping Cai	National University of Defense Technology, China
Ning Cao	Qingdao Binhai University, China
Paolina Centonze	Iona College, USA
Chin-chen Chang	Feng Chia University, Taiwan, China
Han-Chieh Chao	Taiwan Dong Hwa University, Taiwan, China
Bing Chen	Nanjing University of Aeronautics and Astronautics, China
Hanhua Chen	Huazhong University of Science and Technology, China
Xiaofeng Chen	Xidian University, China
Jieren Cheng	Hainan University, China
Lianhua Chi	IBM Research Center, Australia
Kim-Kwang Raymond Choo	The University of Texas at San Antonio, USA
Ilyong Chung	Chosun University, South Korea
Robert H. Deng	Singapore Management University, Singapore
Jintai Ding	University of Cincinnati, USA
Xinwen Fu	University of Central Florida, USA
Zhangjie Fu	Nanjing University of Information Science and Technology, China
Moncef Gabbouj	Tampere University of Technology, Finland
Ruili Geng	Spectral MD, USA
Song Guo	Hong Kong Polytechnic University, Hong Kong, China
Mohammad Mehedi Hassan	King Saud University, Saudi Arabia
Russell Higgs	University College Dublin, Ireland
Dinh Thai Hoang	University Technology Sydney, Australia
Wien Hong	Sun Yat-sen University, China
Chih-Hsien Hsia	National Ilan University, Taiwan, China
Robert Hsu	Chung Hua University, Taiwan, China
Xinyi Huang	Fujian Normal University, China
Yongfeng Huang	Tsinghua University, China
Zhiqiu Huang	Nanjing University of Aeronautics and Astronautics, China
Patrick C. K. Hung	Ontario Tech University, Canada
Farookh Hussain	University of Technology Sydney, Australia
Genlin Ji	Nanjing Normal University, China
Hai Jin	Huazhong University of Science and Technology, China
Sam Tak Wu Kwong	City University of Hong Kong, Hong Kong, China
Chin-Feng Lai	National Cheng Kung University, Taiwan, China
Loukas Lazos	University of Arizona, USA
Sungyoung Lee	Kyung Hee University, South Korea
Chengcheng Li	University of Cincinnati, USA
Feifei Li	Utah State University, USA

Arun Kumar Sangaiah	VIT University, India
Di Shang	Long Island University, USA
Victor S. Sheng	University of Central Arkansas, USA
Zheng-guo Sheng	University of Sussex, UK
Robert Simon Sherratt	University of Reading, UK
Yun Q. Shi	New Jersey Institute of Technology, USA
Frank Y. Shih	New Jersey Institute of Technology, USA
Biao Song	King Saud University, Saudi Arabia
Guang Sun	Hunan University of Finance and Economics, China
Jianguo Sun	Harbin University of Engineering, China
Krzysztof Szczypiorski	Warsaw University of Technology, Poland
Tsuyoshi Takagi	Kyushu University, Japan
Shanyu Tang	University of West London, UK
Jing Tian	National University of Singapore, Singapore
Yoshito Tobe	Aoyang University, Japan
Cezhong Tong	Washington University in St. Louis, USA
Pengjun Wan	Illinois Institute of Technology, USA
Cai-Zhuang Wang	Ames Laboratory, USA
Ding Wang	Peking University, China
Guiling Wang	New Jersey Institute of Technology, USA
Honggang Wang	University of Massachusetts-Dartmouth, USA
Jian Wang	Nanjing University of Aeronautics and Astronautics, China
Jie Wang	University of Massachusetts Lowell, USA
Jin Wang	Changsha University of Science and Technology, China
Liangmin Wang	Jiangsu University, China
Ruili Wang	Massey University, New Zealand
Xiaojun Wang	Dublin City University, Ireland
Xiaokang Wang	St. Francis Xavier University, Canada
Zhaoxia Wang	A*STAR, Singapore
Sheng Wen	Swinburne University of Technology, Australia
Jian Weng	Jinan University, China
Edward Wong	New York University, USA
Eric Wong	The University of Texas at Dallas, USA
Shaoen Wu	Ball State University, USA
Shuangkui Xia	Beijing Institute of Electronics Technology and Application, China
Lingyun Xiang	Changsha University of Science and Technology, China
Yang Xiang	Deakin University, Australia
Yang Xiao	The University of Alabama, USA
Haoran Xie	The Education University of Hong Kong, Hong Kong, China
Naixue Xiong	Northeastern State University, USA
Wei Qi Yan	Auckland University of Technology, New Zealand

Aimin Yang	Guangdong University of Foreign Studies, China
Ching-Nung Yang	Taiwan Dong Hwa University, Taiwan, China
Chunfang Yang	Zhengzhou Science and Technology Institute, China
Fan Yang	University of Maryland, USA
Guomin Yang	University of Wollongong, Australia
Qing Yang	University of North Texas, USA
Yimin Yang	Lakehead University, Canada
Ming Yin	Purdue University, USA
Shaodi You	The Australian National University, Australia
Kun-Ming Yu	Chung Hua University, Taiwan, China
Weiming Zhang	University of Science and Technology of China, China
Xinpeng Zhang	Fudan University, China
Yan Zhang	Simula Research Laboratory, Norway
Yanchun Zhang	Victoria University, Australia
Yao Zhao	Beijing Jiaotong University, China

Organization Committee Members

Xianyi Chen	Nanjing University of Information Science and Technology, China
Yadang Chen	Nanjing University of Information Science and Technology, China
Beijing Chen	Nanjing University of Information Science and Technology, China
Baoqi Huang	Inner Mongolia University, China
Bing Jia	Inner Mongolia University, China
Jielin Jiang	Nanjing University of Information Science and Technology, China
Zilong Jin	Nanjing University of Information Science and Technology, China
Yan Kong	Nanjing University of Information Science and Technology, China
Yiwei Li	Columbia University, USA
Yuling Liu	Hunan University, China
Zhiguo Qu	Nanjing University of Information Science and Technology, China
Huiyu Sun	New York University, USA
Le Sun	Nanjing University of Information Science and Technology, China
Jian Su	Nanjing University of Information Science and Technology, China
Qing Tian	Nanjing University of Information Science and Technology, China
Yuan Tian	King Saud University, Saudi Arabia
Qi Wang	Nanjing University of Information Science and Technology, China

Lingyun Xiang   Changsha University of Science and Technology,
                           China
Zhihua Xia   Nanjing University of Information Science
                           and Technology, China
Lizhi Xiong   Nanjing University of Information Science
                           and Technology, China
Leiming Yan   Nanjing University of Information Science
                           and Technology, China
Li Yu   Nanjing University of Information Science
                           and Technology, China
Zhili Zhou   Nanjing University of Information Science
                           and Technology, China

Contents – Part II

Information Security

Artificial Intelligence

Kernel Fuzzy C Means Clustering with New Spatial Constraints

Limei Wang[1]([✉]), Sijie Niu[1], and Leilei Geng[2]

[1] School of Information Science and Engineering, University of Jinan, Jinan, China
limeiwang@mail.ujn.edu.cn, sjniu@hotmail.com
[2] School of Computer Science and Technology,
Shandong University of Finance and Economics, Jinan, China
leileigeng_njust@163.com

Abstract. Kernel fuzzy c-means clustering with spatial constraints (KFCM_S) is one of the most convenient and effective algorithms for change detection in synthetic aperture radar (SAR) images. However, this algorithm exists problems of weak noise-immunity and detail-preserving on account of the failure to use spatial neighborhood information. In order to overcome above problems, this paper proposed an algorithm using bilateral filtering and large scale median filtering instead of the original spatial constraints. In particular, the approach uses different calculation methods of constraint terms at different locations of image. The bilateral filtering value is used as spatial neighborhood information at the boundary region for preserving the boundary information while the large scale median filtering value is used at the non boundary region for facilitating noise removal. In this paper, 3 remote sensing datasets are used to verify the proposed approach, and the results show that the proposed approach improves the accuracy of remote sensing image change detection.

Keywords: SAR · Change detection · Difference image · KFCM_S

1 Introduction

Image change detection aims to detect regions of change in images obtained from the same scene but at different times, which has been widely used in agricultural surveys [2], environmental monitoring [3,4], urban development studies [5,6], disaster statistics [7] and so on. In terms of remote sensing change detection, SAR [9] images attract widespread attention due to its insensitivity of sunlight and atmospheric conditions. Therefore, we put forward an unsupervised detection technique for reliably highlighting SAR image changes without depending on the manual intervention.

Fuzzy c-means (FCM), desire to maximize the similarity between data points belonging to the same cluster and minimize the similarity between different clusters, is one of the most widely used clustering algorithms [10,11], which

© Springer Nature Singapore Pte Ltd. 2020
X. Sun et al. (Eds.): ICAIS 2020, CCIS 1253, pp. 3–14, 2020.
https://doi.org/10.1007/978-981-15-8086-4_1

retain more detail information by introducing membership. However, the standard FCM algorithm does not consider the influence of spatial neighborhood information on pixels resulting in its noise sensitivity. Hence, researchers have considered compensating the defect of FCM by incorporating local spatial information and local gray information [7].

Ahmed et al. proposed FCM_S by adding spatial constraint term on the basis of the standard FCM objective function, which allows each pixel to consider the influence of its neighborhood pixels. The presented FCM_S1 and FCM_S2 algorithm [12] obtain the neighborhood information of each pixel by calculating median or mean-filtered image in advance, which reduce the running time effectively. The proposed KFCM improves the segmentation by replacing the Euclidean distance of the original FCM algorithm with kernel distance. Noordam et al. Besides, there are a lot of algorithms incorporating local gray information and local spatial information to mitigate the deficiency of standard FCM. Cai et al. [14] proposed a novel fast generalized algorithm (FGFCM) using a new factor to guarantee both noise-immunity and detail-preserving, which enhances the clustering performance. Krindis et al. [15] proposed a fuzzy local information c-means (FLICM) introducing new fuzzy factors into the objective function, which is fully free of the empirically adjusted parameters. [7] et al. presented fuzzy clustering with a modified MRF energy function (MRFFCM) algorithm to modify the membership of each pixel, which reduces the effect of speckle noise.

All algorithms mentioned above mitigate the deficiency of standard FCM via considering local spatial information and local gray information to a certain extent. However, these algorithms have the same shortcoming that the effective removal of speckle noise is usually accompanied by the loss of image detail information, which affects the final detection accuracy of change. Hence, it is necessary to balance noise-immunity and detail-preserving problem for better optimizing the performance of SAR image change detection algorithms.

In this paper, we propose a novel approach on the basis of KFCM_S which not only mitigate the deficiency of standard FCM but also take noise-immunity and detail-preserving into account. First, the approach applies combinatorial difference image composed of differential image and log-ratio image, which constructs relative high-quality difference images facilitating post-processing. Second, bilateral filtering and median filtering are used to substitute for original constraint item in KFCM_S for balancing the noise-immunity and detail-preserving problem. The experiments on 3 SAR image datasets prove that our approach improves the accuracy of change detection to a certain extent.

The rest of this paper is organized as follows: Sect. 2 describes the main procedure of our proposed approach. Section 3 introduce datasets and evaluation criteria. Experimental results on three datasets are described in Sect. 4. Finally, conclusions are drawn in Sect. 5.

2 Motivation and Procedure

The main procedure of SAR images change detection usually consists of three steps: 1) image preprocessing; 2) obtain difference image; 3) analysis of difference image, and the improvements of the proposed algorithm in this paper are mainly reflected in the second and third steps.

2.1 Motivation of Using Combinatorial Difference Image

Given two co-registered SAR images X_1 and X_2 obtained in the same area but at different times, differential image is calculated by subtracting the corresponding elements of the images while log-ratio image use the ratio of the logarithms of the corresponding pixel values as final result, as shown in Fig. 1(a)and(b). It can be seen that the differential image can retain the weak change region of the original image while not suppressing the speckle noise effectively, and the log-ratio image is the opposite. Therefore, inspired by Zhou et al. [16], we take the strategy of combining the differential image and the log-ratio image to generate combinatorial difference image shown in Fig. 1(c). The purpose of combining two kinds of difference images is to reconstruct the relative high-quality combinatorial difference image, which not only can convenient image analysis and but also improve the accuracy of SAR image change detection.

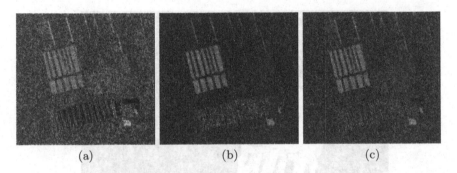

(a)   (b)   (c)

Fig. 1. Comparison of difference images: (a) differential image; (b) log-ratio image; (c) combinatorial difference image.

2.2 Motivation of Using KFCM with New Spatial Constraints

KFCM is an improvement of FCM by substituting kernel distance obtained from kernel function for Euclidean distance, which is equivalent to cluster sample data in high dimensional feature space and improve image segmentation rate. Although the kernel function can improve the performance of KFCM on image segmentation, the noise sensitivity of the algorithm is enhanced without considering the influence of the pixel background in space. Hence, the KFCM_S algorithm is proposed to consider the neighborhood information of pixel as spatial constraints so as to overcome the noise sensitivity problem. KFCM_S1 and KFCM_S2 are two variants of KFCM_S, which use the mean value and median value calculated of neighborhood information in advance at the corresponding position respectively. However, due to the size and density of speckle noise, small scale mean value and median value cannot remove speckle noise while large scale mean value and median value lead to the loss of detail information, which influence the final clustering results.

For the above mentioned problems, we proposed an improved algorithm for mitigating the deficiency of KFCM_S algorithm via "divide and rule" strategy. The whole combinatorial difference image was divided into boundary region and non boundary region through boundary detection, as shown in Fig. 2. Different methods are applied in different regions to balance the noise-immunity and detail-preserving problem. Bilateral filtering value is used to reflect the neighborhood information of the central pixel at the boundary region for preserving detail while the large scale median filter value is used at the non boundary region for remove speckle noise effectively. Compared with traditional median and mean value, bilateral filtering value can reflect the neighborhood information of the pixel without the loss of detail information, and applying large scale median filtering value mainly aims at the characteristics of SAR image with high noise density and large noise size for achieving better noise removal effect.

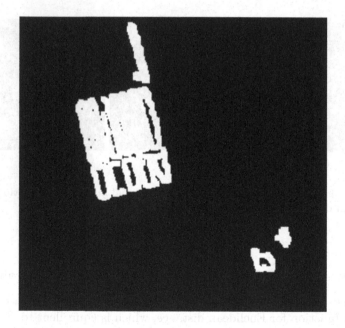

Fig. 2. Boundary image

2.3   Main Procedure

The proposed method in this paper improves KFCM by using combinational difference image and taking the strategy of applying different methods at different regions for considering neighborhood information preferably, which keep as much details as possible on the basis of effective noise removal.

The main procedure of KFCM with new spatial constraints is as follows:

1) Given two SAR images obtained in the same area but at different times, we can get two co-registered SAR images X_1 and X_2 via registration operation aiming to more accurately reflect change situations.

2) Compute differential difference images and log-ratio difference images by using differential operator and log-ratio operator as shown below

$$DI\_d(i,j) = |X_1(i,j) - X_2(i,j)| \tag{1}$$

$$DI\_l(i,j) = \log\left[\frac{X_2(i,j)}{X_1(i,j)}\right] \tag{2}$$

3) Then, combinational difference image (DI) can be calculated by linear combination of DI_d and DI_l, as shown in Eq. (3)

$$DI(i,j) = \lambda_1|X_1(i,j) - X_2(i,j)| + \lambda_2 \log\left[\frac{X_2(i,j)}{X_1(i,j)}\right] \tag{3}$$

4) Obtain boundary image (BI) by applying Canny operator on DI for dividing boundary and region, as shown in (Fig. 1).

5) Compute neighborhood information in advance for facilitating the subsequent clustering operation. Bilateral filtering is applied at boundary region and median filtering is applied at non boundary region as shown in Eq. (4):

$$\bar{x}_k = \begin{cases} S_{ij}W_b & BI(i,j) = 255 \\ S_{ij}W_m & BI(i,j) = 0 \end{cases} \tag{4}$$

where W_b denotes template for bilateral filtering and W_m denotes template for median filtering, and S_{ij} denotes the data matrix around the $DI(i,j)$ position corresponding to the bilateral or median template size. $BI(i,j)$ are the pixel value at position(i,j) in boundary image.

6) Using KFCM with new spatial constraints detect the change area shown below:

The objective function of KFCM with new constraints is

$$JS_m^{\Phi} = \sum_{i=1}^{c}\sum_{k=1}^{N} u_{ik}^m(1 - K(x_k, v_i)) + \alpha \sum_{i=1}^{c}\sum_{k=1}^{N} u_{ik}^m(1 - K(\bar{x}_k, v_i)) \tag{5}$$

where $\bar{x}_k$ represents the neighborhood information of center pixel.

The membership and clustering center is correspondingly update, as formulated in Eq. (6) and Eq.(7), respectively.

$$u_{ij} = \frac{((1 - K(x_k, v_i)) - \alpha(1 - K(\bar{x}_k, v_i)))^{-\frac{1}{(m-1)}}}{\sum_{j=1}^{c}((1 - K(x_k, v_i)) - \alpha(1 - K(\bar{x}_k, v_i)))^{-\frac{1}{(m-1)}}} \tag{6}$$

$$v_i = \frac{\sum_{k=1}^{n} u_{ik}^m (K(x_k, v_i) x_k + \alpha K(\bar{x}_k, v_i) \bar{x}_k)}{\sum_{k=1}^{n} u_{ik}^m (K(x_k, v_i) + \alpha K(\bar{x}_k, v_i))} \tag{7}$$

3   Datasets Description and Evaluation Criteria

3.1   Experimental Datasets

The dataset used in Experiment 1 is Bern dataset [17], as shown in Fig. 3. Among them, Fig. 3 (a) and (b) with the size of 301 × 301 are taken by the European Remote Sensing 2 satellite in the Bern area of Switzerland, which reflect the situation of the Bern area before and after the flood, respectively. Figure 3 (c) is a reference image to reflect the real situation in Bern area.

 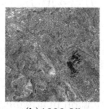 

(a)1994.04   (b)1999.05   (c)reference image

Fig. 3. Bern dataset

As shown in Fig. 4, Experiment 2 used Ottawa dataset [17]. Figure 4 (a) and (b) with the size of 290 × 350 are taken by the Radar-set SAR remote sensing satellite in the Ottawa area of Canada. Among them, Fig. 4 (a) and (b) reflect the situation of the Ottawa area before and after the flood, respectively. Figure 4 (c) is a reference image reflecting the true situation of Ottawa area.

The dataset used in Experiment 3 is the Farmland area [18], as shown in Fig. 5. Figure 5 (a) and (b) with the size of 292 × 306 are all captured by Radarsa-2 satellite. Among them, the image taken in June 2008 is a single view image, and the images taken in June 2009 are four visual images, which makes the noise of the two images very different and increases the difficulty of the change detection. Figure 5 (c) is a reference image reflecting the true surface information.

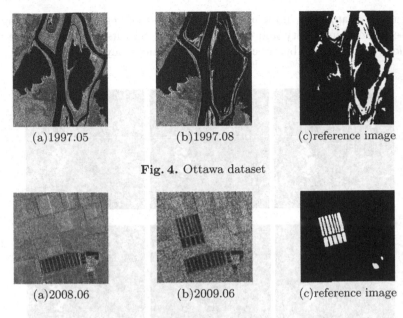

(a)1997.05   (b)1997.08   (c)reference image

Fig. 4. Ottawa dataset

(a)2008.06   (b)2009.06   (c)reference image

Fig. 5. The Farmland dataset

3.2 Evaluation Criteria

This paper evaluates the performance of the different change detection algorithms based on the following criteria: False negatives (FN), false positives (FP), overall error (OE), percentage of correct classification (PCC), and kappa coefficient (KC). The definitions and the calculations of FN, FP, OE, PCC, and KC are same with [20].

4 Experimental Results and Analysis

4.1 Results on the Bern Dataset

Figure 6 shows the results comparison figure of 6 SAR image change detection algorithms in Bern area, and Table 1 shows the performance of these comparison algorithms on certain evaluation criteria. It's easy to see that FCM algorithm is particularly sensitive to the noise of the speckle noise because the influence of spatial neighborhood information is not taken into account, which makes both FN and PN high. Although KFCM_S and MRFFCM aim to remove the speckle noise by using context information, its effect is limited and some noise still exist in the result image. As for FLICM, the limited capability to detect small change areas cause the loss of detail information, which lead to the increasing of PN. Due to deep learning lacks samples in changed area during training process, D_JFCM wrongly classifies changed pixels to unchanged regions, which cause the extremely high of FN. However, the algorithm proposed in this paper takes the strategy of applying different method at different regions for achieving the purpose of noise-immunity and detail-preserving, and its FN and PN are relatively low, which means better change detection accuracy.

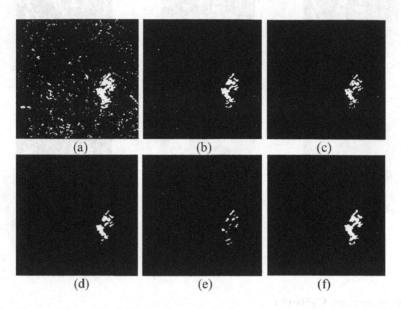

Fig. 6. Comparison of different detection algorithms in Bern area: (a)FCM; (b)$KFCM\_S$; (c)$MRFFCM$; (d)$FLICM$; (e)D_JFCM; (f)*proposed*.

Table 1. Analysis table of Bern regional change detection results

	FN	PN	OE	PCC	$Kappa$
FCM	0	3808	3808	95.74%	60.24
$KFCM\_S$	142	81	223	99.75%	87.15
$MRFFCM$	63	281	344	99.62%	83.37
$FLICM$	36	293	329	99.64%	83.79
D_JFCM	893	52	945	98.96%	35.32
proposed	44	111	155	99.83%	87.37

4.2   Results on the Ottawa Dataset

Results comparison figure of 6 SAR image change detection algorithms in Ottawa area are shown in Fig. 7, and Table 2 shows the performance of these comparison algorithms on certain evaluation criteria. From that, we can see that the effect of speckle noise is not so strong. However, there are many scattered change areas in the detection results of the FCM due to it don't take neighborhood information into account. As for KFCM_S and MRFFCM, their limited ability of noise-immunity causes that boundary areas exist partial speckle noise, which is the reason of high FN. Besides, it can be seen that the limited capability to detect small change areas causes the high PN of FLICM's detection reault. As above mentioned disadvantage of D_JFCM, much changed pixels are classified into unchanged regions, which cause the extremely high of FN. In the proposed approach result image, the boundary of the change area is clear and there are almost no speckle noise due to the combination of two kinds of neighborhood information.

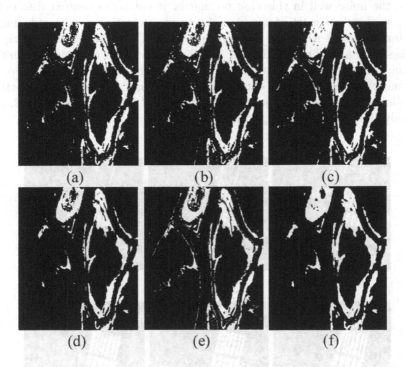

Fig. 7. Comparison of different detection algorithms in Ottawa area: (a)FCM; (b)$KFCM\_S$; (c)$MRFFCM$; (d)$FLICM$; (e)D_JFCM; (f)$proposed$.

4.3 Results on the Farmland Area

Figure 8 shows the results comparison figure of 6 SAR image change detection algorithms in the Farmland area, and we can see that the influence of speckle noise is extremely strong as a result of original farmland images come from different sensor. The FCM, KFCM_S, MRFFCM and FLICM algorithms cannot

Table 2. Analysis Table of Ottawa regional change detection results

	FN	PN	OE	PCC	Kappa
FCM	811	340	1151	98.87%	95.51
KFCM_S	795	449	1244	98.77%	95.15
MRFFCM	1703	666	2639	97.67%	91.46
FLICM	131	2664	2795	97.25%	88.95
D_JFCM	3034	1078	0	95.95%	83.99
proposed	573	58	631	99.38%	97.61

remove the noise well in this case no matter it considers context information or not, so there are a lot of speckle noise in the detection results reducing the detection accuracy. Although the performance of D_JFCM increases obviously, its noise-removal ability still limited. However, as a result of using different calculation methods of constraint term at different regions, the proposed approach can remove the speckle noise effectively and does not affect the information of the boundary area. Hence, the detection results of the proposed algorithm are obviously superior to other algorithms (Table 3).

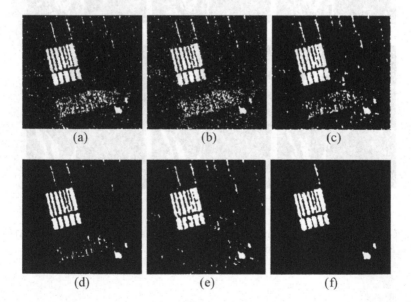

Fig. 8. Comparison of different detection algorithms in Farmland area: (a)FCM; (b)KFCM_S; (c)MRFFCM; (d)FLICM; (e) D_JFCM; (f)proposed.

Table 3. Analysis Table of the Farmland area regional change detection results

	FN	PN	OE	PCC	Kappa
FCM	640	3762	4402	95.06%	71.12
KFCM_S	634	4529	5163	94.20%	68.69
MRFFCM	505	2870	3375	96.21%	72.48
FLICM	960	611	1571	98.24%	84.10
D_JFCM	1296	690	1986	97.77%	81.47
proposed	529	696	1225	98.62%	88.00

5   Conclusion

In this paper, we propose a novel improved KFCM approach that using different calculation methods of constraint terms at different regions on the basis of combinational differential image. Bilateral filtering is used to reflect the neighborhood information of the pixel at the boundary region for preserving detail while the large scale median filter is used at the non boundary region for removing noise, which balances the noise-immunity and detail-preserving problem. Compared with the traditional image change detection algorithm based on FCM and KFCM, experimental results on 3 public datasets show that the proposed approach outperforms other methods.

References

1. Almutairi, A., Warner, T.: Change detection accuracy and image properties: a study using simulated data. Remote Sensing **2**(6), 1508–1529 (2010)
2. Bruzzone, L., Serpico, S.: An iterative technique for the detection of land-cover transitions in multitemporal remote-sensing images. IEEE Trans. Geosci. Remote Sensing **35**(4), 858–867 (1997)
3. Chavez, P., Mackinnon, D.: Automatic detection of vegetation changes in the southwestern United States using remotely sensed images. Photogram. Eng. Remote Sensing **60**(5), 571–582 (1994)
4. Ma, N., Jianhe, G., Pingzeng, L., Ziqing, Z., Gregory, M.P.O.: GA-BP air quality evaluation method based on fuzzy theory. Comput. Mater. Continua **58**(1), 215–227 (2019)
5. Yousif, O., Ban, Y.: Improving SAR-based urban change detection by combining MAP-MRF classifier and nonlocal means similarity weights. IEEE J. Sel. Top. Appl. Earth Observ. Remote Sensing **7**(10), 4288–4300 (2014)
6. Ye, S., Chen, D.: An unsupervised urban change detection procedure by using luminance and saturation for multispectral remotely sensed images. Photogram. Eng. Remote Sensing **81**(8), 637–645 (2015)
7. Gong, M., Su, L., Jia, M., Chen, W.: Fuzzy clustering With a modified MRF energy function for change detection in synthetic aperture radar images. IEEE Trans. Fuzzy Syst. **22**(1), 98–109 (2014)

8. Chapman, B., Blom, R.: Synthetic Aperture Radar. Technol. Past Fut. Appl. Archaeol. (2013)
9. Qi, H., et al.: A weighted threshold secret sharing scheme for remote sensing images based on Chinese remainder theorem. Comput. Mater. Continua **58**(2), 349–361 (2019)
10. Mishra, N., Ghosh, S., Ghosh, A.: Fuzzy clustering algorithms incorporating local information for change detection in remotely sensed images. Appl. Soft Comput. J. **12**(8), 2683–2692 (2012)
11. Ruikang, X., Chenghai, L.: Fuzzy C-means algorithm automatically determining optimal number of clusters. Comput. Mater. Continua **60**(2), 767–780 (2019)
12. Chen, S., Zhang, D.: Robust image segmentation using FCM with spatial constraints based on new kernel-induced distance measure. IEEE Trans. Syst. Man Cybern. **34**(4), 1907–1916 (2004)
13. Noordam J, vandenBroek W, Buydens L.: Geometrically guided fuzzy C-means clustering for multivariate image segmentation. In: 15th IEEE International Conference on Pattern Recognition, vol. 1, pp. 462–465 (2000)
14. Cai, W., Chen, S., Zhang, D.: Fast and robust fuzzy C-means clustering algorithms incorporating local information for image segmentation. Pattern Recogn. **40**(3), 825–838 (2007)
15. Krinidis, S., Chatzis, V.: A robust fuzzy local information C-means clustering algorithm. IEEE Trans. Image Process. **19**(5), 1328–1337 (2010)
16. Zhou, W., Jia, Z., Yang, J., Kasabov, N.: SAR image change detection based on combinatorial difference map and FCM clustering. Laser J. (3) (2018)
17. Gong, M., Zhou, Z., Ma, J.: Change detection in synthetic aperture radar images based on image fusion and fuzzy clustering. IEEE Trans. Image Process. **21**(4), 2141–2151 (2012)
18. Liu, J., Gong, M., Miao, Q., Su, L., Li, H.: Change detection in synthetic aperture radar images based on unsupervised artificial immune systems. Appl. Soft Comput. **34**, 151–163 (2015)
19. Rosin, P., Ioannidis, E.: Evaluation of global image thresholding for change detection. Pattern Recogn. Lett. **24**(14), 2345–2356 (2003)
20. Shang, R., Yuan, Y., Jiao, L., Meng, Y., Ghalamzan, A.M.: A selfpaced learning algorithm for change detection in synthetic aperture radar images. Signal Process **142**, 375–387 (2018)

GSSM: An Integration Model of Heterogeneous Factors for Point-of-Interest Recommendation

Qing Yang[1] , Yiheng Chen[1], Peicheng Luo[1], and Jingwei Zhang[2(✉)]

[1] Guangxi Key Laboratory of Automatic Measurement Technology and Instrument,
Guilin University of Electronic Technology, Guilin 541004, China
gtyqing@hotmail.com
[2] Guangxi Key Laboratory of Trusted Software,
Guilin University of Electronic Technology, Guilin 541004, China
gtzjw@hotmail.com

Abstract. Millions of users prefer to share their locations and social relationships on location-based social networks (LBSNs), such as Gowalla, Foursquare, and etc. It has become an important function to recommend points-of-interest (POIs) for users based on their check-in records. However, the user-location matrix generated by check-in records is often very sparse which causes those traditional methods to present a suboptimal recommendation performance. We proposed a new POI recommendation algorithm named GSSM, which combines multiple factors which can help solve problems in these recommendations and improve recommendation performance. We employ the gaussian mixture model (GMM) to extract geographical factor from user's check-in records. Then we assign a concrete semantics to define social factor. The strength of the connection between users is indicated by the number of visits from associated users. In order to capture the similarity factor between users, we apply the popular cosine similarity to improve recommendation performance for the POI recommendation as the basis of calculating user similarity. Finally, an optimal fusion framework is designed to incorporate the three factors mentioned above, and GSSM is proposed. We conduct experiments on large-scale real data set which is crawled from Gowalla. The experimental results show that the performance of GSSM is better than the baseline and many current popular POI recommendation models.

Keywords: POI recommendation · Geographical factor · Social factor · Fusion framework.

Supported by Guangxi Key Laboratory of Automatic Measurement Technology and Instrument (No. YQ19109) and Guangxi Key Laboratory of Trusted Software (No. kx201915).

X. Sun et al. (Eds.): ICAIS 2020, CCIS 1253, pp. 15–26, 2020.
https://doi.org/10.1007/978-981-15-8086-4_2

1   Introduction

1.1   Background

With the rapid development of mobile devices and wireless networks, location-based social network (LBSN) have entered thousands of households. Different from traditional social networks, LBSN can not only connect people in traditional social networks, but also track them and share their location information at the same time. Typical online LBSNs include Gowalla, Foursquare, Facebook, etc., and they have thousands of users. People prefer to share their traveling experience and evaluation of the places they visit through their check-ins, as well as they show their relationship with friends on LBSNs. These check-in records contain lots of information. In order to improve the user experience of LBSN, a new recommendation technology – point of interest (POI) recommendation is promoted by mining users' check-in records and social relations.

Since the pursuit of novelty is considered a fundamental human activity, people like to explore communities and places that suit their interests [1], and the POI recommendation can help users find new places that they are interested [2]. Nowadays, POI recommendation has became an important task in location-based social networks. It can predict a series of locations that users most likely to go in the future through the analysis of the users' check-in records, such as location information and their social relations. And it also drews users into relationships with LBSNs service providers and it provide potential customers for commercial activities. It can not only provide users with the convenience of life, but also contains great commercial value. The feature that both parties benefit at the same time makes POI recommendation widely concerned. With the support of mass data, POI recommendation has became a hot research topic in recent years, and many location recommendation systems have emerged. POI recommendation is a part of location recommendation. The existing research has a recommendation system that takes geographical and space factors into full consideration [3], and the check-in time of users can also be used as the basis for recommendation [4].

POI recommendation is different from traditional recommendation such as movie and music recommendation [5], it has its own characteristics as follows.

- The Tobler's first law of geography states that "Everything is related to everything else, but near things are more related to each other". It can be seen that the nearby locations have more in common, and people are more willing to go to the POIs which close to them. This is an important reason for the existence of POI recommendation.
- People tend to write down their experience fellings or ratings after watching a movie or listening to music, while people don't usually express their preferences clearly during the check-in process. Therefore, we can only obtain users' preferences with the assistance of information such as the number of check-in times.

- The user's location is dynamic, and they often travel to different locations. In real world, there are a large number of locations, and single user can only check in at a very limited number of locations.

Summing up above, in order to meet the requirements of users, we need to integrate multiple factors reasonably. In this paper, we do this based on preference scores for each location. To get preference scores, we take advantage of three important factors which get from users check-in records. The three factors mentioned here are geographical, social, and user similarity factor. First of all, geographical factors is the most critical of the three factors, and all recommendation questions are based on geographical location. Geographical factor mainly shows that people prefer to go to places closer to each other under similar conditions. The first law of geography also indicates it. For instance, people usually go to a restaurant near their home or company for dinner. Another case, they are likely to go to the cinema near the restaurant which people having meals. Namely, the closer people are to the center, the more likely they are to get there. The second is user social factor. Its a factor that cannot be ignored in real life. When faced with choices in life, people are greatly influenced by their friends, relatives. The choice of location must also be included. Most users tend to go to places where friends and other familiar people have checked in. One more thing to note, people often go out in groups. For example, people often go to the cinema or the bar together. Thus it can be seen that the influence of friends is crucial. The friend mentioned here is two users who follow each other on LBSN. Last but not least, user similarity factor is not negligible. In traditional item recommendation methods, similarity between users or items dominates. In POI recommendation, similarity refers to how many same points of interest each user has visited.

1.2   Challenges

Currently, challenges of POI recommendation can summary as follows.

- There are so many locations in reality, the user-location matrix is very sparse due to the fact. The traditional collaborative filtering recommendation cant be applied directly in the recommendation of geographical location recommendation and it obtains an unsatisfactory effect.
- POI recommendation involves many factors such as geographical and social factors. How to take these factors into consideration to provide services for recommendation is also a big challenge.
- The user check-in data set obtained from LBSN is too large. It contains millions of useless messages. There is a challenge to extracting useful information for recommendations.

1.3 Contributions

In summary, the contributions we made in this research work are four-fold.

- The gaussian mixture model is used to extract geographic factors from user's check-in records. It can accurately find the cluster center of each user's check-in records. Thus, user geographic factors can be captured quickly and effectively. This method can effectively alleviate the sparsity problem of user-location matrix.
- In order to build social relations among users, we propose a unique definition that the strength of the connection between users is indicated by the access score of the associated users.
- The popular cosine similarity algorithm of traditional recommendation is applied to the POI recommendation as the basis for calculating the user similarity.
- We select the optimal framework to integrate geographical, social and similarity factors, and propose GSSM model for POI recommendation. We conduct extensive experiments to evaluate the performance of GSSM using large real data set. We preprocess the jumbled data before the experiment. Experimental results show that the model we proposed performs great.

The structure of this paper is as follows. The second section reviews the development of POI recommendation and related work. In section three and four, we propose the method to capture factors and put forward the framework for POI recommendation. The fifth section is the experimental content of this paper, including the comparison with other recommended methods. The last part is a summary of the full paper.

2 Related Work

When making location-based POI recommendation, the first thing to consider is that the number of similar sites may be large. Therefore, it is a challenge to identify truly relevant sites from among the many candidates. Secondly, the clustering process of large matrix takes a long time. The existing method is making recommendation through memory-based CF or model-based CF collaborative filtering. For instance, Kenneth and Zheng [6,13] were able to obtain the user's time preference from the GPS track through the user's activity, and integrate the user activity into the user-place matrix. [7] used the corating-based similarity measurement for predicting ratings of unknown locations. POI recommendations can also be made based on people's social relationships. Such as friend and POI recommendation based on social trust cluster in location-based social networks. [8] emphasized the importance of social friends in recommendation system and used linear combination to form a probabilistic recommendation model. Wang and Zhu [9,10] proposed a recommendation matrix decomposition model involving trust and distrust.

3   Capturing Recommendation Factors

In this section, we will present our work in detail. We will introduce the research problem and the data needed in the research process. After that we will elaborate how to capture geographical, social and similarity factors.

3.1   Problem Description

Here we define the research problem and explain the data presented in the paper. The purpose of POI recommendation is to recommend locations to users. The process is shown below. The input is the user history check-in records obtained from LBSNs. The method proposed in this paper is used to construct the factor extraction model and establish the relation between factors. After the fusion of various factors, the user can be recommended points of interest based on the output of the result. Table 1 gives the major symbols used in this paper.

Table 1. Major symbols in the paper

Symbol	Meaning
U	*Set of all user in an LBSN*
u	*Subset of the set U.u ∈ U*
L	*Set of all user in an LBSN*
l	*Subset of the set L, l is denoted a pair of latitude and longitude coordinate. l ∈ L*
P	*The probability of the formation of each factor*

3.2   The Capture of Geographical Factor

Each user's check-in location is expressed as a pair of longitude and latitude on LBSNs. When dealing with cold start problems, geographic factors have a more important influence on recommendation. Mapping these pairs of points reveals a phenomenon: each user's check-in record is spread around a fixed number of points [?]. The following figure shows the check-in record distribution of two randomly selected users on LBSN. It can be seen that the check-in records of both users in Fig. 1 shows an obvious geographical clustering phenomenon.

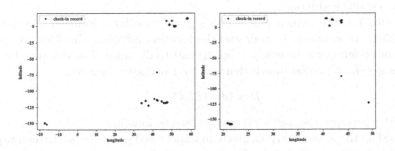

Fig. 1. Check-in distribution of users.

Thus, user's check-in records on LBSN generally have two obvious geographical features [11]: First, the check-in sites generally have several obvious clustering centers, such as the user's residence. The other is that the number of check-in records is inversely proportional to the distance from the nearest cluster center.

As mentioned above, it is particularly important to identify clustering centers based on the user's historical check-in records for effective recommendations. In previous studies, Chen Cheng [12] used a greedy clustering algorithm to do this. Meanwhile, someone use the Kmeans algorithm to accomplish this task. The improbability of Kmeans and its mechanism of judging only according to the distance to the center point of the cluster lead to room for improvement in the model's performance. To overcome this difficulty, we employ gaussian mixture model GMM to model the user's check-in records. GMM can be regarded as an extension of Kmeans, which is a very powerful clustering evaluation tool. Through our analysis of multi-user check-in records, we find that most users have multi-center check-in phenomenon. It greatly fits the model of multi-center gaussian distribution. Each part follows a gaussian mixture distribution $L \sim N(x \,|\, \mu_k, \Sigma_k)$.

According to the proportion of the number of check-ins, a certain coefficient is assigned to each part, which constitutes the gaussian mixture model. Gaussian mixture model is as follow.

$$P(x) = \sum_{k=1}^{K} \pi_k N(x \,|\, \mu_k, \Sigma_k) \tag{1}$$

$N(x \,|\, \mu_j, \Sigma_j)$ is the Kth component in the hybrid model. That is, the Kth cluster center in the users' check-in records. μ_k and Σ_k correspond to the mean and covariance of center k. π_k is mixture coefficient. It's the weight of each component. It represents the probability that each check-in point belongs to each cluster center. Through the historical check-in record of a specific user, the multiple cluster centers that the user checked in can be found out. According to the relationship between the unknown point and the cluster center, the geographic factor of the user's check-in behavior can be well captured.

The expected maximization algorithm (EM) is used to calculate the parameters of the gaussian mixture model. The goal is to create a specific model for each user that belongs only to him. Based on this model, multiple clustering centers are found. Substitute points of interest that are not accessed by the user into the established model.

In addition, the influence of a user's preference for a location will decrease as the distance between the user and the location increases. In other words, the degree of preference is inversely proportional to distance. The distance between them is $dis(L_i, C_i)$. Distance is denoted by Euclidean distance.

$$P \propto (dis(L_i, C_i))^{-1} \tag{2}$$

where P represents the user's preference for the location.

Based on the above analysis, given an unaccessed point $l(x, y)$, we can capture the check-in geographic factor of a user as follows.

1. Gaussian mixture model are calculated according to the probability density, the probability $p(x)$ corresponding to the unvisited point l was calculated.
2. Calculating the Euclidean distance from the point to the nearest center that the user has checked in. The willingness of users to move from one place to another is mainly affected by the distance between two places, and the degree is inversely proportional to the distance.
3. We multiply the above two parameters as factors, and the result is the geographical factor P_{geo} generated under the combined influence of the two factors.

$$P_{geo} = \frac{1}{dis\left(L_i, C_i\right)} \cdot p(x) \tag{3}$$

3.3   The Capture of Social Factor

In real life, people usually go somewhere together or to a place recommended by their friends. Therefore, when it comes to inferring a user's interest in an unvisited location, the behavior of friends should not be ignored. This is the second important factor influencing recommendation – social factor. We call the users who pay attention to each other in LBSNs as friends. It is expressed as $n * 2$ relational list matrix corresponding to a given user. Given U and L, we assume that there is a location l_1 belongs to L, and user u_0 hasn't visited l_1 yet. To capture social impact, we present the following methods.

First of all, we count the check-in times of user u_1 who is related to user u_0 at l_1, we call that N_{11}. And then, we count the check-in times of user u_2 who is also related to user u_0 at l_1, called N_{12}. In the same way, find out the check-in times of all the users related to user u_0 at l_1. Finally, sum it up to get the total number N_{1t}.

As stated, given a set of interest points L which are not visited by user u_0, such as $\{l_1, l_2, ..., l_n\}$. We get N_{1t} using the above method.

$$N_{1t} = N_{11} + N_{12} + ... + N_{1n} = \sum_{i=1}^{n} N_{1i} \tag{4}$$

In the same way, we can get the value of all points. The total number of check-ins for all users associated with u_0 is N_{total}.

$$N_{total} = N_{1t} + N_{2t} + ... + N_{kt} \tag{5}$$

k in the formula means the number of all points.

We can get the user the check-in ratio of all his friends at l_1. That's the social factor that we're talking about. We call it P_{soi} for social factor.

$$P_{soi} = \frac{N_{1t}}{N_{total}} = \frac{N_{1t}}{\sum_{i=1}^{n} N_{kt}} \tag{6}$$

3.4   The Capture of Similarity Factor

Similarity is a key word commonly used in the traditional collaborative recommendation algorithm. As a recommendation system, similarity can be used as one of the evaluation criteria for site recommendation. We use cosine similarity to measure the similarity between users. Here we define an identifier R to determine whether the user has visited a location. The similarity between user i and user k is taken as an example, the process of calculating similarity is as follow.

1. Going through all the points of interest L, and user set $U(i, k \in U)$.
2. Determining whether user i has visited l ($l \in L$). If user i does, then $R_{i,l} = 1$, or $R_{i,l} = 0$.
3. Determining whether user k has visited l ($l \in L$). If user k does, then $R_{k,l} = 1$, or $R_{k,l} = 0$.
4. Using the cosine formula to find the similarity $W_{i,k}$ between user i and k.

$$W_{i,k} = \frac{R_{i,1} \cdot R_{k,1} + R_{i,2} \cdot R_{k,2} + ... + R_{i,n} \cdot R_{k,n}}{\sqrt{\sum_{l \in L} R^2{}_{i,l}} \cdot \sqrt{\sum_{l \in L} R^2{}_{k,l}}} \tag{7}$$

$$= \frac{\sum\limits_{i,k \in U, l \in L} R_{i,l} \cdot R_{k,l}}{\sqrt{\sum_{l \in L} R^2{}_{i,l}} \cdot \sqrt{\sum_{l \in L} R^2{}_{k,l}}} \tag{8}$$

Pseudo-code of similarity capture algorithm is shown in algorithm 1.

Algorithm 1. Similarity Capture Algorithm

Input: The set of users U, and i,k∈U;The set of locations, L.
Output: A series of similarity values $W_{i,k}$.
  for each $l \in L$, l=1 **do**
    for for i=1, k=1 **do**
      if i do ,k do **then**
        $R_{i,l}=1$, $R_{k,l}=1$
      else
        $R_{i,l}=0$, $R_{k,l}=0$
      end if
      i=i+1 ,k=k+1
      return $R_{i,l}$, $R_{k,l}$
    end for
    i=i+1 ,k=k+1
  end for
Calculating $W_{i,k} = \frac{\sum R_{i,l} \cdot \sum R_{k,l}}{\sum R^2{}_{i,l} \cdot \sum R^2{}_{k,l}}$
return A list of $W_{i,k}$ for users i,k.

We obtained the similarity matrix among all users according to the above method. And then, given a location expressed in longitude and latitude pairs

$j(x, y)$ $(j \in L)$. If user k has visited j, then $R_{k,j} = 1$, or $R_{k,j} = 0$. The last step is to figure out the similarity score corresponding to the location. We use P_{pre} to represent it.

$$P_{pre} = \frac{\sum\limits_{k \in U} (W_{i,k} \cdot R_{k,j})}{\sum\limits_{k \in U} W_{i,k}} \tag{9}$$

4   Multiple-Factor Integrating Framework for the POI Recommendation

In this section, we propose a POI recommendation fusion framework, which fuses geographical factor, social factor and similarity factor into a whole. We are aiming at providing users with a list of possible points of interest in the future, rather than simply scoring each point of interest.

Each factor has a impact on the recommendation system. Therefore, we multiply the three factors. In order to unify the data of each behavior in the same value range,three results should be standardized. We divide the result of each part by its maximum value. $S_{\text{geo}} = \frac{P_{geo}}{P_{geo\,\max}}$, $S_{\text{soi}} = \frac{P_{soi}}{P_{soi\,\max}}$, $S_{\text{pre}} = \frac{P_{pre}}{P_{pre\,\max}}$.

S_{geo} , S_{soi} , S_{pre} respectively corresponding to geographical factor, social factor and similarity factor. After that, we will do a multiplication. This is our proposed recommendation algorithm, GSSM. So we have S_{final} as follows.

$$S_{final} = S_{geo} \cdot S_{soi} \cdot S_{pre} \tag{10}$$

5   Experiment Evaluation

In this section, we designed several experiments to evaluate the performance of the GSSM against baseline and current models.

5.1   Experimental Settings

The experimental data include user-location check-in records, geographical information of POI. We use the large data set crawled from Gowalla. The data set contains a total of 107,092 users and 644,2890 check-in records. And there is also a data set about user relationships.

Because the original data set is too jumble, it's necessary to set a threshold to filter out users who check in too few times and POIs which users check in too few times. There are two reasons for filtering. One is that users who check in low times will not usually express their hobbies on LBSNs, and the impact of occasional check-in records on the recommendation results is almost negligible. Another one is the locations with few user check-in records are often remote places or places with low sense of existence. It's clear that users do not want to be recommended for these locations in recommendation results.

To sum up, in terms of users, we filtered out users whose check-in times were less than 50 times and whose associated users are less than 30 times in the list of user relations. In terms of location, we filtered out locations whose total check-in records are less than 50 times. This operation was done only once, and both parts were done at the same time. The number of users after filtering is 25369 and the number of check-ins records is 1664610. We split the check-in data set up into two parts according to the timeline. The first 80% of the data set is used as the training set, and the remaining 20% is used as the test set.

Performance Metrics. The goal of POI recommendation is to recommendation the top-K highest ranked locations to a targeted. To evaluate the quality of POI recommendation, two points should not be ignored. One is that the actual number of places users have gone after recommendation. We call it *precision*.The other is the number of recommended locations that users actually visit. We use the *recall* as the metrics to evaluate it.

$$Precision = \frac{The\ number\ of\ recommended\ POIs\ in\ test\ set}{Number\ of\ POIs\ recommended\ for\ user} \tag{11}$$

$$Recall = \frac{The\ number\ of\ recommended\ POIs\ in\ test\ set}{Number\ of\ POIs\ visited\ by\ user\ in\ test\ set} \tag{12}$$

Comparison. The experiment in this paper is mainly divided into two parts. The comparison of the experimental results is shown below.

Part1: the method of capturing geographic factors.

- Capturing by GMM: this is the paper's method.
- Capturing by K-means: this is a well-known method [12].

Part2: the method of fusing factors.

- KMeans-mul: Fusing by multiplication, and capturing geographic factors by Kmeans.
- KMeans-add: Fusing by linear combination, and capturing geographic factors by Kmeans.
- GMM-add: Fusing by linear combination, and capturing geographic factors by GMM.
- GSSM: Fusing by multiplication, and capturing geographic factors by GMM. This is our method GSSM.

Interpretation of Results. Figure 2 summarizes the only considering geographical factor for recommendation without other two factors. Figure 2(a) is the precision of recommendation and Fig. 2(b) is the recall of recommendation. GMM is significantly better than Kmeans in performance. Figure 3 shows the recommended performance of various fusion methods at different k values. The precision and recall are shown in Figs. 3(a) and 3(b) respectively. It can be seen that our proposed model is obviously superior to others.

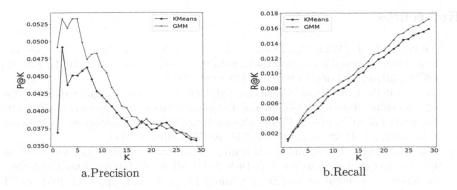

a.Precision   b.Recall

Fig. 2. The influence of geographical factors on recommendation performance.

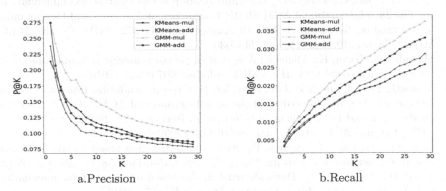

a.Precision   b.Recall

Fig. 3. Performance comparison of different methods under different K values.

6   Conclusions and Future Work

This paper proposes a new POI recommendation model GSSM. It makes recommendation using three factors captured from the users' check-in records. It employs GMM to build relationships between users and locations. And then GSSM establishes a social model to represent the social relationships between users. Based on cosine similarity, GSSM establishes the similarity relationship between users. Finally, GSSM use the best performance framework to combine the three factors into POI recommendations. The experiment on Gowalla with real data shows that the performance of GSSM is more excellent than the currently popular recommendation models. Considering the future work, we plan to add the check-in time factor to make POI recommendation.

Acknowledgements. This study is funded by the National Natural Science Foundation of China (No. 61862013, 61462017, U1501252, U1711263, 61662015), Guangxi Natural Science Foundation of China (No. 2018GXNSFAA281199, 2017GXNSFAA198035), Guangxi Key Laboratory of Automatic Measurement Technology and Instrument (No. YQ19109) and Guangxi Key Laboratory of Trusted Software (No. kx201915).

References

1. Xing, S., Liu, F., Wang, Q., Zhao, X., Li, T.: Content-aware point-of-interest recommendation based on convolutional neural network. Appl. Intell. **49**(3), 858–871 (2018). https://doi.org/10.1007/s10489-018-1276-1
2. Ye, M., Peifeng, Y., Wang-Chien, L., Dik-Lun, L.: Exploiting geographical influence for collaborative point-of-interest Recommendation. In: Proceeding of the 34th International ACM SIGIR Conference on Research and Development in Information Retrieval, 24–28 July, pp. 325–334. ACM, Beijing (2011)
3. Bin, L., Yanjie, F., Zijun, Y.: Learning geographical preferences for point-of-Interest recommendation. In: The 19th ACM SIGKDD International Conference on Knowledge Discovery and Data Mining, 11–14 August, pp. 1043–1051. ACM, Chicago (2013). https://doi.org/10.1145/2487575.2487673
4. Quan, Y., Gao, C., Zongyang, M.: Time-aware point-of-interest recommendation. In: The 36th International ACM SIGIR Conference on Research and Development in Information Retrieval, 28 July–01 August, pp. 363–372. ACM, Dublin (2013). https://doi.org/10.1145/2484028.2484030
5. Shenglin, Z., Irwin, K., Michael.: A survey of point-of-interest recommendation in location-based social networks. CoRR, vol.abs/1607.00647 (2016)
6. Kenneth, Dik.: CLR: A collaborative location recommendation framework based on co-clustering. In: Proceeding of the 34th International ACM SIGIR Conference on Research and Development in Information Retrieval, 25–29 July, pp. 305–314. ACM, Beijing (2011). https://doi.org/10.1145/2009916.2009960
7. Gongshen, L., Kui, M., Jiachen, D.: An entity-association-based matrix factorization recommendation algorithm. Comput. Mater. Continua **58**(1), 101–120 (2019)
8. Gang, W., Mengjuan, L.: Dynamic trust model based on service recommendation in big data. Comput. Mater. Continua **58**(3), 845–857 (2019)
9. Yingjie, W., Guisheng, Y., Zhipeng, C.: A trust-based probabilistic recommendation model for social networks. J. Netw. Comput. Appl. Comput. **55**, 59–67 (2015). https://doi.org/10.1016/j.jnca.2015.04.007
10. Zhu, J., Wang, C., Guo, X., Ming, Q., Li, J., Liu, Y.: Friend and POI recommendation based on social trust cluster in location-based social networks. EURASIP J. Wireless Commun. Netw. **2019**(1), 1–12 (2019). https://doi.org/10.1186/s13638-019-1388-2
11. Liu, Y., Pham, T.A.N., Cong, G., Yuan, Q.: An experimental evaluation of point of interest recommendation in location based social networks. Proc. VLDB Endowment **10**(10), 1010–1021 (2017). https://doi.org/10.14778/3115404.3115407
12. Cheng, C., Yang, H., King, I., Lyu, M.R.: Fused matrix factorization with geographical and social influence in location-based social networks. In: Proceedings of the Twenty-Sixth AAAI Conference on Artificial Intelligence, 22–26 July. AAAI, Canada (2012)
13. Yu, Z., Xing, X., Qiang, Y.: Collaborative location and activity recommendations with GPS history data. In: Proceedings of the 19th International Conference on World Wide Web, 26–30 April, pp. 1029–1038. ACM, Raleigh (2010). https://doi.org/10.1145/1772690.1772795
14. Zhe, L., Bao, X., Qingfeng, L.: An improved unsupervised image segmentation method based on multi-objective particle. Swarm Optim. Clustering Algorithm Comput. Mater. Continua **58**(2), 451–461 (2019)

Contrast Adjustment Forensics Based on Second-Order Statistical and Deep Learning Features

Xinyi Wang, Shaozhang Niu$^{(\boxtimes)}$, and He Wang

Beijing Key Lab of Intelligent Telecommunication Software and Multimedia, Beijing University of Posts and Telecommunications, Beijing, China
xawangxy@163.com, {szniu,fiphoenix}@bupt.edu.cn

Abstract. Contrast adjustment (CA) is one of the most common digital image retouching methods. However, it is often used to hide the traces of tampering, and thus has become an indirect evidence of image forgery. Therefore, CA blind detection has attracted widespread attention in the field of image forensics in recent years. Considering forensic methods based on first-order statistical features are vulnerable to encountering anti-forensic and other operation attacks, an second-order statistical-based CA forensics method using improved Gray-Level Co-occurrence Matrix (GLCM) network is proposed. Different from conventional CNN, which usually takes the image as input, this method can convert input images of different resolution into a uniform size GLCM matrix, in which GLCM adds four more directions to the traditional direction, and then learns the distribution features from GLCM through CNN layers and classifies them. Through active learning the hierarchical feature representation and optimizing the classification results, the proposed network is more suitable for detecting contrast adjustment tampering. Experimental results show that the proposed method can not only detect traditional CA, but also detect the CA image of anti-forensic attacks, and its performance is better than conventional forensic methods.

Keywords: Contrast adjustment tampering · Adversarial image forensics · Gray-Level Co-occurrence Matrix (GLCM) · Convolutional neural networks

1 Introduction

With the spread of information technology, people are no longer limited to things at their fingertips, and they are more willing to share the various things in life through the Internet. Digital images, as a useful digital medium and information carrier, are arbitrarily distributed and disseminated on the Internet. However, in today's society where communication is developed, some malicious falsification and forgery of images have spread in the real world and the online world, causing serious social trust problems. Under such circumstances, image forensics technology has gradually attracted the attention of society and researchers.

Image forensics is a technology to judge whether the image has been tampered and processed by detecting the invisible traces left by human eyes during image tampering

© Springer Nature Singapore Pte Ltd. 2020
X. Sun et al. (Eds.): ICAIS 2020, CCIS 1253, pp. 27–37, 2020.
https://doi.org/10.1007/978-981-15-8086-4_3

and processing. In order to know what processing an image has undergone, it is necessary to perform various processing tests on this image. At present, there are many techniques for detecting manipulated images, such as image contrast adjustment detection [1–5], JPEG compression detection [6, 7], median filter detection [8, 9], resampling detection [10], etc. Among them, contrast adjustment detection has attracted the attention of many scholars. Image contrast enhancement is a tampering operation that improves the visual appearance of an image, which changes the overall distribution of pixel intensities in the image. Although the contrast adjustment operation sometimes only affects the visual quality of the image without changing the image semantics, it may not be a direct result of malicious tampering, but it can hide some traces of other tampering operations (such as splicing[11] and copy-move [12]) to achieve the purpose of reducing tamper detection performance. Such tampering operations are detected to provide advantageous circumstantial evidence in image content tampering operations.

In the past decade, many methods have been proposed to detect contrast adjustment. Early CA forensics methods, such as Stamm et al. [2] and Cao et al. [5] found contrast adjustment operation would cause a significant change in the one-dimensional gray histogram of the image, resulting in significant peaks and intervals for detection, as shown in Fig. 1. However, the features produced in these histograms are easily to change after the image is post-processed, resulting in no difference features, making these CA forensics methods no longer feasible. Those CA detection techniques can obtain good performance when the image is not processed by anti-forensics technology, but paper [13, 14] introduced the universal anti-forensics technology for the enhancement based on histogram forensics technology. The subsequent image was processed to invalidate the existing detection technology. In order to solve these anti-forensic methods, then De Rosa et al. [1] presented a contrast adjustment forensics algorithm that used support vector machine (SVM) training to distinguish between original images, contrast-adjustment and anti-contrast attack images, which can be shown in Fig. 2. In this method, the variance value of each row in the GLCM was extracted, that is, the one-dimensional feature was used for SVM training. This was the first time that the second-order statistical information used in the CA forensics, but since the feature was only a simple one-dimensional, the spatial feature information of the GLCM was not fully utilized.

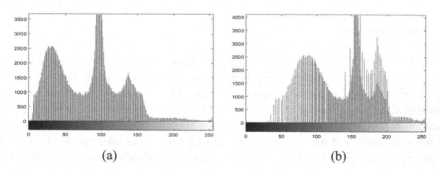

(a)   (b)

Fig. 1. The histogram of (a) an unprocessed image; (b) CA after gamma correction.

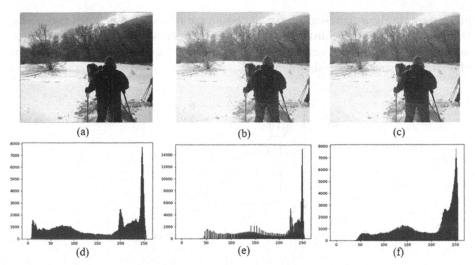

Fig. 2. Images after different operations (the first row) and their corresponding histograms (the second row). (a), (b) and (c) represent original image, contrast-adjustment image by gamma correction and anti-contrast attack image, respectively. (d), (e) and (f) are their histograms.

Therefore, this paper focuses on a forensic method of CA tampering operation based on second-order statistical features. In our paper, a modified convolutional neural network (CNN) is used to detect contrast-adjusted image. we start with the hierarchical structure of CNN, the number and size of feature maps of each layer, and the size of convolution kernels. Since the traces left by the contrast adjustment in the image are not obvious, it is difficult to obtain good results by directly using CNN to learn the image. Therefore, the CNN structure in this paper is different from the traditional CNN structure. In the modified CNN, the first layer is the pre-processing layer, which can convert the input image into a gray level co-occurrence matrix. We design a special CNN network model called G-CNN that combines the GLCM features to tamper with contrast adjustment.

2 Gray-Level Co-occurrence Matrix

In 1973, Haralick et al. [15] proposed the use of gray-scale co-occurrence matrices to describe texture features. This is because textures are formed by alternating gray-scale distributions in spatial locations, so that two distances are separated in the image space. There must be a certain gray-scale relationship between pixels, which is called the spatial correlation property of gray in the image. The texture is described by studying the spatial correlation of gray, which is the ideological basis of the gray-scale co-occurrence matrix [16].

The gray level co-occurrence matrix is defined as the probability that a point from the gray level i leaves a fixed position relationship $d = (D_x, D_y)$ to a gray level of j. The gray level co-occurrence matrix is represented by $P(i, j, d, \theta)$ $(i, j = 0, 1, 2,... L-1)$. Where L represents the gray level of the image, and i, j represent the gray level of the pixel, respectively. d represents the spatial positional relationship between two pixels. Different d determines the distance and direction between two pixels. θ is the direction in which the gray level co-occurrence matrix is generated, usually in the four directions of $0°$, $45°$, $90°$ and $135°$, as shown in Fig. 3.

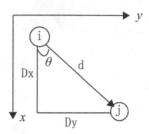

Fig. 3. The Pixel pair of gray level co-occurrence matrix [15].

The texture feature reflects the properties of the image, which is the focus of image analysis, and the gray level co-occurrence matrix (GLCM) is a widely used texture feature extraction method. GLCM is a probability used to count the pixel pairs of a certain gray value in a grayscale image. It reflects the comprehensive information of the image grayscale in the direction, variation amplitude and local neighborhood distribution, and has the macroscopic description characteristics of the image.

3   The Proposed Method

Directly using traditional CNN to learn images will affect the classification effect, so the G-CNN proposed in this paper mainly includes four parts: GLCM layer (pre-processing layer), convolution layer, pooling and classification layer.

3.1   Feature Learning with More Supervisory Information

The convolutional neural networks can not only automatically extract image features, but also can learn the mapping relationship between image input and output autonomously, and can simultaneously extract and classify features. There is no need for precise mathematical expressions between input and output, which makes the extracted features more efficient and helps to classify the next step. In addition, the connection between neurons in the adjacent two layers of the convolutional neural network is not fully connected, and has the characteristics of weight sharing, thus having fewer network connection numbers and weight parameters, greatly reducing the learning complexity of the model. These make the training process easier and the convergence speeds faster. It is only necessary to train the network structure model with a known pattern, and the network has the ability to map between input and output. The traditional CNN mainly consists of three parts: convolutional layer, pooling layer and classification layer. The pre-processing layer can make the traces of contrast adjustment more obvious, which is more conducive to subsequent feature learning and classification.

3.2 The GLCM Layer

A GLCM layer is applied to calculate the gray level co-occurrence matrix of the input image. The detail of calculation steps are as follows:

First, a grayscale image I of size M × N and an offset (Δx, Δy) are calculated, which are obtained by accumulating the pair of gray values *(i, j)* appearing between two pixels.

$$g(i,j) = \sum_{p=1}^{M} \sum_{q=1}^{n} G\{I(p,q) = i \wedge I(p+\Delta x, q + \Delta y) = j\} \qquad (1)$$

In the formula, the value rule of $G\{\cdot\}$ is: when the value of the expression in the brace is true, it is equal to 1; when the value of the expression in the brace is false, it is equal to 0; I (p, q) represents the pixel value of the image in the p-th row and the q-th column; G (i, j) is the value of GLCM in the i-th row and the j-th column, where i, j = 0,..., 255. Since the GLCM does not have any change in the pixel intensity of the input image, and GLCM can represent the relationship between the intensity of each pixel and other pixels in its neighborhood, a useful feature of CE forensics can be extracted.

Figure 4 shows the GLCM image after different operations on the image. In Fig. 4(b), there is CA fingerprint (peak or gap row and column) in GLCM of CE image. On the contrary, the GLCM of unprocessed image (Fig. 4(a)) and anti-forensic image (Fig. 4(c)) has no corresponding trace.

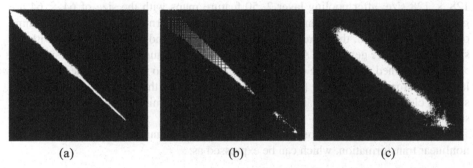

(a)	(b)	(c)

Fig. 4. The GLCM of (a) unprocessed image; (b) contrast-adjusted image after gamma correction (GC) of Fig. 1(a); (c) anti-forensic operation on Fig. 1(b) by method [13];.

For the input images with different resolutions, their GLCM sizes are the same. The eight offsets values of GLCM: (0, −1), (−1, 0), (−1, −1), (−1, 1), (1, 0), (0, 1), (1, 1), (1, −1), these show the relationship between the center and the pixels in its eight directions, finally the cumulative summation of the GLCMs in the eight directions is normalized, and L is equal to 256, that is, 256 gray levels are set. The output of the GLCM layer is the result of its normalization.

3.3 Contrast Adjustment Forensic CNN (G-CNN)

In addition to the pre-processing layer, the CNN structure proposed in this paper is shown as Fig. 5:

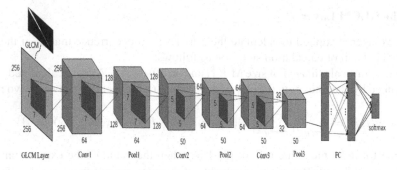

Fig. 5. The architecture of the proposed G-CNN.

As the network shown in Fig. 5. First input an image, after the pre-processing layer, the image is processed into GLCM of 256 × 256 size. The next layer is convolution layer 1, and the convolution kernel size is 7 × 7, each time. Translate one unit, there are 50 convolution kernels, and generate 64 feature maps of 256 × 256 size maps; after pooling layer 1, all pooling layers are pooled with maximum value, the size of the core is 7 × 7, each sub-translation two units, so that 64 feature maps of 128 × 128 size are obtained. The next layer is convolution layer 2, the convolution kernel size is 5 × 5, 1 unit per translation, a total of 50 convolutions The core generates 50 feature maps of 128 × 128 size; after pooling layer 2, 50 feature maps with the size of 64 × 64 are generated. Input to convolution layer 3, the convolution kernel size is 5 × 5, Each time one unit is translated, there are 50 convolution kernels, and 50 feature maps with the size of 64 × 64 are generated. After pooling layer 3, 50 feature maps with the size of 32 × 32 are obtained. Finally, the obtained features are input to the whole. The connection layer uses dropout technology [17] to suppress overfitting; the last layer uses activation softmax classification number, its number of nodes is determined by the number of class samples.

The convolutional layer consists of two parts, a convolutional transformation and a nonlinear transformation, which can be expressed as:

$$x_j^l = f\left(\sum_{i \in M_j} x_i^{l-1} * k_{ij}^l + b_j^l\right) \qquad (2)$$

Where x_j^l is the j-th feature map of the first layer, "$*$" is the convolution operation, M_j is the set of input feature maps, k_{ij}^l is the convolution kernel, and b_j^l is the output j of the first layer. The offset of the feature map, f is a nonlinear transformation. Commonly used nonlinear transformations mainly include sigmoid, tanh, and rectified linear units (ReLUs). The CNN network in this paper uses ReLUs.

The pooling layer is also called the downsampling layer, which is mainly used to reduce the dimension of the features of the convolution layer and suppress over-fitting. Commonly used pooling methods mainly have maximum pooling and averaging pooling, and the maximum pooling is taken. The maximum value in the kernel size area of the previous layer is used as the output, and the mean pooling is to take the average value in the kernel size area of the previous layer as the output.

The classification layer is mainly composed of a fully connected layer, in which the last layer of the fully connected layer is classified by the activation function softmax. In order to adjust the weight and offset of the convolutional layer and the fully connected layer, CNN uses the back propagation algorithm to obtain sufficient training parameters and is used to distinguish between unprocessed images and two types of contrast adjusted images.

4 Experiments

In this paper, all experiments are conducted under Ubuntu 16.04, the operating environment is Intel (R) Core (TM) CPU@ 4.20 GHz i7-7700 K, GeForce GTX 1080Ti, 32 GB memory PC machine.

4.1 Database

In order to evaluate the performance of the proposed network, we use 10, 000 images from the Boss RAW Database [18] to inspect the feasibility of the method. The boss database has the size of 512×512 gray-scale images, which can be used as the original image without any processing. Then, the contrast adjusted (CA) image database is obtained by using gamma correction (GC) and histogram stretching (HS), in which the coefficients of gamma correction are 0.5, 0.8, 1.2, 1.6. Then the formula for gamma correction is as follows:

$$y(i) = F\left(255 \times \left(\frac{x(i)}{255}\right)^{\gamma}\right) \tag{3}$$

Where $x(i)$ is the i-th pixel value of the original image, $y(i)$ is the i-th pixel value after contrast adjustment, γ represents the gamma correction coefficient, and $F(i)$ represents the nearest integer function (Table 1).

"GC-0.5" represents the experimental image obtained with gamma correction and a coefficient of 0.5. In HS, the input pixel value is linearly mapped so that 1% of the total pixel is saturated at the intensity value 0 and another 1% at the intensity value 255. Images obtained using the anti-forensics technique in [13] after GC and HS operations, we use "Anti-CA" represent these types of image and use "Anti-GC, Anti-HS" represent them separately. For the entire eleven types of images, the GLCMs are computed and used as the input images for the proposed network. In total, we obtain 40,000 GLCM data acquired from 10000 unaltered, 15,000 enhanced, and 15,000 anti-attacked images. For each type of GLCM data, we randomly select 80% for training and validation and assign the remaining 20% as the test dataset.

4.2 Experimental Results

In order to test the classification methods of different CNN network, we have done the following experiments. Firstly, an image is directly input to the convolutional network without pre-processing layer for training, and the classification effect is very poor, which indicates that it is difficult for the convolution network to directly extract and distinguish

Table 1. The distribution of experimental dataset.

Type	Detail type	The number of images
Unprocessed	Unprocessed	10000
GC	GC-0.5	2500
	GC-0.8	2500
	GC-1.2	2500
	GC-1.6	2500
HS	HS	5000
Anti-CA [13]	Anti-GC-0.5	2500
	Anti-GC-0.8	2500
	Anti-GC-1.2	2500
	Anti-GC-1.6	2500
	Anti-HS	5000

the contrast adjustment on the image and the corresponding anti-forensic features; After the image is adjusted, its frequency domain features will change significantly. We want to convert the image into a spectrogram first, and then input it to the network for training. The experimental results show a certain effect, but it is still not ideal; According to this idea, we continue to consider the classification of image feature maps. After the image contrast adjustment, especially the anti-forensics method with Gaussian jitter, the high frequency information of the image will be changed to a large extent, so we use the laplacian filter to extract the image. The high-frequency signal is input to the network for training and classification. Experimental results show that the images of the anti-forensic operations added can be better distinguished, but the classification of the original image and the GC-adjusted image is not good. Finally, we continue to extract another second-order statistical feature of the image - GLCM, and input the GLCM statistical feature map to the network, which can get better classification results. Through the above experiments, it can be concluded that GLCM layer has a good classification effect for the contrast adjustment of image corrected by GC and its anti-forensics attack detection (Table 2).

In order to observe the classification accuracy, this section uses the average accuracy (ACC) and the true positive rate (TPR) to evaluate the detection effect. Table 3 shows the comparison of detection performance of the method [1, 2] and proposed method to on the unprocessed image, gamma corrected image, histogram stretched image. Table 3 shows the comparison of detection performance of the method [1, 2] and proposed method to distinguish between the unprocessed image, anti-GC image and anti-HS image. From the experiment results, we can see the proposed method achieved better performance on the entire types of test images, especially in discrimination the images tampered by anti-forensic attack (Table 4).

Table 2. The performance of different CNN-based network.

Network	TPR			ACC
	Unprocessed	GC	Anti-GC	
CNN	0.321	0.295	0.345	0.332
F-CNN	0.472	0.516	0.451	0.475
L-CNN	0.791	0.705	0.857	0.766
G-CNN (proposed)	0.993	0.986	0.996	0.997

Table 3. Comparison of detection performance (Unprocessed, HS, GC).

Method	TPR			ACC
	Unprocessed	HS	GC	
De Rosa [1]	0.967	0.923	0.954	0.948
Stamm [2]	0.956	0.979	1	0.961
G-CNN (proposed)	**0.994**	**0.998**	**0.999**	**0.996**

Table 4. Comparison of detection performance (Unprocessed, Anti-GC, Anti-HS).

Method	TPR			ACC
	Unprocessed	Anti-GC	Anti-HS	
De Rosa [1]	0.642	0.452	0.551	0.587
Stamm [2]	0.827	0.225	0.345	0.476
G-CNN (proposed)	**0.973**	**0.945**	**0.934**	**0.944**

5 Conclusion

The anti-forensic techniques can easily conceal the forensic detectors based on the first-order statistical analysis, so the use of first-order statistical information is inevitably unsafe. When performing high statistical analysis, this anti-forensic technology cannot guarantee that forensic medicine is undetectable. In this paper, a second-order statistical analysis is conducted derived from the image for detecting the footprints left during contrast adjustment and the anti-forensic schemes. We propose a method of contrast adjustment forensics based on a modified CNN. The pre-processed GLCM layer is added in front of the CNN by extracting these second-order statistic features of the image. Experimental results demonstrate this GLCM-CNN can be applied well to contrast adjustment and their anti-forensics techniques detection. Our future work is to study the other statistical features left in the image by contrast adjustment, and then fuse the algorithm proposed in this paper to further improve the comprehensive detection performance of image contrast adjustment.

Acknowledgements. This work was supported by National Natural Science Foundation of China (No. 61370195, U1536121).

References

1. De Rosa, A., Fontani, M., Massai, M., et al.: Second-order statistics analysis to cope with contrast enhancement counter-forensics. IEEE Signal Process. Lett. **22**(8), 1132–1136 (2015)
2. Stamm, M.C., Liu, K.J.R.: Blind forensics of contrast enhancement in digital images. In: Proceedings of the International Conference on Image Processing, ICIP 2008, 12–15 October, San Diego, California, USA. IEEE (2008)
3. Cao, G., Zhao, Y., Ni, R.: Forensic estimation of gamma correction in digital images. In: IEEE International Conference on Image Processing. IEEE (2010)
4. Lin, X., Li, C. T., Hu, Y.: Exposing image forgery through the detection of contrast enhancement. In: 2013 20th IEEE International Conference on Image Processing (ICIP). IEEE (2013)
5. Cao, G., Zhao, Y., Ni, R., Li, X.: Contrast enhancement-based forensics in digital images. IEEE Trans. Inf. Forensics Secur. **9**(3), 515–525 (2014)
6. Chen, C., Shi, Y.Q., Wei, S.: A machine learning based scheme for double JPEG compression detection. In: International Conference on Pattern Recognition (2008)
7. Yi, Z., Luo, X., Yang, C., Ye, D., Liu, F.: A framework of adaptive steganography resisting JPEG compression and detection. Secur. Commun. Netw. **9**(15), 2957–2971 (2016)
8. Liu, A., Zhao, Z., Zhang, C., Su, Y.: Median filtering forensics in digital images based on frequency-domain features. Multimed. Tools Appl. **76**(6), 22119–22132 (2017)
9. Kang, X., Stamm, M.C., Peng, A., Liu, K.J.R.: Robust median filtering forensics based on the autoregressive model of median filtered residual. In: Signal & Information Processing Association Summit & Conference. IEEE (2012)
10. Flenner, A., Peterson, L., Bunk, J., Mohammed, T.M., Nataraj, L., Manjunath, B.S.: Resampling forgery detection using deep learning and a-contrario analysis. Electron. Imaging **7**, 212-1–212-7 (2018)
11. Wang, X., Niu, S., Zhang, J.: Digital image forensics based on CFA interpolation feature and Gaussian mixture model Int. J. Digital Crime Forensics **11**(2), 1–12 (2019)
12. Li, Y., Zhou, J.: Fast and effective image copy-move forgery detection via hierarchical feature point matching. IEEE Trans. Inf. Forensics Secur. **14**(5), 1307–1322 (2019)
13. Cao, G., Zhao, Y., Ni, R., Tian, H.: Anti-forensics of contrast enhancement in digital images. In: Proceedings of the 12th ACM workshop on Multimedia and security, MM&Sec, pp. 25. ACM (2010)
14. Barni, M., Fontani, M., Tondi, B.: A universal attack against histogram-based image forensics. Int. J. Digital Crime Forensics **5**(3), 35–52 (2015)
15. Haralick, R.M., Shanmugam, K., Dinstein, I.H.: Textural features for image classification. Syst. Man Cybern. IEEE Trans. SMC **3**(6), 610–621 (1973)
16. He, J., Zhu, X.: Combining improved gray-level co-occurrence matrix with high density grid for myoelectric control robustness to electrode shift. IEEE Trans. Neural Syst. Rehabil. Eng. **25**(9), 1539–1548 (2017)

17. Hinton, G.E., Srivastava, N., Krizhevsky, A., Sutskever, I., Salakhutdinov, R.R.: Improving neural networks by preventing co-adaptation of feature detectors. Comput. Sci. **3**(4), 212–223 (2012)
18. Bas, P., Filler, T., Pevný, T.: "Break our steganographic system": the ins and outs of organizing BOSS. In: Filler, T., Pevný, T., Craver, S., Ker, A. (eds.) IH 2011. LNCS, vol. 6958, pp. 59–70. Springer, Heidelberg (2011). https://doi.org/10.1007/978-3-642-24178-9_5

Hybrid Low Rank Model Based Deep Neural Network Compression with Application in Data Recovery

Chuanxiang Xu[1], Weize Sun[1(✉)], Lei Huang[1], Jingxin xu[2], and Min Huang[1]

[1] Guangdong Laboratory of Artificial-Intelligence and Cyber-Economics (SZ), College of Electronics and Information Engineering, Shenzhen University, Shenzhen, China
proton198601@hotmail.com
[2] Departmet of Housing and Public Works, Brisbane, QLD, Australia

Abstract. Most deep convolutional neural networks for compressed sensing image reconstruction have large number of parameters. Recently, many deep neural network compression methods based on the low rank characteristics of the network structure are proposed. However, these methods fail to consider the inner similarity structure of the networks, leading to a performance degradation. In this paper, a novel hybrid low rank model based network compression method, which utilizes the similarity structure of the weight matrices and the idea of parameter sharing, is proposed. This network model is then applied to the application of high resolution Synthetic Aperture Radar (SAR) imaging, and experiments show that the proposed method can achieve an outstanding image recovery result comparing to the state-of-the-art methods, with a significant reduction of the number of parameters.

Keywords: Convolutional neural networks · Compressed Sensing (CS) · Network compression · Low rank model

1 Introduction

Deep Neural Network (DNN) is a multi-layer neural network structure widely used in computer vision [1,2], speech signal processing [3,4] and bioinformatics [5,6]. Generally speaking, the deeper the neural network, the richer the representation ability of the input data learned by the model, and the better the performance of the method [7,8]. However, a large network will introduce a huge number of parameters, which are of high redundancy. This leads to a high computational complexity as well as requirement of the storage spaces, and thus restricting the deep neural network models to be deployed on mobile systems.

W. Sun—Corresponding author.
The work described in this paper was supported by the National Natural Science Foundation of China (NSFC) under Grant U1501253 and U1713217.

X. Sun et al. (Eds.): ICAIS 2020, CCIS 1253, pp. 38–50, 2020.
https://doi.org/10.1007/978-981-15-8086-4_4

To overcome this problem, a lot of deep neural network compression methods have been proposed [9–12]. Studies had shown that neural networks tend to have low rank properties on their matrix-based or tensor-based structure. By using matrix decomposition methods such as singular value decomposition (SVD) or a tensor decomposition methods, the principle of low rank approximation can be applied to reorganize the weight matrix or tensor to achieve a significant reduction in the amount of parameters. Denton in [9] used a combination of SVD grading and filter clustering to approximate the weight matrix, and achieved a two-fold acceleration of the computational speed of the convolutional layer. Moreover, to efficiently make use of the tensor structure of the weights, tensor factorization methods are employed for the compression. In [10] and [11], the CP decomposition and Tucker decomposition methods are suggested to perform the low rank structure discovery and both of them achieve good compression effects. Furthermore, [12] achieved network optimization results with a maximum of 30 times compression ratio by utilizing the high compression characteristics of Tensor Train (TT) decomposition. Most of these low rank optimization based methods can achieve appropriate network compression results, but often lead to a serious performance degradation [12].

In recent year, the data recovery problems, such as compressed sensing data recovery, had achieve more and more attentions. Kulkarni proposed to reconstruct the image data using a non-iterative recovery network named as Recon-Net based on CNN [14]. Zhang [16] decomposed the recovered network into an encoder part of feature extraction and a decoder part for recovery. Based on the sparsity hypothesis of the extracted feature and a thresholding operation, a more stable recovery result can be obtained. Motivated by the iterative optimization methods, Yao and Zhang [15,16] combined the idea of iterative optimization and the neural network model, and introduced a large signal recovery network which can be regarded as a cascaded network model. Similarly, Zhang [17] designed multiple sets of similar and/or different small networks and cascaded them into a large one for the purpose of high-resolution imaging. However, when the number of iterations or the cascaded blocks of the network models is large, the whole neural network becomes very complicated, leading to very high computational complexity as well as storage requirement, and thus is not applicable to data processing of the mobile platform. In this case, network optimization becomes very important.

In fact, the stacking or cascading of networks is often accompanied by multiple iterations of similar or identical network structures, and the state-of-the-art compression methods did not take use of such recurring structures, resulting in an unsatisfying compression result. In recent years, the joint matrix decomposition method [18] is proposed to discover the similar structure between several matrices. In this article, we will try to employ the idea of joint low rank property of the weight matrices and design a hybrid optimization network based on this property for better deep neural network compression.

The remainder of this paper is organized as follows. In Sect. 2, the problem of data recovery is first introduced and a baseline network is also presented.

This baseline network is then optimized by the traditional low rank model. In Sect. 3, the proposed hybrid network compression model is described in details. Section 4 presents the experimental results with the application of high resolution Synthetic Aperture Radar (SAR) imaging or compressed sensing SAR image recovery using the SAR dataset. Finally, conclusion is drawn in Section 5.

2   Baseline Models

In this section, we will first introduce the data recovery problem together with one basic network model for the reconstruction process. The state-of-the-art low rank compression model will also be presented.

2.1   Baseline Network

Compressed sensing has attracted much attention as an alternative to the classical sampling paradigm for data compression [19]. Compared to Nyquist sampling theory, the technique of compressed sensing will sample a much less data in a fixed period, and can greatly reduce the requirement of transmission bandwidth as well as storage space. Generally speaking, the compressed sensing technique will first perform a compressed sampling as:

$$y = \Phi x \tag{1}$$

where $x \in R^N$ is the original data, and $\Phi \in R^{N_c \times N}$ is the random projection Gaussian matrix [20] or sampling matrix with $N_c \ll N$. $y \in R^{N_c}$ is the compressed sampled data, and the sampling rate is defined as $MR = N_c/N$. The target now is to recover the original data x from y, yielding

$$\hat{x} = f(W, y) \tag{2}$$

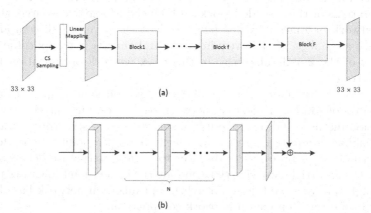

Fig. 1. The network architecture of a typical cascaded recovery network: (a) The whole network; (b) Sub-network of each block.

where $f()$ refers to as the recover process or optimization equation, and W contains all the parameters.

In recent years, many data reconstruction methods had been proposed, including optimization based methods [21,22] and deep neural network based ones [15]. Here we will tackle the latter one only. Firstly, we raise a baseline network for signal recovery. Using this baseline network as an example, the joint compression method will be proposed in the next section. It is worth noting that the compression algorithm introduced in this paper can compress not only this network but others with similar structures. Figure 1 shows the whole network structure for the data reconstruction process using a cascaded deep neural network [15]. Note that the data matrix to be compressed is of dimensions 33×33 [23] and x in (1) is the vectorized result of the data matrix and thus is of dimensions 1089×1. When the actual data is larger than 33×33, we can simply divide it into a lot of sub-matrices during the compressed sensing process.

Under different sampling rates, the output y with different dimensions will be generated and thus is not suitable to be used as the network input. For consistency of the network structure, a linear mapping is applied to y before feeding to the convolutional neural network:

$$z = F^f(y, W^f) \qquad (3)$$

where the network F^f contains one fully-connected layer with 1,089 neurons and W^f is the parameters, then a z with consistence length under different sampling rates can be generated and this can be treated as an initial estimate of the recovered data and thus can be feeded into the network. Therefore, for a very large M, we can use only part of the training data set for this initialization step. It is worth noting that the network contains several blocks and all the blocks have a same structure, which is shown in Fig. 1(b), together with the technique introduced by the residual network [7]. In this case, the output of the f-th block is:

$$x_f = x_{f-1} + f(x_{f-1}, \{W_{n,f}\}) \qquad (4)$$

where $W_{n,f}$, ($n = 0, 1, ..., N + 1$, $f = 1, 2, \cdots, F$) contains all the parameters of all the F blocks, and $x_0 = z$ is the initial estimate of the recovered data. Finally, we output the recovery result of $\hat{x} = x_F$.

2.2   Low-Rank Model

Figure 2 shows a typical low rank model for the neural network compression of the n-th layer of the f-th block of the neural network. As shown in Fig. 2(a), the convolution kernel, or the weight tensor of one single layer, before compression, is of dimensions $L_{n,1} \times L_{n,2} \times P_n \times Q_n$, where $L_{n,1} \times L_{n,2}$ is the filter size, P_n and Q_n are input and output depths, respectively. As the network structure of all the blocks is the same, the weight tensors in the n-th layer of each block had a same structure but different values. The parameter number for this layer is $\#W_{n,f} = L_{n,1}L_{n,2}P_nQ_n$, where $\#A$ refers to as the number of parameters in the tensor A.

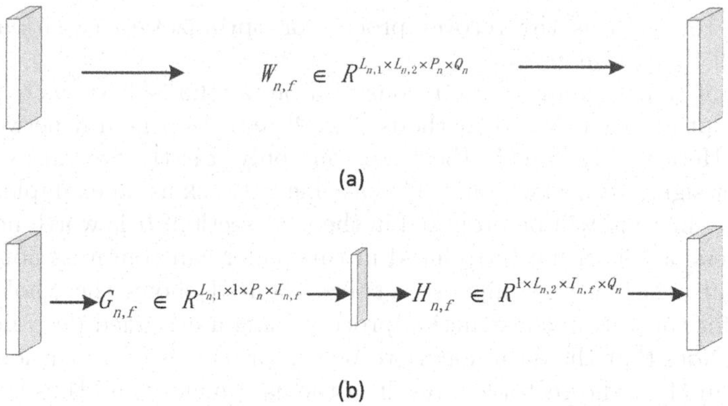

(a)

(b)

Fig. 2. Illustrations of the state-of-the-art low rank model: (a) One layer before compression; (b) The layer after compression.

According to Fig. 2(b), the compression model decomposes this single layer network into two layers, and the new weights tensors $G_{n,f}$ and $H_{n,f}$ are of dimensions $L_{n,1} \times 1 \times P_n \times I_{n,f}$ and $1 \times L_{n,2} \times I_{n,f} \times Q_n$, respectively, where $L_{n,1} \times 1$ and $1 \times L_{n,2}$ are the new filters sizes, and $I_{n,f}$ is the output depth for the first weights tensor as well as the input depth for the second one. Using this technique, the parameter number after compression becomes $\#G_{n,f} + \#H_{n,f} = L_{n,1}P_nI_{n,f} + L_{n,2}I_{n,f}Q_n$. By choosing an $I_n \leq \min\{P_n, Q_n\}$, compression can be achieved, and the compression ratio for this layer can be defined as $CS_{\text{ratio}} = (\#G_{n,f} + \#H_{n,f})/\#W_{n,f}$. It is worth noting that this approach in fact decomposes the original weight tensor into two small sub-tensors and thus is called low rank decomposition with rank $I_{n,f}$.

Since $\#W_{0,i}$ and $\#W_{N+1,i}$ are of dimensions $L_{0,1} \times L_{0,2} \times 1 \times Q_0$ and $L_{N+1,1} \times L_{N+1,2} \times P_{N+1} \times 1$, and the number of parameters of them are usually small because the input and output depths of $\#W_{0,i}$ and $\#W_{N+1,i}$ are 1, respectively, they will not be compressed here. Finally, under this model, the network compression ratio can be defined as:

$$CS_{\text{ratio}} = \frac{\sum_{f=1}^{F}\left[\#W_{0,f} + \#W_{N+1,f} + \sum_{n=1}^{N}(\#G_{n,f} + \#H_{n,f})\right]}{\sum_{f=1}^{F}\sum_{n=0}^{N+1}\#W_{n,f}} \tag{5}$$

3   Proposed Hybrid Compression Method

In this section, we will present the proposed hybrid network compression model in details, including the network structure and the loss function design.

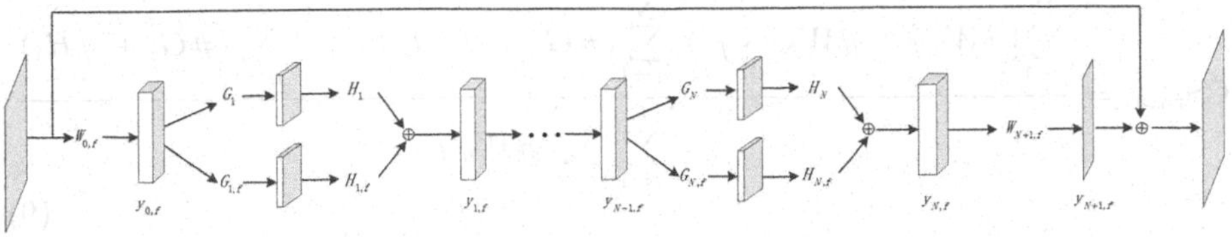

Fig. 3. Illustration of the proposed hybrid low rank model of the f-th block in Fig. 1(a).

3.1 Proposed Network Structure

Figure 3 shows the details of the f-th block of the proposed network compression model. There are totally $(N + 2)$ layers in the original network of this block as shown in Fig. 1, and the output of the n-th layer is defined as $y_{n,f}$, $n = 0, 1, 2, \cdots, N + 1$. Since the parameter number of $\#W_{0,f}$ and $\#W_{N+1,f}$ are small, they are not compressed. Here we focus on the compression of the middle N layers.

In the n-th layer of the f-th block, $n = 1, 2, \cdots, N$, $f = 1, 2, \cdots, F$, the input and output of this layer are $y_{n-1,f}$ and $y_{n,f}$, and we have $y_{n,f} = f(y_{n-1}, W_{n,f})$ where $W_{n,f}$ contains the network parameters of the original model. Here we propose to decompose it into four weight tensors, namely, $G_n \in R^{L_{n,1} \times 1 \times P_n \times I_n}$, $H_n \in R^{1 \times L_{n,2} \times I_n \times Q_n}$, $G_{n,f} \in R^{L_{n,1} \times 1 \times P_{n,f} \times I_n}$ and $H_{n,f} \in R^{1 \times L_{n,2} \times I_{n,f} \times Q_n}$, and obtain:

$$y_{n,f} = y_{n,f,1} + y_{n,f,2} = f(y_{n-1}, W_{n,f,1}) + f(y_{n-1}, W_{n,f,2}) \tag{6}$$

$$y_{n,f,1} = f(y_{n-1}, \{G_{n,f}, H_{n,f}\}) \tag{7}$$

$$y_{n,f,2} = f(y_{n-1}, \{G_n, H_n\}) \tag{8}$$

The main idea of this decomposition is to decompose the original weight tensor $W_{n,f}$ into two sub-tensors $W_{n,f,1}$ and $W_{n,f,2}$. The first weight sub-tensor $W_{n,f,1}$ is then substitute by $G_{n,f}$ and $H_{n,f}$ for $n = 1, 2, \cdots, N$, and $f = 1, 2, \cdots, F$, which is similar to that in Fig. 2. The second weight sub-tensor $W_{n,f,2}$, on the other hand, is substitute by G_n and H_n for all $f = 1, 2, \cdots, F$, which means that in all the F blocks, we will have a same pair of $\{G_n, H_n\}$. This kind of structure is named as 'parameter sharing structure'. To the end, we will refer the parts containing G_n and H_n to as 'sharing part', and the parts containing $G_{n,f}$ and $H_{n,f}$ to as 'non-sharing part',

By introducing the idea of parameter sharing, we embed the similar information between different blocks into the weight tensors $\{G_n, H_n\}$ in all the F blocks, and put the different information between different blocks into the weight tensors $\{G_{n,f}, H_{n,f}\}$. Therefore, this model is named as hybrid compression model. Furthermore, as the weight tensors $\{G_n, H_n\}$ repeat F times in F blocks, the total storage space for them will be reduced by a factor of F, leading to a high compression ratio. To conclude, the final compression ratio of the whole network becomes:

$$\text{CS}_{\text{ratio}} = \frac{\sum\limits_{f=1}^{F}\left[\#W_{0,f} + \#W_{N+1,f} + \sum\limits_{n=1}^{N}(\#G_{n,f} + \#H_{n,f})\right] + \sum\limits_{n=1}^{N}(\#G_i + \#H_i)}{\sum\limits_{i=1}^{F}\sum\limits_{n=1}^{N+1}\#W_{n,f}}$$

(9)

where $\#W_{n,f} = L_{n,1}L_{n,2}P_nQ_n$, $\#G_{n,f} = L_{n,1}P_nI_{n,f}$, $\#H_{n,f} = L_{n,2}I_{n,f}Q_n$, $\#G_n = L_{n,1}P_nI_n$ and $\#H_n = L_{n,2}I_nQ_n$.

3.2   Loss Function Design

In this article, we adopt the loss function $L(\theta)$ in the baseline model as

$$L(\theta) = \frac{1}{M}\sum_{m=1}^{M}\|x_{m,F} - x_m\|_2^2$$

(10)

where $\{x_m\}_{m=1}^{M}$ is the training data set, and M is the number of training samples. The x_m is down sampled into $y_m = \Phi x_m$ according to (1), and transferred to $z_m = \Psi y_m$ under (3), where z_m is the network input, and $x_{m,F}$ is the network output. In another word, the target of this network is to reduce the discrepancy between the recovered data $x_{m,F}$ and the original data x_m.

4   Experiment

In this section, we will first summarize the application of high resolution SAR imaging or SAR imaging data recovery. The implementation details network of

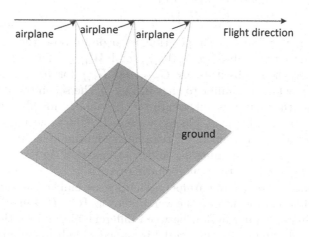

Fig. 4. SAR data acquisition process.

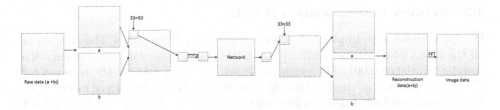

Fig. 5. Experimental flow chart.

the proposed network is then given. In the end, experiments are carried out for the performance comparison between the proposed model and the state-of-the-art ones in terms of reconstruction quality based on the SAR dataset.

4.1 High Resolution SAR Imaging

SAR is a radar system that uses a mobile radar mounted on a satellite or aircraft to continuously scan the ground when passing through an area in the air, which is shown in Fig. 4. During the scan, the data is generated [25]. In our system, these data will be first compressed sampled under a compressed sampling ratio $MR = N_c/N < 1$ using (1) and then transmitted to the receiving device on the ground. In this case, the transmission requirement is reduced by the factor of N/N_c. In the end, the received data is feeded into the network for data recovery, and high resolution SAR imaging is achieved.

In this article, the peak-signal-to-noise ratio(PSNR), one of the most common used measurement for evaluating image quality, is used to evaluate the quality of the restored image. The PSNR is defined as:

$$PSNR = 20 \times log(POXEL\_MAX/\sqrt{MSE}) \qquad (11)$$

where MSE is the mean square error between the reconstruction image and the original image and $POXEL\_MAX$ is maximum value of a grayscale-image. Here we normalized the pixels of the image to get $POXEL\_MAX = 1$.

Experimental flow chart is shown in Fig. 5. The data set in [24] is employed using MATLAB for radar imaging data generation. This data set contains 12 images of dimensions 1024×768, and we selected 10 images for training neural networks and 2 for testing. After scanning, the SAR data is also of dimensions 1024×768. As the scanned data are complex valued, the real part and imaginary part of the data are separated into two sub-matrices. Furthermore, the real and imaginary data matrices are divided into several small matrices of dimensions 33×33 for the compressed sampling. To sum up. one image data can be divided into 1426 training data and a total number of 14260 pieces of data for training. For the testing procedure, we follow the same operation but the evaluation is carried out on the 2 recovered images of dimensions 1024×768.

4.2   Network Implementation Details

We use tensorflow to implement and train the Neural Networks. The weights of all the layers of all the networks are initialised using gaussian distribution with standard variance 0.001. The batch-size is set as 64. We cascade the network for $F = 5$ times, which is, there are totally 5 blocks in all the networks as in Fig. 1(a). The convolution kernel size is unified with $L_{n,1} \times L_{n,2} = 5 \times 5$, $n = 0, 1, \cdots, N+1$ for the baseline model in Fig. 1. The number of layers in each block is $N+2$, and the depths of each layer within one block are $P_n = Q_n = 64$ for any n. For the proposed hybrid compression model, it is assumed that the ranks of the parts with and without parameter sharing are consistent, and we define $I_{n,f} = I$ and $I_n = I'$, for $n = 0, 1, \cdots, N+1$, $f = 1, \cdots, F$.

4.3   Experimental Result

In the first test, we fix the ranks of the 'sharing part' to $I' = 8$ to analysis the effect of 'non-sharing part' under $I = 0, 2, 4, 8, 16, 32$. The situations of $N + 2 = 3, 4, 5$ layers within one block is tested, and the compressed sampling rate is set to be MR = 10%. The experimental results are shown in Table 1. It is shown that the proposed hybrid compression network achieves the best PSNR performance under $(I, I) = (8, 8)$ and $N = 3$. For a larger I, the problem of over fitting is observed. However, when $N = 2$ and $N = 1$, the I with best PSNR performance are 16 and 32, respectively, indicating that a structure with smaller number of layers within one block, more weights are required to achieve a better recovery performance of the network model.

Table 1. SAR image reconstruction result under a fixed $I' = 8$.

(I', I)	(8, 0)	(8, 2)	(8, 4)	(8, 8)	(8, 16)	(8, 32)
N = 1	21.37	24.70	27.16	28.18	22.22	24.94
N = 2	27.12	27.41	28.72	28.79	29.64	28.44
N = 3	24.00	26.99	25.73	29.69	29.04	28.80

Secondly, we fix the ranks of the 'non-sharing part' to $I = 8$ to analysis the effect of 'sharing part' under $I' = 0, 2, 4, 8, 16, 32$. The other parameters are the same as those in the previous test, and the results are shown in Table 2. In this time, the best PSNR performance for $N = 3$ and $N = 2$ are both achieved under $I' = 16$, while for $N = 1$, an $I' = 8$ will give the best recovery result. This means that under a fixed number of parameters or the rank of the weight tensors of the 'non-sharing part', a structure with smaller number of layers within one block contains less similarity information between blocks, thus requiring a smaller I' comparing with the situation of higher number of layers within one block.

Table 2. SAR image reconstruction result under a fixed $I = 8$.

(I', I)	(0, 8)	(2, 8)	(4, 8)	(8, 8)	(16, 8)	(32, 8)
N = 1	21.96	23.08	22.26	28.18	27.14	25.84
N = 2	28.82	29.60	24.50	28.79	29.40	28.86
N = 3	27.43	29.45	28.29	29.68	30.45	29.18

In the end, the PSNR and compression ratio performance of different methods are compared. All the parameters are the same as those in the previous test, and the proposed approach is compared with the baseline model in Fig. 1, the low rank compression model in Fig. 2 [13], and also the DR2 network [15]. The compression ratio of the proposed model is calculated according to (9) under $(I', I) = (16, 8)$ and $N = 2$, and we set the compression ratio of [13] to be slightly larger than the proposed one. The DR2 [15], on the other hand, is a network without low rank structure and thus the compression ratio is not applicable. The results are shown in Table 3 and the imaging result of one recovered test image under MR = 0.25 is shown in Fig. 6. It is shown that the proposed hybrid model gives the better PSNR performance than the low rank model [13], indicating that by considering similarity information between blocks of the network, the compressed model can achieve a better recovery performance comparing with that not considering similarity information between blocks. Furthermore, according to Fig. 6, the image recovered by proposed approach has lighter ripple than the state-of-the-art ones, showing that it is able to capture more detail information than the other algorithms.

Table 3. Average PSNR(dB) and compression ratio performance for test images under different compressed sampling rate (MR).

	MR = 0.25	MR = 0.1	MR = 0.04	Compression ratio
Baseline model	30.37	26.32	15.90	100%
Proposed (16, 8)	32.47	30.45	19.37	11.92%
[13]	31.40	28.62	19.07	12.16%
DR2 [15]	27.45	22.44	11.07	\

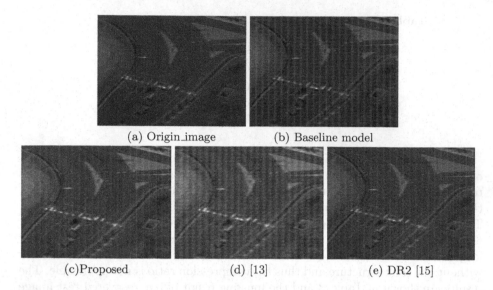

(a) Origin_image   (b) Baseline model

(c)Proposed   (d) [13]   (e) DR2 [15]

Fig. 6. The recovery result of one test image under MR = 0.25: (a) Origin_image; (b) Baseline model (29.83 dB); (c) Proposed (32.96 dB); (d) [13] (30.73 dB); (e) DR2 [15] (27.75 dB).

5   Conclusion

In this article, a hybrid low rank model for network compression is proposed. By employing the idea of parameter sharing between different blocks within one deep neural network, the similarity information is retrieved, and an efficient compression model is generated. Experiments show that the proposed network outperforms the state-of-the-art low rank compression model under a similar compression rate for the SAR image recovery application.

References

1. Karpathy, A., Toderici, G., Shetty, S., Leung, T., Sukthankar, R., Fei-Fei, L.: Large-scale video classification with convolutional neural networks. In: Proceedings of IEEE Conference on Computer Vision and Pattern Recognition (CVPR), pp. 1725–1732, Columbus, USA (2014)
2. Shin, H.K., Ahn, Y.H., Lee, S.H., Kim, H.Y.: Digital vision based concrete compressive strength evaluating model using deep convolutional neural network. Comput. Mater. Continua **61**(3), 911–928 (2019)
3. Oord, A.V.D., et al.: Wavenet: a generative model for raw audio (2016). arXiv preprint arXiv:1609.03499
4. Zhao, Y., et al.: Tibetan multi-dialect speech and dialect identity recognition. Comput. Mater. Continua **60**(3), 1223–1235 (2019)
5. Min, S., Lee, B., Yoon, S.: Deep learning in bioinformatics. Briefings Bioinform. **18**(5), 851–869 (2017)

6. Pastur-Romay, L.A., Cedron, F., Pazos, A., Porto-Pazos, A.B.: Deep artificial neural networks and neuromorphic chips for big data analysis: pharmaceutical and bioinformatics applications. Int. J. Mol. Sci. **17**(8), 1313 (2016)
7. He, K., Zhang, X., Ren, S., Sun, J.: Deep residual learning for image recognition. In: Proceedings of the IEEE conference on computer vision and pattern recognition, pp. 770–778 (2016)
8. Xianyu, W., Luo, C., Zhang, Q., Zhou, J., Yang, H., Li, Y.: Text detection and recognition for natural scene images using deep conVolutional neural networks. Comput. Materi. Continua **61**(1), 289–300 (2019)
9. Denton, E. L., Zaremba, W., Bruna, J., LeCun, Y., Fergus, R.: Exploiting linear structure within convolutional networks for efficient evaluation. In: Advances in neural information processing systems, pp. 1269–1277 (2014)
10. Lebedev, V., Ganin, Y., Rakhuba, M., Oseledets, I., Lempitsky, V.: Speeding-up convolutional neural networks using fine-tuned cp-decomposition (2014). arXiv preprint arXiv:1412.6553
11. Kim, Y.D., Park, E., Yoo, S., Choi, T., Yang, L., Shin, D.: Compression of deep convolutional neural networks for fast and low power mobile applications (2015). arXiv preprint arXiv:1511.06530
12. Garipov, T., Podoprikhin, D., Novikov, A., Vetrov, D.: Ultimate tensorization: compressing convolutional and fc layers alike (2016). arXiv preprint arXiv:1611.03214
13. Zhang, X., Zou, J., Ming, X., He, K., Sun, J.: Efficient and accurate approximations of nonlinear convolutional networks. In: Proceedings of the IEEE Conference on Computer Vision and pattern Recognition, pp. 1984–1992 (2015)
14. Kulkarni, K., Lohit, S., Turaga, P., Kerviche, R., Ashok, A.: Reconnet: non-iterative reconstruction of images from compressively sensed measurements. In: Proceedings of the IEEE Conference on Computer Vision and Pattern Recognition, pp. 449–458 (2016)
15. Yao, H., Dai, F., Zhang, S., Zhang, Y., Tian, Q., Xu, C.: Dr2-net: Deep residual reconstruction network for image compressive sensing. Neurocomputing **359**, 483–493 (2019)
16. Zhang, J., Ghanem, B.: ISTA-Net: interpretable optimization-inspired deep network for image compressive sensing. In: Proceedings of the IEEE Conference on Computer Vision and Pattern Recognition, pp. 1828–1837 (2018)
17. Zhang, F., Cai, N., Cen, G., Li, F., Wang, H., Chen, X.: Image super-resolution via a novel cascaded convolutional neural network framework. Sig. Process. Image Commun. **63**, 9–18 (2018)
18. Jain, P., Murty, S., Chakrabarti, S.: Joint matrix-tensor factorization for knowledge base inference (2017). arXiv preprint arXiv:1706.00637
19. Duarte, M.F., Davenport, M.A., Takhar, D., Laska, J.N., Sun, T., Kelly, K.F., Baraniuk, R.G.: Single-pixel imaging via compressive sampling. IEEE Sig. Process. Mag. **25**(2), 83–91 (2008)
20. Donoho, D.L.: Compressed sensing. IEEE Trans. Inf. Theory **52**(4), 1289–1306 (2006)
21. Sun, W., Chen, Y., Huang, L., So, H.C.: Tensor completion via generalized tensor tubal rank minimization using general unfolding. IEEE Sig. Process. Lett. **25**(6), 868–872 (2018)
22. Sun, W., Chen, Y., So, H.C.: Tensor completion using kronecker rank-1 tensor train with application to visual data inpainting. IEEE Access **6**, 47804–47814 (2018)

23. Dong, C., Loy, C.C., He, K., Tang, X.: Learning a deep convolutional network for image super-resolution. In: Fleet, D., Pajdla, T., Schiele, B., Tuytelaars, T. (eds.) ECCV 2014. LNCS, vol. 8692, pp. 184–199. Springer, Cham (2014). https://doi.org/10.1007/978-3-319-10593-2_13
24. Synthetic Aperture Randar (SAR) Imagery. MiniSAR imagery MiniSAR200 50519p0005image003. http://www.sandia.gov/radar/imagery/index.html
25. Brown, W.M., Porcello, L.J.: An introduction to synthetic-aperture radar. IEEE Spectr. 6(9), 52–62 (1969)

Research on Rail Traffic Safety Factor Model Based on Deep Learning

Ping Zhao[1], Lian-ying Sun[2(⊠)], Shuai Tu[1], Jin-Feng Wang[2], and Ying Wan[1]

[1] Smart City College, Beijing Union University, Beijing 100101, China
[2] College of Urban Rail Transit and Logistics, Beijing Union University, Beijing 100101, China
sunlychina@163.com

Abstract. With the development of urban construction, rail transit has become the main means of transportation for people's daily life. How to effectively improve the efficiency of urban rail transit operations and reduce the occurrence of accidents is very necessary to build a model of rail transit safety global factors. For the cases of rail transit accidents, the characteristics are recorded in the form of text. The CNN-LSTM method based on BERT embedding is used to classify the accident cases. The accuracy of the test set is 90.65%. Based on the deep learning method, the urban rail transit accident cases in the past 20 years were analyzed, and the safety graph of the dominant factors affecting the safe operation of rail transit was constructed. The results show that equipment and facilities factors, circuit signals, and connecting lines are the main factors affecting the safe operation of rail transit. Passengers, management and operators are indirect factors that cause train failure. The constructed safety graph provides a reference for urban rail transit operation management, making rail transit safety from passive emergency to fine prevention possible.

Keywords: Rail transit · Deep learning · Main control factor · Safety graph

1 Introduction

Urban track has developed extremely rapidly in recent years in China, and it is also an irreplaceable element in urban transportation networks. It has become the preferred means of transportation for people's daily life. It is synonymous with no traffic jams and punctuality. Rail transit has not only improved the traffic environment in various places, but also promoted the development of the country. People travel more conveniently and improve the quality of life of our people to a certain extent. By the end of 2018, 35 cities in China had opened 185 urban rail lines, with a total length of 5761.4 km. According to the 2018 statistical bulletin of the Ministry of Transport of China, the national passenger traffic reached 3,075 million in 2018. More and more people like to use rail transit, and safety is the primary task for people's demand for rail transit. However, rail traffic accidents occur frequently, which seriously affects the happiness of people traveling safely. Therefore, the research on the analysis of the leading factors of urban rail transit safety has certain significance. More and more researches have been made on railway

© Springer Nature Singapore Pte Ltd. 2020
X. Sun et al. (Eds.): ICAIS 2020, CCIS 1253, pp. 51–59, 2020.
https://doi.org/10.1007/978-981-15-8086-4_5

rail transit using deep learning methods [1–3]. Based on the case of rail transit accidents, this paper applies the deep learning method to the urban rail transit case analysis and constructs a knowledge graph based on the case analysis of urban rail transit accidents. The map provides reference for urban rail transit operations managers, which makes managers change from passive emergency to active prevention and do active prevention work, which can effectively reduce accident cases.

2 Related Work

The early factors affecting rail transit safety mainly formed some theoretical methods based on the accumulation of instance accidents. China has invested in corresponding security systems in most cities and is constantly researching and improving. In this respect, Chinese experts and scholars have also made outstanding contributions. Researchers have studied the impact on rail transit safety from separate subsystems (risk control, fire, communication systems, rail network, vehicle control) and accident cases. Shi et al. [4] used the calculation model to study the evacuation ability of the station, and simulated the characteristics of the evacuation behavior, evacuation time, and evacuation channel using the Agent model. It has certain research significance for the safe evacuation of urban rail transit design and operation stage. Kyriakidis et al. [5] combined rail transit accidents and related empirical research to control the frequency of rail transit accidents and reduce the unnecessary risk of accidents. Lu et al. [6] analyzed a security risk framework for social technology risk analysis based on social technology system theory, and integrated technical system risk, security practice and security prediction model into the subway system. Zhu Wenya et al. [7] obtained the four major types of accidents in rail transit operations through statistical analysis, and analyzed the specific cases to find the main causes of the accidents. Jiang Linlin [8] et al. used the explanatory structural model to study the direct, indirect and deep-level factors affecting the safety of the rail transit system. Zhang Mingrui [9] et al. proposed a rail transit operational safety evaluation system based on information classification, and studied the influencing factors of multi-level closed-loop management on rail transit safety. Wang Xu [10] proposed using fuzzy Bayesian networks to construct a risk assessment model to improve the safety management of urban rail transit operations.

3 Deep Learning Methods and Model Building

This paper collects the cases of rail transit accidents in the past 20 years at home and abroad, and uses the method of deep learning text analysis to obtain the leading factors and secondary factors affecting rail transit safety. The types of subway operation accidents are divided into: personnel factors; equipment and facilities factors such as trains and power supply equipment; environmental factors such as heavy snow, wind, rain and natural weather disasters; management factors; and other factors such as terrorist attacks.

3.1 Data Preparation

This article has consulted relevant degree dissertations, books, rail transit related news websites, and related academic reports. Cases of urban rail transit from 2001 to 2004 in several major cities in China such as Beijing, Shanghai, Shenzhen, Chongqing, and Tianjin, and related urban rail transit cases from 1963 to 2017 were collected. The data shown in the case section are shown in Tables 1 and 2 below:

Table 1. Foreign accident case (partial)

Time	Country	City	Cause of accident	Result
1971	Canada	Montreal	Circuit failure causes fire	One person died, 36 cars were destroyed
1973	France	Paris	Artificial arson	2 people died, the vehicle was destroyed
1975	UK	London	Train hitting the wall	30 dead
1976	Portugal	Lisbon	Train traction failed	2 people died, 4 cars were destroyed
1976	Canada	Toronto	Train was set on fire	4 cars were destroyed
1977	Russia	Moscow	Terrorist attacks	7 dead and more than 40 injured
1977	Russia	Moscow	Terrorist attacks	6 dead
1978	Germany	Cologne	Cigarette caused fire	Injured 8 people
1979	France	Paris	Short circuit caused fire	Injury 26 people, 1 car was destroyed

Since the processing method in this paper is deep learning, the prediction result of the training model relies heavily on text data and annotation data quality. Therefore, the data acquired needs to be normalized. Proofreading the text, especially the cause of the accident, manually labeling the causes of the rail transit accident according to the "Safety Evaluation Standard for Subway Operation" (GBT 50438-2007), and training set and test set for deep learning.

3.2 Classification Model Based on Deep Learning

Based on CNN [11], this paper proposes a short text classification method BERT-CNN-LSTM embedded in BERT [12] to analyze the influencing factors of urban rail transit accident cases. The overall flow chart is shown in Fig. 1.

First, the first layer of the structure is the process of feature extraction. The process extracts text features using the pre-training language model BERT. As shown in Fig. 2, the text features are extracted through a 12-layer attention mechanism. BERT is based on the fusion of left and right contexts of all layers to pre-train deep two-way representation. Compared with the previous pre-training model, it captures the true context information and can learn the relationship between consecutive text fragments. For each sentence sequence $X = (x_1, x_2, \ldots, x_n)$, it captures the relationship between words and sentences levels, effectively extracting features from the text. Since the data is single text, set the maximum length of the sentence sequence to 20.

Table 2. Domestic urban rail accident case (partial)

Time	City	Reason	Result
2014	Guangzhou	Man spraying irritating gas	Causing an accident
2012	Guangzhou	Turnout failure	Train delay for nearly one hour
2012	Guangzhou	Train failure	Train delay 15 min
2012	Guangzhou	Turnout failure	No
2012	Guangzhou	Door failure	Train delay is about 250 s
2012	Guangzhou	Elevator failure	More than 200 people were stranded
2011	Beijing	Escalator failure	1 person died, 29 people injured
2011	Shanghai	Signal failure	271 injured
2011	Shanghai	Door failure	Line 2 is out of service for one day
2011	Beijing	Water in the tunnel	Bajiao amusement park to the ancient city section is out of service
2011	Beijing	The cable is shorted by rainwater	Section outage
2011	Beijing	Escalator failure	One person died and more than 20 people were injured
2011	Beijing	Cable bare	Out of the outer ring direction for 90 min
2011	Beijing	Train failure	Multi-stop outage for half an hour

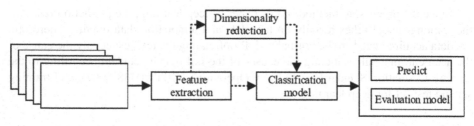

Fig. 1. System flow chart

2) The classification model of the influencing factors is as shown in Fig. 3. The local feature information of the convolutional layer capture semantics is added to the feature feature vector obtained in the first part. The model structure includes a convolutional layer, a pooling layer, an LSTM layer, and the like. The convolution operation of the sentence sequence is as follows (1):

$$Con = f(wx + b) \tag{1}$$

Where w is the convolution kernel, x is the text vector embedded by the BERT, b is the offset term, and function f is the commonly used activation function.

After convolution of the first layer of the model, $Con = [con_1, con_2, \ldots, con_{n-s+1}]$ is obtained, s represents the size of the convolution kernel. In order to reduce the data

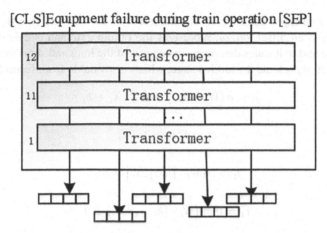

Fig. 2. Feature extraction process based on BERT embedding

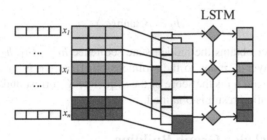

Fig. 3. Classification model

processing capacity of the next layer, the maximum pooling layer is introduced to further extract more abstract information, and the data acquired by the upper layer is maximized by the pooling layer, as shown in the following formula (2):

$$Con_{max} = max\,(con_i) \tag{2}$$

Serialize Con_{max} with a fully connected layer to get the following Z:

$$Z = \{Z_1, Z_2, \ldots, Z_n\} \tag{3}$$

The next layer is the LSTM layer. LSTM [11] was proposed in 1997 and is the most popular recurrent neural network. It is not only sensitive to short-term input, but also preserves long-term state. It mainly controls the input and output of the unit by three switches: forgetting door, input door and output door.

The current time unit state c_t is as follows (5). c_{t-1} indicates the previous unit state. f_t is the forgetting gate. The symbol $°$ indicates multiplication by element. $\widetilde{c}_t$ Indicates the current input unit status. The calculation formula is as shown in (7):

f_t is calculated by the formula as (4), W_{fh} corresponds to the input term h_{t-1}, W_{fx} corresponds to the input term X_t. W_{fh} and W_{fx} constitute the weight matrix m of the forgetting gate W_f, b_f is the offset top, and σ is the activation function.

i_t: denotes an input gate, which is calculated by the formula (6), W_i is a weight matrix, and b_i is an offset top. o_t: represents the output gate and is calculated by (8). The input gate and unit states determine the output of the long and short memory neural network, and h_t represents the hidden state, which is available from formula 9.

$$f_t = \sigma \left(W_{fh} \cdot h_{t-1} + W_{fx} \cdot X_t + b_f \right) \tag{4}$$

$$c_t = f_t^\circ c_{t-1} + i_t^\circ \tilde{c}_t \tag{5}$$

$$i_t = \sigma \left(W_i \cdot \left[h_{t-1}, x_t \right] + b_i \right) \tag{6}$$

$$\tilde{c}_t = \tanh \left(W_c \cdot \left[h_{t-1}, x_t \right] + b_c \right) \tag{7}$$

$$o_t = \sigma \left(W_o \cdot \left[h_{t-1}, x_t \right] + b_c \right) \tag{8}$$

$$h_t = o_t^\circ \tanh(c_t) \tag{9}$$

The LSTM layer obtains the hidden state sequence $h_t = (h_1, h_2, h_3, \ldots, h_n)$, and the linear output layer h_t maps to the s dimension. $L = (l_1, l_2, l_3, \ldots, l_n) \in \mathbb{R}^{n \times s}$, $l_i \in \mathbb{R}^s$, each dimension $l_{i,j}$ is the score of the sequence X corresponds to category label y_j, and the classification result is obtained.

4 Safety Knowledge Graph Building

The classification model is used for the data in 3.1. Since the data volume of urban rail transit accidents at home and abroad has been limited in the past 20 years, this paper uses ten-fold datasets to perform 10-fold cross-validation and then averages them. During training, 10% of the data is randomly selected from the data set each time as a test set. In the performance of each performance indicator, the data set is divided into 10 data sets, and the final performance results are averaged. The results of the ten-fold cross-validation experiment are shown in Table 3 below, and the results of each category verification are shown in Table 4 below. The ten experimental results of the ten-fold division of Table 3 are averaged. The accuracy rate of the classification model for urban rail transit test set is 90.65%.

Category 1 in the table: human factors; category 2: facility equipment factors; category 3: weather factors; category 4: safety management; category 5: other types such as terrorist attacks. Analysis of the results of each category verification shows that the text is more efficient in identifying categories 1 and 2. The recognition efficiency of category 5 is relatively low. Observing the classification results, it can be seen that there is a data imbalance problem in the category 5 accident case, and the abstract features of the text cannot be extracted.

The relationship between each entity is extracted by classification for each influencing factor. The Chinese text similarity embedded in the BERT language model is used to determine the weight relationship between the entities. The knowledge map based on

Table 3. Tenfold cross validation results

n_split	Accuracy	n_split	Accuracy
1	93.20%	6	85.50%
2	97.10%	7	91.30%
3	89.85%	8	94.20%
4	91.60%	9	79.71%
5	91.30%	10	92.75%

Table 4. Verification results for each category

Category	Accuracy
1	97.22%
2	95.90%
3	66.67%
4	70.83%
5	56.16%

the urban rail transit accident case analysis shown in Fig. 4 is constructed. The size of the node label indicates the frequency of occurrence of this type of accident. The color of the node label indicates the influencing factors of different categories of accidents. The thickness of the connecting line between the nodes reflects the influence relationship between the nodes.

It can be seen from Fig. 4 that the dominant factors of urban rail transit accidents are equipment failure and train failure, and the secondary influencing factors are circuit failures. The main factors related to equipment failure are signal failure, power failure, power failure, and information system failure. Therefore, accident cases caused by equipment failures and the like must be regularly checked for signal systems, power supply systems, etc., to reduce the occurrence of such accidents. Factors related to fires caused by circuit failures include connection line fire, fan short circuit, cable immersion in rainwater, failure to touch the power grid, staff error, etc., and trains fail to catch fire, including passenger arson, thus preventing rail traffic fire accidents. The case must strengthen the regular maintenance of the relevant circuits and the strict inspection of the passengers carrying the items. The smallest nodes in the figure are such factors as ambient weather and passenger diving, passenger jumps, extremities, etc., indicating that such factors have less frequent occurrences of accidents throughout the map, but have a certain relationship with train failures. Explain that while improving the maintenance and maintenance of equipment and trains, it is necessary to strengthen the safety awareness of passengers and staff and enhance social public safety education.

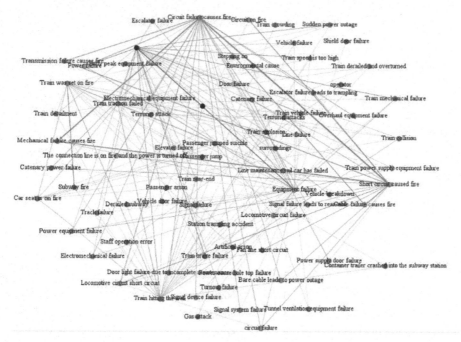

Fig. 4. Knowledge graph of urban rail transit influencing factors

5   Conclusion

Through the deep learning method, the paper analyzes the cases of rail transit accidents in the past 20 years at home and abroad, and builds a safety knowledge map based on the influencing factors affecting the safe operation of urban rail transit. It can be known from the knowledge map that the train equipment factor is the most direct factor affecting the safety of urban rail transit operations. The main factors affecting the train facilities and equipment are train fault equipment faults, signal faults and indirect factors caused by passengers. Circuit faults cause subway fires. The most important factor, and circuit failures are mainly due to circuit facilities, cables, electromechanical circuits, rain and weather, and operator influence. Therefore, it is necessary not only to improve the regular equipment maintenance and circuit maintenance during the train operation, but also to raise the awareness of safety hazards of passengers and operators, to include them in relevant laws and regulations, to ensure public safety, and to do a good job in the prevention of bad weather. The conclusion of this paper provides a reference for urban rail transit operation managers, which can effectively reduce the occurrence of accident cases. With the increase of data volume, the model is continuously optimized, and the traffic safety global factors will be more refined.

References

1. Sun, W., Hongji, D., Nie, S., He, X.: Traffic sign recognition method integrating multi-layer features and kernel extreme learning machine classifier. Comput. Mater. Continua **60**(1), 147–161 (2019)
2. Wu, H., Liu, Q., Liu, X.: A review on deep learning approaches to image classification and object segmentation. Comput. Mater. Continua **60**(2), 575–597 (2019)
3. Wang, Y.: YATA: yet another proposal for traffic analysis and anomaly detection. Comput. Mater. Continua **60**(3), 1171–1187 (2019)
4. Shi, C., Zhong, M., Nong, X., et al.: Modeling and safety strategy of passenger evacuation in a metro station in China. Saf. Sci. **50**(5), 1319–1332 (2012)
5. Kyriakidis, M., Hirsch, R., Majumdar, A.: Metro railway safety: an analysis of accident precursors. Saf. Sci. **50**(7), 1535–1548 (2012)
6. Lu, Y., Li, Q., Song, L.: Safety risk analysis on subway operation based on socio-technical systems. In: 2012 International Conference on Quality, Reliability, Risk, Maintenance, and Safety Engineering, 180–184. IEEE (2012)
7. Zhu, W., Wang, H., Tong, Y., et al.: Analysis and solution of urban rail transit disaster. Build. Saf. **08**, 72–77 (2019)
8. Jiang, L.: Safety evaluation and design of urban rail transit operation based on BP neural network. Dalian Jiaotong University (2014)
9. Zhang Mingrui, M., Yu, M., Pu, Q.: Research on urban rail transit operation safety evaluation system. Urban Rail Transit. Res. **21**(11), 1–4 (2018)
10. Wang, X.: Research on security risk assessment of urban rail transit operation based on fuzzy bayesian network. East China Jiaotong Universit (2018)
11. Zhang, Y., Zheng, J., Jiang, Y., et al.: A text sentiment classification modeling method based on coordinated CNN-LSTM-attention model. Chin. J. Electron. **28**(1), 120–126 (2019)
12. Devlin, J., Chang, M.-W., Lee, K., Toutanova, K.: BERT: pre-training of deep bidirectional transformers for language understanding. ArXiv e-prints (2018)

Research on Pseudo Code Ranging Technology Using Burst DSSS Signal

Jianzhong Qi[1,2(✉)] and Qingping Song[3]

[1] School of Information Science and Technology, North China University of Technology, Beijing 100144, People's Republic of China
qijianzhong2002@aliyun.com
[2] School of Computer and Communication Engineering, University of Science and Technology Beijing, Beijing 100083, People's Republic of China
[3] Science and Technology on Information Systems Engineering Laboratory, Beijing Institute of Control and Electronic Technology, Beijing 100038, People's Republic of China

Abstract. In this paper, a method of ranging high-speed aircraft by using the burst DSSS communication pulse is analyzed. In this algorithm, noncoherent PN code is used for ranging and coherent forwarding is used for carrier. In order to eliminate the error caused by the rapid movement of the aircraft, the relative velocity between the objects is measured and the ranging error is corrected. How to estimate the carrier frequency and pseudo code phase in the burst short pulse spread spectrum communication is discussed. Firstly, PMF + FFT is used to capture the signal and estimate the initial value of carrier frequency and pseudo code phase, then LM algorithm is used to solve the maximum likelihood function, so as to obtain the accurate value of carrier frequency and pseudo code delay.

Keywords: Spread spectrum communication · Pseudo code phase estimation · Carrier frequency estimation · Pseudo code ranging

1 Introduction

Ranging is the basic requirement of aircraft navigation and formation networking. The commonly used means are satellite navigation, laser ranging, radio ranging, etc. Satellite navigation is easy to be interfered, and it can not be used in high orbit satellite formation [1]. Radio ranging methods include voice measurement ranging, pseudo code ranging and so on. Radio ranging is generally used to measure the transmission delay of the radio wave reaching the target. Pseudo code ranging determines the transmission delay by estimating the phase of pseudo code. It has the advantages of high measurement accuracy, large measurement distance without fuzzy and simple system design. It has been widely used in aircraft ranging and deep space ranging.

It is an important research direction to realize the combination of communication and ranging and avoid using special ranging equipment by using wireless communication link ranging [10, 11]. In this paper, the method of short pulse ranging in DSSS communication is studied, which can realize the communication and ranging function

X. Sun et al. (Eds.): ICAIS 2020, CCIS 1253, pp. 60–68, 2020.
https://doi.org/10.1007/978-981-15-8086-4_6

in DSSS communication, and this algorithm can also be used in the ranging of DSSS communication. The algorithm proposed in this paper fully considers the communication situation of high-speed moving carrier, which can be used in the communication ranging between satellites, missiles, aircraft and other high dynamic carriers, and also can be used in the ranging between aircraft and ground stations.

From the point of view of engineering application, this paper discusses the working principle and ranging accuracy of DSSS short pulse ranging, which has certain guiding significance for practical application.

2 Mathematical Model of Pseudo Code Ranging in Response Communication

2.1 Response-Type Incoherent Pseudo-noise Code Ranging Method

The principle of response PN code ranging can be summarized as follows: one terminal A generates local pseudorandom code sequence, modulates data information and carrier, transmits it through antenna, the other terminal B receives the signal, processes the signal and forwards it to terminal A, and terminal A measures the phase delay of the PN code transmitted and received to know the distance.

According to the coherence of the PN code clock transmitted between terminals, it can be divided into coherent PN code ranging and incoherent PN code ranging. The two-way communication link of incoherent PN code ranging can adopt different PN code and rate, and the two-way spread spectrum PN code can be generated independently without coherence. Incoherent PN code ranging has great flexibility and adapts to a wider range of applications. This paper studies the ranging method of incoherent PN code.

The two-way communication link has transmission delay, and the relative distance between high-speed aircrafts will change in the process of two-way communication. Therefore, it is necessary to calculate the relative speed to modify the ranging results, so as to get accurate ranging results. In order to calculate the relative velocity, we need to estimate the carrier Doppler frequency. In this paper, we study the method that the receiver and the transmitter transmit the carrier in proportion to each other, so as to calculate the carrier Doppler frequency shift and estimate the relative velocity [9]. The response-type pseudo-noise code ranging process herein is as follows:

Step 1: communication terminal A transmits downlink DSSS signal at time t_1 (time of frame header of downlink signal);

Step 2: When the communication terminal B receives the synchronous signal of the downlink signal, it starts to transmit the uplink spread spectrum signal at t_0, and the navigation message of the uplink signal includes the delay τ of the forwarding circuit of the communication terminal B, the uplink transmission moment t_0, and the the pseudo-noise code phase Φ_1 from the downlink frame header at t_0, etc.;

Step 3: The communication terminal A receives the uplink signal of each transponder, captures the pseudo code, estimates the pseudo code phase and demodulates the navigation message;

Step 4: At the next sampling time t_2 of communication terminal A, estimate the distance between t_2 time and uplink frame header pseudo code phase Φ_2;

Step 5: According to t_2 time distance uplink frame header pseudo code phase Φ_2, communication terminal circuit delay τ, uplink transmission time distance downlink frame header pseudo code phase Φ_1, calculate the radio wave transmission time to get the distance.

Set the distance between the communication terminal A and the communication terminal B at t_1 as L_1, the distance between the communication terminal A and the communication terminal B at t_2 as L_2, and the distance between the communication terminal A at t_2 from that at t_1 is L_3. Figure 1 of the relationship between the positions is as follows:

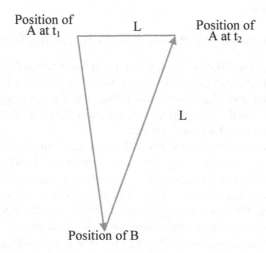

Fig. 1. Diagram of the relative position between terminal A and terminal B

Next is the analysis of the principle of response-type incoherent pseudo-noise code ranging. If the clock correction between the terminal A and terminal B is Δt, the channel delay is τ and the pseudo-noise code rate is Rc, then the transmission moment of the terminal A corresponding to the signal received by the terminal B at t0 is t1 − Φ1. The moment for the signal received by the terminal A at t2 to leave the terminal B is t0 − Φ2. The following equations can be presented:

$$L_1 = (t_0 - (t_1 - \phi_1) - \Delta t - \tau) \times c$$
$$L_2 = (t_2 - (t_0 - \phi_2) + \Delta t - \tau) \times c \tag{1}$$

Obtain:

$$L_1 + L_2 = (t_2 - t_1 + \phi_1 + \phi_2 - \tau_\Sigma) \times c \tag{2}$$

The communication mode of short pulse response is used. Owing to the shorter time, the velocity of the terminal will not change during the response communication, and the radial velocity Vr between the terminal A and the terminal B can be calculated by Doppler frequency. The following equations can be presented:

$$L_1 - L_2 = (t_2 - t_1 + \phi_1 + \phi_2 - \tau_\Sigma) \times V_r \tag{3}$$

Obtain:

$$L_1 = \frac{1}{2}(c + V_r)(t_2 - t_1 + \varphi_1 + \varphi_2 - \tau_\Sigma) \tag{4}$$

2.2 Estimation of Radial Velocity

As shown in the above Eq. (3), in order to obtain the distance L1 between the terminal A and the terminal B, it is necessary to calculate the radial velocity Vr between the terminal A and the terminal B. This system realizes the estimation of the Doppler frequency of communication carrier wave by the communication terminal using the method of carrier wave coherent transponding, and accordingly the radial velocity between the terminal A and the terminal B can be estimated [8]. If the carrier frequency of downlink signal of the terminal A is f_{DOWN}, the carrier Doppler shift of downlink signal is $f_{dopplor}$, the carrier frequency of uplink signal of the terminal B is f_U, and the ratio of uplink carrier frequency to downlink carrier frequency of the terminal B is set as S, then the functional block diagram of the responder is as shown in Fig. 2 below:

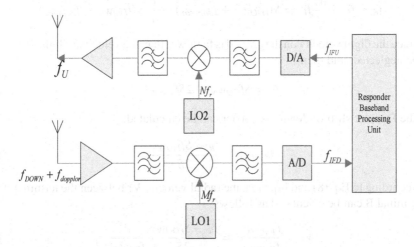

Fig. 2. Block diagram for frequency conversion of terminal responder

The carrier frequency of downlink signal received by the terminal B shall be f_{DOWN} + $f_{dopplor}$, If the responder received radio frequency is converted into intermediate frequency under the channel as f_{IFD}, and then

$$f_{IFD} = f_{DOWN} + f_{dopplor} - Mf_r \tag{5}$$

The value of the intermediate frequency f_{IFD} is accurately estimated in the baseband processing unit of the responder, and the intermediate frequency f_{IFU} of uplink carrier is S times of f_{IFD}, namely coherent transponding.

$$f_{IFU} = Sf_{IFD} = S(f_{DOWN} + f_{dopplor} - Mf_r) \tag{6}$$

Selecting the appropriate local oscillate frequency of reception and transmission frequency channels, making $-SMf_r + Nf_r = 0$, The carrier frequency of the terminal B transmitted uplink signal shall be f_U, as shown in the equation below:

$$f_U = S(f_{DOWN} + f_{dopplor}) \tag{7}$$

It can be seen from the above equation that the responder selects the appropriate local oscillation frequency and performs coherent transponding for the intermediate frequency, and the uplink frequency of the responder will be S times of the reception frequency and unrelated to the local reference oscillator.

According to the formula of Doppler frequency

$$f_{doppler} = \frac{v}{c} f_{DOWN} \tag{8}$$

The communication mode of short pulse response is used. Owing to the shorter time, the velocity of the terminal will not change during the response communication, and the carrier frequency of uplink signal received by the terminal A from the terminal B is:

$$f_R = f_U + \frac{v_r}{c} f_U = S(f_{DOWN} + f_{dopplor}) + \frac{v_r}{c} S(f_{DOWN} + f_{dopplor}) \tag{9}$$

Since the flight velocity on the ground is far lower than the velocity of light, $\frac{v_r}{c} S f_{dopplor}$ can be neglected, and then

$$f_R \approx S f_{DOWN} + 2S f_{dopplor} \tag{10}$$

The Doppler shift of downlink carrier can be calculated.

$$f_{doppler} \approx \frac{f_R - S f_{DOWN}}{2S} \tag{11}$$

According to Eq. (8) and Eq. (11), the radial velocity Vr between the terminal A and the terminal B can be calculated as follows:

$$V_r = \frac{f_{doppler}}{f_{DOWN}} c = \frac{f_R - S f_{DOWN}}{2S} \frac{c}{f_{DOWN}} \tag{12}$$

According to Eq. (12), if the terminal A accurately estimates the frequency of the received uplink signal, the radial velocity between the terminal A and the terminal B can be calculated.

2.3 Estimation of Pseudo-noise Code Phase and Carrier Frequency

As mentioned above, in order to perform ranging calculations, the terminal B shall accurately estimate the carrier frequency and pseudo-noise code phase of the downlink signal, and the terminal A shall also accurately estimate the carrier frequency and pseudo-noise code phase of the uplink signal. Pseudo-noise code phase and carrier frequency can be estimated by coarse estimation and fine estimation in succession. The coarse estimation for the signal pseudo-noise code phase and carrier frequency of DSSS-modulated signal means that the estimated precision of pseudo-noise code phase is less than that of half pseudo-noise code chip, the accuracy of carrier Doppler is 2/Tc, and this process is usually called as signal capturing in spread spectrum communication [2–4].

■ Method of coarse estimation for pseudo-noise code phase and carrier frequency
Common algorithms of pseudo-noise code and carrier capture include sliding correlation method, FFT-IFFT method and partial matched filtering (PMF) + FFT algorithm. Wherein, the PMF + FFT capture algorithm can achieve the capture of pseudo-noise code phase and carrier frequency in a pseudo-noise code cycle, without carrier sweep frequency searching. Therefore, the PMF + FFT capture algorithm is the fastest among the three capture algorithms discussed above, and thus the PMF + FFT capture algorithm is selected for this topic [6, 12].

The partial matched filtering (PMF) method divides a complete sequence of longer period into several smaller sequences to obtain the results of each partially matched filter by segmented matching. The principle structure of PMF + FFT capture method is as shown in Fig. 3. The part in the dotted circle is a partially matched filter (PMF), each PMF outputs a partially coherent accumulation and an FFT operation module for N points at each moment of sliding, the FFT is used to perform spectrum analysis for partial results of matched filtering at each moment, and the capture results are judged based on the frequency spectrum. As long as the input signal contains the same spread spectrum code sequence as the local one, there is always a moment when the two signals are aligned in the code phase during the matching, however, the correlation peak value may not be detected due to the carrier deviation. When the input sequence is aligned with the local sequence, the pseudo-noise code has been relatively offset, and only the carrier deviation is left in the ideal case, and then the fast Fourier transform (FFT) can be used to analyze the frequency component of the carrier deviation.

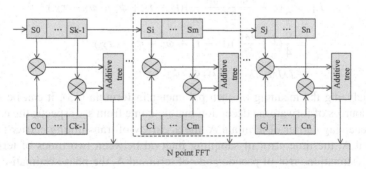

Fig. 3. Diagram for principle structure of PMF + FFT capture method

After the process of spread spectrum capture, the pseudo-noise code phase, carrier frequency difference and navigation message of the received signal can be preliminarily obtained. However, the pseudo-noise code ranging requires an accurate pseudo-noise code phase, because the ranging accuracy is in direct proportion to the estimation accuracy of code phase. This paper discusses a fast and accurate estimation algorithm for pseudo-noise code phase and carrier frequency in the case of short-pulse communication below.

■ Fine estimation of pseudo-noise code phase and carrier frequency

Since the system uses short-pulse communication, fast and accurate estimation is required for the pseudo random sequence code phase. The fine estimation of pseudo-noise code phase and carrier frequency determines the ranging accuracy. For continuous spread spectrum signals, such as GNSS signal and DSSS signal with longer communication pulse duration, the carrier is usually tracked by PLL + FLL, and pseudo-noise code is tracked by DLL loop, so as to achieve the fine estimation of carrier frequency and pseudo-noise code phase. Since the tracking loop requires a certain locking time, it is not suitable for the burst short-pulse communication mode.

In this paper, the latest maximum likelihood joint estimation (MLE) algorithm is used to calculate the carrier Doppler shift and the exact pseudo-noise code phase. Upon completion of signal capture and the rough estimation of carrier and pseudo-noise code phases, the start and end moments for signals in a pseudo-noise code period can be preliminarily determined. The baseband processing unit stores the sample signal in a pseudo-noise code period to construct a Maximum Likelihood Estimation (MLE) value function. For the constructed MLE function, the optimal solutions to the pseudo-noise code phase and carrier frequency can be calculated by the optimization algorithm. The Levenberg-Marquart algorithm is one of the most efficient calculation methods for MLD, and the Levenberg-Marquart algorithm can be used for solution [5, 7].

3 Error Analysis of Ranging

Next, the algorithm is used for ranging, and the source and size of ranging error are analyzed. Substituting Eq. (12) into Eq. (4), the final ranging results are as follows:

$$
\begin{aligned}
L_1 &= \frac{1}{2}(c + \frac{f_{AR} - Sf_A}{2S} \frac{c}{f_A})(t_2 - t_1 + \phi_1 + \phi_2 - \tau_\Sigma) \\
&= \frac{c}{4}(1 + \frac{f_{AR}}{Sf_A})(t_2 - t_1 + \phi_1 + \phi_2 - \tau_\Sigma) \\
&= f(f_{AR}, f_A, t_2 - t_1, \phi_1, \phi_2, \tau_\Sigma)
\end{aligned}
\tag{13}
$$

By analyzing the meaning of each parameter in formula (13), it can be seen that the error sources of forwarding deception mainly come from six aspects: the estimation error of receiving carrier of terminal A, the accuracy of transmitting carrier frequency of terminal A, the time error of sampling interval between two times of terminal A, the phase estimation error of pseudo code of terminal A, the phase estimation error of pseudo code of terminal B, and the delay error of circuit.

The accuracy of transmitting carrier frequency of terminal A can reach 10^{-7} with constant temperature crystal frequency;

The sampling interval time error of terminal a can reach 10^{-7} by using constant temperature crystal frequency;

The circuit time delay can be obtained by ground calibration. The circuit time delay will change slightly with temperature and time. The time delay should be less than 10 ns in the military temperature range and product life;

The phase estimation error of terminal a PN code is mainly affected by the SNR of the received signal;

The phase estimation error of PN code in terminal B is mainly affected by the SNR of received signal in terminal B;

The estimation error of terminal a receiving carrier is relatively complex. From the above, as the carrier frequency of the system is coherent forwarding and terminal B carries out S-TIMES coherent forwarding on the received carrier, the estimation error of terminal B on the received carrier will affect the accuracy of terminal a receiving carrier, and the estimation error of terminal a receiving carrier shall be S-TIMES that of terminal B carrier and itself Sum of carrier estimation errors.

$$df_{AR} = Sf_{\varepsilon B} + f_{\varepsilon A} \tag{14}$$

Where, is the estimation error of terminal B, is the estimation error of terminal a, and is the total estimation error of terminal a for the received carrier.

According to the above Eq. (14), the ranging error can be expressed as:

$$dL_1 = \frac{\partial f}{\partial f_{AR}} df_{AR} + \frac{\partial f}{\partial f_A} df_A + \frac{\partial f}{\partial (t_2 - t_1)} d(t_2 - t_1)$$

$$+ \frac{\partial f}{\partial \varphi_1} d\phi_1 + \frac{\partial f}{\partial \varphi_2} d\phi_2 + \frac{\partial f}{\partial \tau_\Sigma} d\tau_\Sigma \tag{15}$$

In order to analyze the influence of each error term on ranging, the partial derivative of Eq. (13) is calculated for each observation value component, link delay error, sampling interval time and other parameters respectively, including:

$$\begin{cases} \frac{\partial f}{\partial f_{AR}} = \frac{c}{4Sf_A}(t_2 - t_1 + \phi_1 + \phi_2 - \tau_\Sigma) \\ \frac{\partial f}{\partial f_A} = \frac{cf_{AR}}{4Sf_A^2}(t_2 - t_1 + \phi_1 + \phi_2 - \tau_\Sigma) \\ \frac{\partial f}{\partial (t_2 - t_1)} = \frac{c}{4}(1 + \frac{f_{AR}}{Sf_A}) \\ \frac{\partial f}{\partial \phi_1} = \frac{c}{4}(1 + \frac{f_{AR}}{Sf_A}) \\ \frac{\partial f}{\partial \phi_2} = \frac{c}{4}(1 + \frac{f_{AR}}{Sf_A}) \\ \frac{\partial f}{\partial \tau_{\Sigma 1}} = -\frac{c}{4}(1 + \frac{f_{AR}}{Sf_A}) \end{cases} \tag{16}$$

By substituting Eq. (16) into Eq. (15), the total ranging error formula is

$$dL1 = \frac{c}{4Sf_A}(t_2 - t_1 + \phi_1 + \phi_2 - \tau_\Sigma) df_{AR}$$

$$+ \frac{cf_{AR}}{4Sf_A^2}(t_2 - t_1 + \phi_1 + \phi_2 - \tau_\Sigma) df_A$$

$$+ \frac{c}{4}(1 + \frac{f_{AR}}{Sf_A}) d(t2 - t1) + \frac{c}{4}(1 + \frac{f_{AR}}{Sf_A}) d\phi_1$$

$$+ \frac{c}{4}(1 + \frac{f_{AR}}{Sf_A}) d\phi_2 - \frac{c}{4}(1 + \frac{f_{AR}}{Sf_A}) d\tau_\Sigma \tag{17}$$

4 Conclusion

In this paper, we discuss the technology of ranging by using the burst DSSS communication pulse. We propose a method of fast pseudo code phase and carrier frequency estimation, as well as the method of solving the relative speed. The error sources of using this method are analyzed, and the influence of each kind of error is calculated. The ranging method discussed in this paper can be realized by communication link and applied to the ranging between high-speed aircrafts.

References

1. Parkinson, B.W., Spilker, J.J.: Global ositioning system: theory and applications, vol. I. American Institute of Aeronautics and Astronautics, Reston (1996)
2. Lin, Y., Zhu, Y.B.: A FLL-PLL cooperative GNSS weak signal tracking framework. Appl. Mech. Mater. 470–477 (2014). https://doi.org/10.4028/www.scientific.net/AMM.551.470
3. Liu, Y., Zhang, J., Zhu, Y.: Weak satellite signal tracking loop based on traditional tracking framework. Wirel. Pers. Commun, 1761–1775 (2013). https://doi.org/10.1007/s11277-012-0779-z
4. Ma, W.Z., Wang, Z., Li, Y.R., Zhang, W.: Research on code tracking loop algorithm of GPS. Appl. Mech. Mater. **229–231**, 1556–1559 (2012)
5. Rezeanu, S.-C., Ziemer, R.E., Wickert, M.A.: Joint maximum-likelihood parameter estimation for burst DS spread-spectrum transmission. IEEE Trans. Commun. 45(2), 227–238 (1997). https://doi.org/10.1109/26.554371
6. Qi, J., Luo, F., Song, Q.: Fast acquisition method of navigation receiver based on folded PMF-FFT. In: 2014 IEEE Computers, Communications and IT Applications Conference, ComComAp (2014). https://doi.org/10.1109/comcomap.2014.7017171
7. Won, J.H., Pany, T., Eissfeller, B.: Iterative maximum likelihood estimators for high-dynamic GNSS signal tracking. IEEE Trans. Aerosp. Electron. Syst. 48(4), 2875–2893 (2012). https://doi.org/10.1109/taes.2012.6324667
8. Wang, Y., Zhang, X., Zhang, Y.: Joint spectrum partition and performance analysis of full-duplex D2D communications in multi-tier wireless networks. Comput. Mater. Continua 61(1), 171–184 (2019)
9. Bing, H., Xiang, F., Fan, W., Liu, J., Sun, Z., Sun, Z.: Research on time synchronization method under arbitrary network delay in wireless sensor networks. Comput. Mater. Continua 61(3), 1323–1344 (2019)
10. Liu, W., Luo, X., Liu, Y., Liu, J., Liu, M., Shi, Y.Q.: Localization algorithm of indoor wi-fi access points based on signal strength relative relationship and region division. Comput. Mater. Continua 55(1), 071–093 (2018)
11. Hui, H., Zhou, C., Shenggang, X., Lin, F.: A novel secure data transmission scheme in industrial internet of things. China Commun. 17(1), 73–88 (2020)
12. Gong, C., Lin, F., Gong, X., Yueming, L.: Intelligent cooperative edge computing in the internet of things. IEEE Internet Things J. (2020). https://doi.org/10.1109/JIOT.2020.2986015

A Study on PN Code Phase and Carrier Frequency Fast Estimation Technology for DSSS Signal

Jianzhong Qi[1,2(✉)] and Qingping Song[3]

[1] School of Information Science and Technology, North China University of Technology, Beijing 100144, People's Republic of China
qijianzhong2002@aliyun.com
[2] School of Computer and Communication Engineering, University of Science and Technology Beijing, Beijing 100083, People's Republic of China
[3] Science and Technology on Information Systems Engineering Laboratory, Beijing Institute of Control and Electronic Technology, Beijing 100038, People's Republic of China

Abstract. This paper mainly discusses the method of fast and accurate estimation of carrier frequency and pseudo code phase for burst short pulse DSSS communication signal. In this algorithm, PMF + FFT is used to acquisition the signal and estimate the coarse value of carrier frequency and pseudo code phase. Then LM algorithm is used to solve the maximum likelihood function of the signal, so as to obtain the accurate estimation of carrier Doppler frequency and pseudo code delay. Using this algorithm, the carrier frequency and pseudo code phase can be estimated accurately in a pseudo code period.

Keywords: Spread spectrum communication · Pseudo code phase estimation · Carrier frequency estimation · Pseudo code ranging

1 Introduction

In satellite navigation and other pseudo code ranging systems, it is necessary to accurately estimate the pseudo code phase and carrier frequency of DSSS signals [1, 2]. In the continuous communication system, such as GPS or Beidou satellite navigation system, the carrier frequency is estimated by PLL loop, and the pseudo code phase is estimated by pseudo code feedback tracking DLL loop. The algorithm and circuit are simple and reliable, but the feedback tracking loop needs a certain locking time and a certain dynamic range. Therefore, the frequency and pseudo code phase estimation method based on carrier tracking loop and pseudo code tracking loop is not suitable for the signal estimation of burst short pulse communication system or the fast signal estimation of high-speed and high acceleration mobile carrier [3–5].

In this paper, an algorithm for accurate estimation of PN code phase and carrier is discussed. It can complete the accurate estimation of PN code phase and carrier in one PN code period, and is suitable for the reception and estimation of burst short pulse

© Springer Nature Singapore Pte Ltd. 2020
X. Sun et al. (Eds.): ICAIS 2020, CCIS 1253, pp. 69–76, 2020.
https://doi.org/10.1007/978-981-15-8086-4_7

spread spectrum signal. This algorithm does not use the feedback tracking method to estimate the pseudo code and carrier, but uses the PMF + FFT acquisition algorithm to realize the rough estimation of the signal, then constructs the maximum likelihood function and uses the optimization method to solve the precise pseudo code phase and carrier frequency of the signal [17–19].

2 Principle of Fast PN Code Phase and Carrier Frequency Coarse Estimation

2.1 Mathematical Model of DSSS Signal

In this paper, m sequence, gold sequence or M sequence are used for the pseudo-random sequence of DSSS signal. The period of pseudo code is less than or equal to the length of a data symbol. BPSK modulation is used for the signal. The output DSSS signal of transmitter can be expressed as follows [6]:

$$s_T(t) = A_T \cdot C(t) \cdot D(t) \cdot \cos(2\pi f t) \tag{1}$$

Here, A_T represents the amplitude of the transmitted signal;
$C(t)$ represents spread spectrum sequence;
$D(t)$ is the data bit of navigation message (± 1);
f is the center frequency of transmitter RF signal.

If signal of receiving channel after RF amplification and down conversion can be expressed as follows:

$$
\begin{aligned}
r(t) &= s_R(t) + n(t) \\
&= A_t \cdot C(t - \tau_t) \cdot D(t - \tau_t) \cdot \cos(2\pi(f_{IF} + f_d)t + \varphi_t) + n(t)
\end{aligned} \tag{2}
$$

Here, $s_R(t)$ is the received signal without noise;
A_t is Signal amplitude;
$D(t)$ is Data bit (± 1);
f_{IF} is IF frequency of receiver;
τ_t is PN code delay;
f_d is Carrier Doppler shift;
φ_t is carrier phase;
$r(t)$ is IF signal of receiver
$n(t)$ is the additive band limited white Gaussian noise.

For a data bit, the data is not changed to +1 or −1, and the sampled IF signal can be expressed as:

$$r(k) = A \cdot C(k - \tau) \cos(2\pi T(f_{IF} + f_d)k + \varphi) + n(k) \tag{3}$$

The estimation of pseudo code phase and carrier frequency is to calculate the values of τ and f_d [6, 8].

2.2 Coarse Estimation of Pseudo Code Phase and Carrier Frequency

The estimation of PN code phase and carrier frequency can be divided into two steps, the first step is coarse estimation, the second step is fine estimation. For DSSS modulation signal, the accuracy of PN code phase estimation is less than half of PN code chip, and the accuracy of carrier Doppler is less than 2/TC. This process is also called signal acquisition in spread spectrum communication [3, 4].

Commonly used PN code and carrier acquisition algorithms include sliding correlation method, FFT-IFFT method and partial matched filter (PMF) plus FFT algorithm. The acquisition algorithm of PMF + FFT can realize the acquisition of PN code phase and carrier frequency in a PN code cycle, without carrier sweep search. Therefore, PMF + FFT acquisition algorithm is the fastest of the three acquisition algorithms discussed above. In this paper, PMF + FFT acquisition algorithm is selected [7].

Matched filter (MF) is a correlation receiver with the best signal-to-noise ratio, which can be used to realize the correlation dispreading operation of spread spectrum communication. The principle structure of a digital matched filter (DMF) is shown in Fig. 1.

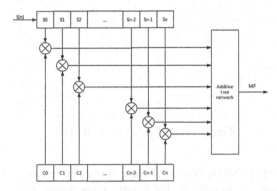

Fig. 1. Block diagram for matched filter

The process of applying matched filter to acquisition of DSSS signal is as follows: if sampling signal of receiver is mixed with local carrier, then I and Q signals I[n] and Q[n] are obtained. After passing I and Q signals through decimation filter, the rate of I and Q signals is transformed to twice pseudo code rate. Let s[n] = I[n] + Q[n] j, the input sequence s[n] is a complex sequence. The s[n] sequence is continuously input and shifted, at the same time, it multiplies the stored local pseudo code, and the related results are output by the adder tree network.

As long as the input signal contains the same spreading code sequence as the local signal, there will always be a time when the two signals are aligned in the code phase, but due to the carrier deviation, it may not be able to detect the correlation peak. When the input sequence is aligned with the local sequence, the pseudo code has been correlated and cancelled. Ideally, only the carrier wave frequency deviation is left. Then the frequency component of the carrier deviation can be analyzed by fast Fourier transform

(FFT). According to the magnitude value of FFT operation result, we can judge whether the signal is captured or not.

It is very difficult to realize the structure of the complete matched filter, and the hardware resource consumption is too much. The method of partial matched filter (PMF) can be adopted to divide the complete pseudo code sequence with a long period into several smaller sequences, and the results of each partial matched filter can be obtained by piecewise matching. The principle structure of PMF + FFT capture method is shown in Fig. 2. The part circled by the dotted line is a partial matched filter (PMF). At each sliding moment, each PMF outputs a partial coherent accumulation sum to the FFT operation module of n points. The FFT is used to analyze the partial results of the matched filter at each time and judge the captured results according to the spectrum. PMF + FFT acquisition method is a code phase and carrier frequency dual parallel acquisition method, which can complete signal acquisition in a complete pseudo code cycle [9–16].

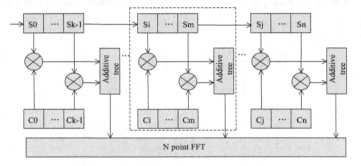

Fig. 2. Block diagram for PMF+FFT

The fundamental of PMF is FIR filter with constant coefficient. Suppose s(n), h(n), L is input signal, tap coefficient and PN length, respectively, then the output can be expressed by:

$$y(i) = \sum_{n=0}^{L-1} s(i-n)h(n) \tag{4}$$

However, in the case of long PN code, inverted FIR filter consumes lots of hardware resources. To overcome this disadvantage, folded PMF uses the faster processing speed to exchange for less hardware resources consumption. The above Eq. (4) also can be represented by:

$$y(i) = \sum_{n=0}^{L-1} s(i-n)h(n)$$
$$= \sum_{n=0}^{p-1} s(i-n)h(n) + \sum_{n=p}^{2p-1} s(i-n)h(n)$$

$$+ \ldots + \sum_{n=(M-1)p}^{L-1} s(i-n)h(n) \tag{5}$$

Where $L = M * p$, M is fold ratio, p is the number of taps, L is PN length. The local PN code of PMF is folded M times so that the number of taps reduced from L to p. Each tap connect a ROM with depth of M and width of one bit.

From Fig. 2 in order to reduce the consumption of hardware resources, folded PMF divides the whole correlation calculation into p parts and the sampling rate adopts n. When folded PMF receives one sampling data, each part carries out M times addition operation where M is folded ratio. Use the zero-padding method for local PN code, if the length of local PN code cannot be divided exactly by M. Because the spread PN code sequence only has two values including −1 and 1, the multiplier can be replaced by adder. The output values of each adder are saved in delay units which length of n * M. There have n sampling data per code. Those sampling data perform correlation calculation with local PN code separately. For this reason, each PN period get n correlation peaks. The process of folded PMF algorithm as follows:

Step 1: When the 1st clock cycle arrives, each tap loads the first register's values including h0, h1… hp−1 from the connected ROM and inserts zero into the first adder. At the same time, each adder performs addition shifting operation and output value of the last delay unit puts into the holding register. The details of addition shifting operation as follows: If the tap coefficient is 1, the result of adder is the sum of former adder's result and received signal value. But if the coefficient is 0, the result of adder is the difference between former adder's result and received signal value.

Step 2: When the 2nd clock cycle arrives, load the second registers' values including hp, hp + 1… h2p−1 from the connected ROM to each tap. The input value of first adder comes from holding register. Meanwhile each adder performs addition shifting operation and puts the output value of last delay unit to the holding register.

Step 3: Next, the operations of the 3rd, 4th… Mth clock cycles are same as step 2. When the Mth clock cycle is over, the value of the last register of the last delay unit saves to the capturing register.

Step 4: Repeat the above steps for the next sampling data.

Through the acquisition process of spread spectrum signal, the pseudo code phase and carrier frequency difference of the received signal can be obtained preliminarily, but the pseudo code ranging requires accurate pseudo code phase, because the ranging accuracy is directly proportional to the estimation accuracy of the code phase. In the case of short pulse communication, the following paper discusses the fast and accurate estimation algorithm of maximum likelihood estimation value function.

3 Fine Estimation of Pseudo-noise Code Phase and Carrier Frequency

As mentioned above, the DSSS signal modulated by BPSK is in one data bit, $D(t)$ value is +1 or −1, If signal after sampling is shown in formula (3) above. IF signal of receiver without noise is:

$$r(k) = A \cdot C(k - \tau) \cos(2\pi T (f_{IF} + f_d)k + \varphi) \tag{6}$$

After correlation with carrier signal and pseudo code signal of local estimation, the signal is:

$$I(k) = A \cdot \frac{\sin(\pi \Delta fT)}{\pi f_d T} R(\tau) \cos(\frac{\pi \Delta fT}{2} + \varphi) \tag{7}$$

In the formula (7), $R(\tau)$ is the correlation value between pseudo code C(t) and $\overset{\Lambda}{C}(t - \tau)$, the autocorrelation function of pseudo-random sequence is similar to the impact function, and $R(\tau)$ is strictly convex function in the range of $(-\frac{\tau}{2}, \frac{\tau}{2})$. After the rough estimation of the signal, the phase estimation of the PN code can be accurate to less than half of the PN code chips, and the carrier Doppler frequency to less than 2/Tc. Therefore, the correlation function between the received signal and the estimated signal can be used to form the maximum likelihood estimated value function, and the maximum value of this function can be calculated by using the optimization theory, so as to accurately estimate the pseudo code phase error τ and the carrier frequency error Δf.

For the additive band limited white Gaussian noise channel, N sampling points of the received signal can be expressed as follows:

$r_N = [r(0), r(1), \cdots, r(N - 1)]$, represents a given N-dimensional observation vector;

$\hat{r}_N = [\hat{r}(0), \hat{r}(1), \cdots, \hat{r}(N - 1)]$, denotes the estimate of r_N.

The joint probability density of the first N samples of the received signal can be expressed:

$$\Lambda(A, \tau, f_d, \varphi | r_N) = -\frac{1}{N_0} \sum_{k=0}^{N-1} \left| r(k) - r(\hat{k}) \right|^2 \tag{9}$$

where Λ is the log-likelihood cost function for the various signal parameters. Thus, the MLE of the signal parameters is obtained by maximizing the log-likelihood cost function in (9), based on the observation vector r_N satisfying

$$\frac{\partial \Lambda(\theta | r_N)}{\partial \theta} = 0 \tag{10}$$

where $\theta = [A, \tau, f_d, \phi]^T$ represents the signal parameter vector.

The Levenberg-Marquardt (LM) method is known as one of the most effective optimization methods for the determination of MLEs [6]. This algorithm requires the computation of the gradient and the Hessian matrices of the log-likelihood function and has the form [8]:

$$\overset{\Lambda}{\theta}_{ML}^{i+1} = \overset{\Lambda}{\theta}_{ML}^{i} - (H_i + d_i)^{-1} G_i \quad for \quad i = 0, 1 \ldots \tag{11}$$

where i represents the iteration index, θ_{ML} is the 2-by-1 MLE state vector, G_i and H_i are the 2-by-1 gradient vector and the 2-by-2 pseudo-Hessian matrix, respectively, defined as follows:

$$G_i = \left[\frac{\partial \Lambda(\theta | r_N)}{\partial \theta} \right]_{\theta = \hat{\theta}^i} \tag{12}$$

and

$$H_i = \left[\frac{\partial^2 \Lambda(\theta|r_N)}{\partial \theta^2} \right]_{\theta=\hat{\theta}^i} \tag{13}$$

with

$$\frac{\partial \Lambda}{\partial \theta} = \begin{bmatrix} \frac{\partial \Lambda}{\partial \tau} \\ \frac{\partial \Lambda}{\partial f_d} \end{bmatrix} \tag{14}$$

and

$$\frac{\partial^2 \Lambda}{\partial \theta^2} = \begin{bmatrix} \frac{\partial^2 \Lambda}{\partial \tau^2} & \frac{\partial^2 \Lambda}{\partial \tau \partial f_d} \\ \frac{\partial^2 \Lambda}{\partial f_d \partial \tau} & \frac{\partial^2 \Lambda}{\partial f_d^2} \end{bmatrix} \tag{15}$$

The diagonal matrix d_i is chosen such that $H_i + d_i$ is always positive definite, resulting in $(H_i + d_i)^{-1}$ always being computable. The $(H_i + d_i)^{-1} G_i$ term represents a correction value at each iteration. The calculation steps of LM algorithm are as follows [8]:

① Calculate Gi and Hi, and update $\hat{\theta}^0$;
② Compute the MLE cost function, and compare it with the previous one.
③ If $\Lambda(\hat{\theta}^i) < \Lambda(\hat{\theta}^{i-1})$, increase di and try again. If $\Lambda(\hat{\theta}^i) \geq \Lambda(\hat{\theta}^{i-1})$, accept this iteration and go to step 4.

④ Check the convergence. If there is no convergence, proceed to compute $\hat{\theta}^{i+1}$, using step 2 until convergence is achieved.

4 Conclusion

In this paper, a new fast pseudo code phase and carrier frequency estimation method is proposed. In this algorithm, FFT + PMF is used to capture the signal and estimate the coarse value of carrier frequency and pseudo code phase. Then LM algorithm is used to solve the maximum likelihood function of the signal, so as to obtain the accurate estimation of carrier Doppler frequency and pseudo code delay. The algorithm can accurately estimate the carrier frequency and the phase of PN code in a period of PN code. This algorithm can be used in pseudo code ranging system and other spread spectrum communication systems as design guidance and reference.

References

1. Parkinson, B.W., Spilker, J.J.: Global Ositioning System: Theory and Applications, vol. I. American Institute of Aeronautics and Astronautics, Reston (1996)
2. ICD-GPS-200C Navstar GPS space segment/Navigation User Interfaces. ARINC Research Corporation, Segundo (2000)

3. Lin, Y., Zhu, Y.: A FLL-PLL cooperative GNSS weak signal tracking framework. In: Applied Mechanics and Materials, pp. 470–477 (2014). https://doi.org/10.4028/www.scientific.net/AMM.551.470

4. Liu, Y., Zhang, J., Zhu, Y.: Weak satellite signal tracking loop based on traditional tracking framework. Wirel. Pers. Commun. **70**, 1761–1775 (2013). https://doi.org/10.1007/s11277-012-0779-z

5. Ma, W.Z., Wang, Z., Li, Y.R., Zhang, W.: Research on code tracking loop algorithm of GPS. Appl. Mech. Mater. **229–231**, 1556–1559 (2012). https://doi.org/10.4028/www.scientific.net/AMM.229-231.1556

6. Rezeanu, S.-C., Ziemer, R.E., Wickert, M.A.: Joint maximum-likelihood parameter estimation for burst DS spread-spectrum transmission. IEEE Trans. Commun. **45**(2), 227–238 (1997). https://doi.org/10.1109/26.554371

7. Qi, J., Luo, F., Song, Q.: Fast acquisition method of navigation receiver based on folded PMF-FFT. In: 2014 IEEE Computers, Communications and IT Applications Conference, ComComAp (2014). https://doi.org/10.1109/ComComAp.2014.7017171

8. Won, J.-H., Pany, T., Eissfeller, B.: Iterative maximum likelihood estimators for high-dynamic GNSS signal tracking. IEEE Trans. Aerosp. Electron. Syst. **48**(4), 2875–2893 (2012). https://doi.org/10.1109/TAES.2012.6324667

9. Hui, H., Zhou, C., Shenggang, X., Lin, F.: A novel secure data transmission scheme in industrial Internet of Things. Chin. Commun. **17**(1), 73–88 (2020)

10. Borio, D., Camoriano, L., Presti, L.L.: Impact of GPS acquisition strategy on decision probabilities. IEEE Trans. Aerosp. Electron. Syst. **44**(3), 996–1011 (2008)

11. Xu, F., Shao, D., Li, S.: Fast PN code acquisition for DNSS receiver in high dynamic situation. J. Beijing Univ. Aeronaut. Astronaut. **33**(6), 672–676 (2007)

12. Gang, X.: Principles of GPS and Receiver Design. Publishing House of Electroing Industry, Beijing (2009)

13. Lin, F., Zhou, Y., An, X., You, I., Choo, K.-K.R.: Fair resource allocation in an intrusion-detection system for edge computing: ensuring the security of Internet of Things devices. IEEE Consum. Electron. Mag. **7**(6), 45–50 (2018)

14. Liu, T., Qin, Z., Xu, R., Chen, H.: Research of rapid code acquisition method based on folded-structure matched filter and FFT. J. Acad. Equip. Command Technol. **21**(4), 93–96 (2010)

15. Gong, C., Lin, F., Gong, X., Yueming, L.: Intelligent Cooperative Edge Computing in the Internet of Things. IEEE Internet of Things Journal (2020). https://doi.org/10.1109/JIOT.2020.2986015

16. Spangenberg, S.M., Scott, I., Mclaughlin, S., et al.: FFT-based approach for fast acquisition in spread spectrum communication systems. Wirel. Pers. Commun. **13**(1), 27–56 (2000)

17. Wang, Y., Zhang, X., Zhang, Y.: Joint spectrum partition and performance analysis of full-duplex D2D communications in multi-tier wireless networks. Comput. Mater. Continua **61**(1), 171–184 (2019)

18. Hu, B., Xiang, F., Wu, F., Liu, J., Sun, Z., Sun, Z.: Research on time synchronization method under arbitrary network delay in wireless sensor networks. Comput. Mater. Continua **61**(3), 1323–1344 (2019)

19. Liu, W., Luo, X., Liu, Y., Liu, J., Liu, M., Shi, Y.Q.: Localization algorithm of indoor Wi-Fi access points based on signal strength relative relationship and region division. Comput. Mater. Continua **55**(1), 071–093 (2018)

Research of Software Information Hiding Algorithm Based on Packing Technology

Zuwei Tian[(⊠)] and Hengfu Yang

Hunan First Normal University, Changsha 410205, China
35568625@qq.com

Abstract. This paper presents a software information hiding technique based on packing under Windows. The main function of the system includes identifying PE files, PE file packing, PE file code encryption, PE file information implantation, PE file information extraction, etc. The system uses the dynamic link library as a shell program, implants the end of the target PE file, implants the given information into the code segment, and encrypts the code segment with the information to be hidden by using shelling technology to complete the information hiding. The paper encrypts the information with the code segment, mixing the two. Even if adversary obtains this piece of data, it can't distinguish between the effective information, effectively reduces the density of information, and increases the difficulty of information recognition, so as to achieve the purpose of information hiding.

Keywords: Information hiding · Packing technology · PE file · Dynamic link

1 Introduction

With the rapid development of computer technology and Internet technology, the application of computer is increasingly expanding. People are more and more demanding of information security. How to effectively carry out the secure transmission and storage of digital information has attracted widespread attention. Encryption technology can easily expose the importance of information itself, and can't solve this problem well. Information hiding technology has emerged. It has become a research hotspot in the field of information security, providing a new way of thinking and method for the secure storage and communication of digital information.

PE file is standard format for executable files in win32 environments and is applied widely [1–5]. The diversity of PE file, the uncertainty of file size, the complexity of file structure and the singleness of file format, which make PE file easy to be a carrier of information hiding, especially for that of large hiding capacity. Existing information technologies based on PE file often utilize redundant space or fields [6–10]. Those approaches are not related to program functions or instruction codes. Therefore there exists some disadvantages, such as exceeding convergence, bad concealment and unsatisfied robust of hidden information [11–14]. In view of this problem, the system starts from another angle, which hides the location of the information while encrypting. On the other hand, using shelling technology to embed information into the Windows executable file, rather than storing the file. It makes information as part of a program, and then realizes information hiding. Information hiding technology based on shelling technology overcomes this to some extent, when the adversary cannot distinguish the carrier object's data and secret information data, theoretically makes the hidden capacity can reach the maximum PE file level, at the same time, encryption makes the statistical law become meaningless, increases concealment, anti-aggressiveness and robustness.

2   Load of PE File

PE program can be divided into the header area, data area two parts. The operating system does not load all PE in memory when it starts to load PE, but first load the header table area into memory intact. It follows these steps.

1. Allocate memory space, create process and main thread.
2. Verify the legitimacy of the PE file, if it is not a legitimate PE file, will terminate subsequent reads and give prompt information.
3. Load the program head according to the ImageBase recommended in Optional-Header. Reallocate space if occupied.
4. Read the block table, each block is loaded into the memory in turn. Because the memory and file alignment is generally different, the loader according to the file offset and memory offset corresponding loading in the block table. In a multiprogramming operating system, blocks may not be loaded all at once.
5. Read the resource directory, initialize the resource data table (import table, resource table, relocation table, etc.), such as read INT (if present), load the dynamic link library that is not loaded according to INT and update the IAT to point to the correct physical address.
6. Load the code segment into memory according to the base address of the program entry, and then give control to the program.

The relative position of each block in memory is logically consistent with the relative position in the file, but the alignment is different. Windows operating system default file alignment is 0x200, memory is aligned to 0x1000. Generally, the "gap" of each block in memory will be greater.

3   PE File Shelling Technology

A shell is a protection program that is attached to the original program. There are usually two types, compression shell and encryption shell, with different emphasis. However, both shells change the static structure of the original PE file.

Compression shell is like compressed file. Generally, compression and decompression of the compressed files are relative to the disk. After the compressed file is decompressed in memory, it is written back to disk to form the decompressed file. The packed shell is decompressed in memory, do not need to write back to disk, so the speed of decompression is faster.

The encryption shell usually does not compress the original file, the important data in the file is encrypted, such as the code segment data. Static disassembly of the original program will get wrong data, which will prevent code data from being stolen. In the process of operation, the shell first decrypts the original code data, and then executes the original code.

Software shelling is to attach the shell to the original PE file, the shell as part of the PE program, and let the shell take control of the program. Decrypting the code segment when the program is running, repairing the import table, relocation table and other data directory. The shell also needs to correct the import table and the relocation table after completing its own tasks, and the shelling program is responsible for the shelling.

This system uses dynamic link library as a shell, which has the characteristics of simple realization and good compatibility. During the shelling process, the system simulates the PE loader to load the target PE file into memory, and then load the dynamic link library. It saves the critical data in the original PE file to the dynamic link library. Finally, the set-up dynamic link library is added to the end of the target PE file as an additional segment. The windows API is called directly in the shell, eliminating the need for import table corrections. When the shell is loaded, the shell has been relocated, so the relocation data is restored. The restored data address is relative to the dynamic link library default base address (0x10000000), so address correction of data is required. The address offset is based on the default base address of the executable file (0x400000). Finally, the relocation directory is pointed to the shell relocation table, which is initialized by using the windows loading system when the program is loaded, and the relocation data and import table of the original program are corrected by the shell program at runtime.

4 Proposed Method

The system involves four modules: PE files as hidden carriers of information, shell procedure responsible for decryption, hidden information, and overall control procedure.

4.1 Shell Structure

The shell uses a dynamic link library, which defines a data structure SHELL_DATA, as shown in Table 1. It holds important data in the target PE file. The initialization of data is carried out in the data transfer of the process control module. The shell and the shelling program belong to two systems, the interface unification is very important in the process of data transfer, and some redundant data is helpful to the expansion of the program.

4.2 Working Process of Shell

The shell runs the process control function using the keyword _declspec (naked) to declare it as a naked function. Let the compiler generate pure assembly code without function framework, otherwise it will affect the execution of JMP instructions. It is necessary to maintain the stack within the function. The main processing processes are as follows:

Table 1. SHELL_DATA

Type	Identity	Description
DWORD	dwStartFun	Shell Start Function
DWORD	dwPEOEP	Entry of target PE
DWORD	dwXorKey	Encryption key
DWORD	dwBaseOfCode	Target PE code segment base address
DWORD	dwXorSize	Size of encrypted data of code segment
DWORD	dwPEBaseOfImage	Image base address of target PE
IMAGE_DATA_DIRECTORY	PERelocDir	Relocation table directory
IMAGE_DATA_DIRECTORY	PEImportDir	Import table directory
DWORD	dwIATSectionBase	Import table segment base address
DWORD	dwIATSectionSize	Import table segment size

1. Register push to stack. The compiler will not automatically generate the function framework in the naked function, and the stack needs to be maintained manually.
2. Gets the current program image base address. Using the windows API GetModule-HandleA (NULL) to obtain the base address of the current program image, and cast it to DWORD type, as the program base address used for subsequent relocation repair, import address table, switch program entry, submit control right, and decryption.
3. Decrypt the original PE file code segment. Call the decryption module, the decrypted information is saved in the SHELL_DATA structure, and the decryption algorithm can be replaced as needed.
4. Fix the import table for the original PE file. Call the repair import table submodule.
5. Register pop-up stack.
6. Calculate the original PE file code entry to submit control. Use the jmp instruction to make unconditional adjustments to complete the shell operation.

4.3 Decrypt the Original PE File Code Segment

Using a simple increment XOR encryption algorithm, the original data of the program is restored. The main processing processes are as follows:

1. The physical address of the code segment is obtained by adding the relative offset address of image to the base address of code segment.
2. Get memory permission. In Windows, due to program security concerns, different segments are usually not directly accessible, and shell programs and original PE code segments do not belong to the same segment. So use the Windows API VirtualProtect() to get memory read and write permissions before accessing.

3. Decrypt. Perform decryption with saved information such as code data size, decoding keys, and so on. This part can be replaced by other algorithms as needed.
4. Restore memory permission.

4.4 Repair Import Table

The program's import table will be corrected when the PE file is loaded into memory by the operating system. Nevertheless, the shelling will point the import table directory to the shell's import table directory, loading the shell's import table data, so it is necessary to repair the import table of the original program during the execution of the shell. The main processing processes are as follows:

1. Get the PE program import table pointer. Calculate the sum of image base address and saved import table directory.
2. Get the actual physical address.
3. Get memory page read and write permission.
4. Get the name of the link library you want to import. If it is empty, the module process is ended. The name field is a pointer to an array of names, and also requires to get physical address through base address conversion.
5. Load the link library. Load the link library into memory with the Windows API LoadLibraryA() function.
6. Get the IAT pointer.
7. Get AddressOfData. If it is empty, jump to step 13.
8. Determine import mode of import function d. If it is function name import method, skips to step.
9. Get the function serial number. Jump to step 10.
10. Get the function name.
11. Get the physical address of the function. Get the function address with API GetProcaddress().
12. Fix the IAT. Using IAT pointer to make IAT table point to physical address of function.
13. The IAT pointer moves back. Jump to step 6.
14. Import the table pointer backward. Jump to step 3.
15. Restore memory page read and write permission.

4.5 Information Hiding Module

Information file is from the outside world, the type is unlimited. Bytecode is stored in the carrier PE file. If the information introduced is less than redundant within the code segment in page, there is no need to correct the address information for the later segments of the code segment in the chunk table.

Opening the information to be hidden from the file, handing the information to the PE file for implantation, giving a warning and stop the program in case of file opening error. The main processing processes are as follows:

1. Open the information file. A universal file dialog box encapsulated with MFC, and give error feedback.

2. Information delivery. Load the information data into the cache of the control module and wait for the PE module to receive it.
3. Close the file. Get the memory page to get the correction data of the PE file based on the information size.

After loading the information, the information is used to correct the space required for the code segment, and adjust the location information of the subsequent segments to ensure the normal operation of the program. The main processing processes are as follows:

1. Define variable of segment table. Get the segment table in the PE information.
2. Traverse section table.
3. Compare the current segment offset with the code segment base address.
4. Record the location and size of the information.
5. Calculate the new page size.
   In order to achieve a better hiding effect, the hidden information needs to be next to the code data, not another page and obvious segmentation. The smallest unit of memory that exists in the program is a memory page, usually is 0x1000, so increasing the size of the page must be a full multiple of this value. The number of new pages required is determined by the inside of the last page of the code area and the information size. No new page is required when the information is filled with redundancy in the page, otherwise the new page size is calculated based on the amount of excess information.
6. Encrypting information is still using incremental differences or algorithms.
7. Give the processed information to the PE module for processing.

4.6 Packing Program Module

The control module is responsible for packing. Its main functions include reading the target file, recording information, loading the shell program, attaching the shell program to the end of the original PE file, correcting the header table information of the original PE file, and inventory. In the shelling process, there is no need to perform file operation. Instead, the data is copied and transferred directly by code. It shows the advantages of using DLL as shell. The only drawback is the need to correct the relocation table information. The main processing processes are as follows:

1. Read the target PE file and verify the legitimacy of the file.
2. Initialize the PE file. Call initialization sub module.
3. Load the shell link library and give feedback if it fails. The shell uses a dynamic link library that simply calls the API to load memory without manual initialization.
4. Get the data structure of the shell. Use the API to get it by name. No manual positioning is required.
5. Initialize the shell data structure. Save the information obtained in the PE file. Save the RVA of code segment base address and data directory to the shell.
6. Repair the relocation table of the shell to an unloaded state.
7. Get shell information. Use the API to get module information.
8. Copy the shell to the end of the target PE file.

9. Call the PE module's relocation repair sub module. When the shell is loaded into memory, it has been fixed to relocate, so the relocation directory should be fixed to the state when it is not loaded.
10. Set up a new entrance to the program.
11. Merge the shell with the original PE file. Call the combined sub module of the PE module and complete the header correction operation in the sub module.
12. Save in file alignment. Finally release the resource.

4.7 PE Module

First, the system checks whether it is a PE file, and then records the header table data. The most important thing is to load the PE file into memory in memory format and simulate the PE loader. The relative offset RVA in each segment is used directly without the need to fix offset inconsistencies caused by the different alignment between the file and the memory. The main processing processes are as follows:

1. Open the target PE file. Open the file and load the target PE file into memory.
2. Verify the legitimacy of the PE file. Call the previous module. If it is illegal, give feedback and exit from the function.
3. Extract header table information. Get segment table information. The main areas are segment size, file offset, memory offset, etc.
4. Mount each segment from the file offset to the memory offset as per memory. The simulated windows loader is prepared to load each segment in memory. Facilitate subsequent operations.
5. Free the old memory.
6. Initialize the PE file information for the memory format. Call the PE information acquisition module to update the PE control block data structure.

4.7.1 Get PE File Information

To obtain the location of the corresponding block of the required data, you can only compare the relative offset address of the data in turn with the starting and ending locations of the chunks, which are included in it, which means that the data belongs to the block. The main processing processes are as follows:

1. Initialize data structure of PE file. The PE file in this case is expanded in memory format, and all RVAs plus cache base addresses can be accessed to the correct address.
2. Save the relocation directory and import table catalog information.
3. Save the information in the area where the IAT is located. Compare the RVA of the desired data catalog with the segment range, and if the directory offset is included in the range, the record is logged and exited, otherwise look for the next segment. This method uses the same algorithm as the previous method to find the code segment number, and only this method can locate the segment of the data.

4.7.2 Repair Shell Relocation Table

The shell is loaded from memory, its relocation table is corrected when loaded into memory. The relocation table points to a specific physical address, and the remediation of the relocation table is also possible in the operating system page replacement, which is designed to ensure that the relocation information points to the correct physical address. But as a shell, it must be the data when it is not loaded, and he needs to wait for the packed program to be loaded when the information is relocated. The main processing processes are as follows:

1. Define a temporary structure. That is, the definition of the relocation address structure, the data structure occupies 2 bytes, where the high 4 bits represent the type of the relocation data, the low 12 bits is the data in-page offset address. The different bits of the data are bound with different identifiers, which can simplify the program.
2. Get the shell's relocation directory table. The method is the same as the operation PE file.
3. Get relocation table items. The relocation table items are immediately followed by the relocation table structure, which constitutes a repositioning structure. The VA represents the starting address of the data that needs to be relocated, and SizeOfBlock represents the size of the entire structure. So the real data needs to subtract the space occupied by VA and SizeOfBlock.
4. Calculate the number of relocated items.
5. Fix the relocation item. The relocation table entry records the address of the data that needs to be relocated, the data in the shell is offset by the base address at the time of loading, and now the real data is reduced to the shell base address when not loaded, plus the base address of the target PE, because the shell is in the original PE end, so, also need to add the size of the PE image.
6. Fix the shell to reposition the base address of the directory. The base address of the target PE needs to be added.
7. Fix the relocation directory of the PE file. Make the target PE file relocation directory point to the shell's relocation directory table while modifying the size.

4.7.3 Merge Shell

When merging, you should add area table information, set the properties of the new block segment, modify the segment characteristics, add executable properties, and prepare for the subsequent inventory. The main processing processes are as follows:

1. Fix the Nt header information. Increase the number of blocks.
2. Calculate the file alignment size. Calculate the file alignment offset information, divide the total size of the shell by the alignment size, get the number of pages, and add one page if there is a surplus.
3. Calculate the memory alignment size.
4. Modify block table information, include alignment, size, name, attributes, and so on.
5. Merge. The shell program and the original PE program are combined into one file to prepare for the final save.

4.7.4 Change Image Size

Adjust the space of the final program according to the new page size calculated by information hiding to reduce the control difficulty of merging and saving. Although the windows default code segment is the first segment, it is still necessary to calculate the code section for increasing the robustness of the program. The main processing processes are as follows:

1. Request a new PE space. After the information content is added to the code segment, in order to avoid moving, the previous module initialization can be called again in order to avoid moving, using the overall reconstruction method.
2. Load the sections. Scan the code segment using the code segment number saved earlier.
3. Modify offset. When a code segment is found, the information is attached to the end of the code, and the subsequent segments are moved back to address, and the corresponding segment file offsets in the header table information are corrected.
4. Correct the block and image size. In the previous step, it needs to read before loading, so block correction is not allowed.
5. Update the information of the PE file.

4.7.5 Information Extraction Module

When the information is extracted, the location information stored in the redundant information is read, the information in the hidden carrier of the information is extracted according to the location information, and then the information is decrypted to the information file to complete the information extraction.

5 Experiments

The program before and after being packed is shown in Fig. 1 and Fig. 2. After shelling, the code segment data is all encrypted, and the static disassembled code is not the same as the original code.

The program before and after hiding the information is shown in Fig. 3 and Fig. 4.

The size of information data in the sample program is larger than the redundancy in the code segment. Therefore, the length of the code segment after hiding the information needs to be expanded, and all segments after the code segment need to be moved back.

```
         0  1  2  3  4  5  6  7  8  9  a  b  c  d  e  f
00000f90h: 00 00 00 00 00 00 00 00 00 00 00 00 00 00 00 00
00000fa0h: 00 00 00 00 00 00 00 00 00 00 00 00 00 00 00 00
00000fb0h: 00 00 00 00 00 00 00 00 00 00 00 00 00 00 00 00
00000fc0h: 00 00 00 00 00 00 00 00 00 00 00 00 00 00 00 00
00000fd0h: 00 00 00 00 00 00 00 00 00 00 00 00 00 00 00 00
00000fe0h: 00 00 00 00 00 00 00 00 00 00 00 00 00 00 00 00
00000ff0h: 00 00 00 00 00 00 00 00 00 00 00 00 00 00 00 00
00001000h: 68 38 70 40 00 E8 AC 00 00 00 68 30 70 40 00 E8
00001010h: 0C 00 00 00 83 C4 08 33 C0 C3 90 90 90 90 90 90
00001020h: 55 8B EC 83 EC 10 56 68 D8 60 40 00 E8 21 06 00
00001030h: 00 59 33 F6 8B 4D 08 89 45 F0 3B CE 75 18 3B C6
00001040h: 75 04 33 C0 EB 6D 56 50 E8 C1 05 00 00 F7 D8 59
00001050h: 1B C0 59 40 EB 5D 3B C6 C7 45 F4 D4 60 40 00 89
00001060h: 4D F8 89 75 FC 74 24 8D 4D F0 56 51 50 56 E8 01
00001070h: 04 00 00 83 C4 10 83 F8 FF 75 38 8B 0D EC 78 40
00001080h: 00 83 F9 02 74 05 83 F9 0D 75 28 F6 05 F9 78 40
00001090h: 00 80 C7 45 F0 C8 60 40 00 75 07 C7 45 F0 C0 60
000010a0h: 40 00 8D 45 F0 56 50 FF 75 F0 56 E8 5F 01 00 00
```

Fig. 1. Original program code segment data

```
         0  1  2  3  4  5  6  7  8  9  a  b  c  d  e  f
00000f90h: 00 00 00 00 00 00 00 00 00 00 00 00 00 00 00 00
00000fa0h: 00 00 00 00 00 00 00 00 00 00 00 00 00 00 00 00
00000fb0h: 00 00 00 00 00 00 00 00 00 00 00 00 00 00 00 00
00000fc0h: 00 00 00 00 00 00 00 00 00 00 00 00 00 00 00 00
00000fd0h: 00 00 00 00 00 00 00 00 00 00 00 00 00 00 00 00
00000fe0h: 00 00 00 00 00 00 00 00 00 00 00 00 00 00 00 00
00000ff0h: 00 00 00 00 00 00 00 00 00 00 00 00 00 00 00 00
00001000h: 68 39 72 43 04 ED AA 07 08 09 62 3B 7C 4D 0E E7
00001010h: 1C 11 12 13 97 D1 1E 24 D8 DA 8A 8B 8C 8D 8E 8F
00001020h: 75 AA CE A0 C8 35 70 4F F0 49 6A 2B C4 0C 28 2F
00001030h: 30 68 01 C5 BF 78 3E BE 7D C9 01 F5 49 25 05 F9
00001040h: 35 45 71 83 AF 28 10 17 A0 88 4F 4B 4C BA 96 16
00001050h: 4B 91 0B 13 BF 08 6D 91 9F 1C AE 8F 3C 1D 5E D6
00001060h: 2D 99 EB 16 98 11 42 EA 25 99 3C 3A 3C 3B 86 6E
00001070h: 74 71 72 F0 B0 65 F5 8F 87 0C 42 F0 71 91 06 3F
00001080h: 80 02 7B 81 F0 80 05 7E 85 FC A2 7D 89 74 F6 CF
00001090h: 90 11 55 D6 64 5D F6 D7 98 EC 9D 5C D9 6D 5E FF
000010a0h: E0 A1 2F E6 54 F3 F6 58 DD 59 FC 43 F3 AC AE AF
```

Fig. 2. Packed program code segment

```
          0  1  2  3  4  5  6  7  8  9  a  b  c  d  e  f
00005ed0h: 01 74 05 83 FF 02 75 16 6A 02 E8 75 FF FF FF 6A
00005ee0h: 01 8B E8 E8 6C FF FF FF 59 3B C5 59 74 1C 57 E8
00005ef0h: 60 FF FF FF 59 50 FF 15 6C 60 40 00 85 C0 75 0A
00005f00h: FF 15 14 60 40 00 8B E8 EB 02 33 ED 57 E8 C8 FE
00005f10h: FF FF 8B 03 59 80 64 30 04 00 85 ED 74 09 55 E8
00005f20h: 75 D3 FF FF 59 EB 15 33 C0 EB 14 83 25 F0 78 40
00005f30h: 00 00 C7 05 EC 78 40 00 09 00 00 00 83 C8 FF 5F
00005f40h: 5E 5D 5B C3 56 8B 74 24 08 8B 46 0C A8 83 74 1D
00005f50h: A8 08 74 19 FF 76 08 E8 00 CC FF FF 66 81 66 0C
00005f60h: F7 FB 33 C0 59 89 06 89 46 08 89 46 04 5E C3 CC
00005f70h: FF 25 58 60 40 00 00 00 00 00 00 00 00 00 00 00
00005f80h: 00 00 00 00 00 00 00 00 00 00 00 00 00 00 00 00
00005f90h: 00 00 00 00 00 00 00 00 00 00 00 00 00 00 00 00
00005fa0h: 00 00 00 00 00 00 00 00 00 00 00 00 00 00 00 00
00005fb0h: 00 00 00 00 00 00 00 00 00 00 00 00 00 00 00 00
00005fc0h: 00 00 00 00 00 00 00 00 00 00 00 00 00 00 00 00
00005fd0h: 00 00 00 00 00 00 00 00 00 00 00 00 00 00 00 00
00005fe0h: 00 00 00 00 00 00 00 00 00 00 00 00 00 00 00 00
00005ff0h: 00 00 00 00 00 00 00 00 00 00 00 00 00 00 00 00
00006000h: EC 65 00 00 FE 65 00 00 0C 66 00 00 1A 66 00 00
```

Fig. 3. End of original program code segment

```
          0  1  2  3  4  5  6  7  8  9  a  b  c  d  e  f
00005ed0h: D1 A5 D7 50 2B D7 A3 C1 B2 DB 32 AE 23 22 21 B5
00005ee0h: E1 6A 0A 0B 88 1A 19 18 B1 D2 2F B2 98 F1 B9 07
00005ef0h: 90 0E 0D 0C AD A5 09 E2 94 99 BA FB 79 3D 8B F5
00005f00h: FF 14 16 63 44 05 8D EF E3 0B 39 E6 5B E5 C6 F1
00005f10h: EF EE 99 10 4D 95 72 27 1C 19 9F F6 68 14 4B F7
00005f20h: 55 F2 DD DC 7D CE 33 14 E8 C2 3E A8 09 DD 56 6F
00005f30h: 30 31 F5 36 D8 4D 76 37 31 39 3A 3B BF F5 C1 60
00005f40h: 1E 1C 19 80 12 CE 32 63 40 C2 0C 47 E4 CE 3A 52
00005f50h: F8 59 26 4A AB 23 5E BF 58 95 A5 A4 3A DC 38 53
00005f60h: 97 9A 51 A3 3D EC 60 EE 2E 61 E3 2D 68 33 AD A3
00005f70h: 8F 54 2A 13 34 75 BC C6 C8 C1 B5 BB 34 35 3A 29
00005f80h: 69 63 65 63 6F B3 D7 DB D0 A2 AA 27 24 25 38 7A
00005f90h: 72 72 72 7C A2 D8 EA E3 93 9D 16 17 14 07 4B 41
00005fa0h: 43 45 4D 91 E9 E5 F2 80 8C 01 06 07 16 54 50 50
00005fb0h: 54 5A 80 FA F4 FD F1 FF 70 71 76 65 25 2F 21 27
00005fc0h: 2B F7 8B 87 8C FE EE 63 60 61 74 36 3E 3E 36 38
00005fd0h: E6 9C 96 9F EF E1 52 53 50 43 07 0D 0F 09 09 D5
00005fe0h: AD A1 AE DC D0 5D 42 43 52 10 1C 1C 18 16 C4 BE
00005ff0h: B0 B9 CD C3 4C 4D B2 A1 E1 EB ED EB E7 3B 4F 43
00006000h: 48 3A 32 BF BC BD B0 F2 FA FA FA F4 2A 50 52 5B
```

Fig. 4. Code segment after hiding information

6 Experiments

Based on the combination of shelling and information hiding, this paper elaborates the implementation principle of these two technologies, analyzes the feasibility of combining the two technologies, and describes the implementation and results of the combination of the two technologies with encryption as an auxiliary technology. It introduces the windows operating system program startup logic and the role of kernel and user dynamic link library. The experimental results show that the information hiding technology based on the shell technology has good imperceptibility and anti-attack.

References

1. Liu, Y., Liu, D., Chai, X.: MFC and windows program. Comput. Knowl. Technol. **11**(32), 64–65 (2015)
2. Jiao, L., Luo, L.: Research and implementation of PE file shell technology. Inf. Netw. Secur. (01), 38–43 (2013)
3. Li, X.: Research on Information Hiding Model and some problems. Beijing University of Posts and Telecommunications (2012)
4. Wu, Z.: Windows Assembly Language Programming. Tsinghua University Press, Beijing (2004)
5. Wang, B.: Information Hiding Technology. National Defense Industry Press, Beijing (2007)
6. Qi, L.: Windows PE Authoritative Guide. Mechanical Industry Press, Beijing (2011)
7. Yosifovich, P.: Windows Internals, 7th edn. Posts and Telecommunications Press, Beijing (2017)
8. Biondi, F., Enescu, M.A., Given-Wilson, T., Legay, A., Noureddine, L., Verma, V.: Effective, efficient, and robust packing detection and classification. Comput. Secur. **85**, 436–451 (2019)
9. Namanya, A.P., Awan, I.U., Disso, J.P., Younas, M.: Similarity hash based scoring of portable executable files for efficient malware detection in IoT. Future Gener. Comput. Syst. **110**, 824–832 (2019)
10. Darshan, S.L.S., Jaidhar, C.D.: Performance evaluation of filter-based feature selection techniques in classifying portable executable files. Proc. Comput. Sci. **125**, 346–356 (2018)
11. Zaidan, A.A., Zaidan, B.B., Naji, A.W., et al.: Approved undetectable-antivirus steganography for multimedia information in PE-file. In: International Conference on Advanced Management Science (ICAMS 2009), Singapore, pp. 437–441 (2009)
12. Alanazi, H., Jalab, H.A., Zaidan, A.A., et al.: New framework of hidden data with in non multimedia file. Int. J. Comput. Netw. Secur. **2**(1), 46–53 (2010)
13. Zaidan, B.B., Zaidan, A.A., Othman, F., et al.: Novel approach of hidden data in the unused area 1 within exe files using computation between cryptography and steganography. In: Proceeding of the International Conference on Cryptography, Coding and Information Security, Paris, pp. 1–22 (2009)
14. Islam, M.R., Naji, A.W., Zaidan, A.A., et al.: New system for secure cover file of hidden data in the image page within executable file using statistical steganography techniques. Int. J. Comput. Sci. Inf. Secur. **7**(1), 273–279 (2009)
15. Zaidan, B.B., Zaidan, A.A., Othman, F.: New technique of hidden data in PE-file with in unused area one. Int. J. Comput. Electr. Eng. (IJCEE) **1**(5), 669–678 (2009)
16. Wang, X., Jiang, J., Zhao, S., Bai, L.: A fair blind signature scheme to revoke malicious vehicles in VANETs. Comput. Mater. Continua **58**(1), 249–262 (2019)

17. Wang, J., Wang, H., Li, J., Luo, X., Shi, Y.-Q., Jha, S.Kr.: Detecting double JPEG compressed color images with the same quantization matrix in spherical coordinates. IEEE Trans. CSVT. https://doi.org/10.1109/tcsvt(2019)
18. Wang, J., Li, T., Luo, X., Shi, Y.-Q., Jha, S.: Identifying computer generated images based on quaternion central moments in color quaternion wavelet domain. IEEE Trans. CSVT **29**(9), 2775–2785 (2018)

A Free-Space Quantum Secure Direct Communication Scheme Based on Prefixed-Threshold Real-Time Selection Method

Hao Yu[1], Qianqian Hu[2,3]([✉]), Zhenwei Li[1], and Bao Feng[2,3]

[1] State Grid Information & Telecommunication Branch, NARI Group Corporation,
Hefei 230009, China
[2] NRGD Quantum CTek., LTD., NARI Group Corporation, Nanjing 210000, China
huqianqian@sgepri.sgcc.com.cn
[3] State Grid Electric Power Research Institute, NARI Group Corporation, Nanjing 210000,
China

Abstract. Quantum secure direct communication (QSDC) is a secure communication method that uses the quantum state as an information carrier to directly transmit the message between two remote anticipators. In the free-space quantum communication, atmospheric turbulence causes fluctuations in transmittance, which further affects the quantum bit error rate (QBER) and signal-to-noise ratio (SNR). Under such circumstances, the intensity of some optical signals arriving at the remote end may be weak, which makes it difficult to meet the requirements of secure communication. In order to solve this problem, a free-space QSDC scheme based on prefixed-threshold real-time selection (P-RTS) method is proposed. In this scheme, the sender transmits all photons in the pulse way, and the remote end receives these pulses responding to the optical threshold which is calculated by the P-RTS method. It shows that the proposed scheme has lower QBER and higher SNR than other QSDC scheme through analysis.

Keywords: Quantum communication · Mobile communication · QSDC

1 Introduction

In the modern social environment where the Internet is rapidly developing, information and communication security is receiving more and more attention now. Compared with the classical communication protocol, the unconditional security of the quantum communication protocol has attracted people's attention. There are different forms of quantum communication, such as quantum key distribution [1–3], quantum secret sharing [4, 5], quantum direct security communication [6–10], etc. Besides, some exciting developments such as entanglement based QKD over 144 km [11] and entanglement distribution over 100 km in free space channels [12], have been achieved, which have laid the foundation for future long-distance quantum communication.

© Springer Nature Singapore Pte Ltd. 2020
X. Sun et al. (Eds.): ICAIS 2020, CCIS 1253, pp. 90–98, 2020.
https://doi.org/10.1007/978-981-15-8086-4_9

Among these quantum communication protocol, quantum secure direct communication (QSDC) transmit secret message over a quantum channel directly without setting up a private key session. In this protocol, the sender and receiver share the prearranged entangled photon pair first, thus setting up the communication channel. After the receiver obtains one photon of the pair, the sender encodes the remaining photon with one of the four unitary operations I, σ_z, σ_x, σ_{iy}, which correspond to the encoding information 00, 01, 10, and 11, respectively. Finally, the receiver performs a Bell-state measurement for photons to decode the information after receiving the second photon. The first QSDC protocol exploited the properties of Bell states and used a block transmission technique [6], and the standard criterion for QSDC was explicitly clarified in 2003 using the EPR pair [7]. Furthermore, a QSDC protocol based on single photons is also proposed [8]. Recently, QSDC is practical verified by Hu et $al.$ [9] and Wei et $al.$ [10] and an efficient controlled quantum secure direct communication and authentication protocol is discussed [13]. These experimental demonstration marks a huge advance in actual application of QSDC. And recently, Full-Blind Delegating Private Quantum Computation is analyzed by Liu et $al.$ [14].

Except practical realization of QSDC, quantum communication in free space also developed. The first demonstration of free-space quantum communication was published by Bennett et $al.$ from IBM research in 1992 over 32 cm of free-space channel [15]. And in 2007, two successful experimental ground-to-ground free-space QKD experiments based on BB84 and E91 protocol were implemented over a 144-km link between the Canary Island of La Palma and Tenerife [11, 16]. In 2012, Yin et $al.$ and Ma et $al.$ respectively performed quantum teleportation over 100 and 143 km [12, 17]. In recent years, free-space QKD has also seen much development over rapidly moving platforms, with an air-to-ground experiment in 2013 by Nauerth et al. [18], and in 2017, Liao et $al.$, Yin et $al.$ and Ren et $al.$ complete satellite-based quantum communication experiments respectively [19–21].

Free-space quantum communication is an optical communication technology that uses photon in free space to transmit data wirelessly for telecommunications. "Free space" means air, outer space, vacuum, or something similar. In free-space communications, background photons and detector noise are unavoidable sources of quantum bit error rate (QBER), which limits the range of quantum protocols, and typically, the disturbance are fluctuating. This fluctuation due to turbulence can be modeled as a probability distribution, called the probability distribution of the transmission coefficient (PDTC) [22], being the transmitted intensity constant, follows the log-normal distribution, given by $p(\eta; \eta_0, \sigma^2) = \frac{1}{\sqrt{2\pi}\sigma} \frac{1}{\eta} \exp\left(-\left(ln\frac{\eta}{\eta_0} + \frac{1}{2}\sigma^2\right)^2 / 2\sigma^2\right)$, where p is the probability density, η is the the the transmittance, and η_0 and σ are the mean and variance. The distribution is determined by the two parameters η_0 and σ, which are inherent to the channel itself, η_0 is the expected atmospheric transmittance, with a typical value of 10^{-3} to 10^{-4} (corresponding to 30–40 dB for loss) for a 100-km channel, while σ typically taking a value between zero and one, in determined by the amount of turbulence, the larger the amount of turbulence, the larger the bariance. Hence the real-time transmittance η is a random time-dependent variable that can be described by the PDTC. Vallone et $al.$ proposed a method named adaptive real-time selection (ARTS) [23] that acquires information about real-time transmittance fluctuation due to turbulence, and makes use of this information to perform post-selection and improve the key rate of QKD. And a similar proposal by Erven *et al.* called the signal-to-noise-ratio filter (SNRF) [24] also discusses the idea of using a threshold to post-select high-transmittance periods, but uses the quantum data themselves rather than a secondary classical channel. Recently, Wang *et al.* proposed a prefixed-threshold real-time selection method (P-RTS) [25] base on the ARTS method, which explored the character of the PDTC and proved that an optical threshold could be prefixed before transportation. This method can effectively solve the atmospheric interference existing in free space quantum communication, effectively improve the signal-to-noise ratio of the channel, and provide a lower error rate for the security of the protocol.

In this paper, we apply the prefix-threshold real-time selection method to meet with the problem in free-space quantum direct secure communication, and use the optical signal according to the pulse of a certain length of time at the transmitting end, and preset the intensity threshold at the receiving end. If the received pulse intensity does not reach the threshold, it will be abandoned. In this way, the quantum bit error rate of the received signal is reduced, which provides a guarantee for protocol security. The rest of the paper is organized as follows, the basic knowledge of quantum computation, QSDC and free space communication is introduced in Sect. 2. Section 3 give a detailed explanation to the prefix threshold real-time selection method and the free-space P-RTS scheme based on P-RTS method. And last conclusion is given.

2 Preliminary

2.1 Quantum Computation

As we know, the classic bit is the smallest unit in information processing, and its value is either 0 or 1. In quantum computing, the quantum bit (namely qubit) is quantum analogue of the classical bit, but it has two possible values $|0\rangle$ and $|1\rangle$ with a certain probability,

$$|\varphi\rangle = \alpha|0\rangle + \beta|1\rangle, \tag{1}$$

Where $\|\alpha\|^2 + \|\beta\|^2 = 1$, $\alpha, \beta \in C$. Since the vectors $|0\rangle$ and $|1\rangle$ can be represented as follows,

$$|0\rangle = \begin{pmatrix} 1 \\ 0 \end{pmatrix} \quad \text{and} \quad |1\rangle = \begin{pmatrix} 0 \\ 1 \end{pmatrix}, \tag{2}$$

the qubit $|\varphi\rangle$ can be expressed in vector form $|\varphi\rangle = \begin{pmatrix} \alpha \\ \beta \end{pmatrix}$.

Quantum operators over a qubit are represented by 2×2 unitary matrices. An $n \times n$ matrix U is unitary if $UU^\dagger = U^\dagger U = I$, where $U^\dagger$ is the transpose conjugate of U. For instance, Pauli X, Pauli Z, and the Hadamard H operators are important quantum operators over one qubit and they are described in Eq. (3).

$$X = \begin{pmatrix} 0 & 1 \\ 1 & 0 \end{pmatrix} \quad Z = \begin{pmatrix} 1 & 0 \\ 0 & -1 \end{pmatrix} \quad H = \frac{1}{\sqrt{2}} \begin{pmatrix} 1 & 1 \\ 1 & -1 \end{pmatrix}. \tag{3}$$

The operator described in Eq. (4) is *CNOT* operator that flips the second qubit if the first (the controlled qubit) is the state $|1\rangle$.

$$CNOT = \begin{bmatrix} 1 & 0 & 0 & 0 \\ 0 & 1 & 0 & 0 \\ 0 & 0 & 0 & 1 \\ 0 & 0 & 1 & 0 \end{bmatrix} \qquad (4)$$

In Quantum Physics, if a system is in a state which is a superposition $|\varphi\rangle = \alpha_0|1\rangle + \alpha_1|1\rangle$, upon measurement the system collapses to one of its basis state $|i\rangle$, probabilistically:

$$p(|i\rangle) = \frac{|\alpha_i|^2}{\||\varphi\rangle\|^2} = \frac{|\alpha_i|^2}{\sum_j |\alpha_j|^2}, \qquad (5)$$

which is the probability that the system will be found in the ground state $|i\rangle$ after a measurement. After the first measurement of a state $|\varphi\rangle$ if one performs another measurements will get the same result. The collapse of the state after measurement says that one cannot see all the results generated by the quantum parallelism. The challenge in quantum computation is how to take advantage of the quantum parallelism before performing a measurement.

2.2 Prefix-Threshold Real-Time Selection Method and Free-Space Communication

An important characteristic of a turbulent channel is the time-dependent transmittance, which follows a probability distribution called the *PDTC*. There have been multiple efforts to accurately characterize the PDTC, and a widely accepted model is the log-normal distribution

$$p(\eta)_{\eta_0,\sigma} = \frac{1}{\sqrt{2\pi}\sigma}\frac{1}{\eta}\exp\left(-\frac{\left(ln\frac{\eta}{\eta_0} + \frac{1}{2}\sigma^2\right)^2}{2\sigma^2}\right) \qquad (6)$$

Then, we can calculate the number of secure key bits from each bin, according to their respective η, and add all bins together. In the limit of $\eta \to 0$, this is an integration of $R(\eta)$ over η, with $p(\eta)_{\eta_0,\sigma}$ being the weight (i.e., the proportion of signals in each bin). We call this model the ratewise *integration model*. Its rate $R^{Ratewise}$ satisfies

$$R^{Ratewise} = \int_0^1 R(\eta)p_{\eta_0,\sigma}(\eta)d\eta \qquad (7)$$

To keep the consistency of notations with following discussions we will use parameters which is also used as the channel model for decoy-state discussion, where detector dark count/background count rate is Y_0, basis misalignment is $e_d\psi$, and total system transmittance is η_{sys}

$$R_{S-P} = (Y_0 + \eta_{sys})(1 - 2h_2(e(\eta_{sys}))) \qquad (8)$$

$$e(\eta_{sys}) = \frac{\frac{1}{2}Y_0 + e_d \eta_{sys}}{Y_0 + \eta_{sys}} \tag{9}$$

A point worth noting is that ψR_{S-P} has the unique property of having an $\eta_{critical}$ such that $R_{S-P}(\eta) = 0$ for all $\eta < \eta_{critical}$, and R_{S-P} for $\eta_{critical}$. This critical position can be expressed as

$$\eta_{critical} = \frac{Y_0}{\eta_d} \frac{\frac{1}{2} - e_{critical}}{e_{critical} - e_d} \tag{10}$$

3   A Free-Space Quantum Secure Direct Communication Scheme Base on P-RTS Method

In the free-space quantum direct communication protocol, the QBER of the channel is relatively high and change frequently because of the atmospheric disturbances in the free space. If the lowest transmission rate is used as the channel transmission rate, that means we assume the transmission rate of channel much lower than the expectation of transmission rate, and this will result in the message transmission efficiency of the protocol is low (but in fact mainly because of we do not make full use of the communication channel), and what's more, this may cause the insecurity of the protocol itself. In response to such problems, we have used the P-RTS method to select the sequence of transmitted light pulses, which can effectively solve such problems. The specific content of the program is as follows:

a)   Alice and Bob measure the expected atmospheric transimittance η_0 and its variance σ before the communication, and Bob uses formula to get the prefix threshold η_T. The channel information can be determined by the atmospheric conditions. The threshold η_T is a prior knowledge. Alice and Bob communicate by the Bell states $|\phi^{\pm}\rangle = \frac{(|H\rangle|H\rangle \pm |V\rangle|V\rangle)}{\sqrt{2}}$, $|\psi^{\pm}\rangle = \frac{(|H\rangle|V\rangle \pm |V\rangle|H\rangle)}{\sqrt{2}}$, where state $|H\rangle$ and $|V\rangle$ represent horizontally polarized and vertically polarized photons respectively. And the four Bell states $|\phi^+\rangle, |\phi^-\rangle, |\psi^+\rangle, |\psi^-\rangle$ are encode into 00, 01, 10 and 11, respectively.

b)   Alice prepares Bell states with two single photon pulse on microphoton operating platform. And the pulse length is Δt_1, intensity is η and contains N pair of Bell states $|\phi^+\rangle = \frac{(|H|H + |V|V\rangle)}{\sqrt{2}}$. After operation, Alice sends the first sequence of pulses to Bob. Bob receive these pulses and check the remaining intensity η_i. If $\eta_i > \eta_T$, then check the missing photon and continue protocol, else Bob abandon this pulse and inform Alice to resend.

c)   Alice and Bob perform channel security detection. Bob randomly selects different base to measure the first pulse. Then Bob tells Alice which base he uses and results he gets respectively. Last Alice measures the other pulse and compares the results. These results should be exactly the same within the tolerance of channel disturbance. If not, it means there is an eavesdropper, and they discard their transmission and abort the communication.

d) In remaining photons, Alice randomly chooses k photons as check states and chooses
    one of four unitary operations I, σ_z, σ_x, σ_{iy} to perform on the check states. For the
    other message states, Alice performs one of four unitary operations I, σ_z, σ_x, σ_{iy} to
    transform states $|\phi^+\rangle$, $|\phi^-\rangle$, $|\psi^+\rangle$, $|\psi^-\rangle$, respectively. These operations correspond
    to the encoding information 00, 01, 10, and 11 respectively. Besides, in order to deal
    with channel errors, Alice needs to use a reasonable code such as the Shor code.
    After that Alice sends the other pulses to Bob.

Bob receive the other pulses and Alice tell Bob the position and operation of check
states. Bob performs measurement on each Bell states and compares it with responding
operation. If error rate is small than the channel error rate, then Bob can makes an
measurement on every message states and get the information, otherwise we think there
is an eavesdropper, and the protocol should be abandoned and restart a new commutation
protocol.

Here we give the graphic process of the scheme.

4 Analysis

As shown in Fig. 1 (a), Alice uses two single photon source to prepare two pairs of Bell
states $|\phi^+\rangle = \frac{(|H\rangle|H\rangle + |V\rangle|V\rangle)}{\sqrt{2}}$, Laser1 and Laser2 emit single photon pulse in state $|0\rangle$. After
operation H and $CNOT$, Bell states $|\phi^+\rangle = \frac{(|H\rangle|H\rangle + |V\rangle|V\rangle)}{\sqrt{2}}$ are got. And these two photon
pulse sequences, namely S_c and S_m, are respectively stored in the photonic memory, in
which Alice can not only do unitary operation on photon but emit the sequences.

In Fig. 1 (b), Alice sends the photon pulse sequence S_c (for example, a part of
the 10 pairs of Bell states) to Bob through the atmospheric channel. Bob receives the
photon of sequence S_c and checks the total intensity of received photon (i.e., the number
of photons). Because of atmospheric turbulence and other uncontrollable reason, Bob
receives a total of 8 photons, and the other photons are lost. The intensity $\eta = 0.8$ (we
can calculate for the received photon intensity) satisfies the prefix threshold, after Alice
and Bob confirm that the fourth photon and the eighth photon are lost, the protocol can
be continued.

In Fig. 1(c), Alice and Bob perform channel security detection. Using the security
features of the Bell state, Bob randomly selects two photons to measure using σ_x base or
σ_z base, and the third and seventh pairs of photons are chosen. The measured results are
$|V\rangle$ and $|H\rangle$ respectively. Bob tells Alice the base, photon position, and measurement
results. Alice measures the corresponding photons in the selected two pairs of Bell states
based on Bob's published measurements and measurements and compares them with
Bob's results. If the measurement is the same as Bob, $|V\rangle$ and $|H\rangle$, it means that there
is no eavesdropper in the communication process, the agreement continues, otherwise
it means there is an eavesdropper and the agreement is aborted.

In Fig. 1(d), among the remaining photons, Alice randomly selects 2 photons as the
detection state, and the rest as the message state. Alice selects the first pair and the fifth
pair of photons as the measurement states. Alice randomly selects one of the unitary
operators I, σ_z, σ_x, σ_{iy} respectively: σ_z is used for the first pair of photons, and state
is transformed into $|\phi^-\rangle$, σ_x is used for the fifth pair of photons, which is transformed

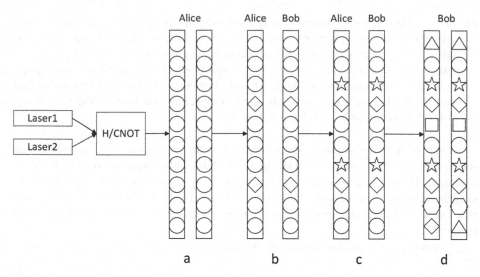

Fig. 1. Process of free-space QSDC scheme based on prefix real-time threshold selection method. The name upon the sequence represent the possessor, Each shape in the figure represents the four different kind of Bell state, and the shape of a circle, a triangle, a square, and a hexagon represent the transmission $|\phi^+\rangle$, $|\phi^-\rangle$, $|\psi^+\rangle$, $|\psi^-\rangle$ respectively, and the diamond represents the lost state, and the pentagon represents the state that has been used for detection.

into $|\psi^+\rangle$; the remaining Bell states have the second, sixth, ninth, and tenth pairs of photons that can be used to transmit messages. Here Alice uses $I, I, \sigma_{iy}, \sigma_z$ to encode the message in order to transmit the message 00001101. After the encoding is completed, Alice sends another sequence of photon pulses S_m to Bob. And after Bob receives the call, Alice tells Bob the location and operation of the detection states. Bob measures the detection states to evaluate the error rate. Bob measures the state of the first pair and the fifth pair of photons as $|\phi^-\rangle$ and $|\psi^+\rangle$, and by calculation the error rate is less than the threshold, where the threshold is the setting needs to be selected according to the actual application environment, not only related to the preset preset-threshold η_T, but also related to the transmission rate of free space and the photon frequency. At this point, Alice begins to measure each message state to measure and obtains the information, in which the 2nd, 6th, and 9th pairs of photons were successfully measured, the message 000011 was successfully transmitted; and by classical communication Bob knows the 10th pair of photons was lost in the second transmission, and information was lost, Bob Notifies Alice the message that it needs to be resent.

By means of free-space QSDC scheme based on P-RTS method, we can use quantum to transport message in free-space directly, securely and efficiently. With the safety guarantee of QSDC, an eavesdropper can hardly get any information from this communication process. And P-RTS method is significantly more convenient than protocols which perform optimization of threshold after the experiment is done. It will substantially reduce the amount of data storage requirements and calculation resource in the experiment (also in practical communication), since Bob does not need to store all data and wait until communication is over, and optimization is done before the communication, so real-time calculation capability is saved. In real-time communication service, reduce of real-time calculation capability will greatly reduce communication delay, and help improve service quality. And this method is especially effective for regions of high turbulence and high loss, and can even "salvage something out of nothing," when the secure key rate could have been zero without the P-RTS method. This make quantum mobile communication realizable, and may provide a new way of communication.

5 Conclusion

In this paper, we discuss the protocol of quantum direct secure communication in free space, and we also analyze the implementation and give a detail explanation of the protocol using and 10-pair-photon example. The photon transmission rate in free space has fluctuating interference, which has a great influence on the interference of the channel, and because of it is difficult to obtain a good QBER that meets the security requirements if we just use the lowest transmission rate. In response to such problems, we use the P-RTS method to select the sequences of transmitted optical pulses and only retain the high-transmitting optical pulses sequences and abandon the low-rate sequence and retransmission, this provides a small QBER for QSDC, ensuring the safety of QSDC in actual implementation. This method is good not only because the safety of the protocol, but also the efficiency. In the protocol we can calculate an optimal threshold and this can help improve the utilization efficiency of qubit, and a prefix threshold prevents calculating threshold during communication protocol, this save real-time computation capability, and can reduce the communication delay. However, when considering the actual use of free-space quantum direct secure communication as a solution for quantum mobile communication, some specific implementation details are not considered. In addition, in terms of code rate and communication speed, technical improvements are still needed to be put into practice.

Acknowledgement. The paper is supported by the project of the key technology projects of Anhui State Grid Information & Telecommunication Branch, project number: B1120718003P.

References

1. Ekert, A.K.: Quantum cryptography based on Bell's theorem. Phys. Rev. Lett. **67**(6), 661–663 (1991)
2. Bennett, C.H., Brassard, G.: Quantum cryptography: Public key distribution and coin tossing. Theoret. Comput. Sci. **560**, 7–11 (2014)
3. Sasaki, T., Yamamoto, Y., Koashi, M.: Practical quantum key distribution protocol without monitoring signal disturbance. Nature **509**, 475 (2014)
4. Hillery, M., Bužek, V., Berthiaume, A.: Quantum secret sharing. Phys. Rev. A **59**(3), 1829–1834 (1999)
5. Schmid, C., et al.: Experimental single qubit quantum secret sharing. Phys. Rev. Lett. **95**(23), 230505 (2005)

6. Long, G.L., Liu, X.S.: Theoretically efficient high-capacity quantum-key-distribution scheme. Phys. Rev. A **65**(3), 032302 (2002)
7. Deng, F.-G., Long, G.L., Liu, X.-S.: Two-step quantum direct communication protocol using the Einstein-Podolsky-Rosen pair block. Phys. Rev. A **68**(4), 042317 (2003)
8. Deng, F.-G., Long, G.L.: Secure direct communication with a quantum one-time pad. Phys. Rev. A **69**(5), 052319 (2004)
9. Hu, J.-Y., et al.: Experimental quantum secure direct communication with single photons. Light: Sci. Amp; Appl. **5**, e16144 (2016)
10. Zhang, W., et al.: Quantum secure direct communication with quantum memory. Phys. Rev. Lett. **118**(22), 220501 (2017)
11. Ursin, R., et al.: Entanglement-based quantum communication over 144 km. Nat. Phys. **3**, 481 (2007)
12. Yin, J., et al.: Quantum teleportation and entanglement distribution over 100-kilometre free-space channels. Nature **488**, 185 (2012)
13. Zhong, J., Liu, Z., Xu, J.: Analysis and improvement of an efficient controlled quantum secure direct communication and authentication protocol. CMC: Comput. Mater. Continua **57**(3), 621–633 (2018)
14. Liu, W., et al.: Full-blind delegating private quantum computation. CMC: Comput. Mater. Continua **56**(2), 211–223 (2018)
15. Bennett, C.H., Bessette, F., Brassard, G., Salvail, L., Smolin, J.: Experimental quantum cryptography. J. Cryptol. **5**(1), 3–28 (1992). https://doi.org/10.1007/BF00191318
16. Schmitt-Manderbach, T., et al.: Experimental demonstration of free-space decoy-state quantum key distribution over 144 km. Phys. Rev. Lett. **98**(1), 010504 (2007)
17. Ma, X.-S., et al.: Quantum teleportation over 143 kilometres using active feed-forward. Nature **489**, 269 (2012)
18. Nauerth, S., et al.: Air-to-ground quantum communication. Nat. Photonics **7**, 382 (2013)
19. Liao, S.-K., et al.: Satellite-to-ground quantum key distribution. Nature **549**, 43 (2017)
20. Ren, J.-G., et al.: Ground-to-satellite quantum teleportation. Nature **549**, 70 (2017)
21. Yin, J., et al.: Satellite-based entanglement distribution over 1200 kilometers. Science **356**(6343), 1140 (2017)
22. Bourgoin, J.-P.: Experimental and theoretical demonstration of the feasibility of global quantum cryptography using satellites. Ph.D. thesis, University of Waterloo (2014)
23. Vallone, G., et al.: Adaptive real time selection for quantum key distribution in lossy and turbulent free-space channels. Phys. Rev. A **91**(4), 042320 (2015)
24. Erven, C., et al.: Studying free-space transmission statistics and improving free-space quantum key distribution in the turbulent atmosphere. New J. Phys. **14**(12), 123018 (2012)
25. Wang, W., Xu, F., Lo, H.-K.: Prefixed-threshold real-time selection method in free-space quantum key distribution. Phys. Rev. A **97**(3), 032337 (2018)

Internet of Things

Design of Intelligent Mobile Robot Control System Based on Gesture Recognition

Dong Dai[1], Wei Zhuang[2], Yixian Shen[2], Lu Li[2], and Haiyan Wang[3]([✉])

[1] School of Cyber Science and Engineering, Southeast University, Nanjing 210096, China
daidong@seu.edu.cn
[2] School of Computer and Software, Nanjing University of Information Science and Technology, Nanjing 210044, China
{zw,syx}@nuist.edu.cn, lilu7qi@163.com
[3] School of Economic and Management, Southeast University, Nanjing 210096, China
hywang@seu.edu.cn

Abstract. At present, technologies such as smart home and intelligent wearable devices are developing, bringing convenience and enjoyment to our daily lives, while also avoiding a series of potential hidden dangers. This study aims to design an intelligent mobile robot control system based on gesture recognition which allows people to control the forward, backward and steering of the mobile robot through simple gestures. For gesture recognition, this paper uses the MPU6050 accelerometer to detect and recognize human gestures. The system adopts the control chip STM32 MCU to collect the acceleration data. The results of the experiments have shown that the proposed gesture recognition device can control the mobile robot maneuvering well and complete the function of forward and backward and steering.

Keywords: MPU6050 · Smart home · Wearable equipment · Mobile robot

1 Introduction

In the field of intelligent wearable devices, some have become very popular, such as smart bracelets. But these smart bracelet devices are limited to body temperature, heart rate, and step counting and other functions. In the field of smart home, the technology of using mobile phone APP, computers and other electronic devices to detect temperature and humidity and set accident alarms in real time has been relatively advanced [1–4]. As in the market, there are already off-the-shelf products that can control the rotation angle of blinds with mobile phone APP. However, there are few cases that the home robot is directly controlled by gestures.

Gesture recognition is an important research field in recent years. The solutions for gesture recognition are also diverse. In 2016, G. Luh et al. [5] proposed a muscle gesture-computer interface for controlling a five-fingered robotic based on a commercial wearable MYO gesture armband. The average recognition accuracy of 89.38% was achieved by the proposed system. Before that, Chen S. et al. [6] developed a practical

© Springer Nature Singapore Pte Ltd. 2020
X. Sun et al. (Eds.): ICAIS 2020, CCIS 1253, pp. 101–111, 2020.
https://doi.org/10.1007/978-981-15-8086-4_10

and effective hand gesture based robot control system using leap motion. Z. Ju et al. [7] proposed a new method to segment hand gestures in RGB-depth images in an order to reduce the error of Kinect sensing. At the same time, many researchers try to apply gesture recognition technology into improving the life quality of the elderly. Kundu et al. [8] presented a hand gesture based control system of wheelchair utilizing wearable sensors including inertial measurement unit (IMU) and myoelectric units in. The DSVM was used for classification and the accuracy while operating the wheelchair was 90.5%. In 2016, S. Jiang et al. [9] introduced a wristband for detecting eight air gestures and four surface gestures utilizing the fusion of sEMG and IMU which resulting in a total average recognition rate of 92.6% for air gestures and 88.8% for surface gestures. In 2017, N. Siddiqui et al. [10] investigated a novel hand gesture recognition method based on the acoustic measurements at wrist. A prototype with 5 microphone sensors was designed and Linear Discriminant Analysis (LDA) was selected for classification. In 2018, H. Kosawa and S. Konishi [11] introduced a new type of wearable motion capture device for detecting the motion of fingers based on an air cylinder. In 2018, J. Sun et al. [12] achieved 98.3% hand gesture recognition accuracy with convolution neural network by establishing the skin color model based on computer vision. Q. Yu et al. [13] proposed a human-robot interface based on two wireless standalone sensing system IMU sensors, among which, one IMU sensor fixed on human hand and another IMU sensor fixed on the mobile robot. The robot can move smoothly according to human's hand motion. In 2016, C. Assad et al. [14] designed a biosleeve which enables intuitive control of robotic platforms. In that paper, they demonstrated control of several small mobile robots using the biosleeve. It is worth mentioning that L. Anusha et al. [15] proposed a system in 2016 which aims to help dumb persons communicate with people who do not understand gestures. This system consists of MPU6050 for sensing gesture movement, Raspberry pi for processing, speaker for showing. The Raspberry convert the gesture data collected from MPU6050 to voice which can be of great benefit. In 2017, H. Basanta et al. [16] proposed a system to control the home appliances based on recognition of voice and gesture in an order to facilitate the life of elderly. In 2014, O. Sidek and M. Abdul Hadi [17] presented the development of wireless Bluetooth hand gesture recognition system using 3-axis accelerometers embedded in a glove and a database system which can recognize any sampled data saved in the database. In 2019, Zhuang, W. and Chen, Y et al. [18] proposed a new human activity recognition system only with a single wearable motion sensor which can accurately identify the daily activity of the human body.

The technology used in human gesture recognition field can be divided mainly into two categories, one of which is a video-based gesture recognition scheme. Although there are many gesture recognitions in the video direction, its requirements for the external environment are relatively high. Because the data acquisition part is all handled by the camera, the external light and background have a great influence on the data acquisition. In addition, the collected data is large, the gesture recognition delay is high and the software and hardware cost requirements are also high. Therefore, the video-based gesture recognition method has many limitations.

The other category is a sensor-based gesture recognition scheme. There are also a variety of solutions for gesture recognition using specific sensors, such as using infrared to perform gesture recognition, and this scheme mainly uses four directional diodes to sense infrared energy, and converts infrared energy data into distance information of four directions, and then matches the algorithm to determine the human gesture through artificial neural network, dynamic time warping, hidden Markov model HMM and so on. However, the limitations of the algorithm and the external environment are relatively large. Gesture recognition using the angular velocity accelerometer MPU6050 is also a scheme. Since the MPU6050 has its own digital motion processor (DMP), the raw data of the human gesture is processed and output in quaternion form, and then the quaternion is converted into Euler angle to further solve the attitude information. DMP only requires a less complex trigonometric function to obtain Euler angles, which is not only simple but also highly accurate.

2 Overall Design of the System

The process of the implementation of this system design is shown in the Fig. 1. According to the flow in the Fig. 1, we can know that the MPU6050 angular acceleration sensor worn on the human hand collects the raw angle data of the human hand and sends it to the STM32 main control chip 1 to solve the attitude angle. The MPU6050 mainly uses the IIC protocol to communicate with the main control chip. Since the STM32 integrates the IIC bus, the MPU6050 can communicate with the main control chip through a simple connection.

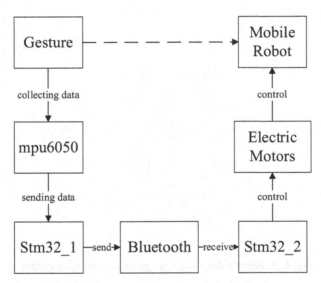

Fig. 1. System design implementation flow chart

After the master chip solves the attitude raw data, the data is converted into a corresponding control command and sent to another main control chip 2 which is used to control the shutter. Since the two main control chips need to communicate wirelessly, the two need to realize the transmission of control commands through the Bluetooth communication.

The main control chip 2 drives the motor to control the shutter flip according to the received command. According to the above process, the direct control of the mobile robot by human body gestures is finally realized (which is indicated by a dotted line in the Fig. 1).

3 System Hardware Design

3.1 Gesture Recognition System Hardware Design

The gesture recognition system is used to collect the raw data of the human gesture, and obtains the attitude angle of the human gesture according to the raw data which is through filtering processing, quaternion calculation, and so on. This part is mainly consisted of three parts: MPU6050 angular acceleration sensor, STM32f103C8T6 and Bluetooth HC05. The MPU6050 collects human gesture data and sends it to the STM32C8T6. The STM32C8T6 processes the data to obtain command control information and send them to the mobile robot control system module through the Bluetooth HC05 module.

The schematic diagram of the gesture recognition system and the PCB diagram are shown in the Fig. 2.

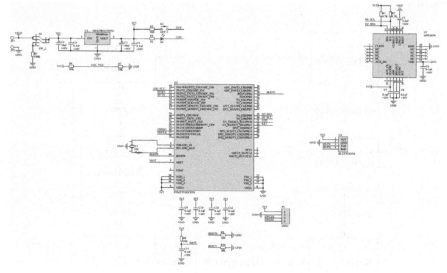

Fig. 2. Schematic diagram of the gesture recognition system

Stabilized Source Circuit. When designing the stabilized source circuit, this system refers to the STM32 minimum development board commonly used in the market, and selects the ME6206A33M3G circuit shown in the Fig. 3.

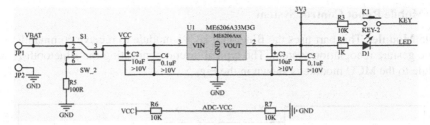

Fig. 3. Stabilized source circuit

MPU6050. The connection graph of the MPU6050 module is shown in Fig. 4.

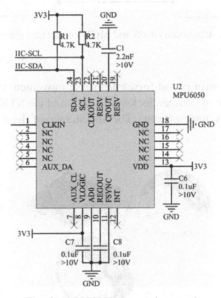

Fig. 4. MPU6050 connection graph

The commonly used typical circuits are provided in the official document of the MPU6050. According to the typical circuit, it is only necessary to connect the SDA and SCL pins of the chip to the serial data line and the serial clock line. Since the STM32F103C8T6 integrates the IIC internally, it is only needed to connect the GPIO pins with SDA and SCL multiplexing functions of the MPU6050 and the STM32F103C8T6. After consulting the official document of the STM32F103C8T6, it can be known that the PB8 and PB9 of the chip have SDA and SCL multiplexing functions respectively.

STM32F103C8T6. There are no overly complicated peripherals for this part. Because the system only uses two modules: the MPU6050 module and the Bluetooth HC05 module, and these two modules only need a simple pin connection. Therefore, the most important part of the design schematic diagram is to find out which of the GPIO ports of the STM32F103C8T6 is connected to the communication interface of the peripheral.

3.2 Mobile Robot Control System

HC05 Module. This part uses the Bluetooth HC05 module to receive commands sent by the gesture recognition system. The typical circuit connecting the Bluetooth HC05 module to the MCU module is shown in the Fig. 5.

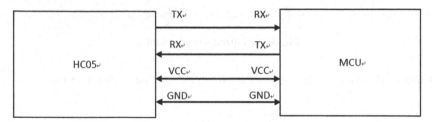

Fig. 5. Bluetooth HC05 and MCU connection diagram

Robot Module. The control of the forward/reverse movement of the mobile robot is realized by the clockwise or counterclockwise rotation of the STM32 direct drive motor which is driven by the system software. The appearance of the robot module is shown in the Fig. 6.

Fig. 6. Mobile robot module structure

4   System Software Design

The mobile robot control system based on hand gesture recognition mainly includes hand gesture recognition system software design and mobile robot system software design. The MPU6050 data collection, attitude calculation and sending control command are managed by hand gesture recognition system software. And the mobile robot system are responsible for receiving control command and control the motor.

System software design of hand gesture recognition system and mobile robot control are detailed in this section.

4.1 Hand Gesture Recognition Control System Design

The hand gesture recognition control system design can be divided into the following few steps: Firstly, connect the hardware circuit appropriately. Secondly, read the original data from MPU6050. Thirdly, calculate the attitude angle using the collected data. Fourthly, send the attitude angle to Bluetooth HC-05 module.

Reading Data from MPU6050 Using STM32. The STM32 reads the original data measured by gyroscope and accelerometer from MPU6050 using I2C. The reading process is shown in Fig. 7.

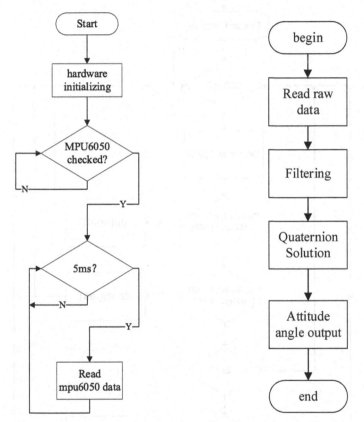

Fig. 7. The reading flow chart of MPU6050   **Fig. 8.** Attitude angle calculation procedure.

The delay function is initialized by system to achieve a high accuracy software's delaying. In this study, IIC is simulated using software. The SCL and SDA pin are configured in the initialization of IIC. Writing data into some registers to configure the sampling frequency, measurement range and working pattern of gyroscope and accelerometer. The timer is configure to produce an interruption every 5 ms in order to read data from MPU6050 in the interrupt handler.

Attitude Calculation. Attitude angle is calculated utilizing the data after filtering and quaternion calculation due to the original data read from MPU6050 cannot directly reflect hand gestures. The attitude angle calculation is shown in Fig. 8.

Converting the Hand Gesture Command. The hand gesture recognition algorithm flow is described as Fig. 9.

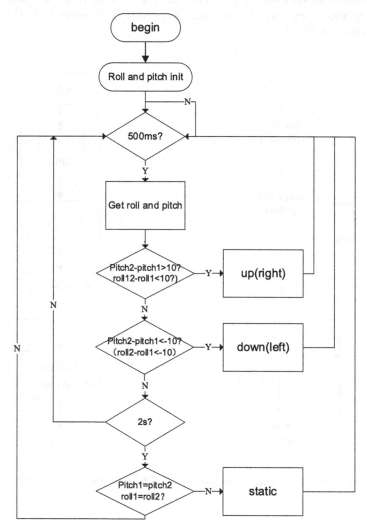

Fig. 9. Flow diagram of hand gesture recognition algorithm

5   Experimental Results

Because the STM32C8T6 used in this system is small and difficult to solder, the circuit scheme and PCB diagram are designed firstly and the PCB board is then produced. The real prototype of hand gesture recognition system is shown in Fig. 10 and Fig. 11.

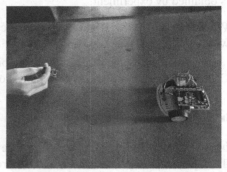

Fig. 10. Prototype of experimental mobile robot

Fig. 11. Controlling with hand gesture

The hand gesture definition and related control command are shown in Table 1.

Table 1. Hand gesture definition and related command

Gesture	Definition	Command
Turn up y degrees in x milliseconds	Wave up	Up
Turn down y degrees in x milliseconds	Wave down	Down
No action in z seconds	Static	Null
Turn left y degrees in x milliseconds	Wave left	Left
Turn right y degrees in x milliseconds	Wave right	Right

The attitude angle is calculated every 5 ms from the original data which is read from MPU6050 using STM32C8T6. Considering the high extraction speed compared with human hand movement, the data can be considered approximately as continuous. Thus, the specific hand gesture movement should be identified from the collected information. With the purpose of controlling the forward and backward movement of robot, wave up, wave down and static was identified in this study. The wave up and wave down was judged using the angle of pitch. The concrete method used is detailed as follows.

Wave Up. Time window size 0.1 s is selected in this study, which can better identify the hand gesture. Supposing the time window size is much bigger, some behaviors are likely to be ignored which will decrease the system sensitivity. If the time window size is much smaller, it won't be of any benefit but increase the system power consumption. Considering the low battery capacity in the wearable device, lowering the system power consumption is necessary.

Wave Down. The basic principle of identifying wave down is just like wave up.

Static. The static means the attitude angle of hand gesture has no big change in a period of time. Due to the variance can represent the dispersion degree, it is used in this design in order to evaluate the change of attitude angle in a period of time. Based on the variance of eight consecutive pitch angles, we can judge whether the hand is static. The threshold is obtained by experiment.

Wave Left and Wave Right. The identification of wave left and wave right is similar with wave up and wave down.

The final prototype of experiment mobile robot is shown in the following Fig. 10. Controlling the car with hand gesture is shown in Fig. 11.

6 Conclusion

In this study, a hand gesture recognition device based on MPU6050 has been built and the experiment result has shown that the proposed hand gesture recognition device can control the mobile robot successfully. Since the mobile robot in the experiment is an off-the-shelf module, it turned out the feasibility of controlling more complex robot with hand gesture. In this paper, three gestures are supported for controlling the robot, which can make the mobile robot go forward, go backward and turning. Considering there exists many operations in a complex robot system, more gestures should be supported and recognized in the future.

Acknowledgements. This work was supported by the National Natural Science Foundation of China (Grant No. 61972207), Jiangsu Provincial Government Scholarship for Studying Abroad and the Priority Academic Program Development of Jiangsu Higher Education Institutions (PAPD).

References

1. Wang, J., Gao, Y., Liu, W., Wu, W., Lim, S.-J.: An asynchronous clustering and mobile data gathering schema based on timer mechanism in wireless sensor networks. Comput. Mater. Continua **58**(3), 711–725 (2019)
2. Chin, H.-C., Pang, X., Wang, Z.: Analysis of bus ride comfort using smartphone sensor data. Comput. Mater. Continua **60**(2), 455–463 (2019)
3. Sun, Y., Gao, Q., Du, X., Gu, Z.: Smartphone user authentication based on holding position and touch-typing biometrics. Comput. Mater. Continua **61**(3), 1365–1375 (2019)
4. Su, J., Wen, G., Hong, D.: A new RFID anti-collision algorithm based on the Q-ary search scheme. Chin. J. Electron. **24**(4), 679–683 (2015)
5. Luh, G., Ma, Y., Yen, C., Lin, H.: Muscle-gesture robot hand control based on sEMG signals with wavelet transform features and neural network classifier. In: 2016 International Conference on Machine Learning and Cybernetics (ICMLC), Jeju, pp. 627–632 (2016)
6. Chen, S., Ma, H., Yang, C., Fu, M.: Hand gesture based robot control system using leap motion. In: Liu, H., Kubota, N., Zhu, X., Dillmann, R., Zhou, D. (eds.) ICIRA 2015. LNCS (LNAI), vol. 9244, pp. 581–591. Springer, Cham (2015). https://doi.org/10.1007/978-3-319-22879-2_53

7. Ju, Z., Ji, X., Li, J., Liu, H.: An integrative framework of human hand gesture segmentation for human-robot interaction. IEEE Syst. J. **11**(3), 1326–1336 (2017)
8. Kundu, A.S., Mazumder, O., Lenka, P.K., et al.: Hand gesture recognition based omnidirectional wheelchair control using IMU and EMG sensors. J. Intell. Robot. Syst. **91**, 529 (2018)
9. Jiang, S., Lv, B., Sheng, X., Zhang, C., Wang, H., Shull, P.B.: Development of a real-time hand gesture recognition wristband based on sEMG and IMU sensing. In: 2016 IEEE International Conference on Robotics and Biomimetics (ROBIO), Qingdao, pp. 1256–1261 (2016)
10. Siddiqui, N., Chan, R.H.M.: A wearable hand gesture recognition device based on acoustic measurements at wrist. In: 2017 39th annual International Conference of the IEEE Engineering in Medicine and Biology Society (EMBC), Seogwipo, pp. 4443–4446 (2017)
11. Kosawa, H., Konishi, S.: Wearable hand motion capture device. In: 2018 IEEE CPMT Symposium Japan (ICSJ), Kyoto, pp. 129–130 (2018)
12. Sun, J., Ji, T., Zhang, S., Yang, J., Ji, G.: Research on the hand gesture recognition based on deep learning. In: 2018 12th International Symposium on Antennas, Propagation and EM Theory (ISAPE), Hangzhou, China, pp. 1–4 (2018)
13. Yu, Q., Lu, Z., Liu, C., Wang, H., Tang, W.: Human-robot interface based on WSSS IMU sensors. In: 2015 IEEE International Conference on Cyber Technology in Automation, Control, and Intelligent Systems (CYBER), Shenyang, pp. 846–849 (2015)
14. Assad, C., et al.: Live demonstration: BioSleeve, a wearable hands-free gesture control interface. In: 2016 IEEE Sensors, Orlando, FL, p. 1 (2016)
15. Anusha, L., Devi, Y.U.: Implementation of gesture based voice and language translator for dumb people. In: 2016 International Conference on Communication and Electronics Systems (ICCES), Combatore, pp. 1–4 (2016)
16. Basanta, H., Huang, Y., Lee, T.: Assistive design for elderly living ambient using voice and gesture recognition system. In: 2017 IEEE International Conference on Systems, Man, and Cybernetics (SMC), Banff, AB, pp. 840–845 (2017)
17. Sidek, O., Abdul Hadi, M.: Wireless gesture recognition system using MEMS accelerometer. In: 2014 International Symposium on Technology Management and Emerging Technologies, Bandung, pp. 444–447 (2014)
18. Zhuang, W., Chen, Y., Su, J., Wang, B., Gao, C.: Design of human activity recognition algorithms based on a single wearable IMU sensor. Int. J. Sens. Netw. **30**(3), 193–206 (2019)

Multimodal Biometric Recognition Based on Convolutional Neural Networks

Hui Xu[1], Jun Kong[1,3], Miao Qi[1,2(✉)], and Yinghua Lu[3(✉)]

[1] School of Computer Science and Information Technology, Northeast Normal University, Changchun 130117, China
qim801@nenu.edu.cn
[2] Key Laboratory of Applied Statistics of MOE, Northeast Normal University, Changchun 130024, China
[3] College of Humanities and Sciences, Institute for Intelligent Elderlycare, Northeast Normal University, Changchun 130117, China
luyh@nenu.edu.cn

Abstract. In the traditional biometrics system, all stages are interacted and it is difficult to achieve a balance among pre-processing, feature extraction and classifier design. To address this issue, we propose an end-to-end trainable convolutional neural networks (CNN) model for multimodal biometric recognition, where high-level feature can be abundantly extracted by convolution operation. In order to improve the recognition performance by feature level fusion, two types of network structures and a two-layer fusion mechanism are put forward. Moreover, the fused features pass through convolutional and pooling layers for generating more informative feature representation. Specifically, the robustness of proposed method is also test on degraded image set. Experimental results demonstrate the proposed CNN model not only can achieve recognition rate of 98.84% in testing, but also is robust to conventional image degradation and applicable to identity recognition task.

Keywords: Multimodal biometrics · CNN · Two-layer fusion

1 Introduction

Biometrics have been widely used in identity recognition because of its stability, uniqueness and reliability. At present, unimodal biometric technology has achieved very good research results, such as palmprint [1], face [2] and iris [3]. However, along with the increasing expanded application of biometrics, identity recognition based on single modality has many disadvantages and limitations in real application. For example, forged biometric features increase potential safety hazard in the unimodal identification system. The loss, damage and lesions of biometric features will affect the performance of biometric system directly. To this end, multimodal biometrics are put forward, which can improve the robustness and safety by integrating a variety of biometric features. Some defects of unimodal features are made up by complementary relationship between different types of biometric features. For example, Krishneswari et al. [4] proposed

© Springer Nature Singapore Pte Ltd. 2020
X. Sun et al. (Eds.): ICAIS 2020, CCIS 1253, pp. 112–123, 2020.
https://doi.org/10.1007/978-981-15-8086-4_11

a multimodal biometrics method using palm print and fingerprint, where the discrete cosine transform and information gain were applied for feature extraction and selection. Chin et al. [5] proposed a 3-stage hybrid template protection method for fingerprint and palmprint verification, and bank of 2D Gabor filters were used for feature extraction. An adaptive bimodal recognition framework using PCA and sparse coding technologies for face and ear was proposed in [6], which is robust to various kinds of image degeneration. Group Sparse Representation based Classifier (GSRC) was presented for multimodal multi-feature biometric recognition [7]. Recently, Walia et al. [8] proposed a multimodal biometric system based on iris, finger vein and fingerprint using an optimal score level fusion model to resolve the conflict among discordant classifiers.

It can be seen that multimodal is the inevitable trend of biometrics. However, most of the literatures use statistics-based or texture-based methods for feature extraction. Although these methods can reach satisfying results, they are hard to discover deep features. What's more, it is hard to coordinate each stage since that the pre-processing, feature extraction and classifier design are independent in traditional models. To deal with this problem, many convolutional neural network (CNN) models has been applied in the field of biometrics, such as iris segmentation [9] and verification [10], face detection [11] and verification [12], fingerprint recognition [13]. Experimental results show the better performance compared with the methods based on hand-crafted representation. Nevertheless, little research has been done about multimodal biometric system based on CNN. Zhang et al. [14] proposed a Deep Convolutional Neural Network (DCNN) for contactless palmprint/palmvein recognition. However, the feature extraction and classification are separated by two stages. That is to say, this is not a end-to-end model and inconvenient to task processing. Koo et al. [15] presented a multimodal human recognition method based on face and body using VGG-16 and ResNet-50 for indoor human recognition. Although this method can recognize part of the body and twisted face, the network structure needs more layers to implement feature representation, resulting in the training process of CNN model is complicated. To deal with this issue, we propose an end-to-end multimodal model based on CNN. As we know, face and palmprint recognition are two popular biometric technologies, both of which are characterized by non aggression, reliability and acceptability. The multimodal system based on the combination of these two biometric features has good maneuverability and broad application prospects. Consequently, multimodal biometrics based on face and palmprint recognition is studied using CNN model in this work. Specifically, we realize feature level fusion by single-layer and two-layer fusion methods for improving the performance. Moreover, the discriminant feature is further represented by convolution and pooling operations after shallow fusion. In addition, the robustness of the proposed model is also evaluated on various image degeneration.

The three contributions of this paper are as follows:

(1) We propose an end-to-end CNN model for multimodal recognition task. The model can be easily extended to other modality recognition.
(2) The influence of model structures and fusion methods on recognition performance is investigated in detail and a group of optimal combination is recommended.
(3) The robustness of CNN model is evaluated by degrading biometric image. As far as we know, there is no related reported on CNN-based multimodal recognition.

The paper is organized as follows: Sect. 2 presents the detailed implementation of our algorithm. We show results of experiments conducted on two public benchmark datasets to verify our algorithm in Sect. 3. A brief conclusion will be made in Sect. 4.

2 The Proposed Method

In recent years, the rapid development of deep learning has attracted the attention of the academia, and has achieved good results in the fields of image recognition [16], behavior recognition [17] and scene analysis [18]. In the framework of depth learning, the output of lower level is used as the input of adjacent higher level, and the learning features from the bottom to the high-level are extracted step by step. Since deep learning model has shown good performance in the field of image processing, we proposed a CNN framework for multimodal biometrics, whose architecture is shown in Fig. 1.

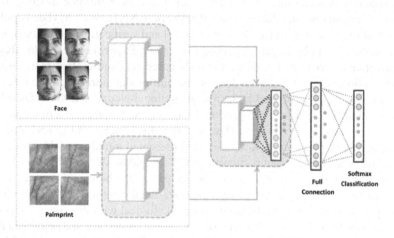

Fig. 1. The structure of the proposed CNN.

The CNN involves both 2D convolutional and pooling layers. The 2D convolutional layer extracts features for jointly capturing the appearance, The main function of the max-pooling layer is to reduce the spatial size of the convolutional layers' output representations, and it produces a limited form of the translational invariance. The detailed parameters of the CNN is shown in Table 1, where the parameters in bracket represent the size of kernel, the stride of pooling and the number of kernels.

In summary, the proposed CNN model contains 5 convolutional layers, 3 max-pooling layers, 2 fully connected layers (Fc). In Fc2, there is a Softmax layer for classification. Using this network, we can complete the following three tasks:

- Face recognition: the upper part can be adopted for face recognition, the architecture of this sub-network can be adjusted for improving the recognition performance, such as the number of convolutional layers, the size and number of filters.

Table 1. The parameter setting of the proposed CNN.

Input face(64×64 Grey image)	Input palmprint(64×64 Grey image)
Conv(3×3,1,16)	Conv(3×3,1,16)
ReLU	ReLU
Conv(3×3,1,16)	Conv(3×3,1,16)
ReLU	ReLU
Max-pooling	Max-pooling
Fusion	
Conv(3×3,1,32)	
ReLU	
Max-pooling	
Fc1	
Fc2	

- Palmprint recognition: the lower part also can be adopted for palmprint recognition by adjusting the network structure as face recognition. The structures of two sub-network may be not the same since their tasks are different.
- Multimodal recognition: this network can realize multimodal recognition task based on face and palmprint, which can reach the better performance compared with single modal recognition. Of course, this network architecture can be expanded to other modality.

The whole architecture of the proposed network can be divided three stages: feature extraction, feature fusion and classification. In the first stage, the input face and palmprint images are first normalized and reshaped to 64 × 64 grey scale images. Then they pass through a set of filters in the first convolutional layer, respectively. There are 16 filters which have a size of 3 × 3 kernel in this convolutional layer, and the filtered images are rectified by Rectified Linear Unit (ReLU) function to introduce non-linearity mapping. Next, another 16 filters are applied on this mapped results for obtaining high-level features. Finally, the max-pooling operation is adopted on feature maps for enhancing the robustness. At this point, 16 feature maps of size 32 × 32 are generated for face and palmpints, respectively.

The second stage is feature fusion. Information fusion is a key step in multimodal biometric systems. The feature-level fusion is more effective than the score-level and decision-level method owing to the fact that the original feature set contains richer information about the biometric data. So, the two sets of feature maps are fused and pass through 32 filters with size of 3 × 3 followed by max-pooling operation for encoding the feature maps into a more compressed representation. Thus, two types of discriminative feature is extracted and regarded as the input of fully connected layer. In particular, hierarchical fusion mechanism is designed to improve the recognition performance. To be specific, two-layer fusion structure is adopted in information fusion. The first layer is to fuse each feature map pair using three fusion methods for achieving feature extraction level fusion, as shown in Eq. (1). The first fusion method is to add two corresponding feature maps of different modalites. The second is multiplication of corresponding elements of two feature maps. The last one is to concatenate each feature map directly. The second layer is the feature response level fusion for achieving complementarity of three fusion methods, which is realized by fusing the results generated from the first layer.

$$
\begin{aligned}
f_i^1 &= f_{f_i} + f_{p_i}, \\
f_i^2 &= f_{f_i} \circ f_{p_i}, \qquad i = 1, 2, \cdots, k \\
f_i^3 &= [f_{f_i}, f_{p_i}],
\end{aligned}
\tag{1}
$$

where f_{f_i} and f_{p_i} represents the ith feature maps of face and palmprint images respectively. And $\circ$ is the product of corresponding elements, $[\cdot]$ represents to concatenate two feature maps directly, k is the number of feature maps.

The stage of classification is composed of two fully connected layers with one Softmax layer. The number of neurons of the Fc1 and Fc2 layers are set to 256 and the number of categories, respectively. The Softmax layer in the output of the network is used to compute a multinomial logistic loss during training as following:

$$
f(z_j) = \frac{e^{z_j}}{\sum_{i=1}^{n} e^{z_i}} \qquad j = 1, 2, \cdots, n
\tag{2}
$$

where z_i is the actual output of each neuron and n is the number of categories.

3 Experimental Results and Analysis

3.1 Database

The AR database is a facial verification standard dataset [19], which consists of over 400 color face images from 126 individuals (70 men and 56 women) and each individual contains 26 face images. In our experiment, a sub-set of this database contains 1400 face images corresponding to 100 subjects (50 men and 50 women) are selected as one type of modality for multi-modal biometric system.

The palmprint images come from partial Hong Kong Polytechnic University (http://www4.comp.polyu.edu.hk/~biometrics). In our study, 1000 palmprint from 100 individuals are selected as another type of modality. Each individual provides ten images. The size of all the original palmprint images is 384×284 pixels. In our experiments, sub-region(ROI, named palmprint in our study) of each original palmprint is cropped with the normalized size of 128×128.

3.2 Single Modal Recognition

For validating the performance of CNN in the filed of biometrics, we design different CNN models for face and palmprint recognition, respectively. Each time, we take half samples randomly from each class to construct the training set, and leave the rest as the test set of each database. The random sample selection is repeated 10 times and the average result is regarded as final testing performance. Table 2 lists the average recognition rate with different CNN networks, where 4 layer represents the structure of network is composed of two convolutional layers, one max-pooling layer and one fully connected layer. Specifically, one biometric image will first pass through 16 filters with size of 3 × 3 in the first convolutional layers. And then pass through another 16 filters with size of 3 × 3 in the second convolutional layer and followed by max-pooling operation with 2 × 2 window. Finally, the pooling results are input the full connected layer followed by softmax layer. In addition, the dropout is used to the fully connected layers for avoiding over-fitting and the probability is set at 50%.

Table 2. The average recognition rate of different modalities with various CNN models (%).

Databases	4 layers	5 layers	6 layers	7 layers	8 layers
Face	97.10	97.34	97.37	97.22	97.71
Palmprint	95.84	97.34	96.92	97.40	97.36

Table 2 illustrates that the depth of network has a certain effect on the recognition results. For different modalities, the depth is also discrepant for archiving better result. For face database, the CNN model with 8 layers reaches the highest recognition rate with 97.71%. However, the CNN model with 7 layers exhibits best results on palmprint database. That is to say, the structure of CNN model should be changed for different tasks. Moreover, the number of layers should not be too many for reducing the number of parameters and real-time identification.

For further verifying the efficiency and effectiveness of deep learning algorithm, we compare the accuracy of our CNN algorithm on face classification task with other methods using five standard face databases, including AR [19], Extended YaleB [20], CMU PIE [21], Yale [22] and LFW [23]. The details of each database are shown in Table 3 and the comparable results are given in Table 4. For fairness, we compare the results provided by the authors, which has the same running implementation process as us for recognition. For the structure of CNN, the number of layers is set as 6 and the number of iterations for training is set as 150. The results indicate that both neural network and non-neural network based methods can obtain relatively good results. However, the CNN method improve the recognition rate evidently. Extended YaleB in particular, it higher than LC-GODR by 6.77%. LFW is a challenging database, where the face images are collected from the web and take on great changes within the class. Although CNN method only reaches the recognition rate with 50.80%, it still higher than SFL-LBP by 3.39%. This table illustrates that the CNN can reach better performance due to the strong ability of extracting high-level feature and the pooling operation can improve the robustness of biometric system.

3.3 Multimodal Recognition

In general, multimodal recognition can reach better performance than single modality since multimodal data contains more discriminant information. In this experiments, we select 10 images for each person from AR database to match the palmprint database. In the same way as single biometric, half images are chosen randomly as training set and

Table 3. Detailed information of each face database.

Databases	Number of samples	Dimension	Class
AR	1400	64 × 64	100
Extended YaleB	2414	64 × 64	38
CMU PIE	1632	64 × 64	68
Yale	165	64 × 64	15
LFW	1580	32 × 32	158

Table 4. The comparable results on different face databases.

Methods	AR	Extended YaleB	CMU PIE	Yale	LFW
SFL-LBP [24]	93.93(7:7)	/	93.24(12:12)	96.40(6:5)	47.41(7:3)
LC-GODR [25]	92.9(7:7)	92.39(20:44)	93.45(12:12)	/	/
FNDC [26]	/	84.9(20:40)	/	93.60(6:5)	/
CNN	97.71(7:7)	99.16(20:44)	97.81(12:12)	98.13(6:5)	50.80(7:3)

The brackets represent the number ratio of training and test samples

the rest is used for testing in each time. The recognition rate can reach 96.74% with 6 layer network on selected AR face database. As we know, the structure of deep learning model is a very important for classification task. To investigate the effect of structure of network on recognition performance, we design two types of structures for multimodal biometrics, which are shown in Fig. 2. For each structure, we set the learning rate as 0.01. Similarly, we run the whole system 10 times and the average recognition rate is shown in Table 5.

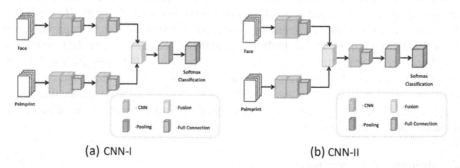

(a) CNN-I   (b) CNN-II

Fig. 2. Two network structures of CNN.

As shown in Table 5, both the structure of network and fusion method effect the recognition performance. From the point of network structure, CNN-II achieves the best

Table 5. The comparable results of different structures of CNN with single-layer fusion (%).

Structure	Addition	Multiplication	Concatenation
CNN-I	98.24	98.04	98.10
CNN-II	98.68	98.06	98.34

recognition rate with 98.68%, which is higher than face and palmprint recognition by 1.94% and 1.48%, respectively. This can be attributed to the addition of convolutional and pooling layers after fusion, which makes the two types of biometric feature further better represent and be more discriminative for classification. Although CNN-I also adds the convolutional and pooling layers before fusion, the recognition rate is not the best. This may be caused by over-extraction of feature for each modality. In other words, excessive feature extraction is not conducive to classification. Therefore, the design of model is very significant for specific task.

Seen from the perspective of fusion, the way of addition obtains comparatively better results followed by concatenation. Multiplication may widen the difference between the features and weaken the discriminant information between classes, so the recognition rate is relatively low compared with another two fusion methods. What's important is that both of these two networks obtain higher recognition rate than unimodal recognition.

According to Table 5, we can conclude that the single-layer fusion can improve the performance compared with unimodal recognition. And addition fusion give the best result. In view of this conclusion, we put forward a two-layer fusion mechanism. Based on the results of single-layer fusion, the second layer of two-layer fusion is designed with three ways as shown in Eq. 3.

$$F_i^1 = f_i^1 + f_i^2,$$
$$F_i^2 = [f_i^1, f_i^2], \qquad i = 1, 2, \cdots, k$$
$$F_i^3 = [f_i^1, f_i^3], \tag{3}$$

where F^j ($j = 1, 2, 3$) is the fused result of the first layer and input into the convolutional layer. The comparable results is list in Table 6.

Table 6. The comparable results of CNN-II with two-layer fusion (%).

Structure	CNN-II-F1	CNN-II-F2	CNN-II-F3
Recognition rate	98.64	98.84	98.62

We can see that the recognition rate can reach 98.84% by two-layer fusion, which is higher the single-layer fusion with 98.68% by 0.16%. This illustrates the proposed two-layer fusion method is effective and can improve the recognition performance to a certain degree. Although the rate of another two ways is lower than single-layer fusion with addition, they are still higher than another two single-layer fusion methods. That is to say, hierarchical fusion realizes the complementary advantages of single-layer fusion. Therefore, the structure of CNN-II-F2 is commended for this multimodal recognition task. Without doubt the structure can be lightly adjusted for accommodating other recognition task.

3.4 Robustness Test

Although biometrics system plays a significant role in kinds of safety area, biometric images may suffer from various degradation during the stage of data acquisition, such as blur, noise and compression. Ideally, we hope the conventional degraded images will not affect the biometrics system. In order to test the robustness of proposed CNN, we generated the degraded versions of each testing images as the following:

Low Resolution: We down-sample the biometric image with a scale factor r to formulate the quality degradation. Here, we set $r \in \{0.9, 0.8, 0.7, 0.6, 0.5, 0.4, 0.3\}$. In addition, the low resolution image is resized to 64×64 by using the nearest neighbor interpolation method for adapting the input of CNN model.

Gaussian Blurring: The biometric image is filtered by using a circular-symmetric 2-D Gaussian kernel of size $w \times w$ pixels. For generating different blur quality, we set the size of Gaussian kernel $w \times w \in \{3 \times 3, 5 \times 5, 7 \times 7, 9 \times 9\}$ and the standard deviation $\sigma \in \{0.01, 0.1, 1, 5, 10\}$. It can be observed that the blurring operation weakens the detailed quality of biometric image as shown in Fig. 3(b).

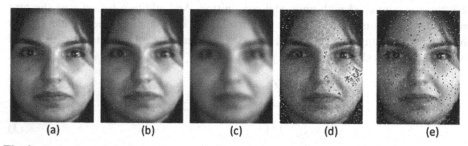

| (a) | (b) | (c) | (d) | (e) |

Fig. 3. Examples of degraded face images. (a) The original image, (b) Low-resolution (c) Gaussian blurring, (d) Gaussian noise, (e) Salt and pepper noise.

Gaussian Noise: In the process of capturing image, the Gaussian noise may be often introduced, whose strength is controlled by mean μ and standard deviation σ. In this work, we set $\mu = 0$ and $\sigma \in \{1, 5, 10, 15, 20\}$.

Salt and Pepper Noise: Besides Gaussian noise, salt and pepper noise might often occur in image. This type of noise changes the some pixels to black or white with a certain density d. Empirically, we set $d \in \{0.001, 0.005, 0.01, 0.03, 0.05, 0.07\}$.

As a result, 38 degraded versions $(7 + 4 \times 5 + 5 + 6)$ are generated for each testing image. For the first two kinds of degradation, the image loses some details. For the latter two kinds of degradation, some pixel values are changed. The curves of testing recognition rate under CNN-II with addition fusion are shown in Fig. 4.

Seen from Fig. 4, the recognition rate is not much affected with small interference. For low resolution, the recognition rate declines very slowly with increasing the scale

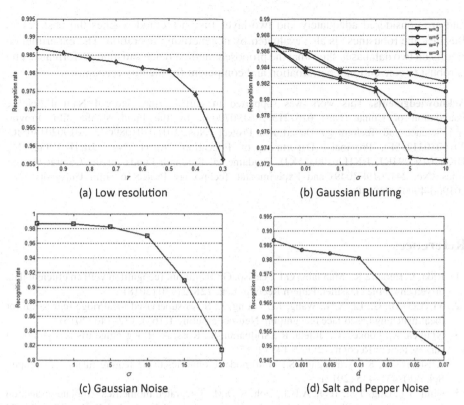

(a) Low resolution

(b) Gaussian Blurring

(c) Gaussian Noise

(d) Salt and Pepper Noise

Fig. 4. The recognition rate curves under different kind of degradation.

factor. Moreover, it still maintains a recognition rate of 98.06% when $r = 0.5$. Overall, the curves take on descending trend with increasing the size of window and standard variance for Gaussian blurring. The recognition rate still can keep above 98.20% with $w = 5$ and $\sigma = 1$. Even we add Gaussian noise with $\sigma = 5$, the recognition rate only descends 0.44%. With the increase of interference, the recognition rate is decreasing rapidly. For salt and pepper noise, the recognition rate descends to 98.34% with the density of 0.001. This figure illustrates the proposed method is robust to common degradation operation, which is due to the characteristics of CNN itself. As we known, the function of convolution operation is to highlight features and pooling operation not only can reduce the number of parameters, but also can enhance the robustness of the network. Therefore, the proposed CNN model is robust to certain degree of degeneration and is applicable to identity recognition task.

4   Conclusion

We have proposed an effective CNN network for multimodal recognition task. By fusing two types of features, the recognition performance is improved evidently compared with unimodal recognition. Moreover, the effect of different fusion methods on recognition rate are considered adequately and two-layer fusion method reaches the best result. Besides, the robustness is also evaluated by degenerating operation. The experimental results on two databases show that the proposed method reach satisfied performance and is robust to conventional perturbation and competent for identity recognition.

Acknowledgments. This work was supported in part by the National Natural Science Foundation of China (Nos. 61672150, 61907007), by the Fund of the Jilin Provincial Science and Technology Department Project (Nos. 20180201089GX, 20190201305JC, 20190303129SF), Provincial Department of Education Project (Nos. JJKH20190291KJ, JJKH20190294KJ, JJKH20190355KJ), Fundamental Research Funds for the Central Universities (No. 2412019FZ049) and Experimental Technology Project of Jilin University (No. 201906-409020720180).

References

1. Rida, I., Herault, R., Marcialis, G.L., Gasso, G.: Palmprint recognition with an efficient data driven ensemble classifier. Pattern Recogn. Lett. **126**, 21–30 (2018)
2. Yi, Y.G., Bi, C., Li, X.H., Wang, J.Z., Kong, J.: Semi-supervised local ridge regression for local matching based face recognition. Neurocomputing **1**(167), 132–146 (2015)
3. Nguyen, K., Fookes, C., Jillela, R., Sridharan, S., Ross, A.: Long range iris recognition: a survey. Pattern Recogn. **72**, 123–143 (2017)
4. Krishneswari, K., Arumugam, S.: Multimodal biometrics using feature fusion. J. Comput. Sci. **3**(8), 431–435 (2012)
5. Chin, Y.J., Ong, T.S., Teoh, A.B.J., Goh, K.O.M.: Integrated biometrics template protection technique based on fingerprint and palmprint feature-level fusion. Inf. Fusion **18**, 161–174 (2014)
6. Huang, Z., Liu, Y., Li, X., Li, J.: An adaptive bimodal recognition framework using sparse coding for face and ear. Pattern Recogn. Lett. **1**(563), 69–76 (2015)
7. Goswami, G., Mittal, P., Majumdar, A., Vatsa, M., Singh, R.: Group sparse representation based classification for multi-feature multimodal biometrics. Inf. Fusion **32**, 3–12 (2016)
8. Walia, G.S., Singh, T., Singh, K., Verm, N.: Robust multimodal biometric system based on optimal score level fusion model. Expert Syst. Appl. **116**, 364–376 (2019)
9. Bazrafkan, S., Thavalengal, S., Corcoran, P.: An end to end Deep Neural Network for iris segmentation in unconstrained scenarios. Neural Netw. **106**, 79–95 (2018)
10. Liu, N.F., Zhang, M., Li, H.Q., Sun, Z.N., Tan, T.N.: DeepIris: learning pairwise filter bank for heterogeneous iris verification. Pattern Recogn. Lett. **15**(82), 154–161 (2016)
11. Sun, X.D., Wu, P.C.S., Hoi, C.H.: Face detection using deep learning: an improved faster RCNN approach. Neurocomputing **19**(299), 42–50 (2018)
12. Schroff, F., Kalenichenko, D., Philbin, J.: FaceNet: a unified embedding for face recognition and clustering. Presented at the IEEE Computer Society Conference on CVPR (2015)
13. Sun, Y., Gao, Q.Y., Du, X.F., Gu, Z.: Smartphone user authentication based on holding position and touch-typing biometrics. Comput. Mater. Continua **3**(61), 1365–1375 (2019)
14. Zhang, L., Che, Z.X., Shen, Y., Wang, D.Q.: Palmprint and palmvein recognition based on DCNN and a new large-scale contactless palmvein dataset. Symmetry **10**, 78 (2018)
15. Koo, J.H., Cho, S.W., Baek, N.R., Kim, M.C., Park, K.R.: CNN-based multimodal human recognition in surveillance environments. Sensors **9**(18), 1–34 (2018)
16. Fang, W., Zhang, F.H., Sheng, V.S., Ding, Y.W.: A method for improving CNN-based image recognition using DCGAN. Comput. Mater. Continua **1**(57), 167–178 (2018)

17. Wang, Y., Long, M., Wang, J.: Spatiotemporal pyramid network for video action recognition. In: Proceedings of the IEEE Conference on Computer Vision and Pattern Recognition (2017)
18. Maamar, A., Benahmed, K.: A hybrid model for anomalies detection in AMI system combining K-means clustering and deep neural network. Comput. Mater. Continua 1(60), 15–39 (2019)
19. Martinez, A., Benavente, R.: The AR Face Database. CVC Technical Report 24, CVC (1998)
20. Lee, K.C., Ho, J., Kriegman, D.J.: Acquiring linear subspaces for face recognition under variable lighting. IEEE Trans. Pattern Anal. Mach. Intell. 5(27), 684–698 (2005)
21. Sim, T., Baker, S., Bsat, M.: The CMU pose, illumination, and expression (PIE) database. In: Proceedings of the IEEE International Conference on Automatic Face and Gesture Recognition, pp. 46–51 (2002)
22. Georghiades, A.: Yale face database. Center for computational Vision and Control at Yale University (1997). http://cvc.yale.edu/projects/yalefaces/yalefa
23. Huang, G.B., Ramesh, M., Berg, T., Miller E.: Labeled faces in the wild: a database for studying face recognition in unconstrained environments. Technical Report 07–49, University of Massachusetts, Amherst (2007)
24. Bi, C., et al.: Supervised filter learning for representation based face recognition. PLoS ONE 7(11), 1–16 (2016)
25. Wang, J.Z., Zhao, R., Wang, Y., Zheng, C.X., Kong, J., Yi, Y.G.: Locality constrained graph optimization for dimensionality reduction. Neurocomputing 5(245), 55–67 (2017)
26. Tang, Z.J., Wu, X.C., Fu, B., Chen, W.W., Feng, H.: Fast face recognition based on fractal theory. Appl. Math. Comput. 15(321), 721–730 (2018)

Multiple Graph Regularized Non-negative Matrix Factorization Based on L2,1 Norm for Face Recognition

Minghai Yao[✉], Jinsong Li, and Changyu Zhou

School of Information Science and Technology, BoHai University, Jinzhou 121001, China
yao_ming_hai@163.com

Abstract. In order to solve the problem that most non-negative matrix decomposition methods are sensitive to noise and outliers, resulting in poor sparsity and robustness, a multiple graph regularized non-negative matrix factorization based on L2,1 norm is proposed in this paper, and its performance is verified by face recognition. Firstly, the texture rich area is selected in the preprocessing stage. Secondly, L2,1 norm is used to improve the sparsity and robustness of decomposition results. Then, in order to better maintain the manifold structure of the data, the multi-graph constraint model is constructed. Furthermore, the corresponding multiplicative updating solution of the optimization framework is given, and the convergence proof is given. Finally, a large number of experimental results show that the superiority and effectiveness of the proposed approach.

Keywords: Non-negative matrix factorization · Graph regularization · Feature extraction · Face recognition

1 Introduction

As one of the most challenging classification tasks in computer vision and pattern recognition, face recognition have attracted much researchers' attentions [1–4]. Many face recognition techniques have been proposed in the past few decades. A face image of size pixels is usually represented by a dimensional vector. However, excessive high dimensionality has an impact on the efficiency and accuracy of face recognition. In the face of this situation, the method of feature extraction or data dimensionality reduction is generally adopted. The classic dimensionality reduction methods mainly include PCA, LDA, etc. Although these methods can reduce the dimension of the original data well, there is no non-negative requirement for the decomposition factor, so there are negative values in the decomposed components. These negative values have no physical significance in practical problems. Therefore, NMF is generated by operation.

In 1999, Non-negative matrix decomposition (NMF) algorithm was first proposed by Lee in Nature [5]. Its purpose is to approximate decompose the original nonnegative data matrix into the product of two matrices with nonnegative elements, namely basis matrix and coefficient feature matrix. This part-based, purely additive nature of the

© Springer Nature Singapore Pte Ltd. 2020
X. Sun et al. (Eds.): ICAIS 2020, CCIS 1253, pp. 124–135, 2020.
https://doi.org/10.1007/978-981-15-8086-4_12

NMF method can enhance the partial to overall interpretation of the data. Because of its non-negative constraints, sparse local expression and good interpretability, the NMF has been widely used in many real world problems such as face recognition, text clustering, feature recognition and information retrieval [6–8].

Many scholars have improved NMF and applied it in the field of face feature extraction and classification recognition. In 2002, Hoyer [9] integrated the idea of sparse coding into NMF, using L1 norm as sparse penalty term, and using Euclidean distance to calculate the error between the original data and the reconstructed data. To use the data geometric structure, Cai et al. [10] proposed a graph regularization non-negative matrix factorization (GNMF). In the GNMF algorithm, the geometrical structure of data is encoded by a k-nearest neighbor graph. In order to maintain the internal structure of the original data, Qing et al. proposed another variant of NMF, which is called a graph regularization non-negative matrix factorization (GNMF) method to describe the internal manifold structure of data points in the data matrix by constructing the neighborhood graph [11]. In order to improve the sparsity of the decomposition results and transmit the effective information, Jiang Wei et al. Proposed the sparse constraint graph NMF method (SGNMF) [12]. Zhou et al. Proposed the NMF algorithm based on Gabor wavelet by combining wavelet change and manifold [13].

With single figure to constraints of the internal structure of the original data, although to a certain extent to meet the demand of feature vector, but the results were not intellectual and meet the requirements of the single, while there are double or more constraints of the NMF algorithm, but while in measuring loss function based on L2 norm, existing algorithms are sensitive to noise and outliers caused by sparse decomposition results, and poor robustness problems. Therefore, this paper proposes a multi-graph regularized non-negative matrix factorization method based on L2,1 norm (L2,1-MGNMF). The method uses the line sparse property of L2,1 norm as the loss function. On the basis of the single graph regularization structure, the manifold structure of the original data is represented by fusing multiple graphs, and the constraints and decomposition results of the original structure of the original data are considered. Increased sparsity and robustness. The proposed L2,1-MGNMF method is finally tested on ORL and other face databases. A lot of experimental results show that our L2,1-MGNMF approach is effective and feasible, which surpasses some existing methods.

The remainder of the paper is organized as follows: Sect. 2 introduces the basic ideas of the existing NMF and GDNMF methods. Section 3 proposes our L2,1-MGNMF and gives theoretic analysis. Experimental comparisons are reported in Sect. 4. Finally, conclusions are given in Sect. 5.

2   A Brief Review of NMF

This section describes NMF and GNMF algorithms briefly. Let X be a training data matrix of $m \times n$-dimensional samples $x_1, x_2, \cdots, x_n$, $i.e.$, $x \in \mathcal{R}^{m \times n}$ with nonnegative entries. Each column of X represents a face image with m dimensions.

2.1 Non-negative Matrix Factorization(NMF)

NMF aims to approximately decomposes the training sample matrix X into a product of two non-negative matrices $A \in \mathcal{R}^{m \times r}$ and $S \in \mathcal{R}^{r \times n}$ (r ≪ min (m, n)), i.e., X ≈ AS. Matrices A and S are called basis matrix and coefficient matrix, respectively. In general, NMF is based on minimizing the Euclidean distance between X and AS. The corresponding optimization problem is as follows:

$$\min_{A,S} \|X - AS\|_F^2, \ s.t. A \geq 0, S \geq 0 \tag{1}$$

where $\|\bullet\|_F$ is the matrix Frobenius norm of a matrix. The optimization problem can be solved using gradient descent method. The well-known multiplicative update rules are as follows:

$$S^{(t+1)} \leftarrow S^{(t)} \frac{\left(A^{(t)^T} X\right)}{\left(A^{(t)^T} A^{(t)} S^{(t)}\right)} \qquad A^{(t+1)} \leftarrow A^{(t)} \frac{\left(X S^{(t)^T}\right)}{\left(A S^{(t)} S^{(t)^T}\right)} \tag{2}$$

The convergence of these multiplicative update rules have been proved in [14].

2.2 Graph Regularized Non-negative Matrix Factorization (GNMF)

To find a compact representation which uncovers the hidden semantics and simultaneously respects the intrinsic geometric structure, the graph regularized non-negative matrix factorization (GNMF) was proposed in [10]. GNMF solved the following optimization problem:

$$\min_{A,S} \|X - AS\|_F^2 + \lambda Tr\left(SLS^T\right), \ s.t. A \geq 0, S \geq 0 \tag{3}$$

where $Tr(\bullet)$ is the trace of a matrix and $L = D - W$ is called the graph Laplacian matrix, regularization parameter $\lambda \geq 0$ controls the smoothness of the new representation. The W denotes the weight matrix, and D is a diagonal matrix. The corresponding multiplicative update rules for solving Eq. (3) are as follows:

$$S^{(t+1)} \leftarrow S^{(t)} \frac{\left(X^{(t)^T} A + \lambda WS\right)}{\left(A^{(t)^T} A^{(t)} S^{(t)}\right)} \qquad A^{(t+1)} \leftarrow A^{(t)} \frac{\left(X S^{(t)^T}\right)}{\left(A S^{(t)} S^{(t)^T}\right)} \tag{4}$$

3 Multiple Graph Regularized Non-negative Matrix Factorization Based on L2,1 Norm (L2,1-MGNMF)

Although the existing NMF-based improved methods have achieved good results, they still have some limitations. In this section, we will describe our Multiple Graph Regularized Non-negative Matrix Factorization based on L2,1 Norm (L2,1-MGNMF). Further we formulate our optimization problem by adding supervised label information to the objective function of L2,1-MGNMF. The definition and update rules of L2,1-MGNMF are given below.

3.1 $L_{2,1}$-MGNMF Model

In order to maintain the original structure of the data as much as possible, this paper uses the neighborhood weighting, weight weighting, and sparse weighting to constrain the structure of the original data. The three weight matrices are defined as follows:

1. Neighborhood weighting. $W_{ij}^N = 1$ if and only if sample j is the nearest neighbor of sample i. This is the simplest weighting method and is very easy to compute.
2. Weight weighting. If sample j is the neighbor of sample i, then

$$W_{ji}^W = exp(\frac{-\|x_i - x_j\|^2}{2\sigma^2}) \qquad (5)$$

3. Sparse weighting. Sparse weight graphs can represent the sparse structure of the original data, and the sparse constraint is added to make the base image obtained by the decomposition represent the original image with as few features as possible, the weight matrix defined by:

$$W^S = s.t. \|x - D\varphi\|_p \leq \varepsilon, \qquad (6)$$

where φ is the sparse coefficient.

The $L_{2,1}$-MGNMF solves the following optimization problem:

$$\min_{A,S} \|X - AS\|_{2,1} + \alpha \sum_{x=1}^{X} \mu_x \left(\sum_{i,j=1}^{m} \|s_i - s_j\|_2^2 w_{ij}^x \right) + \beta \|\mu\|_2^2,$$

$$s.t. A \geq 0, S \geq 0, \sum_{x=1}^{X} \mu_x = 1, \mu \geq 0 \qquad (7)$$

where, W^X represents the x-th weight graph, and α and β are balance parameters. The discrimination ability of different graphs is very different. The weight μ should be set according to the graph, and the balance parameter α determines the influence of the integrated manifold structure on the objective function.

3.2 The Update Rules of $L_{2,1}$-MGNMF

Though the objective function in Eq. (7) is not jointly convex in the pair (A, S, μ), it is convex with respect to one variable in the (A, S, μ) while fixing the others. Therefore it is unrealistic to expect an algorithm to find the global minima. In the following, we can use the iterative solution of fixing two variables to update another variable which can achieve local minima. The solution process is as follows:

1. Fix μ and S, update A. To remove the irrelevant items, the optimization problem of A can be transformed into the following:

$$\min \|X - AS\|_{2,1} = tr((X - AS)D(X - AS)^T)$$

$$= tr\left(XDX^T - 2ASDX^T + ASDS^TA^T\right)$$

$$s.t.\, A \geq 0 \tag{8}$$

where D is a diagonal matrix $d_{ii} = 1/\|x_i - As_i\|$.

2. Let Λ be the Lagrange multiplier, the Lagrange ℓ is:

$$\ell(A, \Lambda) = tr(XDX^T) - 2tr(ASDX^T) + tr(ASDX^TA^T) + \lambda tr(\Lambda A). \tag{9}$$

3. The partial derivatives of ℓ with Eq. (9) is:

$$\frac{\partial \ell(A, \Lambda)}{\partial A} = -2XDS^T + 2ASDS^T + \lambda\Lambda = 0 \tag{10}$$

4. Using the KKT conditions $\Lambda_{ij}A_{ij} = 0$, we get the following equations:

$$\left(-2XDS^T + 2ASDS^T\right)A_{ij} = 0 \tag{11}$$

5. Fix μ and A, update S. To remove the irrelevant items, the optimization problem of S can be transformed into the following:

$$min\|X - AS\|_{2,1} + \alpha \sum_{x=1}^{X} \mu_x \left(\sum_{i,j=1}^{m} \|s_i - s_j\|_2^2 w_{ij}^x\right). \quad s.t.\, S \geq 0 \tag{12}$$

6. Similarly, we get the following equations:

$$\left(-2A^TXD + 2A^TASD + \alpha SL\right)S_{ij} = 0 \tag{13}$$

Where $L = \sum_{x=1}^{X} \mu_x L^x$.

7. Therefore, according to Eq. (11) and Eq. (13), we have the following updating rules:

$$A^{(t+1)} \leftarrow A^{(t)} \frac{(XDS^T)^{(t)}}{(ASDS^T)^{(t)}} \tag{14}$$

$$S^{(t+1)} \leftarrow S^{(t)} \frac{(A^TXD)^{(t)}}{(A^TASDS + \alpha SL)^{(t)}} \tag{15}$$

Theorem 1: The objective function O_1 in Eq. (7) is non-increasing under the updating rules in Eq. (14), and (15).

We can iteratively update A and S until the objective value of O_1 does not change or the number of iteration exceed the maximum value. Theorem 1 also guarantees that the multiplicative updating rules in Eq. (14) and (15) converge to a local optimum.

We summarize our Multiple Graph Regularized Non-negative Matrix Factorization based on $L_{2,1}$ Norm ($L_{2,1}$-MGNMF) algorithm in Table 1.

4   Experimental Results

In this section, we compare the proposed L2,1-MGNMF with four representative algorithms, which are NMF, SGNMF, LGNMF [15], and SPGNMF [16], on three face datasets, i.e., ORL [17], Yale [18], and PIE [19].

Table 1. The algorithm of L2,1-MGNMF

Input: Data matrix $X \in \mathfrak{R}^{m \times n}$, balance parameters α and weight μ ,convergence condition

Initialization: Randomly initialize two non-negative matrices $A \in \mathfrak{R}^{m \times r}$ and $S \in \mathfrak{R}^{r \times n}$

Repeat: 1. Update A by rule(14)

2. Update S by rule(15)

Until Convergence

Output: Basis matrix A

4.1 Dataset

Three datasets are used in the experiment. The important statistics of these data sets are summarized in Table 2. Figure 1 shows example images of ORL, Yale, and PIE datasets. Before the experiment, face image should be preprocessed. We think that the texture region contains more information, and the rest of the region is redundant. Therefore, the texture rich region is reserved for future experiments (see Fig. 2). Then, each face image is represented as a column vector and the features (pixel values) are then scaled to [0, 1] (divided by 255).

For each sample, we randomly select half of the images as the training set and the rest as the test set. Repeat random selection l times to ensure that 95% of the images have participated in the training and testing. The performance of L2,1-MGNMF is measured by Accuracy (ACC) and False Acceptance Rate (FAR).

Table 2. Statistics of the four datasets

Dataset	Number of samples (P)	Dimensionality (N)	Number of classes (K)
ORL	400	112*92	40
Yale	165	64*64	15
PIE	1632	64*64	68

4.2 Parameter Selection

The main parameters in the algorithm model are the dimension rafter dimension reduction, the iteration number Lit which affects the convergence speed of the algorithm, and balance parameters α which affects the decomposition error.

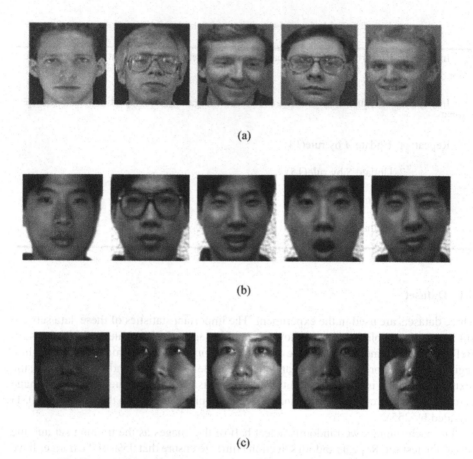

(a)

(b)

(c)

Fig. 1. Face image examples of the (a) ORL, (b) Yale, and (c) PIE datasets

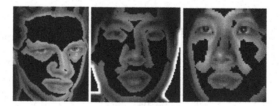

Fig. 2. Pre-processed image examples

Figure 3 shows the accuracy curve when Lit values 100, 300, 500, 800 and 1500 respectively. It can be seen from the figure that the performance of the algorithm increases with the number of iterations. Considering the relationship between accuracy and computational efficiency, Lit is set to 1500.

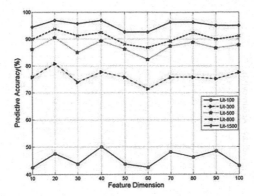

Fig. 3. The ACC with different Lit

It can be seen from the figure that the performance of the algorithm increases with the decrease of the balance factor α. when $\alpha < 0.01$, the performance of the algorithm fails to further improve, so the balance parameters in this paper is 0.01 (Fig. 4).

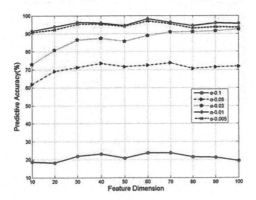

Fig. 4. The ACC with different α

4.3 Compared Algorithms

To demonstrate how our approach improves performance, we compared the following four popular algorithms: NMF, SGNMF, LGNMF, and SPGNMF.

Figure 5 gives that the average accuracy versus the dimension of the subspace. Figure 6 gives that the average FAR versus the dimension of the subspace. According to Fig. 5 and 6, it can be seen that the performance of the proposed method on three face databases is significantly higher than that of other methods.

Finally, we compared the sparsity of the matrix decomposition results of these five algorithms, and selected the base image obtained by the decomposition of the original data X. The feature dimension of the base image was set at 30, and the sparsity is defined

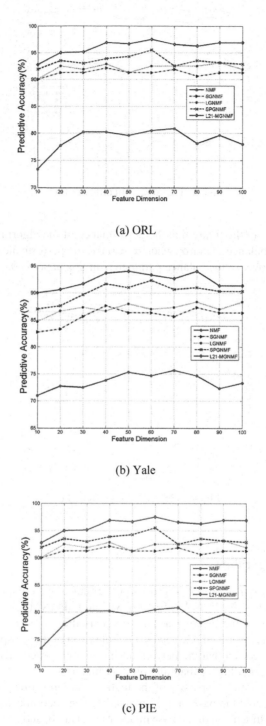

(a) ORL

(b) Yale

(c) PIE

Fig. 5. Face predictive accuracy on the (a) ORL, (b) Yale, and (c) PIE datasets

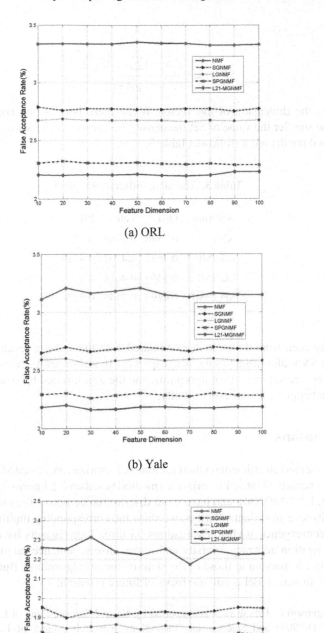

(a) ORL

(b) Yale

(c) PIE

Fig. 6. The FAR on the (a) ORL, (b) Yale, and (c) PIE datasets

by:

$$SP(x) = \frac{\sqrt{m} - (\sum |x_i|)/\sqrt{\sum x_i^2}}{\sqrt{n} - 1} \tag{16}$$

where m is the dimension of the vector. When there is only one non-zero element, $SP = 1$, the smaller the value of SP, the denser the vector x, otherwise, the sparser. The experimental results are as follows (Table 3):

Table 3. The SP of different algorithm

Algorithm	ORL	Yale	PIE
NMF	0.3546	0.3789	0.3762
SGNMF	0.4632	0.4762	0.4785
LGNMF	0.4469	0.4618	0.4539
SPGNMF	0.4793	0.5149	0.5278

It can be seen from the table that compared with the sparsity results of these algorithms, the NMF algorithm has the worst sparsity. In this paper, L2,1-mgnmf algorithm has the highest result than other algorithms, and the decomposed base image is the most sparse with better local expression ability.

5   Conclusions

We have presented an efficient method for matrix factorization, called Multi-graph regularized Non-negative Matrix Factorization method based on L2,1 norm (L2,1-MGNMF). As a result, L2,1-MGNMF can have more discriminative power than the conventional NMF and its several variants. Further, we show the corresponding multiplicative update rules and convergence studies. Evaluations on three face datasets have revealed both higher recognition accuracy, sparsity and lower false acceptance rate of the proposed algorithm in comparison to those of the state-of-the-art algorithms. But how to build a multi-graph fusion model is still the focus of future research.

Acknowledgements. This work was supported by Natural Science Fund of Liaoning Province (No. 2019-ZD-0503) and Science and Technology Research project of Liaoning Province Education Department (No. LQ2017004).

References

1. Luo, X., Xu, Y., Yang, J.: Multi-resolution dictionary learning for face recognition. Pattern Recogn. (93), 283–292 (2019)

2. Li, S., Liu, F., Liang, J.Y., Cai, Z.H., Liang, Z.Y.: Optimization of face recognition system based on azure IoT edge. Comput. Mater. Continua 3(61), 1377–1389 (2019)
3. Wang, X., Xiong, C., Pei, Q.Q., Qu, Y.Y.: Expression preserved face privacy protection based on multi-mode discriminant analysis. Comput. Mater. Continua 1(57), 107–121 (2018)
4. Yu, X., Tian, Z.H., Qiu, J., Su, S., Yan, X.R.: An intrusion detection algorithm based on feature graph. Comput. Mater. Continua 1(61), 255–274 (2019)
5. Lee, D.D., Seung, H.S.: Learning the parts of objects by non-negative matrix factorization. Nature 401(6755), 788–791 (1999)
6. Li, S.Z., Hou, X.W., Zhang, H.J.: Learning Spatially Localized, Parts-Based Representation. IEEE Computer Society (2001)
7. Yu, N., Gao, Y.L., Liu, J.X., Shang, J., Zhu, R., Dai, L.Y.: Co-differential gene selection and clustering based on graph regularized multi-view NMF in cancer genomic data. Genes 9(12), 586 (2018)
8. Su, Y.R., Niu, X.X.: An improved random seed searching clustering algorithm based on shared nearest neighbor. Appl. Mech. Mater. 3749(719), 1160–1165 (2015)
9. Hoyer, P.O.: Non-negative sparse coding. In: Proceedings of Neural Networks for Signal Processing, pp. 557–565 (2002)
10. Cai, D., He, X., Han, J., Huang, T.: Graph regularized nonnegative matrix factorization for data representation. IEEE Trans. Pattern Anal. Mach. Intell. 33(8), 1548–1560 (2011)
11. Liao, Q., Zhang, Q.: Local coordinate based graph-regularized NMF for image representation. Signal Process. 124, 103–114 (2016)
12. Zhou, J., Zhang, S., Mei, H., Wang, D.: A method of facial expression recognition based on Gabor and NMF. Pattern Recogn. Image Anal. 26(1), 119–124 (2016). https://doi.org/10.1134/S1054661815040070
13. Yang, Y.S., Ming, A.B., Zhang, Y.Y., Zhu, Y.S.: Discriminative non-negative matrix factorization (DNMF) and its application to the fault diagnosis of diesel engine. Mech. Syst. Signal Process. 3(26), 158–171 (2017)
14. Lee, D., Seung, H.: Algorithms for non-negative matrix factorization. Adv. Neural. Inf. Process. Syst. 13, 556–562 (2001)
15. Jia, X., Sun, F., Li, H.J.: Image feature extraction method based on improved nonnegative matrix factorization with universality (2018)
16. Jiang, J.H., Chen, Y.J., Meng, X.Q., Wang, L.M., Li, K.Q.: A novel density peaks clustering algorithm based on k-nearest neighbors for improving assignment pro-cess. Physica A: Stat. Mech. Appl. 3(12), 702–713 (2019)
17. Samaria, F.S., Harter, A.C.: Parameterisation of a stochastic model for human face identification. In: Proceedings of the Second IEEE Workshop on Applications of Computer Vision, pp. 138–142 (1994)
18. Belhumeur, P.N., Hespanha, J.P., Kriegman, D.J.: Eigenfaces vs. fisherfaces: recognition using class specific linear projection. IEEE Trans. Pattern Anal. Mach. Intell. 19(7), 711–720 (1997)
19. Sim, T., Baker, S., Bsat, M.: The CMU pose, illumination, and expression database. IEEE Trans. Pattern Anal. Mach. Intell. 25(12), 1615–1618 (2003)

Facial Expression Recognition Method Based on Convolution Neural Network Combining Attention Mechanism

Peizhi Wen[1], Ying Ding[1], Yayuan Wen[2], Zhenrong Deng[1(✉)], and Zhi Xu[1]

[1] School of Computer Science and Information Security, Guilin University of Electronic Technology, Guilin 541004, China
zhrdeng@guet.edu.cn
[2] College of Electronic Engineering, Guangxi Normal University, Guilin 541004, China
wenyy@gxnu.edu.cn

Abstract. Facial expression recognition is one of the research hotspots in the field of computer vision. Aiming at the problems that the current machine learning method extracts facial features are less robust and the traditional convolutional neural network can not fully extract the expression features, a residual network model integrating CBAM attention mechanism is proposed. Given an intermediate feature map, a attention map is generated on the channel domain and the spatial domain of the feature map respectively by our module, and multiplied by the original feature map to obtain a recalibrated feature map. In the training process, the improved loss function A-Softmax is used to generate the angular interval by manipulating the feature surface, so that the different class features learned have angular intervals in the angular space, and the similar features are more closely clustered. Experiments on FER2013 and JAFFE dataset show that the proposed method effectively improves the feature expression ability of the network, enhances the ability to distinguish different facial expression features, and achieves good recognition performance.

Keywords: Facial expression recognition · Residual network · Attention mechanism · CBAM · A-Softmax

1 Introduction

Human emotion information is mainly expressed through rich facial expressions. With the rapid development of artificial intelligence, intelligent computing technology is becoming more and more popular in people's lives. The recognition of facial expressions has more and more obvious application research value in human-computer interaction, interactive games, wisdom education and criminal investigation. Facial expression recognition can make computer understand human emotion better, make human-computer interaction not only stay at the level of instruction interaction, but also help computer to move forward to the level of intelligent interaction.

This work was supported by the National Natural Science Foundation of China (No. 61662014).

In the traditional machine learning research, the feature extraction of expressions has always been a difficult problem. Most of them use the method of artificially extracting features, and then use the artificially extracted features to train the shallow classifier to classify the expressions. Classic expression extraction methods include Histograms of Oriented Gradients (HOG [1]), Gabor wavelet transform [2], Local Binary Pattern (LBP [3]).

However, the manual feature extraction method can't explain the expression information efficiently, and the human interference factors will directly affect the feature extraction, so the shallow classifier trained by this method will have the problem of insufficient generalization ability. And in complex environments, such as the intensity of light, whether there is occlusion or posture transformation, the traditional machine learning method would be less robust.

In recent years, neural networks technology have been developed rapidly and have shown great advantages in the field of facial expression recognition. Neural networks automatically extract and learn the characteristics of samples, and can be classified by classifiers. This not only gets rid of the cumbersomeness of the artificial extraction feature, but also greatly improves the accuracy of the recognition and the robustness of the algorithm.

After that, the neural network is also used in facial expression recognition. For example, Tang [4] proposed to combine Convolutional Neural Networks (CNN [5]) with Support Vector Machine (SVM [6]), and gave up the cross entropy loss minimization method used by ordinary CNN, instead of using standard hinge loss to minimize margin-based loss. His method achieved a 71.2% recognition rate on the private test set and won the FER2013 [7] Face Expression Recognition Challenge. Zhang [8] adopted a stacked hybrid self-encoder expression recognition method. The network structure is composed of a Denoising AutoEncoder (DAE), a Sparse Auto-Encoder (SAE), and an Auto-Encoder (AE). The feature extraction is performed by DAE. SAE are cascaded to extract more abstract sparse features. Experiments show that the average recognition rate on JAFFE [9] dataset reaches 96.7%. Pramerdorfer [10] et al. analyzed the structural defects of facial expression recognition in deep convolutional neural networks, improved the structure of the classical convolutional neural network, and extracted the features of the face with a single face image as input, in the FER2013 dataset. A 72.4% recognition rate was achieved.

In addition, the combination of attention mechanism [11] and image processing further enhances the performance of the network. Attention mechanism can ignore irrelevant information and focus on effective information. For example, Jaderberg [12] and others proposed a spatial transformer module through the attention mechanism, and the spatial domain information of the image is transformed into a corresponding space, thereby extracting the region of interest in the image. Hu Jie et al. [13] proposed a novel architecture unit Squeeze-and-Excitation (SE) module. The SE module starts with the relationship between feature channels and adopts a new feature recalibration strategy. The way to automatically obtain the importance of each feature channel, and then to enhance the useful features according to this degree of importance and suppress features that are of little use to the current task.

To sum up, this paper proposes a convolution neural network method for facial expression recognition based on attention mechanism. Firstly, the depth residual network - residual neural network (ResNet [14]) is used as the basic model to avoid the gradient disappearance, the network model is too large and the accuracy is reduced with the deepening of the network. Then, the attention mechanism module of Convolutional Block Attention Module (CBAM [15]) is introduced to generate attention on the channel domain and the spatial domain of the feature map at the same time. That is to say, for a given feature map, CBAM module will calculate attention through independent learning along channel dimension and spatial dimension. Then, the attention map and the input feature map are multiplied to get a new and more detailed feature map, which improves the feature expression ability of the network model without significantly increasing the amount of parameters and calculation. At the same time, the improved loss function Angular Softmax [16] (A-Softmax) is used to manipulate the feature surface to generate the angular interval, so that the convolutional neural network can learn the angle discrimination feature, so as to increase the distance between classes, reduce the distance within classes, and further improve the network classification effect. The experimental results show that the method can prevent the gradient from disappearing, fully extract facial expression features, and effectively improve the expression recognition rate.

The remainder of the paper is organized as follows. In Sect. 2, we introduce the main techniques used in this paper; Sect. 3 introduce the methods we proposed in detail; Sect. 4 discusses the experiment setup and results. Section 5 concludes the work.

2   Related Technology

2.1   Residual Neural Network (ResNet)

ResNet was proposed in Microsoft Research Institute in 2015 and won the title of classification task in Imagenet competition. ResNet can quickly speed up the training of neural network to prevent the gradient from disappearing or exploding due to the deepening of network layers. It is also widely used in image recognition, segmentation and other fields. ResNet's main idea is to use residual learning to add identity short connection in the network and connect the original input directly to the later network layer. The residual learning module is shown in Fig. 1. The input is x, the output of fast connection is also x, and $H(x)$ is the ideal mapping. Originally, the learning is $h(x)$ only obtained through convolution layer. Now, the learning is the part of the difference between the input and output, i.e. the residual $H(x) - x$, which effectively prevents information loss and loss in information transmission. ResNet's residual module is divided into two types. The first one is a residual block with two 3 * 3 convolution layers connected in series, and the second is a residual block with two 1 * 1 convolution layers and one 3 * 3 convolution layer connected in series.

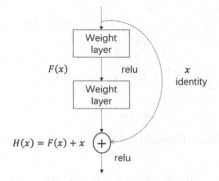

Fig. 1. Basic structure of residual network.

2.2 Convolutional Block Attention Module (CBAM)

In order to improve the feature extraction ability of the network model, this paper introduces the attention mechanism, which is to add the efficient attention module-CBAM to the network. CBAM is divided into a Channel Attention Module and a Spatial attention module. The overall structure is shown in Fig. 2.

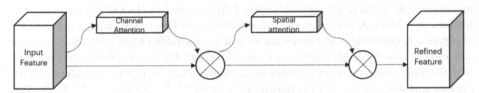

Fig. 2. The overview of CBAM.

The channel attention module is similar to the structure of SeNet, and the structure diagram is shown in Fig. 3. Firstly, the given feature map is compressed along the spatial dimension to get a one-dimensional vector and each two-dimensional feature channel becomes a real number, which has a global receptive field to some extent, and the output dimension matches the input feature channel number. It represents the global distribution of the response on the characteristic channel. The difference with senet is that the average pooling is not only considered in the spatial dimension compression of the input feature map, but also Max pooling is introduced as a supplement. After two pooling functions, two one-dimensional vectors can be obtained. Global average pooling has feedback to every pixel on the feature map, while global Max pooling only has gradient feedback in the most responsive part of the feature map, which can be a supplement to gap. The specific methods are as follows: input feature map as F, and F_{avg}^c and F_{max}^c represent the features calculated by global average pooling and global Max pooling respectively. W_0 and W_1 represent the two-layer parameters in the multi-layer perceptron model. The calculation in this part can be expressed as follows:

$$M_C(F) = \sigma(MLP(AvgPool(F)) + MLP(MaxPool(F)))$$

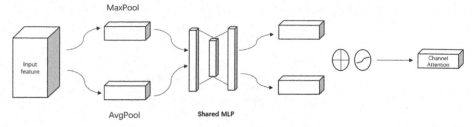

Fig. 3. Diagram of channel attention module.

$$= \sigma(W_1(W_0(F_{avg}^c)) + W_1(W_0(F_{max}^c))) \tag{1}$$

Where σ represents the sigmoid activation function to obtain a normalized weight between 0 and 1. MLP stands for multi-layer perceptron, and the feature between W_0 and W_1 in the perceptron model needs to be processed using ReLU as an activation function. ReLU function can largely solve the gradient dissipation problem of back propagation algorithm in optimizing neural network. In addition, the spatial attention module extracts attention from the spatial domain. Its structure is shown in Fig. 4. First, it compresses the input feature map through average pooling and Max pooling, which is different from channel attention. Here, it compresses along the channel dimension, averaging and maximizing the input features on the channel dimension. Finally, two two-dimensional features are obtained, which are spliced together according to the channel dimensions to obtain a feature map with two channels, and then a hidden layer containing a single convolution kernel is used to convolute it, so as to ensure that the final feature is consistent with the input feature map in the spatial dimension. Define the feature map after the max pooling and average pooling operations, $F_{avg}^s \in \mathbb{R}^{1*H*W}$ and $F_{max}^s \in \mathbb{R}^{1*H*W}$. The mathematical formula of this part is as follows:

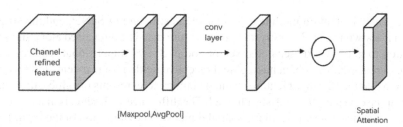

Fig. 4. Diagram of spatial attention module.

$$M_S(F) = \sigma(f^{7\times7}([AvgPool(F); MaxPool(F)]))$$
$$= \sigma(f^{7\times7}([F_{avg}^s; F_{max}^s])) \tag{2}$$

Where σ represents the sigmoid activation function and uses a 7 * 7 convolution kernel for extraction. CBAM is an efficient attention module that can be embedded into the mainstream CNN model. In this paper, we embed the CBAM module multiple times in the ResNet-based network model to extract facial expressions and obtain significant features.

3 Convolutional Neural Network Combining CBAM

3.1 Network Model Building

This paper takes ResNet as the basic network model, improves ResNet and introduces CBAM attention module to improve the feature extraction ability of the network. The schematic diagram of the network model is shown in Fig. 6. The network consists of 17 convolution layers, an average pooling layer and a full connection layer (FC). Among them, the convolution kernel is 3 * 3. After each convolution layer, Batch Normalization (BN [17]) and ReLU [18] are used. In addition, eight groups of residual modules (Res-Block) are set. Each residual module is composed of two 3 * 3 convolutions in series. The residual module is shown in Fig. 5.

Each two residual modules form a layer. The number of convolution channels in each layer is 64, 128, 256, 512. Each group of residual module is added with a CBAM module to re-calibrate the feature, and then the dimension is adjusted to 1 * 1 through an average pooling layer with a window size of 4 and a stride size of 4. Finally, a 7-dimensional fully connected layer is connected and seven facial expressions are classified using the A-softmax loss function.

3.2 Improved Loss Function

At present, due to the complex environment factors such as illumination, occlusion, posture deviation, etc., facial expressions of the same kind have large differences, while expressions of different classes have small differences. The traditional softmax loss function cannot solve this problem. Therefore, this paper proposes an improved loss function-Angular softmax (A-softmax) to increase the distance between classes and reduce the distance within classes, thus further improving the accuracy of expression recognition. When A-softmax was first proposed, it was applied to face recognition and won the first place in the 2017 MegaFace dataset recognition rate. Facial expression

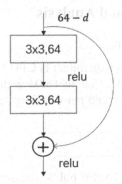

Fig. 5. ResBlock diagram.

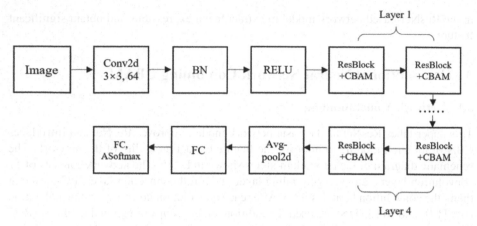

Fig. 6. The schematic diagram of the network.

recognition is essentially a multi-class problem. It is assumed that the feature vector of the last fully connected layer output is x_i, the corresponding label is y_i, and the A-softmax loss function is expressed as

$$L_{ang} = \frac{1}{N} \sum -\log \left(\frac{e^{||xi||\psi(\theta_{yi,i})}}{e^{||xi||\psi(\theta_{yi,i})+\sum_{j\neq y_i} e^{||xi||\cos(\theta_{j,i})}}} \right) \tag{3}$$

Where we define $\theta_{yi,i}$ as the angle between vector w_{yi} and vector x_i, $\Psi(\theta_{yi,i}) = -1^k \cos(m\theta_{y_i,i}) - 2k$, $\theta_{y_i,i} \in \left[\frac{k\pi}{m}, \frac{(k+1)\pi}{m} \right]$ and $k \in [0, m-1]$, m is an integer greater than or equal to 1, which is used to control the size of angle interval. On the basis of softmax, A-softmax increases the limit of angle by m times. At the same time, the weight (w) and bias (b) of full connection layer are set to 1 and 0 respectively. Therefore, the classification process depends on the angle between weight and bias. The loss function of A-softmax takes angle as the measurement standard of distance, which can learn the characteristics of angle boundary, and combine angle characteristics with learned characteristics. It improves the feature recognition ability of different facial expressions.

4 Experimental Results and Analysis

4.1 Experimental Environment

The hardware environment of this experiment is CPU E5-2698 V4, GPU Nvidia P100, memory 32G, video memory 16G. Ubuntu 16.04 is the operating system in the software environment, and python 3.6 and pytorch deep learning framework are used for programming.

4.2 Dataset Introduction

In this experiment, Fer2013 and JAFFE public datasets are used to train the network and analyze the experimental results. The Fer2013 dataset is the official dataset of the

2013 kaggle facial expression recognition competition. Because most of the pictures are downloaded from the online crawler, including pictures of different ages, different angles, partial occlusion, etc., it will be closer to the facial expression in the natural environment, but there will be some errors. Fer2013 contains 35887 pictures in total, and the dataset is divided into three parts: training set, public test set and private test set. The training set contains 28709 pictures, and both the public test set and private test set contain 3589 pictures. Fer2013 divides facial expressions into seven basic expressions: anger, disgust, fear, happiness, sadness, surprise and neutrality.

The JAFFE dataset is a dataset used by Japanese ATR institutions to study expression recognition. The dataset selects 10 Japanese women, each of which makes 7 basic expressions, including a total of 213 images. The JAFFE dataset are all face portraits. And the position in the image is roughly the same, the face size is basically the same, and it belongs to the standard expression data set.

4.3 Data Preprocessing and Data Enhancement

In the experiment, the images of the two datasets are normalized to 48 * 48 pixels. In order to enhance the robustness of the model to noise and slight transformation, data enhancement is used. In the training stage, we randomly cut the image into 44 * 44 pixels, and horizontally flip the image according to the probability of 0.5. In the test stage, we cut the image up, down, left, right and center, and then all horizontally flip, so that we can get 10 pictures, the size of the dataset will become 10 times the original, and the test accuracy is to average 10 pictures.

4.4 Experimental Results Analysis of Facial Expression Recognition

The experiment adopts the method of this paper and the existing methods to train, test and compare the two datasets respectively. Firstly, 28709 training sets in FER2013 dataset are used to train the model, 3589 public test sets are used as verification sets to adjust the super parameters of the model, and finally 3589 private test sets are used to test the model. During the training, we randomly initialize the weight and bias and perform 300 epoch training with the batchsize set to 64. The model pre-trains FER2013 and then adjusts the parameters of the JAFFE dataset, which can speed up the network convergence and improve the overall performance of the model. Due to the small amount of JAFFE data, we used a 5-fold crossvalidation method to train and test the network. The dataset is divided into five parts, four of which were taken as training set in turn, and the remaining one is used as test set validation. The average of the five results is used as the accuracy estimation of the entire dataset. All networks train only 30 epochs to prevent overfitting caused by the limited training set. In order to prove the effectiveness of the proposed method, the proposed model and a series of other models are compared on two datasets. The average recognition rate of different models on two datasets is shown in Table 1.

In this paper, we first make a comparative experiment on whether to add CBAM to ResNet. From Table 1, we can see that after adding CBAM, the recognition rate on FER2013 reach 73.1%, which is 0.7% higher than that of ResNet [10], and 1.9% higher than that of Tang [4], the champion of 2013 kaggle facial expression recognition competition, the recognition rate of JAFFE is 98.4%, 0.8% higher than that of ResNet [10],

Table 1. Comparison of average recognition rate of different models on two datasets

Model	FER2013	Model	JAFFE
Tang [4]	71.2%	Zhang [8]	96.7%
Resnet [10]	72.4%	Resnet [10]	97.6%
CBAM+ResNet+softmax	73.1%	CBAM+ResNet+softmax	98.4%
CBAM+ResNet+Asoftmax (Our)	73.5%	**CBAM+ResNet+Asoftmax (Our)**	98.9%

and higher than that of other classical models, which proves that CBAM can effectively improve the network's feature expression ability and recognition rate. In addition, this paper makes a comparative experiment between the non improved loss function and the improved loss function. It can be seen that compared with the traditional softmax loss function on the two dataset, the replacement of the Asoftmax loss function improves the recognition rate by 0.4% and 0.5% respectively, which proves that the Asoftmax loss function can effectively improve the feature recognition ability of expression and then improve the recognition rate. The method in this paper achieves 73.5% and 98.9% on FER2013 and JAFFE respectively, and achieves good recognition performance. Finally, this paper makes a comparative experiment on the sequence of channel attention module and spatial attention module in the network, and the experimental results are shown in Table 2.

Table 2. Comparison of average recognition rate of attention module sequence

Description	FER2013	JAFFE
Channel-first (Our)	73.5%	98.9%
Spatial-first	73.4%	98.7%
Channel and spatial in parallel	73.2%	98.6%

It can be seen from Table 2 that the channel-first order can achieve the best recognition effect. Table 3 and Table 4 show the confusion matrix of this model on Fer2013 and JAFFE dataset respectively. Table 3 shows that the recognition rate of happiness is the highest, reaching 91%, followed by the expression of surprise reaching 83%. However, the recognition rate of fear, sadness, neutrality and anger is lower than 70%. It can be seen from the Table 2 that the four expressions are easy to be confused. For example, anger and neutrality are easy to be confused into sadness, and fear and sadness are easy to be confused with each other.

Figure 7 shows an example of these four expressions with low recognition rate in Fer2013 dataset. It can be seen that in real life, these four kinds of expressions are very similar in themselves, especially when they don't know each other, and it is difficult to distinguish these expressions manually. As can be seen from the confusion matrix in Table 4, the recognition rate of the model in this paper has reached a high level, and the

Table 3. Confusion matrix of FER2013 recognition result

Real expression categories	Predict expression categories						
	Angry	Disgust	Fear	Happy	Sad	Surprise	Neutral
Angry	0.68	0.00	0.10	0.03	0.11	0.02	0.06
Disgust	0.11	0.75	0.05	0.01	0.02	0.04	0.01
Fear	0.08	0.00	0.63	0.02	0.13	0.08	0.05
Happy	0.00	0.00	0.01	0.91	0.02	0.02	0.03
Sad	0.08	0.00	0.14	0.02	0.64	0.01	0.11
Surprise	0.01	0.00	0.08	0.04	0.02	0.83	0.03
Neutral	0.05	0.00	0.06	0.06	0.15	0.01	0.67

Table 4. Confusion matrix of JAFFE recognition result

Real expression categories	Predict expression categories						
	Angry	Disgust	Fear	Happy	Sad	Surprise	Neutral
Angry	0.98	0.01	0.01	0.00	0.00	0.00	0.00
Disgust	0.00	0.98	0.01	0.00	0.01	0.00	0.00
Fear	0.00	0.01	0.99	0.00	0.00	0.00	0.00
Happy	0.00	0.00	0.00	1.00	0.00	0.00	0.00
Sad	0.00	0.01	0.00	0.00	0.98	0.01	0.00
Surprise	0.00	0.00	0.00	0.00	0.00	1.00	0.00
Neutral	0.00	0.00	0.01	0.01	0.00	0.00	0.98

overall recognition rate has reached 98.9%, among which the recognition rate of happy and surprised has reached 100%. This is because the JAFFE is a dataset specially used to study expression recognition, expression calibration standards, and all are positive faces.

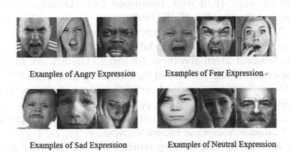

Examples of Angry Expression   Examples of Fear Expression

Examples of Sad Expression   Examples of Neutral Expression

Fig. 7. Four examples of confusing expression.

5 Conclusion

In this paper, we propose a residual network model which integrates the attention mechanism of CBAM. In this model, attention mechanism is introduced into the channel domain and the spatial domain of the feature graph, which effectively improves the feature expression ability of the model. The improved loss function A-softmax is used to increase the distance between expression classes and reduce the distance within expression classes. Experiments are carried out on Fer2013 and JAFFE expression dataset to verify the effectiveness of this method. The experimental results show that the method proposed in this paper achieves better expression recognition effect. In the future work, we will further improve the basic residual network structure, so that the network has better feature extraction ability, and further improve the expression recognition rate.

References

1. Dahmane, M., Meunier, J.: Emotion recognition using dynamic grid-based HoG features. In: IEEE International Conference on Automatic Face & Gesture Recognition & Workshops. IEEE Gesture Recognition (FG 2011). Face and Gesture 2011, Santa Barbara, CA, USA, 21–25 Mar 2011, pp. 884–888. IEEE (2011)
2. Wold, S.: Principal component analysis. Chemometr. Intell. Lab. Syst. **2**(1), 37–52 (1987)
3. Guoying, Z., Matti, P.: Dynamic texture recognition using local binary patterns with an application to facial expressions. IEEE Trans. Pattern Anal. Mach. Intell. **29**(6), 915–928 (2007)
4. Tang, Y.: Deep learning using linear support vector machines. arXiv preprint arXiv:1306.0239 (2013)
5. Fang, W., Zhang, F., Sheng, V.S., Ding, Y.: A method for improving CNN-based image recognition using DCGAN. CMC: Comput. Mater. Continua **57**(1), 167–178 (2018)
6. Li, R., Liu, Y., Qiao, Y., Ma, T., Wang, B., Luo, X.: Street-level landmarks acquisition based on SVM classifiers. CMC-Comput. Mater. Continua **59**(2), 591–606 (2019)
7. Goodfellow, I.J., et al.: Challenges in representation learning: a report on three machine learning contests. In: International Conference on Neural Information Processing, pp. 117–124. Springer (2013)
8. Zhang, Z.Y., Wang, R.Q., Wei, M.M.: Stack hybrid self-encoder facial expression recognition method. Computer Engineering and Application, pp. 1–8, 09 April 2019. http://kns.cnki.net/kcms/detail/11.2127.tp.20180920.1759.010.html
9. Lyons, M., Akamatsu, S., Kamachi, M., Gyoba, J.: Coding facial expressions with Gabor wavelets. In: Proceedings Third IEEE International Conference on Automatic Face and Gesture Recognition, pp. 200–205. IEEE (1998)
10. Pramerdorfer, C., Kampel, M.: Facial expression recognition using convolutional neural networks: state of the art. arXiv preprint arXiv:1612.02903 (2016)
11. Wang, F., et al.: Residual attention network for image classification. In: Proceedings of the IEEE Conference on Computer Vision and Pattern Recognition, pp. 3156–3164 (2017)
12. Jaderberg, M., Simonyan, K., Zisserman, A., et al.: Spatial transformer networks. In: Advances in Neural Information Processing Systems, pp. 2017–2025 (2015)
13. Hu, J., Shen, L., Sun, G.: Squeeze-and-excitation networks. In: Proceedings of the IEEE Conference on Computer Vision and Pattern Recognition, pp. 7132–7141 (2018)
14. He, K., Zhang, X., Ren, S., Sun, J.: Deep residual learning for image recognition. In: Proceedings of the IEEE Conference on Computer Vision and Pattern Recognition, pp. 770–778 (2016)

15. Woo, S., Park, J., Lee, J.-Y., Kweon, I.S.: CBAM: convolutional block attention module. In: Ferrari, V., Hebert, M., Sminchisescu, C., Weiss, Y. (eds.) ECCV 2018. LNCS, vol. 11211, pp. 3–19. Springer, Cham (2018). https://doi.org/10.1007/978-3-030-01234-2_1
16. Liu, W., Wen, Y., Yu, Z., Li, M., Raj, B., Song, L.: SphereFace: deep hypersphere embedding for face recognition. In: Proceedings of the IEEE Conference on Computer Vision and Pattern Recognition, pp. 212–220 (2017)
17. Ioe, S., Szegedy, C.: Batch normalization: Accelerating deep network training by reducing internal covariate shift. arXiv preprint arXiv:1502.03167 (2015)
18. Krizhevsky, A., Sutskever, I., Hinton, G.E.: ImageNet classification with deep convolutional neural networks. In: Advances in Neural Information Processing Systems, pp. 1097–1105 (2012)

Behavior Compatibility Analysis for Service Mashup with Model Checking

Zhongyi Zhai[1,2], Guibing Lai[1], Lingzhong Zhao[1(✉)], and Junyan Qian[1(✉)]

[1] Guangxi Key Laboratory of Trusted Software, Guilin University of Electronic Technology, Guilin 541004, Guangxi, China
zhaizhongyi@guet.edu.cn, laiguibing521@163.com,
zhaolingzhong163@163.com, qjy2000@gmail.com
[2] State Key Laboratory of Networking and Switching,
Beijing University of Posts and Telecommunications, Beijing 100876, China

Abstract. In existing mashup environment, end-users take charge of the behavioral compatibility of mashup services. Actually, because of the limited ability of end-users in both programming technique and domain knowledge, they cannot always find the mismatch of services' behavior. We present an automatic approach for analyzing the behavioral compatibility of service mashup with verification techniques of Communication Sequence Processes (CSP). The feature of this approach is that if a service process includes some incompatibilities, the counterexample would be returned to end-users to track the source of errors. In this approach, a Service Behavior Model (SBM) is presented to facilitate the modeling of services with CSP, and an automatic modeling approach is proposed for service processes through a modular way. Furthermore, two types of behavioral compatibility are introduced based on the development practice, and an automatic specification approach is presented for each type of compatibility properties. Finally, a case study is presented to analyze the behavioral compatibility based on our approach with PAT checker.

Keywords: Service mashup · CSP · Behavioral compatibility analysis

1 Introduction

In recent years, service mashup is proposed to generate applications quickly by combining web services together. A comprehensive check for syntax compatibility, semantic compatibility and behavioral compatibility during development is necessary to ensure the correct execution of the mashup application [1, 2]. Syntax compatibility is resolved by existing service mashup frameworks and tools [3]. The correctness of the interaction can be guaranteed by learning service function semantics to solve semantic compatibility

This work was supported by the National Nature Science Foundation of China (Nos. 61562015, 61572146, 61862014, 61902086), Guangxi Natural Science Foundation of China (No. 2018GXNSFBA281142), Innovation Project of young talent of Guangxi (AD18281054), Guangxi Key Laboratory of Trusted Software (kx201718).

© Springer Nature Singapore Pte Ltd. 2020
X. Sun et al. (Eds.): ICAIS 2020, CCIS 1253, pp. 148–159, 2020.
https://doi.org/10.1007/978-981-15-8086-4_14

[4]. Currently, formal verification method is an effective way to identify behavioral compatibility in service systems [5–8]. A compatibility analysis method based on Petri net is proposed to detect behavioral compatibility between two interactive services described by Business Process Execution Language (BPEL) [9]. In [10], the authors proposed a chor-calculus model to describe the Web Service Choreography Description Language (WS-CDL) service process. In [11], the authors proposed a service composition timing compatibility analysis method based on Petri net, which can be used to analyze state timing errors in the service mashup process. However, these behavior compatibility analysis methods can apply only to traditional service mashup, which can easily convert BPEL into a formal model. In contrast, service mashup usually uses a coarse-grained mashup and implicitly describes the logical relationship between services. To make better use of formal analysis techniques, a proper behavior model needs to be constructed for the service mashup model to convert between BPEL and formal model conveniently.

In this paper, we propose a service behavioral model compatibility analysis framework to complete compatibility analysis based on CSP model checking [12]. In addition, we divide the compatibility of service behavior into two types of compatibilities: structural compatibility and logical compatibility. Then, we use Linear Temporal Logic (LTL) to describe the properties of service behavior formally. Finally, we use CSP to verify whether the service processes satisfy the expected properties.

The paper is structured as follows. Section 2 proposes a service behavior compatibility framework based on model checking. In Sect. 3, we define the service behavior model and the behavioral semantics of the service process and then use CSP to formalize the process. Section 4 introduces two types of behavior incompatibility and proposes a compatibility analysis theory. Section 5 introduces the testing process of a case and evaluates it. Finally, Sect. 6 concludes the paper.

2 Behavioral Compatibility Analysis Framework Based on Model Checking

In order to assist the formal modeling of service processes, we construct a behavioral compatibility analysis framework based on model checking, which uses SDM and Service Relationship Model (SRM) in Lightweight Service Creation Environment (LSCE) [12] as the meta-model, in turn, LSCE can modify the incompatibilities in the service process by the results of formal analysis.

Figure 1 shows the framework. The framework mainly includes the following four parts: formal modeling of service process, analysis and specification of behavior compatibility, instantiation of models, and compatibility verification based on PAT. Formal modeling of service process provides an abstract method for service process with CSP. The basic components of the compatibility property are provided in the behavioral compatibility specification, which can be utilized to assist in the generation of behavioral property specifications for service process instances. In the instantiation of the model, we generate a CSP model of the service process instance and then generate a property specification for the service process instance. In compatibility verification based on PAT, the compatibility analysis is summarized as a process that satisfies the decision, and

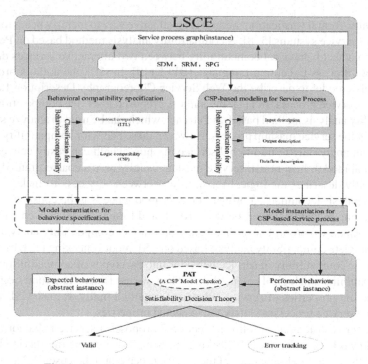

Fig. 1. Service behavior compatibility analysis framework

then the PAT detector can be used to verify whether the model conforms to the expected properties.

The verification framework defines a new set of basic models and transformation strategies to ensure the automation of compatibility analysis, such as service behavior models, compatible classifications and specifications. The following sections will explain the core theory separately.

3   Service Behavior Model and CSP Representation

This paper adopts a *data-driven* service mashup method, named, and the service component also uses *data attributes* as the basic features of service interaction. In the previous study, we have defined a standardized Service Data Model (SDM), which provides a valuable form of human-computer interaction for end users. However, behavior information is rough and not suitable for machine analysis. To accurately describe behavioral model of the service, we propose SBM based on SDM to comprehensively represent the basic elements for service behavior calculation.

3.1   Service Behavior Model

SBM is a service behavior representation model evolved from SDM, which removes the visual elements of SDM and extends the attributes and transformation information in SDM, and most importantly, it adds structure and logical information between attributes.

Definition 1 (*Service Behavior Model, SBM*). A Service Behavior Model can be abstractly represented as a 6-tuple, $<Inputs, Outputs, Op, f_{Inputs}, f_{Op}, R_{Outputs}>$, where,

$Inputs = \{inputs_1, inputs_2, \ldots, inputs_n\}$ represents a collection of input attribute sets related to the operation, and $inputs_i = \{a_1, a_2, \ldots, a_n\}$ is a collection of input properties related to operation Op_i. $Op = \{op_1, op_2, \ldots, op_n\}$ represents the set of operations contained in the service. $f_{Inputs} : Inputs \rightarrow Op$ means the mapping of input attribute set to operation set. $R_{Outputs} = \{R_{Outputs1}, R_{Outputs2}, \ldots, R_{Outputsn}\}$ represents the logical relationship information contained in each output attribute set.

SBM adopts data attributes as the basic feature elements of behavior, and the sequence of attributes formed by them is the specific performance of service behavior. For example, We give an abstract service S_i in Fig. 2, which contains two operations Op_1 and Op_2. Two output attributes belongs to the selection relationship. The SBM description of S_i is shown in Fig. 2(b). In Fig. 2(c), we list some of the possible behavioral sequences of S_i.

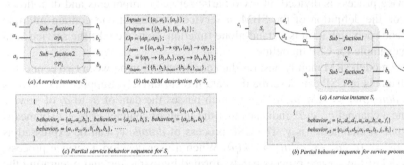

Fig. 2. Service behavior model instance and its behavior representation

Fig. 3. Service process instance and its behavior representation

A service process consists of a service component and a data flow, and its behavior can be abstracted as a sequence of attributes. The sequence is constructed based on the start input, data flow, and service component properties. For example, the single operations S_l, S_m and S_k are respectively connected with S_i to form a service instance. As showed in Fig. 3(a), the initial input is c_i, and the service has multiple possible execution sequences, as shown in Fig. 3(b).

3.2 Service Mashup Modeling Method Based on CSP

This section describes the service mashup process with CSP, including formalization of the service behavior model and formalization of the data flow. CSP is an abstract high-level language model that provides a series of operators and grammar rules to describe processes.

Definition 2 (*CSP syntax*). A capital letter is usually employed to represent a process. a$\rightarrow$P indicates the behavior of the process P after the execution of the event a. We assume that there are processes P and Q, and the other syntax of the process can be expressed as Table 1.

Table 1. CSP syntax rules

Expression	Rules
P;Q	P then Q
P□Q	P choice Q
PΠQ	P or Q (non-deterministic)
c?x:A → P	Channel c then P
P‖Q	P in parallel with Q
P‖‖Q	P interleave Q

Some basic CSP grammar and semantic rules are given below. More formal definitions of grammar and semantics can be found in [13].

The service process is divided into two parts: service components and data flows. Depending on the definition of the SBM, a service component can contain multiple operations, and each operation is a stand-alone function. Here we take the service S_i in Fig. 2 as an example for CSP modeling.

Data flow model-SRM mainly ensures data communication between two connected services. Channels in CSP can describe the data flow intuitively. Suppose that there is a data flow $dataflow_1 = <S_j, a_j, a_i, S_i>$, which passes the data of a_j to a_i of service S_i. We define a channel c_1, $c_1?x$ indicates that the input of channel c_1 is x. $c_1!y$ means that the output of channel c_1 is y. The CSP process of $dataflow_1$ can be expressed as $dataflow_{1(CSP)} = (c_1?a_j \rightarrow c_1!a_i \rightarrow Skip)$. When a user develop a service process, the CSP model of the service process can be formed by extracting and integrating the relevant service components and the data flow (Table 2).

Table 2. CSP modeling instance

Process	CSP expression
Inputs of Op_1	$Inputs_{op1} = (a_1 \rightarrow Skip)\|\|\|(a_2 \rightarrow Skip)$
Outputs of Op_1	$Outputs_{op1} = (b_1 \rightarrow c_1?b_1(x)\|a_2 \rightarrow c_2?b_2(y))$
Sequence process of Op_1	$Op_1(CSP) = Inputs_{Op1}; Outputs_{Op1}$
Inputs of Op_2	$Inputs_{op2} = (a_3 \rightarrow Skip)$
Outputs of Op_2	$Outputs_{op2} = (b_3 \rightarrow c_1?b_1(x))\|\|\|(b_4 \rightarrow c_2?b_2(y))$
Sequence process of Op_2	$Op_2(CSP) = Inputs_{Op2}; Outputs_{Op2}$
Service of S_i	$S_i(CSP) = Op_2(CSP)\|\|\|Op_2(CSP)$

4   Behavioral Compatibility Analysis Method for Service Mashup

In this section, we introduce two types of behavior incompatibility in detail, and then we describe the compatibility analysis theory based on model checking.

4.1   Classification of Behavioral Compatibility of Services

Structural behavior compatibility is primarily to prevent incomplete or incorrect connection of input/output attributes in the service process, as shown in Fig. 4. In addition, the service process may have input/output connection errors, such as the mismatch of data formats between input and output. In this case, the actual execution of the service process will stop in halfway. For service processes of behavior compatibility, the services should meet the following structural constraint rules:

1) Each element of the set of service operation input attributes connected to the data flow appears either simultaneously on the service's behavior trajectory or not simultaneously. It can be obtained from service behavior document.
2) If the output attributes of a service operation is a synchronous, the relevant output attributes must appear in the sequence of service actions at the same time.
3) If the output attributes of a service operation is a selective, then only one of the associated output attributes can appear in the sequence of service actions.

The above three rules can be described by LTL and can be used for judgement by generating the attributes to be verified during the design of service processes.

Logical behavior compatibility is primarily to prevent probable behavior conflicts between multiple services, as well as logical design errors. The description of the deadlock can be described using the assertion expression of the CSP validation tool. In addition, behavior-compatible service processes need to conform to the following rules:

1) If there is a selective relationship between data flows, then subsequent service behavior can only occur in one of the branches.
2) If the data flows are in a synchronous relationship, the branching behaviors should occur simultaneously in the subsequent process behaviors.

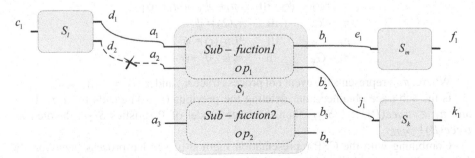

Fig. 4. Incomplete connection of service process instance behavior

These two rules can be described using LTL and generated validating properties adaptively during service process development.

4.2 Compatibility Analysis Theory Based on Model Checking

In order to facilitate the automatic analysis of service behavior, not only formal modeling of service behavior is needed, but also the compatible properties of behavior needs to be standardized. Here we introduce relative compatibility properties in LTL. The grammatical structure is $\psi ::= p \in A|\neg\psi|\psi_1 \wedge \psi_2|\psi_1 \vee \psi_2|G_\psi|X_\psi$ [14].

For the sake of brevity, only three tense operators G, F, X are adopted here. Among them, G operator means all future states, F operator means some future state and X operator means next state. The behavior compatibility rules can be represented by LTL as Table 3. The satisfaction of the CSP model for the above rules can be determined by its trace model. In CSP theory, there is a set of LTL satisfiability semantics based on trace model to solve the properties above recursively.

Table 3. LTL expression of behavior compatibility rules

Types	Rules	LTL expression
Structural	Rule(1)	$(Fa_1 \wedge \ldots \wedge Fa_n) \vee (\neg Fa_1 \wedge \ldots \wedge \neg Fa_n)$
	Rule(2)	$(Fd_1 \wedge \ldots \wedge Fd_n) \vee (\neg Fd_1 \wedge \ldots \wedge \neg Fd_n)$
	Rule(3)	$(Fb_1 \wedge \ldots \wedge Fb_n) \vee (\neg Fb_1 \wedge \ldots \wedge \neg Fb_n)$
logical	Rule(1)	$(Fa_1 \wedge Fa_2 \wedge \neg Fa_3 \wedge \neg Fa_4) \vee (\neg Fa_1 \wedge \neg Fa_2 \wedge Fa_3 \wedge Fa_4)$
	Rule(2)	$(Fa_1 \wedge Fa_2 \wedge Fa_3 \wedge Fa_4) \vee (\neg Fa_1 \wedge \neg Fa_2 \wedge \neg Fa_3 \wedge \neg Fa_4)$

Definition 3 (*LTL properties based on trace model can satisfy judgment* ($traces(P) \models S_{LTL}$)). There are process P and arbitrary LTL properties S_{LTL}, π_t is the longest trace extracted by $traces(P)$, and π_t satisfies the definition of S_{LTL} (denoted as $\pi_t \models S_{LTL}$) as:

$$
\begin{aligned}
\pi_t \models p & \quad \text{iff} \quad \exists i.p = \pi_{t(i)} \\
\pi_t \models \neg p & \quad \text{iff} \quad \pi_t \nvDash p \\
\pi_t \models \psi_1 \wedge \psi_2 & \quad \text{iff} \quad \pi_t \models \psi_1 \text{ and } \pi_t \models \psi_1 \\
\pi_t \models \psi_1 \vee \psi_2 & \quad \text{iff} \quad \pi_t \models \psi_1 \text{ or } \pi_t \models \psi_1 \\
\pi_t \models X_\psi & \quad \text{iff} \quad \pi_t(2) \models \psi \\
\pi_t \models F_\psi & \quad \text{iff} \quad \exists i.\pi_t(i) \models \psi \\
\pi_t \models G_\psi & \quad \text{iff} \quad \pi_t \models \neg F \neg \psi
\end{aligned}
$$

Where, $\pi_{t(i)}$ represents the event i of process trace π_t, and $\pi_t(i) = \pi_{t(i)} \to \pi_{t(i+1)} \to \ldots$ is the sub-trace obtained after deleting the previous (i − 1) events from π_t. If for any $\pi_t \in trace(P)$, $\pi_t \models S_{LTL}$, then the trace model of P satisfies S_{LTL}, denoted as: $trace(P) \models S_{LTL}$.

Combining with the CSP representation method of service process behavior, the *LTL* specification of behavior compatibility, and the above determination method, if $trace(P) \models S_{LTL}$, i.e., process $P \models S_{LTL}$, the following conclusions can be proved.

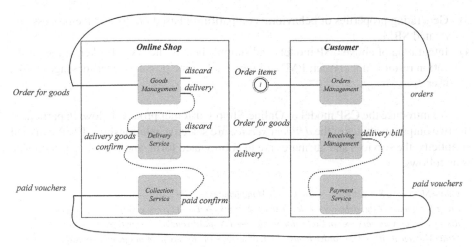

Fig. 5. An Online-Shop/Customer service process case

Theorem 1: If $SPG_{i(CSP)} \vDash R_{LTL}$, then service process instance SPG_i meets the behavior compatibility rule R, where, $SPG_{i(CSP)}$ represents the CSP model of SPG_i and R_{LTL} represents the LTL specification of R.

Proof: If $SPG_{i(CSP)} \vDash R_{LTL}$, $traces(SPG_{i(CSP)}) \vDash R_{LTL}$ can be obtained. According to Sect. 4, trace model of $SPG_{i(CSP)}$ is equivalent to service behavior execution sequence of SPG_i. Therefore, the service behavior of SPG_i meets the properties of SPG_i, and the service behavior of SPG_i meets the compatibility rule R.

According to Theorem 1, compatibility verification of the service can be transformed into the satisfiable verification of the corresponding model. Our core work is to generate the CSP model of service processes and the specification of compatibility properties to reduce end-user involvement.

5   Case Analysis and Verification

5.1   Service Process Instance Analysis

In this section, we use the Customer/Online Shop service process as an example to discuss the verification of service mashup. Figure 5 shows the internal structure of the service and its business relationship. The *Customer Service* required users pay bills after they received the goods, the *Online Shop* needs users pay first. For this service process, the above verification methods can be utilized to assist in the discovery of errors. The verification of service instances can be roughly divided into four steps:

1) Generating SBM and automatically transforming into CSP model after the service is accessed.
2) Generating a CSP model of the data flow after a service process is designed.

3) Generating properties of behavioral compatibility based on the service process and related SBM.
4) Integrating of above CSP models and submit them to the PAT checker. If the verification result is not correct, PAT will feed back some possible error messages to the user.

We introduce the CSP model of Online-Shop/Customer process below. In particular, the two output attributes of the *delivery service* are selective relationships. For the sake of simplicity, the services and attributes are in abbreviated form, and their correspondence is as follows:

$OnlineShop \rightarrow OS$, $Customer \rightarrow Cu$, $Goods\ Management \rightarrow GM$,
order for goods $\rightarrow og$, *delevery* $\rightarrow de$, *Delivery Service* $\rightarrow DS$, *delivery goods* $\rightarrow dg$, *confirm* $\rightarrow co$,
discard $\rightarrow di$, *vouchers* $\rightarrow vo$, *CollectionService* $\rightarrow CS$, *paid vouchers* $\rightarrow pvl$, *paid confirm* $\rightarrow pc$,
OrderManagement $\rightarrow OM$, *order items* $\rightarrow oi$, *orders* $\rightarrow or$, *ReceivingManagement* $\rightarrow RM$,
goods $\rightarrow go$, *delivery bill* $\rightarrow dbl$, *PaymentService* $\rightarrow PS$, *delivery bill* $\rightarrow db$, *paid vouchers* $\rightarrow pv$.

//Service S and its internal data flow

$Inputs_{GM} = (og \rightarrow Skip). Outputs_{GM} = (de \rightarrow c_1?de). GM_{(CSP)} = Inputs_{GM}; Outputs_{GM}$.
$Inputs_{DS} = (dg \rightarrow Skip)||||(co \rightarrow Skip). Outputs_{DS} = (di \rightarrow Skip|del \rightarrow c_4?del)$
$DS_{(CSP)} = Inputs_{DS}; Outputs_{DS}.Inputs_{CS} = (pvl \rightarrow Skip). Outputs_{CS} = (pc \rightarrow c_1?pc). CS_{(CSP)} = Inputs_{CS};$
$Outputs_{CS}.dataflow_{1(CSP)} = (c_1?de \rightarrow c_1!dg \rightarrow Skip). dataflow_{2(CSP)} = (c_2?pc \rightarrow c_2!co \rightarrow Skip)$.
$OS = GM_{(CSP)}||dataflow_{1(CSP)}||CS_{(CSP)}||dataflow_{2(CSP)}||DS_{(CSP)}$.

//Service Cu and its internal data flow

$Inputs_{OM} = (oi \rightarrow Skip).Outputs_{OM} = (or \rightarrow c_5?or).OM_{(CSP)} = Inputs_{OM}; Outputs_{OM}$.
$Inputs_{RM} = (go \rightarrow Skip).Outputs_{RM} = (db1 \rightarrow c_3?db).RM_{(CSP)} = Inputs_{RM}; Outputs_{RM}$.
$Inputs_{PS} = (db \rightarrow Skip).Outputs_{PS} = (pv \rightarrow c_6?pv).PS_{(CSP)} = Inputs_{PS}; Outputs_{PS}$.
$dataflow_{3(CSP)} = (c_3?db1 \rightarrow c_3!db \rightarrow Skip).Cu = (RM_{(CSP)}||dataflow_{3(CSP)}||PS_{(CSP)})||||OM_{(CSP)}$.

//Service *OS&Cu* and their internal data flow

$dataflow_{4(CSP)} = (c_4?del \rightarrow c_4!go \rightarrow Skip).dataflow_{5(CSP)} = (c_5?or \rightarrow c_5!og \rightarrow Skip)$.
$dataflow_{6(CSP)} = (c_6?pv \rightarrow c_6!pvl \rightarrow Skip)$.
$Cu\_OS = OS||dataflow_{4(CSP)}||dataflow_{5(CSP)}||dataflow_{6(CSP)}||Cu$.

//start process & complete service process

$$In(CSP) = oi \rightarrow Skip.In(CSP)||Cu\_OS.$$

//Online-Shop/Customer compatibility specification

$(F\ di \wedge \neg F\ de) \vee (\neg F\ di \wedge F\ de)$.
$F\ oi.F\ or.F\ go.F\ db1.F\ db.F\ pv.F\ pv1.F\ pc.F\ dg.F\ di.F\ og.F\ de$.

The Online-Shop/Customer process will be deadlocked due to the conflict between the internal behavior of the two services *Online-Shop* and *Customer*. So, it results in the relevant service components can't execute.

5.2 Experimental Argumentation

In this paper, the CSP verification tool-Process Analysis Toolkit (PAT) developed by Nation University of Singapore [15] is adopted as the experiment platform, which provides a rich language expression, not only accept some extended CSP models, but also provides a variety of property specifications. In addition, PAT can simulate the execution of a process to give users with an intuitive dynamic execution process. If the situation is not satisfied, PAT can also provide relevant counterexamples to facilitate user tracking errors.

We take the Online-Shop/Customer as an example. The verification experiment is divided into two steps: one is to verify the description of the example in Fig. 5, the next is to refer to the returned results of PAT to modify the service process. We re-express the examples using the PAT language because the input language specification of PAT has a distinct format specification for CSP.

Figure 6 shows the verification results of the example with PAT. Obviously, this instance has a deadlock situation. At the same time, a corresponding counterexample {*orders*− > *order for goods*− > *delivery*− > *delivery goods*} is provided by PAT.

Fig. 6. Deadlock verification effect   **Fig. 7.** Deadlock verification effect after modified

Analyzing the counterexample, the instance is lack of shopping service conflicts with the payment and sales agreement. The end user can select other services with the same function but different internal behavior constraints to replace it. For example, the user can select an Online-shop service with similar functionality, and its internal delivery service can be shipped directly according to the order (no need for the user to pay first), that is, the data flow <*paid confirm, confirm*> limit in Fig. 5 is removed. We can redesign the service process based on the above analysis and revalidated its CSP model. As can be seen from Fig. 7, there is no deadlock problem in the design modified according to the counterexample.

We have introduced the rules on service dataflow behavior compatibility in above, which can help generate multiple LTL property specifications to verify the correctness of the service dataflow graph. Figure 8 shows the verification results of the modified process on the LTL behavior compatibility specification. Here, we introduce a composite structural specification because the service flow does not contain a logical selection structure: *F del ^ F or* means events *del* and *or* will take place. The events *del* and *or* are the actions that must be performed in the process. If Online-Shop/Customer is executed correctly, then the process must satisfy the property $F\ del \ ^\wedge\ F\ or$. As can be seen from Fig. 8, the verification result satisfies this property, that is, the modified procedure is safe for the property.

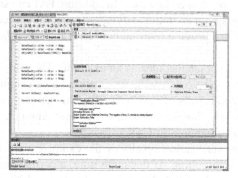

Fig. 8. The effect of the LTL behavior compatibility specification of the Online-Shop/Customer process after modified.

6 Conclusion

Aiming at the problem of business correctness in service mashup development, this paper have proposed a service behavior compatibility analysis method based on model checking. This method transforms the compatibility problem of service behavior into the model verification problem, which realizes the automatic analysis of service behavior and reduces the developer's task and technical threshold. Referring to the characteristics of the Service Data Model and the Service Relationship Model, this paper adopts CSP as the service process modeling language, which not only can abstractly represent the top level of the process, but also intuitively provide the behavior characteristics of the service.

In the future work, we will further refine and classify the compatibility of service behaviors to make the compatibility of service behaviors more complete.

References

1. Cubo, J., Pimentel, E.: On the service discovery using context-awareness, semantic matching and behavioural compatibility, pp. 259–266 (2012)
2. Li, X., Fan, Y., Sheng, Q.Z., Maamar, Z., Zhu, A.H.: A petri net approach to analyzing behavioral compatibility and similarity of web services. IEEE Trans. Syst. Man Cybern. - Part A: Syst. Hum. **41**, 510–521 (2011)
3. Ali, S.A., Roop, P.S., Warren, I., Bhatti, Z.E.: Unified management of control flow and data mismatches in web service composition. In: IEEE 6th International Symposium on Service Oriented System Engineering. SOSE 2011, Irvine, CA, USA (2011)

4. Yang, W., et al.: A MPTCP scheduler for web transfer. Comput. Mater. Continua **57**, 205–222 (2018)
5. Bi, J., Yuan, H., Zhou, M.: A petri net method for compatibility enforcement to support service choreography. IEEE Access **4**, 8581–8592 (2016)
6. Jin, J., Hu, J., Cao, Y.: Behavioral compatibility analysis for context-independent service substitution. In: 2012 Seventh ChinaGrid Annual Conference, ChinaGrid, pp. 121–127. IEEE Computer Society (2012)
7. Cheng, J., Liu, C., Zhou, M.C.: Automatic composition of semantic web services based on fuzzy predicate petri nets. IEEE Trans. Autom. Sci. Eng. **12**(2), 680–689 (2015)
8. Graiet, M., Lahouij, A., Abbassi, I.: Formal behavioral modeling for verifying SCA composition with event-B. In: IEEE International Conference on Web Services, pp. 17–24 (2015)
9. Tan, W., Fan, Y., Zhou, M.: A petri net-based method for compatibility analysis and composition of web services in business process execution language. IEEE Trans. Autom. Sci. Eng. **6**(1), 94–106 (2009)
10. Khaled, A., Miller, J.: Using π-calculus for formal modeling and verification of WS-CDL choreographies. IEEE Trans. Serv. Comput. **10**(99), 1 (2015)
11. Du, Y., Tan, W., Zhou, M.C.: Timed compatibility analysis of web service composition: a modular approach based on petri nets. IEEE Trans. Autom. Sci. Eng. **11**(2), 594–606 (2014)
12. Zhai, Z., Cheng, B., Tian, Y., Chen, J., Zhao, L., Niu, M.: A data-driven service creation approach for end-users. IEEE Access **4**, 9923–9940 (2016)
13. Roscoe, A.W.: The Theory and Practice of Concurrency, pp. 1–40. Prentice Hall, Upper Saddle River (1998)
14. Baier, C., Katoen, J.P.: Principles of Model Checking, pp. 89–120. The MIT Press, Cambridge (2010)
15. Jiang, J., Mao, H., Shao, R., Xu, Y.: Formal verification and improvement of the PKMv3 protocol using CSP. In: 2018 IEEE 42nd Annual Computer Software and Applications Conference (COMPSAC). IEEE Computer Society (2018)
16. Yao, J., et al.: Data based violated behavior analysis of taxi driver in metropolis in China. Comput. Mater. Continua **60**(3), 1109–1122 (2019)
17. Wang, G., Liu, M.: Dynamic trust model based on service recommendation in big data. Comput. Mater. Continua **58**(3), 845–857 (2019)

Study on Practical IoT Applications in Civil Aviation Industry

Yuanqing He[✉]

Civil Aviation Flight University of China, Guanghan 618307, China
2422932028@qq.com

Abstract. The introduction of the current technologies such as the Internet of things, big data, and cloud computing have helped the civil aviation industry to improve its business value as well as management level. For passengers, they can experience more additional quality services. For airline companies, if a commercial air plane is connected to the Internet of things, then the various sensors of the airplane system can be used to constantly provide the ground tower with accurate and real time tracking information about the air plane through the information relay by intermediate airplanes. In this article, some advanced practical IoT applications in nowadays civil aviation industry are studied ranging from IoT aviation infrastructures, IoTs based flight tracking system, to IoT based flight communication. And several related insightful literatures are also surveyed, introduced, and analyzed, which could help more practitioners to better understand the IoT applications in reshaping the modernization of current civil aviation industry.

Keywords: Internet of Things · Practical applications · Civil aviation

1 Introduction

The introduction of the current technologies such as the Internet of things, big data, and cloud computing have helped the civil aviation industry to improve its business value as well as management level. For passengers, they can experience more additional quality services. For airline companies, if a commercial air plane is connected to the Internet of things, then the various sensors of the airplane system can be used to constantly provide the ground tower with accurate and real time tracking information about the air plane through the information relay by intermediate airplanes. In this article, some advanced practical IoT applications in nowadays civil aviation industry are studied ranging from IoT aviation infrastructures, IoTs based flight tracking system, to IoT based flight communication. And several related insightful literatures are also surveyed and introduced, which could help more practitioners to better understand the IoT applications in reshaping the modernization of current civil aviation industry.

2 IoT in Aviation

Flight 4.0, which represents a fast expanding study field in aviation industry, brings IoT technology into the aviation industry. By using the current technologies such as Wireless Sensor Networks and embedded systems, Flight 4.0 systems are characterized by high degree of heterogeneity such as communication, hardware, and software solutions [1, 2]. However, in order to be accepted by the final end users, it is of importance to present high degree of configurability and flexibility such that they can be used in diverse application circumstances. To address such issues, the authors in [3] try to identify the chief aspects and trends toward a holistic end-to-end communication infrastructure for Flight 4.0 systems, and their research act as a milestone for providing a homogeneous support to a wide range of WSN communication technologies and protocols while they can also support time constrained monitor, control, and configuration of critical components of Flight 4.0 infrastructures. According to [3], as is shown in Fig. 1, Fight 4.0 systems architecture pays close attention to the usage of distributed components and these components can offer enhanced fault tolerance performance to some extent.

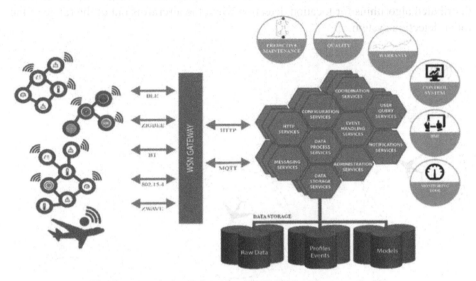

Fig. 1. IoT aviation infrastructures in Flight 4.0 system in [3]

In the above infrastructure system, according to the authors, each component has its own self-controlled power supply, and these components should work at the time, or else, the whole system might be out of function. But to satisfy these objective is no easy job which needs many critical perspectives of a wireless communication platform relating with both hardware and software [4, 5].

In addition, some essentially important technologies are also discussed in [3] regarding the Flight 4.0 systems. For example, IEEE 802.15.4 [6–10] is based on significant advantages when dealing with very low-power, low-complexity; Bluetooth technology [11–13] is a wireless radio standard used to provide data and voice signals among various electronic devices. Such a standard is defined by the Bluetooth Special Interest Group and has more than 1000 electronics' manufacturers.

To precisely track and identify the location of airplanes during its entire flight time is a difficult yet challenging task. By utilizing the current radar and other technologies, it is relatively easy to locate the flights over the land, but regarding the long distance of intercontinental flying in which most of the flight route is over sea or water bodies, e.g., in Fig. 2, how to identify the location of airplane in by real time turns out to be almost infeasible [14] even with the help of modern radar systems. According to the findings of [15, 16], there have been enhancements for radar detection by using certain advanced technologies such as LIDAR systems, but these improved radar techniques only work when the airplanes are flying over land mass. Hence, this situation brings about a huge social and financial influence over the airlines and civil aviation [17, 18]. To this end, the authors in [14] study the problem of location detection for commercial aircraft and methods to improve the location detection over any terrain that the flight route covers. The proposed method is based on the Internet of things framework [17, 18] for aircraft, e.g., in Fig. 3, where the aircraft can communicate with each other within a certain range or through certain intermediate ones. The proposed method also introduces some distributed algorithms for location detection when the aircraft is out of the range of the radar detection system.

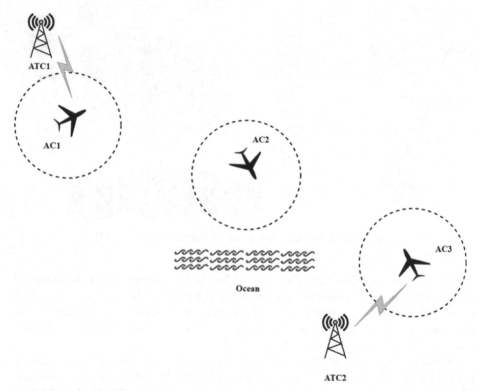

Fig. 2. Traditional flight tracking over the ocean in [14]

There are a variety of sensors installed on an aircraft, and many of these sensors are essential for the full functioning of the aircraft. With the sensors being used throughout the flight duration, a large quantity of data is collected which can be transferred during the flight between the aircraft and an air traffic control or ATC tower serving as a

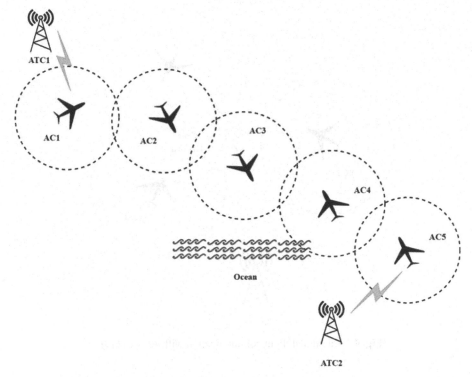

Fig. 3. IoTs flight tracking in [14]

base station. Thus, the aircraft equipped with all these electronica sensors can form a framework of Internet of things [19]. Then, these data sets can be analyzed later for valuable information for enhancing the process of efficiency about flight operations [20–22].

In [19], the authors proposed a framework for IoT with regards to aircraft and associated sensor and communication devices. The proposed method focuses on detection and avoidance of turbulence in commercial aviation, and it is also intended for clear air turbulence (CAT) avoidance [23]. The authors believed that, in general, direct communication between aircraft using IoT framework is the most efficient technique of avoiding CAT and the same principles can also be applied to detect and avoid the other types of turbulence as well. The traditional flight communication scenario and the proposed IoT based communication scenario in [19] are presented respectively in Fig. 4 and Fig. 5.

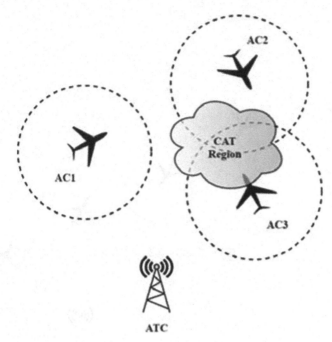

Fig. 4. Traditional flight communication with ACT in [19]

Airports are of complex environments and situations, and some recent advances in IoTs have made it viable to implement real-time passengers aid tools for cell phones, which will be especially important for the older people or disabled ones, or people with other constraints that need help in the airports [24].

To address this problem, the authors in [24] designed such tools that can cover the necessary path from the airport to the flight and they also allow the travelers to spend the waiting time through discovering the close by facilities. As is shown in Fig. 6, the proposed method uses cloud node [25–30] and fog computing nodes [32–38] that are placed inside an airport and it also provides the airport with user heat maps which can highlight the traffic situation and other situations that need manual handling. According to [31], the relationship between fog nodes and cloud data centers is shown in Fig. 7.

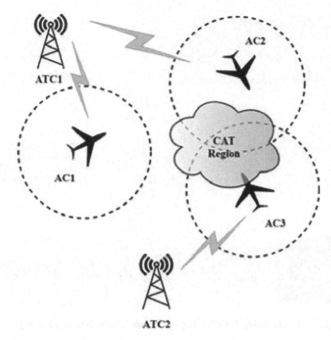

Fig. 5. IoT based flight communication with ACT in [19]

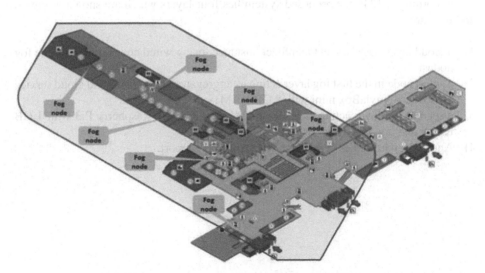

Fig. 6. Fog nods allocation at an airport in [24]

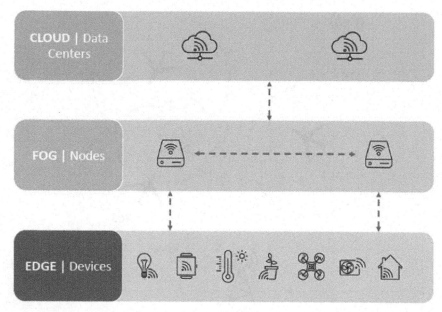

Fig. 7. Relationship between fog nodes and cloud data centers in [31]

According to [24], the proposed system has four layers which are shown in Fig. 8, and they are:

1) a cloud layer based on an OpenStack instance, using wired connection with the fog nodes;
2) a smart node in the first fog layer acting as aggregator, based on a local cloud service hosted in a NuvlaBox mini with 8 GB RAM;
3) a second fog layer acting as access nodes, based on six Raspberry Pi3 with 1 GB RAM, and hosting at each wireless point;
4) Android smartphones at the edge with Android support.

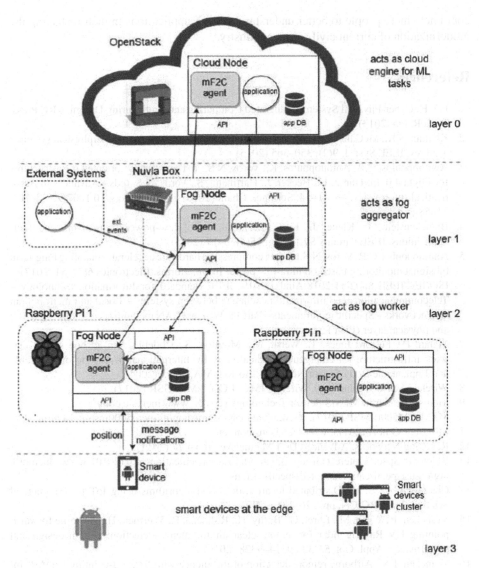

Fig. 8. Four layers for system implementation in [24]

3   Conclusion

The introduction of the current technologies such as the Internet of things, big data, and cloud computing have helped the civil aviation industry to improve its business value and management level. In this article, some practical IoT applications and successful instances in current civil aviation industry are introduced and studied ranging from IoT aviation infrastructures, IoTs based flight tracking system, to IoT based flight communication. Some related insightful literatures are also surveyed and analyzed, which could help more people to better understand the IoT applications in their reshaping the modernization of current civil aviation industry.

References

1. Hu, F.: Cyber-Physical Systems: Integrated Computing and Engineering Design. CRC Press, Boca Raton (2013)
2. Khaitan, S.K., McCalley, J.D.: Design techniques and applications of cyberphysical systems: a survey. IEEE Syst. J. **9**(2), 350–365 (2015)
3. Antonopoulos, C.P., Antonopoulos, K., Voros, N.S.: IoT and service oriented infrastructures for Flight 4.0. In: Durak, U., Becker, J., Hartmann, S., Voros, N.S. (eds.) Advances in Aeronautical Informatics, pp. 41–54. Springer, Cham (2018). https://doi.org/10.1007/978-3-319-75058-3_4
4. Blanckenstein, J., Klaue, J., Karl, H.: A survey of low-power transceivers and their applications. IEEE Circuits Syst. Mag. **15**(3), 6–17 (2015)
5. Antonopoulos, C.P., Voros, N.S.: A data compression hardware accelerator enabling long-term biosignal monitoring based on ultra-low power IoT platforms. Electronics **6**(3), 54 (2017)
6. ISO/IEC/IEEE 8802-11:2018/Amd 1:2019: IEEE Standard for Information technology – Telecommunications and information exchange between systems – Local and metropolitan area networks – Specific requirements – Part 11: Wireless LAN medium access control (MAC) and physical layer (PHY)
7. Malan, D., Fulford-Jones, T., Welsh, M., Moulton, S.: Codeblue: an ad hoc sensor network infrastructure for emergency medical care. In: International Workshop on Wearable and Implantable Body Sensor Networks, Boston, MA, vol. 5 (2004)
8. Wireless Sensor Technology, Wireless IMU, ECG, EMG, GSR (2017)
9. Memsic Leader in MEMS Sensor Technology (2017). www.memsic.com/
10. MTM-CM5000-MSP (2017). www.advanticsys.com/shop/mtmcm5000msp-p-14.html
11. Movisens GmbH (2017). www.movisens.com/en
12. Revoking Networks, Advanced User Manual Version 4.77 (2011)
13. Bluetooth Special Interest Group, Bluetooth Core Specification v4.0 (2010). www.bluetooth.org/en-us/specification/adopted-specifications
14. Chatterjee, A., et al.: Distributed location detection algorithms using IoT for commercial aviation. In: ICRCICN, pp. 126–131 (2017)
15. Vrancken, P., Wirth, M., Ehret, G., Barny, H., Rondeau, P., Veerman, H.: Airborne forward-pointing UV Rayleighlidar for remote clear air turbulence detection: system design and performance. Appl. Opt. **55**(32), 9314–9328 (2016)
16. Vrancken, P.S.: Airborne remote detection of turbulence with forward-pointing LIDAR. In: Sharman, R., Lane, T. (eds.) Aviation Turbulence: Processes, Detection, Prediction, pp. 443–464. Springer, Cham (2016). https://doi.org/10.1007/978-3-319-23630-8_22
17. Suresh, M., Saravana Kumar, P., Sundararajan, T.V.P.: IoT based airport parking system. In: Innovations in Information, Embedded and Communication Systems (2015)
18. Ye-Won, L., Yong-Lak, C.: Proposal for air-baggage tracing system based on IoT. In: 2015 9th International Conference on Future Generation Communication and Networking (FGCN), pp. 25–28, November 2015
19. Chatterjee, M., et al.: Efficient clear air turbulence avoidance algorithms using IoT for commercial aviation. In: 2017 Recent Development in Control, Automation & Power Engineering, pp. 28–33 (2017)
20. Chatterjee, A., Radhakrishnan, S., Antonio, J.K.: Data structures and algorithms for counting problems on graphs using GPU. Int. J. Netw. Comput. (IJNC) **3**(2), 264–288 (2013)

21. Chatterjee, A., Radhakrishnan, S., Antonio, J.K.: On analyzing large graphs using GPUs. In: 2013 IEEE 27th International Symposium on Parallel and Distributed Processing, Workshops & PhD Forum (IPDPSW), pp. 751–760. IEEE (2013)
22. Chatterjee, A., Radhakrishnan, S., Antonio, J.K.: Counting problems on graphs: GPU storage and parallel computing techniques. In: 2012 IEEE 26th International Symposium on Parallel and Distributed Processing, Workshops & PhD Forum, pp. 804–812. IEEE (2012)
23. Williams, J.K.: Using random forests to diagnose aviation turbulence. Mach. Learn. **95**(1), 51–70 (2013). https://doi.org/10.1007/s10994-013-5346-7
24. Salis, A., et al.: Anatomy of a fog-to-cloud distributed recommendation system in airports. In: 2018 IEEE/ACM International Conference on Utility and Cloud Computing Companion, pp. 272–277 (2018)
25. Hou, X., et al.: Vehicular fog computing: a viewpoint of vehicles as the infrastructures. IEEE Trans. Veh. Technol. **65**(6), 3860–3873 (2016)
26. Zhu, C., et al.: Folo: latency and quality optimized task allocation in vehicular fog computing. IEEE Internet Things J. **6**(3), 4150–4161 (2019)
27. Zhang, Y., et al.: Parking reservation auction for parked vehicle assistance in vehicular fog computing. IEEE Trans. Veh. Technol. **68**(4), 3126–3139 (2019)
28. Xiao, M.: A hybrid scheme for fine-grained search and access authorization in fog computing environment. Sensors (Switz.) **17**(6), 1423 (2017)
29. Jalali, F., et al.: Cognitive IoT gateways: automatic task sharing and switching between cloud and edge/fog computing. In: Proceedings of the 2017 SIGCOMM Posters and Demos, SIGCOMM Posters and Demos 2017, Part of SIGCOMM 2017, 22 August 2017, pp. 121–123 (2017)
30. Chen, H., et al.: Indoor formaldehyde monitoring system based on fog computing. In: 2nd International Conference on Advanced Materials, Intelligent Manufacturing and Automation - Automatic Control and Systems, IOP Conference Series: Materials Science and Engineering, 9 August 2019, vol. 569, no. 4 (2019)
31. Tedeschi, P., Sciancalepore, S.: Edge and fog computing in critical infrastructures: analysis, security threats, and research challenges. In: 2019 IEEE European Symposium on Security and Privacy Workshops (2019)
32. Sun, L., Ma, J., Wang, H., et al.: Cloud service description model: an extension of USDL for cloud services. IEEE Trans. Serv. Comput. **11**(2), 354–368 (2018)
33. Sun, L., Dong, H., Hussain, O., Hussain, F., Liu, A.X.: A framework of cloud service selection with criteria interactions. Future Gener. Comput. Syst. **94**, 749–764 (2019)
34. Su, J., Sheng, Z., Xie, L., Li, G., Liu, A.: Fast splitting based tag identification algorithm for anti-collision in UHF RFID system. IEEE Trans. Commun. **67**(3), 2527–2538 (2019)
35. Su, J., Sheng, Z., Liu, A., Han, Y., Chen, Y.: A group-based binary splitting algorithm for UHF RFID anti-collision systems. IEEE Trans. Commun. **68**(2), 998–1012 (2019)
36. Kou, L., Shi, Y., Zhang, L., Liu, D., Yang, Q.: A Lightweight three-factor user authentication protocol for the information perception of IoT. Comput. Mater. Continua **58**(2), 545–565 (2019)
37. Kim, D.-Y., Min, S.D., Kim, S.: A DPN (Delegated Proof of Node) mechanism for secure data transmission in IoT services. Comput. Mater. Continua **60**(1), 1–14 (2019)
38. Badshah, A., Ghani, A., Qureshi, M.A., Shamshirband, S.: Smart security framework for educational institutions using Internet of Things (IoT). Comput. Mater. Continua **61**(1), 81–101 (2019)

Study on IoT Solutions in Smart Airports

Huan Zhang$^{(\boxtimes)}$

Civil Aviation Flight University of China, Guanghan 618307, China
papergood@qq.com

Abstract. The function of Internet of things, or IoTs can be referred to as the collection of any object that needs to be constantly tracked, connected and interacted through various means such as RFID technology, global positioning system, and other communication devices and technologies. The Internet of Things enable all ordinary physical objects to be independently form an intelligent interconnected network. Thus, the IoT is becoming a more and more important component to the new generation of information technology with many concrete applications in various fields especially in the solutions of smart airports which need modern technologies to solve many real problems and issues. In this research, several typical IoT concrete cases as partial solutions to smart airport are discussed and introduced ranging from IoT based baggage automated self check-in system to IoT based airport parking applications, aiming to enlighten more and more insightful ideas and proposals about the solutions to smart airports.

Keywords: Internet of Things · Solutions · Smart airports

1 Introduction

Through all kinds of possible network access, IoTs carry out the ubiquitous connection between objects and people. To some extent, the Internet of things is an information carrier based on the Internet and or traditional telecommunication network. The function of Internet of things, or IoTs can be referred to as the collection of any object that needs to be constantly tracked, connected and interacted through various means such as RFID technology, global positioning system, and other communication devices and technologies. The Internet of Things enable all ordinary physical objects to be independently form an intelligent interconnected net-work. Thus, the IoT is becoming a more and more important component to the new generation of information technology with many concrete applications in various fields especially in the solutions of smart airports which need modern technologies to solve many real problems and issues. In this research, several typical IoT concrete instances as partial solutions to smart airport are discussed and introduced ranging from IoT based baggage automated self check-in system to IoT based airport parking applications, aiming to enlighten more and more insightful ideas and proposals about the solutions to smart airports.

© Springer Nature Singapore Pte Ltd. 2020
X. Sun et al. (Eds.): ICAIS 2020, CCIS 1253, pp. 170–179, 2020.
https://doi.org/10.1007/978-981-15-8086-4_16

2   IoT Solutions

RFID or radio frequency identification uses wireless sensor network or WSN technology and is applied within the IoTs in many practical applications such as inventory level management, product identification, healthcare monitoring, and security surveillance [1–5]. Some larger airports with a considerable yearly number of customers traveling usually confronts with some delaying issues at the baggage check-in [6]. In [6], the authors tried to alleviate such a problem by introducing the automation of the check-in process through using self-service counters connecting to the airport system and servers, and all the airport counters can be activated immediately to serve more customers and thus to reduce the delay resulted from the long waiting hours. According to [6], the service scenario is started when the passenger arrives at the baggage check-in area as shown in Fig. 1, then the automated system generate a certain tag data based on the information received from the passenger, and the proposed detail steps are shown as follows [6]:

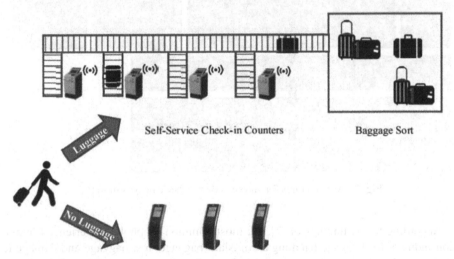

Fig. 1. Illustrations for automated self check-in system in [6].

1) A passenger without luggage will head to the self-service machine to scan his or her passport or print the boarding pass;
2) A passenger with luggage will go to the self service check-in counters;
3) The RFID related machine has a scanner, tag printer, boarding pass printer, and camera for passenger identification which attaches to the convey or to transport the luggage;
4) The passenger is to place each luggage next to the machine to start the automated check-in process;
5) The passenger uses the machine to scan his passport to generate the RFID data based on passport number, travel information, luggage weight and size, and payment

terminal for additional charges. The passenger will answers some questions about the baggage. The camera takes a photo of the passenger on the top of RFID data for further verification;

6) When the passenger's data is captured, the machine prints out the RFID tag and prints the boarding pass for the passenger.

7) The baggage will move further through the conveyor and the RFID reader on the conveyor scans the tags and finally reach the sorting room to be later loaded on the carriers.

In addition, the architectures in [6] is presented in Fig. 2.

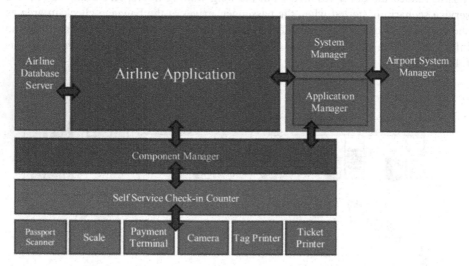

Fig. 2. Architectures for automated self check-in system in [6]

According to the findings of [7], the most common loopholes experienced in aviation industry for baggage handling are mislaid baggage, lost baggage and damage to belongings. In order to provide a better and secure system to the passengers, similar to the methods used in [6], the authors in [7] proposed a design of baggage tracing and handling system using smart RFID tags and IoTs, which are based on the cloud server. The proposed method designed a prototype at two locations that has both check-in and check-out processes, and a secured algorithm is proposed for generating tags that are attached to printed baggage label with the detail information about the passenger and airlines.

The details of the proposed method are as follows [7]: RFID readers in the check-out areas help with the step tracking of baggage in order to avoid baggage loss; the baggage's real time position is tracked and stored in a cloud server and the unique ID can be retrieved by the passengers wherever and whenever necessary; the same ID is to be used for the baggage collection at check-out counters. In addition, the proposed method also ensures less time consumption and more baggage security. The processes of baggage check-in system and baggage off-loading system in the proposed method are respectively presented in Fig. 3 and Fig. 4. Figure 5 and Fig. 6 respectively illustrate the system implementation and IoTs based baggage sorting in the proposed method.

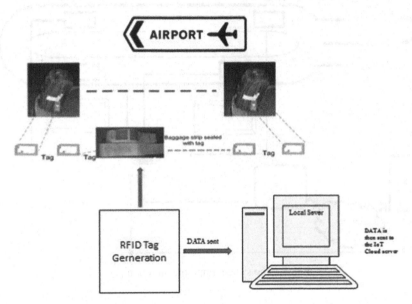

Fig. 3. Processes of baggage check-in system in [7]

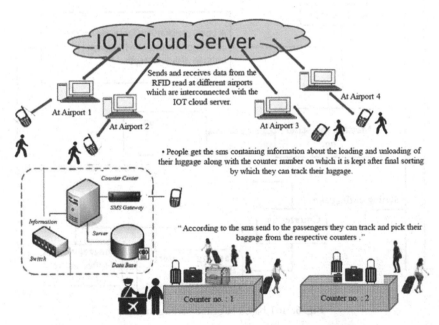

Fig. 4. Processes of baggage off loading system in [7]

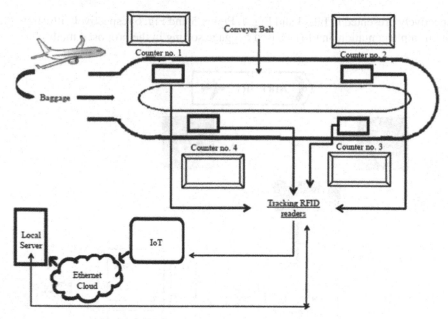

Fig. 5. The system implementation in [7]

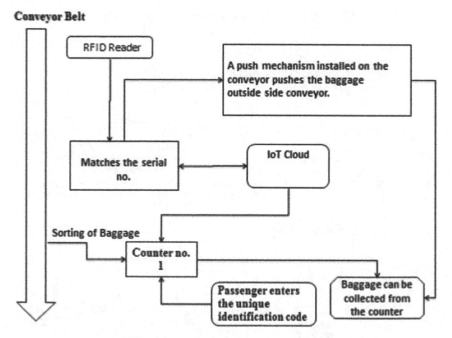

Fig. 6. IoT based baggage sorting in [7]

The authors in [8] proposed an IoT based airport-parking system. The proposed parking service can display all user details to the related administrator, and every passenger can also view the details of parking location in a smartphone through the cloud server in the airport. Accoding the methods used in [8], Arduino UNO board with ATmega328 is used as shown in Fig. 7 as an embedded controller to interact with the Ethernet shield along with PC.

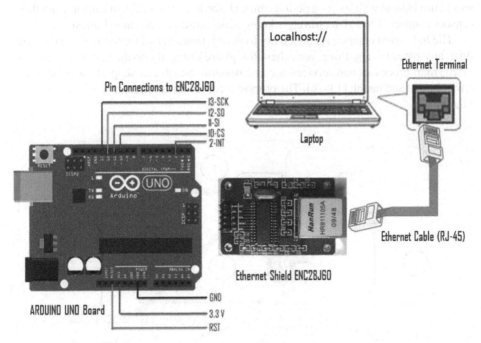

Fig. 7. Arduino based parking as an Iot solution in [8]

According to the techniques used in [8], the Arduino board is from an open-source computer hardware and software company which designs and manufactures kits for building digital devices and interactive objects; the board is based on a family of microcontroller board designs manufactured mainly by Smart Projects in Italy, and also by several other vendors, through using various 8-bit Atmel AVR microcontrollers or 32-bit Atmel ARM processors; these systems also provide digital and analog I/O pins that can be interfaced to various extension boards and other circuits; the boards feature serial communications interfaces, including USB on some models, primarily for loading programs from PCs; for programming the microcontrollers, the Arduino platform provides an integrated development environment based on the processing project, which includes C and C++ programming languages support [8–12].

The authors in [13] proposed an airport management system based on the IoT standards, where passengers, baggage, airplane or the departure lounge are to some degree treated as things. The proposed smart airport management system aims to automate passengers processing and flight management steps, to improve services, facilitate airport agents' tasks, and to provide passengers a safe travel. The proposed IoT-based smart airport solution enables the remote controlling and monitoring many systems unlike the traditional airports. The proposed method also helps to provide a safer environment for the travelers as well as the workers, and any fault occurrence can be dealt immediately. Besides, in the proposed method, the lighting and air conditioning systems can be set based on the demand to reduce the energy consumption resulting in more reduce cost. Smart airports in [13] also provide better service for travelers and those the travelers would not have to wait for long periods through the help of intelligent sensors, and these sensors connected to IoT let travelers know which waiting lines are shortest.

The IoT vision enhances connectivity from any-time, any-place for any-one into any-time, any-place for any-thing, once these things are plugged into the network, more and more smart processes and services become possible which can support the economies, environment and health [13–16]. The proposed communication interface is presented in Fig. 8.

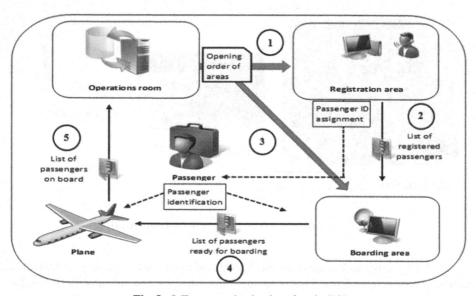

Fig. 8. IoT communication interface in [13]

Aviation is pervasive in everyday life, and most aviation applications are safety-critical system and any failure can directly or indirectly lead to the loss of life, or property damage [17–20]. On average, about 100,000 daily flights originate from approximately 9000 airports around the world [21]. While air travel is still considered one of the safest forms of travel, there are still small but present dangers in air travel.

In [17], the authors demonstrated some potential benefits of edge computing using a high-impact IoT use-case [22–28] which is shown in Fig. 9. The proposed method uses an IoT edge computing framework in a high-impact safety critical use-case, aviation safety and can analyze the collected data so as to reduce transmitted data and only transmit actionable information for faster response in emergencies.

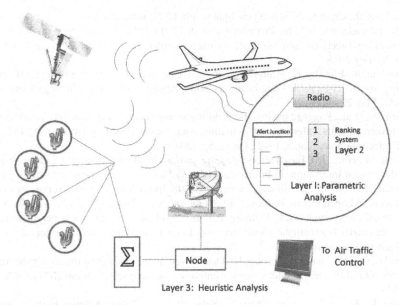

Fig. 9. A high level illustration of the proposed method in [17]

3 Conclusion

Through all kinds of possible network access, IoTs carry out the ubiquitous connection between objects and people. The Internet of things is an important component of the new generation of information technology especially in the smart airports. In this research, several typical IoT concrete instances as partial solutions to smart airport are discussed and introduced ranging from IoT based baggage automated self check-in system to IoT based airport parking applications, aiming to enlighten more and more insightful ideas and proposals about the solutions to smart airports.

References

1. Vales-Alonso, J., et al.: Conditions for rate stability in constrained RFID networks. In: 2018 6th International EURASIP Workshop on RFID Technology, EURFID, 2 July 2018 (2018)
2. Merenda, M., et al.: Design principles of a fully-passive RFID-based IoT sensing node. In: 24th European Wireless 2018 Wireless Futures in the Era of Network Programmability, EW 2018, pp. 162–167 (2018)
3. Hu, G., et al.: Human activity recognition based on hidden Markov models using computational RFID. In: 2017 4th International Conference on Systems and Informatics, ICSAI 2017, 28 July 2017, pp. 813–818 January 2018
4. Gu, Q., Yin, K., Niu, B., Chen, H.: RFID networks planning using BF-PSO. In: Huang, D.-S., Ma, J., Jo, K.-H., Gromiha, M.M. (eds.) ICIC 2012. LNCS (LNAI), vol. 7390, pp. 181–188. Springer, Heidelberg (2012). https://doi.org/10.1007/978-3-642-31576-3_24

5. Yin, Y., et al.: Cryptanalysis of a new lightweight RFID mutual authentication protocol with cache in reader for IoT. In: Proceedings of the 2017 IEEE 2nd Information Technology, Networking, Electronic and Automation Control Conference, ITNEC, 2 July 2017, pp. 909–913, January 2018
6. Baashirah, R., Elleithy, K.: Automation of the baggage check-in process using RFID system in airports. In: 2019 IEEE Long Island Systems, Applications and Technology Conference, LISAT, May 2019 (2019)
7. Singh, A., et al.: Baggage tracing and handling system using RFID and IoT for airports. In: 2016 International Conference on Computing, Analytics and Security Trends (CAST) College of Engineering Pune, India, 19–21 December (2016)
8. Suresh, M., et al.: IoT Based airport parking system. In: IEEE Sponsored 2nd International Conference on Innovations in Information Embedded and Communication Systems(2015)
9. Granjal, J., Monteiro, E., Silva, J.: Security for the Internet of Things: a survey of existing protocols and open research issues. IEEE Commun. Surv. Tutor. **17**(3), 1294–1312 (2015)
10. Doukas, C., Maglogiannis, I.: Bringing IoT and cloud computing towards pervasive healthcare. In: Sixth International Conference on Innovative Mobile and Internet Services in Ubiquitous Computing (2012)
11. Han, W., Gu, Y., Zhang, Y., Zheng, L.: Data driven quantitative trust model for the internet of agricultural things. In: International Conference on Internet of Things (IOT), OCT 2014 (2014)
12. Zhang, K., Liang, X., Lu, R., Shen, X.: Sybil attacks and their defenses in the internet of things. IEEE Internet Things J. **1**(5), 372–383 (2014)
13. Bouyakoub, S., et al.: Smart airport: an IoT-based airport management system. In: Proceedings of the International Conference on Future Networks and Distributed Systems, ICFNDS 2017, ACM International Conference Proceeding Series, Part F130522, 19 July 2017 (2017)
14. Mattern, F., Floerkemeier, C.: From the internet of computers to the internet of things. In: Sachs, K., Petrov, I., Guerrero, P. (eds.) From Active Data Management to Event-Based Systems and More. LNCS, vol. 6462, pp. 242–259. Springer, Heidelberg (2010). https://doi.org/10.1007/978-3-642-17226-7_15
15. Daskala, B., Clarke J., Nilson, D.K.: Looking through the crystal ball: identifying future security, privacy and social risks in a prospective IoT scenario. In: First International Workshop on the Security of Internet of Things, Tokyo, Japan (2010)
16. Li, H., Su, X., Jiang, H.: Modelling landing control system of carrier based aircraft on Internet of Things. In: International Conference on Software Intelligence Technologies and Applications & International Conference on Frontiers of Internet of Things, Hsinchu, Taiwan (2014)
17. Pate, J., Adegbijai, T.: AMELIA: an application of the Internet of Things for aviation safety. In: 15th IEEE Annual Consumer Communications & Networking Conference (CCNC) (2018)
18. Sundmaeker, H., Guillemin, P., Friess, P., Woelffl'e, S.: Vision and challenges for realising the Internet of Things. Cluster Eur. Res. Proj. Internet Things Eur. Comm. **20**, 34–36 (2010)
19. McKinsey: Disruptive technologies: advances that will transform life, business, and the global economy (2016). http://www.mckinsey.com. Accessed Jan 2016
20. Adegbija, T., Rogacs, A., Patel, C., Gordon-Ross, A.: Enabling right provisioned microprocessor architectures for the internet of things. In: International Mechanical Engineering Congress and Exposition, ASME (2015)
21. How it's possible to lose an airplane in 2014. http://www.wired.com/2014/03/malaysia-air/. Accessed Aug 2016
22. Sun, L., Ma, J., Wang, H., et al.: Cloud service description model: an extension of USDL for cloud services. IEEE Trans. Serv. Comput. **11**(2), 354–368 (2018)
23. Sun, L., Dong, H., Hussain, O., Hussain, F., Liu, A.X.: A framework of cloud service selection with criteria interactions. Future Gen. Comput. Syst. **94**, 749–764 (2019)

24. Su, J., Sheng, Z., Xie, L., Li, G., Liu, A.: Fast splitting based tag identification algorithm for anti-collision in UHF RFID system. IEEE Trans. Commun. **67**(3), 2527–2538 (2019)
25. Su, J., Sheng, Z., Liu, A., Han, Y., Chen, Y.: A group-based binary splitting algorithm for UHF RFID anti-collision systems. IEEE Trans. Commun. **68**, 1–14 (2019)
26. Kou, L., Shi, Y., Zhang, L., Liu, D., Yang, Q.: A lightweight three-factor user authentication protocol for the information perception of IoT. Comput. Mater. Continua **58**(2), 545–565 (2019)
27. Kim, D.Y., Min, S.D., Kim, S.: A DPN (Delegated Proof of Node) mechanism for secure data transmission in IoT services. Comput Mater. Continua **60**(1), 1–14 (2019)
28. Badshah, A., Ghani, A., Qureshi, M.A., Shamshirband, S.: Smart security framework for educational institutions using Internet of Things (IoT). Comput. Mater. Continua **61**(1), 81–101 (2019)

MultiSec: A Bionics Security Architecture of Ad-hoc Network

Muyao Wang[1(⊠)], Yun Yang[2] , and Zongtao Duan[2]

[1] Xidian University, Xi'an 710071, Shaanxi, China
tiferking@xidian.edu.cn
[2] Chang'an University, Xi'an 710064, Shaanxi, China
yangyun@chd.edu.cn

Abstract. Advanced in IoT (Internet-of-Things) technology recently, it is more popular to make things connect with each other, like wearable device, home appliance, transportation, etc. There's no doubt that internet will finally connect everything together. An ad-hoc network is suitable for extending the coverage of the Internet. However, the security of the ad-hoc network is the main problem to solve. It is hard to engage an anti-virus software on a power-limited device or a low-cost device with limited computing power. Even it is hard to defend the attacks by one device, it is possible to defend attacks by the entire ad-hoc network.

In this paper, we came up with a new architecture that combined software and hardware called MultiSec, inspired by the method of how animal immune pathogens. With a new protocol stack called SecPath and a special anti-virus engine called SecGuard working on the ad-hoc network. It is easier to reduce the power consumption in this way but with a powerful anti-virus software working on it. Then with the control of SecGuard, the network will only accept the trusted devices and make it take part in the defense work. SecGuard will move randomly in the ad-hoc network, gathering working feature of the entire ad-hoc network. It will detect the suspicious data transport in network and abnormal device status then block data or ban device to keep the network safe. SecPath is independent of the TCP/IP protocol stack and can work together with it. We evaluated some basic features of MultiSec on STM32 platform and it works well. The evaluate system can show as a hardware demo. And we think the architecture is worth to share.

Keywords: MultiSec · Bionics security architecture · Hardware-Software cooperative security

1 Introduction

In recent years, IoT technology becomes more and more popular. Not only for the device used in everyday life, but also for the device in industrial and medical use. With growth of the quantity of IoT device. It is a challenge for the wireless access point to deal with so many devices. To make more device connect to

© Springer Nature Singapore Pte Ltd. 2020
X. Sun et al. (Eds.): ICAIS 2020, CCIS 1253, pp. 180–188, 2020.
https://doi.org/10.1007/978-981-15-8086-4_17

internet and with a stable access, devices can forward data onto others. Ad-hoc network is a method that organizes devices as a network. Data can forward from a device to another and finally transmit to internet. These are a good way of extending the coverage of internet. But ad-hoc network is not a perfect solution, and security is one of the important problem [1,2,7,8]. The ad-hoc network does not have a constant network topology, and so that it is hard to setup a firewall or a fixed device to ensure the ad-hoc network was secure. Meanwhile it is hard to engage an advanced firewall or anti-virus software on a single device for power consumption, compute power limitation, custom hardware device or so on [3]. So, we came up with an idea that may help ad-hoc network become secure and become more practical.

MultiSec is a brand new architecture that combines all the devices in ad-hoc network. It gathers all the compute resource, device information, device working status, etc. Then it will use this data to cognize the environment and defense the invasion. The main idea came from how animal immune pathogens. Suppose that every device is a cell, and when animal get sick, a cell never get over it by itself. Indeed every cell should take part in the invisible fight. We came up with a new architecture called MultiSec consisted with three parts, which is SecPath, SecDevice and SecGuard. SecPath is a new protocol stack which has a low level trust chain and different transfer method to connect all the devices with a trusted channel [4,6]. It wiped out the route function and only have the broadcast and regioncast[1]. So the protocol stack will be lite and efficient. The SecDevice is a hardware which supplies the trusted compute, process the data over SecPath [5]. And SecGuard is a software which working on the device in ad-hoc network, and it can move from one device to another randomly. It can take control of the whole ad-hoc network adding or delete device, monitor the network working status and filter out abnormal data. Combine with machine learning it will learn the working status of ad-hoc network and even facing unknown attack. And all these part consists in MultiSec architecture working together to make the ad-hoc network secure.

The principle map of SecPath is shown in Fig. 1. The firewall can protect the ad-hoc network from internet attack, but not from ad-hoc network attack. The device firewall can protect every device, but cost too much. MultiSec can protect the entire ad-hoc network with few cost.

The remainder of this paper is organized as follows. SecPath, SecDevice and SecGuard will be described in detail. Then some application scenarios will be mentioned to analysing the feasibility of this architecture. Finally, there is some testing result of basic function we made so far.

2   SecPath Outline

To provide a trusted communication channel efficiently. In our design, it should have a totally trusted mechanism from bottom to top. And this protocol stack

---

[1] Regioncast: The frame only send to the receivers which sender can reach directly, and do not need forward.

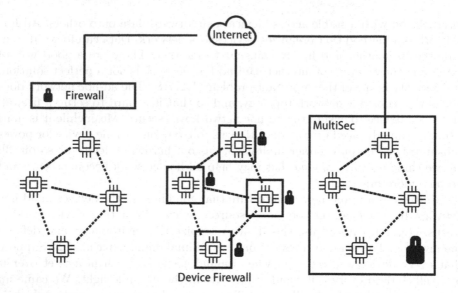

Fig. 1. Network Firewall vs Device Firewall vs MultiSec, MultiSec is more secure and efficient.

is designed only to transmit data packet, not data flow, which means it needn't to hold a link. The whole protocol stack is divided into four layers.

The bottom layer is physical layer, it is a wireless channel under most conditions. As we consider, the physical layer is not a specific channel or transfer method. Due to the difference between ethernet frame and SecPath frame, it is easy to separate SecPath frame from ethernet frame. So, it is possible to use single physical channel to transmit double frame type.

The second layer is link layer. In this layer data should pack in a frame structure. For SecPath frame, a unique frame id is in the head of frame. Every frame should contain a unique device id which considered to generate from the device PUF (Physical Unclonable Function) circuit as a device fingerprint. And a transmits mode selection for select between broadcast and regioncast. Broadcast means every device should forward this frame once in order to make all the device in this ad-hoc network receive this frame. Regioncast means device should not forward this frame, and this frame can only be received by the device near by the source device. A digital signature should follow after the frame data, in order to prove the information in frame is trusted.

The third layer is encryption layer. The data can be encrypted in this layer, using the encryption principle such as AES (Advanced Encryption Standard), DES (Data Encryption Standard), etc. The encryption method and key is controlled by SecGuard, which will be describe later. In this layer, data are transmitted in ciphertext except the new device which in authentication period. Once the device is permitted, the encryption information of this network will be sent to this device in asymmetric encryption.

The top layer is application layer, which is the SecGuard working layer. In this layer, the SecGuard can request the working status from nearby devices, move SecGuard database to nearby device and broadcast filter option, etc.

The sketch map of SecPath is shown in Fig. 2.

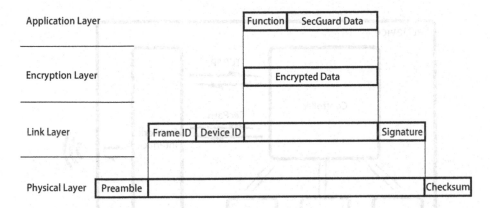

Fig. 2. SecPath Protocol Stack provide a secure communication channel for devices.

In this way, we can make sure that every packet of data could be trusted through the SecPath and most of them are encrypted. This will be the first step to connect all the device in an ad-hoc network and deal with the internet attack together. And because of the independence of SecPath protocol stack, it will be work with TCP/IP protocol as dual stack. So the application relies on TCP/IP can run as usual. And the MultiSec can ensure the security of TCP/IP.

3   SecDevice Outline

SecDevice plays an important role in MultiSec architecture. For it should be able to provide hardware unique ID and trusted compute ability. Besides, a SecDevice should be authenticated by a CA (certificate authority). And a digital certificate should be stored in the device memory. And the certificate should contain the device unique ID, device manufacturer, device hardware information, etc. When the device is adding into a new ad-hoc network, a certificate exchange will take place between the device and the network. After an authenticate period, a packet of network encryption information will be sent to device. Then the device will have the right to access the MultiSec network.

In order to keep the data transmit over TCP/IP secured. A low-level filter should be added into SecDevice, which be better placed in the datalink layer of TCP/IP. With this filter, all the data coming in or sending out from the device can be monitored and abnormal data can be filtered. Consider to the efficiency, this filter shouldn't be too complex to apply. The rule of this filter is controlled by SecGuard, which will broadcast the rule of filter.

SecDevice should have the ability to monitor the device working status with workload, error message, energy consumption, etc. All the information can be gathered by SecGuard and this will help to find out an invisible tendency towards security status.

The sketch of SecDevice is shown in Fig. 3.

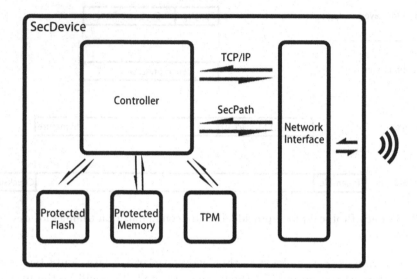

Fig. 3. SecDevice make sure the compute and application runing on a trusted platform

With the SecDevice, all the device which authenticated adding into ad-hoc network can be trusted. And SecGuard will run on the device in the ad-hoc network without threatening.

4   SecGuard Outline

The previous two sections described the protocol and hardware based on the MultiSec architecture. They are focusing on how to make a network fully trusted, which means all the device on the network can be trusted and all the frame transmits over the SecPath can be trusted. And that can make a network working together in trust. The SecGuard is a software working on the trusted network, and it will control the entire network and gathering the network resource to protect entire network just like a guarder.

The SecGuard is not a software working on a specific device. It is working like a guarder, moving around the entire network. The SecGuard working on a device for a short time and then request for a move to nearby device, transmit the database to the destination, start up the new thread. In this way, the software can balance the power consumption and performance.

The sketch of SecGuard is shown in Fig. 4.

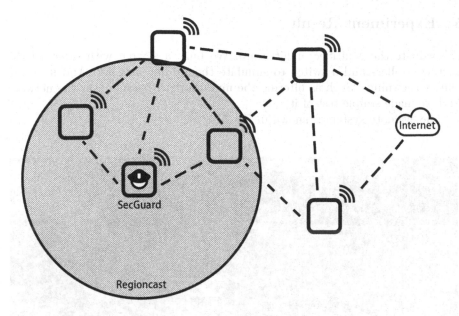

Fig. 4. SecGuard can move in the ad-hoc network randomly, and manage the entire network by regioncast to gather the device information and broadcast to filter the threaten.

When SecGuard is running, it is in charge of all the network. A device adding into this network should authenticate by SecGuard, and the key and encryption method is delivered to the device. Then the device can get access to the ad-hoc network. SecGuard will maintain the encryption and trust list of this network, renew them and broadcast them. Due to the uncertainty of ad-hoc network. A heartbeat packet of SecGuard will be broadcasting timed. And if some of the device gets offline or in fatal error. The network can recover a SecGuard using the snapshot. This will ensure the network always working.

SecGuard can gather the working status of devices nearby. The information is used to analyze the condition of network and status of device. The SecGuard can carry the module of machine learning, which will learn the working status of every device in ad-hoc network continuously. And the data packet pass through the network can be learned too. The SecGuard can use this to judge the security of this network and take the action accordingly. For example, If there is a device reported a list of fetal errors. There may have someone trying to attack it. Then the data coming in the device should be analyzed. A rule of filtering this abnormal data will be broadcast to entire network soon. The similar data can not pass through the ad-hoc network. In case that some of the device had be hacked. And there have some abnormal task running on the device. With the information of device working status. The SecGuard will cancel the authentication of this device and broadcast to entire network, renew the encryption key and force the device offline to protect other device in network.

5   Experiment Result

To evaluate the MultiSec architecture. We built a system with some STM32 microcontrollers and a switch to simulate the Ad-hoc network. And it can do some basic things. Such as filtering the unauthorized packets over the network. And we made simple test of it.

The evaluate system is shown in Fig. 5.

Fig. 5. MultiSec evaluate system consist with PC, STM32, Raspberry Pi and Switch to simulate the ad-hoc network.

We built a network with 6 hosts (3 STM32 Microcontroller, 1 Raspberry Pi, 2 PC). 5 of them are organized in MultiSec method. We use wireshark to capture the frames pass through the network. And we use ping packet to test the effect of MultiSec.

First we test the filter function of the system. We use the unauthorized device to send the ping packet to the other device, and other device sends ping packet with each other. As shown in Fig. 6, we can see the unauthorized packets are filtered by network and even can't get the ARP (Address Resolution Protocol) response. Even it is physically connected with each other. Meanwhile, for the authorized device, they can ping each other freely. Then we captured the packet over network. It shows the SecGuard is sending packet over SecPath and moving

Fig. 6. All the device are pinging 192.168.120.101, but only 192.168.120.100 is unauthorized. So all the device can get success ping except 192.168.120.100. And the ARP request without response can be captured on the ad-hoc network. It means MultiSec is working well.

from one device to another. And the SecGuard we use to test can light up a blue led on device which can show the position of it. We can also see the blue light moving from one device to another. (The SecGuard are set to move only between STM32 platform, to prove the low cost of it.)

6 Conclusion

We brought up a new ad-hoc network security architecture called MultiSec which can protect ad-hoc network with low cost and high security. The main idea are to defend against the attack using the entire power of a network not some specific device or every device itself. The architecture consists in three parts, which is SecPath, SecDevice and SecGuard. We evaluated them on prototype of ad-hoc network we built. It worked nicely. It does bring a new way to solve the problem which the ad-hoc network used by IoT device really facing. And we will build up the real MultiSec system as we design in the future. So far, the evaluate system shows that the system can work in the way we design, and keep the prototype of ad-hoc network secure. We hope it can bring some new thoughts in this research field.

Acknowledgment. Thanks to Xidian University who supported me with all those devices, I can finally take a test of the design. This work was also supported by the Key Scientific and Technological Innovation Team of the Shaanxi Province, China, under grant no. 2017KCT-29, and the Key Research Item for the Industry Shaanxi Province under grant no. 2018GY-136. Thanks all the anonymous reviewers for their attentions and constructive comments.

References

1. Badshah, A., Ghani, A., Qureshi, M.A., Shamshirband, S.: Smart security framework for educational institutions using internet of things (IoT). Comput. Mater. Continua **61**(1), 81–101 (2019)
2. Bhatt, D., Agrawal, B.: Major challenges of mobile adhoc networks. Orient. J. Comput. Sci. Technol.: Int. Open Access Peer Rev. Res. J. **10**(2), 417–421 (2017)
3. Ruxanayasmin, B., Krishna, B., Subhashini, T.: Minimization of power consumption in mobile adhoc networks. Int. J. Comput. Netw. Inf. Secur. (IJCNIS) **6**(2), 38–44 (2014)
4. Jie, C., YuPu, H., YueYu, Z.: Impossible differential cryptanalysis of advanced encryption standard. Sci. China Ser. F-Inf. Sci. (in English) **50**(3), 342–350 (2007). https://doi.org/10.1007/s11432-007-0035-4
5. Padma, E., Rajalakshmi, S.: An efficient architecture for handling IoT in trusted environment. Adv. Comput. Sci. Technol. **10**(2), 295–307 (2017)
6. Qi, N., et al.: Analysis and research of the RSA algorithm. Inf. Technol. J. **12**(9), 1818–1824 (2013)
7. Qiaoyang Zhang, Z.L., Cai, Z.: Developing a new security framework for bluetooth low energy devices. Comput. Mater. Continua **59**(2), 457–471 (2019)
8. Jiang, X., Liu, M., Yang, C., Liu, Y., Wang, R.: A blockchain-based authentication protocol for WLAN mesh security access. Comput. Mater. Continua **58**(1), 45–59 (2019)

A Large-Scale Parallel Network Intrusion Detection Model Based on K-Means in Security Audit System

Xueming Qiao[1], Yuan Zhang[1], Yanhong Liu[1], Hao Hu[2], Dongjie Zhu[2(✉)], Zhi Qiu[3],
and Chenglin Liu[1]

[1] State Grid Weihai Power Supply Company, Weihai, China
[2] School of Computer Science and Technology, Harbin Institute of Technology, Weihai, China
zhudongjie@hit.edu.cn
[3] State Grid Rushan County Electric Power Supply Company, Weihai, China

Abstract. With the gradual entry of 5G communication technology into the commercial stage, the era of the Internet of Thing is coming, bringing great convenience to people's lives. However, there are potential threats to security audit data interaction in the IoT environment. Traditional network intrusion detection methods cannot meet the requirements of parallel processing of massive data. Therefore, network intrusion detection should consider parallelizing data processing and predicting abnormal behavior ahead. In this paper, we propose a large-scale parallel network intrusion detection method based on k-means. Firstly, the Isolation Forest algorithm is used to filter and segment the sample data; Secondly, the clusters is obtained by the k-means algorithm in a distributed manner; Finally, the generated cluster is weighted and voted for abnormality determination. The experimental results of KDDCUP dataset shows that the algorithm improves the recognition accuracy and speeds up the training time and prediction time compared with the traditional k-means algorithm.

Keywords: K-means · Isolated forest · Parallel processing · Network security

1 Introduction

Network security and information security have become the subject of increasing concern. Network security and data leakage incidents caused by network intrusion occur frequently. Traditional network security monitoring methods mostly use rule matching to judge network security intrusion. A large amount of prior knowledge is needed as a basis to establish relevant matching rules or knowledge bases. Each time there is a network request, the decision program takes the data related to the network request as input and uses the established rules or knowledge base to determine whether it is a threat request, so such schemes do not have logical reasoning ability. For new exception information that is not covered by the rule, it cannot be detected as an exception request, which is a fatal flaw for network security. Because cybercriminals have been generating new viruses or other means of attack, monitoring methods without learning and reasoning capabilities

© Springer Nature Singapore Pte Ltd. 2020
X. Sun et al. (Eds.): ICAIS 2020, CCIS 1253, pp. 189–198, 2020.
https://doi.org/10.1007/978-981-15-8086-4_18

will be difficult to ensure data security. With the continuous development of data mining technology, the hidden information and value in the massive data generated by daily life are more and more excavated and displayed. Some researchers begin to use data mining technologies to conduct network security intrusion detection. Data mining technologies solve the problem that traditional methods are too dependent on prior knowledge. The network security intrusion detection technology based on this method has strong reasoning and learning ability. Therefore, this method can predict new security threat requests based on previous historical information, thus protecting against security threats.

In recent years, there are some experts and scholars who are committed to the research of network anomaly detection. Chandola et al. [1]. have a structured and comprehensive overview of anomaly detection research and classify according to the methods used by technology to provide different types of technology. Understand and discuss its strengths, weaknesses and complexity. Eskin et al. [2]. proposed a new geometric framework based on unsupervised anomaly detection, which is an algorithm for processing unlabeled data. M.H. Bhuyan et al. [3]. compared a large number of anomaly detection methods and systems, discussed the tools and data sets that network defenders can use, and emphasized the future direction of network anomaly detection. L. Akoglu et al. [4]. briefly introduced the framework of unsupervised and semi-supervised methods, static and dynamic graphs, attribution and general graphs in anomaly detection, starting from four aspects: effectiveness, scalability, versatility and robustness. Further analysis and understanding. Kim et al. [5]. proposed a new hybrid intrusion detection method, which showed that using decision trees to construct misuse detection models to decompose training data into smaller subsets before anomaly detection would improve accuracy and significantly reduce training and time complexity. Kulariya et al. [6]. proposes a large data processing tool based on Apache spark to detect intrusions, evaluating processing tools from training time, prediction time, sensitivity and specificity on the KDD'99 dataset. Belouch et al. [7]. showed that the random forest classifier is superior to SVM and decision tree classification algorithm in detecting accuracy, construction time and prediction time. Zhang et al. [8]. proposed a set of extensible rules and a reliable spark-based anomaly detection mechanism for the temporal association of IP spoofing characteristics and transport layer connection status. R. Kumari et al. [9] proposed a machine learning method based on k-means clustering to detect intrusions using big data analysis methods. Sinanc Terzi et al. [10]. analyzed the network anomaly detection data using a new unsupervised anomaly detection method on the big data cluster and used the PCA algorithm to perform the dimensionality reduction analysis. J Mathew et al. [11] proposed a firefly-based k-means clustering algorithm to parallelize data. They compared their methods with existing methods and found that their performance is better than existing algorithms. Wang et al. [12]. proposed a method for determining traffic anomaly based on a cloud model. A cloud conversion algorithm was used to fuse the collected quantitative values into the qualitative of the anomaly, which can quickly and directly understand network traffic. Tan et al. [13]. improved on the basis of SOM neural network. They proposed an adaptive neural network method based on k-means, which relatively improves the accuracy of network intrusion detection and reduces the number of cluster iterations. Xiao et al. [14]. Addressed the problem of slow anomaly detection in massive data. They proposed an improved outlier detection algorithm, which combined the simulated annealing algorithm and k-means algorithm to reduce the number of iterations and improve the accuracy of clustering.

In this paper, we propose a k-means-based parallel anomaly detection model for data auditing and verify it on the KDD CUP 1999 dataset. The experimental results show that the optimization and improvement of k-means with Isolation Forest algorithm can improve the anti-interference ability of the initial cluster center. In addition, this model has the advantages of high data processing speed and resource saving and has the ability to parallelize data.

2 The Design of Intrusion Detection Model

The overall structure of the proposed method is shown in Fig. 1. The Isolation Forest algorithm is used to calculate the abnormality coefficient, which reduces the interference ability of the anomaly data to the initial clustering center of k-means. The processed data is divided into different spark nodes by using the fragmentation strategy, and the data is clustered by k-means algorithm to obtain an optimal detection model.

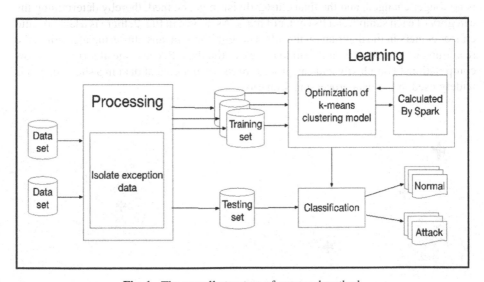

Fig. 1. The overall structure of proposed method.

$$\min(x_{ij}, j = q, x_{ij} \in X') < p < \max(x_{ij}, j = q, x_{ij} \in X') \tag{1}$$

(3) a hyperplane is generated at the cutting point p, and the current space is divided into two subspaces, and the sample points whose degree is less than p are placed in the left child node, and the right child node is greater than or equal to p. Repeat (2) until all leaf nodes have only one sample point or the isolated tree has reached the end of the specified height. Loop (1), (2), (3), (4) operations until t isolated trees are generated. For each data point, iterate through each isolated tree, calculate the average height $h(x_i)$ of

the data points in the forest, and normalize the average height of all points. The Eq. (2) for calculating the outlier score is as follows:

$$s(x, \psi) = 2^{\frac{E(h(x))}{c(\psi)}} \qquad (2)$$

Where $c(\psi)$ is defined as shown in Eq. (3).

$$c(\psi) = \begin{cases} \frac{2H(\psi-1)-2(\psi-1)}{\psi}, \psi > 2 \\ 1, \psi = 2 \\ 0, otherwise \end{cases} \qquad (3)$$

Where $c(\psi)$ is the average path length of the binary search tree, $H(\psi - 1)$ represents the total path length of the binary tree.

K-means is an unsupervised learning algorithm that determines the final clustering class number K in advance, a given data set $D = \{x_1, x_2, \ldots, x_n\}$, and randomly selects $d_{ij} = ||x_i - \mu_j||_2$ between each sample and the centroid. Based on the Euclidean distance, the sample points are classified into the nearest cluster by the equation $r = \arg\min_{j \in K} d_{ij}$, the centroid of each cluster is recalculated, and the operation is repeated until the centroid is no longer changed, and the final cluster division is obtained, thereby determining the category of each sample and Its center of mass. As shown in Fig. 2, there is a lack of valid cluster centers in the diagram on the left. Through the k-means clustering algorithm, the resulting cluster center is sufficient to represent the data. Because the algorithm has low computational complexity and can process massive amounts of data in a short time, it is widely used in big data processing scenarios.

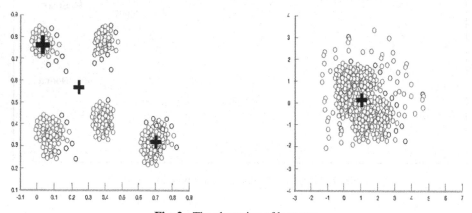

Fig. 2. The clustering of k-means.

3   The Implementation and Experiment

3.1   Experiment Platform

The system platform is Centos 7, the processor is Xeon E5-2620 v4, the memory is 64 GB, the hard disk is 2 TB, and the Apache Spark version used is 2.2.1.

3.2 Data Set

The KDDCUP1999 dataset is derived from the simulated US Air Force LAN environment established by Lincoln Labs. It collects 9 weeks of network connectivity and system audit data, simulating various user types, various network traffic and attack methods. The identification type of the dataset is shown in Table 1. This article divides existing data sets into training sets, cross-validation sets, and test sets. Use the training set for machine learning, then use the cross-validation set to adjust to improve the parameters, and finally use the test set to test the accuracy of the model.

Table 1. The identification type of dataset.

Identification type	Description	Specific classification identifier
Normal	Normal record	Normal
Dos	Denial of service attack	back, land, neptune, pod, smurf, teadrop
Probing	Surveillance and other detection activities	ipsweep, nmap, portsweep, satan
R2L	Illegal access from remote machines	ftp_write, guess_passwd, imap, multihop, phf, spy, warezclient, warezmaster
U2R	Ordinary user's illegal access to local superuser privileges	italic buffer_overflow, loadmodule, perl, rootkit

3.3 Experiment Processing

Among the traditional anomaly detection methods, SVM, NaiveBayes, decision trees and random forests have been widely used, but these algorithms are difficult to parallelize for large-scale and high-latitude data processing. This paper proposes an algorithm that can easily process large-scale network intrusion data in parallel.

Firstly, the data is read in a 2 s time window, and then these data is pre-processed. For discrete features, numerical processing is performed, for example: yes and no converted to 0 and 1. The missing features are also to be supplemented. In order to avoid the dependence on the selection of the measurement unit, eliminate the impact of differences in attribute metrics on clustering.

Secondly, the Isolation Forest algorithm is used to calculate the sample anomaly coefficient, which reduces the interference ability to the initial cluster center. The Isolation Forest algorithm uses a binary tree to segment the data. The depth of the data point in the binary tree reflects the degree of dispersion of the data in the set. The algorithm flow can be roughly divided into two steps: (1) Build. Extract data samples build multi-class binary trees and combine them into forests; (2) Calculate. Integrate each binary tree result to calculate the outliers for each data point in the set. Algorithm 1 shows our build tree algorithm.

Alogrithm1 Building tree

Inputs: Data collection $D=\{x_1, x_2, \cdots, x_n\}$, current tree height c, limit tree height l

Output: A Tree

1   If $c>l$ or $|D|\leq 1$

2   return node { $Size \leftarrow |D|$ }

3   else

4   let P be a list of attributes in D

5   random select an attribute $p\in P$

6   random select a parameter β from max and min values of attribute P in D

7      $D_l \leftarrow filter(D, p<\beta)$

8      $D_r \leftarrow filter(D, p\geq\beta)$

9   return input Node ($Left \leftarrow tree(D_l, c+1, l)$,

10     $Right \leftarrow tree(D_r, c+1, l)$

11     $Att \leftarrow p$

12     $value \leftarrow \beta$

13   )

14   end if

The abnormality coefficient calculation process uses the Eq. (4):

$$S(x, n) = 2^{-\frac{E(h(x))}{C(n)}} \tag{4}$$

$E(h(x))$ represents the average path length of x in each tree, and $C(n)$ represents the correction value, $C(n) = 2H(n-1) - (2(n-1)/n)$, $H(m) = \ln m + \delta$. Especially, $\delta = 0.5772156649$. Sample filtering is performed by setting a reasonable outlier threshold. Select the required cluster number k and the outlier filtering ratio r, r defaults to 0.1, and formulate the abnormality coefficient threshold equation $t = S_{max} - (S_{max} - S_{min}) \times r$. Isolation of data with abnormality coefficients greater than t to avoid errors due to excessively large number of isolated data. The processed data is fragmented, and the parallelization strategy diagram is shown in Fig. 3.

In the data fragmentation phase, the raw data of the total N is divided into m slices by using a hash function on each node, and each slice has a size of $n = N/m$. The initial value is uniformly selected inside the data set to reduce the influence of the boundary value on the initial cluster center selection. For the attribute T with the value range $[i, j]$, according to the required cluster number k, the Eq. (5) is applied to calculate the initial cluster center.

$$K_n = T_i + \frac{(T_j - T_i)}{k+1}, 0 < n \leq k \tag{5}$$

Finally, use the spark platform for clustering calculations. Apache spark is a general-purpose big data processing engine built around the principles of speed, complexity, and

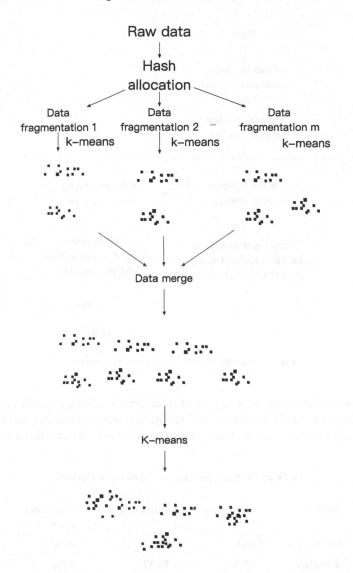

Fig. 3. Implementation of the parallelization prototype.

ease of use. The system increases the speed of applications in the Hadhoop cluster by up to 100 times in memory and can even increase the speed by 10 times on disk.

Using spark-k-means for local clustering analysis, since the previous step has already processed the data, it is possible to apply the fragmentation strategy directly to Spark, and then use spark to perform localization on each machine. Clustering to achieve the purpose of parallelization processing.

The cluster center obtained after clustering on each computer will be used as the data point of the next cluster, as shown in Fig. 4.

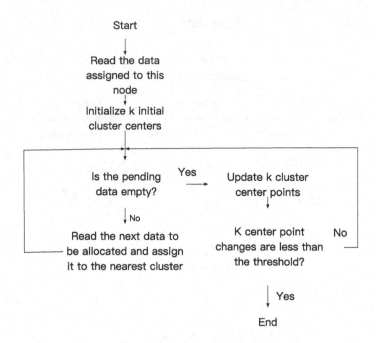

Fig. 4. Implementation of the clustering process.

In addition, the voting method is used to determine whether a node in the corresponding cluster is an abnormal request. This method was verified on KDD CUP 1999. Spark created a Driver node and four worker nodes. The results are shown in Table 2.

Table 2. Compare performance with other methods.

Methods	Accuracy (%)	Training time(s)	Prediction time(s)
Our results	99.6	28.37	0.48
K-means	87.5	76.52	1.34
SVM	69.52	30.46	4.82
Decision trees	81.05	10.56	0.15
AdaBoost	90.31	25.93	1.45

4   Conclusion

This paper proposes a k-means-based parallel anomaly detection method for data auditing. By using the Isolation Forest algorithm to improve and optimize k-means, the anti-interference ability to isolated points, noise points and initial cluster centers is significantly improved. In addition, the fragmentation strategy is used to allocate request data to different spark processing nodes. Processing and analysis on the other greatly improve the processing capacity of massive data and the real-time performance of network detection. The performance of these algorithms was evaluated by experiments on the KDD Cup 1999s dataset to evaluate performance. The proposed method is superior in terms of accuracy and timeliness.

Acknowledgement. This work is supported by State Grid Shandong Electric Power Company Science and Technology Project Funding under Grant no. 520613180002, 62061318C002, the Fundamental Research Funds for the Central Universities (Grant No. HIT. NSRIF.201714), Weihai Science and Technology Development Program (2016DX GJMS15) and Key Research and Development Program in Shandong Provincial (2017GGX90103).

References

1. Chandola, V., Banerjee, A., Kumar, V.: Anomaly detection: a survey. ACM Comput. Surv. (CSUR). Statistical Report on the Development of China's Internet 2018, vol. 41, no. 3, p. 15. Plosone, Beijing (2018)
2. Eskin, E., Arnold, A., Prerau, M., Portnoy, L., Stolfo, S.: A Geometric Framework for Unsupervised Anomaly Detection. In: Barbará, D., Jajodia, S. (eds.) Applications of Data Mining in Computer Security Advances in Information Security, vol. 6. Springer, Boston (2002). https://doi.org/10.1007/978-1-4615-0953-0_4
3. Bhuyan, M.H., Bhattacharyya, D.K., Kalita, J.K.: Network anomaly detection: methods, systems and tools. IEEE Commun. Surv. Tutor. **16**(1), 303–336 (2013)
4. Akoglu, L., Tong, H., Koutra, D.: Graph based anomaly detection and description: a survey. Data Min. Knowl. Disc. **29**(3), 626–688 (2014). https://doi.org/10.1007/s10618-014-0365-y
5. Kim, G., Lee, S., Kim, S.: A novel hybrid intrusion detection method integrating anomaly detection with misuse detection. Expert Syst. Appl. **41**(4), 1690–1700 (2014)
6. Kulariya, M., Saraf, P., Ranjan, R., Gupta, G.P.: Performance analysis of network intrusion detection schemes using Apache Spark. In: 2016 International Conference on Communication and Signal Processing (ICCSP), pp. 1973–1977. IEEE, England (2016)
7. Belouch, M., El Hadaj, S., Idhammad, M.: Performance evaluation of intrusion detection based on machine learning using apache spark. Procedia Comput. Sci. **127**, 1–6 (2018)
8. Zhang, J., Zhang, Y., Liu, P., He, J.: A spark-based DDoS attack detection model in cloud services. In: Bao, F., Chen, L., Deng, R.H., Wang, G. (eds.) ISPEC 2016. LNCS, vol. 10060, pp. 48–64. Springer, Cham (2016). https://doi.org/10.1007/978-3-319-49151-6_4
9. Kumari, R., Singh, M.K., Jha, R., Singh, N.K.: Anomaly detection in network traffic using k-mean clustering. In: 2016 3rd International Conference on Recent Advances in Information Technology (RAIT), pp. 387–393. IEEE, Dhanbad (2016)
10. Terzi, D.S., Terzi, R., Sagiroglu, S.: Big data analytics for network anomaly detection from netflow data. In: 2017 International Conference on Computer Science and Engineering (UBMK), pp. 592–597. IEEE, Dubai (2017)

11. Mathew, J., Vijayakumar, R.: Scalable parallel clustering approach for large data using parallel k means and firefly algorithms. In: 2014 International Conference on High Performance Computing and Applications (ICHPCA), pp. 1–8. IEEE, Bhubaneswar (2014)
12. Wang, Y., Cao, Y., Zhang, L.: YATA: yet another proposal for traffic analysis and anomaly detection. Comput. Mater. Cont. **60**(3), 1171–1187 (2019)
13. Tan, L., Li, C., Xia, J.: Application of self-organizing feature map neural network based on k-means clustering in network intrusion detection. Comput. Mater. Cont. **61**(1), 275–288 (2019)
14. Xiao, B., Wang, Z., Liu, Q.: SMK-means: an improved mini batch k-means algorithm based on mapreduce with big data. Comput. Mater. Cont. **56**(3), 365–379 (2018)

Task Offloading Strategy in Cloud Collaborative Edge Computing

Wenli Wang, Yanfeng Bai, and Suzhen Wang$^{(\boxtimes)}$

Hebei University of Economics and Business, Shijiazhuang, Hebei 050061, China
wsuz@163.com

Abstract. With the development of 5G and IOT technology, data processed by intelligent mobile terminals grows explosively. Due to the limited computing power of the intelligent terminal, which can not meet the requirements of low task delay, an edge computing with cloud collaborative task offloading method is proposed to solve the problem. This method applies to computing intensive applications. In the cloud center, the resources are scheduled and terminal tasks are offloaded to the edge nodes in using the method. At the same time, considering the offloading needs of the terminal users and the load of the edge server, the improved artificial bee colony algorithm is adopted to provide the offloading scheme that meets the requirements of each task's delay. The simulation results show that the method can improve the load balance of the cluster, and reduce the task processing delay compared with the random offloading method and the task local processing method.

Keywords: Edge computing · Cloud - edge synergy · Task offload

1 Introduction

Since cloud computing was put forward, it has changed the way of daily life, work and learning. In recent years, with the rapid development of Internet of things technology and 5 g communication, a number of emerging applications have emerged, such as driverless, virtual augmented reality, smart city, etc. [1]. Most of the emerging applications are computing intensive or data intensive applications, which require high processing delay. However, cloud computing requires data to be uploaded to the cloud center and complete the calculation. High data transmission cost will cause high delay. Therefore, the traditional cloud architecture is difficult to meet the delay requirements of emerging applications. The purpose of edge computing [2, 3] is to process data close to the edge of the network generated by the data, so as to meet the needs of users in terms of low delay, low energy consumption, security and privacy. The emergence of edge computing extends cloud services to the edge of the network, and processing near the edge of data generation has become a trend of technology development. According to Gartner's top 10 strategic technology trends for 2018: cloud to the edge, 75% of the data generated by enterprises will be generated and processed outside the cloud in 2022, but only 10% in 2018 [4]. Cloud computing and edge computing have their own advantages, and they

© Springer Nature Singapore Pte Ltd. 2020
X. Sun et al. (Eds.): ICAIS 2020, CCIS 1253, pp. 199–209, 2020.
https://doi.org/10.1007/978-981-15-8086-4_19

are complementary to each other. In November 2018, the Edge Computing Consortium released the white paper on edge computing and cloud collaboration [5], which believes that edge computing and cloud computing collaboration can meet the matching of various demand scenarios and maximize the application value of edge computing and cloud computing.

Task offloading is one of the research hotspots of edge computing, which has been explored by academia and industry. Literature [6–8] summarizes the task offloading strategies of mobile edge computing. Wu et al. [9] studied the service request in mobile edge computing, modeled the problem of task assignment to edge computing server and cloud server as optimization problem, and proposed gamec algorithm for this problem. Chen et al. [10] use the idea of software defined network to abstract the task offloading problem into a mixed integer nonlinear programming problem. Aiming at this optimization problem, task offloading is divided into two problems: task distribution and resource allocation. Based on this, a new offloading scheme is proposed to reduce the total duration and energy consumption of the task. Dong et al. [11, 12] proposed a scheduling strategy based on task priority, which considered the priority and delay constraints comprehensively, and provided an efficient solution for users with different priority in edge network to offload tasks.

The edge computing industry alliance believes that from the perspective of market, edge computing is mainly divided into three categories and six main business forms. Huawei, Cisco, Siemens and other companies in the industry already have solutions for edge computing. Huawei's EC lot and Cisco's fog computing are typical Edge Computing solutions of the Internet of things, which make the original business field extend to the Internet of things, and can promote the value mining of E2E data.

In this paper, the task offloading problem of edge computing is studied. Considering the offloading requirements of mobile users and the load deviation degree of the cluster to be offloaded, the task offloading model of edge computing and cloud collaboration is proposed. The task offloading problem is transformed into the optimization problem, and the improved artificial bee colony algorithm is used for optimization. We named this offloading approach ECBL.

2 Problem Description

2.1 Edge Computing

At present, European Telecommunications Standards Institute(ETSI), International organization for standardization ISO/IEC JTC1/SC38 and Edge Computing Consortium(ECC) give many different definitions. There is a consensus on these concepts: Process and provide services near the place where data is generated. In fact, industry and academia have not given a unified definition in a strict sense.

Shi et al. [13] review the development of edge computing, and think that the basic idea of edge computing is function cache. Besides, the divide the development of edge computing into three stage, and present the typical events for each period. Ding et al. [14] believe that edge computing is an enabling technology. By providing storage, bandwidth and other resources on the edge of the network, it can meet the needs of the industry in agile connection, security and privacy. Wei et al. [15] proposed the edge computing unloading strategy based on deep learning. Li et al. [16] proposed a collaborative regression learning for edge computing. Guo et al. [17] proposed a resource allocation method for micro data center.

Cloud computing relies on cloud rich computing, storage and other resources to carry out a large number of complex operations on the cloud. Therefore cloud computing requires data to be stored or uploaded to the cloud. However, with the growth of the number and types of mobile terminals, the increase of data volume in recent years, limited by the high cost of data transmission and privacy issues, stakeholders rarely share data and cooperate less [3]. The edge serves as a small, independent data center connected to both end users and the cloud. Edge computing provides a new cooperation opportunity for these stakeholders. The overall architecture of cloud edge collaboration is shown in Fig. 1.

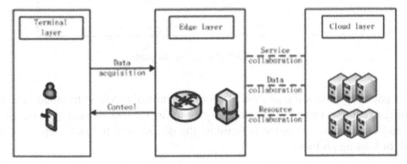

Fig. 1. Cloud edge collaboration.

Considering that in practice, the priority of different user task offloading requests is different, and the resources that the edge layer servers can provide are often different at different times. Therefore, considering the user demand and the load of the edge server at the same time, which can improve the efficiency of task offloading, reduce the service time and energy consumption.

This paper focuses on the resource collaboration in cloud edge collaboration, and the task offloading of mobile end firstly selects the edge server cluster closer to it. The cloud is responsible for task offloading scheduling, offloading decision-making, processing terminal offloading request, matching the best edge server for offloading task, as shown in Fig. 2.

When the mobile terminal cannot meet the computing, storage and bandwidth resources required by the task, the mobile terminal initiates an offloading request to the cloud center, which processes the received offloading request. The cloud center listens to the resource surplus of the edge server at all times to form a resource queue. When receiving the task offloading request from the mobile terminal, the task is added to the request queue and sorted according to the user priority. The cloud center schedules the requested tasks in descending priority order to match the most edge servers. When there is no suitable edge server to provide services for tasks in the task queue, the cloud center will give the best solution to offload some tasks from the edge server to the cloud center.

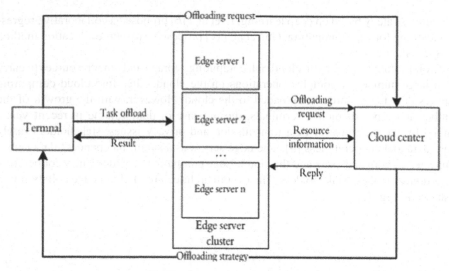

Fig. 2. Task offloading diagram.

This paper optimizes the process of mobile terminal's request to cloud center and offloading to edge service in edge computing, ignoring the task offloading between edge server and cloud center. In order to facilitate the description, the next step is to model the task offloading problem.

2.2 Model Building

The content of this paper is the process of the terminal user offloads the task to the edge server. Edge computing server is closer to data generator, but its resource is still limited compared with cloud center. Therefore, it is the key to find a suitable edge computing server for the task of user offloading.

When the terminal user initiates the offloading request, this section abstracts the offloading problem of the edge computing task to the cloud center, gives the following definitions and formal descriptions.

Definition 1(Offload Request)
A Offload request is represented as a 5-tuples(K, e, t, S, D),where:

(1)   K represents the set of tasks that are ready to be offloaded;
(2)   e represents the cloud server that processing offloading requests;
(3)   t is the time when e receives the offload request;
(4) $S = \{S_i | S_i = \{K_i\}_{i=1}^n\}$, indicates the possible correspondence between tasks and processors. N indicates the number of currently idle edge computing servers;
(5)   D represents the offloading request structure, including the offloading request structure data volume and other information describing the offloading request.

Definition 2(Task)

A Task is represented as a 6-tuples $K_i(m, c, b, d, t_{max}, MOB)$, where:

(1) m represents the memory requirements of the task;
(2) c represents the CPU requirements of the task;
(3) b represents the bandwidth requirement of the task;
(4) d represents the amount of data to be offloaded for the task;
(5) t_{max} represents the latest acceptable completion time;
(6) MOB represents the terminal computing capacity that generates the task.

Definition 3(Edge Server)

A Edge server is represented as a 4-tuples $E_i(m, c, b, t_0)$, where:

(1) m represents the memory resources that the edge server can provide;
(2) c represents the CPU resources that the edge server can provide;
(3) b represents the bandwidth resources that the edge server can provide;
(4) t_0 represents the estimated time of task processing.

Definition 4(Delay)

In this paper, the total task offloading delay is defined as follows:

$$T = t_c + t_0 + t_w \tag{1}$$

(1) $t_c = \frac{K_i(b)}{B_j}$, represents the transmission delay, and B_j represents the bandwidth of task I offloading to edge server j;
(2) $t_0 = \frac{d_i}{E_j(c)}$ represents the expected processing time on edge server i;
(3) t_w represents the waiting delay after task offloading.

Definition 5(Center Cloud)

A Center cloud is represented as a 5-tuples $ECloud_i, m, c, b, R, Ans$, where:

(1) m represents the memory resources that the cloud server can provide;
(2) c represents the CPU resources that the cloud server can provide;
(3) b represents the bandwidth resources that the cloud server can provide;
(4) R is center cloud receives the offload request;
(5) Ans is center cloud returned to offload the terminal user's reply;

Definition 6(Load Deviation Degree)

Define load deviation degree to measure the load balance degree of edge server
cluster:

$$\beta = \sqrt{\frac{\sum_{i=1}^{N} (R_i - R_{ave})^2}{N}} \tag{2}$$

R_i represents the resource utilization of the i-th server and the R_{ave} represent average
the resource utilization of the edge server cluster. Considering the different weight of
memory, CPU and bandwidth resources in task processing, the load factor is introduced.
The load factor of edge server i is L_i:

$$L_i = \xi_1 R_{im} + \xi_2 R_{ic} + \xi_3 R_{ib}$$
$$S.t. \xi_1 + \xi_2 + \xi_3 = 1 \tag{3}$$

ξ_1, ξ_2, ξ_3 are used to represent the utilization of server memory, CPU and bandwidth
resources respectively. In this paper, 0.2, 0.7 and 0.1 are used.

Define the standard deviation of weighted load deviation:

$$\beta L = \sqrt{\frac{\sum_{i=1}^{N} (L_i - L_{ave})^2}{N}} \tag{4}$$

In order to further measure the change of load deviation, the change rate of load
deviation is defined. The change rate of load deviation CR L is defined as follows:

$$CR\beta L = \frac{\beta L^{after} - \beta L}{\beta L} \tag{5}$$

When CRβL is less than 0, it is proved that unloading the task to server I will improve
the load balance of the whole cluster, otherwise it will reduce the load balance, and the
unloading strategy tends to choose the direction of CRβL reduction.

3   ECBL Approach

In this paper, the minimum delay is taken as the optimization objective, and the load
deviation is considered. We make the following constraints on the model, that the task
is only offloaded to one server at a time, and that the edge server meets the offloading
conditions. We named this approach ECBL. There is the process of ECBL in Fig. 3.

In the process of finding edge server, we use the optimized artificial bee colony
algorithm. The heuristic algorithm has good performance in the process of searching
optimization. At present, the main heuristic algorithms are particle swarm algorithm,
genetic algorithm, ant colony algorithm and artificial swarm algorithm. The artificial
bee colony algorithm, which mimics bees gathering honey in nature, is a kind of group
intelligence heuristic algorithm. It has excellent local search capability and strong robustness. However, it is easy to fall into the local optimization in the early stage of search,
and has the phenomenon of early maturity.

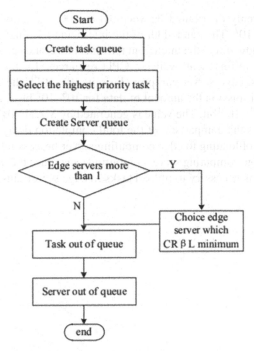

Fig. 3. ECBL approach.

Simulated annealing algorithm is a general optimization algorithm. The idea is derived from the similarity between solid material annealing process and combination optimization. It is robust to initial value. However, it requires sufficient sampling for different temperatures, so the convergence rate is slow.

4 Experiment

In this paper, MATLAB simulation tool was selected to conduct experimental verification on the proposed algorithm optimization under the Windows platform to prove the effectiveness of the algorithm. The local computation of the task is compared with the random offloading and fair scheduling of the computational task and the offloading algorithm based on load balancing proposed in this paper.

Experimental design: Firstly, the total time of task local processing and offloading processing is compared, which proves the necessity of offloading. By comparing the local processing and random offloading strategies with the offloading strategies proposed in this paper, the maximum completion time of this group of tasks is selected as the completion time of this group of tasks, which proves the effectiveness of the ECBL method.

The task processing delay of selection of comparative measurement index has been defined in Sect. 2.2 of this paper. Since there is currently no unified experimental platform and data for edge computing, according to experience [11, 12], we selected self-assembled data for experimental proof. Simulation parameters and values are described as follows.

Task amount evenly distributed between 10 to 100, the amount of data for task ranges from in 10^6–10^7. The bandwidth of the intelligent terminal and the edge server for 108 bit/s, the bandwidth of the intelligent terminal and cloud center for 10^7 bit/s. Use computing capacity to represent available CPU resources, for the mobile computing capacity is 10^7 bit/s, edge server can provide is in 10^9–10^{10}, the center of the cloud computing was 1011 mission the amount of data for 10^6–10^7 bit/s. And the memory of edge server is in 10^{10}–10^{11} bit. The value is generated by MATLAB's random function.

The Fig. 4 shows the comparison of the total completion delay between task local processing and task offloading to edge computing server processing. It can be seen that task offloading to edge computing server computing can reduce the task delay by 73.8%, which proves that it is necessary to offload tasks to edge server cluster.

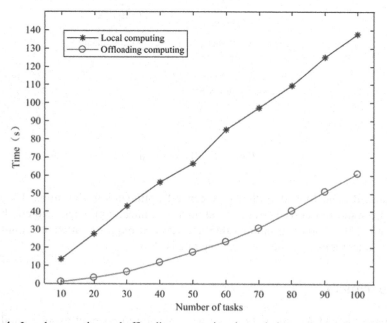

Fig. 4. Local computing and offloading computing time relative to the number of tasks.

After comparing the task processing time of data local processing and offloading to edge computing server, the paper compares the data local processing, random offloading edge server and the offloading scheme proposed in this paper, and selects the maximum completion delay of reorganization task as the completion delay of the scheme. The task processing delay of the three strategies is shown in the Fig. 5. The offloading scheme proposed in this paper has better delay reduction effect than the data local processing and random processing.

Then we compare the task processing delay between the random offload strategy and the proposed strategy in different number of edge servers. The results are shown in Fig. 6.

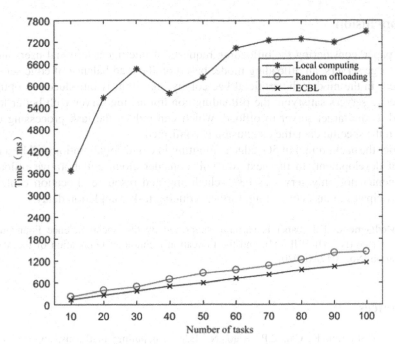

Fig. 5. Comparison of time consumption of each strategy.

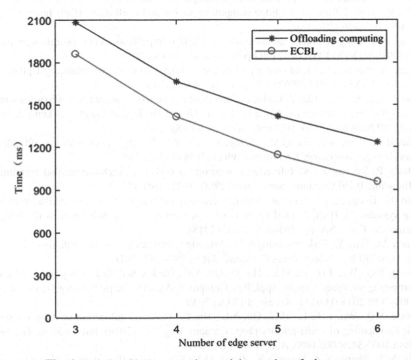

Fig. 6. Relationship between time and the number of edge servers.

5 Conclusion

In this paper, considering the offloading requests of intelligent terminal users and the load of edge servers, an offloading model based on the load balance of edge servers is proposed. In the model, the artificial bee colony algorithm is introduced to optimize. In the edge servers satisfying the offloading conditions, the server with better load is selected as the target server to offload, which can reduce the task processing delay. Through the specific data, the conclusion is confirmed.

Under the background of 5G, edge computing in cloud collaboration will be a major trend of development. In the next, we will consider cloud collaborative offloading. Cloud center not only serves as task scheduling and resource allocation center, but also participates in task computing, further reducing task completion delay.

Acknowledgement. This paper is partially supported by the Social Science Foundation of Hebei Province (No. HB19JL007), and the Education technology Foundation of the Ministry of Education (No. 2017A01020).

References

1. Zhao, Z.M., Liu, F., Cai, Z.P., Xiao, N.: Edge computing: platforms, applications and challenges. J. Comput. Res. Dev. **55**(2), 327–337 (2018)
2. Shi, W., Dustdar, S.: The promise of edge computing. Computer **49**(5), 78–81 (2016)
3. Shi, W., IEEE Fellow, et al.: Edge computing: vision and challenges. IEEE Internet Things J. **3**(5), 637-646 (2016)
4. Edge computing reference architecture 3.0 (2018). http://www.ecconsortium.org/Uploads/file/20190225/1551059767474697.pdf. Accessed 26 Oct 2019
5. Edge computing and cloud synergy white paper, http://www.ecconsortium.org/Uploads/file/20190221/1550718911180625.pdf. Accessed 5 Oct 2019
6. Dong, S.Q., Li, H.L., Qu, Y.B., Hu, L.: Survey of research on computation offloading strategy in mobile edge computing. Comput. Sci. 1–12 (2019). http://kns.cnki.net/kcms/detail/50.1075.TP.20190814.1150.037.html. Accessed 17 Oct 2019
7. Xie, R.C., Lian, X.F., Jia, Q.M., Huang, T., Liu, Y.J.: Survey on computation offloading in mobile edge computing. J. Commun. **39**(11), 138–155 (2018)
8. Mach, P., Becvar, Z.: Mobile edge computing: a survey on architecture and computation offloading. IEEE Commun. Surv. Tutor. **19**(3), 1628–1656 (2017)
9. Wu, H., Deng, S., Li, W., et al.: Service selection for composition in mobile edge computing systems. In: IEEE 2018 IEEE International Conference on Web Services (ICWS), San Francisco, CA, USA, pp. 355–358. IEEE (2018)
10. Chen, M., Hao, Y.: Task offloading for mobile edge computing in software defined ultra-dense network. IEEE J. Select. Areas Commun. **36**(3), 287–597 (2018)
11. Dong, S.Q., Wu, J.H., Li, H.L., Hu, L., Qu, Y.B.: Task scheduling policy for mobile edge computing with user priority. Appl. Res. Comput. 1–5 (2019). https://doi.org/10.19734/j.issn.1001-3695.2019.03.0131. Accessed 17 Oct 2019
12. Dong, S.Q., Wu, J.H., Li, H.L., Qu, Y.B., Hu, L.: Resource allocation strategy for mobile edge computing of multi-priority tasks. Comput. Eng. 1–7 (2019). https://doi.org/10.19678/j.issn.1000-3428.0054490. Accessed 24 Oct 2019
13. Shi, W.S., Zhang, X.Z., Wang, Y.F., Zhang, Q.Y.: Edge computing: state-of-the-art and future directions. J. Comput. Res. Dev. **56**(1), 69–89 (2019)

14. Ding, C.T., Cao, J.N., Yang, L., Wang, S.G.: Edge computing: applications, state-of-the-art and challenges. ZTE Technol. J. **25**(3), 2–7 (2019)
15. Wei, Y., Wang, Z., Guo, D., Yu, F.R.: Deep Q-learning based computation offloading strategy for mobile edge computing. Computers, Materials & Continua **59**(1), 89–104 (2019)
16. Li, Y.Y., Wang, X., Fang, W.W., Xue, F., Jin, H., Zhang, Y., Li, X.W.: A distributed ADMM approach for collaborative regression learning in edge computing. Comput. Mater. Continua **59**(2), 493–508 (2019)
17. Guo, Y.T., Liu, F., Xiao, N., Chen, Z.G.: Task-based resource allocation bid in edge computing micro datacenter. Comput. Mater. Continua **61**(2), 777–792 (2019)

A Review of Wireless Sensor Network Simulation Tools

Ning Cao[1](✉) and Pingping Yu[2]

[1] College of Information Engineering, Sanming University, Sanming, Fujian, China
`ning.cao2008@hotmail.com`
[2] School of Information Science and Engineering, Hebei University of Science and Technology,
Shijiazhuang, Hebei, China

Abstract. Simulation results rely not only on the environment but also on the physical layer assumptions, which are not that accurate. Although this problem exists, simulation is still a good approach for the deployment of real sensors. This paper will compare several popular simulations tools for wireless sensor networks and analyze nthe advantages and dis-advantages for different simulation tools.

Keywords: Simulation tool · Wireless sensor networks

1 Introduction

A wireless sensor network consists of a number of sensors deployed either randomly or in a pre-determined state in a given space. Such sensors are designed to measure one or more physical quantities in the space, such as location or temperature. The sensors need to transmit this collected data to the manager or end-user via internet. Since the sensors concerned are wireless they are typically powered by a battery with a finite lifetime and power output; it may be impossible to recharge or replace such batteries. A wireless sensor network (WSN) consists of spatially distributed autonomous sensors to cooperatively monitor physical or environmental conditions, such as temperature, sound, pressure, motion. The sensor node transmits the data to the related sensors, and finally the aggregated data arrives at the gateway sensor node or sink node which is connected to the terminal device through internet or satellite. (The terminal device can be used to collect data from the sink node or transmit data to the sink node. It can also be used to interact with manager. A computer is normally working as the terminal device, but a tablet or a smart phone can be the terminal device as well.) Then the manager (end-user) can do analysis. Owing to the limited number of sensors that can be distributed in a real experimental network means that much research in this area is based on an over-simplified analysis, and therefore only limited confidence can be placed on predictions arising from such experiments. Thus simulation has become a common way to test new applications Xie et al. (2019) and new protocols Wang et al. (2019) before real deployment Pham et al. (2007).

Figure 1 is a general model of a simulation tool Egea-Lopez et al. (2005). The model includes several sensor nodes, a radio channel, environment, agents and sink nodes.

A detailed description of the components in this figure is as follows:

© Springer Nature Singapore Pte Ltd. 2020
X. Sun et al. (Eds.): ICAIS 2020, CCIS 1253, pp. 210–220, 2020.
https://doi.org/10.1007/978-981-15-8086-4_20

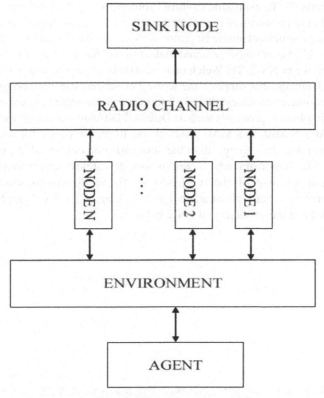

Fig. 1. Simulation model

(a) Nodes: Nodes are basic devices in this model. Each node can communicate with each other through the radio channel. There also exists a protocol stack to control these communications.

(b) Environment: The environment component models the generation and propagation of events that are sensed by the sensor nodes, which can lead to other sensor actions.

(c) Radio channel: This component characterizes the propagation of radio signals among the nodes in the network.

(d) Sink nodes: The sink nodes will receive data from common sensor nodes.

(e) Agents: Agents play a role as a generator of events of interest for the nodes.

Based on this simulation model, several examples of popular simulation tools will be analyzed below.

2   NS-2

Network simulator version 2 Downard (2004) (NS-2) is a discrete event simulator targeted at networking research, which is developed in C++. C++ is one of the most popular general-purpose programming languages and is implemented on a wide variety of hardware and operating system platforms.

NS-2 supports the Transmission Control Protocol (TCP). TCP Mogul (1992) is one of the original core protocols of the internet protocol suite and resides at the transport layer; it provides routing and multicast protocols over wired and wireless networks. OTcl Hegedus et al. (2005), an object-oriented dialect of Tcl has been used as configuration and script interface in NS-2. Tcl Welch et al. (2003) is a scripting language, which is a programming language that supports the writing of scripts; these are programs written for a special runtime environment that can interpret and automate the execution of tasks.

NS-2 can implement protocols such as Directed Diffusion or sensor medium access control (S-MAC). S-MAC is a MAC protocol specifically designed for wireless sensor networks, which uses less energy than the standard protocol. In addition, there exist some projects like SensorSim, which plan to provide wireless sensor support to NS-2. One of NS-2's disadvantages is that it is based on a flat-earth model in which it assumes that the environment is flat without any bulge or sinking. Also, NS-2 graphical support is not very good and the scalability of NS-2 is limited.

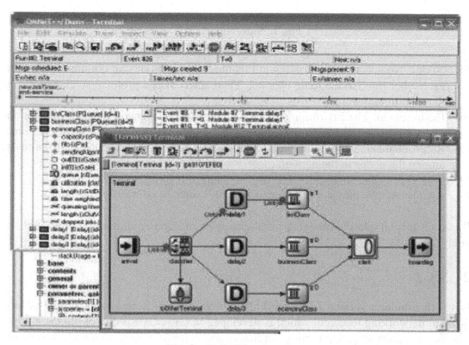

Fig. 2. OMNET++ interface

3 Omnet++

OMNET++ Kaage et al. (2001) is an extensible, modular discrete event simulator written in the C++ language. The framework of OMNET++ provides a very strong functionality as it supports queuing networks, performance evaluation and communication networks. It also provides support for real-time simulation, network emulation, database integration and many other functions. Compared to NS-2, OMNET++ provides a better graphical user interface (GUI) library for tracing and debugging support, see Fig. 2 Varga and Hornig (2008). In addition the MAC protocol has been implemented in OMNET++ and it can simulate power consumption.

The disadvantage of this simulation tool is that it doesn't provide many protocols in its library. However, OMNET++ has become a popular simulation tool for wireless sensor networks. This thesis will select a Java-based simulation tool,so OMNET++ will not be the choice.

4 Tossim

TOSSIM Levis et al. (2003) is a discrete event simulator for TinyOS sensor networks. Users can compile TinyOS code (nesC) into the TOSSIM framework, which runs on a PC. Thus, users can debug and test different algorithms in a repeatable and controlled environment.

TinyViz is the user-interface of TOSSIM, which provides users with a convenient and highly efficient running environment. This means that there is no need for a user to go through all the commands. Figure 3 illustrates the TinyViz interface.

TOSSIM is designed to simulate TinyOS networks instead of the real world. In other words, TOSSIM will just focus on the behaviour of TinyOS. The TOSSIM framework can simulate a huge number of sensors; in addition TOSSIM has a good radio model. Thus many simulation results can be obtained by using TOSSIM. On the other hand, TOSSIM cannot provide users with a good energy consumption simulation, which is the main disadvantage of this simulator. So this thesis will not choose TOSSIM as its simulation tool. A second disadvantage is that the programming language NesC (the dialect of C previously mentioned) should be run on all the sensor nodes, so TOSSIM can only simulate homogeneous applications.

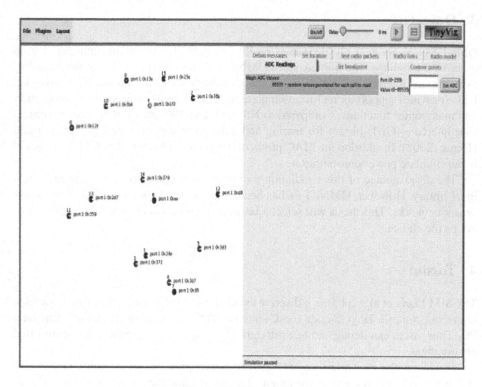

Fig. 3. TinyViz interface

5   Atemu

ATEMU Polley et al. (2004) is a C-based simulation tool for wireless sensor networks, which operates under Linux. The processor of ATEMU is called AVR, which is used in MICA2 sensors. The GUI for ATEMU is named XATDB, which provides a good interface for users to know the actions of sensor nodes. Figure 4 shows an example of a six sensor node simulation. ATEMU is designed to bridge the gap between real sensors and simulation, as it can not only be implemented for real sensors but also provides users with a simulation for the interactions among the sensor nodes.

The main advantage of ATEMU is that it supports a heterogeneous sensor network. That is to say it is possible not only to simulate on the MICA2 nodes, but also on other platforms. Based on the ATEMU simulation a lot of useful and accurate results can be obtained, which assists users to find unbiased comparisons. The main disadvantage of ATEMU is that it only supports a limited number of routing protocols, so, for example, it doesn't provide any routings Kaddi et al. (2019) regarding the clustering problem. This thesis will not select a real-time only simulation tool as a discrete-event simulator can run for as long as necessary to complete the simulation. Thus ATEMU is not the choice of simulation tool in this thesis.

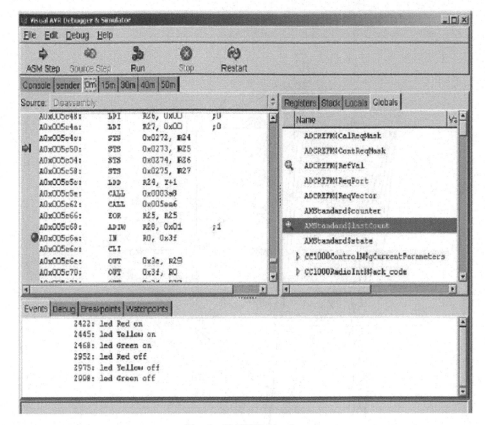

Fig. 4. XATDB interface

6 EmStar

EmStar is a C-based simulation tool for wireless sensor networks, which operates under Linux. EmStar provides the users with a GUI (Fig. 5) with which users control the devices directly Girod et al. (2007). The main advantage for EmStar is that the debug operation for EmStar is very convenient and users can switch the simulation and deployment of sensors freely. The main disadvantage of EmStar is that it can only run in real-time. However, a discrete-event simulator can run for as long as necessary in order to complete the simulation. So EmStar will not be selected as the simulation tool.

Figure 5 is a screen shot of EmView, the Emstar visualizer.

7 J-Sim

J-Sim Sobeih et al. (2005) (formerly known as JavaSim) is an open-source, component-based compositional network simulation environment. The system is based on the IEEE 802.11 Crow et al. (1997) implementation provided with J-Sim. IEEE 802.11 is the first wireless LAN (WLAN) standard proposed in 1997. J-Sim provides a script interface that

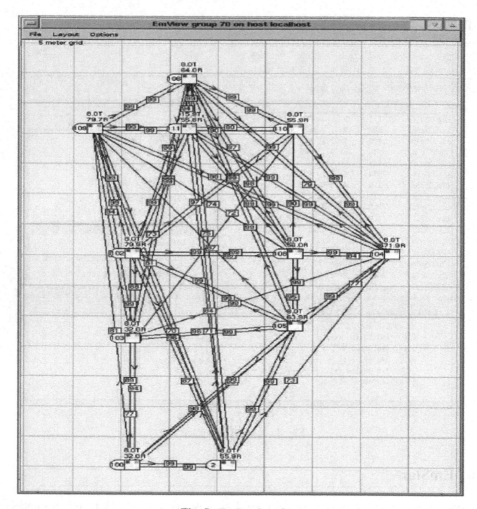

Fig. 5. EmStar interface

allows its integration with Tcl and has been developed entirely in Java. Java is a general purpose object-oriented computing language that is specifically designed to have as few implementation dependencies as possible.

The main advantage of J-Sim is that it provides some basic routing protocols, such as Greedy Perimeter Stateless Routing Karp and Kung (2000) and Directed Diffusion Intanagonwiwat et al. (2000), and it also provides the user with a wireless sensor network simulation framework with a very detailed model of a WSN.

In the J-Sim framework a five-layer sensor stack and a power model are basic components for the key component, the sensor node. A diagram explaining the structure of the sensor node is (Fig. 6):

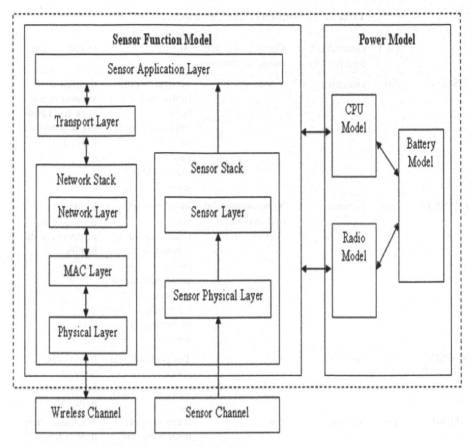

Fig. 6. Sensor node

8   Comparison of Simulation Tools

The following table compares some popular simulation tools Yu and Jain (2014) (Include: NS-2, OMNET++, TOSSIM, ATEMU, EmStar, and J-Sim) and illustrates their advantages and disadvantages (Table 1).

Table 1. Comparison of simulation tools for WSNs

	GUI	General OS or Specific OS	Open-source and online documents	Advantages	Disadvantages
NS-2	No	General	Yes	Several routing protocols have been implemented. It supports randomly placement of sensors	Graphical support is not very good and the scalability is limited
OMNET++	Yes	General	Non-commercial or commercial license	MAC protocol has been implemented. It can simulate power consumptions. It supports randomly placement of sensors	It doesn't provide many protocols in its library
TOSSIM	Yes	Specific	Yes	The scalability is good	It can only simulate homogeneous networks
ATEMU	Yes	Specific	Yes	It can support heterogeneous networks. The power consumption model is good	The simulation time is long
EmStar	Yes	Specific	Yes	The debug operation is very convenient	It can only run in real-time

(continued)

Table 1. (*continued*)

	GUI	General OS or Specific OS	Open-source and online documents	Advantages	Disadvantages
J-Sim	Yes	General	Yes	It provides some routing protocols. It has a good GUI. The power consumption model has been implemented. The scalability is good. It is a Java-based simulation tool. It supports randomly placement of sensors	The simulation time is long

9   Conclusions

Some of the existing WSN simulation tools has been described in this paper. NS-2 and OMNET++ are most popular simulation tools. TOSSIM, ATEMU and EmStar simulation tools provide specific OS. The scalability of J-sim is good and it is a Java based simulation tool. Users can select the most suitable simulation tool as needed.

Acknowledgement. This research is based upon works supported by the Grant 19YG02, Sanming University.

References

Xie, Y., Xu, F., Li, X., Zhang, S., Zhang, X., Israr, M.: EIAS: an efficient identity-based aggregate signature scheme for WSNS against coalition attack. Comput. Mater. Continua **59**(3), 903–924 (2019)

Wang, J., Gao, Y., Liu, W., Wu, W., Lim, S.: An asynchronous clustering and mobile data gathering schema based on timer mechanism in wireless sensor networks. Comput. Mater. Continua **58**(3), 711–725 (2019)

Crow, B.P., Widjaja, I., Kim, J.G., Sakai, P.T.: IEEE 802.11 wireless local area networks. Commun. Mag. **35**(9), 116–126 (1997)

Downard, I.: Simulation sensor networks in NS-2, Technical report NRL/FR/5522-04-10073, Naval Research Laboratory, Washington DC, USA (2004)

Egea-Lopez, E., Vales-Alonso, J., Martinez-Sala, A.S., Pavón-Mariño, P., García-Haro, J.: Simulation tools for wireless sensor networks. In: Proceedings of the International Symposium on Performance Evaluation of Computer and Telecommunication Systems (SPECTS 2005), Article 24, Philadelphia, USA, 24–28 July (2005)

Kaddi, M., Benahmed, K., Omari, M.: An energy-efficient protocol using an objective function & random search with jumps for WSN. Comput. Mater. Continua **58**(3), 603–624 (2019)

Girod, L., Ramanathan, N., Elson, J., Stathopoulos, T., Lukac, M., Estrin, D.: Emstar: a software environment for developing and deploying heterogeneous sensor-actuator networks, ACM Trans. Sens. Netw. **3**(3), Article 13 (2007)

Hegedus, A., Maggio, G.M., Kocarev, L.: A NS-2 simulator utilizing chaotic maps for network-on-chip traffic analysis. In: IEEE International Symposium on Circuits and Systems, pp. 3375–3378 (2005)

Intanagonwiwat, C., Govindan, R., Estrin, D.: Directed diffusion: a scalable and robust communication paradigm for sensor networks. Proceedings of the 6th Annual International Conference on Mobile Computing and Networking, pp. 56–67 (2000)

Kaage, U., Kahmann, V., Jondral, F: An OMNET++ TCP model. In: Proceedings of the European Simulation Multiconference, pp. 409–413 (2001)

Karp, B., Kung, H.T.: GPSR: greedy perimeter stateless routing for wireless networks. In: The Sixth Annual International Conference on Mobile Computing and Networking, pp. 243–254, Massachusetts, USA, 6–11 August. ACM (2000)

Levis, P., Lee, N., Welsh, M., Culler, D.: TOSSIM: accurate and scalable simulation of entire TinyOS applications. In: 1st International Conference on Embedded Networked Sensor Systems, pp. 126–137 (2003)

Mogul, J.C.: Observing TCP dynamics in real networks. ACM SIGCOMM Comput. Commun. Rev. **22**(4), 305–317 (1992)

Pham, H.N., Pediaditakis, D., Boulis, A.: From simulation to real deployments in WSN and back. In: World of Wireless, Mobile and Multimedia Networks, pp. 1–6 (2007)

Polley, J., Blazakis, D., McGee, J., Rusk, J., Baras, J.S.: ATEMU: a fine-grained sensor network simulator. In: First Annual IEEE Communications Society Conference on Sensor and Ad Hoc Communications and Networks, pp. 145–152 (2004)

Sobeih, A., et al.: J-Sim: a simulation environment for wireless sensor networks. In: Proceedings of the 38th Annual Symposium on Simulation, pp. 175–187 (2005)

Varga, A., Hornig, R.: An overview of the OMNET++ simulation environment. In: Proceedings of the 1st International Conference on Simulation Tools and Techniques for Communications, Networks and Systems & Workshops, Article 60, ICST, Marseille, France, 3–7 March, ACM. (2008)

Welch, B.B., Jones, K., Hobbs, J.: Practical Programming in Tcl and Tk. Prentice Hall Professional (2003)

Yu, F., Jain, R.: A survey of wireless sensor network simulation tools. Washington University in St. Louis, Department of Science and Engineering 2009 (2014)

Research on Ozone Prediction Based on Genetic Neural Network for Multi-city Collaboration

Haichuan Li[1], Haoran Xu[2(✉)], Qi Gao[3], and Yaning Nie[2]

[1] Meteorological Detection Center, Cangzhou Meteorological
Services Authority, Cangzhou 061001, China
[2] School of Information Science and Engineering, Hebei University of Science and Technology,
Shijiazhuang 050018, China
xuhaoran25@126.com
[3] Shijiazhuang Meteorological Services Authority, Shijiazhuang 050011, China

Abstract. Aiming at the problems of low prediction accuracy of traditional ozone prediction models, a BP neural network model based on genetic algorithm is proposed to solve the problem of single source and low accuracy of atmospheric ozone prediction algorithm. At the same time, in order to further improve the accuracy, the model added the weather data of several cities around Shijiazhuang. Six meteorological factors and four main pollution factors (NO_2, SO_2, NO, VOC) in Shijiazhuang and its satellite cities were used as input data to estimate the wind speed and direction of the target city. The ozone data were output after 24 h. The results show that, on the basis of compensating for the local optimum problem of BP neural network, the prediction results of the model are better than those of Shijiazhuang meteorological data alone in terms of correlation and absolute deviation, which can further improve the prediction accuracy of ozone.

Keywords: Ozone · Genetic algorithm · BP neural network · Collaborative prediction

1 Introduction

With the rapid development of the contemporary Chinese economy and the rapid population growth, a series of environmental problems are inevitably brought about, especially the frequent occurrence of smog weather. One of the reasons for the occurrence of smog weather is the high ozone concentration in the environment [1–3]. Excessive ozone concentration will affect people's body and cause a variety of respiratory diseases. If the forecast of atmospheric ozone can be realized, it can not only can it provide a basis for government agencies to take action in advance, but also provide a reasonable reference for the public's outbound activities. From the perspective of ozone prediction method, the initial ozone prediction method is to use numerical regression method, by establishing the relationship between ozone and meteorological factors and pollutant factors to predict [4–8]. Liu Bingchun et al. [9] used regression models to predict the air quality index of major cities in the Beijing-Tianjin-Hebei region. With the rise of deep learning,

© Springer Nature Singapore Pte Ltd. 2020
X. Sun et al. (Eds.): ICAIS 2020, CCIS 1253, pp. 221–231, 2020.
https://doi.org/10.1007/978-981-15-8086-4_21

Kaminski W et al. [10] Established an artificial neural network model to predict the air quality index. Most neural networks use the BP algorithm, but they have problems such as too slow convergence and are easily trapped in local minimums. Wang Chongjun and Wu Chen et al. [11, 12] used genetic algorithms to optimize the BP neural network.

At the same time, many scholars began to use neural networks to build ozone prediction models. For example, West et al. [13] used the source of ozone to analyze how to predict ozone and used a multilayer perceptron to predict changes in ozone concentration, demonstrating an average error of 2 to 7% using a multilayer perceptron model. Meng Gao et al. [14] used artificial neural networks to predict urban areas where ozone is concentrated, using six meteorological factors and a time variable as predictors, and Monte Carlo techniques for model analysis. Fabio et al. [15] used recurrent neural networks to analyze near-surface ozone concentrations and predicted ozone concentrations in Italian coastal towns, proving that artificial neural networks have higher performance than multiple regression equations, proving that neural networks can be used to carry out ozone for the next few hours. Prediction. Liu Huan et al. [16] used weather forecast and community multi-scale air quality model (WRF-CMAQ) to simulate changes in ozone concentration in China. The results showed that the ozone concentration in most parts of China was too high, and revealed the relationship between excessive ozone concentration and lung disease. Luna et al. [17] used principal component analysis and support vector machine (SVM) artificial neural network to predict ozone in Rio de Janeiro. Principal component analysis can reduce data and reduce computational complexity. Victor et al. [18] used neural networks to predict the daily ozone concentration in Houston, proving superiority to the traditional ARIMA model. There are many other methods used to predict or analyze the cause of ozone [19–23]. The ozone concentration values of several neighboring cities in the target city are of reference significance. The concentration values of several cities can be used to predict the concentration values of the target city, making the prediction more accurate [24, 25].

2 Data Acquisition

Ozone is one of the important factors that can represent the quality of atmospheric environment and one of the evaluation indexes of air pollution. Scholars at home and abroad have obtained that the ozone of the atmosphere is correlated with wind speed, relative humidity, dew point temperature, air temperature, air pressure, sunshine hours, SO_2, NO_2, CO, NO, VOC, air pollutant concentration under the precondition of eliminating extreme weather such as heavy rain and snow, typhoon. Therefore, Six meteorological factor factors, such as daily mean pressure (hpa), daily mean temperature (C), average relative humidity (%), daily mean total cloud amount (%), sunshine hours (h), daily mean wind speed (m/s) and the daily average concentration of NO_2, SO_2, NO, VOC are used as input variables. In this paper, we select Shijiazhuang City as the target city. Shijiazhuang City is located in the North China Plain. In view of the topographical features of the Shijiazhuang area, the four cities of Jinzhou, Zhengding, Jingxing and Yuanshi counties are selected as the collaborative city with a radius of 50 km, as shown in Fig. 1. The meteorological data of the cities studied in this paper were obtained from the Central Meteorological Observatory, and the air pollutant concentration data was obtained from the China National Environmental Monitoring Center. 320 meteorological data from January 1, 2017 to November 30, 2017 in Shijiazhuang were selected as training data. Thirty groups of data from December 1, 2017 to December 30, 2017 in four cities of Jinzhou, Xingtang, Jingxing and Yuanshi were selected as the test data to be processed.

Fig. 1. Geographical orientation map

3 BP Neural Network Model Optimized by Genetic Algorithm

3.1 BP Neural Network

BP neural network is a multilayer feedforward neural network trained based on error back propagation algorithm. It uses a back propagation learning algorithm to adjust the weight between different neurons. Since it was proposed in 1986, BP neural network has become one of the most mature and widely used neural networks due to its excellent multi-dimensional function mapping ability, classification ability for complex patterns and small computational complexity. This paper chooses a three-layer BP network, including input layer, hidden layer and output layer. The network topology is shown in Fig. 2.

Ten atmospheric ozone influence factor parameters were selected as input variables of the model, and the visibility prediction value was the output variable. Therefore, the number of neurons in the input layer of the BP neural network is determined to be 10, and the number of output layers is determined to be 1. The number of neurons in the hidden layer is directly related to the number of input and output units. We generally consider the formula (1) to select the number of neurons with optimal hidden layers.

$$m = \sqrt{n+q} + \alpha \tag{1}$$

In formula (1), n is the number of neurons in the input layer, q is the number of neurons in the output layer, α is an integer in $[1, 10]$, and m is the number of neurons in the hidden layer. Therefore, the number of neurons in the hidden layer can be selected from 4 to 13. Using the same sample for testing, this paper determines the number of hidden layer neurons to be 6 under the conditions of the highest accuracy and the minimum error. In

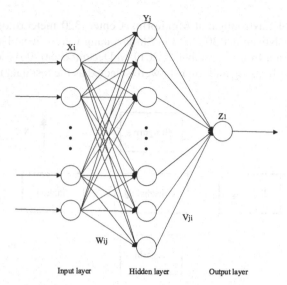

Fig. 2. Three-layer BP neural network structure

the hidden layer, the neuron transfer function uses the logsig function, and the output layer neuron transfer function uses the purelin function. In order to avoid the network instability caused by excessive learning rate, the gradient descent momentum learning function is used in the choice of learning function.

3.2 Implementation of BP Neural Network Model Optimized by Genetic Algorithm

BP neural network adjusts the weights and thresholds between the hidden layer and the output layer, and between the input layer and the hidden layer with the error of actual output and expected output as the adjustment signal. Therefore, in the BP neural network, there will be problems in the training that are easy to fall into the local minimum and terminate the training early.

In order to improve the stability of BP algorithm and solve the problem of local optimal solution, this paper constructs a BP neural network model based on genetic algorithm optimization. The genetic algorithm does not rely on the gradient information, and uses the advantages of its global search to optimize the BP neural network to get the best solution. The genetic algorithm uses binary encoding to assign a real number string to each individual of the population, which represents all the weights and thresholds of the BP neural network layer. According to the fitness value of the design, the coded individual is used for the training of the BP neural network, and then the selected optimal fitness individuals are determined through processes such as selection, crossover and mutation. The specific design is as follows:

(1) Initialization population
   Since the genetic algorithm can not directly deal with the parameters of the problem, this paper uses the binary coding method to represent the weight and threshold of

each connection layer of the BP neural network as the individual of the genetic algorithm structure.

(2) Fitness function

The fitness function F, also known as the evaluation function, can measure the pros and cons of individuals in a group. It can be expressed by the sum E of the predicted output of the BP neural network and the absolute value of the error of the actual output. The calculation formula is

$$F(x) = k(\sum\nolimits_{i=1}^{n} abs(y_i - o_i)) \tag{2}$$

k is the coefficient; n is the number of output neurons; y_i is the actual output value of the ith neuron of the BP neural network; o_i is the predicted output value of the ith neuron.

(3) Select operation

After the evaluation in (2) is completed, a selection operation is performed. The commonly used selection methods of genetic algorithms are fitness proportionality method, local selection method and roulette selection method. This paper chooses the roulette selection method. The probability that an individual in this method is selected is proportional to the value of the fitness calculated in (2). Let the fitness of individual i be f_i.

$$p_i = f_i / \sum\nolimits_{j=1}^{n} f_i \tag{3}$$

Among them, n is the size of the group, and p_i is the probability that the individual i is selected.

(4) Cross operation

Cross-operation refers to the operation of forming a new individual by selecting the two first-generation individuals according to the principle of cross-interchange of biological chromosomes. In this paper, binary encoding is used, then the binary crossover algorithm in the way of a single point crossover, randomly select a crossover point in the individual string, two individuals at this point before and after the structure of the exchange.

(5) Mutation operation

The binary mutation operator is used to improve the random search ability of genetic algorithm. The variation process in the binary code string is as follows:

The mutation operator first judges the mutation probability of the individual in the group, and then randomly selects the mutation position of the mutant.

$$(A)10\,0\,1\,1\,001 \overset{Variation}{\rightarrow} 10\,1\,1\,0\,001(New\ A) \tag{4}$$

Individual to obtain the result of the mutation. The parameter settings are shown in Table 1:

The overall design process is as follows (Fig. 3):

Table 1. Genetic algorithm parameters

Parameter	Numerical value
Genetic algebra	10
Population size	100
Cross rate	0.2
Mutation rate	0.1

7

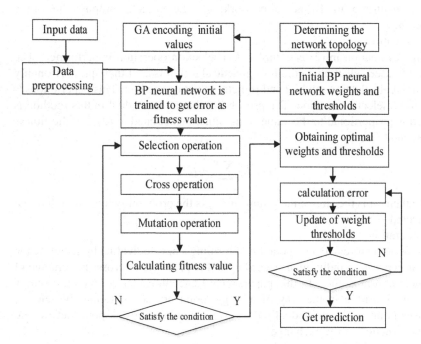

Fig. 3. Genetic algorithm optimization BP neural network flow chart

4   Experimental Methods

4.1   Data Preprocessing

In the statistical preprocessing methods of data, there are generally harmonic mean method, arithmetic mean method, geometric mean method and characteristic binary method. In this paper, the average method is adopted, which is based on the wind direction (based on the geographical location of Shijiazhuang). The mean value of the meteorological data of the associated area and the meteorological data of the target city are used as the input and output variables of the training set. For convenience, Shijiazhuang City, Jinzhou City, Zhengding County, Jingxing County and Yuanshi County were replaced by T, A, B, C and D respectively. The specific city combination and its corresponding team number are shown in Table 2:

Table 2. City combination and group number

Wind direction	City combination	Group number
East	T+A	1
Northeast	T+A+B	2
North	T+B	3
Northwest	T+B+C	4
West	T+C	5
Southwest	T+C+D	6
South	T+D	7
Southeast	T+A+D	8

4.2 Experimental Steps

The prediction of Atmospheric ozone concentration in Shijiazhuang is divided into five steps.

The meteorological data and air pollutant data of Shijiazhuang are taken as input variables separately, and the "d+1" daily ozone concentration value is taken as output variable. 320 data from January 1, 2017 to November 30, 2017 are selected as training set of neural network.

Thirty data of Shijiazhuang from December 1, 2017 to December 30, 2017 are selected as the test set of neural network, and the predicted results are obtained. This is experiment 1.

Thirty sets of data from December 1, 2017 to December 30, 2017 in Shijiazhuang and four surrounding cities were selected and processed with reference to Tables 2.

The daily average value of meteorological data and air pollutant data of the combined city in step 3 is calculated as the input variable of the test set, and the forecast result is obtained. This is experiment 2.

The prediction results of Experiment 1 and Experiment 2 were compared with the actual ozone results, and the conclusions were drawn.

5 Forecast and Result Analysis

In this paper, we use the 2014a MATLAB Neural Network Toolbox and the Sheffield Genetic Algorithm Toolbox to perform experiments according to experimental procedures. The predicted values of Experiment 1 and Experiment 2 are compared with the real values as shown in Figs. 4 and 5 respectively.

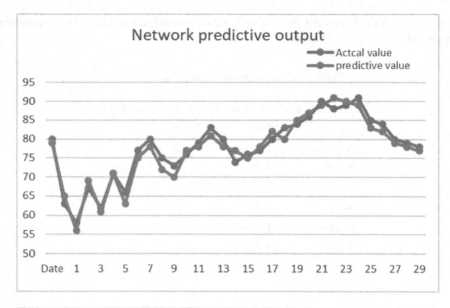

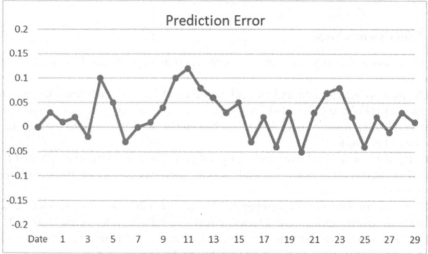

Fig. 4. Comparison of the predictive value and true value in experiment 1

In order to verify the accuracy of the experimental prediction, this study compared and analyzed the predicted and real atmospheric ozone concentration data. Figure 4 and Fig. 5 are the predicted results and error percentages of a single selected target city data scheme in Experiment 1 and Experiment 2, respectively. The accuracy of predicting ozone in Experiment 1 was 83.76%, and the correlation coefficient was 0.7365 and in Experiment 2, they were 88.53% and 0.7563. From the comparison and analysis of the forecasting results, we can see that the latter is about 5% points lower than the former in the accuracy of ozone, and its forecasting ability has been greatly improved. In order to

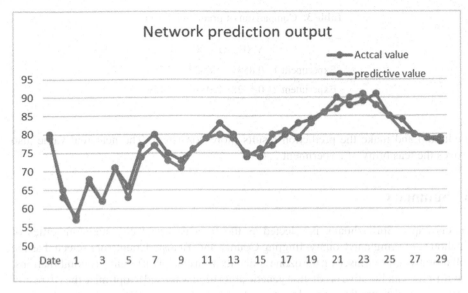

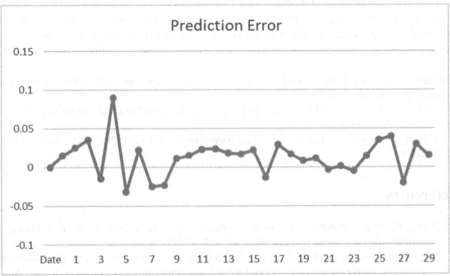

Fig. 5. Comparison of the predictive value and true value in experiment 2

evaluate the predictive stability of the two experimental schemes more accurately, MSE (Mean Square Error), RMSE (Root Mean Square Error) and MAE (Mean Absolute Error) were selected as the error evaluation indexes. The comparison results are shown in Table 3.

By comparison, we can find that the error values of Experiment 1 are higher than those of experiment 2. It shows that the prediction data of Experiment 2 have smaller deviation and error values than those of experiment 1. This indicates that the multicity coordination scheme can improve the effect of atmospheric ozone concentration

Table 3. Comparison of prediction results

	MSE	RMSE	MAE
Experiment 1	0.8537	3.8524	2.5766
Experiment 2	0.5728	2.9815	2.1459

prediction and make the prediction results more consistent. The near real value also proves the feasibility of Experiment 2.

6 Summary

In this paper, Shijiazhuang is selected as the forecast target city, and four cities of Jinzhou City, Xingtang County, Jingjing County and Yuanshi County are selected as the collaborative cities. Based on the ozone concentration data of different city combinations, a multi-city collaborative prediction genetic algorithm was used to optimize the BP neural network visibility prediction model. On the basis of improving BP neural network, which is easy to be trapped in local optimum problem, through the analysis of wind direction and wind force of target city, the prediction result is better than that of single target city. At the same time, it also verifies the regional relevance of the atmospheric environment.

Funding. This research was funded by Science and Technology Support Plan Project of Hebei Province, grant number 17210803D.

This research was funded by Science and Technology Support Plan Project of Hebei Province, grant number 19273703D.

This research was funded by Education Department of Hebei Province, grant number QN2018095.

References

1. Zanis, P., et al.: Summertime free-tropospheric ozone pool over the eastern Mediterranean/Middle East. Atmos. Chem. Phys. **14**, 115–132 (2014)
2. Ainsworth, E.A., Yendrek, C.R., Sitch, S., Collins, W.J., Emberson, L.D.: The effects of tropospheric ozone on net primary productivity and implications for climate change. Ann. Rev. Plant Biol. **63**, 637–661 (2012)
3. Blanchard, C.L., Fairley, D.: Spatial mapping of VOC and NOx-limitation of ozone formation in central California. Atmos. Environ. **35**, 3861–3873 (2001)
4. Sun, W., Zhang, H., Palazoglu, A.: Prediction of 8 h-average ozone concentration using a supervised hidden Markov model combined with generalized linear models. Atmos. Environ. **81**, 199–208 (2013)
5. Abdul-Wahab, S.A., Bakheit, C.S., Al-Alawi, S.M.: Principal component and multiple regression analysis in modelling of ground-level ozone and factors affecting its concentrations. Environ. Model Softw. **20**, 1263–1271 (2005)
6. Zhang, H., Zhang, W., Palazoglu, A., Sun, W.: Prediction of ozone levels using a hidden Markov model (HMM) with gamma distribution. Atmos. Environ. **62**, 64–73 (2012)

7. Rasmussen, D.J., Fiore, A.M., Naik, V., Horowitz, L.W., McGinnis, S.J., Schultz, M.G.: Surface ozone-temperature relationships in the Eastern US: a monthly climatology for evaluating chemistry-climate models. Atmos. Environ. **47**, 142–153 (2012)
8. Jiang, W., Qian, Y., Du, K., Gu, X.: Changes and predictions of ozone concentration in the near-surface layer of Ningbo City. J. Meteorol. Environ. **32**(01), 53–59 (2016)
9. Liu, B., Zheng, H., Zhang, B.: Research on cooperative prediction of air quality index based on multidimensional urban information: a case study of Beijing-Tianjin-Shijiazhuang. Environ. Sci. Technol. **40**(07), 9–13 (2017)
10. Kaminski, W., Skrzypski, J., Jach-Szakiel, E.: Application of artificial neural networks (ANNs) to predict air quality classes in big cities: systems engineering. In: 19th International Conference, ICSENG 2008 (2008)
11. Wang, C., Yu, W., Chen, Z., Xie, J.: A BP neural network algorithm based on genetic algorithm and its application. J. Nanjing Univ. (Nat. Sci.) **39**(05), 459–466 (2003)
12. Wu, C., Wang, H.: Optimization of BP neural network based on improved adaptive genetic algorithm. Electron. Des. Eng. **24**(24), 29–32, 37 (2016)
13. Fontes, T., Silva, L.M., Silva, M.P., Barros, N., Carvalho, A.C.: Can artificial neural networks be used to predict the origin of ozone episodes? Sci. Total Environ. **488–489**, 197–207 (2014)
14. Gao, M., Yin, L., Ning, J.: Artificial neural network model for ozone concentration estimation and Monte Carlo analysis. Atmos. Environ. **184**, 129–139 (2018)
15. Biancofiore, F., et al.: Analysis of surface ozone using a recurrent neural network. Sci. Total Environ. **514**, 379–387 (2015)
16. Liu, H., et al.: Ground-level ozone pollution and its health impacts in China. Atmos. Environ. **173**, 223–230 (2018)
17. Luna, A.S., Paredes, M.L.L., de Oliveira, G.C.G., Corrêa, S.M.: Prediction of ozone concentration in tropospheric levels using artificial neural networks and support vector machine at Rio de Janeiro, Brazil. Atmos. Environ. **98**, 98–104 (2014)
18. Prybutok, V.R., Yi, J., Mitchell, D.: Comparison of neural network models with ARIMA and regression models for prediction of Houston's daily maximum ozone concentrations. Eur. J. Oper. Res. **122**(1), 31–40 (2000)
19. Taylan, O.: Modelling and analysis of ozone concentration by artificial intelligent techniques for estimating air quality. Atmos. Environ. **150**, 356–365 (2017)
20. Wang, W., Lu, W., Wang, X., Leung, A.Y.: Prediction of maximum daily ozone level using combined neural network and statistical characteristics. Environ. Int. **29**, 555–562 (2003)
21. Bandyopadhyay, G., Chattopadhyay, S.: Single hidden layer artificial neural network models versus multiple linear regression model in forecasting the time series of total ozone. Int. J. Environ. Sci. Technol. **4**(1), 141–149 (2007). https://doi.org/10.1007/BF03325972
22. Cobourn, W.G., Dolcine, L., French, M., Hubbard, M.C.: A comparison of nonlinear regression and neural network models for ground-level ozone forecasting. J. Air Waste Manage. Assoc. **50**, 1999–2009 (2000)
23. Ning, M., Guan, J., Liu, P., Zhang, Z., O'Hare, G.M.P.: GA-BP air quality evaluation method based on fuzzy theory. Comput. Mater. Continua **58**(1), 215–227 (2019)
24. Bin, S., et al.: Collaborative filtering recommendation algorithm based on multi-relationship social network. Comput. Mater. Continua **60**(2), 659–674 (2019)
25. Jiang, W., et al.: A new time-aware collaborative filtering intelligent recommendation system. Comput. Mater. Continua **61**(2), 849–859 (2019)

The Shape Classification of Snowflakes Based on BP Neural Network

Haichuan Li[1], Xu Zhang[2]($\boxtimes$), Shuhai Wang[2], and Shikun Song[2]

[1] Meteorological Detection Center,
Cangzhou Meteorological Services Authority, Cangzhou 061001, China
[2] School of Information Science and Engineering, Hebei University of Science and Technology,
Shijiazhuang 050000, China
1035164243@qq.com

Abstract. In view of the problem of snowflake shape classification in the basic research of meteorology, a kind of snow flower shape classification method based on BP neural network is proposed in this paper. First we preprocess the snowflake images and extract the contour characteristics of the snowflake; on the basis of the contour characteristics of the snowflake, we can obtain six morphological parameters such as the axis ratio, rectangularity, convexity area, convexity perimeter, form parameter and density of snowflakes, and the parameters will be divided into three kinds of snowflake shape categories; finally we analyze the nonlinear relationship between the shape features and classification results, to design the BP neural network classifier that can divide the snowflake images into 3 types. Experiments show that the recognition rate of this classifier can reach 91.67%, which can provide reliable data support for subsequent research on the relationship between snowflake physical structure and artificial intervention in snowfall.

Keywords: BP neural network · Image preprocessing · Feature extraction · Shape feature parameters · Classifier

1 Introduction

With the approach of the Beijing Winter Olympics in 2022 and the continuous development of the ski tourism industry, skiing has become more and more popular and loved. The domestic ski resorts are mostly artificial snow fields, ski resorts, skis, snowboards, etc. In terms of choice, skiers know very little. Most skiers pay more attention to the length, width and slope of the trail [1], but there is little attention and research on snow quality. Different snow quality feedbacks give skiers different speeds of sliding and pushing snow, which brings different skiing pleasures. Snow quality plays a vital role in skiing, and the shape of snowflakes is largely related. The quality of snow is good. The study of the classification of snowflake shape has an impact on the quality of snow, artificial snow and even artificial snowfall.

At home and abroad, relevant technologies in the field of shape classification are actively carried out, but there are not many researches on the classification of snowflake

© Springer Nature Singapore Pte Ltd. 2020
X. Sun et al. (Eds.): ICAIS 2020, CCIS 1253, pp. 232–242, 2020.
https://doi.org/10.1007/978-981-15-8086-4_22

shapes. The existing research on snowflake is about the physical structure of snowflakes, but there are certain difficulties in the automatic classification of snowflake shapes. Therefore, the automatic classification algorithm for snowflake shapes is still blank. It is of great significance to study the classification of snowflake shapes.

Snowflake shape classification is based on the specific snowflake shape, and the snowflake shape classification process [2, 3] is shown in Fig. 1. The image preprocessing technique is used to extract the feature parameters of the snowflake image, analyze the parameter feature values, and use the reasonable classifier to realize the automatic classification of the snowflake image shape [4–8]. This paper is based on the snowflake image library [9], using image processing technology for binarization [10] image combined with contour tracking method for the aspect ratio of the snowflake image, rectangularity, perimeter to convex ratio, area to convex ratio, shape parameters and density six morphological parameters were extracted, and BP neural network [11–13] was used as a classifier to nonlinearly classify snowflake shapes.

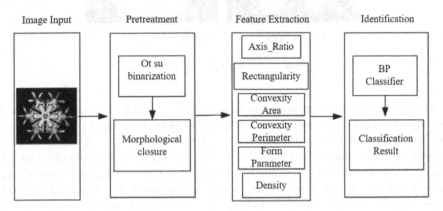

Fig. 1. Snowflake shape classification process

2 Image Preprocessing

In this paper, the preprocessing work on the snowflake image firstly grayscales the snowflake image, sets the threshold value to perform the binarization operation of the image, and then divides the target region image by threshold segmentation method [14], and performs the segmental image morphology operation, and finally the operation is to detect the edges of the image and extract the contour. Perform edge detection and extract outlines. The preprocessing of snowflake image is an important basis for feature extraction of snowflake image. The preprocessing of snowflake image directly affects the accuracy of feature extraction of snowflake image.

2.1 Image Binarization

The image in the snowflake image library used in this paper is a grayscale image, and the snowflake library image is shown in Fig. 2.

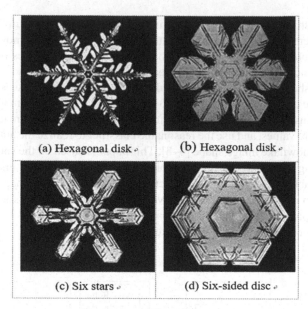

(a) Hexagonal disk   (b) Hexagonal disk

(c) Six stars   (d) Six-sided disc

Fig. 2. Snowflake original map

Firstly, there are thirteen histogram-based images global binarization algorithm. In this paper, the maximum inter-class variance method (Otsu) is applied to image binarization. This method is based on the gray histogram of the image. The maximum deviation between the target and the background is used as the threshold selection criterion. The image to be processed is divided into two groups (target and background), and the relevant parameters of the two sets of pixel values are recorded. The mathematical model of the variance between classes is established, and a set of segmentation thresholds with sequential changes is obtained. When the ratio of the inter-class variance and the intra-class variance of the two sets of data reaches the maximum, the optimal image segmentation threshold is obtained. Figure 3 shows the results of threshold segmentation using the maximum inter-class variance method.

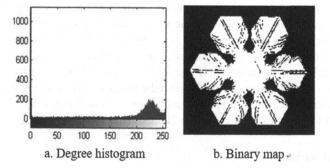

a. Degree histogram   b. Binary map

Fig. 3. Snowflake image binarization

2.2 Image Morphology Operation

The relevant shape parameters of the snowflake can be calculated by the outer edge contour of the snowflake, but due to the texture distribution inside the snowflake, the inner texture will be smoothed out before the full edge contour is extracted. Using the closed operation in morphological processing, A is closed by B, and the result of A being expanded by B is then corroded by B, as shown in Eq. 1. The closed operation can fill the small holes inside the image object, connect adjacent objects, and smooth the inner and boundary of the object without changing the area and shape of the object, as shown in Fig. 4.

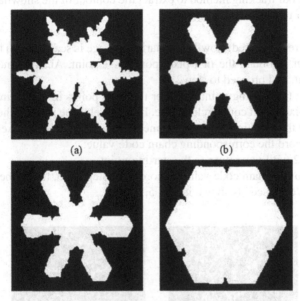

(a)   (b)

Fig. 4. Closed operation result

defined as:

$$A \bullet B = (A \oplus B) \ominus B \tag{1}$$

Where: A--original image, B--structural element image.

3 Shape Feature Parameter Extraction

The snowflake image contains a large number of effective feature information, such as shape features, texture features, etc. According to the relevant theory of shape classification, this paper selects the more effective shape features as the basis for snowflake classification research. For the geometric shape characteristics of snowflake, because the size of the snowflake is different, the classification of the snowflake shape cannot be effectively performed by using the commonly used feature values such as circumference and area as the classification basis. In this paper, the shape description is obtained by using the snowflake outline, the snowflake convex hull and the minimum bounding box. The shape description is used to calculate the vertical and horizontal axis ratio, the rectangularity, the perimeter to convex ratio, the area to convex ratio, the shape parameter and the density relative state parameters.

3.1 Snowflake Contour Extraction

For the snowflake analysis, the contour feature analysis of the snowflake can extract the effective feature quantity. This paper first extracts the outer contour of the snowflake, and uses the contour tracking method to extract the contour of the snowflake image. The specific algorithm steps are as follows:

1. The image pre-processed snowflake binarized image is scanned in a top-down, left-to-right order to obtain the first pixel point as 1 point. At this time, use it as the starting point, and proceed to step 2.
2. After getting the starting point, look for the field points in the 8 directions around the current pixel point counterclockwise. If the pixel value is 1 and the field contains 0 pixels, and the pixel has not been scanned before, then use this pixel as the current point and record the corresponding chain code value.
3. Repeat step 2 until you return to the starting point.
4. According to the chain code values recorded in steps 2, 3, the shape outline of the snowflake is obtained, as shown in Fig. 5.

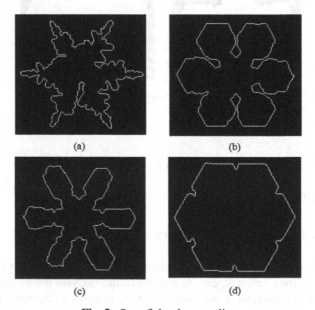

Fig. 5. Snowflake shape outline

3.2 Find a Snowflake Convex Hull

In this paper, the Graham scan method is used to obtain the minimum convex hull. The convex hull is to find some points as a polygon in the snowflake image, so that the polygon can include all points. This convex polygon is called convex hull. Figure 6 shows the snowflake shape convex hull. The Graham scanning process is described as follows:

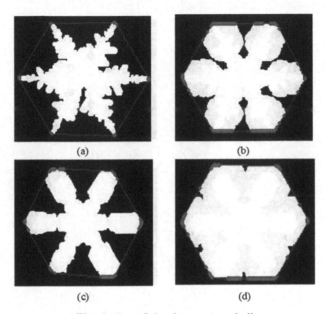

Fig. 6. Snowflake shape convex hull

1. Place the image in a two-dimensional coordinate system, select the point with the smallest ordinate as the point, and move the coordinate point to make it the origin.
2. Calculate the relative angle of each point, sort the points according to the order from small to large. When they are the same, the distance is closer to the front.
3. The above steps can find the first point and the second point on the convex hull, put these points on the stack, and now from the result obtained in step 2, use the back point as the starting point, find the next point.
4. Connect and point at the top of the stack to get a straight line L. Determine if the current point is on the right or left side of line L. If you are on the right side of the line, go to step 5. If it is on a straight line, or on the left side of the line, go to step 6.
5. If on the right side, the element at the top of the stack is not the point on the convex hull, and the top element of the stack is popped. Perform step 4.
6. If the current point is a point on the convex hull, push it onto the stack and go to step 7.
7. Check if the current point is the last element of the result obtained in step 3. If it is the last element, it will end. If not, then the latter point will be used as the current point, and return to step 4.
8. Finally, the elements in the stack are the points on the convex hull. Connect these points to get the minimum convex hull.

3.3 Find the Minimum Bounding Box

Minimum bounding box: A minimum rectangle containing all the pixels in a certain area. Because one edge of the minimum bounding box coincides with one side of the convex hull, the convex hull of the snowflake can be used to obtain the minimum by using this overlapping edge. Enclose the rectangle. Figure 7 shows the snowflake shape minimal bounding box diagram.

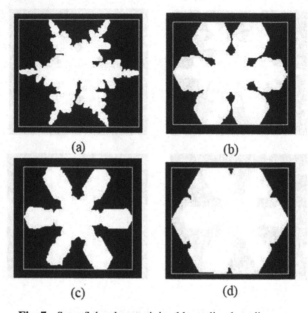

Fig. 7. Snowflake shape minimal bounding box diagram

The algorithm process is described as follows:

1. Using a parallel line to detect the vertices on both sides of the convex hull, it is found that the line between the vertices of a convex hull coincides with the parallel line, record the position of the two parallel lines, and then make two perpendicular to this Line segments of parallel lines, starting from the bulge vertices on both sides of this direction. The last 4 segments can form a rectangle and calculate the area of the rectangle.
2. Repeat the above process until all the snowflake hull vertices have been traversed. The smallest rectangle is the minimum bounding box.

3.4 Shape Feature Parameter Extraction

1. Axis_Ratio
   Aspect ratio: The ratio of the width D of the minimum bounding box of the snowflake image to the length L.

$$AR = \frac{D}{L} \tag{2}$$

2. Rectangularity
   Rectangularity: The ratio of S_{SNOW} to $S_{trangle}$.

$$R = \frac{S_{SNOW}}{S_{trangle}} \tag{3}$$

3. Convexity Area
   Convexity Area: The ratio of S_{SNOW} to S_{out}.

$$CA = \frac{S_{SNOW}}{S_{out}} \tag{4}$$

4. Convexity Perimeter
   Convexity Perimeter: The ratio of L_{SNOW} to L_{out}.

$$CA = \frac{L_{SNOW}}{L_{out}} \tag{5}$$

5. Form parameter
   Form parameter: The ratio of S_{SNOW} to S_{Lout}, reflects the tightness of the snow area.

$$F_P = \frac{S_{SNOW}}{L_{SNOW}} \tag{6}$$

6. Density
   Density: The indicator used to describe the complexity of the image boundary reflects the extent to which the image tends to be round.

$$D_e = \frac{L_{SNOW}^2}{S_{SNOW}} \tag{7}$$

3.5 Shape Feature Parameter Data

See Table 1.

Table 1. Sample picture feature values

	Figure 2(a)	Figure 2(b)	Figure 2(c)	Figure 2(d)
Axis_Ratio	0.8505	0.8339	0.9133	0.8700
Rectangularity	0.4247	0.7704	0.5552	0.5575
Convexity area	0.5159	0.8657	0.6088	0.6697
Convexity perimeter	2.2879	1.9379	1.0092	1.1439
Form parameter	0.1113	0.2573	0.2051	0.5698
Density	112.9097	48.8385	61.2480	22.0536

4   BP Neural Network Classifier

The BP neural network [15] is a multi-layer feedforward neural network. The main feature is the forward transmission of the input signal and the back propagation of the error. If the output layer does not get the expected output, it will turn to the back propagation and adjust the network weight according to the prediction error. Adjust network weights and thresholds through prediction errors to make the predicted output continuously approach the expected output. As a nonlinear function, BP neural network expresses the function mapping relationship from n input independent variables to m output dependent variables. The BP neural network used in this paper is 3 layers, and the sigmod function is activated.

The snowflake shape classification process based on BP neural network includes three steps of BP neural network construction, training and classification. The algorithm flow is shown in Fig. 8.

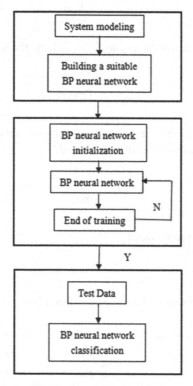

Fig. 8. Algorithm flowchart

1. Determine the number of network nodes. According to the characteristics of input and output data, determine the construction of the network. In this paper, six shape features are used as the number of input layer nodes, that is, the number of output

layer nodes corresponds to the number of snowflake shape classifications, that is, the number of hidden layer nodes. Make sure to refer to the following formula:

$$l < \sqrt{(m+n)} + a \qquad (8)$$

Where a takes a constant, determines the approximate range, and determines the optimal number of nodes by using the trial and error method.

2. Network initialization. In the initialization phase, the weight coefficient is given a random number (), the learning rate is 0.01, and the target error is 0.001.
3. Training algorithm selection. This paper uses gradient correction method and reverse error propagation algorithm.

There are three types of snowflake snowflakes: hexagonal disk, six star-shaped and star-shaped snowflake images. There are 500 images, 100 randomly selected as the training samples, and the remaining 200 are classified. Test sample, the recognition rate reached 91.67%. The network training results are shown in Fig. 9.

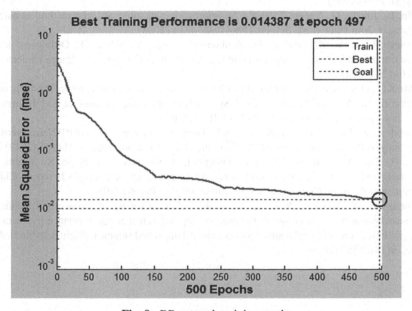

Fig. 9. BP network training results

Funding. This research was funded by Science and Technology Support Plan Project of Hebei Province, grant number 17210803D.

References

1. Yiteng, W., Fengyue, M.: Effects of different snow quality on skiers. West. Leather **8**, 269 (2017)
2. Wei, L., Fenglian, C., Lin-xi, G.: Plant recognition method based on blade shape feature. Comput. Appl. **36**(S2), 200–202, 226 (2016)
3. Yuvaraj, D., Sivaram, M., Karthikeyan, B., Abdulazeez, J.: Shape, color and texture based CBIR system using fuzzy logic classifier. Comput. Mater. Continua **59**(3), 729–739 (2019)
4. Yang, L., Yueyang, L., Haichi, L., Gaoming, J., Honglian, C.: On-line identification method of plant leaves based on shape feature. Comput. Eng. Appl. **53**(02), 162–165, 171 (2017)
5. Ning, Z., Wenping, L.: Review of plant leaf recognition technology based on image analysis. J. Comput. Appl. **28**(11), 4001–4007 (2011)
6. Lei, W., Dongjian, H., Yongliang, Q.: Research on plant leaf classification based on image processing and SVM. J. Agric. Mech. Res. **35**(05), 12–15 (2013)
7. Xiaofeng, W., Deshuang, H., Jixiang, D., et al.: Research on feature extraction and recognition of leaf image. Comput. Eng. Appl. **42**(3), 190–193 (2006)
8. Lijun, W., Yongjian, H., YuCheng, P.: Identification of foliage plant species based on multi-feature fusion of leaf images. J. Beijing Forest. Univ. **37**(1), 55–61 (2015)
9. Kenneth, L., Patricia, R., Philippe, M.B.: The snowflake: winter's secret beauty. Am. J. Phys. **72**(8), 1134 (2004)
10. Mu, L., Jihong, Q., Yanhe, Z., et al.: An improved application of Dajin method in machine vision. J. Jilin Univ. (Eng. Sci. Ed.) **38**(4), 913–918 (2008)
11. Yingke, L., Jiwei, Z., Tianbao, D., Zhuhong, Y., Yuan, Y., Yihua, H.: Orthogonal locally discriminant spline embedding for plant leaf recognition. Comput. Vis. Image Underst. **119**, 116–126 (2014)
12. Wu, S.G., et al.: A leaf recognition algorithm for plant classification using probabilistic neural network. In: 2007 IEEE International Symposium on Signal Processing and Information Technology, Giza, Egypt, pp. 2162–7843. IEEE (2007)
13. Guodong, Z., Yuewei, Z., Yiqi, S., Haiyan, L., Qing, Y.: The application of BP Neural networks to analysis the national vulnerability. Comput. Mater. Continua **58**(2), 421–436 (2019)
14. Qi, H., Shui, Yu., Huifang, X., Jia, L., Dongmei, H., Guohua, L., Fangqin, X., Yanling, D.: A weighted threshold secret sharing scheme for remote sensing images based on Chinese remainder theorem. Comput. Mater. Continua **58**(2), 349–361 (2019)
15. Zhenzhou, W., Wei, H., Pingping, Y., et al.: Hebei university of science and technology researchers add new findings in the area of applied sciences (performance evaluation of regionbased convolutional neural networks toward improved vehicle taillight detection). Appl. Sci. **9**(18), 3753 (2019)

Fabric Hair Ball Pilling Detection Based on Memristive Cell Neural Network

Jingyun Wang[1], Jincan Yin[2(✉)], Wenjie Duan[2], and Yang Li[2]

[1] National Cashmere Product Quality Supervision an Inspection Center,
Shijiazhuang 050091, China

[2] School of Information Science and Engineering, Hebei University of Science and Technology,
Shijiazhuang 050000, China
936651615@qq.com

Abstract. Aiming at the low detection rate of traditional detection methods in complex environments and the long time of experimenters, a test method of textile pilling initiation under complex environment based on memristive cell neural network was proposed. The memristor is used as the connection weight of the cellular neural network, and the connection weight is flexibly adjustable. Through the adaptive adjustment of network parameters, the image-denoising and edge extraction of the memristive cell neural network is realized, the image processing speed is improved, the noise interference is effectively filtered out, and the image edge information is highlighted. Through the adaptive adjustment of network parameters, the image-denoising and edge extraction of the memristive cell neural network is realized, the image processing speed is improved, the noise interference is effectively filtered out, and the image edge information is highlighted. It can be seen from the experiment that the method is beneficial to alleviate the experimental task of the inspection mechanism, and the pilling of the textile can achieve better detection effect, which is beneficial to improve the detection rate and the detection speed.

Keywords: Membrane cell neural network · Fabric ball pilling · Fast Hough transform

1 Introduction

The pilling performance of textiles is a very complex indicator due to its many influencing factors, including the type of fiber and its blended product, the size of the fiber, the structure of the yarn and fabric, and the finishing of the fabric. Since many kinds of spherical particles are formed on the surface of the human body through various wrinkles and frictions, we usually call it "pilling." At present, pilling has become one of the important indicators for assessing the performance of fabrics. The significance of this experiment is that it predicts the condition of the pilling ball before it is put on the market, and then rationally improves and evades.

In recent years, convolutional neural networks in deep learning have been widely used in the field of image detection and recognition [1]. However, convolutional neural networks need different training to perform different functions, and cannot use the

© Springer Nature Singapore Pte Ltd. 2020
X. Sun et al. (Eds.): ICAIS 2020, CCIS 1253, pp. 243–254, 2020.
https://doi.org/10.1007/978-981-15-8086-4_23

same convolutional neural network to complete multiple tasks. Detecting fabric pilling requires a large amount of data to be calculated, making it difficult to achieve real-time requirements. The cellular neural network is a large-scale nonlinear analog circuit with real-time signal parallel processing. The appropriate memristor model is used as the connection weight of the cellular neural network, so that the fine neural network realizes the programmable connection weight when performing image processing, and the same network can be used to accomplish different tasks [2].

At present, the commonly used detection method is the standard sample comparison rating, but this method has great subjectivity. Due to the individual differences, it is impossible to make an objective, accurate and quantitative analysis of the fabric pilling. Liu Jing et al. performed mathematical modeling of two-dimensional discrete wavelet transform on fabric hair ball image processing according to the wavelet transform method, and designed the analysis efficiency and corresponding analysis scale process of increasing wavelet transform [3]. At the same time, using the square wave simulation of Haar wavelet and the related relationship of the weaving pattern of the machine fabric, the scientific estimation method of fabric pilling is studied. The watershed image segmentation algorithm can obtain ideal image segmentation results, and has been widely concerned and applied due to its fast calculation speed and accurate image edge information positioning [4]. However, this algorithm has the phenomenon of over-segmentation, which leads to the disadvantage that the image to be segmented is too thin and the segmentation area is too large [5, 6].

Although all of the above methods have achieved certain results, most of them are not conducive to hardware implementation, and the detection rate is low and the detection time is long. Therefore, in view of the shortcomings of the existing detection methods, this paper proposes a textile ball pilling detection method based on memristive cell neural network (MCNN), extracts the image of the gray image, and uses MCNN to denoise and extract the gray image. The method of fast Hough transform is used to detect the circular and elliptical shape of the image after edge extraction, and the precise position of the pilling of the textile ball is obtained.

2   MCNN

2.1   Cellular Neural Network (CNN)

CNN is a neural network model that is easy to implement in hardware. It combines the advantages of Hopfiled neural network and cellular automata, and has symmetry in the structure of the network [7, 8]. When CNN is used for image processing, the signal space of the image is mapped to the cell space of the CNN, and the pixel range is mapped into $[-1, 1]$. Each pixel in the image corresponds to a cell at the same position, the pixel gray value corresponds to the input of the cell, and the network energy function corresponds to the connection weight. Each cell of CNN is only connected to its neighboring cells, and the state of each cell changes to the lowest energy direction through multiple iterations until convergence. The minimum value of the network energy function corresponds to the optimal solution of the problem, and the binary image formed by the output matrix of the network is the result of CNN processing.

CNN [9] has the characteristics of local interconnection, and each cell is only connected to adjacent cells. This structure enables CNN to better process grayscale images and binary images. In the CNN model, cells C(i, j) in row i and column j are only connected to cells in their neighborhood, where r is the neighborhood radius, as shown in Fig. 1.

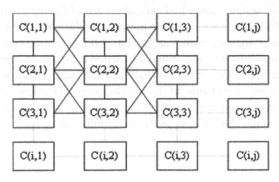

Fig. 1. CNN model

In CNN, there are both output feedback and input control. The output feedback template A(i, j; k, l) indicates that the central cell is affected by the output of surrounding neighbor cells, and the input control template B(i, j; k, l) Indicates that the central cell is affected by the input of surrounding neighborhood cells. The state equation [10] of CNN is:

$$C\frac{dv_{xij}(t)}{dt} = -\frac{1}{R}v_{xij}(t) + \sum_{C(k,l)\in N_r(i,j)} A(i,j;k,l)v_{ykl}(t) + \sum_{C(k,l)\in N_r(i,j)} B(i,j;k,l)v_{ukl}(t) + I \tag{1}$$

$$1 \leq i \leq M, 1 \leq j \leq N$$

The output equation is:

$$v_{yij}(t) = \frac{1}{2}(|v_{xij}(t) + 1| - |v_{xij}(t) - 1|) \tag{2}$$

$$1 \leq i \leq M, 1 \leq j \leq N$$

The output equation is:

$$v_{uij} = E_{ij}, \ 1 \leq i \leq M, 1 \leq j \leq N \tag{3}$$

2.2 MCNN

In traditional CNN, in order to implement different applications, it is usually necessary to reset the connection weight of the clone template. The connection weight needs to be implemented by a multiplier, the circuit structure is complex, and it is fixed in the template of a certain network, if it is to be performed. In this paper, the HP memristor model [11] is used as the connection weight of the cellular neural network to realize the update of the connection weight. The memristor is a nonlinear component, which changes the memristor value of the memristor by applying a constant voltage, and has a memory function [12], which is beneficial to realize CNN hardware circuit integration.

In this paper, the voltage-controlled current source of the memristor [13] is used to replace the controlled current source in the traditional CNN. When the switch is closed, the resistance value of the memristor can be changed by the time and amplitude of the voltage applied across the two ends. When the switch is turned off, the resistance value of the memristor remains unchanged, so that the controlled current source outputs the desired current to realize the change of the weight, wherein the left 8 diamonds and the right 8 diamonds respectively correspond to the input. Control template B (i, j; k, l) and output feedback template A (i, j; k, l), as shown in Fig. 2 and Fig. 3.

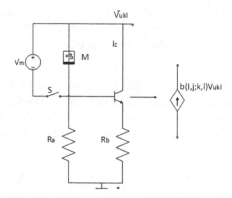

Fig. 2. Voltage controlled current source equivalent diagram

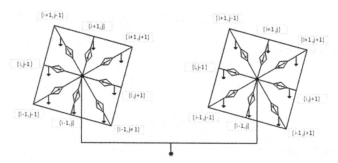

Fig. 3. Circuit template equivalent diagram

3   Fabric Ball Pilling Detection Based on MCNN

In the traditional CNN method, denoising and edge extraction need to be implemented by different circuits. The hardware circuit is large in scale and space utilization is low. The

MCNN method can use the same circuit to change the template by using the memory and rewritable function of the memristor. Parameters to achieve denoising and edge extraction to improve hardware circuit integration.

The flow chart of the fabric pilling detection method based on MCNN in the complex environment proposed in this paper is shown in Fig. 4.

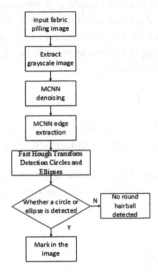

Fig. 4. Flow chart of the fabric pilling detection method based on MCNN

3.1 Image Preprocessing

The image is detected in the HSV space, and the collected RGB image of the fabric hairball is converted into a Gray image. The original image and the Gray image are shown in Fig. 5.

Original image   Gray image

Fig. 5. Original image and Gray image

3.2 Denoising Based on MCNN

The image is disturbed by noise in the external environment during shooting and transmission. In order to reduce the noise in the image and improve the efficiency of subsequent edge detection, the image needs to be denoised and preprocessed.

The key to the denoising performance of MCNN [14] is the selection of output feedback template A and input control template B parameters. In this paper, the linear matrix inequality (LMI) method is used to obtain the template parameters. In the solution process, the constraints of each cell are expressed as inequalities. Using LMI to solve the inequality, the required template parameters can be obtained. The general form of LMI is shown by the following inequality:

$$F(x) = F_0 + x_1 F_1 + \cdots + x_m F_m < 0 \tag{4}$$

F_i is a given set of symmetric matrices, x_i is the decision variable of LMI, $x = [x_1, \cdots, x_m]^T$ is the decision vector composed of decision variables, where i = 0,1,2,…,m.

Taking the noisy image as the input and the noise-free ideal image as the output, the inequality is solved by LMI, and the template parameters required for denoising can be obtained, as shown in Fig. 6.

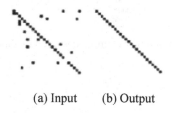

(a) Input   (b) Output

Fig. 6. Denoising training image

The denoising template parameters can be obtained by the LMI solution inequality:

$$
\begin{aligned}
t = \{ & 425.2515, -157.5837, -177.4233, \\
& -168.5389, -104.5283, -63.3847, \\
& -163.1437, -127.9893, 383.5728, \\
& 31.4781, 57.9852, 51.9853, \\
& 59.8985, 185.9387, 58.1425, \\
& 27.8953, 136.2133, 21.3421, 560.5135 \}
\end{aligned}
\tag{5}
$$

The extracted gray image denoising process is performed using a memristive cell neural network, and the output feedback template A and the input control template B are used as follows:

$$
A = \begin{bmatrix} 425.2515 & -157.5837 & -177.4233 \\ -168.5389 & -104.5283 & -63.3847 \\ -163.1437 & -127.9893 & 383.5728 \end{bmatrix}, B = \begin{bmatrix} 31.4781 & 57.9852 & 51.9853 \\ 59.8985 & 185.9387 & 58.1425 \\ 27.8953 & 136.2133 & 21.3421 \end{bmatrix}
\tag{6}
$$

$I = 560.5135$

Among the traditional denoising methods, Gaussian filtering, mean filtering, and median filtering are widely used. The MCNN denoising method and the traditional denoising method are shown in Fig. 7.

Gaussian filtering   Mean filtering   Median filtering   MCNN filtering

N=27424 N=25113 N=23664 N=28376

Fig. 7. Denoising comparison image

In order to compare the effects of MCNN denoising and traditional denoising methods, this paper compares the denoising results of various methods with the original image, and counts the number of white points in the difference image (i.e. the number of removed noise points), which is recorded as N, the value of N represents the strength of the denoising ability. The comparison shows that the MCNN-based denoising method can better preserve the original image information and remove most of the noise, which is beneficial to improve the integrity of edge extraction.

3.3 Edge Extraction Based on MCNN

The edge extraction based on MCNN [15] is calculated in the same way as the denoising template. The image before edge extraction is used as input, and the image after edge extraction is used as output. According to the constraints of input and output, the template with edge detection function can be obtained. The parameters are shown in Fig. 8.

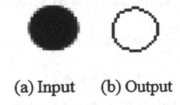

(a) Input   (b) Output

Fig. 8. Edge detection training image

In a typical 3 * 3 system, the required parameters are $9 + 9 + 1 = 19$, which are expressed as:

$$t = \{a_{-1,-1}, a_{-1,0}, a_{-1,1}, a_{0,-1}, a_{0,0}, a_{0,1}, a_{1,-1}, a_{1,0}, a_{1,1},$$
$$b_{-1,-1}, b_{-1,0}, b_{-1,1}, b_{0,-1}, b_{0,0}, b_{0,1}, b_{1,-1}, b_{1,0}, b_{1,1}, I\} \quad (7)$$

As can be seen from the cell neural network template library, templates A and B can be simplified in the form:

$$A = \begin{bmatrix} 0 & 0 & 0 \\ 0 & a & 0 \\ 0 & 0 & 0 \end{bmatrix}, B = \begin{bmatrix} c & c & c \\ c & b & c \\ c & c & c \end{bmatrix} \tag{8}$$

At the same time, t can be reduced to:

$$t = \{a, b, c, I\} \tag{9}$$

Solving the equation by LMI can be found:

$$t = \{3.9488, 8.0148, -0.9916, -0.5414\} \tag{10}$$

On the basis of denoising, the MCNN is used for edge extraction [16]. The output feedback template A and the input control template B are both 3*3 templates with a threshold of I, as shown below:

$$A = \begin{bmatrix} 0 & 0 & 0 \\ 0 & 3.9488 & 0 \\ 0 & 0 & 0 \end{bmatrix}, B = \begin{bmatrix} -0.9916 & -0.9916 & -0.9916 \\ -0.9916 & 8.0148 & -0.9916 \\ -0.9916 & -0.9916 & -0.9916 \end{bmatrix} \tag{11}$$

$I = -0.5414$

In order to achieve adaptive adjustment of network parameters, the stability conditions of the network [17] are analyzed, and the formula (1) is changed to:

$$\frac{dx_{ij}(t)}{dt} = -\frac{1}{R}x_{ij}(t) + A(i, j; i, j)y_{ij}(t) + q \tag{12}$$

$$q = \sum_{k,l \neq i,j} A(i, j; k, l)y_{kl}(t) + \sum_{c(k,l) \in N(i,j)} B(i, j; k, l)u_{kl}(t) + I \tag{13}$$

Where $u_{kl}(t)$ is the input, $x_{ij}(t)$ is the state of c(i, j), and $y_{ij}(t)$ is the output of c(i, j).

$$\frac{dx_{ij}(t)}{dt} = -x_{ij}(t) + 2y_{ij}(t) + p \tag{14}$$

$$P = B * u + I \tag{15}$$

The stability of the MCNN is achieved by determining the value of I. When the pixel (i, j) is an edge point, it should satisfy $P = B * u + I > a - 1/Rx = 1$, when $I = 2 - B * u$, the stability condition of $P > 1$ is satisfied. When the pixel (i, j) is a non-edge point, it should satisfy $P = B * u + I < -a + 1/Rx = -1$, and satisfy the stability of $P < -1$ when $I = -2 - B * u$. Since B*u is a change value and $I = -B * u \pm 2$, I can change according to the change of $B * u$, and satisfy the stability condition of the network.

Sobel operator [18], prewitt operator, and log operator are frequently used edge extraction methods. In this paper, the traditional five edge extraction methods are compared with the MCNN-based edge extraction method. By comparing the graphs, it can be seen that the edge extraction based on the memristive cell neural network is obviously better than other traditional edge extraction algorithms. The obtained edge information of the fabric ball pilling image is more complete, the continuity is better, and the clearness can be more clearly Highlighting the shape of the hair ball facilitates fast Hough transform detection, as shown in Fig. 9.

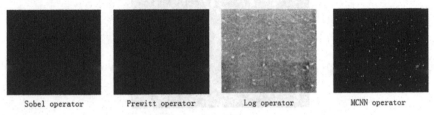

| Sobel operator | Prewitt operator | Log operator | MCNN operator |

Fig. 9. Edge extraction comparison image

3.4 Fast Hough Transform Detection

The edge image of the fabric ball pilling image is circular or elliptical in different shooting angles, and the Hough transform [19] is widely used for shape detection due to its good noise immunity and insensitivity to occlusion. In this paper, the method of fast Hough transform [20] is used to detect the circular and elliptical shapes, and the coordinates and radius of the center of the circle and the central coordinate, long axis and short axis of the ellipse are obtained. The time complexity of the traditional Hough transform is reduced by approximating iteration. Compared with the traditional Hough transform, the operation speed is increased by 18 times, which can minimize the missed detection rate and improve the detection efficiency. The fast Hough transform result is shown in Fig. 10.

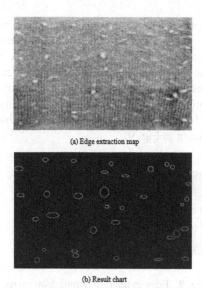

(a) Edge extraction map

(b) Result chart

Fig. 10. Fast Hough transform result

4 Experimental Results and Analysis

In order to test the effectiveness of the method proposed in this paper, cotton, hemp and wool fabric Pilling images were selected for hair ball detection. Watershed segmentation detection, wavelet transform detection and this detection method are compared. In the experiment, Halcon was selected as the platform. The experimental image is shown in Fig. 11 below.

Cotton   Hemp   Wool Fabric

Fig. 11. Experimental image

The watershed segmentation detection, wavelet transform [21] and the detection rate and average time of this method in 400 test images are compared. As can be seen from the table, this method has a significant improvement in the detection rate and speed, compared with other methods for the detection of fabric pilling has a better performance, as shown in Table 1.

The false detection rate of other methods is compared with that of this method. From the table, it can be seen that this method has better robustness than other methods, and

Table 1. Comparison of detection rate and average time

Test method	Detection rate/%	Average time/s
Watershed segmentation	96.16	0.61
Wavelet transform	97.44	0.55
Article method	98.2	0.44

the false detection rate of fabric hair pilling is lower. It is proved that this method has a good adaptability to fabric hair pilling detection, and can realize the accurate detection of fabric hair pilling, as shown in Table 2.

Table 2. Comparison of false detection rates

Test method	Noise factor/%
Watershed segmentation t	3.4
Wavelet transform	2.8
Article method	1.8

5 Conclusion

In this paper, a fabric hair pilling detection method based on memristor cell neural network is proposed. The flexible variability of different applications of MCNN in image processing is verified by experiments, and it is proved that MCNN is combined with traditional fabric hair pilling detection technology. It can greatly improve the detection rate and speed of fabric hair pilling. In the experiment, it is found that although the detection effect is good, but there is also the situation of missed detection, the missed image is generally similar to the color of the fabric, in the next study will explore these situations, to find a solution.

Funding. This research was funded by Science and Technology Support Plan Project of Hebei Province, grant number 17210803D.

This research was funded by Science and Technology Support Plan Project of Hebei Province, grant number 19273703D.

This research was funded by Science and technology spark project of Hebei Seismological Bureau, grant number DZ 20180402056.

References

1. Feng, X., Zhang, X., Xin, Z., Yang, A.: Investigation on the Chinese text sentiment analysis based on convolutional neural networks in deep learning. Comput. Mater. Continua **58**(3), 697–709 (2019)

2. Zhong, S.: Heterogeneous memristive models design and its application in information security. Comput. Mater. Continua **60**(2), 465–479 (2019)
3. Priyanka, D., Dharani, K., Anirudh, C., Akshay, K., Sunil, M.P., Hariprasad, S.A.: Traffic light and sign detection for autonomous land vehicle using raspberry Pi. In: International Conference on Inventive Computing and Informatics, pp. 160–164 (2017)
4. Shen, J., Yang, X.Z.: A new edge preserving watershed image segmentation algorithm. J. Eng. Graph. **30**(5), 8088 (2009)
5. Zhang, Y.: Research on the Application of Watershed Algorithm in Image Segmentation. Guangdong University of Technology, Guangzhou (2013)
6. Xu, W., Liu, Z.Q., Liu, Q.: Research on image segmentation method based on improved watershed algorithm. Comput. Simul. **28**(9), 272–274 (2013)
7. Chua, L.O., Yang, L.: Cellular neural networks: theory. IEEE Trans. Circ. Syst. **10**, 1257–1272 (1998)
8. Fang, W., Zhang, F., Sheng, V.S., Ding, Y.: A method for improving CNN-based image recognition using DCGAN. Comput. Mater. Continua **57**(1), 167–178 (2018)
9. Deng, S.J., Tian, Y., Hu, X.P., et al.: Application of new advanced CNN structure with adaptive thresholds to color edge detection. Commun. Nonlinear Sci. Numer. Simul. **7**(4), 1637–1648 (2012)
10. Mazumder, P., Li, S.R., Ebong, I.E.: Tunneling-based cellular nonlinear network architectures for image processing. IEEE Trans. Very Large Scale Integr. (VLSI) Syst. **17**(4), 487–495 (2009)
11. Strukov, D., et al.: The missing memristor found. Nature **453**, 80–83 (2008)
12. Williams R.S., Stewart D.: How we found the missing memristor. IEEE Spectrum 29–35 (2008)
13. Zhang, X.H., Miao, L.Y., Yu, L.H.: Modeling and circuit simulation of a novel memristive cell neural network. J. Syst. Simul. **28**(08), 1715–1724 (2016)
14. Gao, S.Y., Duan, S.K., Wang, L.D.: Membrane cell neural network and its application in image denoising and edge extraction. J. Southwest Univ. (Nat. Sci. Ed.) **33**(11), 63–70 (2011)
15. Ting, Y., Shukai, D., Lidan, W.: Color image edge extraction based on improved memristive cell neural network. Chin. Sci.: Inf. Sci. **47**(07), 863–877 (2017)
16. Baştürk, A., Günay, E.: Efficient edge detection in digital images using a cellular neural network optimized by differential evolution algorithm. Exp. Syst. Appl. **36**(2), 2645–2650 (2009)
17. Zhang, Y., Wang, T.Y., Huang, G.L.: Gray image edge detection based on parameter adaptive CNN. Comput. Eng. Appl. **44**(18), 160–162 (2008)
18. Li, Z.H., Jin, H.Y., Xing, X.H.: Edge detection algorithm for fractional order Sobel operator with integer order filtering. Comput. Eng. Appl. **54**(04), 179–184 (2018)
19. Houben S.A.: Single target voting scheme for traffic sign detection. In: IEEE Intelligent Vehicles Symposium, pp. 124–129 (2011)
20. Qiu, S.M., Xia, Y.R.: A fast Hough transform algorithm. Comput. Eng. **30**(2), 148–150 (2004)
21. Zhang, Y., Ma, J., Deng, Z.M.: Detection of fabric hairball based on wavelet transform and morphology. Knitting Ind. **64**–66 (2015)

Propagator Method Based on Virtual Array Manifold Matching Algorithm for 2D DOA Estimation

Sheng Liu$^{(\boxtimes)}$, Jing Zhao, Weizhi Xiong, and Xiangjun Dai

Tongren University, Tongren 554300, China
liushengtrxy@126.com

Abstract. In this paper, a propagator method (PM) based on virtual array manifold matching (AMM) algorithm for two-dimensional (2D) direction of arrival (DOA) estimation is proposed by using a two-parallel linear array. The used array consists of two parallel linear arrays that are symmetric around the x-axis. The conjugate of cross-covariance matrix of received data from the two linear arrays is exploited to construct a virtual cross-covariance matrix. Then a virtual AMM algorithm is presented to estimate the 2D DOA combining with PM. Compared with some other PM algorithms, the proposed algorithm shows many specific advantages in estimation precision, computational complexity and the number of distinguishable signals. Complexity analysis and simulation results can testify the property of proposed approach.

Keywords: AMM · 2D DOA estimation · Two-parallel linear array · PM

1 Introduction

Direction of arrival (DOA) estimation of multiple space signal sources is one of core technologies in mobile communication [1–4]. Multiple signal classification (MUSIC) algorithm [5], estimation of signal parameters via rotational invariance technique (ESPRIT) [6] and propagator method (PM) [7] are three classical one-dimensional (1D) DOA estimation algorithms, and have been improved and extended over the years.

In fact, compared with the one dimensional (1D) DOA estimation algorithm based on linear array, two-dimensional (2D) DOA estimation algorithm based on planar array is more realistic to simultaneously estimate the elevation angles and azimuth angles of space signals. L-shaped array [8–12] and cross array [13] are two kinds of common planar array which consists two orthogonal linear arrays. Many effective (2D) DOA estimation algorithm algorithms have been proposed by the two kinds of array construction. The construction of cross-covariance is an important key process to get the estimations of elevation angles and azimuth angles. In [14], author use the conjugate of cross-covariance based on T-shaped array to construct an extended cross-covariance which can be seen as the cross-covariance based on a virtual cross array.

Multiple-parallel linear array [15–20] that consists of two or more parallel linear arrays is another widely used planar array. In [15], a polynomial rooting algorithm was

X. Sun et al. (Eds.): ICAIS 2020, CCIS 1253, pp. 255–264, 2020.
https://doi.org/10.1007/978-981-15-8086-4_24

proposed to estimate the elevation angles and azimuth angles based on two-parallel linear array. Although this algorithm has higher estimation accuracy, it requires eigenvalue decomposition (EVD), calculation of determinant and polynomial rooting which are high-complexity processes. In [16], a rank-reduction 2D DOA estimation algorithm based on three-parallel linear array was proposed. But it still needs EVD and calculation of determinant. Computational complexity is an important index for evaluating an algorithm. PM algorithm is widely used for DOA estimation, because it doesn't need EVD of covariance matrix. In [17], a 2D PM algorithms based on two-parallel linear array was proposed. In [18], an improved 2D PM algorithm has been proposed and shows higher estimation accuracy and lower complexity than the PM algorithm [17]. A 2D PM algorithm based on a special two-parallel linear array was presented in [19]. But the estimation precision of angles is unstable to the position of the array. In order to reduce complexity and obtain automatic pairing 2D angles, a unilateral array manifold matching (AMM) was proposed in [20]. When AMM algorithm is used with PM algorithm, the computation complexity is lower than the PM algorithms [17–19] under the same number of sensors. But unilateral AMM algorithm is based on more than three linear arrays, and the accuracy also is lower than the PM algorithm [17–19] when it is used with PM algorithm [20].

In this paper, a propagator method (PM) based on virtual unilateral AMM is introduced. A special two-parallel linear array is placed on $x-z$ plane, and is symmetric around the x-axis. The conjugate of the cross-covariance matrix is used to construct a virtual cross-covariance matrix. PM algorithm is used with the virtual unilateral AMM to get the 2D DOA estimation. Compared with PM algorithm based unilateral AMM [20], the computational complexity of proposed algorithm has the same level of computational complexity. But the proposed algorithm can distinguish more signals and has higher estimation accuracy. Compared with PM [17, 18], the proposed algorithm has lower complexity, and higher estimation accuracy in the condition of low SNR.

Notation: The symbol $[\bullet]^+$, $[\bullet]^T$ and $[\bullet]^H$ is the Moore-Penrose generalized inverse, the transpose, the conjugate transpose, respectively. The operator $E[\bullet]$ is the statistical expectation. The superscript $[\mathbf{A}]_{i:j,:}$ denotes a matrix consisting of the ith column to the jth column of matrix $\mathbf{A}$.

2 Data Model

Suppose that K $(K < M)$ far-field sources imping the two-parallel linear array located in the $x-z$ plane as shown in Fig. 1. The spacing between the two linear arrays is $d/2$, where $d = \lambda/2$ is the wavelength of signal. An M-element uniform linear array located on the z-axis , where M is odd number and the inter-element spacing is d. The other N-element linear array doesn't have to be uniform linear array, but all the sensor positions are symmetric around the x-axis. Assume that θ_k and β_k are the elevation and azimuth angles of the kth signal, respectively.

Denote the received vectors of the two parallel linear arrays as $z(t) = [z_1(t), z_2(t), \cdots, z_M(t)]$ and $x(t) = [x_1(t), x_2(t), \cdots, x_N(t)]$. Suppose that $\theta =$

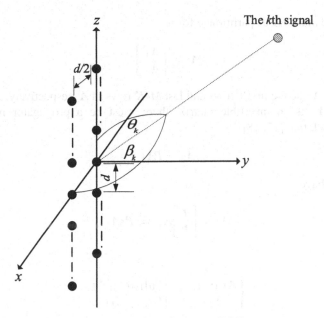

Fig. 1. The construction of two-parallel linear array

$[\theta_1, \cdots, \theta_K]$, $\boldsymbol{\beta} = [\beta_1, \cdots, \beta_K]$, then $\boldsymbol{z}(t), \boldsymbol{x}(t)$ can be written as [20]

$$\begin{cases} \boldsymbol{z}(t) = \boldsymbol{A}(\boldsymbol{\theta})\boldsymbol{s}(t) + \boldsymbol{n}_z(t) \\ \boldsymbol{x}(t) = \boldsymbol{B}(\boldsymbol{\theta})\boldsymbol{\Omega}(\boldsymbol{\beta})\boldsymbol{s}(t) + \boldsymbol{n}_x(t) \end{cases}, \ t = 1, 2 \cdots T \qquad (1)$$

where $\boldsymbol{s}(t) = [s_1(t), s_2(t), \cdots, s_K(t)]^T \in C^{K \times 1}$ is signal data vector; $\boldsymbol{A}(\boldsymbol{\theta}) = [\boldsymbol{a}(\theta_1), \boldsymbol{a}(\theta_2), \cdots, \boldsymbol{a}(\theta_K)] \in C^{M \times K}$ is array manifold matrix with $\boldsymbol{a}(\theta_k) = [e^{\frac{j\pi(M-1)d\,\cos\theta_k}{\lambda}}, \cdots, e^{\frac{j2\pi d\,\cos\theta_k}{\lambda}}, 1, e^{-\frac{j2\pi d\,\cos\theta_k}{\lambda}}, \cdots, e^{-\frac{j\pi(M-1)d\,\cos\theta_k}{\lambda}}]^T \in C^{M \times 1}$; $\boldsymbol{B}(\boldsymbol{\theta})\boldsymbol{\Omega}(\boldsymbol{\beta})$ is the other array manifold matrix, where $\boldsymbol{\Omega}(\boldsymbol{\beta}) = \text{diag}\{e^{-\frac{j\pi d\,\cos\beta_1}{\lambda}}, e^{-\frac{j\pi d\,\cos\beta_2}{\lambda}}, \cdots, e^{-\frac{j\pi d\,\cos\beta_K}{\lambda}}\}$ and $\boldsymbol{B}(\boldsymbol{\theta}) = [\boldsymbol{b}(\theta_1), \boldsymbol{b}(\theta_2), \cdots, \boldsymbol{b}(\theta_K)] \in C^{N \times K}$ with $\boldsymbol{b}(\theta_k) = [e^{\frac{j2\pi d_{N/2}\,\cos\theta_k}{\lambda}}, \cdots, e^{\frac{j2\pi d_1\,\cos\theta_k}{\lambda}}, \cdots, e^{-\frac{j2\pi d_1\,\cos\theta_k}{\lambda}}, \cdots, e^{-\frac{j2\pi d_{N/2}\,\cos\theta_k}{\lambda}}]^T \in C^{N \times 1}$; $\boldsymbol{n}_z(t) = [n_{z,1}(t), n_{z,1}(t), \cdots, n_{z,M}]^T \in C^{M \times 1}$ and $\boldsymbol{n}_x(t) = [n_{x,1}(t), n_{x,2}(t), \cdots, n_{x,N}]^T \in C^{N \times 1}$ are white noise vector with zeros mean and covariance matrix $\delta^2 \boldsymbol{I}_M$ and $\delta^2 \boldsymbol{I}_N$, respectively.

3 Algorithm Description

In this section, we firstly use the PM [17, 18] to estimate the elevation angles. Denote a cross-correlation matrix as $\boldsymbol{R}_{zx} = E[\boldsymbol{z}(t)\boldsymbol{x}^H(t)]$, where $\boldsymbol{R}_{zx}$ can be estimated by $\hat{\boldsymbol{R}}_{zx} = \frac{1}{T} \sum_{t=1}^{T} \boldsymbol{z}(t)\boldsymbol{x}^H(t)$, where T is snapshots. According to (1), $\boldsymbol{R}_{zx}$ can be expressed as

$$\boldsymbol{R}_{zx} = \boldsymbol{A}(\boldsymbol{\theta})E\{\boldsymbol{s}(t)\boldsymbol{s}^H(t)\}\boldsymbol{\Omega}^*(\boldsymbol{\beta})\boldsymbol{B}^H(\boldsymbol{\theta}) \qquad (2)$$

Divide the matrix A as partitioned form

$$A = \begin{bmatrix} A_1 \\ A_2 \end{bmatrix} \tag{3}$$

where A_1 and A_2 be the first k rows and last $M\text{-}K$ rows of A, respectively.

Because A_1 is an invertible matrix, there must be a propagator matrix $P \in C^{(M-K) \times K}$ such that [17, 18]

$$A_2 = PA_1 \tag{4}$$

Then, we have

$$A = \begin{bmatrix} I \\ P \end{bmatrix} A_1 = P_0 A_1 \tag{5}$$

and

$$\begin{cases} A_{1:M-1,:} = [P_0]_{1:M-1,:} A_1 \\ A_{2:M,:} = [P_0]_{2:M,:} A_1 \end{cases} \tag{6}$$

According to (6), we have

$$[P_0]_{1:M-1,:}^{+}[P_0]_{2:M,:} = A_1 \boldsymbol{\Phi}(\theta) A_1^{-1} \tag{7}$$

where $\boldsymbol{\Phi}(\theta) = \text{diag}\{e^{-\frac{j2\pi d \cos\theta_1}{\lambda}}, \cdots, e^{-\frac{j2\pi d \cos\theta_K}{\lambda}}\}$.

Then, we can get the estimation of $\theta_k, k = 1, 2, \cdots, K$ by eigenvalue decomposition (EVD) of $[P_0]_{1:M-1,:}^{+}[P_0]_{2:M,:}$ as [17, 18, 20].

From (2), we can obtain the R_{zx}^*

$$\begin{aligned} R_{zx}^* &= (A(\theta)E\{s(t)s^H(t)\}\boldsymbol{\Omega}^*(\beta)B^H(\theta))^* \\ &= A^*(\theta)E\{s(t)s^H(t)\}\boldsymbol{\Omega}(\beta)B^T(\theta) \end{aligned} \tag{8}$$

According to (8), we can get

$$J_M R_{zx}^* J_N = A(\theta)E\{s(t)s^H(t)\}\boldsymbol{\Omega}(\beta)B^H(\theta) \tag{9}$$

where J_M and J_N are two matrices with 1 on the back-diagonal and 0 on the other positions.

From (9), $J_M R_{zx}^* J_N$ can be seen as the cross-covariance matrix of received signals from the firstly array and a virtual array being symmetric with the second array around the z-axis.

Denote a partitioned matrix R as

$$R = [J_M R_{zx}^* J_N \ \ R_{zx}] \tag{10}$$

Combining (2) and (9), we can get

$$R = A(\theta)[R_s\boldsymbol{\Omega}(\beta)B^H(\theta) \ \ R_s\boldsymbol{\Omega}^*(\beta)B^H(\theta)] \tag{11}$$

Denote the estimations of k elevation angles as $\hat{\theta}_{e1}, \hat{\theta}_{e2}, \cdots, \hat{\theta}_{eK}$, and the estimation of $A(\theta)$ as $\hat{A} = [a(\hat{\theta}_{e1}), a(\hat{\theta}_{e2}), \cdots, a(\hat{\theta}_{eK})] \in C^{M \times K}$, then we can get

$$\left[\hat{A}^+\right]_{k,:} R = [J_M R_{zx}^* J_N \ R_{zx}]$$

$$= [q_k e^{\frac{j\pi d \cos \beta_k}{\lambda}} b^H(\theta_k) \ q_k e^{-\frac{j\pi d \cos \beta_k}{\lambda}} b^H(\theta_k)] \tag{12}$$

According to (12), we can get

$$e^{\frac{j\pi 2d \cos \beta_k}{\lambda}} = \frac{1}{N} \sum_{i=1}^{N} \frac{([\hat{A}^+]_{k,:}R)_i}{([\hat{A}^+]_{k,:}R)_{N+i}} \tag{13}$$

Then, β_k can be estimated by

$$\hat{\beta}_k = \arccos\{\frac{1}{\pi} angle(\frac{1}{N} \sum_{i=1}^{N} \frac{([\hat{A}^+]_{k,:}R)_i}{([\hat{A}^+]_{k,:}R)_{N+i}})\} \tag{14}$$

As [20], we can know that $\hat{\beta}_k$ is paired with $\hat{\theta}_k$.

Remark: From the estimation process presented above, we can see the proposed algorithm as an improved unilateral array manifold matching (AMM) algorithm [20]. A key is that there must be two correlation matrices without noise. So the unilateral AMM only can be used for the array consisting of more than three linear arrays. For the proposed algorithm, by using the conjugate symmetry of manifold matrix, a virtual cross-correlation matrix can be got. Hence we can get two different cross-correlation matrices without noise, which extend the application scope of unilateral AMM.

4 Complexity Analysis

In this subsection, we compare the complexity of 2D PM algorithm [18], PM algorithm [20] and proposed PM algorithm. Suppose that a two-parallel array consisting of an L-element linear array and an L-1-element linear array is used for the 2D PM algorithm [18] and proposed PM algorithm. A three-parallel array consisting of L-element linear array and two $(L - 1)/2$-element linear arrays is used for PM algorithm [20], where L is an odd number. The complexity of main steps for PM algorithms involves the construction of cross-covariance matrix. The complexity of PM [18] is $O\{(2L - 1)^2 T\}$. The complexity of PM algorithm [20] and proposed algorithm is $O\{L(L - 1)T\}$.

5 Simulation Results

In this subsection, several simulations are presented to prove the effectiveness of proposed algorithm. We compare the proposed 2D PM algorithm with the PM algorithm [18] and PM algorithm [20]. A two-parallel array consisting of an 11-element uniform linear array and a 10-element uniform linear array is used for the proposed 2D PM algorithm and PM algorithm [18]. For the PM algorithm [20], we use a three-parallel array consisting of an 11-element uniform linear array and two 5-element uniform linear arrays. The root-mean-square error (RMSE) of 2D DOA estimation is defined as

$$\text{RMSE} = \sqrt{\frac{1}{JK} \sum_{k=1}^{K} \sum_{j=1}^{J} (\hat{\theta}_{jk} - \theta_k)^2 + (\hat{\beta}_{jk} - \beta_k)^2} \tag{15}$$

where $J = 1000$, and $\hat{\theta}_{jk}$, $\hat{\beta}_{jk}$ are the elevation angle and azimuth angle estimations of the kth target in the jth Monte Carlo trial.

Firstly, suppose that the second linear array also is uniform linear array with half-wavelength spacing. Figure 2 shows the result of 100 times DOA estimation by proposed 2D PM algorithm, where $[\theta_1, \theta_2, \theta_3, \theta_4, \theta_5, \theta_6] = [60°, 70°, 80°, 90°, 110°, 120°]$, $[\beta_1, \beta_2, \beta_3, \beta_4, \beta_5, \beta_6] = [110°, 120°, 130°, 140°, 150°, 160°]$, SNR is 5 dB and the number of snapshots is 1000. From Fig. 2, we can see clearly that the proposed PM can distinguish six signals without parameter mismatch. But PM [20] based on the 21-element three-parallel linear arrays can only distinguish no more than five signals under the same complexity.

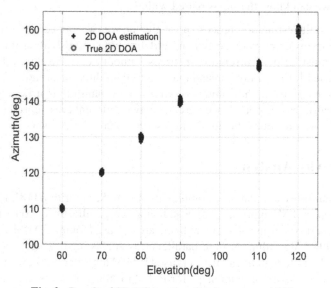

Fig. 2. Result of 2D DOA estimation by proposed PM.

Then, suppose that the second linear array is a non-uniform linear array with the x-coordinates being $-8\lambda, 7\lambda, -5\lambda, -3\lambda, -\lambda, \lambda, 3\lambda, 5\lambda, 7\lambda, 8\lambda$, respectively. Fix the SNR at 5 dB and number of snapshots at 1000. Figure 3 shows the result of 100 times DOA estimation by proposed 2D PM algorithm, where $[\theta_1, \theta_2, \theta_3, \theta_4, \theta_5] = [70°, 80°, 90°, 110°, 120°]$ and $[\beta_1, \beta_2, \beta_3, \beta_4, \beta_5] = [130°, 120°, 140°, 150°, 160°]$. Figure 4 shows the result of 100 times DOA estimation by proposed 2D PM algorithm, where $[\theta_1, \theta_2, \theta_3, \theta_4, \theta_5] = [70°, 80°, 90°, 100°, 110°]$ and

$[\beta_1, \beta_2, \beta_3, \beta_4, \beta_5] = [130°, 120°, 140°, 130°, 150°]$. For the PM algorithm [17–19], the employed linear array must be uniform linear arrays.

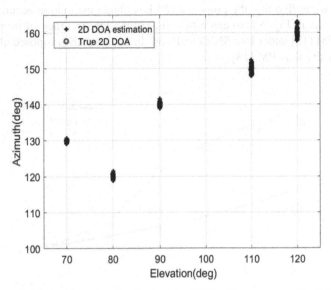

Fig. 3. Result of 2D DOA estimation by proposed PM with one non-uniform linear array

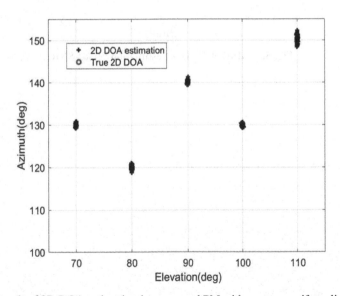

Fig. 4. Result of 2D DOA estimation by proposed PM with one non-uniform linear array

At last, suppose that the second sub-array also is uniform linear array with half-wavelength spacing, $[\theta_1, \theta_2, \theta_3, \theta_4, \theta_5] = [60°, 70°, 80°, 90°, 110°]$ and

$[\beta_1, \beta_2, \beta_3, \beta_4, \beta_5] = [110°, 120°, 130°, 140°, 150°]$. Figure 5 shows the RMSE comparison versus SNR for three PM algorithms with T = 500. Figure 6 shows the RMSE comparison versus snapshots for three PM algorithms with SNR = 2.5 dB. From Fig. 5 and Fig. 6, we can find that the proposed PM has higher estimation accuracy than PM [20]. The results in Fig. 5 also can reflect the estimation accuracy of proposed PM is higher than PM [18] under low-SNR condition. In addition, the proposed algorithm has lower complexity than PM [18].

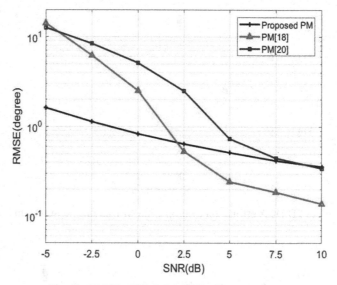

Fig. 5. RMSE of 2D DOA estimation versus SNR

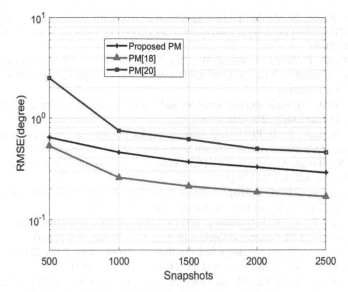

Fig. 6. RMSE of 2D DOA estimation versus snapshots

6   Conclusions

In this paper, a 2D PM algorithm based on a virtual unilateral AMM algorithm by using a symmetric two-parallel linear array is proposed. The conjugate of the cross-covariance matrix is used to construct a virtual cross-covariance matrix. PM algorithm is used with the virtual unilateral AMM to get the 2D DOA estimation. Complexity analysis proves that the computation complexity of proposed algorithm is lower than some existing PM algorithms. Simulation results certify the estimation accuracy of proposed algorithm is higher than some existing PM algorithm, particularly in the low-SNR condition.

Acknowledgments. This work was supported by the Cooperation Agreement Project by the Department of Science and Technology of Guizhou Province of China (LH [2017]7320, LH [2017]7321), the Foundation of Top-notch Talents by Education Department of Guizhou Province of China (KY [2018]075), the nature and science fund from the Education Department of Guizhou province the Innovation Group Major Research Program Funded by Guizhou Provincial Education Department (KY [2016]051) and PhD Research Startup Foundation of Tongren University (trxyDH1710).

References

1. Min, S., Seo, D.K., Lee, B.H., Kwon, M., Lee, Y.H.: Direction of-arrival tracking scheme for DS/CDMA systems: direction lock loop. IEEE Trans. Wireless Commun. **3**(1), 191–202 (2004)
2. Yu, S., Liu, J., Zhang, X., Wu, S.: Social-aware based secure relay selection in relay-assisted D2D communications. Comput. Mater. Continua **58**(2), 505–516 (2019)

3. Wang, Y., Zhang, X., Zhang, Y.: Joint spectrum partition and performance analysis of full-duplex D2D communications in multi-tier wireless networks. Comput. Mater. Continua **61**(1), 171–184 (2019)
4. Huang, Z., Su, J., Wen, G.J., Zheng, W., Chu, C., Zhang, Y.: A physical layer algorithm for estimation of number of tags in UHF RFID anti-collision design. Comput. Mater. Continua **61**(1), 399–408 (2019)
5. Schmidt, R.O.: Multiple emitter location and signal parameter estimation. IEEE Trans. Antennas Propag. **34**(3), 276–280 (1986)
6. Roy, R., Kailath, T.: ESPRIT-estimation of signal parameters via rotational invariance techniques. IEEE Trans. Acoust. Speech Signal Process. **37**(7), 984–995 (1989)
7. Marcos, S., Marsal, A., Benidir, M.: The propagator method for source bearing estimation. Signal Process. **42**(2), 121–138 (1995)
8. Tayem, N., Kwon, H.M.: L-shape 2-dimensional arrival angle estimation with propagator method. IEEE Trans. Signal Process. **53**(5), 1630–1662 (2005)
9. Gan, L., Gu, J.F., Wei, P.: Estimation of 2-D DOA for noncircular sources using simultaneous SVD technique. IEEE Antennas Wireless Propag. Lett. **7**, 385–388 (2007)
10. Nie, X., Li, L.: A computationally efficient subspace algorithm for 2-D DOA estimation with L-shaped array. IEEE Signal Process. Lett. **21**(8), 971–974 (2014)
11. Liu, S., Yang, L., Li, D., Cao, H.: Subspace extension algorithm for 2D DOA estimation with L-shaped sparse array. Multidimen. Syst. Signal Process. **28**(1), 315–327 (2016). https://doi.org/10.1007/s11045-016-0406-3
12. Elbir, A.M.: L-shaped coprime array structures for DOA estimation. Multidimen. Syst. Signal Process. **31**(1), 205–219 (2019). https://doi.org/10.1007/s11045-019-00657-4
13. Liu, S., Yang, L.S., Wu, D.C., Huang, J.H.: Two-dimensional DOA estimation using a coprime symmetric cross array. Progress Electromagnet. Res. C **54**, 67–74 (2014)
14. Nie, X.: Research on 2D DOA estimation algorithm for array signal, Ph.D. thesis, University of Electronic Science and Technology of China (2015)
15. Xia, T., Zheng, Y., Wan, Q., Wang, X.G.: Estimation of 2-D angles of arrival using two parallel uniform linear arrays. IEEE Trans. Antennas Propag. **55**(9), 2627–2632 (2007)
16. Zhang, Y., Xu, X., Sheikh, Y.A., Ye, G.F.: A rank-reduction based 2-D DOA estimation algorithm for three parallel uniform linear arrays. Signal Process. **120**, 305–310 (2016)
17. Wu, Y., Liao, G., So, H.C.: A fast algorithm for 2-D direction-of-arrival estimation. Signal Process. **83**(8), 1827–1831 (2003)
18. Li, J., Zhang, X., Chen, H.: Improved two-dimensional DOA estimation algorithm for two-parallel uniform linear arrays using propagator method. Signal Process. **92**(12), 3032–3038 (2012)
19. Luo, J., Zhang, G., Yu, K.: An automatically paired two-dimensional direction-of-arrival estimation method for two parallel uniform linear arrays. AEU-Int. J. Electron. Commun. **72**, 46–51 (2017)
20. Yang, L., Liu, S., Li, D., Cao, H.L., Jiang, Q.P.: Fast 2D DOA estimation algorithm by an array manifold matching method with parallel linear arrays. Sensors **16**(3), 274 (2016)

Two-Dimensional Seismic Data Reconstruction Method Based on Compressed Sensing

Caifeng Cheng[1,2], Xiang'e Sun[1], and Deshu Lin[3(✉)]

[1] School of Electronics and Information, Yangtze University, Jingzhou 434023, Hubei, China
ccf_cheng@126.com
[2] College of Engineering and Technology, Yangtze University, Jingzhou 434020, Hubei, China
[3] School of Computer Science, Yangtze University, Jingzhou 434023, Hubei, China
lindeshu@yangtzeu.edu.cn

Abstract. Compressive sensing theory mainly includes the sparsely of signal processing, the structure of the measurement matrix and reconstruction algorithm. Reconstruction algorithm is the core content of CS theory, that is, through the low dimensional sparse signal recovers the original signal accurately. This thesis based on the theory of CS to study further on seismic data reconstruction algorithm. We select Orthogonal Matching Pursuit algorithm as a base reconstruction algorithm. Then do the specific research for the implementation principle, the structure of the algorithm of AOMP and make the signal simulation at the same time. In view of the OMP algorithm reconstruction speed is slow and the problems need to be a given number of iterations, which developed an improved scheme. We combine the optimized OMP algorithm of constraint the optimal matching of item selection strategy, the backwards gradient projection ideas of adaptive variance step gradient projection method and the original algorithm to improve it. Simulation experiments show that improved OMP algorithm is superior to traditional OMP algorithm of improvement in the reconstruction time and effect under the same condition.

Keywords: Compressive sensing · Sparse · Seismic data reconstruction

1 Introduction

For the collected seismic data, we hope to collect more data in order to get better reconstruction effects, and hope that with the demand for large data compression, we can achieve the expected results with less data. The Nyquist sampling theorem requires that the sampling frequency should be guaranteed to be more than twice the signal bandwidth, which greatly limits the development of information technology [1–3]. The theory of compressed sensing developed in recent years has greatly improved the development space of information technology. It shows that if the incomplete data has compressibility, it is possible to obtain the ideal reconstruction effect [4–7]. Compressed sensing theory saves the acquisition cost and provides a new theoretical basis for seismic data reconstruction.

© Springer Nature Singapore Pte Ltd. 2020
X. Sun et al. (Eds.): ICAIS 2020, CCIS 1253, pp. 265–277, 2020.
https://doi.org/10.1007/978-981-15-8086-4_25

2 Sparse Representation of Seismic Data

The precondition for reconstruction of seismic data using CS theory is that the seismic signal has sparse or compressible characteristics, but most of the characteristics of this signal cannot be satisfied by itself. If the seismic signal to be reconstructed can meet this requirement in a certain transform domain, then the CS theory can be applied [8, 9]. Currently used sparse transform methods are: discrete cosine transform, Fourier transform, wavelet transform and later proposed curvelet transform.

Discrete cosine transform is a widely used transform. After the seismic signal is subjected to discrete cosine transform, most of the energy data in the transform domain is concentrated in the low frequency part, so that the original signal can be expressed with few transform coefficients [10]. And thus the signal has sparse characteristics. However, the attribute of the discrete cosine transform is a global transform, and the local characteristics of the signal cannot be efficiently recognized and read [11]. The Fourier transform, which also has good applicability, can link the time domain and frequency domain characteristics of the signal, and can analyze the characteristics of the signal from the frequency domain. The time domain and frequency domain of the signal can be arbitrarily selected. Perform mutual transformation. The integral of the Fourier transform in a complete time domain is also a global transform. The spectrum of a certain time cannot be read very well. Because the seismic data signal has obvious mutation characteristics, the Fourier transform is also the seismic signal cannot be expressed sparsely. The gradually developed wavelet transform makes up for the shortcomings of the above two changes, belonging to the local transform, which can effectively identify the local information of the signal, and the point singular feature, so that the transform coefficient in the wavelet transform domain of the signal to be reconstructed has The faster the attenuation near the discontinuous feature, the more the representation signal can be rendered more sparse. Since the seismic data is generally composed of curved seismic waves, the above three transformations cannot represent the ideal sparse representation of the signal, and the sparsely transformed base of the gradually evolved curvelet transform is composed of curved elements of different directions and sizes. The ability to recognize is multi-scale and multi-directional. According to the above analysis, the curvelet transform is selected to sparsely represent the seismic wave field signal, thereby reconstructing the seismic data [12–15].

Curvelet transform is a sparse transform method that performs optimal sparse representation of high-dimensional signals. Its appearance succeeds in compensating for the limitations of contours and edges, such as contours and edges, which can only be limited by wavelet transform. The transform has multi-resolution characteristics and multi-directionality [16]. Since the seismic data is generally composed of curved seismic waves, the curvelet transform is selected as the sparse representation of the seismic signal. This transformation can provide a good sparse representation of the seismic signal to a certain extent. The core idea of curvelet transform is based on the multi-scale geometric analysis method [17]. By constructing the support interval to satisfy the basis of the anisotropic scale relationship, then extending and expanding it, so that the signal can be sparsely represented. The basis function used by the curvelet transform has no correlation with the content of the reconstructed signal, is very simple and easy to operate in parameter selection, and can perform an optimal and non-adaptive sparse representation of the edge portion of the seismic signal to be reconstructed [18].

The expression form of the curvelet transform is similar to other sparse representation methods. The sparse representation of the signal to be reconstructed can be realized by the sparse transform basis function and the inner product of the original signal or function [19–22]:

$$c(j, l, k) = \langle f, \varphi_{jlk} \rangle \tag{1}$$

In formula (1), c denotes the sparse transform coefficient in the curvelet transform domain, the transform coefficient contains the parameter values of the scale, position and angle, f represents the signal to be recovered, and j, l, k represent at different scales [23]. The position is based on a curved wave in a certain direction. Since the curved wave can form a compact frame structure, the above decomposition form can be inversely processed, and the following reconstruction algorithm with stable values can be obtained:

$$f = \sum_{jlk} c_{jlk} \varphi_{jlk} = \sum_{jlk} \langle f, \varphi_{jlk} \rangle \varphi_{jlk} \tag{2}$$

According to the above expression (2), it can be seen that after the inverse signal is inversely transformed, the curvelet transform coefficient c can reconstruct the original signal to be recovered f.

The main reason for choosing the curvelet transform as the sparse representation of the reconstructed seismic signal is that the transform has the characteristics of common discrete cosine transform, Fourier transform and wavelet transform. The curvelet transform has good directivity and is a kind of Multi-resolution, band pass and multi-scale transformation [24, 25]. According to the following analysis of the characteristic properties of the curvelet transform, it can be clearly seen that the curvelet transform can represent the seismic data to be recovered very well.

(1) Tight frame. The curvelet transform and any binary function can be similar to a standard orthogonal base decomposition, which belongs to the tight frame of appropriate redundancy, and this function $f(x_1, x_2) \in L^2(R^2)$ can use a series of fucitons. The wave function is expressed in the form of a weighted summation:

$$f = \sum_{jlk} \langle f, \varphi_{jlk} \rangle \varphi_{jlk} \tag{3}$$

(2) Anisotropy. When the scale of the curvelet transform is 2^{-j}, the length is $2^{-j/2}$, and the width is 2^{-j}, then there is the following formula (4).

$$width \approx length^2 \tag{4}$$

3 Wave Field Reconstruction of Seismic Data Based on Improved OMP Algorithm

3.1 Seismic Data Reconstruction Using OMP Algorithm

The greedy iterative algorithm based on the l_0 norm minimization in the reconstruction algorithm mainly represents two algorithms for matching chasing (Matching pursuit, MP) and Orthogonal Matching Pursuit (OMP) algorithm. The OMP algorithm is based on the MP algorithm, so the MP algorithm is introduced first.

The core idea of the MP algorithm is to select an atom from the atom library that best matches the structural performance of the target signal at each iterative operation, and finally perform iterative approximation one by one [26]. After a certain number of iterations, the convergence can be achieved, and the original signal to be recovered can be reconstructed by only requiring a small number of atoms. The entire flow of the MP algorithm is shown as Fig. 1.

Suppose $\Gamma = \{s_y\}$ is an over complete item library. All items' norms contained in this library are 1. The initial value of the signal is $B_0 = a$. The signal will be decomposed below.

$$B_0 = \langle s_{y_0}, B_0 \rangle s_{y_0} + B_1 \tag{5}$$

In formula (5), $\langle s_{y_0}, B_0 \rangle s_{y_0}$ represents the projection value obtained by B_0 to s_{y_0}, B_1 represent the residual component of the signal [27, 28]. Since there is orthogonal relationship between s_{y_0} and B_0, it can have the following expressions.

$$\|B_0\|^2 = |\langle s_{y_0}, B_0 \rangle|^2 + \|B_1\|^2 \tag{6}$$

In order to obtain the ideal reconstruction effect, it is necessary to control the residual component B_1 of the signal as much as possible within the minimum range, so it can be seen from the above formula that the projection value $\langle s_{y_0}, B_0 \rangle$ must be maximized. Maximizing the projection value of $\langle s_{y_0}, B_0 \rangle$ is equivalent to s_{y_0} is a unit vector that can be optimally matched to the original signal in an over complete item library [29]. The content expressed in the whole process is the true meaning of matching. The residual component B_1 is then processed and has the following requirements:

$$|\langle s_{y_m}, B_m \rangle| = \sup|\langle s_{y_0}, B_0 \rangle| \tag{7}$$

$$a_{m+1} = a_m + |\langle s_{y_{m+1}}, B_{m+1} \rangle| s_{y_{m+1}} \tag{8}$$

$$B_{m+1} = a - a_{m+1} \tag{9}$$

The above operation process is iterated sequentially, and when iterating to the N step, there is an approximation as in formula (10).

$$a = \sum \langle s_{y_m}, B_m \rangle s_{y_m} + B_N \tag{10}$$

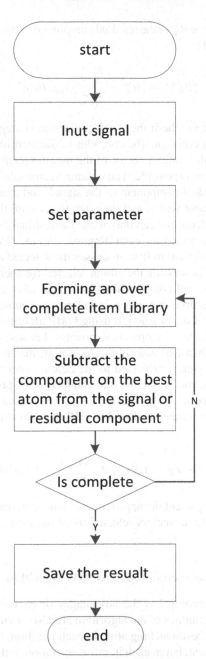

Fig. 1. MP algorithm flow diagram

The approximation error B_N of the residual component in the formula (10) can satisfy the following formula (11).

$$\|B_N\|^2 = \|a\|^2 - \sum_{M-0}^{N-1} |\langle s_{y_m}, B_m \rangle|^2 \tag{11}$$

The OMP algorithm can inherit the atomic selection strategy in the MP algorithm, that is, the atom matching criterion. The core idea of the algorithm is to select the iterative method in selecting the column vector of the measurement matrix, and make each iteration operation as much as possible. The column vector selected in the correlation is related to the current residual component of the signal, and then the relevant portion is removed in the measurement vector, and then iteratively until the signal is undistorted. The MP algorithm has defects that can only make the residual components of the signal orthogonal to the atoms selected for each iteration, and the OMP algorithm is a good improvement. The OMP algorithm first processes the selected atom using the Schmidt orthogonal method when processing the atoms selected for each iteration. The purpose of this is to make the residual component of the signal after each iterative operation. Atomic orthogonal speeds up convergence and improves computational efficiency.

In the process of signal reconstruction using OMP algorithm, it is better to choose iterative framework to realize the operation process, because the operation speed of this algorithm is faster than MP algorithm. Assuming that the original signal to be reconstruction is x, the signal is projected to the column vector ϕ_M orthogonal of the measurement matrix, and the projection set obtained after projection is P. After M orthogonal, the channel approximates the signal $x_{cs} = P(x)$, and the residual component $b = x - x_{cs}$, then the iteration framework of the OMP algorithm has the following formula (12).

$$x_{M+1} - x_M = (\phi_M \phi_1) \begin{pmatrix} \Delta Y_m \\ Y_1 \end{pmatrix} = P_{\phi_m \phi_1} B_M \tag{12}$$

In formula (12), x_M represent the approximate signal obtained after the N iterations. ϕ_M is matrix set of M column vectors selected by M iterations, and B_M is the residual component in the signal.

3.2 Seismic Data Reconstruction Using AOMP Algorithm

The traditional OMP algorithm has the advantages of easy to understand and wide application, but the shortcomings of the algorithm are also obvious. Although the OMP algorithm can choose the best matching atom in each iteration, the number of iterations is reduced to a certain extent, but in each iterative operation, only one optimal atom can be selected to update the support set, and all the atoms in the support set are subjected to Schmidt orthogonalization. Doing so will increase the amount of computation of the algorithm. This operation process increases the number of iterations invisibly, because the number of iterations has a certain correlation with the sparsely and the number of samples, which restrict each other. The increase of the above two parameters will inevitably greatly extend the operation time.

When the data to be recovered is seismic wave field data, the reconstruction effect is unsatisfactory, and the OMP algorithm is also very demanding on the selection requirements of the measurement matrix. The OMP algorithm is needed to reconstruct the seismic signal when the number of iterations is known. This will greatly increase the data of the measured values.

The OOMP algorithm is used to constrain the optimal matching atom selection strategy. This method can avoid the defect that the original selection strategy does not have optimality for the current signal margin in the original algorithm, so the new selection strategy can be used. The selected atom in each iteration of the operation selection may cause the modulus of the current signal margin to be in a minimum range. However, because the constraints of the number of iterations are not explicitly given, this leads to the wrong selection of atoms, so the idea of backward projection in the AVSGP algorithm is introduced into the improved algorithm. The AVSGP algorithm mentioned here actually proposes the adaptive concept in the selection step size of the Gradient Projection for Sparse Reconstruction (GPSR) algorithm. Since the original GPSR algorithm is ideal for processing small-scale data, applying the algorithm to a large number of seismic data reconstructions will affect the reconstruction performance and make it worse because the original GPSR algorithm is the fastest in the optimal theory. The law is the theoretical basis, so it has the drawback of prolonging the calculation time. The introduction of this idea takes the sparsely of the original signal as a criterion for the number of iterations in the iterative operation, and then uses a specific atomic matching criterion to post-process the iterative vector after the iterative operation. Since the number of iterations of the original GPSR algorithm is not subject to any restrictions, it will lead to the wrong selection of atoms. The idea of backward projection can gradually eliminate the selected wrong atoms, and the residual components of the signal are greatly reduced. Accurately and ideally recover the original seismic wave field data.

Suppose that there is a complete set as $\{h_i | i = 1, 2, \ldots . N\}$, h_{L_1} represents an item selected from the complete set, and has the following definition: $H_1 = h_{L_1}$, $H_{k+1} = H_k \oplus h_{L_{k+1}}$, W_{k+1} is the orthogonal complement of space H_{k+1}, then we can show that the orthogonal projection operator on H_{k+1} is:

$$P_{H_{k+1}} = P_{H_k} + P_{W_{k+1}} \tag{14}$$

According to the formula (14), the formula satisfies the relation $h_{L_{k+1}} \in H_{k+1}$, the result $\alpha^{(k+1)}$ of $h_{L_{k+1}}$ orthogonal projection on W_{k+1} can be expressed as:

$$\alpha^{(k+1)} = P_{W_{k+1}} h_{L_{k+1}} = P_{H_{k+1}} h_{L_{k+1}} - P_{H_K} h_{L_{k+1}} \tag{15}$$

The $\alpha^{(k+1)}$ in the above formula (15) is normalized, and the expression $\alpha^{\sim(k+1)}$ s:

$$\alpha^{\sim(k+1)} = \frac{\alpha^{(k+1)}}{\left\| \alpha^{(k+1)} \right\|_2} \tag{16}$$

Then we can project the measurement signal y on the W_{k+1} of the orthogonal complement space as follows:

$$P_{W_{k+1}} y = \alpha^{\sim(k+1)} \langle \alpha^{\sim(k+1)}, y \rangle \tag{17}$$

Next, the expression of the operation symbol H_{k+1} to which the orthogonal projection operation is performed on the space $P_{H_{k+1}}$ will be listed. First assume that the function satisfies the conditional expression $\beta_{L_1}^{(1)} = h_{L_1}$, at the same time, the function expression can make the formula.

$$\beta_{L_1}^{(k+1)} = \frac{\alpha^{(k+1)}}{\left\|\alpha^{(k+1)}\right\|_2} \tag{18}$$

The core idea of the item selection strategy of AOMP algorithm: in the k + 1th iterative operation, the modulus of the selected signal after the selected item $h_{L_{k+1}}$ can be the smallest; the whole process can satisfy the following expression:

$$\left\|r^{k+1}\right\|_2^2 = \|y\|_2^2 - \left\langle P_{H_{k+1}} y, y \right\rangle \tag{19}$$

Next, assume that the coefficients obtained in the k + 1 iterative operation can be expressed as $b_{L_1}^{(k+1)}$, then the following expression can be established.

$$P_{H_{k+1}} y = \sum_{i=1}^{k+1} b_{L_1}^{(k+1)} h_{L_1} \tag{20}$$

The following results can be calculated by the formula (21).

$$b_{L_{k+1}}^{(k+1)} = \left\langle \frac{\alpha^{\sim(k+1)}}{\left\|\alpha^{(k+1)}\right\|}, y \right\rangle \tag{21}$$

We can find the approximate signal $\bar{x}$ to be recovered by the OOMP algorithm. The approximate estimate of the initial coefficient is $b = \left[b_{L_1}^{(k)}, b_{L_2}^{(k)}, \cdots, b_{L_k}^{(k)} \right]^T$, At the same time, this initial coefficient is close to the original value of the estimated value, which is $\left\{ h_{L_1} | i = 1, 2, \cdots, k \right\}$.

During the operation, the signal is orthogonally projected to the column vectors of all selected atoms, so that the participation vector of the signal can be reduced, and the item selected in the previous operation are successively eliminated one by one, until it can be matched. The limitation of the sparsely makes the remaining atomic number and the signal sparsely numerically the same, so that the original to be recovered signal can be reconstructed without distortion.

3.3 AOMP Algorithm Operation Steps

Using sparsely as the true standard of adaptive iterations, a particularly simple atomic selection mechanism is given to post-process the results of the iterative operations obtained earlier, so that the extra atoms are eliminated backwards, then they can be reconstructed. The original seismic data signal is derived, and the number of measurements is also reduced to some extent.

Assume that the sparseness is K of the sparsely signal x in the algorithm, the perceptual matrix is H, the signal margin error threshold is δ, the compression measurement is $y \in R^M$, the output is the optimal approximate solution $\bar{x}$ of the N-dimensional signal x, and the recovery error is r.

(1) Initialization signal input is expressed as $r^{(0)} = y$, the index set is $\Lambda^{(0)} = \varnothing$, $\gamma_i = h_i$, Adaptive value c, the feasible area boundary in the calculation process is $\frac{y^T y}{2\tau}$, the feasible area boundary in the calculation process is $k = 1$.

(2) This formula represents the calculation of the index value as $L_1 = \underset{i=1,2,\cdots N}{\arg\max} |\langle h_i, y \rangle|$.

And update the index set to $\Lambda^{(1)} = \{L_1\}$, the function vector after orthogonal projection is $\alpha^{(1)} = h_{L_1} = \beta_1$, and the decomposition coefficient is $b_1 = \langle h_{L_1}, y \rangle$.

(3) For $i = 1, 2, \ldots, N$, the following expressions are calculated.

$$\gamma_i = \gamma_i - \alpha^{(k)} \langle \alpha^{(k)}, h_i \rangle, \, c_i = \langle \gamma_i, y \rangle \tag{22}$$

$$d_i = d_i - \left| \langle \alpha^{(k)}, h_i \rangle \right|^2, \, e_i = |c_i|^2 / d_i \tag{23}$$

(4) Calculate the gradient and step size, if $\alpha_k^{BB1} / \alpha_K^{BB2} < c$, set $c = b$, and update the constant number $c = c \times 0.9$; otherwise, execute $\alpha_k = \alpha_k^{BB1}$ and update the constant number $c = c \times 1.1$.

(5) Introducing the backward projection, make iterations $k \leftarrow k+1$, and calculate the index value $L_1 = \underset{i=1,2,\cdots N}{\arg\max} \, e_i$, thus updating the index set to $\Lambda^{(k)} = \Lambda^{(k-1)} \cup \{L_k\}$, thereby ensuring that the new iteration point belongs to the feasible area and at the same time obtaining a more suitable iteration point.

(6) When it is determined that the current function value does not change, a line search is performed, the objective function is determined, and the signal margin is updated so that it can satisfy $\left\| r^{(k)} \right\|_2^2 = \left\| r^{(k)} \right\|_2^2 - e_{L_k}$, and the following formula is calculated.

$$\alpha^{(k)} = \frac{\gamma_{L_k}}{\sqrt{d_{L_k}}}, \, \beta^{(k)} = \frac{\gamma_{L_k}}{d_{L_k}} \tag{24}$$

(7) Update the projection vector and the coefficient, that is, when $i = 1, 2, \ldots, k-1$, calculate the projection vector as $\beta_i = \beta_i - \beta_k \langle h_{L_k}, \beta_i \rangle$, and the coefficient as $b_i = b_i - b_k \langle h_{L_k}, \beta_i \rangle$.

(8) Determining whether the condition of the iteration stop has been met. If the condition has been met, proceed to step (7) and output $\bar{x}$, otherwise repeat step (3) until the condition is met.

(9) When $i = 1, 2, \ldots, k$, the normalized form of k coefficients is calculated, the result is expressed as $\bar{b} = \left[b_{L_1}^{(k)} / \|b\|_2, b_{L_2}^{(k)} / \|b\|_2, \cdots, b_{L_k}^{(k)} / \|b\|_2 \right]^T$. Then remove the $k-K$ smallest normalization coefficients and the item corresponding to the respective coefficients, so a new coefficient vector $\bar{b}_{new} = \left[b_1^{(k)}, b_2^{(k)}, \cdots b_k^{(k)} \right]^T$, and a set $H_{\Lambda^{(K)}} = \left[h_{L_1}, h_{L_2}, \cdots h_{L_k} \right]$ are obtained, thereby outputting the last result.

3.4 Experimental Results and Performance Analysis

In order to verify the improvement of reconstruction effect and recovery time based on AOMP algorithm, a simulation experiment platform was built, and the original and improved algorithms were used to reconstruct the two-dimensional image. The effective application of the improved algorithm was verified by comparison. The second is the original and improved. The algorithm is applied to the seismic wave field data for reconstruction simulation. After comparison, the improved algorithm is used as the reconstruction algorithm to recover the seismic wave field data successfully and with high precision.

The seismic data used in the simulation test forms a contrast between color and black, and the curvelet transform is selected as the sparse representation method, and the Gauss matrix is used as the measurement matrix.

The sparseness of the signal after sparse transformation is K = 23. Finally, the selected seismic data is subjected to compressed sensing reconstruction. The results are shown in the following Fig. 2 and Fig. 3.

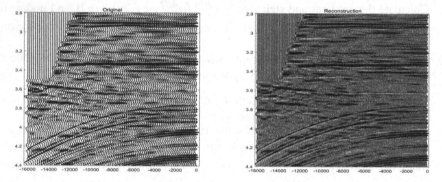

Fig. 2. Data reconstruction comparison chart in black

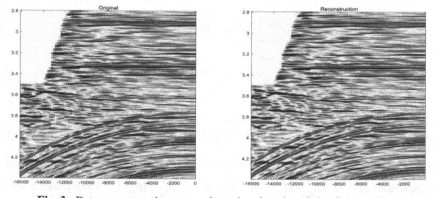

Fig. 3. Data reconstruction comparison chart in color (Color figure online)

In the whole simulation process, the original algorithm reconstructed the seismic wave field data for 50 s, and the improved algorithm reconstructed the seismic wave field data for about 25 s as shown in Table 1. It can be seen that the improved algorithm has greatly improved the processing time. From the reconstruction effects shown in Fig. 2 and Fig. 3, it can be seen that the improved algorithm has a great improvement in reconstruction accuracy compared with the original algorithm. When the actual seismic wave field data is missing a lot of tracks, the compressed sensing theory combined with the improved OMP algorithm can recover the seismic wave field data almost completely, which proves that it is very good both theoretically and practically based on the AOMP algorithm. Practical applicability, can successfully recover the seismic wave field signal.

Table 1. Test processing time(s) and PSNR

Algorithm	OMP		AOMP	
Sampling Rate	0.3	0.5	0.3	0.5
PSNR	25.422	38.788	29.476	45.235
Processing time	50.424	54.342	25.345	28.126

4 Conclusions

In this paper, the sparse representation selected in the seismic field reconstruction of seismic data using the theory of compressed sensing is the curvelet transform and the Gaussian matrix is used as the measurement matrix. The focus of this problem is on the selection of the reconstruction algorithm. The OMP algorithm was chosen in the selection of reconstruction algorithm. The algorithm has the advantages of easy to understand and wide application. However, when dealing with a large amount of seismic wave field data, it will be very large in time consumption and resource utilization, and lead to reconstruction accuracy. And the effect is greatly affected. In order to make up for the above defects, this paper will constrain the optimal matching atom selection strategy by AOMP algorithm, and construct a recovery algorithm with high reconstruction precision, strong anti-noise ability and short processing time. The improved algorithm is proved to be very effective by the simulation experiment model of the two-dimensional image. When applying the improved OMP algorithm to reconstruct the seismic wave field data, it can be seen from the simulation experiment comparison model that the reconstruction effect of the improved OMP algorithm is better than the original OMP algorithm, which can better approximate the true sparseness of the original seismic wave field data, and thus The high-precision recovery of seismic wave field data effectively compensates for the defects of the original algorithm, and the reconstructed effect is excellent while reducing the processing time by shortening the seismic signal.

Acknowledgements. This study was supported by the Scientific Research Project of Hubei Provincial Department of Education (NO: B2018029).

References

1. Li, C., Mosher, C.C., Kaplan, S.T.: Seg technical program expanded abstracts 2012. Soc. Explor. Geophys. s(1), 1–6 (2012)
2. Janiszewski, F., Mosher, C., Li, C., et al.: Seg technical program expanded abstracts 2017. Soc. Explor. Geophys. s(1), 47–51 (2017)
3. Sun, Y., Jia, R., Sun, H., et al.: Reconstruction of seismic data with missing traces based on optimized poisson disk sampling and compressed sensing. Comput. Geosci. 117(1), 32–40 (2018)
4. Li, X., Guo, M., Li, W., et al.: Seg technical program expanded abstracts 2019. Soc. Explor. Geophys. s(1), 132–136 (2019)
5. Chen, Y., Huang, W., Zhang, D., et al.: An open-source matlab code package for improved rank-reduction 3d seismic data denoising and reconstruction. Comput. Geosci. 95(1), 59–66 (2016)
6. Hennenfent, G., Fenelon, L., Herrmann, F.J.: Nonequispaced curvelet transform for seismic data reconstruction: a sparsity-promoting approach. Geophysics 75(6), 1–12 (2010)
7. Huang, X., Zhang, J., Zhu, Z., et al.: Seg technical program expanded abstracts 2019. Soc. Explor. Geophys. S(1), 303–307 (2019)
8. Nianmin, G., Meng, C., Xuemei, F., et al.: Seismic data reconstruction method based compressed sensing theory. In: 2016 International Geophysical Conference, pp. 20–22. Society of Exploration Geophysicists and Society of Petroleum Geophysicists, Beijing (2016)
9. Mosher, C., Li, C., Williams, L., et al.: Seg technical program expanded abstracts 2017. Soc. Explor. Geophys. S(1), 127–131 (2017)
10. Mansour, H., Wason, H., Lin, T.T., et al.: Randomized marine acquisition with compressive sampling matrices. Geophys. Prospect. 60(4), 648–662 (2012)
11. Li, C., Mosher, C., Keys, R., et al.: Seg technical program expanded abstracts 2017. Soc. Explor. Geophys. S(1), 4241–4245 (2017)
12. Gan, S., Wang, S., Chen, Y., et al.: Seg technical program expanded abstracts 2015. Soc. Explor. Geophys. S(1), 3814–3819 (2015)
13. Baraniuk, R.G., Steeghs, P.: Compressive sensing: a new approach to seismic data acquisition. Lead. Edge 36(8), 642–645 (2017)
14. Gholami, A.: Non-convex compressed sensing with frequency mask for seismic data reconstruction and denoising. Geophys. Prospect. 62(6), 1389–1405 (2014)
15. Li, C., Mosher, C.C., Morley, L.C., et al.: Seg technical program expanded abstracts 2013. Soc. Explor. Geophys. S(1), 82–87 (2013)
16. Mosher, C.C., Keskula, E., Kaplan, S.T., et al.: Seg technical program expanded abstracts 2012. Soc. Explor. Geophys. S(1), 1–5 (2012)
17. Jiang, T., Eick, P., Jiang, Y., et al.: Seg Technical Program Expanded Abstracts 2019. Society of Exploration Geophysicists, pp. 4505–4509 (2019)
18. Brown, L., Mosher, C.C., Li, C., et al.: Application of compressive seismic imaging at lookout field, Alaska. Lead. Edge 36(8), 670–676 (2017)
19. Jiang, T., Gong, B., Qiao, F., et al.: Seg technical program expanded abstracts 2017. Soc. Explor. Geophys. S(1), 4272–4277 (2017)
20. Pawelec, I., Sava, P., Wakin, M.: Seg technical program expanded abstracts 2019. Soc. Explor. Geophys. S(1), 147–151 (2019)
21. Lu, P., Xiao, Y., Zhang, Y., et al.: Deep learning for 3d seismic compressive-sensing technique: a novel approach. Lead. Edge 38(9), 698–705 (2019)
22. Bai, L., Lu, H., Liu, Y.: High-efficiency observations: compressive sensing and recovery of seismic waveform data. Pure. Appl. Geophys. 19(1), 1–17 (2019)

23. Zhang, D., Gan, S., Chen, Y.: Seg technical program expanded abstracts 2016. Soc. Explor. Geophys. **S**(1), 14–21 (2016)
24. Yang, J., Li, W., Jie, M., et al.: Application of data reconstruction techniques based on compressive sensing in onshore acquisition. In: Conference and Exhibition 2016, pp. 316–322. Society of Exploration Geophysicists and American Association of Petroleum, Barcelona (2016)
25. Huang, X., Xue, D., Zhu, Z., et al.: Seismic data interpolation based on compressive sensing and its applications. In: International Geophysical Conference 2018, pp. 1723–1726. Society of Exploration Geophysicists and Chinese Petroleum Society, Beijing (2018)
26. López, K.L., Ramírez, J.M., Agudelo, W., et al.: Regular multi-shot subsampling and reconstruction on 3d orthogonal symmetric seismic grids via compressive sensing. In: 2019 XXII Symposium on Image, Signal Processing and Artificial Vision, pp. 11–17. Society of Exploration Geophysicists, Beijing (2019)
27. Liu, Z., Xiang, B., Song, Y., Lu, H., Liu, Q.: An improved unsupervised image segmentation method based on multi-objective particle. Swarm Optim. Clustering Algorithm Comput. Mater. Continua **58**(2), 451–461 (2019)
28. Xiao, D., Liang, J., Ma, Q., Xiang, Y., Zhang, Y.: High capacity data hiding in encrypted image based on compressive sensing for nonequivalent resources. Comput. Mater. Continua **58**(1), 1–13 (2019)
29. Jayashree, N., Bhuvaneswaran, R.S.: A robust image watermarking scheme using z-transform, discrete wavelet transform and bidiagonal singular value decomposition. Comput. Mater. Continua **58**(1), 263–285 (2019)

Optimal Location for Electric Vehicles Charging Stations Based on P-Median Model

Daxin Tian[1,2], Huiwen Yan[1,2], Xuting Duan[1,2(✉)], Yue Cao[1,2], Jianshan Zhou[1,2], Wei Hao[3], Kejun Long[3], and Jian Gu[3]

[1] Beijing Advanced Innovation Center for Big Data and Brain Computing, Beijing, China
duanxuting@buaa.edu.cn
[2] School of Transportation Science and Engineering, Beihang University, Beijing 100191, China
[3] School of Traffic and Transportation Engineering,
Changsha University of Science and Technology, Changsha 410114, China

Abstract. To some certain extent, the development of electric vehicles relies on the availability of infrastructure, especially charging facility. There have been a large amount of studies on the location of electric vehicle charging stations before. In this paper, we establish an improved p-median model that aims to minimize the time costs. This model has some constraints such as the capacity of charging stations and the demand of customers, etc. All of these constraints should be satisfied at the same time. In order to solve this problem, a greedy heuristic algorithm is proposed. Then, we use MATLAB to simulate the case of a real-city charging station layout, and the result indicates that our method is effective and reasonable.

Keywords: Electric vehicle · Charging station · P-median model · Greedy heuristic algorithm

1 Introduction

In recent two decades, the challenge from the expectation of energy depletion and environmental issues urge automobile industry to speed up its energy transition [1]. The depletion of fossil fuels and the desire to reduce city pollutant emissions have given impetus to the development of electric vehicles [2]. In electric vehicles, battery is one of the most expensive and inefficient components. In particular, most electric vehicles have very limited travel ranges without recharging the battery [3]. Limited by travel range, electric vehicles often need to be charged during traveling. After parking, the vehicle can automatically connected the network of the target charging station through radio frequency electronic label (RFID), and realize automatic bow selection by tag identification [4–6]. At present, many builders have relied too much on increasing the number of charging facilities to increase their service levels, resulting in uneven distribution. Some of the charging facilities have been idle for a large amount of time causing waste of resources and unmatched partial charging requirements. This situation thus motivates a design problem to determine optimal locations for recharging stations.

© Springer Nature Singapore Pte Ltd. 2020
X. Sun et al. (Eds.): ICAIS 2020, CCIS 1253, pp. 278–289, 2020.
https://doi.org/10.1007/978-981-15-8086-4_26

The charging station layout problem is essentially a location issue. In previous literature, there are two main approaches to model charging stations: point-based demand model and path-based demand model. The first model assumes that the demand only appears on the static node of road network, typically including p-median model, p-center model. The demand for the second model is supposed to occur on the fixed path. The flow-based approach captures electric vehicle traffic by inserting recharging stations on traffic routes. Hodgson has proposed a flow capturing location model in the 1990s, which maximizes flow-through service facilities [7]. There are some charging station layout studies based on queuing theory [8], game theory [9], and so on.

In this paper, the deployment of charging stations in the city is the focus of attention, and charging demands in the city are mainly concentrated on densely populated areas, such as hospitals, schools, shopping malls, etc. So an improved p-median model is applied which can meet the requirement of charging in the city. For every customer, Dijkstra's algorithm seeks the shortest route to a candidate location for charging station. Then, a concept called speed classification with the conversion factor is introduced since the speeds are diverse on many roads in the city. In this way, the driving time to different charging station candidate locations is generated. Afterward, the queueing theory is combined with service reliability and requirement because the station has limited charging piles. Because this problem is an NP-hard problem, it is not easy to get accurate solution [10]. Therefore, a greedy heuristic algorithm is adopted which always effective and suitable. At last, a simulation is conducted to confirm that our model and algorithm can achieve a good performance.

2 Formulation

In this section, a model based on p-median problem is established to obtain the optimum.

2.1 Problem Description and Hypothesis

The essence of this problem is a location problem. We consider the location problem as a point-based demand and extend the applicability of p-median model. The destination is to find the least and the most reasonable location of charging station to balance the demand of customers and the set-up strategies. The drivers who need to charge are called customers, and they all come from demand points. In this letter, our concern is the ideal minimization problem, so some minor factors will not affect our analysis. Main simplifying assumptions are listed below:

(1) Demand only occurs at the demand points, and the demand quantity can represent all demands in this district.
(2) The candidate locations of charging station are known and abstract to the edge of the road topology.
(3) The electric vehicle receives a fast-charging service in the charging station. In other words, quick charging piles are set in the charging station.
(4) Assuming that electric vehicles can always reach the charging station, and ignoring the influence of state of charge (SOC).

In this way, we already have the proper conditions for modeling.

2.2 Model Establishment

Symbolic notations used throughout this paper are summarized in Table 1.

Table 1. Symbolic notations

Symbolic	Meaning
N	The set of demand points, $i \in N$
M	The set of charging station candidate locations, $j \in M$
m	The amount of charging station candidate locations
p	The amount of charging stations built, $p < m$
λ_j	Average arrival rate
μ_j	Average service ability
ρ_j	Service intensity
ρ_0	Utilization rate of charging facility
d_i	The amount of demand for the customer i
t_h	Average servicing hours of charging piles in charging station per day
n_j	The amount of charging piles in charging station
n_j'	The amount of charging piles in charging station based on redundant design
t_s	Average charging time
P_j	The probability of all charging piles idle
M_j	The expectation time of waiting in line
C	The unit price for building a charging pile
α, β	The linear weighting factor of queuing time and time costs, respectively
x_j	A variable indicates whether to establish a charging station at j
y_{ij}	A variable indicates whether to assign the demand to j

Dijkstra's Algorithm

Given a directed graph $G = (V, E)$, in which there are origins (probable demand points) $N = \{v_n, v_{n+1} \dots\}$ to destination (charging station candidate locations)$M = \{v_m, v_{m+1} \dots\}$, and $V = (N, M)$. All the distances of every two adjacent nodes from the topology map will be obtained.

Step 1. First, let $S = \{v_0\}$, $v_0 \in V$, $T = \{$other nodes$\}$. If $v_0 \in N$ and $v_i \in M$, v_0, v_i is an OD pair, $d(v_0, v_i)$ is the weight on v_0, v_i. Otherwise, $d(v_0, v_i) = \infty$.
Step 2. Select a node $W \notin S$ from T, whose distance with v_0 is shortest, then put W into S.
Step 3. Modify the distance of nodes in T: add W as mid-node, and modify the distance if the distance from v_0 to v_i is shorter than the path without W.

Repeat the above *Step 2* and *Step 3* until $S = T$. Figure 1 is a flow chart of this algorithm.

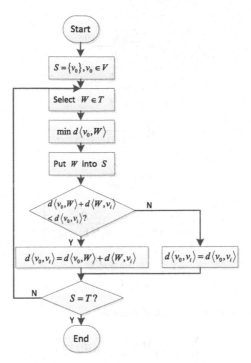

Fig. 1. Flow chart of Dijkstra's algorithm.

In addition, a factor δ is introduced based on the difference of busyness in the city. The range of δ is (0.4, 1), representing the most crowded to unimpeded driving conditions. v is the fastest speed that can be achieved in the urban road section. Then the shortest time matrix is indicated as follow:

$$T = \left[\frac{s_{ij}}{\delta v}\right] \tag{1}$$

For a single user, Dijkstra's algorithm can produce the shortest path. Furthermore, the queuing theory is needed for the design of the charging station itself.

Queuing Theory
Because the capacity of the charging station is limited, customers cannot be charged immediately when they reach the charging station in most cases. The waiting of customers can be considered as a queuing behavior. Customers arrive at the charging station independently, and only one customer arrives in an absolutely short period time. Therefore, the charging process conforms to an M/M/c model, which refers to an input process

obeyed the Poisson distribution and the service time obeyed the negative exponential distribution [5].

$$\lambda_j = \frac{\sum_{i \in N} d_i y_{ij}}{t_h} \tag{2}$$

$$\mu_j = \frac{1}{t_s} \tag{3}$$

$$\rho_j = \frac{\lambda_j}{n_j \mu_j} \tag{4}$$

$$\rho_0 = \frac{\lambda_j}{\mu_j} \tag{5}$$

$$P_j = \left[\sum_{n=0}^{n_j-1} \frac{\rho_0^n}{n!} + \frac{\rho_0^{n_j}}{n_j!(1-\rho_j)} \right]^{-1} \tag{6}$$

$$M_j = \frac{\rho_0^{n_j} \rho_j P_j}{\lambda_j n_j! (1-\rho_j)^2} \tag{7}$$

Then calculated waiting time of customers is

$$\sum_{j \in M} \left[M_j \left(\sum_{i \in N} d_i y_{ij} \right) \right] \tag{8}$$

P-Median Model

Based on p–median model, an improved model is raised, which aims to attain the minimal time cost of customers and the balance between charging pile costs and total queuing time of customers. The objective functions demonstrate as follows:

$$Min \sum_{i \in N} \sum_{j \in M} d_i y_{ij} \frac{S_{ij}}{\delta v} \tag{9}$$

$$Min \alpha \sum_{j \in M} \left[\frac{\rho_0^{n_j} \rho_j P_j}{\lambda_j n_j! (1-\rho_j)^2} \left(\sum_{i \in N} d_i y_{ij} \right) \right] + \beta \sum_{j \in M} n_j p C \tag{10}$$

s.t.

$$\sum_{j \in M} y_{ij} = 1, \forall i \in N \tag{11}$$

$$y_{ij} \leq x_j, \forall i \in N, j \in M \tag{12}$$

$$\sum_{j \in M} x_j = p \tag{13}$$

$$x_j \in \{0, 1\}, \forall j \in M \tag{14}$$

$$y_{ij} \in \{0, 1\}, \forall i \in N, j \in M \tag{15}$$

$$3 \leq n_j \leq 10 \tag{16}$$

To ensure service reliability, the redundant design of charging piles is necessary [11]. Thus we add the charging piles following the rule below:

$$n_j' = \lceil 1.1 n_j \rceil \tag{17}$$

The first objective function aims to find the minimum time of customers spending on the finding way and determine the location of charging station. Next, ensure the minimum queuing time for customers and minimum land costs and construction costs by satisfying the second objective function. Multi-objective function linear weighting method is used to balance the importance of the influence. Queuing time weight is assigned α and costs weight is assigned β. Constraint (11) stipulates that every demand node is assigned to a charging station, so every demand at demand node is satisfied. Constraint (12) indicates that if there was not a charging station built, customers will not come to this candidate location. Constraint (13) limits the total number of charging stations that can be built. Constraint (14) and (15) restrict the decision variables to be binary. In the end, Constraints (16) shows that the amount of fast charging piles is 3 and more. Considering land restrictions and cost restrictions in cities, charging piles installed in the charging station generally do not exceed 10 [12]. Next, we need a suitable algorithm to solve this model.

Greedy Heuristic Algorithm
In view of the fact that p-median problem is an NP-hard problem, a greedy heuristic algorithm is proposed to solve it [13, 14]. When solving problems, this algorithm always makes the best choice at the moment. In other words, without considering the overall optimality, what is currently obtained is a local optimal solution in a certain sense. Specific steps are as follows:

Step 1. Make the number of facilities currently selected $k = m$, that is, all m candidate locations are selected.
Step 2. Assign each customer to the nearest one of the m candidate locations and calculate the total transportation cost.
Step 3. If $k = p$, output the k facilities and the assignment result of each customer, and stop; otherwise, go to *Step 4*.
Step 4. Determine a take-away point from the k facility candidate points to satisfy: if it is taken away and its customers are assigned to other nearest facilities, the total costs increase is minimal.
Step 5. Delete the removal point from the candidate point set and let $k = k - 1$, go to *Step 2*.

Finally, after comparing multiple minimum increases in costs, the best p locations were found.

3 Case Study

In this section, this model is applied to real planning cases in a small city to verify the practicability and effectiveness of this proposed model. We select an area as our study district with an area of approximately 4.33 km^2 as shown in Fig. 2. The goal is to use the method proposed above to plan the site for charging stations and further the amount of charging piles in charging stations.

Fig. 2. Research area and road network.

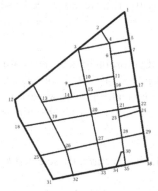

Fig. 3. Research area and road network.

It is a preparation to extract road network topology and mark the intersection as nodes 1–36. In this area, there are schools, shopping malls, residential areas and other densely populated places where more intensive charging requirements will be generated. Assume that the charging demands generate at 10 points. In addition, 5 candidate location points of charging station are given. For the convenience of expression, we relabel demand points and candidate points in Fig. 4, respectively. Triangle marks represent demand points, while round marks represent candidate points. By investigating the demand of each point, the charging demands are shown in Table 2 (Fig. 3).

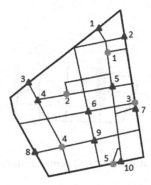

Fig. 4. Demand points and candidate points.

Table 2. Amount of demands at demand points.

Demand point	Amount of charging demand
1	11
2	7
3	9
4	6
5	10
6	9
7	10
8	4
9	6
10	8

In this case, the basic speed v for roads is 40 km/h, and the actual speed v_{ij} of each road is multiplied by a certain conversion factor δ. Among the 36 nodes in the topology, the distances of every two adjacent nodes are measured on a digital map and form an adjacency matrix s_{ij}. In the p-median model proposed above, $t_{ij} = s_{ij}/v_{ij}$ is an adjacency time matrix. Then Dijkstra's algorithm provides a measure to obtain the minimum time from any demand point to the candidate point. In this paper, the time costs replaces the distance of every two adjacency nodes, since the degree of congestion in urban environments largely affects accessibility. A greedy heuristic algorithm is used to solve this problem. In formula (2) and (3), t_h is 18 h and t_s is 1/3 h. According to the actual situation in this area, select two to four locations to set up charging stations among the five candidate points, respectively $p = 2, p = 3, p = 4$, and the address of the charging pile and the allocated demand are shown in Fig. 5 and Table 3.

When the amount of charging stations is larger, the demand allocated by each charging station is less. Different p depends on the plan of the decision-makers. Moreover, for

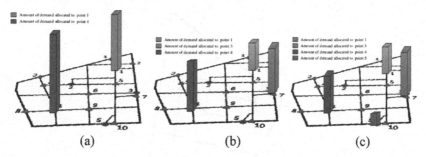

Fig. 5. Charging station position and allocated demand with (a) $p = 2$, (b) $p = 3$, (c) $p = 4$.

Table 3. The demand point for each charging station service under different p.

Charging station number p	Amount of charging demand
$p = 2$	Candidate point 1: demand point 1, 2, 5, 7
	Candidate point 4: demand point 3, 4, 6, 8, 9, 10
$p = 3$	Candidate point 1: demand point 1, 2
	Candidate point 3: demand point 5, 6, 7
	Candidate point 4: demand point 3, 4, 8, 9, 10
$p = 4$	Candidate point 1: demand point 1, 2
	Candidate point 3: demand point 5, 6, 7
	Candidate point 4: demand point 3, 4, 8, 9
	Candidate point 5: demand point 10

different p, the amounts of charging piles in the charging station are different. Generally, customer queuing time is related to the number of charging piles: the more charging piles, the smaller time and probability of customers waiting in line. However, taking into account the charging pile construction costs, the number of charging piles should not be too large. Specifically, the service experience is much more important than costs in the early stage of electric vehicle promotion. In this paper, queuing time weight α is set to 0.8 and costs weight β is set to 0.2. The numbers of optimal charging piles n_j at different p are shown in Fig. 6.

When the number of charging stations p increases, the amounts of charging piles show a decrease tend, and different allocations determine different number of charging piles. It is in line with our understanding. From $p = 2$ to 4, customers are allocated dispersedly, so the number of charging piles in a single charging station can be reduced appropriately. However, the situation does not always meet our expectations. For example, when p increases from 3 to 4, the numbers of charging piles at points 1, 3, 4 do not change at all. That may because in this paper, the volume of the customer group is relatively small and the increase of p is relatively flat. Currently, due to limited research methods and research area, the total number of charging customers and charging stations in this

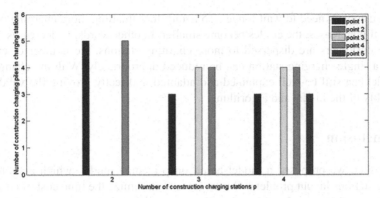

Fig. 6. The number of charging piles with different p.

study can only reach this level. When the total quantity of customers and the value of p are large, and the p increases rapidly, the number of charging piles will be significantly reduced. This needs to be further explored and verified.

In the above, we set average charging time t_s to $1/3$ h. However, due to grid level and battery SOC effects, charging time can be changed [15]. At three different average charging times ($t_s = 1/3$ h, $t_s = 2/3$ h, $t_s = 1$ h), the change of the number of charging piles is shown in Fig. 7.

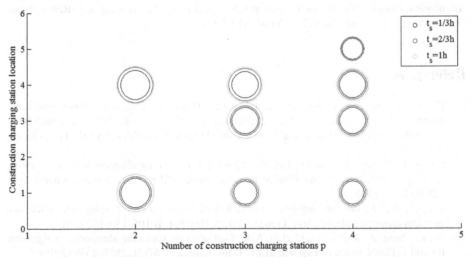

Fig. 7. The number of charging piles with three different average charging times ($t_s = 1/3$ h, $t_s = 2/3$ h, $t_s = 1$ h). (Color figur online)

Figure 7 shows n_j with different p at different charging stations. The area of circles indicates the number of charging piles. It can be seen that t_s has a significant impact on n_j. In Fig. 7, the green circle is greater than the red circle while the red circle is greater than the blue circle. n_j is on the increase with the increase of t_s. When charging time becomes longer, customers need to wait longer. To avoid this situation, more charging piles are needed. If p increases, the circles become smaller. In other words, n_j decreases slightly. Because customers are dispersed to more charging stations, the number of charging piles in a single charging station can be reduced appropriately. With the change of t_s, our model can still be well explained and adapted, indirectly proving the validity and practicality of the model and algorithm.

4 Conclusion

In this paper, we proposed a model based on p-median model, which aims to solve charging stations layout problem. Our target is to minimize the time cost of customers, including travel time and waiting time, by rationally positioning the charging station and the number of charging piles. We go through a series of algorithms, like Dijkstra's algorithm and greedy heuristic algorithm, and get the result of the charging station layout and charging piles setting.

Also, our results have some limitations. Customers may have different charging choices, so they will not always go to the nearest charging station. This involves the problem of probability distribution. In addition, it is worth further investigating the capacity of charging station and the effect of charging behavior on the power grid both. In the future, a charging guide will be one of the key development directions in Intelligent Vehicle Infrastructure Cooperative Systems.

Acknowledgement. This research was supported in part by the National Key Research and Development Program of China (2018YFB1601302).

References

1. Cramer, A., Miller, I., Eichenberg, N., Jesus, J.D., Daniel, L., Longo, M.: Power grid simulation considering electric vehicles and renewable energy sources. In: 2019 Fourteenth International Conference on Ecological Vehicles and Renewable Energies (EVER), pp. 1–3, May 2019
2. Cheng, L., Chang, Y., Wu, Q., Lin, W., Singh, C.: Evaluating charging service reliability for plug-in EVs from the distribution network aspect. IEEE Trans. Sustain. Energy **5**(4), 1287–1296 (2014)
3. Lee, C., Han, J.: Benders-and-price approach for electric vehicle charging station location problem under probabilistic travel range. Transp. Res. Part B **106**, 130–152 (2017)
4. Su, J., Sheng, Z., Xie, L., Li, G., Liu, A.X.: Fast splitting-based tag identification algorithm for anti-collision in uhf rfid system. IEEE Trans. Commun. **67**(3), 2527–2538 (2019)
5. Su, J., Sheng, Z., Liu, A.X., Han, Y., Chen, Y.: A group-based binary splitting algorithm for UHF RFID anti-collision systems. IEEE Trans. Commun. **68**(2), 998–1012 (2019)
6. Su, J., Sheng, Z., Leung, V.C.M., Chen, Y.: Energy efficient tag identification algorithms for RFID: survey, motivation and new design. IEEE Wirel. Commun. **26**(3), 118–124 (2019)
7. Hodgson, M.: A flow-capturing location-allocation model. Geograph. Anal. **22**(3), 270–279 (1990)
8. Zhu, J., Li, Y., Yang, J., Li, X., Zeng, S., Chen, Y.: Planning of electric vehicle charging station based on queuing theory. J. Eng. **2017**(13), 1867–1871 (2017)

9. Meng, W., Kai, L.: Optimization of electric vehicle charging station location based on game theory. In: Proceedings 2011 International Conference on Transportation, Mechanical, and Electrical Engineering (TMEE), pp. 809–812, December 2011

10. Jia, S.: An efficient greedy heuristic for warehouse-retailer network design optimization. Transp. Sci. **44**(2), 183 (2010)

11. Liu, W., Tang, Y., Yang, F., Dou, Y., Wang, J.: A multi-objective decision-making approach for the optimal location of electric vehicle charging facilities. Comput. Mater. Continua **60**(2), 813–834 (2019)

12. GB 50966-2014: Code for Design of Electric Vehicle Charging Station. China Planning Press, Beijing (2014)

13. Mohammed, B., Naouel, D.: An efficient greedy traffic aware routing scheme for internet of vehicles. Comput. Mater. Continua **60**(3), 959–972 (2019)

14. Deng, M., Liu, F., Zhao, M., Chen, Z., Xiao, N.: GFCache: a greedy failure cache considering failure recency and failure frequency for an erasure-coded storage system. Comput. Mater. Continua **58**(1), 153–167 (2019)

15. Malik, F.H., Lehtonen, M.: Minimization of queuing time of electric vehicles at a fast charging station. In: 2017 IEEE PES Innovative Smart Grid Technologies Conference Europe (ISGT-Europe), pp. 1–6, September 2017

A Succinct Power Management Circuit for Wireless Sensor Network Nodes

Gang Li[1,3], Wenxian Zheng[2,3], Zhenbing Li[1,3], Zhong Huang[1,3], Yongjun Yang[1,3], and Guangjun Wen[1,3(✉)]

[1] Centre for RFIC and System, School of Information and Communication Engineering, University of Electronic Science and Technology of China, Chengdu, Sichuan, P.R. China
wgj@uestc.ed
[2] Tsinghua Shenzhen International Graduate School, Shenzhen 518055, P.R. China
[3] Shenzhen Intellifusion Technologies Co., Ltd., Shenzheng 518000, China

Abstract. In wireless sensor networks, radio frequency identification (RFID) is one of the key technologies for data transmitted by the sensor node. In the RFID system, tags convert RF energy to DC through antennas and rectifying circuits, and supply power to other circuits. The sensor and signal conditioning circuit require high energy, so it is difficult to make the sensor node work normally by using the traditional energy harvest and power management circuits. Moreover, since the power management circuit is charged and discharged at the same time, when the converted RF energy is close to the energy consumed by circuit, the sensor and signal conditioning circuit may not work normally. In order to improve the performance of the power management circuit of the sensor node, a succinct power management circuit based on double capacitance is proposed in this paper. Compared with the classical commercial BQ25570 devices, the proposed power management circuit is easier to realize and integrate into the sensor node chip, thus reducing the power consumption of the sensor node. In the paper, the different charging time constants of two capacitor circuits are used to provide power for the subsequent circuits after enough energy is collected. This mode of operation enables the sensor nodes to work stably. The proposed circuit is succinct and easy to implement, and the energy transfer efficiency is about 87% after the capacitor is charged.

Keywords: Wireless sensor networks · RFID · Energy harvest · BQ25570 · Double capacitance

1 Introduction

Radio Frequency Identification (RFID) technology is currently used in many applications, such as wireless sensor networks, supply chain management, biometric recognition, target tracking, automatic positioning and so on [1–7]. According to the energy supply methods, RFID sensor tags can be divided into three types: active, semi-active, and passive. Passive sensor tags have no batteries, and they harvest energy from surrounding RF signals [8]. At present, passive RFID tags are widely used in various fields due to their advantages of durability, low cost and miniaturization.

© Springer Nature Singapore Pte Ltd. 2020
X. Sun et al. (Eds.): ICAIS 2020, CCIS 1253, pp. 290–299, 2020.
https://doi.org/10.1007/978-981-15-8086-4_27

Energy harvest and management circuits play an important role in passive RFID tags, especially in sensor nodes with higher energy requirements, which puts forward higher requirements for the stability of power supply voltage. Passive RFID tags harvest energy from surrounding RF signals and convert them into DC. Due to the large variation of RF energy density in the environment, the RFID sensor node may not work when the RF signal power is very weak. In general, the greater the distance between the tag and the RF transmitter, the less energy the tag captures. In order to enlarge the effective working distance of wireless sensor networks, RFID sensor nodes need to adopt better performance power management technology to maximize power supply capacity.

In [9], a two-stage wake up circuit topology is proposed to supply power to an active RFID tag. The advantage of this topology is that it can effectively reduce power consumption, however, an accurate bandgap reference voltage source is needed. In [10], dual-power-path RF-DC topology is adopted to supply power to the load through two different energy paths. When this topology works, higher input power is required to charge the standby capacitor, and more leakage current is consumed when switching the power supply path. When the transmission power of signal source is limited, ZigBee is used to realize the intermediate transmission function, thus increasing the communication distance [11]. This is a good solution for applications with strict communication distance requirements, but it increases system cost and complexity and is not suitable for low-power application environments. In [12], there are three operating modes for tags based on the communication distance between the tags and reader, and power management is carried out through a wake-up mechanism, which is too much complexity to calculate in tags. A rectifying scheme using diode-connected NMOS rectifier to convert RF signals into DC output is proposed in [13], and the output voltage can be as low as 1 V. A comparator is used in [14] to compare the reference voltage with the rectified output voltage to determine whether to charge the energy storage device, in which the comparator and the current controlled oscillator (CCO) consume a large amount of electric energy. In [15], a rectifier circuit based on an initial Dickson RF-DC is proposed, where an LC oscillator and an ultra-low voltage integrated booster converter were connected to realize the function of energy management. In that work, the circuit must also harvest more energy than consumed, which is suitable for higher input power, but also limit the working distance of the tag.

In this paper, a dual-capacitor power management circuit is proposed to realize the energy control function of the wireless sensor node, in order to obtain enough energy even when the input power is very low, providing stable working voltage for the active circuit, and indirectly improving the power sensitivity of the sensor node.

The remaining parts of the paper are organized as follows: Sect. 2 describes the overall design of the two stages power management. The proposed power management circuit design and simulation are presented in Sect. 3. Section 4 analyzes the power of proposed circuit. Section 5 discusses the conclusion and future research about the proposed power management.

2 Overview of the Proposed Power Management Circuit

The maximum effective radiated power specified by the Federal Communications Commission is 4 W in 902–928 MHz [16]. When the reader transmits fixed RF power, the power received by the tag is inversely proportional to the distance between the tag and the reader. When the tag is close to the reader, it continues to work normally. However, when the tag is far away from the reader, it may not work properly because it may harvest less energy than it consumes. In this paper, a power management circuit based on double capacitors is proposed to solve the problem of the tag not being able to work normally because the energy harvest speed is less than the consumption speed. This circuit can make the tag harvest enough energy before power to the subsequent circuit. The circuit structure and the connection relationship of the front and rear stages are shown in Fig. 1.

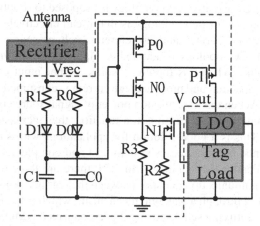

Fig. 1. The structure of tag with proposing power management circuit (Color figure online)

The rectifier converts the energy of the RF signal into DC, the output voltage is V_rec, and the LDO is universal Low Dropout Regulator. Rectifier and LDO can be implemented in a general circuit, so this paper will not discuss them in detail. The Tag Load is the key module of tag energy consumption. The circuit structure proposed in this paper is shown in the red dotted box in Fig. 1.

The energy storage circuit is composed of a diode (D0), resistance (R0) and capacitor (C0), and C0 provides voltage to inverters (PMOS, P0, and NMOS, N0) and MOS switches (PMOS, P1). The wake-up circuit is composed of a diode (D1), resistor (R1), capacitor (C1), inverter and MOS switches (PMOS, P1). After the charging of C0, if the voltage of C1 is higher than the threshold voltage of the inverter, the inverter outputs a low voltage so that P1 can be conducted and C0 begins to supply power to subsequent circuits. If the voltage of C1 is lower than the threshold voltage of the inverter, the inverter outputs a high voltage so that P1 is cut off. The energy-saving circuit includes an MOS switches (NMOS, N1) and a resistor (R2). When the load completes all the functions, C1 is discharged through N1 and R2, which will disconnect P1 and store C0's energy for later use. We need to adjust the charging time of the capacitor so that the charging time of the energy storage capacitor is less than the charging time of the wake-up circuit. This is the core idea of the dual-capacitor power management circuit proposed in this paper. It is necessary to ensure that the energy storage capacitor has enough energy before the wake-up circuit passes through P1. Since the output stage of the rectifier circuit is usually connected with a diode, D0 and D1 can be disconnected to reduce the power consumption. However, if the energy saving function is to be realized, D0 needs to be connected so that C0 will not discharge through N1 in the energy saving mode.

3 Proposed Power Management Circuit Design and Simulation

This section discusses how to select component parameters to make the proposed power management circuit work properly. First, the diode is used to prevent C0 charge to C1, and the threshold voltage of the diode should be as low as possible to reduce circuit power consumption. The diode threshold voltage selected in this design is 0.2034 V, the conduction current is 200 mA, and the reverse breakdown voltage (BV) is 33 V. R0, R1 and R2 are current limiting resistors, respectively 20 ohms, 2000 ohms and 2000 ohms. In order to meet the charging time requirements of energy storage circuit and wake-up circuit, the capacitance values of C0 and C1 are 2 uF and 200 nF, respectively. The product of R0 and C0 determines the charging time of C0, and similarly, the product of R1 and C1 determines the charging time of C1. The calculation formula of capacitor charging time constant is as follows.

$$T = R * C \tag{1}$$

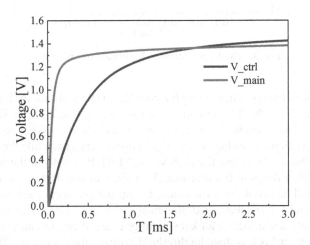

Fig. 2. The charging time of C0 and C1

When the voltage of C1 reaches the threshold voltage of the inverter, the inverter outputs a low voltage to conduct P1. The simulation waveform is shown in the blue waveform in Fig. 3. The V_out is the output voltage of the energy management circuit. At the position indicated by mark M1, the V_out output starts supplying power for the load at high. Because when the V_out is high means the power supply (V_main) has been charged, so as long as the sensor node can charge, it can work normally, which can effectively improve the working distance between the sensor node and the reader. It can be seen from the rise time of V_out and the voltage value of V_ctrl that the voltage value of V_ctrl is about 0.8 v, slightly higher than the threshold value of traditional MOSFET of 0.7 v. In traditional MOSFET circuits, we always hope that the lower the threshold voltage is, the better it can reduce the power consumption of the system. However, this often requires more complex threshold voltage compensation technology. The proposed energy management circuit structure can be implemented by common MOSFET, and the high threshold voltage can reduce R1 value accordingly, thus reducing the power consumption and design complexity of the circuit (Fig. 2).

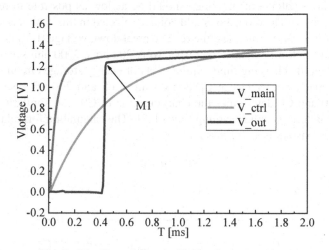

Fig. 3. The V_out becomes high and powers to load

In order to save energy, when the tag has completed all functions, the load can conduct N1 to discharge C1, so that P1 is cut off and saving energy of C0. The working process is shown in Fig. 4. The V_dis is the energy-saving signal from the node's protocol function module. As you can see from Fig. 4, The V_ctrl drops very fast, while the V_main drops slowly. When the V_ctrl is less than 0.8 V, MOSFET P1 works in the truncated zone, and V_out quickly drops to 0. After that, V_main will not decline in theory, and the energy in C0 will be saved, so as to achieve the purpose of energy saving.

When C0 and C1 are recharged, the energy management circuit must be able to function normally again. As we all know, a fully charged circuit can work for a period of time. When V_ctrl is less than the threshold voltage, the energy in C0 can be saved. Then, a DC voltage is once again applied to the V_rec and the energy management circuit continues to be charged. When the V_ctrl voltage rises to about 0.8 v, the V_out quickly becomes a high level and continues to supply power to the load. The process of recharging the energy management circuit is shown in Fig. 5.

The simulation waveform of the continuous charge and discharge process of the energy management circuit is shown in Fig. 6. At 150 ms, when V_rec is changed to 0 V, V_main, V_out, and V_ctrl will decrease. Setting V_dis to high, the V_ctrl voltage drops quickly. When V_ctrl drops below 0.8 V, V_out quickly becomes 0 V, and V_main maintains a constant voltage (ideally).

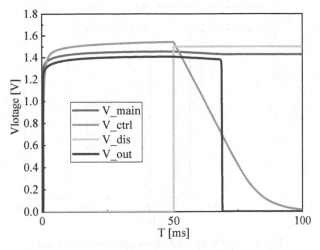

Fig. 4. Energy saving process of the C0

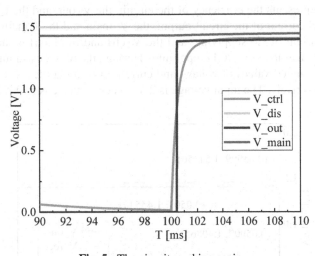

Fig. 5. The circuit working again

4 Power Analysis

Ideally, we don't need components R0, R1, D0, and D1. Therefore, in order to reflect the power consumed by key circuit elements, we calculate the power conversion efficiency of the circuit after charging is completed, so as to indirectly obtain the power consumed by other key elements. The power conversion efficiency formula of the energy management circuit is presented as follows.

$$\eta = \frac{V_{\_out} * I_{\_out}}{V_{\_main} * I_{\_main} + V_{\_out} * I_{\_ctrl}} * 100\% \tag{2}$$

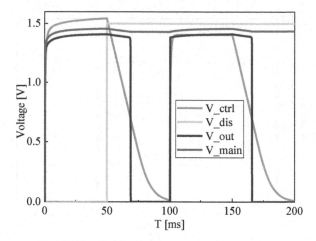

Fig. 6. The circuit continuous operation waveform

Where η represents the efficiency of the circuit, the V_out, and the I_out represent the voltage and current of the circuit output, the V_main and the I_main represent the voltage and current of C0 supplying, and the V_ctrl and the I_ctrl is the voltage and current of the wake-up circuit (C1) supplying. Through the previous simulation, we can obtain the determined values of voltage and current in formula (2), as shown in Fig. 7 and Fig. 8 respectively. The input voltage is 2 V, load resistance is 500 KΩ.

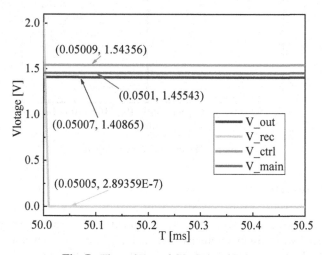

Fig. 7. The voltage of C0, C1, and V_out

In Fig. 8, the I_ctrl is similar to a sawtooth wave, so it's not possible to calculate power directly. However, we can calculate it by calculating the average power in a period.

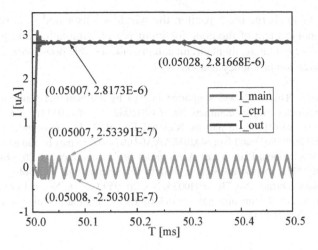

Fig. 8. The current of the varies branch

The calculation process is as follows.

$$V_{\_ctrl} * I_{\_ctrl} = \left(\left(\int_0^{T/2} V_{\_ctrl} * i\right)dt\right)/(T/2) \tag{3}$$

We can calculate T by the numbers in Fig. 8, and the formula is as follows.

$$T = 2 * (t_2 - t_1) \tag{4}$$

Where t_2 is 0.05008 s and t_1 is 0.05007 s, so we can get the T is $2*10^{-5}$ s.

As can be seen from Fig. 8, the current is symmetric and equal in one cycle, therefore, we can calculate the average power consumption of half a cycle. We can also calculate the instantaneous i_ctrl by the numbers in Fig. 8, and the formula is as follows.

$$i\_ctrl = \frac{I_2 - I_1}{t_2 - t_1}t \tag{5}$$

Where I_2 is $-2.50301*10^{-7}$ A and I_1 is $2.53391*10^{-7}$ A, so we can get the formula for i_ctrl as follows.

$$i\_ctrl = -5.03692 * 10^{-2}t \tag{6}$$

According to the formula (2), (3), (4), (5) and (6), we can calculate that the circuit transfer efficiency is 87.43%.

5 Conclusions

The main advantage of the succinct power management circuit proposed in this paper is the dual capacitor operation mode (main capacitor and wake capacitor), when the wake-up event exists, the main capacitor has stored enough energy. Therefore, as long as the rectifier circuit can charge the capacitor, the wireless sensor node can work normally, reducing the requirement of the node for input power. Simulation and power analysis show that the energy management circuit can provide a stable power supply voltage, and the power conversion efficiency is about 87%.

Acknowledgment. This work was supported in part by the National Natural Science Foundation of China under project contracts No. 61701082, No. 61701116, No. 61601093, No. 61971113 and No. 61901095, in part by National Key R&D Program under project contract No. SQ2018YFB180088-02 and No. SQ2018AAA010074-03, in part by Guangdong Provincial Research and Development Plan in Key Areas under project contract No. 2019B010141001 and No. 2019B010142001, in part by Sichuan Provincial Science and Technology Planning Program under project contracts No. 2018HH0034, No. 2019YFG0418, No. 2019YFG0120 and No. 2018JY0246, in part by the fundamental research funds for the Central Universities under project contract No. ZYGX2016J004.

References

1. Finkenzeller, K.: RFID Handbook. Wiley, Chichester (2003)
2. A Power Management System Architecture for LF Passive RFID tags
3. Fang, W., Zhang, W., Zhao, Q., Ji, X., Chen, W., Assefa, B.: Comprehensive analysis of secure data aggregation scheme for industrial wireless sensor network. Comput. Mater. Continua **61**(2), 583–599 (2019)
4. Hussien, F.A., Turker, D.Z., Srinivasan, R., Mobarak, M.S., Cortes, F.P., Sanchez-Sinencio, E.: Design considerations andtradeoffs for passive RFID tags. In: Proceedings of SPIE VLSICircuits and Systems Conference, Sevilla, Spain, 9–11 May 2005
5. Paret, D.: RFID and Contactless Smart Card Applications. Wiley, Chichester (2005)
6. Jin Wang, Yu., Gao, W.L., Wenbing, W., Lim, S.-J.: An asynchronous clustering and mobile data gathering schema based on timer mechanism in wireless sensor networks. Comput. Mater. Continua **58**(3), 711–725 (2019)
7. Gao, D., Zhang, S., Zhang, F., Fan, X., Zhang, J.: Maximum data generation rate routing protocol based on data flow controlling technology for rechargeable wireless sensor networks. Comput. Mater. Continua **59**(2), 649–667 (2019)
8. Han, Y., Zheng, W., Wen, G., et al.: Multi-rate polling: improve the performance of energy harvesting backscatter wireless networks. Cmc-computers Mater. Continua **58**(2), 795–812 (2019)
9. Che, W., et al.: Power management unit for battery assisted passive RFID tag. Electron. Lett. **46**(8), 589–590 (2010)
10. Yi, J., Ki, W.H., Mok, P.K.T., et al.: Dual-power-path RF-DC multi-output power management unit for RFID tags. 200–201 (2009)
11. Chen, L., Ba, H., Heinzelman, W., et al.: RFID range extension with low-power wireless edge devices. In: International Conference on Computing, Networking and Communications, pp. 524–528. IEEE (2013)
12. Janek, A., Steger, C., Preishuber-Pfluegl, J., et al.: Power management strategies for battery-driven higher class UHF RFID tags supported by energy harvesting devices. In: 2007 IEEE Workshop on Automatic Identification Advanced Technologies. IEEE, pp. 122–127 (2007)
13. Hassouni, S, Qjidaa, H.: A design of power management for passive UHF RFID tag in 90 nm CMOS process. In: Intelligent Systems and Computer Vision, pp. 1–4. IEEE (2015)

14. Sun, M., Al-Sarawi, S.F., Ashenden, P., et al.: A fully integrated hybrid power management unit for passive UHF RFID in 130-nm Process. IEEE J. Radio Freq. Ident. **1**, 90–99 (2017)
15. Pasca, M., Catarinucci, L., Colella, R., et al.: A UHF-RFID power management circuit for body sensor networks. In: Microwave Symposium, pp. 1–4. IEEE 2015
16. Sasaki, A., Kotani, K., Ito, T.: Differential-drive CMOS rectifier for UHF RFIDs with 66% PCE at −12 dBm Input[C]. In: 2008 IEEE Asian Solid-State Circuits Conference A-SSCC 2008, pp. 105–108. IEEE (2008)

Survival Analysis of a Stochastic Single-Species System with Diffusion Under the Effect of Environmental Toxins in Polluted Environments

Xiangjun Dai[1], Suli Wang[2], Sheng Liu[1(✉)], and Weizhi Xiong[1]

[1] Tongren University, Tongren 554300, China
liushengtrxy@126.com
[2] Tongren Preschool Education College, Tongren 554300, China

Abstract. In this paper, a stochastic single-species population model with diffusion under the effect of environmental toxins in polluted environments is proposed and studied. Firstly, by constructing a suitable Lyapunov function, the existence and uniqueness of global positive solutions are analyzed, and the stochastic ultimate boundedness of solution is discussed. Finally, sufficient conditions for the stochastic persistence, persistence in the mean and extinction are established, and some simulations are used to illustrate our main results.

Keywords: Environmental pollution · Persistence in the mean · Extinction · Diffusion

1 Introduction

Diffusion is a common phenomenon in the natural environment, it is closely related to human activities, such as, migration of animals. There are many scholars to study the effect of diffusion on population in patch environment by establishing bio-mathematical models [1–5].

In addition, with the rapid development of modern industry and agriculture, a large number of toxic pollutants are transited into the environment, environmental pollution is becoming more and more serious, therefore, More and more scholars pay attention to the problem of environmental pollution [6–8]. And then, due to the influence of human activities, the habitats of many species are divided into several small patches, which pollute many patch environments also. Then, the population of polluted patches will increase their dispersal to other non-polluting or lightly polluted patches. Obviously, it depends on the concentration of toxins in the environment, there are few literatures to discuss the effect of environmental toxins on population diffusion. In this paper, we will consider the effect of environmental toxin concentration on diffusion. We thus propose the following single-population model with diffusion under the effect of environmental toxins:

© Springer Nature Singapore Pte Ltd. 2020
X. Sun et al. (Eds.): ICAIS 2020, CCIS 1253, pp. 300–311, 2020.
https://doi.org/10.1007/978-981-15-8086-4_28

$$
\begin{cases}
\frac{dx_1(t)}{dt} = x_1[r_1 - r_{10}c_{10}(t) - a_1 x_1(t)] + [d_{21}e^{-m_{12}c_{1e}(t)+m_{22}c_{2e}(t)}x_2(t) - d_{12}e^{m_{11}c_{1e}(t)-m_{21}c_{2e}(t)}x_1(t)] \\
\frac{dx_2(t)}{dt} = x_2[r_2 - r_{20}c_{20}(t) - a_2 x_2(t)] + [d_{12}e^{m_{11}c_{1e}(t)-m_{21}c_{2e}(t)}x_1(t) - d_{21}e^{-m_{12}c_{1e}(t)+m_{22}c_{2e}(t)}x_2(t)] \\
\frac{dc_{10}(t)}{dt} = k_1 c_{1e}(t) - (g_1 + m_1)c_{10}(t), \quad \frac{dc_{1e}(t)}{dt} = -h_1 c_{1e}(t) + u_1(t) \\
\frac{dc_{20}(t)}{dt} = k_2 c_{2e}(t) - (g_2 + m_2)c_{20}(t), \quad \frac{dc_{2e}(t)}{dt} = -h_2 c_{2e}(t) + u_2(t)
\end{cases}
$$

$$(1)$$

where $x_i(t)$ represents the population density of patch i at time t, r_i stands for the population growth rate of patch i, $i = 1, 2$. $c_0(t)$ and $c_e(t)$ represent the concentration of toxicant in the organisms and environment at time t, r_{i0} denotes the population x_i response to the toxicant, d_{ij} stands for the dispersal rate of from the i-th patch to j-th patch, $i, j = 1, 2$, $i \neq j$; k_i represents the organism's net uptake rate of toxicant from the environment; $(g_i + m_i)c_{i0}(t)$ denotes the egestion and deputation rates of the toxicant in x_i, and h_i denotes the toxicant's loss rates from the environment by volatilization and so on; $u_i(t)$ stands for the exogenous rate of toxicant input into the environment; Function $e^{m_{ii}c_{ie}(t)}$ represents a "driving force", that is, the population x_i in patch i accelerates to disperse to patch j under the influence of toxins in patch i environment, and function $e^{-m_{ij}c_{ie}(t)}$ denotes a "resistance", namely, the population x_j in patch j slows down the diffusion to patch i under the influence of toxins in patch i environment, where $m_{ij}(0 \leq m_{ij} < 1, i, j = 1, 2.)$ denotes the extent to which toxicant in the patch i affect the dispersal rate of population x_j; $r_1, r_2, a_1, a_2, k_i, g_i, \lambda_{ij}, h_i$ are positive constants.

On the other hand, due to the population growth will inevitably be disturbed by environmental noise, hence, it is very meaningful to study the effect of white noise on population [9–12], for example, Zu, et al. [9] discussed a stochastic logistic population system with dispersal, the stochastic persistence, persistence in the mean and extinction are discussed of the solution to the system. May [13] pointed out that the birth rates, carrying capacity, competition coefficients and other parameters involved in the system can be infected by environmental noise. Motivated by the above works, in this paper, we suppose that the environmental noise mainly affected the growth rate r, according to the central limits theorem, we usually use an average value plus an error term satisfying the standard normal distribution to estimate a value, that is,

$$
r_i \rightarrow r_i + \sigma_i \frac{dB_i(t)}{dt}, \quad i = 1, 2.
$$

where $\frac{dB_i(t)}{dt}$ is a Gaussian white noise process, $B_i(t)$ denotes a standard Brownian motion, σ_i^2 is the intensity of the noise, $i = 1, 2$. Motivated by the facts mentioned above, we will discuss the following stochastic single- population model with diffusion under the effect of environmental toxins in polluted environments:

$$
\begin{cases}
dx_1(t) = x_1[r_1 - r_{10}c_{10}(t) - a_1 x_1(t)]dt \\
\quad + [d_{21}e^{-m_{12}c_{1e}(t)+m_{22}c_{2e}(t)}x_2(t) - d_{12}e^{m_{11}c_{1e}(t)-m_{21}c_{2e}(t)}x_1(t)]dt + \sigma_1 x_1(t)dB_1(t) \\
dx_2(t) = x_2[r_2 - r_{20}c_{20}(t) - a_2 x_2(t)]dt \\
\quad + [d_{12}e^{m_{11}c_{1e}(t)-m_{21}c_{2e}(t)}x_1(t) - d_{21}e^{-m_{12}c_{1e}(t)+m_{22}c_{2e}(t)}x_2(t)]dt + \sigma_2 x_2(t)dB_2(t) \\
dc_{10}(t) = [k_1 c_{1e}(t) - (g_1 + m_1)c_{10}(t)]dt, \ dc_{1e}(t) = [-h_1 c_{1e}(t) + u_1(t)]dt \\
dc_{20}(t) = [k_2 c_{2e}(t) - (g_2 + m_2)c_{20}(t)]dt, \ dc_{2e}(t) = [-h_2 c_{2e}(t) + u_2(t)]dt
\end{cases}
\tag{2}
$$

Remark 1. In model (2), since $c_0(t)$ and $c_e(t)$ are the concentration of toxicant in pollute environment, thus $0 \le c_0(t) \le 1$ and $0 \le c_e(t) \le 1$ must hold for all $t \ge 0$. To this end, we need the following constraints [14],

$$
k_i \le g_i + m_i, \ 0 \le u_i(t) \le u_i < h_i, \ i = 1, 2.
$$

Because the latter four equations of model (2) are linear in $c_{i0}(t)$ and $c_{ie}(t), i = 1, 2.$, and $c_{i0}(t)$ and $c_{ie}(t)$ are bounded and continuous function, we thus need actually only to consider the subsystem (3) consisting of the first two equations in system (2)

$$
\begin{cases}
dx_1(t) = x_1[r_1 - r_{10}c_{10}(t) - a_1 x_1(t)]dt \\
\quad + [d_{21}e^{-m_{12}c_{1e}(t)+m_{22}c_{2e}(t)}x_2(t) - d_{12}e^{m_{11}c_{1e}(t)-m_{21}c_{2e}(t)}x_1(t)]dt + \sigma_1 x_1(t)dB_1(t) \\
dx_2(t) = x_2[r_2 - r_{20}c_{20}(t) - a_2 x_2(t)]dt \\
\quad + [d_{12}e^{m_{11}c_{1e}(t)-m_{21}c_{2e}(t)}x_1(t) - d_{21}e^{-m_{12}c_{1e}(t)+m_{22}c_{2e}(t)}x_2(t)]dt + \sigma_2 x_2(t)dB_2(t)
\end{cases}
\tag{3}
$$

with the initial value $x_i(0) > 0, \ i = 1, 2.$

2 Preliminaries

For convenience, we define some notations.

$$
R_+^n = \left\{(a_1, a_2, \ldots, a_n)^T | a_i > 0, i = 1, 2, \ldots, n\right\}, \ f^*(t) = \sup_{t \ge 0} f(t), \ f_*(t) = \inf_{t \ge 0} f(t),
$$

$$
\langle f(t) \rangle = t^{-1} \int_0^t f(s)ds, \ \breve{a} = \frac{\min\{a_1, a_2\}}{2}, \ \hat{r} = \max\{r_1 - r_{10}(c_{10})_*, r_2 - r_{20}(c_{20})_*\}, \ \sigma^2 = \frac{\sigma_1^2 \sigma_2^2}{\sigma_1^2 + \sigma_2^2},
$$

$$
A = r_1 - r_{10}c_{10}^* - d_{12}e^{m_{11}c_{1e}^* - m_{21}(c_{2e})_*} - 0.5\sigma_1^2, \ B = r_2 - r_{20}c_{20}^* - d_{21}e^{-m_{12}(c_{1e})_* + m_{22}c_{2e}^*} - 0.5\sigma_2^2.
$$

Lemma 2.1 [14]. Suppose that $x(t) \in C[\Omega \times [0, +\infty)]$.

(1) If there exist λ and positive constants λ_0, T such that

$$\ln x(t) \leq \lambda t - \lambda_0 \int_0^t x(s)ds + \sum_{i=1}^n \beta_i B_i(t), \quad t \geq T,$$

where $\beta_i (1 \leq i \leq n)$ is constant, then

$$\begin{cases} \lim\limits_{t \to +\infty} \sup t^{-1} \int_0^t x(s)ds \leq \dfrac{\lambda}{\lambda_0}, & a.s., \ \lambda \geq 0. \\ \lim\limits_{t \to +\infty} x(t) = 0 & a.s., \ \lambda < 0. \end{cases}$$

(2) If there exist positive constants λ, λ_0 and T such that

$$\ln x(t) \geq \lambda t - \lambda_0 \int_0^t x(s)ds + \sum_{i=1}^n \beta_i B_i(t), \ t \geq T.$$

Then $\lim\limits_{t \to +\infty} \inf t^{-1} \int_0^t x(s)ds \geq \frac{\lambda}{\lambda_0}$, a.s.

Lemma 2.2 [15]. Stochastic single population system $dx = x[r - ax]dt + \sigma x(t)dB(t)$, where r, a and σ are positive constants, if $r > 0.5\sigma^2$, have

$$\lim_{t \to +\infty} \langle x(t) \rangle = \frac{r - 0.5\sigma^2}{a}, \quad \lim_{t \to +\infty} \frac{\ln x(t)}{t} = 0, \ a.s.$$

3 Main Results

Theorem 3.1. For any given initial value $(x_1(0), x_2(0))^T \in R_+^2$, there exists a unique global positive solution $x(t) = (x_1(t), x_2(t))^T$ to the first two equations of system (2), and the solution will remain in R_+^2 almost surely.

Proof. The proof is a similar to [15] by defining function

$$V(x) = \sum_{i=1}^2 (x_i - 1 - \ln x_i).$$

Applying *Itô's* formula, have

$$dV(x) = \sum_{i=1}^2 \left((1 - \frac{1}{x_i})dx_i + \frac{1}{2x_i^2}(dx_i)^2 \right) = LV(x)dt + \sum_{i=1}^2 \sigma_i(x_i - 1)dB_i(t),$$

where

$$LV(x) = \left\{(x_1 - 1)[r_1 - r_{10}c_{10}(t) - a_1x_1 + d_{21}e^{-m_{12}c_{1e}(t)+m_{22}c_{2e}(t)}\frac{x_2}{x_1} - d_{12}e^{m_{11}c_{1e}(t)-m_{21}c_{2e}(t)}] + 0.5\sigma_1^2\right\}$$

$$+ \left\{(x_2 - 1)[r_2 - a_2x_2 + d_{12}e^{m_{11}c_{1e}(t)-m_{21}c_{2e}(t)}\frac{x_1}{x_2} - d_{21}e^{-m_{12}c_{1e}(t)+m_{22}c_{2e}(t)}] + 0.5\sigma_2^2\right\}$$

$$\leq \left\{(r_1 + a_1 + d_{12}e^{m_{11}c_{1e}^* - m_{21}(c_{2e})*})x_1 - a_1x_1^2 + 0.5\sigma_1^2 + r_0c_0(t) + d_{12}e^{m_{11}c_{1e}^* - m_{21}(c_{2e})*}\right\}$$

$$+ \left\{(r_2 + a_2 + d_{21}e^{-m_{12}(c_{1e})*+m_{22}c_{2e}^*})x_2 - a_2x_2^2 + 0.5\sigma_2^2 + d_{21}e^{-m_{12}(c_{1e})*+m_{22}c_{2e}^*}\right\},$$

obviously, there is a $K > 0$, such that $LV(x) \leq K$. The next proof is similar to [ ], hence it is omitted.   ∎

Lemma 3.1. Let $(x_1(t), x_2(t))^T$ is the solution of system (3) with the initial value $(x_1(0), x_2(0))^T \in R_+^2$, there exists a positive constant $L(p)$, have

$$\lim_{t \to +\infty} \sup E(\sum_{i=1}^{2} x_i(t))^p \leq L(p)$$

Proof. Defining function $V(x) = \left(\sum_{i=1}^{2} x_i(t)\right)^p$, applying Itô's formula, have

$$dV(x) = p\left(\sum_{i=1}^{2} x_i\right)^{p-1} d\left(\sum_{i=1}^{2} x_i\right) + \frac{p(p-1)}{2}\left(\sum_{i=1}^{2} x_i\right)^{p-2}\left(d\left(\sum_{i=1}^{2} x_i\right)\right)^2$$

$$= LV(x)dt + p\left(\sum_{i=1}^{2} x_i\right)^{p-1}\sum_{i=1}^{2} \sigma_i x_i dB_i(t) \qquad (4)$$

where

$$LV(x) = p\left(\sum_{i=1}^{2} x_i\right)^{p-1}(r_1 - r_{10}c_{10} - a_1x_1 + r_2 - r_{20}c_{20} - a_2x_2) + \frac{p(p-1)}{2}\left(\sum_{i=1}^{2} x_i\right)^{p-2}\sum_{i=1}^{2} \sigma_i^2 x_i^2,$$

$$\leq \left(\sum_{i=1}^{2} x_i\right)^p\left(\alpha - \beta\sum_{i=1}^{2} x_i\right)dt$$

where $\alpha = p[\max\{r_1, r_2\} + 0.5(p+1)\max\{\sigma_1^2, \sigma_2^2\}]$ and $\beta = \frac{p\min\{a_1, a_2\}}{2}$.

Integrating on both sides of the above inequality (4) from 0 to t and take expectations, have

$$EV(x(t)) - EV(x(0)) \leq p\alpha\int_0^t E\left(\sum_{i=1}^{2} x_i(s)\right)^p ds - p\beta\int_0^t E\left(\sum_{i=1}^{2} x_i(s)\right)^{p+1} ds.$$

Let $z(t) = E\left(\sum_{i=1}^{2} x_i\right)^p$, have $\frac{dz(t)}{dt} \leq pz(t)(\alpha - \beta z^{\frac{1}{p}}(t))$, by comparison theorem,

have $z^*(t) \leq \left(\frac{\beta}{\alpha}\right)^p$, that is, $\lim_{t\to\infty} \sup E(\sum_{i=1}^{2} x_i(t))^p \leq \left(\frac{\beta}{\alpha}\right)^p = L(p)$.

This ends the proof. ∎

Theorem 3.2. System (2) is stochastically ultimate bounded, that is, for all $\varepsilon > 0$, there is a positive constant $\delta = \delta(\varepsilon)$, for any given initial value $(x_1(0), x_2(0))^T \in R_+^2$, have

$$\lim_{t\to+\infty} \sup P(|x(t)| = \sqrt{x_1^2 + x_2^2} > \delta) < \varepsilon.$$

Proof. By Lemma 3.1 and Chebyshev's inequality it is easy to obtain, hence it is omitted in here. ∎

Next, we will mainly discuss the extinction and the persistence in the mean of system (2).

Let us consider the following auxiliary system:

$$\begin{cases} dX_1(t) = X_1[r_1 - r_{10}c_{10}^* - d_{12}e^{m_{11}c_{1e}^* - m_{21}(c_{2e})_*} - a_1X_1(t)]dt + \sigma_1X_1(t)dB_1(t) \\ dX_2(t) = X_2[r_2 - r_{20}c_{20}^* - d_{21}e^{-m_{12}(c_{1e})_* + m_{22}c_{2e}^*} - a_2X_2(t)]dt + \sigma_2X_2(t)dB_2(t) \\ X_1(0) = x_1(0), X_2(0) = x_2(0). \end{cases}$$

$$(5)$$

By comparison theorem of stochastic differential equations, have

$$X_i(t) \leq x_i(t), \quad i = 1, 2.$$

Lemma 3.2 [9]. Suppose $A > 0$, $B > 0$ are hold, there are positive constants H_1, H_2 and θ, such that

$$r_1 - r_{10}c_{10}^* - d_{12}e^{m_{11}c_{1e}^* - m_{21}(c_{2e})_*} - 0.5(1 + \theta)\sigma_1^2 > 0, \quad r_2 - r_{20}c_{20}^* - d_{21}e^{-m_{12}(c_{1e})_* + m_{22}c_{2e}^*} - 0.5(\theta + 1)\sigma_2^2 > 0$$

and satisfy

$$\lim_{t\to+\infty} \sup E\left[\frac{1}{x_i^\theta(t)}\right] \leq \lim_{t\to+\infty} \sup E\left[\frac{1}{X_i^\theta(t)}\right] \leq H_i \quad a.s., i = 1, 2.$$

$$\lim_{t\to+\infty} \inf \frac{\ln x_i(t)}{\ln t} \geq \lim_{t\to+\infty} \inf \frac{\ln X_i(t)}{\ln t} \geq -\frac{1}{\theta} \quad a.s., i = 1, 2.$$

Theorem 3.2. If $A > 0$ and $B > 0$, system (2) is stochastically permanent.

Proof. By Lemma 3.2, there are positive constants H_1, H_2 and θ, such that

$$\limsup_{t\to+\infty} E\left[\frac{1}{x_i^\theta(t)}\right] \le \limsup_{t\to+\infty} E\left[\frac{1}{X_i^\theta(t)}\right] \le H_i \ a.s., \ i=1,2.,$$

for all $\varepsilon > 0$, let $\chi_i = \left(\frac{\varepsilon}{H_i}\right)^{\frac{1}{\theta}}$, we easy obtain that

$$P(x_i(t) < \chi_i) = P\left(\frac{1}{x_i^\theta} > \frac{1}{\chi_i^\theta}\right) \le \frac{E\left(x_i^{-\theta}\right)}{\chi_i^{-\theta}} \le \varepsilon, \ i=1,2.$$

Hence, $\limsup\limits_{t\to+\infty} P(x_i(t) < \chi_i) \le \varepsilon$, it is easy imply that,

$$\liminf_{t\to+\infty} P(x_i(t) \ge \chi_i) \ge 1-\varepsilon, \ i=1,2.$$

By Theorem 3.2, there exists $\delta_i > 0$ such that

$$\liminf_{t\to+\infty} P(x_i(t) \le \delta_i) \le 1-\varepsilon, \ i=1,2.$$

The proof is complete.   ∎

Lemma 3.3. Let $(x_1(t), x_2(t))^T$ is the solution of system (2) for any given initial value $(x_1(0), x_2(0))^T \in R_+^2$, If $A > 0, B > 0$, have

$$\lim_{t\to+\infty} \frac{\ln x_i(t)}{t} = 0, \ i=1,2, \ a.s.$$

Proof. Since $A > 0, B > 0$, by Lemma 2.1 and Eq. (5), have

$$\lim_{t\to+\infty} \langle X_1(t)\rangle = \frac{A}{a_1} = L_1, \ \lim_{t\to+\infty} \langle X_2(t)\rangle = \frac{B}{a_2} = L_2, \ \lim_{t\to+\infty} \frac{\ln X_i(t)}{t} = 0, \ a.s., \ i = 1, 2.$$

By virtue of comparison theorem, have $x_i(t) \ge X_i(t)$, thus,

$$\liminf_{t\to+\infty} \langle x_i(t)\rangle \ge L_i, \tag{6}$$

$$\liminf_{t\to+\infty} \frac{\ln x_i(t)}{t} \ge 0, \ i=1,2, \ a.s. \tag{7}$$

Defining function $V(x) = \ln(x_1(t) + x_2(t))$, applying *Itô's* formula

$$dV(x) = \frac{1}{x_1 + x_2} d(x_1 + x_2) - \frac{1}{2(x_1 + x_2)^2}(d(x_1 + x_2))^2$$

$$= \left(\frac{x_1[r_1 - r_{10}c_{10} - a_1 x_1] + x_2[r_2 - r_{20}c_{20} - a_2 x_2]}{x_1 + x_2} - \frac{\sigma_1^2 x_1^2 + \sigma_2^2 x_2^2}{2(x_1 + x_2)^2}\right)dt + \frac{\sigma_1 x_1 dB_1(t) + \sigma_2 x_2 dB_2(t)}{x_1 + x_2}$$

$$\le \left(\hat{r} - \check{a}(x_1 + x_2) - \frac{\sigma_1^2 x_1^2 + \sigma_2^2 x_2^2}{2(x_1 + x_2)^2}\right)dt + \frac{\sigma_1 x_1 dB_1(t) + \sigma_2 x_2 dB_2(t)}{x_1 + x_2}. \tag{8}$$

Applying *Itô's* formula for $e^t V(x)$, we have

$$de^t V(x) \leq e^t \left(V(x) + \hat{r} - \breve{a}(x_1 + x_2) - \frac{\sigma_1^2 x_1^2 + \sigma_2^2 x_2^2}{2(x_1 + x_2)^2} \right) dt + e^t \frac{\sigma_1 x_1 dB_1(t) + \sigma_2 x_2 dB_2(t)}{x_1 + x_2}$$

Integrating on both sides of the above inequality from 0 to t, have

$$e^t V(x(t)) \leq V(x(0)) + \int_0^t e^s \left(\ln(x_1(s) + x_2(s)) + \hat{r} - \breve{a}(x_1(s) + x_2(s)) \right) ds$$

$$- \int_0^t e^s \frac{\sigma_1^2 x_1^2(s) + \sigma_2^2 x_2^2(s)}{2(x_1(s) + x_2(s))^2} ds + M_1(t) + M_2(t), \tag{9}$$

where

$$M_1(t) = \int_0^t \frac{\sigma_1 e^s x_1(s)}{x_1(s) + x_2(s)} dB_1(s), \quad M_2(t) = \int_0^t \frac{\sigma_2 e^s x_2(s)}{x_1(s) + x_2(s)} dB_2(s).$$

Because $\breve{a} > 0$, there is a positive constant K, such that

$$\ln(x_1(t) + x_2(t)) + \hat{r} - \breve{a}(x_1(t) + x_2(t)) \leq K. \tag{10}$$

Let $M(t) = M_1(t) + M_2(t)$, It is easy to see that $M(t)$ is a local martingale, thus, the quadratic form of $M(t)$ is

$$\langle M(t), M(t) \rangle = \int_0^t e^{2s} \frac{\sigma_1^2 x_1^2(s) + \sigma_2^2 x_2^2(s)}{(x_1(s) + x_2(s))^2} ds.$$

By virtue of the exponential martingale inequality, for any positive constants T, α and β, we have

$$P \left\{ \sup_{0 \leq t \leq T} \left[M(t) - \frac{\alpha}{2} \langle M(t), M(t) \rangle \right] > \beta \right\} \leq e^{-\alpha\beta},$$

choose $T = k$, $\alpha = e^{-k}$ and $\beta = \theta e^k \ln k$, have

$$P \left\{ \sup_{0 \leq t \leq T} \left[M(t) - \frac{e^{-k}}{2} \langle M(t), M(t) \rangle \right] > \theta e^k \ln k \right\} \leq k^{-\theta},$$

where $k \in N$ and $\theta > 1$.

Because $\sum_{k=1}^{\infty} k^{-\theta} < +\infty$, by virtue of Borel-Cantalli Lemma, for almost all $\omega \in \Omega$, there is a $k_1(\omega) > 0$, for all $k \geq k_1(\omega)$,

$$M(t) \leq \frac{e^{-k}}{2} \langle M(t), M(t) \rangle + \theta e^k \ln k, \ 0 \leq t \leq k.$$

By inequality (9) and (10), for all $k \geq k_1(\omega)$, we can obtain that

$$e^t V(x(t)) \leq V(x(0)) + K(e^t - 1) - \int_0^t e^s \frac{\sigma_1^2 x_1^2(s) + \sigma_2^2 x_2^2(s)}{2(x_1(s) + x_2(s))^2} ds + \int_0^t e^s e^{s-k} \frac{\sigma_1^2 x_1^2(s) + \sigma_2^2 x_2^2(s)}{2(x_1(s) + x_2(s))^2} ds + \theta e^k \ln k$$

$$\leq V(x(0)) + K(e^t - 1) + \theta e^k \ln k, \ 0 \leq t \leq k.$$

Then, for all $t \in [k-1, k]$, have

$$\frac{\ln(x_1(t) + x_2(t))}{t} \leq \frac{\ln(x_1(0) + x_2(0))}{e^t t} + \frac{K(e^t - 1)}{te^t} + \frac{\theta e \ln k}{(k-1)},$$

when $k \to +\infty \ (t \to +\infty)$,

$$\lim_{t \to +\infty} \sup t^{-1} \ln(x_1(t) + x_2(t)) \leq 0, \ a.s.$$

so

$$\lim_{t \to +\infty} \sup \frac{\ln x_i(t)}{t} \leq \lim_{t \to +\infty} \sup \frac{\ln(x_1(t) + x_2(t))}{t} \leq 0, \ i = 1, 2. \ a.s. \qquad (11)$$

By virtue of (7) and (11), we get

$$\lim_{t \to +\infty} t^{-1} \ln x_i(t) = 0, \ i = 1, 2, \ a.s.$$

The proof is complete. ■

Theorem 3.3. Let $(x_1(t), x_2(t))^T$ is solution of system (2) with any initial value $(x_1(0), x_2(0))^T \in R_+^2$. If $A > 0, B > 0$, then

$$L_i \leq \langle x_i(t) \rangle_* \leq \langle x_i(t) \rangle^* \leq M, \ i = 1, 2., \ a.s.$$

where $L_1 = \frac{A}{a_1}, L_2 = \frac{A}{a_2}, M = \frac{\hat{r} - 0.5\sigma^2}{\breve{a}}$. That is, system (2) is persistent in the mean.

Proof. Let $V(x) = \ln(x_1 + x_2)$, by (8), we get

$$d \ln(x_1 + x_2) \leq \left(\left(\hat{r} - \frac{\sigma^2}{2} \right) - \breve{a}(x_1 + x_2) \right) dt + \frac{\sigma_1 x_1 dB_1(t) + \sigma_2 x_2 dB_2(t)}{x_1 + x_2}.$$

Integrating on both sides of the above inequality from 0 to t, have

$$t^{-1} \ln(x_1 + x_2) \leq \left(\hat{r} - 0.5\sigma^2 - \breve{a} \langle x_1 + x_2 \rangle \right) dt + t^{-1} M(t), \qquad (12)$$

where $M(t) = \int_0^t \frac{\sigma_1 x_1(s) dB_1(s) + \sigma_2 x_2(s) dB_2(s)}{x_1(s) + x_2(s)}$, the quadratic form of $M(t)$ is

$$\langle M(t), M(t) \rangle = \int_0^t \frac{\sigma_1^2 x_1^2(s) + \sigma_2^2 x_2^2(s)}{(x_1(s) + x_2(s))^2} ds \leq \max\{\sigma_1^2, \sigma_2^2\} t,$$

According to the strong law larger numbers theorem, have $\lim\limits_{t\to+\infty} t^{-1}M(t) = 0$, $a.s.$
By virtue of (12), we can observed that

$$\left[t^{-1}\ln(x_1(t)+x_2(t))\right]^* + \breve{a}\langle x_1(t)+x_2(t)\rangle^* \le \left(\hat{r}-0.5\sigma^2\right), \tag{13}$$

by Lemma 3.3, we get $\langle x_i(t)\rangle^* \le \langle x_1(t)+x_2(t)\rangle^* \le \frac{\hat{r}-0.5\sigma^2}{\tilde{a}}$, $i = 1, 2$. According to the proof of Lemma 3.3, have

$$L_1 \le \langle x_1(t)\rangle_* \le \langle x_1(t)\rangle^* \le M, \ L_2 \le \langle x_1(t)\rangle_* \le \langle x_1(t)\rangle^* \le M.$$

Theorem 3.4. If $\hat{r} - 0.5\sigma^2 < 0$, population $x_i (i = 1, 2.)$ will goes to extinction almost surely, namely, $\lim\limits_{t\to+\infty} x_i(t) = 0$, $a.s.$, $i = 1, 2$.

Proof. By (13), we get

$$\lim\limits_{t\to+\infty}\sup\left[t^{-1}\ln(x_1(t)+x_2(t))\right] \le \left(\hat{r}-0.5\sigma^2\right) < 0, \ a.s.,$$

hence, $\lim\limits_{t\to+\infty} x_i(t) = 0$, $a.s.$, $i = 1, 2$. ■

4 Simulation

We use the famous Milstein method developed in [16] to illustrate our mainly results. We consider the discretization equation:

$$\begin{cases} x_{1,k+1} = x_{1,k} + x_{1,k}[r_1 - r_{10}c_{10,k} - a_1x_{1,k}]\Delta t + \left[d_{21}e^{-m_{12}c_{1e,k}+m_{22}c_{2e,k}}x_{2,k} - d_{12}e^{-m_{21}c_{2e,k}+m_{11}c_{1e,k}}x_{1,k}\right]\Delta t \\ \quad + \sigma_1 x_{1,k}\sqrt{\Delta t}\xi_k + 0.5\sigma_1^2 x_{1,k}^2(\xi_k^2 - 1)\Delta t \\ x_{2,k+1} = x_{2,k} + x_{2,k}[r_2 - r_{20}c_{20,k} - a_2x_{2,k}]\Delta t + \left[d_{12}e^{-m_{21}c_{2e,k}+m_{11}c_{1e,k}}x_{1,k} - d_{21}e^{-m_{12}c_{1e,k}+m_{22}c_{2e,k}}x_{2,k}\right]\Delta t \\ \quad + \sigma_2 x_{2,k}\sqrt{\Delta t}\eta_k + 0.5\sigma_2^2 x_{2,k}^2(\eta_k^2 - 1)\Delta t \end{cases}$$

Let $r_1 = 0.5$, $r_2 = 0.6$, $a_1 = 0.4$, $a_2 = 0.3$, $r_{10} = 0.3$, $r_{20} = 0.2$, $d_{12} = 0.3$, $d_{21} = 0.4$, $m_{11} = 0.3$, $c_{10}(t) = 0.3+0.2\sin t$, $c_{20}(t) = 0.3+0.1\sin t$, $c_{1e}(t) = 0.3+0.1\cos t$, $c_{2e}(t) = 0.3+0.1\cos t$, $m_{12} = 0.2$, $m_{21} = 0.2$, $m_{22} = 0.3$. The only difference of Fig. 1 and 2 is that the values of σ_1 and σ_2 are different.
In Fig. 1, we choose $\sigma_1 = 0.2$, $\sigma_2 = 0.2$, then

$$A = r_1 - r_{10}c_{10}^* - d_{12}e^{m_{11}c_{1e}^* - m_{21}(c_{2e})_*} - 0.5\sigma_1^2 = 0.0146 > 0,$$

$$B = r_2 - r_{20}c_{20}^* - d_{21}e^{-m_{12}(c_{1e})_* + m_{22}c_{2e}^*} - 0.5\sigma_2^2 = 0.0579 > 0.$$

By virtue of Theorem 3.3, population x and y are persistent in the mean, see Fig. 1.
In Fig. 2, we choose $\sigma_1 = 1.4$, $\sigma_2 = 1.5$, we have $\hat{r} - 0.5\sigma^2 = -0.0538 < 0$, by Theorem 3.4, the population x and y will be die out, see Fig. 2.

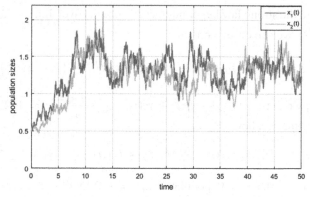

Fig. 1. Solution of system (2) of $\sigma_1 = \sigma_2 = 0.2$, $(x_1(0), x_2(0))^T = (0.5, 0.5)^T$.

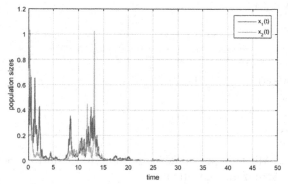

Fig. 2. Solution of system (2) of $\sigma_1 = 1.4$, $\sigma_2 = 1.5$, $(x_1(0), x_2(0))^T = (0.5, 0.5)^T$.

5 Conclusions

In the natural ecosystem, due to the pollution of the patch environment, some species of the contaminated patches will spread to the lightly polluted patch, hence, it is very significance to study the effects of environmental toxins on population diffusion in polluted patch environment. In this paper, we have studied a stochastic single- population model with diffusion under the effect of environmental toxins in polluted environments. If $A > 0, B > 0$, the population is stochastic persistent and persistent in the mean (see Fig. 1). If $\hat{r} - 0.5\sigma^2 < 0$, the single-species will dies out (see Fig. 2).

There are many interesting question for this system need to further investigation, such as, stationary distribution of this system. And, one may establish more realistic but complex models. We leave these questions for future consideration.

Acknowledgments. This work was supported by the Cooperation Agreement Project by the Department of Science and Technology of Guizhou Province of China (LH [2016]7300), the nature and science fund from the Education Department of Guizhou province the Innovation Group Major Research Program Funded by Guizhou Provincial Education Department (KY [2016]051, ([2015]456).

References

1. Levin, S.A.: Dispersion and population interactions. Am. Nat. **108**(960), 207–228 (1974)
2. Freedman, H.I., Takeuchi, Y.: Global stability and predator dynamics in a model of prey dispersal in a patchy environment. Nonlinear Anal. Theory Methods Appl. **13**(8), 993–1002 (1989)
3. Allen, L.: Persistence and extinction in single-species reaction-diffusion models. Bull. Math. Biol. **45**(2), 209–227 (1983)
4. Cui, J., Takeuchi, Y., Lin, L.: Permanence and extinction for dispersal population systems. J. Math. Anal. Appl. **298**, 73–93 (2004)
5. Zhu, C., Yin, G.: Asymptotic properties of hybrid diffusion systems. SLAM J. Control Optim. **46**, 1155–1179 (2007)
6. Hallam, T.G., Clark, C.E., Jordan, G.S.: Effects of toxicants on populations: a qualitative approach II. First order kinetics. J. Math. Biol. **18**, 25–37 (1983)
7. Hallam, T.G., Deluna, J.T.: Effects of toxicants on populations: a qualitative approach III. Environment and food chain pathways. J. Theor. Biol. **109**, 411–429 (1984)
8. Liu, M., Wang, K., Liu, X.W.: Long term behaviors of stochastic single-species growth models in a polluted environment II. Appl. Math. Model. **35**, 752–762 (2011)
9. Zu, L., Jiang, D.Q., Donal, O.: Stochastic permanence, stationary distribution and extinction of a single-species nonlinear diffusion system with random perturbation. Abstr. Appl. Anal. Article ID 320460, 14 (2014)
10. Aadil, L., Adel, S.: A note on stochastic Gilpin-Ayala population model with dispersal. Differ. Equ. Dyn. Syst. **25**(3), 417–430 (2013)
11. Zhang, L., Teng, Z.D.: The dynamical behavior of a predator–prey system with Gompertz growth function and impulsive dispersal of prey between two patches. Math. Methods Appl. Sci. **39**(13), 3623–3639 (2016)
12. Zou, X.L., Fan, D.J., Wang, K.: Effects of dispersal for a logistic growth population in random environments. Abstr. Appl. Anal. Article ID 912579, 9 (2013)
13. May, R.M.: Stability and Complexity in Model Ecosystems. Princeton University Press, Princeton (2001)
14. Liu, M., Wang, K.: Survival analysis of stochastic single-species population models in polluted environments. Ecol. Model. **220**, 1347–1357 (2009)
15. Liu, M., Wang, K., Wu, Q.: Survival analysis of stochastic competitive models in a polluted environment and stochastic competitive exclusion principle. Bull. Math. Biol. **73**(9), 1969–2012 (2011)
16. Higham, D.J.: An algorithmic introduction to numerical simulation of stochastic differential equations. SIAM Rev. **3**(43), 525–546 (2001)

Precipitation Phase Inversion Algorithm for Extremely Unbalanced Data

Shengchun Wang[1], Chengcheng Jiang[1], Jingui Huang[1(✉)], Jinyu Xu[2], Hong Deng[1], Long Huang[1], and Xiaozhong Yu[1]

[1] College of Information Science and Engineering, Hunan Normal University,
Changsha 410081, China
hjg@hunnu.edu.cn
[2] Hunan Meteorological Observatory, Changsha, China

Abstract. Precipitation phase inversion has important significance for agricultural production, flood mitigation, human activities and power. Due to the high uncertainty of precipitation phase, traditional physical models and, statistical models are difficult to meet the requirements of real-time and accuracy. In the actual inversion process, there are very few samples of a few types, which leads to the poor inversion of a few classes. Aiming at the challenge of data imbalance in precipitation phase inversion, this paper proposes an improved hybrid sampling method ADASYN Borderline-Tomek Link, which uses boundary location and reduces redundancy for most types of large-density regions. After a comparison of several sets of experiments, a few types of G-mean and F-value have been improved, which effectively improved the data imbalance in precipitation phase inversion.

Keywords: Precipitation phase · Minority category · Mixed sampling · Inversion

1 Introduction

The precipitation phase state inversion problem [1] is to infer the precipitation phase state from the data of known meteorological elements. The supercomputer of the Central Meteorological Observatory predicts the current or future time meteorological data in various regions of the country. The meteorological element data used this time are various meteorological factors that greatly affect the phase of precipitation, mainly including temperature, atmospheric pressure, and humidity at different altitudes, Wind speed, wind direction, cloud cover, dew point, etc. [2]. The model in this paper uses machine learning to invert the meteorological element data, and finally obtains the precipitation phase classification of each region [3].

Precipitation phase inversion is a multi-classification problem. The main difficulty is that the data of each type is extremely unbalanced, and the sample size of a few types is very small. When the machine learning classification is performed, the accuracy of the minority samples is extremely low. this paper starts to study the processing methods of unbalanced data [4] and improve the accuracy of a few samples.

© Springer Nature Singapore Pte Ltd. 2020
X. Sun et al. (Eds.): ICAIS 2020, CCIS 1253, pp. 312–323, 2020.
https://doi.org/10.1007/978-981-15-8086-4_29

Chawla [5] et al. proposed the SMOTE algorithm. The algorithm makes the data set balance by artificially constructing a few kinds of samples. Since this method does not consider the phenomenon of uneven distribution within a few class samples, they later consider the phenomenon of uneven distribution within a few class samples, they later proposed ADASYN [6], an adaptive integrated oversampling algorithm, based on the SMOTE method. According to the proportion of the nearest neighbor majority samples of a few class samples, the number of synthetic samples is assigned, and the higher the proportion of samples, the more synthetic samples are generated. However, because these algorithms only oversample a small number of samples, it may eventually lead to over-fitting in the sample set classification. Under sampling ENN [18] and Tomek Link [6] methods can effectively reduce the repeated samples among classes, the phenomenon of over-fitting, but will make the data set samples lose important information, the combination of these two methods [7, 8] was proposed, Gustavo [9] and others proposed SMOTE+Tomek Line and SMOTE+ENN combination method to solve the data imbalance problem.

Based on the idea of boundary location and mixed sampling, this paper proposes the ADASYN Borderline-Tomek Link algorithm, combined with the ADASYN algorithm and the Borderline-Tomek Link algorithm to improve and improve the classification performance of minority species and prevent the impact of severe weather on human life and such as traffic [10].

2 Related Work

2.1 Introduction to Rainfall Phase Data Set

This precipitation phase data set uses some meteorological data samples from the China Meteorological Observatory for the past two years, which is more representative than other scholars' small-scale data samples [11].

The statistics of the precipitation phase data are shown in Table 1. The precipitation phase is divided into six categories: rain, snow, sleet, freezing rain, ice particles and other weather. Among them, sleet, freezing rain and ice particles are three types of sample data. Very few, for a small number of samples, while rain, snow and other weather are mostly samples. The data set is described in Table 2, where the imbalance between most class samples and minority samples exceeds 300:1.

Table 1. Statistics by category

Classification	Rain	Snow	Rain and snow mixed	Frozen rain	Ice particles	Other weather
Quantity	36253	5094	588	252	73	308697

Table 2. Dataset description

Data set	Dimension	Majority classes/minority classes	Imbalance ratio
Rainfall phase	38	308697/913	338.11281

2.2 Processing Method for Local Density and Density Reduction in Spatial Domain

This article uses the Euclidean distance (L2). Let the sample space X be a subspace of the n-dimensional real vector space Rn. For any two n-dimensional vector $x = (x_1, x_2, \ldots, x_n)$, $y == (y_1, y_2, \ldots, y_n)$ s, in X, the Euclidean distance d between them is defined as:

$$d(x,y) = |x - y| = \left(\sum\nolimits_{i=1}^{n} (x_i - y_j)^2\right)^{1/2} \tag{1}$$

Suppose the sample to be classified is x Î X, and its k-nearest neighbor refers to the set of k samples closest to it. This set is called the spatial domain, that is, the n-dimensional hypersphere spatial domain, which is recorded as. The hypersphere radius r is expressed as $\omega(x, k)$

$$r = \max_{y \in \omega(x,k)} |y - x| \tag{2}$$

The local density of each category in the spatial domain can be calculated by the average number of samples per unit area formed by the category in the spatial domain, and the category is c_i used. The number of neighbor samples in the sample set is Num (x_i, r, c_i). Then, the density of each category in the spatial domain $\omega (x_i, k, r)$ is:

$$\rho(x, k, c_i) = \frac{Num(x, r, c_i)}{k} \tag{3}$$

Since the local density is generally different in each class space domain, in order to reduce the local high-density category, we uniformly divide the high-density area pass. When the local density is greater than the overall density of this category, we judge it to be a high-density region $\rho_w < \rho_p$, define a collection Q of high-density regions.

To prevent the data sample category from being excessively reduced, a class imbalance degree $IB = \frac{M_s}{M_L}$ is introduced, where $IB \in (0, 1]$, M_s is the majority sample size, and M_L is the minority sample number.

2.3 Basic Methods for Unbalanced Data Set Classification

In solving the problem of unbalanced data classification, many experts have proposed improvements based on data and algorithms. For the improvement of the algorithm, there are classifier integration methods [1, 12, 13], cost-sensitive methods [14], feature selection [15, 16] methods and so on. The integrated learning method improves the generalization performance of the classifier by integrating the classification results of multiple base classifiers in a specific way, thereby obtaining a higher classification effect. The basic idea of the cost-sensitive method is to introduce a cost-sensitive factor based on the traditional learning algorithm, so that the classifier based on the minimum error rate is transformed into a cost-sensitive classifier based on the least cost. Feature selection can eliminate redundant features, thereby reducing the number of features and improving the accuracy of the model. For data, the methods are under sampling method [17], over sampling method [18], mixed sampling method [19], etc. Under sampling method improves the accuracy of a small number of samples by regularly reducing the number of majority samples. In contrast to under sampling method, oversampling increases the number of samples of a few classes to improve the classification performance of a small number of samples. Hybrid sampling method is a combination of under sampling and oversampling. When the ratio of positive and negative samples is large [20], the single sampling method is not effective. This paper proposes the ADASYN Borderline-Tomek Link hybrid sampling method to solve the unbalanced data problem.

2.4 ADASYN

The ADASYN algorithm is an adaptive oversampling algorithm. The method adaptively synthesizes a small number of data samples according to the distribution probability of a few types of data samples, and then adds the synthesized new samples to the original data set, so that the various data samples reach a relative balance to solve the data imbalance problem.

Input: Assume that the entire training sample set D contains m samples $\{x_i, y_i\}$, i = 1, 2, ..., m. Where is x_i a sample of the n-dimensional feature space X, $y_i \in Y = \{1, 2, 3, 4, 5, 6\}$ is a class label, $y_i = 2, 3, 4$ are small class samples, $y_i = 1, 4, 6$ are majority Class sample. Here, use m_s and to m_l indicate the number of samples of minority and x_i majority classes, respectively. Therefore, there are $m_s \leq m_l$ and $m_l + m_s = m$.

The algorithm steps are as follows:

Step 1: Calculate the class imbalance, $d = m_s/m_l$, $d \in (0, 1]$

Step 2: Calculate the total number of samples of the few classes that need to be synthesized: $G = (m_l - m_s) \times \beta$, where $\beta \in [0, 1]$ represents the desired degree of imbalance after the addition of the synthetic sample.

Step 3: For each sample x_i of a few classes, find their K-nearest neighbors in n-dimensional space, and calculate the ratio $r_i = \Delta_i/K$, (i = 1, 2, ..., m) where is the multi-sample in the K-nearest neighbor Number of $r_i \in (0, 1]$.

Step 4: According to $\hat{r} = \sum_{i=1}^{m_s} r_i$ regularization r_i, then the probability distribution $(\sum r_i = 1)$.

Step 5: Calculate the number of samples that need to be synthesized for each minority class sample x_i: $g_i = \hat{r}_i \times G$ where G is the total number of synthetic samples.

Step 6: randomly select a minority class x_i from the K-nearest neighbors of each of g_i the small sample samples x_i according to the following steps; According to s_j synthesis sample, where: λ is a random number, $\lambda \in (0, 1]$.

2.5 Tomek Link

The Tomek Link algorithm is under sampling, which algorithm used to reject approximate and overlapping boundary point data.

Input: Assume that the entire training sample set D contains m samples $\{x_i, y_i\}$, i = 1, 2, ..., m. Where is x_i a sample of the n-dimensional feature space X, $y_i \in Y = \{1, 2, 3, 4, 5, 6\}$ is a class label, $y_i = 2, 3, 4$ are small class samples, $y_i = 1, 4, 6$ are majority.

Class sample. Here, use m_s and to m_l indicate the number of samples of minority and majority classes.

The algorithm steps are as follows:

Step 1: In sample set D, find sample points m_i and m_l.
Step 2: Calculate the Euclidean distance d (m_i, m_l) between the two sample points of m_i and m_l. If there is no third m_k. Majority class sample point k such that d$(m_i, m_k) <$ d(m_i, m_l) or d$(m_l, m_k) <$ d(m_i, m_l) holds, then (m_i, m_l) is a Tomek link pair.
Step 3: Delete most of the class samples in the Tomek link pair.
Step 4: Repeat step 1 until you find all the Tomek link pairs.

3   ADASYN Borderline-Tomek Link Hybrid Sampling Method

3.1   Introduction to the Method

For the unbalanced data set, the ADASYN algorithm is used to adaptively augment the minority samples, and the extended samples are added to the original data set to obtain the data set N. In the data set N, using the improved algorithm Borderline-Tomek Link algorithm, the data set N is divided into four types of data, from which the majority samples of the neighbors and some of the majority samples of the high-density region and the isolated majority samples are eliminated, reducing the imbalance, get the data N'. The algorithm flow chart is shown in Fig. 1.

3.2   Borderline-Tomek Link Algorithm

This method adds boundary mechanism and high-density area deletion mechanism on Tomek Links, protects valid data boundary information and deletes redundant data, avoiding unintentional deletion.

The original Tomek Links algorithm treats all minority samples equally, but in the actual process, it is found that the data samples at the boundary position are more likely to be misclassified. Therefore, the data sample information at the boundary position is used to delete the data, which is better. Protecting the effective information while adding redundant information for high-density areas effectively solves the problem of unbalanced data. The algorithm steps are Table 3.

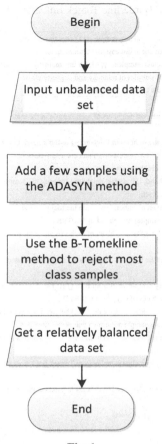

Fig. 1.

4 Experimental Analysis

4.1 Evaluation Criteria

In the general classification method, the classification accuracy is used as the evaluation index, that is, the number of samples with the correct classification as a percentage of the total number of samples. However, the classification accuracy does not consider the difference between the minority sample and the majority sample in the unbalanced sample, which causes the evaluation index to be inconsistent with the actual situation. Therefore, scholars have proposed new evaluation methods and indicators. The typical confusion matrix combined with F-value and G-mean achieves scientific evaluation indicators for the performance of unbalanced data classification.

In Table 4, T_P indicates that the positive class sample prediction is still positive, T_N indicates that the negative class prediction is still negative, F_P indicates that the negative class sample is positive, and F_N indicates that the positive sample is negative. Usually a few classes are defined as positive and most are negative.

Table 3. Borderline Tomek link algorithm steps

Input: Assume that the entire training sample set D contains m samples $\{x_i,y_i\}$, i = 1, 2, …, m. Where is x_i a sample of the n-dimensional feature space X, $y_i \in Y = \{1,2,3,4,5,6\}$ is a class label, y_i=2,3,4 are small class samples, y_i=1,4,6 are majority Class sample. Here, use m_s and to m_i indicate the number of samples of minority and majority classes.
Output: Data set D' after the expanded sample.

step 1:

step 1.1: Calculate the k nearest neighbors of each sample in the minority sample set F in the training sample set D.

step 1.1.2: Then classify the samples in F according to the k nearest neighbors:

step 1.2.1: Assuming that the k nearest neighbors are a few class samples, we define the sample as a safe sample and place it in the N set.

step 1.2.2: On the other hand, if k nearest neighbors are majority samples, the sample is a noise sample and is placed in the S set.

step 1.2.3: The last k nearest neighbors have both the majority and the minority, and are considered to be boundary samples and placed in the B set.

step 1.3.1: Calculate the k nearest neighbors of each sample in the majority sample set M in the training sample set D.

step 1.3.2: Assuming that the k nearest neighbors are all majority samples, we put it in the G set.

Step 2:

Step 2.1: Set the boundary sample set B from B to $\{f_1, f_2, f_i... f_n\}$. Select samples f_i in sample set B. Find multiple types of samples m_i from D.

Step 2.2: Calculate the Euclidean distance $d(f_i, m_l)$ between the two sample points f_i and m_l. If there is no third majority class sample point such that $d(m_i, m_k)<d(f_i, m_l)$ or $d(m_l, m_k)<d(f_i, m_l)$ holds, then (f_i, m_l) is a Tomek link pair. Then the sample pairs form a Tomek links. These Tomek links join the collection F.

Step 2.3: Remove the majority class samples from Tomek links from set F. Repeat the 2 process to find all the Tomek links.

Step 2.4: After the goal of the balanced sample set is reached, the algorithm ends.

Step 3:

Delete the majority sample of all S sets

Step 4:

Sample Set $D' = N \cup B \cup G$

Step 5:

Step 5.1: Calculate the average global density ($\bar{\rho}_{y_1}, \bar{\rho}_{y_2} \bar{\rho}_{y_3} ... \bar{\rho}_{y_s}$) and quantity ($Num_{y_1}, Num_{y_2}, Num_{y_3} ... Num_{y_s}$)of each category on the training data set D'.

Step 5.2: Calculate the local density of the class in the k-nearest neighbor space ω (x_i, k, r) of the sample x_i: $\rho(x,k,c_i) = \dfrac{Num(x,r,c_i)}{k}$. space information ω(x_i, k, r) sample information deleted from data set G after each calculation) (space domainω (x_i, k) sample information deleted from data set D', after each calculation)

Step 5.3: Calculate the local density by Step 5.2. When the partial local density is greater than the global density of this class, put this part of the sample into the set s_i. and mark the high-density region set Q_{ij}.

Step 5.4: Sort from the set Q_{ij} in a certain class s_i, from large to small ($Q_{i1}, Q_{i2}, Q_{i3} ... Q_{in}$), start from the region with the highest density from the highest density set, randomly remove part of the data x_i through the unbalanced degree IB, and obtain the set s_i'.

Step 5.5: After the purpose of sample equalization is reached, the algorithm ends.

Step 5.6: Find the union G of s_i'.

Table 4. Confusion matrix

Category	Predictive positive class	Predictive negative class
The actual positive class	T_P	F_N
The actual negative class	F_P	T_N

(1) F-value is an evaluation criterion for unbalanced data classification problems. It is mainly used to evaluate the classification accuracy of positive categories, which is defined as:

$$\text{F-value} = \frac{\left(1+\beta^2\right) \times \text{Re}call \times \text{Precision}}{\beta^2 \times \text{Re}call + \text{Precision}} \tag{4}$$

$$\text{Re}call = T_P/(T_P + F_N) \tag{5}$$

$$\text{Precision} = T_P/(T_P + F_p) \tag{6}$$

Recall is the recall rate; Precision is the precision; β indicates the relative importance, usually $\beta = 1$, F-value can reasonably evaluate the classification performance of the classifier for the unbalanced data set.

G-mean reflects the degree of balance between the classification ability of positive and negative samples, and is an evaluation index for measuring the overall classification performance of data sets. It is defined as:

$$\text{G-means} = \sqrt{P_A \times N_A} \tag{7}$$

$$P_A = T_P/(T_P + F_N) \tag{8}$$

$$N_A = T_N/(F_P + T_N) \tag{9}$$

This paper uses G-mean, F-value, Recall, Precision indicators to evaluate the unbalanced data processed by the algorithm.

4.2 Experimental Design

Before the experiment, because the feature measurement methods vary from each other, the data types are different, so the data set needs to be preprocessed: the missing data is deleted, and the data is standardized. The data set is divided into 2 parts, 80% of which are used as training data sets and 20% are used as verification data sets. This experiment converts multiple classifications into two-category problems.

Four sets of experimental data sets, namely, the original data set, the data set after ADASYN method, the data set after ADASYN+Tomek Line method, and the data set of this method, are compared in this paper Use classifiers for decision trees and random forests.

4.3   Analysis of Results

It is not difficult to see from Table 5 that the algorithm of this paper has a good performance in the precipitation phase prediction problem after comparison by two classifiers. Recall and Precision are better than the first three methods. In the random forest classifier, the method of this method is 19.1%, 13.5%, and 6.8% higher than the other methods. The accuracy of this method was 6.8%, 7.6%, and 6.5% higher than other methods.

Table 5. Evaluation and performance comparison

Dataset	Classifier	Recall	Precision
Original dataset	Decision tree	0.286	0.247
	Random decision forest	0.275	0.355
ADASYN	Decision tree	0.314	0.287
	Random decision forest	0.331	0.347
ADASYN+B-Tomek Line	Decision tree	0.348	0.219
	Random decision forest	0.398	0.358
ADASYN+B-Tomek Line	Decision tree	0.370	0.298
	Random decision forest	0.466	0.423

In Figs. 2 and 3, the method in this paper is greatly improved on F-value and G-mean compared to other methods. In the random forest classifier, the method of this method is 13.4%, 10.5%, and 6.7% higher than other methods in F-value. The accuracy of this method was increased by 10.0%, 8.1%, and 5.0%, respectively, compared with other methods. Through the comparison of these four types of indicators on the classifier, the classification errors of a few types of samples are reduced, and it is obvious that the method performance is better than the Tomek link method.

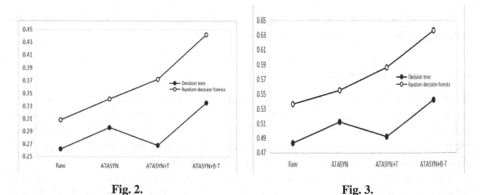

Fig. 2.   Fig. 3.

Figure 4, 5, 6 and 7 shows a two-dimensional view of partial data a is a majority sample, and b is a minority sample.

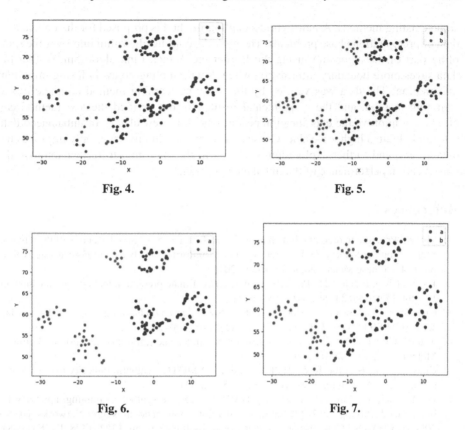

Fig. 4.   Fig. 5.

Fig. 6.   Fig. 7.

Figure 4 shows the original partial data set. There is a problem of data imbalance in the figure, and most of the classes invade into a few classes, which makes the classification of a few classes difficult. Figure 5 shows that after the ADASYN algorithm, the original data set increases the number of samples, which reduces the imbalance between the majority class and the minority class. Figure 6 and Fig. 7 respectively use the Tomek Link algorithm and improve the data set after the ADASYN algorithm. The viewable by the Borderline-Tomek Link algorithm, after comparison with Fig. 6 and Fig. 7, shows that some of the boundary samples are deleted in Fig. 6, which causes most of the boundary sample information to be lost, with the loss of a lot of important sample information. Figure 7 shows the data set after using the algorithm. After the improvement of the boundary algorithm, the boundary information of most types of samples is protected, the important samples of most classes are not lost, and the density of most samples as well as the redundancy of most classes are reduced. and the redundancy of most classes is reduced. The imbalance has also been reduced.

5 Summary

This paper mainly explores the imbalance data in the precipitation phase problem, explores the problems faced by unbalanced data in machine learning, and summarizes some existing methods. A new hybrid sampling method is proposed for the unbalanced data of precipitation phase problems. The hybrid sampling algorithm improves the sampling part of the algorithm, using the Borderline Tomek-Link algorithm, so that the data saves more boundary information when downsampling, to avoid losing important information. The data was verified by the machine learning method after the mixed sampling method, and the experimental results further verified the text method can effectively improve the classification performance of a few classes of unbalanced data sets, and obtain a higher F-value, G-mean. The method in this paper only improves the data aspect, and further exploration is needed in the algorithm to further improve the classification performance of the imbalance problem.

References

1. Mu, X.: Progress in precipitation phase analysis. In: The 35th Annual Meeting of the Chinese Meteorological Society S1 Disaster Weather Monitoring, Analysis and Forecasting, vol. 6, pp. 1–4. Chinese Meteorological Society (2018)
2. Jia, X., Chen, L., Gao, H.: Progress in short-term climate prediction technology in China. Q. J. Appl. Meteorol. **24**(06), 641–655 (2013)
3. Chawla, N., Japkowicz, N., Kotcz, A., et al.: Special issue on learning from imbalanced data sets. ACM SIG SIGKDD Explor. Newsl. **6**(1), 1–6 (2004)
4. You, F., Guo, L., Shi, Y., Jian, Z.: Discrimination index and test of precipitation in Beijing. J. Meteorol. Environ. **29**(05), 49–54 (2013)
5. Chawla, N.V., Bowyer, K.W., Hall, L.O., et al.: SMOTE: synthetic minority over sampling technique. J. Artif. Intell. Res. **16**(1), 321–357 (2002)
6. He, H., Bai, Y., Garcia, E.A., et al.: ADASYN: adaptive synthetic sampling, approach for imbalanced learning. In: IEEE International Joint Conference on Neural Networks, IJCNN 2008 (IEEE World Congress on Computational Intelligence), pp. 1322–1328. IEEE (2008)
7. Ha, J., Lee, J.S.: A new under-sampling method using genetic algorithm for imbalanced data classification. In: International Conference on Ubiquitous Information Management & Communication (2016)
8. Tomek, I.: Twomodi fications of CNN. IEEE Trans. Syst. Man Cybern. **6**, 769–772 (1976)
9. Seiffert, C., Khoshgoftaar, T.M., van Hulse, J.: Hybrid sampling for imbalanced data. In: IEEE International Conference on Information Reuse and Integration, pp. 202–207 (2008)
10. Gazzah, S., Hechkel, A., Amara, N.E.B.: A hybrid sampling method for imbalanced data. In: 2015 IEEE 12th International Conference on Systems, Signals & Devices, pp. 1–6 (2015)
11. Gustavo, E.A., Batista, P.A., Ronaldo, C., et al.: A study of the, pp. 1–8 (2009)
12. Zhang, C., Yang, X., Zhang, W.: The learning and typical application of meteorological big data ultra-short-precision precision precipitation machine. J. Agric. Big Data **1**(01), 78–87 (2019)
13. Yu, S.: Feature selection and classifier ensembles: a study on hyperspectral remote sensing data. University of Autwerp, Flanders (2003)
14. Kim, D.-Y., Kim, S.: A data download method from RSUs using fog computing in connected vehicles. Comput. Mater. Continua **59**(2), 375–387 (2019)
15. Ciraco, M., Rogalewski, M., Weiss, G.: Improving classifier utility by altering the misclassification cost ratio. In: Proceedings of the 1st International Workshop on Utility-based Data Mining, pp. 46–52. ACM, New York (2005)
16. Mladenic, D., Grobenik, M.: Feature selection for unbalanced class distribution and Naive Bayes. In: Proceedings of the 16th International Conference on Machine Learning, pp. 258–267. Morgan Kaufmann, San Francisco (1999)

17. Tao, Q., Wu, G., Wang, F.Y., et al.: Posterior probability support vector machines for unbalanced data. IEEE Trans. Neural Netw. **16**(6), 1 561–1 573 (2005)
18. Maloof, M.A.: Learning when data sets are imbalanced and when costs are unequal and unknown. In: Workshop on Learning from Imbalanced Data Sets II, ICML 2003. AAAI Press, Washington DC (2003)
19. Xiao, D., Liang, J., Ma, Q., Xiang, Y., Zhang, Y.: High capacity data hiding in encrypted image based on compressive sensing for nonequivalent resources. Comput. Mater. Continua **58**(1), 1–13 (2019)
20. Liu, Z., Xiang, B., Song, Y., Lu, H., Liu, Q.: An Improved unsupervised image segmentation method based on multi-objective particle, swarm optimization clustering algorithm. Comput. Mater. Continua **58**(2), 451–461 (2019)

Vehicular Trajectory Big Data: Driving Behavior Recognition Algorithm Based on Deep Learning

Xiaorun Yang[1,2], Fei Ding[2], Dengyin Zhang[2(✉)], and Min Zhang[1,2]

[1] College of Telecommunications and Information Engineering,
Nanjing University of Posts and Telecommunications, Nanjing 210003, China
[2] Jiangsu Key Laboratory of Broadband Wireless Communication and Internet of Things,
Nanjing University of Posts and Telecommunications, Nanjing 210003, China
zhangdy@njupt.edu.cn

Abstract. Vehicular trajectory data contains a wealth of geospatial information and human activity information. This paper proposes a method that uses only a time series, including latitude and longitude information, to classify drivers into four types: dangerous, high-risk, low-risk, and safe. The main contribution of this paper is the creative approach that uses Convolutional Neural Networks (CNNs) in extracting trajectory features and processing raw trajectories into inputs of CNN. After training the CNN network and combining results predicted by segments, the study described in this paper achieved a classification accuracy of 77.3%.

Keywords: GPS trajectory · Security analysis · CNN

1 Background

According to China's 2018 traffic report, human error accounted for 90% of all traffic accidents. Therefore, it is of great practical significance to study the driving styles of different drivers and analyze the safety of driving styles in order to reduce the occurrence of traffic accidents. A low traffic accident rate will bring huge commercial value to many companies, including taxi companies, car rental companies, and bus groups. In addition, Usage-based insurance (UBI) can use different driving styles to customize stepped premiums.

At the same time, as a result of the developments in the automotive electronics industry, such as vehicle GPS (Global Positioning System), mobile terminal GPS positioning, and vehicle networking communication technology, the acquisition and transmission of vehicle location information has become easier. The improvement of computer performance, the rapid development of cloud computing technology, and massive data storage technology make it possible to apply deep learning to extracting useful information from large-scale vehicle trajectory data.

Vehicle trajectory analysis aims to analyze the degree of driving safety of the drivers through floating vehicle trajectory data. The degree of safety of the driver's behavior is an important factor that affects traffic accidents independently of the vehicle's hardware status.

© Springer Nature Singapore Pte Ltd. 2020
X. Sun et al. (Eds.): ICAIS 2020, CCIS 1253, pp. 324–336, 2020.
https://doi.org/10.1007/978-981-15-8086-4_30

Using vehicle GPS to collect vehicle trajectories has an irreplaceable cost advantage over installing sensors on a vehicle to detect its motion status. GPS sensors have become broadly popular as providers of the needed vehicle navigation. Therefore, the use of the vehicle GPS trajectory information for driving style analysis has the advantages of wide coverage, low cost, and rich location information. However, the accuracy of the GPS signal is greatly affected by the environment, and the sampling frequency is low. This is a challenge when using GPS track information to analyze driving styles.

2 Related Research

Analysis of the vehicle trajectory can assist with determining the driver's driving style, which can in turn lead to a reduction in traffic accidents. Available research in this area can roughly be divided into three categories.

The first category is traditional unsupervised learning. Constantinescu [1] used cluster and principal component analysis to classify drivers into five levels of driving safety. Hong [2] used the data collected by multiple sensors for the Naive Bayes classification and created a classifier for driving style. Eboli [3] conducted an analysis of the risk of traffic accidents using road environment and driving speed.

The second category is the pattern-matching method. This type of research usually pre-defines dangerous driving behaviors and analyzes driver's driving style and driving behavior safety by matching these dangerous driving behaviors. Johnson & Trivedi [4] used a trajectory time series to match predefined driving behavior templates for driving analysis. Li [5] used a camera to monitor the shifting of various maneuvering states and used a random forest algorithm to classify the driving styles.

The third category is a direct modeling analysis. Vaiana et al. [6] developed an algorithm for evaluating aggressiveness based on g-g graphs, which are plotted using longitudinal and lateral acceleration. In their study, a "safe area" was defined on the g-g map, and the driver's aggression was assessed by calculating the percentage of external points. Since then, Joubert, de Beer, and de Koker [7], as well as Eboli, Mazzulla, and Pungillo [8] continued to improve the introduction of regional weights and speeds within the g-g diagram to enhance the analytical capabilities of the g-g map. In addition, Chen [9] proposed a method based on a behavioral map to evaluate driving safety, which could further the understanding of the characteristics of driving behavior and provide suggestions for targeted optimization.

In recent years, there has been an increase in the number of research components of trajectory data acquisition and an analysis based on smart phones [10]. Montanino [11] attempted to reconstruct the trajectory data and verify the simulation macro traffic model. Zadeh [12] created a warning system for vulnerable roads based on smart phones, and Efekhari [13] developed a driver behavior recognition system based on adaptive neuro-fuzzy reasoning. Yujie [14] used clustering methods to extract moving trajectory individuals from the trajectory stream. Jiao [15] analyzed violation probability of taxi drivers in metropolis and found they more dangerous than normal drivers. Huiyu [16] used semi-supervised and active learning to analysis New York's transportation data.

3 Research Methods

Compared to previous studies, the use of Convolutional Neural Networks (CNNs) has the advantage of providing more objective information and making it possible to create strong model generalizations. In addition, CNN provides access to large-scale data, which can help with the issue of a somewhat low accuracy of the vehicle trajectory information and a relatively low density of the information.

Choosing CNN instead of the Recurrent Neural Network (RNN) or its variant - Long and Short-Term Memory network (LSTM) - allows researchers to extract local features of the convolution network. Although RNN has advantages in global feature extraction, driving style is better reflected in the local feature of the data track. CNN can show the frequency of driving behaviors by extracting local features and collecting further local information. In this study, the factors, such as vehicle performance, driver's driving age, traffic conditions, and weather were ignored when driving style was considered.

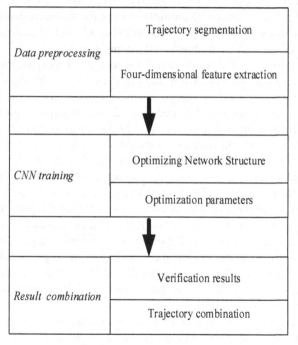

Fig. 1. Processing framework

The method proposed in this paper is divided into three steps:

The first step is the data preparation phase. A two-dimensional time series of trajectory data for each driver is converted into a sequence containing a plurality of kinematic features, while the feature sequence is cut into a plurality of small sequences of fixed length.

The second step is the network training phase. Network structure is designed and adjusted, network parameters are adjusted, and the tagged data is used to train the network.

Finally, the last step is the result-integration phase. The model trained in the second step is used to re-convert the fixed-length sequence with the predicted results back to the original sequence and predict results of the fixed-length small sequence (Fig. 1).

3.1 Data Preprocessing

Vehicle trajectory data is essentially a two-dimensional time series, $x = (x_1, x_2, \ldots, x_t)$, $x_i = (lat_i, long_i)$. The latitude and longitude data form is a human-defined knowledge concept, and it is difficult to extract the information directly from the convolutional neural network. Therefore, real-world rules need to be incorporated into the data, providing CNN with more information and assisting it in reducing learning difficulty and improving learning efficiency.

The Vincenty formula [17] was used to calculate the distance between the two track points x_i, x_{i+1}. Then the time interval ΔT between x_i, x_{i+1} was used to calculate the velocity V_i of track points x_i. The formula is as follows:

$$V_i = \frac{Vinceny(x_i, x_{i+1})}{\Delta T}, \Delta T = t_{i+1} - t_i \tag{1}$$

Where t_i, t_{i+1} are respectively the time when the track point coordinates x_i, x_{i+1} are recorded. Speed V_i and time difference ΔT were then used to calculate acceleration A_i and jerk J_i of point x_i.

$$A_i = \frac{V_{i+1} - V_i}{\Delta T} \tag{2}$$

$$J_i = \frac{A_{i+1} - A_i}{\Delta T} \tag{3}$$

Finally, the change rate of steering angle B_i was calculated. This article improves the steering angle formula provided in Dabiri [18]. Dabiri used the latitude and longitude to calculate the angle between the trajectory point and the magnetic north (or true north) and find the difference between the two trajectory points and the magnetic north (or true north). In this paper, the rate of change of steering angle between two track points was further calculated to characterize the magnitude and rate of change of the vehicle's direction of transition.

$$y = \sin[x_{i+1}(long) - x_i(long)] * \cos[x_{i+1}(lat)] \tag{4}$$

$$x = \cos[x_i(lat)] * \sin[x_{i+1}(lat)] - \sin[x_i(lat)] * \cos[x_{i+1}(lat)] * \cos[x_{i+1}(long) - x_i(long)] \tag{5}$$

$$B_i = \arctan(y, x) \tag{6}$$

$$BC_i = \frac{B_{i+1} - B_i}{\Delta T} \tag{7}$$

For the study, the trajectory sequence was cut into segments of fixed length M since CNN requires the same input size. For a track segment of length L < M, if L < a * M, the segment was discarded. If L > a * M, the segment was subjected to a zero-filling operation (a is a coefficient between [0, 1]). Another benefit of trajectory cutting was that it increased the number of samples and reduced the possibility of over-fitting of the CNN model.

Additionally, an important aspect of trajectory data preprocessing was the driving stroke segmentation. In an effort to ensure the integrity of the GPS track flow, the driving stroke segmentation provided an effective way to eliminate the disturbance caused by sudden breakpoints. Since the dataset used in this study contained the passenger order ID, the journey of the vehicle could be segmented with the passenger's order. In addition, due to the truncation of the dataset to the urban area of Xi'an, the trajectory points of some orders were incomplete, and these parts of the trajectories were discarded.

3.2 CNN Architecture

Compared with the trajectory data collected by other technical solutions, the GPS trajectory data of the vehicle has the characteristics of large positioning deviation and low sampling frequency. At the same time, the GPS trajectory acquisition cost is low and the amount of trajectory data is huge. This results in the low effective information density of GPS trajectory data, which brings difficulties to trajectory analysis methods based on feature analysis of professional knowledge. The neural network can be used to automatically extract and characterize the hard-to-perceive features of humans. The use of neural networks to analyze the driving characteristics of GPS trajectories avoids the defect that the features extracted based on professional knowledge fail in GPS trajectory information.

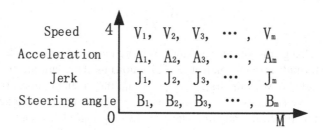

Fig. 2. A four channel track segment

The key idea in a Convolutional Neural Network (CNN) is similar to that of a normal Multi-Layer Perceptron (MLP), but the difference is that each node of the MLP is fully connected to the node in the previous layer. While the CNN passes the neurons, only small areas (also known as receptive fields) of the previous layer are connected to take advantage of the spatial local correlation. This local connection between nodes results in a smaller number of weights, which alleviates the catastrophic and over-fitting problems of the dimensions.

CNN has various types of layers. This paper focuses only on the layers used in this model, including the input layer, convolution layer, pooling layer, fully-connected layer, dropout layer, and the selected loss function.

CNN usually requires that the input sample contain three dimensions: height, width, and a number of channels. In the study, a sequence of track points from one sequence was processed into four dimensions and treated as four channels in the CNN input sample. At the same time, in order to meet the requirements of consistent input sample size, the track node was intercepted as a segment of fixed length M. For segments with a length less than M after interception, 0 fill or discard processing was performed according to the rules mentioned above. Figure 2 shows a four-dimensional track channel.

Dropout is proposed in order to prevent model over-fitting. Dropout can be used as a kind of trick for selection. Hinton [19] pointed out that by ignoring half of the feature detectors in each training batch (letting half of the hidden layer node values to be 0), the over-fitting phenomenon could be significantly reduced. This way, the interaction between feature detectors can be reduced as well. Detector interaction means that some detectors rely on other detectors to work.

Pooling, which is actually a form of down-sampling, is another important concept related to CNN. There are many different forms of nonlinear pooling functions, among which "Max pooling" is the most common. It divides input data into several rectangular regions, outputting the maximum value for each sub-region. Intuitively, the reason why this mechanism works is that after finding a feature, its exact position becomes far less important than the relation of its position to its other features. The pool layer continually reduces the spatial size of the data, so the number of parameters and the amount of calculations decreases as well, which to a certain extent helps to control over-fitting. Generally speaking, the convolution layer of CNN is periodically inserted into the pooling layer.

Fully-connected layer (FC) plays the role of a "classifier" within CNN. Original data is mapped to the hidden layer feature space by the convolution layer, pooling layer, and the activated function layer, and then the learned "distributed feature representation" is mapped to the sample marker space by the fully-connected layer.

The nonlinear activation function $f(x) = \max(0, x)$ is selected in the convolution layer, which is one of many types of activation functions. This function (called ReLU) replaces all negative values in the feature map with zeros. Compared with other functions (such as $\tanh(x)$ and Sigmoid functions), ReLU improves the learning speed of CNN.

In this study, the cross entropy loss function was chosen in several types of loss functions. This can effectively avoid the shortcomings of the slow update of parameters caused by the mean square error function (MSE). Cross entropy was used to evaluate the difference between the probability distribution and the real distribution obtained from the current training.

$$L = -\frac{1}{N} \sum_{i=0}^{N-1} \sum_{k=0}^{K-1} y_{i,k} \log p_{i,k} \tag{8}$$

where y is the real label of the sample (x, y). Suppose there are K label values and N samples. If the i-th sample belongs to the k-th label, in this case $y_{i,k} = 1$, in other cases $y_{i,k} = 0$. The probability that the ith sample is predicted to be the k-th tag value is $p_{i,k}$.

3.3 Segment Result Combination

In the course of data preprocessing within this study, the trajectory data of each driver was cut into n small tracks of m length in order to achieve the purpose of adapting the input of CNN and expanding the number of CNN networks. The trained CNN generated prediction results for the segmented trajectories in the verification set. In this step, we used the prediction result of the segmented trajectory to predict the classification result of the trajectory before segmentation.

$$S = (\frac{1}{2k}) * a_1 + (\frac{3}{2k}) * a_2 + \cdots + (\frac{2k-1}{2k}) * a_k \tag{9}$$

where S is the classification score, k is the classification category number, and a_k indicates that the fixed length trajectory after the division is predicted as the ratio of the kth category to the total number of divisions.

$$\frac{n}{k} < S \le \frac{n+1}{k}, n \in N, 0 \le n \le k-1 \tag{10}$$

When S fell into the above range, the driver was assigned to the nth driving style.

The above prediction combination method represented average prediction results of the trajectory segments after each driver was assigned a driving style. Interference caused by the feature offset of the segmented segment being segmented by this averaging.

4 Experiment and Results

All the experimental codes are written in Python language, and the training and application of CNN are supported by Keras framework and using TensorFlow as backend framework with GPU.

4.1 Data Set Description

The data set selected in this paper comes from the data set published by the Didi Chuxing GAIA Initiative to the research community, including driver id, order id, time and latitude and longitude. The accuracy of the GPS trajectory is 3 s, and it is processed by the tying road. Select the data of the drip taxi for one month in October 2016 in Xi'an, China. According to the Fazeen paper [20], the frequency of rapid acceleration, rapid deceleration (±0.3 g) was calculated, and our data set was labeled with a simplified scoring system. We randomly selected 80% of the data set as the training set and the rest as the test set. The final performance evaluation of the CNN model is only performed on test sets that do not work during training.

4.2 Training Process

The goal of the training process is to learn the parameters of the filters at each level in a way that minimizes the loss function. The error in the output layer is calculated using the classification cross entropy as a loss function. Use the Adam optimizer to update model parameters during backpropagation, which is ideal for working with large data sets. Batch size equals 64, learning rate $= 0.001$, $\beta_1 = 0.9$, $\beta_2 = 0.999$, $\varepsilon = 10^{-8}$. We apply the early stop method to train the CNN, which determines the depth of the network and the choice of parameters, which avoids the problem of overfitting. In the early stop method, the training and verification scores (e.g., accuracy) are calculated after each training session. The number of periods generated selects the maximum verification score as the best value for the period.

4.3 Experiment Configuration and Analysis

Table 1 lists the typical configurations in the process of exploring CNN network structure and parameters. Accuracy1 is the prediction accuracy of the fixed long track segment and accuracy2 is the prediction accuracy of the driver's track with the combination of the prediction results of the fixed long track segment. We can observe that the accuracy of

Table 1. CNN configuration.

	A	B	C	D	E	F	G
Input layer	A pool of ($M \times 4$) GPS segments						
Convolutional	32	32	32	32	32	32	32
Convolutional	32	32	32	32	32	32	32
Max-pooling	No	No	No	Yes	Yes	Yes	Yes
Dropout	No	No	No	Yes	Yes	Yes	Yes
Convolutional	No	64	64	64	64	64	64
Convolutional	No	64	64	64	64	64	64
Max-pooling	No	No	No	Yes	Yes	Yes	Yes
Dropout	No	No	No	Yes	Yes	Yes	Yes
Convolutional	No	No	128	128	128	128	128
Convolutional	No	No	128	128	128	128	128
Max-pooling	No	No	No	Yes	Yes	Yes	Yes
Dropout	No	No	No	Yes	Yes	Yes	Yes
Convolutional	No	No	No	No	No	256	256
Convolutional	No	No	No	No	No	256	256
Max-pooling	No	No	No	No	No	Yes	Yes
Dropout	No	No	No	No	No	Yes	Yes
FC	No	No	No	Yes	Yes	Yes	Yes
Dropout	No	No	No	Yes	No	Yes	No
FC	Yes	Yes	Yes	Yes	Yes	Yes	Yes
Accuracy1	65.3%	68.2%	71%	74.4%	70.3%	70.2%	69.3%
Accuracy2	68.1%	70.9%	74%	77.3%	73%	73.1%	72.2%

classification increases by 3% on average (the accuracy 2 is greater than the accuracy1 3%) with the application of our segment trajectory results combination strategy. As shown in Table 1, the effect of model D is the most outstanding, reaching the highest of 74.4% for accurate1 and 77.3% for accurate2.

In the configuration of A, B, C and F, we only use the volume accumulation layer. As this convolution layer increases from 2 layers in model A to 8 layers in model F, the accuracy in model B reaches the maximum of these three models. This proves that the 6-layer convolution layer is a suitable depth. Adding a convolution layer before the depth reaches 6 layers can improve the accuracy by 3%. However, when the network depth increases to 8 layers, the accuracy does not increase.

Through the comparison of models C and D, we find that adding the maximum pooling layer and dropout layer between the convolution layers will improve the accuracy by 3%. Compared with the models D and E, we found that the accuracy could not be improved by simply increasing the full connection layer. The key to improve the accuracy is to insert dropout layer and pool layer between convolution layers to reduce over fitting. We specify the range of P values for both dropout layers in the model D from 0.2 to 0.8. Finally, it is found that the best result is obtained when the P value is 0.5.

Figure 3 shows the trend of accuracy1 change of training set and test set in each epoch during CNN network training. The data shows that the accuracy of CNN test set is stable in the 30th epoch, but it is still rising in the training set. This shows that the network has a certain degree of over fitting, which maybe due to the fact that the trajectory cut into segments can not fully reflect all the characteristics of the trajectory and the driving style of some drivers is not completely stable.

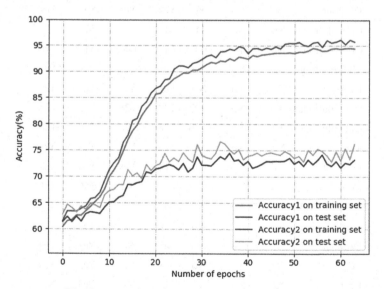

Fig. 3. Accuracy of training and test set on model D

Table 2 provides the best experimental results for driver's driving style type prediction, including confusion matrix, recall rate and prediction accuracy of each type of driving style. Through the confusion matrix as shown in Fig. 4, we can observe that even if the network prediction is wrong, the classification of errors is also the adjacent category of the correct category. This is a good property, because in the task of judging the danger of driving style, we are very sensitive to classify a driver with dangerous driving style as safe, but not so sensitive to classify a safer driving style as safe.

Table 2. Confusion matrix, recall rate and prediction of model D

Model D evaluation		Predicted class					
		Dangerous	High-risk	Low-risk	Safe	Sum	Recall%
Actual class	Dangerous	46	16	8	0	70	65.7%
	High-risk	6	930	461	23	1420	65.5%
	Low-risk	1	131	2371	160	2663	89.0%
	Safe	0	10	367	760	1137	66.8%
	Sum	53	1087	3207	943	5290	–
	Precision%	86.8%	85.5%	73.9%	80.6%	–	–

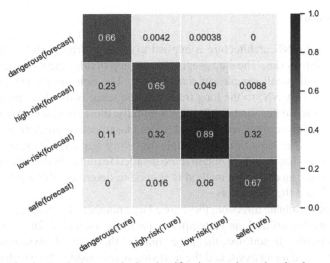

Fig. 4. Confusion matrix for classification results and real values

4.4 Comparison with Traditional Machine Learning Algorithm

In order to evaluate our CNN model, we compare it with the most effective random forest (RF) algorithm. To make a fair comparison, the traditional algorithm is trained and tested by using the same training and test track segment as CNN model. The input features of RF need to be designed manually. We use the same features as Dong's paper

Table 3. Comparison between our method and RF

Model	Test accuracy	Average precision	Average recall	Average F-score
RF	67.4%	67.2%	66.5%	66.9%
MLP	59.1%	58.8%	59.4%	59.1%
CNN-A	65.3%	66.1%	66.5%	66.3%
CNN-D	73.9%	74.4%	73.1%	73.7%

[21], including speed norm, difference of speed norm, acceleration norm, difference of acceleration norm, *angular speed* (Table 3).

Comparing RF with CNN, we find that RF is better than CNN using only two layers of convolution, but it is still 6% lower than our best CNN network. In addition, we compared CNN with MLP, and set the number of neurons in the hidden layer after MLP to twice that in the previous layer. However, the experimental results of MLP are far away from CNN. As mentioned before, CNN algorithm is superior to traditional supervised learning algorithm based on Feature Engineering fitting due to its ability to extract higher level features through multi-layer nonlinear processing units.

5   Conclusion

In this paper, the CNN architecture is applied to classify driving styles using only the original GPS trajectories. The data preprocessing step divides the data segments of different lengths into small samples of fixed length. The rich sample size greatly helps the performance of CNN, so the long trajectory sequence is divided into small sample sequences to increase the number of samples. Finally, these fixed-length trajectory classification prediction results are combined into a classification prediction result for the driver's safety. At the same time, the sample trajectory sequence is expanded from one dimension to four dimensions to obtain more detailed features. In the process of training the CNN network, an early stop method is applied to determine the depth and structure of the network and the parameters.

In the future graduate direction, there are a large number of unlabeled raw data in the data set that are not utilized, and attempts to use these unlabeled data sets using unsupervised algorithms. In addition, this paper ignores the external environmental factors during driving for data analysis, and the next step is to consider the weather, road, time and other factors into the impact on the driver's driving safety.

Acknowledgements. This work was partially supported by National Natural Science Foundation of China (No. 61571241 and 61872423), Industry Prospective Primary Research & Development Plan of Jiangsu Province (No. BE2017111), the Scientific Research Foundation of the Higher Education Institutions of Jiangsu Province (No. 19KJA180006), Six talent peaks project of Jiangsu Province (No. DZXX-008), the Postdoctoral Science Foundation, China (Nos. 2019K026 and 2019M661900), and the Postgraduate Research & Practice Innovation Program of Jiangsu Province (No. KYCX18_0912).

References

1. Constantinescu, Z., Marinoiu, C., Vladoiu, M.: Driving style analysis using data mining techniques. Int. J. Comput. Commun. Control **5**(5), 654–663 (2010)
2. Hong, J.H., Margines, B., Dey, A.K.: A smartphone-based sensing platform to model aggressive driving behaviors. In: Proceedings of the 32nd Annual ACM Conference on Human Factors in Computing Systems, pp. 4047–4056 (2014)
3. Eboli, L., Guido, G., Mazzulla, G., Pungillo, G., Pungillo, R.: Investigating car users' driving behaviour through speed analysis. Promet-Traffic Transp. **29**(2), 193–202 (2017)
4. Johnson, D.A., Trivedi, M.M.: Driving style recognition using a smartphone as a sensor platform. In: 14th International IEEE Conference on IEEE Intelligent Transportation Systems (ITSC), pp. 1609–1615 (2011)
5. Li, G., Li, S.E., Cheng, B., Green, P.: Estimation of driving style in naturalistic highway traffic using maneuver transition probabilities. Transp. Res. Part C: Emerg. Technol. **74**, 113–125 (2017)
6. Vaiana, R., et al.: Driving behavior and traffic safety: An acceleration-based safety evaluation procedure for smartphones. Mod. Appl. Sci. **8**(1), 88 (2014)
7. Joubert, J.W., de Beer, D., de Koker, N.: Combining accelerometer data and contextual variables to evaluate the risk of driver behaviour. Transp. Res. Part F: Traffic Psychol. Behav. **41**, 80–96 (2016)
8. Eboli, L., Mazzulla, G., Pungillo, G.: Combining speed and acceleration to define car users' safe or unsafe driving behaviour. Transp. Res. Part C: Emerg. Technol. **68**, 113–125 (2016)
9. Chen, C., Zhao, X., Zhang, Y., et al.: A graphical modeling method for individual driving behavior and its application in driving safety analysis using GPS data. Transp. Res. Part F: Traffic Psychol. Behav. **63**, 118–134 (2019)
10. Wahlström, J., Skog, I., Handel, P.: Smartphone-based vehicle telematics: a ten-year anniversary. IEEE Trans. Intell. Transp. Syst. **18**(10), 2802–2825 (2017)
11. Montanino, M., Punzo, V.: Trajectory data reconstruction and simulation-based validation against macroscopic traffic patterns. Transp. Res. Part B: Methodol. **80**, 82–106 (2015)
12. Zadeh, R.B., Ghatee, M., Efekhari, H.R.: Tree-phases smartphone-based warning system to protect vulnerable road users under fuzzy conditions. IEEE Trans. Intell. Transp. Syst. **19**(7), 2086–2098 (2018)
13. Efekhari, H.R., Ghatee, M.: Hybrid of discrete wavelet transform and adaptive neuro fuzzy inference system for overall driving behavior recognition. Transp. Res. Part F Traffic Psychol. Behav. **58**, 782–796 (2018)
14. Zhang, Y., Ji, G., Zhao, B., Sheng, B.: An algorithm for mining gradual moving object clusters pattern from trajectory streams. Comput. Mater. Continua **59**(3), 885–901 (2019)
15. Yao, J., et al.: Data based violated behavior analysis of taxi driver in metropolis in China. Comput. Mater. Continua **60**(3), 1109–1122 (2019)
16. Sun, H., McIntosh, S.: Analyzing cross-domain transportation big data of New York City with semi-supervised and active learning. Comput. Mater. Continua **57**(1), 1–9 (2018)
17. Vincenty, T.: Direct and inverse solutions of geodesics on the ellipsoid with application of nested equations. Surv. Rev. **23**, 88–93 (1975)
18. Dabiri, S., Heaslip, K.: Inferring transportation modes from GPS trajectories using a convolutional neural network. Transp. Res. Part C: Emerg. Technol. **86**, 360–371 (2018)

19. Hinton, G.E., Srivastava, N., Krizhevsky, A., Sutskever, I., Salakhutdinov, R.: Improving neural networks by preventing co-adaptation of feature detectors. CoRRabs/1207.0580. http://arxiv.org/abs/1207.0580 (2012)
20. Fazeen, M., Gozick, B., Dantu, R., Bhukhiya, M., González, M.C.: Safe driving using mobile phones. IEEE Trans. Intell. Transp. Syst. **13**(3), 1462–1468 (2012)
21. Dong, W., Li, J., Yao, R., Li, C., Yuan, T., Wang, L.: Characterizing driving styles with deep learning. arXiv preprint arXiv:1607.03611 (2016)

Measurement-Device-Independent Quantum Identity Authentication Based on Single Photon

Yu Cheng, Xiaoping Lou(✉), Wensheng Tang, Zehong Liu, Yu Wang, and Guan Huang

School of Information Science and Engineering, Hunan Normal University,
410081 Changsha, China
louxiaoping@hunnu.edu.cn

Abstract. To overcome the channel attacks of the detector side, a measurement-device-independent quantum identity authentication based on single photon is proposed. The participants authenticate the identity of each other based on a relay measurement result. The technique of measurement-device-independent enhances the distance in the communication. Moreover, the analysis results show that our scheme has the higher security under the general attacks.

Keywords: Measurement-device-independent · Quantum identity authentication · Bell state measurement

1 Introduction

As a combination of classical cryptography and quantum mechanics, quantum cryptography has attracted much attention. Since quantum key distribution (QKD) [1] was proposed in 1984 by Bennett et al. QKD [1, 2] had become one of the important research topics. With the QKD technique, any two communication parties (or many communication parties) share secret key. Many scholars also proposed kinds of schemes to solve the other security problems such as arbitrated quantum signature (AQS) [3, 4], quantum secret sharing (QSS) [5, 6], quantum secure direct communication (QSDC) [7–10] and so on. Quantum identity authentication (QIA) serves as a scheme, which guarantees the participant's identities. Recently, many QIA schemes [11–18] have been proposed. We can simply classify those schemes as single party quantum identity authentication (S-QIA) and multi-party quantum identity authentication (M-QIA) according to the numbers of participants. For example, Zhang et al. [14] introduced a S-QIA scheme in 2006. In the same year, a multiparty simultaneous QIA [15] was proposed based on entanglement swapping by Wang et al. However, the most of existing QIA schemes use entanglement particles. In fact, single photons are ideal source for quantum communication, compared

This work was supported in part by the National Natural Science Foundation of China under Grant 61602172 and Grant U1636106, in part by the Natural Science Foundation of Hunan Province under Grant 2017JJ3223, in part by the Science and Technology Project of Hunan province Department of Education under Grant 16B179, and in part by the Hunan Province's Strategic and Emerging Industrial Projects under Grant 2018GK4035.

© Springer Nature Singapore Pte Ltd. 2020
X. Sun et al. (Eds.): ICAIS 2020, CCIS 1253, pp. 337–345, 2020.
https://doi.org/10.1007/978-981-15-8086-4_31

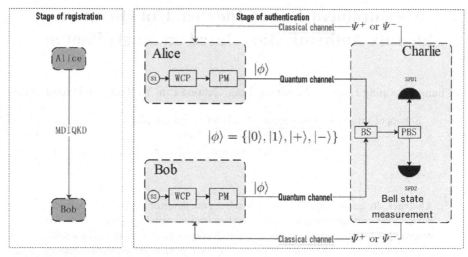

Fig. 1. The experiment devices of our scheme. S1 and S2: Two independent laser sources; WCP: phase randomized weak coherent pulses; PM: polarization modulator; BS: a 50:50 beam splitter; PBS: polarization beam splitter; SPD1 and SPD2: Two single-photon detectors. Firstly, Alice and Bob share secret key in registration stage. Then they prepare four BB84 states by there device respectively. Finally, they send those photons to Charlie who performs Bell state measurement and publics outcomes. The Charlie's device can only identify two of the four Bell states. Alice or Bob can complete identity authentication according the measurement outcome. We will describe the details of the scenario in a later section.

with those schemes using entangled state, the schemes without entanglement are more practical within the present technology [5]. Therefore, Hong proposed a QIA protocol based on the single photons [11].

In addition, the detector side channel attack also is a vital problem. To overcome this attack, a measurement-device-independent QIA (MDI-QIA) scheme was proposed [13], but it still use entanglement photon source. We propose a MDI-QIA scheme in this paper. Firstly, four single photons are used rather than entanglement states. Secondly, it eliminates security loopholes with the measurement device. In addition, the measurement-device-independent (MDI) technique doubles the communication distance. It is shown that our scheme has the higher security under the impersonation attack [6], measure resend attack [11], entangle and measure attack [11].

The rest of this paper is organized as follows. Firstly, we introduce two sections in the scheme: Stage of registration and authentication. Secondly, we make an analysis on the correctness and security. Finally, we sum up this paper.

2 Scheme of Quantum Identity Authentication Based on Bell State Measurement

There is two sections in our scheme: Stage of registration and stage of authentication. Firstly, we give a presentation about four polarization states:$|0\rangle|1\rangle|-\rangle$. Where $|+\rangle = \frac{1}{\sqrt{2}}(0\rangle + |1\rangle)$, $|-\rangle = \frac{1}{\sqrt{2}}(|0\rangle - |1\rangle)$. Alice and Bob prepare four polarization states and send them to Charlie located in the middle, who performs a Bell state measurement [2]. The experiment devices can be described in Fig. 1.

2.1 Stage of Registration

In this section, Alice and Bob share the authentication keys using the measurement-device-independent QKD technique [2]. Firstly, the relationship of single photons and classical message can be shown in Table 1. The process of QKD can be described in Table 2.

Table 1. Relationship of single photons and classical message, Alice and Bob will randomly prepare four BB84 polarization states and encode classical message according to this regulation.

Classical bit	0	1	0	1
Single photon	$|0\rangle$	$|1\rangle$	$|+\rangle$	$|-\rangle$

Table 2. Specific procedure of MDI-QKD, Alice and Bob prepare photons and send Charlie, they will share secret key:1101.

Alice	Polarization	0°	45°	90°	135°	0°	45°	90°	135°
	Basis	Rect	Diag	Rect	Diag	Rect	Diag	Rect	Diag
	Classical bit	0	0	1	1	0	0	1	1
Bob	Polarization	90°	135°	45°	0°	0°	90°	45°	135°
	Basis	Rect	Diag	Diag	Rect	Rect	Rect	Diag	Diag
	Classical bit	1	1	0	0	0	1	0	1
Charlie's outcome		ψ^+	ψ^+	×	×	ψ^-	×	×	ψ^-
Alice's bit flip		1	1			0			1
Bob's bit		1	1			0			1
Authentication key		1	1			0			1

Step1: Alice and Bob randomly prepare a string of BB84 polarization states: $|0\rangle|1\rangle|+\rangle|-\rangle$, then they send them to Charlie respectively.
Step2: Charlie performs the Bell state measurement when he received all photons, he publics those measurement results.
Step3: Alice and Bob publish their basis and discard the data of those different basis.
Step4: Either Alice or Bob performs a bit flip to the datas when the measurement result is Ψ^+.
Step5: Alice and Bob get the authentication key according to measurement results of Charlie.

2.2 Stage of Authentication

Alice verifies the Bob's identity based on a secret key that is shared between them in this section. Where Alice and Bob use a regulation. The regulation as follows in Table 3.

Table 3. Regulation of encoding form Alice and Bob. Alice and Bob prepare specified photons according the key. If their identities are legitimate, Charlie get the correct measurement outcomes.

Authentication key	00	01	10	11
Alice's photon	$|0\rangle$	$|1\rangle$	$|+\rangle$	$|-\rangle$
Bob's photon	$|1\rangle$	$|0\rangle$	$|+\rangle$	$|-\rangle$
Charlie's outcome	ψ^+	ψ^+	ψ^-	ψ^-

Step1: Alice and Bob prepare specific polarization states based the authentication key and send those photons to Charlie.

Step2: Charlie performs the Bell state measurement and publics the measurement results. If their identities are legal, they have identical key and generate related photons. When two photons from Alice and Bob enter the 50:50 beam splitter, Charlie always gets the specific measurement result: Ψ^+ or Ψ^-.

Step3: Alice verifies the Bob's identity. If the measurement results is correct, Bob's identity is legitimate, they go to the next step. Otherwise, they stop the communication.

2.3 An Example of MDI-QIA Protocol

In this section, we give a simple example about our scheme.

Step1: The authentication keys is shared by Alice and Bob in registration stage: 01100011.

Step2: Alice and Bob prepare their photons according to the regulation respectively as shown in Table 3. Alice prepares a string of polarization states: $|1\rangle|+\rangle|0\rangle|-\rangle$. Bob also prepares a string of polarization state: $|0\rangle|+\rangle|1\rangle|-\rangle$. Then they send those photons to Charlie.

Step3: Charlie performs the Bell state measurement and publics the measurement results. If their identities are legal, Charlie get measurement results: $\Psi^+\Psi^-\Psi^+\Psi^-$. It is shown that the identity authentication is successful. Otherwise, there are two possible scenarios: Bob is fake or there is an eavesdropper who is named Eve generally.

3 Analysis of MDI-QIA Protocol

3.1 Analysis of Correctness and Feasibility

The basic principle behind our scheme is based on the Hong–Ou–Mandel effect when two indistinguishable photons enter a 50:50 beam splitter.

The Hong–Ou–Mandel effect is when two identical single-photon waves enter a 50:50 beam splitter, the photons extinguish each other. Without loss of generality, when a photon enters a beam splitter, it will either be reflected or refracted. The probabilities of refection and refraction are determined by the reflectivity of this beam splitter [2].

In particular, if two identical photons enter a 50:50 beam splitter, they always exit the beam splitter together in the same output mode (refection and refraction). While they are prepared in orthogonal polarizations, they will exit the beam splitter in the same output arm, both photons always reach the same detector. When a photon enters a beam splitter, there are two possibilities: it is either reflected or transmitted [2]. The relative probabilities of transmission and reflection are determined by the reflectivity of the beam splitter. Here, we assume a 50:50 beam splitter, in which a photon has equal probability of being reflected and transmitted.

It is indicated that we can observe stable Hong–Ou–Mandel interference when two in- distinguishable photons from two independent laser sources enter 50:50 beam splitter [2]. Therefore, our scheme can be realized with the current technology.

3.2 Analysis of Security

In the authentication process, a photon is sent to Charlie from Alice or Bob. A malicious eavesdropper named Eve forges identity in this communication. We analyze the security of the scheme under the impersonation attack, measure resend attack, entangle and measure attack.

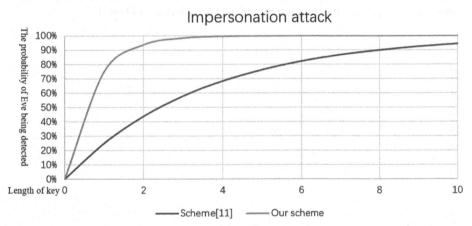

Fig. 2. The probability of Eve being detected of scheme [11] and our scheme in impersonation attack.

Impersonation Attack

Firstly, we assume a malicious eavesdropper Eve who impersonates Bob. She prepares randomly a string of polarization states in the situation without the correct key. As we all know, if two photons are different or nonorthogonal, Charlie can't get a successful measurement outcome. The probability that Charlie gets a successful measurement outcome is 1/4. This means the probability that Eve passes Alice's test is 1/4, while the probability that Eve passes the security mode is 3/4 in scheme [11]. The probability of Eve being detected is P_1 when the length of the key is N. The probability of Eve being detected in scheme [11] is P_2.

Where $P_1 = 1 - \left(1 - \frac{3}{4}\right)^N$, $P_2 = 1 - \left(1 - \frac{1}{4}\right)^N$. Our scheme has the higher security under the impersonation attack according to Fig. 2.

Measure Resend Attack

Secondly, Eve wants to intercept the photons from Bob and analyze some information about the correct key. All the photons are prepared by Bob based on the key, Eve measures those photons in the situation without the correct key, she selects the basis randomly. The probability that she guesses the measurement basis correctly is 1/2.

Eve resends the photons to Charlie. Charlie can't get a successful measurement. Alice finds the eavesdropper in time. The probability of Eve being detected is P_3. While the probability of Eve being detected in scheme [11] is P_4.

$$P_3 = 1 - \left(1 - \frac{1}{2}\right)^N. \tag{1}$$

$$P_4 = 1 - \left(1 - \frac{1}{4}\right)^N. \tag{2}$$

It is shown that Alice finds the Eavesdropper under the measure resend attack when the length of the key is long enough according to Eq. (1). Our scheme is more secure than scheme [11] under the measure resend attack as follows in Fig. 3.

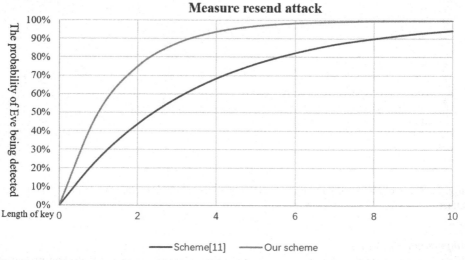

Fig. 3. The probability of Eve being detected of scheme [11] and our scheme in Impersonation attack.

Entangle and Measure Attack

Under the entangle and measure attack, Eve prepares a string of ancilla particles. Eve intercepts a photon from Bob and performs operation U on this photon and ancilla particle, she wish to get some information about the key. The operation U is described as in Eq. (3).

$$U|0, \delta\rangle = a|0, \delta_{00}\rangle + b|1, \delta_{01}\rangle.$$

$$U|1, \delta\rangle = b|0, \delta_{10}\rangle + a|1, \delta_{11}\rangle.$$

$$U|+, \delta\rangle = \frac{1}{2}|+\rangle(a|\delta_{00}\rangle + b|\delta_{01}\rangle + b|\delta_{10}\rangle + a|\delta_{11}\rangle)$$
$$+\frac{1}{2}|-\rangle(a|\delta_{00}\rangle + b|\delta_{01}\rangle + b|\delta_{10}\rangle + a|\delta_{11}\rangle). \qquad (3)$$

$$U|-, \delta\rangle = \frac{1}{2}|+\rangle(a|\delta_{00}\rangle - b|\delta_{10}\rangle + b|\delta_{01}\rangle - a|\delta_{11}\rangle)$$
$$+\frac{1}{2}|-\rangle(a|\delta_{00}\rangle - b|\delta_{10}\rangle - b|\delta_{01}\rangle + a|\delta_{11}\rangle).$$

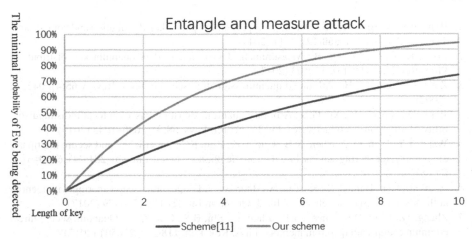

Fig. 4. The probability of Eve being detected of scheme [11] and our scheme in Entangle and measure attack.

Eve extracts some information after Charlie's measurement, while Eve's operation changes Charlie's measurement outcome. Alice finds the eavesdropper. The probability of Eve being detected is P_5, which is decided by b^2. The probability of Eve being detected in scheme [11] is P_6.

$$P_5 = \frac{1}{4}\left(\frac{1}{2} + \frac{1}{2} + b^2 + b^2\right) = \frac{1}{2}b^2 + \frac{1}{4}.$$

$$P_6 = \frac{1}{4}\left(\frac{1}{4} + \frac{1}{4} + b^2 + b^2\right) = \frac{1}{2}b^2 + \frac{1}{8}. \qquad (4)$$

The probability of Eve being detected is D when the length of the key is N. $D_1 = 1 - (1 - P_5)^N$. $D_2 = 1 - (1 - P_6)^N$. We can show that our scheme is more secure than scheme [11] under the entangle and measure attack from Fig. 4.

In this section, we analyze our scheme is secure under the impersonation attack, measure resend attack, entangle and measure attack. Eve want to personate Bob or obtain information about the key, her actions influence Charlie's measurement, and Alice determines the identity failure based on this phenomenon. It is shown that our scheme has the higher security from what has been discussed above.

4 Conclusion

We propose a MDI-QIA scheme in this paper, which has the higher security and can be realized with the current technology. In addition, our scheme introduces the idea of independent measurement equipment and uses single photons as the photon source. Compared with the exiting schemes, the safe transmission distance and the security under the general attacks have been significantly increased.

References

1. Bennett, C.H., Brassard, G.: Quantum cryptography: public key distribution and coin tossing. Theoret. Comput. Sci. **560**(12), 7–11 (2014)
2. Lo, H.K., Curty, M., Qi, B.: Measurement-device-independent quantum key distribution. Phys. Rev. Lett. **108**(13), 130503 (2012)
3. Zeng, G., Keitel, C.H.: Arbitrated quantum-signature scheme. Phys. Rev. A **65**(4), 042312 (2002)
4. Jiang, D.H., Xu, Y.L., Xu, G.B.: Arbitrary quantum signature based on local indistinguishability of orthogonal product states. Int. J. Theoret. Phys. **58**(3), 1036–1045 (2019)
5. Wang, T.Y., Wen, Q.Y., Chen, X.B., Guo, F.Z., Zhu, F.C.: An efficient and secure multiparty quantum secret sharing scheme based on single photons. Opt. Commun. **281**(24), 6130–6134 (2008)
6. Abulkasim, H., Hamad, S., Khalifa, A., Bahnasy, K.E.: Quantum secret sharing with identity authentication based on bell states. Int. J. Quantum Inf. **15**(04), 175–179 (2017)
7. Zhang, W., Ding, D.S., Sheng, Y.B., Zhou, L., Shi, B.S., Guo, G.C.: Quantum secure direct communication with quantum memory. Phys. Rev. Lett. **118**(22), 220501 (2017)
8. He, Y.-F., Ma, W.-P.: Multiparty quantum secure direct communication immune to collective noise. Quantum Inf. Process. **18**(1), 1–11 (2018). https://doi.org/10.1007/s11128-018-2119-z
9. Deng, F.G., Long, G.L.: Secure direct communication with a quantum one-time pad. Phys. Rev. A **69**(5), 052319 (2004)
10. Hu, J.Y., et al.: Experimental quantum secure direct communication with single photons. Light: Sci. Appl. **5**(9), e16144 (2016)
11. Hong, Ch., Heo, J., Jang, J.G., Kwon, D.: Quantum identity authentication with single photon. Quantum Inf. Process. **16**(10), 1–20 (2017). https://doi.org/10.1007/s11128-017-1681-0
12. Zawadzki, P.: Quantum identity authentication without entanglement. Quantum Inf. Process. **18**(1), 1–12 (2018). https://doi.org/10.1007/s11128-018-2124-2

13. Dong, Y.D., Peng, J.Y., Zhang, X.B., Zhang, Z.L.: Quantum identity authentication scheme based on measurement-device-independent quantum key distribution protocol. J. Commun. (2016)
14. Zhang, Z., Zeng, G., Zhou, N., Xiong, J.: Quantum identity authentication based on ping-pong technique for photons. Phys. Lett. A **356**(3), 199–205 (2006)
15. Jian, W., Quan, Z., Chao-Jing, T.: Multiparty simultaneous quantum identity authentication based on entanglement swapping. Chin. Phys. Lett. **23**(9), 2360 (2006)
16. Yang, Y., Wen, Q., Zhang, X.: Multiparty simultaneous quantum identity authentication with secret sharing. Sci. China Ser. G: Phys. Mech. Astron. **51**(3), 321–327 (2008). https://doi.org/10.1007/s11433-008-0034-5
17. Chen, Z., Zhou, K., Liao, Q.: Quantum identity authentication scheme of vehicular ad-hoc networks. Int. J. Theor. Phys. **58**(1), 40–57 (2019). https://doi.org/10.1007/s10773-018-3908-y
18. Liu, B., Gao, Z., Xiao, D., Huang, W., Liu, X., Xu, B.: Quantum identity authentication in the orthogonal-state-encoding QKD system. Quantum Inf. Process. **18**(5), 1–16 (2019). https://doi.org/10.1007/s11128-019-2255-0

Quantifying Community Detection Algorithms in Student Networks of Book Borrowing via Demographic Characterists

Fanjing Kong[1(✉)], Zhiqiang Meng[2], and Songtian Che[3]

[1] Library, Northeast Normal University, Changchun 130012, China
kongfj505@nenu.edu.cn
[2] Library System Department, Jilin University, Changchun 130117, China
mengzq@jlu.edu.cn
[3] Department of Ocular Fundus Disease of the Second Clinical Hospital, Jilin University, Changchun 130012, China
20688938@qq.com

Abstract. Students borrow books in university libraries with diverse motivations that associated with individual demographic characterists and therefore group into communities of students. In this paper, we analyze the relationship between demographic characterists and network communities of student borrowing behaviors using CDM. Taking the library system of Jilin University as a case study, we construct network with students as nodes and the connections between them as edges weighted by the number of shared borrowing books. The communities identify the group of students with borrowing similar books. The communities identify the group of students with borrowing similar books. Demographic characterists are mapped into nodes in the network and serve as independent variables to classify the community categories of students.

Keywords: Community detection · Student networks of book · Demographic factors

1 Introduction

Students study in a university, generating borrowing records in university libraries. Knowledge of the clusters of students with respect to reading books in a university is particularly beneficial for diverse practical applications, such as to develop the curriculum of optional courses and to capture the similarity and disparity of colleges [4]. Previous studies have applied community detection methods (CDMs) to unveil individual relationships with demographic characterists to understand the underlying behaviors of book borrowing [3, 6, 7, 13–15].

To analyze the book loan behaviors of university students, we construct a book-loan network with students as nodes and the connections between them as edges weighted by the number of shared borrowing books. The community in this co-loan network is applied for further analysis of book-loan behaviors as it offers a interpretation of

© Springer Nature Singapore Pte Ltd. 2020
X. Sun et al. (Eds.): ICAIS 2020, CCIS 1253, pp. 346–353, 2020.
https://doi.org/10.1007/978-981-15-8086-4_32

relational clusters, where a community is a set of students with more readily shared books among themselves than other groups. There are myriad available CDMs with the representatives of fast unfolding [1], infomap [9] and Combo [10], are applied to detect network community structures. Actually, there are underlying motivations (perhaps for courses, exams, traveling, and entertainment) when students borrow books in university libraries, which are associated with individual demographic characterists and therefore group into communities of students [5, 12]. For example, shared courses (e.g., computer science and English) connect students in different colleges and motivate them to borrow the same category of books in university libraries. This means book borrowing behaviors are not random but rooted in students' activities and demographic characterists (e.g., courses or entertainment) [2, 11]. Therefore, revealing the inherent consistency between network communities and demographic characterists would provides new insight for understanding motivations of book-loan behaviors in university students.

In this paper, we have three contribution: (1) We construct book-loan network with university students as nodes and connections between nodes as edges weighted by the volume of shared borrowing books in the study period. (2) We apply Combo CDM to detect communities to group students with heterogeneous demographic characterists. We consider the consistency between student communities and their demographic characterists (college, enrollment year, gender, original residence province, and original residence city) as a multi-class classification problem by adopting a stepwise logistic regression. (3) We further analysis the relationship between colleges with respect to Combo's results. We construct the feature vector for each college by counting the relative ratio of students in different communities. Using the method of hierarchical cluster tree, we cluster colleges to reveal their similarity and disparity in the perspective of students' book loan behaviors.

2 Methods

We construct a book-loan network, detect the co-loan communities, and analyze the relationship between demographic characterists and the detected communities to characterize the driving factors of book-loan behavior. With respect to the best results of identified communities, we inversely cluster college. First, we depict the construction of the book-loan network, and then present the CDMs used to identify co-loan communities associated with the classification method of stepwise logistic regression. Finally, we show how to construct and cluster the feature vectors for colleges with respect to identified communities.

2.1 Book-Loan Data

We collect 2,766 freshman of Jilin University, China in 2017 with 17,048 book loan records during the period from September 2017 to May 2018 across 42 colleges (School of Clinical Medicine, Jiaotong University, Instrument and Electrical, Sports Academy, public health, Public diplomacy, Animal Medical School, Animal Academy, School of Chemistry, Stomatology School, Zheshe College, Business School, Geodetic College, Geoscience Academy, Foreign Language School, Building School, Nursing School,

Mathematics Institute, art college, news and propagation, Mechanical Institute, Materials Institute, Plant Science, Botanical Academy, Automotive Institute, law school, Physics Institute, Environmental school, Life Science Academy, Biology and Agriculture, Electronics Institute, Bethune Medicine, School of Management, School of Economics, Art Academy, College of Pharmacy, Limton College, Administration College, IT Academy, Software College, Communication College, Food Academy). For each student, we also collect his/her demographic characterists (college, enrollment year, gender, original residence province, and original residence city).

2.2 Book-Loan Network and CDMs

To construct the book-loan network in this research, we take each student as a node. The edge between nodes is weighted by the number of shared books in the studied period between the two nodes.

In network science, we can cluster nodes into tightly connected groups (henceforth communities) and reveal the network clustering characteristics. Three representative community detection methods are adapt to our constructed networks with the traditional metric of modularity Q to measure the performance of network community detection [8]:

$$Q = \sum_{k=1}^{m} \left(\frac{w_k}{w} - \frac{w_k^{in} w_k^{out}}{w} \right) \tag{1}$$

Here, w_k is the total weight of edges connecting nodes in community k, w_k^{in}, and w_k^{out} are the total in- and out-weight of edges in community k, and w is the total weight of all edges in the network.

There are many CDMs, such as fast unfolding [1], infomap [9] and Combo [10]. Specifically, the method of fast unfolding takes value of strategies of moving nodes and merging communities [1]. The modularity is updated according the change of modularity by moving node i in community C:

$$\Delta Q = \left(\frac{\sum_C + w_{i,in}}{2m} - \left[\frac{\sum_{tot} + w_i}{2m} \right]^2 \right) - \left(\frac{\sum_{in}}{2m} - \left[\frac{\sum_{tot}}{2m} \right]^2 - \left[\frac{w_i}{2m} \right]^2 \right)$$

where P_C is the total weight of edges in community C, P_{tot} is the total weight of edges incident to nodes in community C, w_i is the total weight of edges incident to node i, $w_{i,in}$ is the total weight of the edges from i to nodes in community C, and m is the total weight of edges in the whole network.

Another method is infomap – a kind of random walk based algorithm – by adopting the Huffman code to enumerate a succession of locations visited by a random walker [9]. The objective function is:

$$\begin{cases} L(M) = q_\frown H(Q) + \sum_i^k p_\circlearrowright^i H(p^i) \\ p_\circlearrowright^i = q_{i\frown} + \sum_{\alpha \notin C_i} p_\alpha \end{cases} \tag{2}$$

where q_y is the total travelling probability from community i to another community. p_α denotes the probability of visiting nodes in community is the fraction of within module movements that occur in community i, plus the probability of exiting community i. $H(Q)$ and $H(P_i)$ denote the entropy of the community code book and the entropy of nodes in the i-th community.

Combo involves all three methods to optimize modularity with an upper bound of the execution time as $O(N^2 log(N_C))$ [10]. Here N is the number of nodes, and N_C is the number of communities in the network. Thus we mainly consider Combo in this analysis.

2.3 College Clusters

With respect to the best results of identified communities, we inversely cluster colleges. For the i-th college, its feature vector is denoted as $d_i = (d_1, d_2,..., d_k,..., d_{NC})$. Here N_C is the number of communities in the network. d_k is the percentage of students in the i-th college, who are in the k-th community. Using the method of hierarchical cluster tree, we can cluster colleges to find their similarity and disparity (Fig. 1).

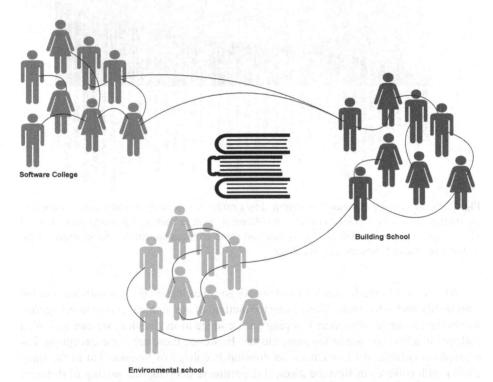

Fig. 1. Overview of book-loan network. We construct a book-loan network with students across colleges as nodes and the connections between them as edges weighted by the number of shared borrowing books.

3 Results

With respect to Combo community detection method, we begin to study the relationship between colleges and communities. We estimate the percentage of each of the four communities in different colleges as shown in Fig. 2. Different communities are marked by different colors. For the i-th college, its feature vector of percentages is denoted as $d_i = (d_1, d_2, d_3, d_4)$. Intuitively, we can find some colleges are similar, for example of the building school and communication college (Fig. 3).

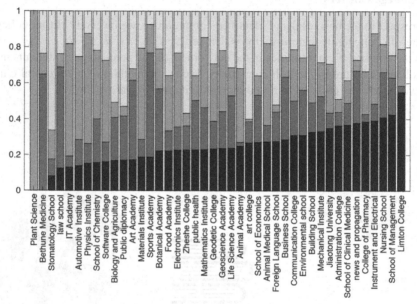

Fig. 2. Distribution of communities identified by Combo across colleges. Different communities are marked by different colors. For the i-th college, its feature vector of percentages is denoted as $d_i = (d_1, d_2, d_3, d_4)$. Intuitively, we can find some colleges are similar, for example of the building school and communication college.

With respect to the feature vectors for colleges, we cluster colleges with input of the community vector for each college using the method of hierarchical cluster tree. Figure 4 shows the cluster results. After mapping each college to its division, we can find most colleges in a division are in the same cluster. However, there are some exception. For example of college of life sciences, its division is college of Science, but in the same cluster with colleges in Bethune medical department, denoting the mixing of different divisions.

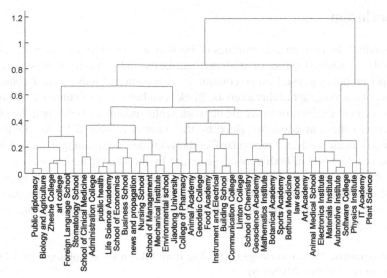

Fig. 3. College clusters. With respect to the feature vectors for colleges, we cluster colleges with input of the community vector for each college using the method of hierarchical cluster tree. Figure 4 shows the cluster results.

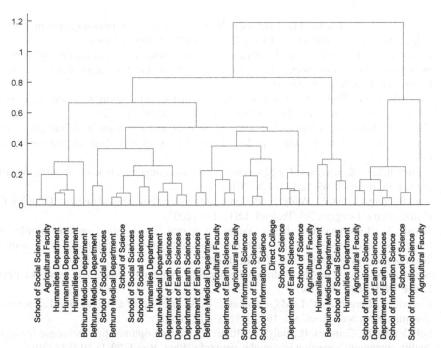

Fig. 4. Division clusters. There are nine divisions in Jilin university. Each division involves several colleges. We review the cluster results in Fig. 4 by checking each college's division.

4 Conclusion

Understanding the co-loan communities of book-loan behaviors in university libraries is valuable for understanding of students' similarity and disparity across colleagues. This paper proposes to use Combo community detection methods by their consistency with students' demographic characterists. Book-loan behaviors of students in university libraries are collected to construct the network with students as nodes and the connections between them as edges weighted by the number of shared books. Taking Jilin university as a case study, we recognize Combo is the best community detection method with good explanation of both network structure by modularity and social meaning by relationship with students' demographic factors. In summary, Combo could identify co-loan communities that are best explained by the demographic features. This paper may provide some insights for future application of redesign divisions, each of which involve similar colleges.

Acknowledgments. We acknowledge the funding from Jilin province philosophy social science planning fund project (no. 2019wt39).

References

1. Blondel, V.D., Guillaume, J.L., Lambiotte, R., Lefebvre, E.: Fast unfolding of communities in large networks. J. Stat. Mech. Theory Exp. **2008**(10), P10008 (2008)
2. Bussaban, K., Kularbphettong, K.: Analysis of users' behavior on book loan log based on association rule mining. World Acad. Sci. Eng. Technol. Int. J. Comput. Electric. Autom. Control Inf. Eng. **8**(1), 18–20 (2014)
3. Chowdhury, G.: Building environmentally sustainable information services: a green is research agenda. J. Am. Soc. Inf. Sci. Technol. **63**(4), 633–647 (2012)
4. Dillon, J.: Towards a Convergence Between Science and Environmental Education: The Selected Works of Justin Dillon, p. 269 (2016). 17 on scientific literacy and curriculum reform
5. Gambrell, L.B.: Seven rules of engagement: What's most important to know about motivation to read. Read. Teach. **65**(3), 172–178 (2011)
6. Gao, F., Xing, C., Du, X., Wang, S.: Personalized service system based on hybrid filtering for digital library. Tsinghua Sci. Technol. **12**(1), 1–8 (2007)
7. Jomsri, P.: Book recommendation system for digital library based on user profiles by using association rule. In: 2014 Fourth International Conference on Innovative Computing Technology (INTECH), pp. 130–134. IEEE (2014)
8. Newman, M.E., Girvan, M.: Finding and evaluating community structure in networks. Phys. Rev. E **69**(2), 026113 (2004)
9. Rosvall, M., Bergstrom, C.T.: Maps of random walks on complex networks reveal community structure. Proc. Natl. Acad. Sci. **105**(4), 1118–1123 (2008)
10. Sobolevsky, S., Campari, R., Belyi, A., Ratti, C.: General optimization technique for high-quality community detection in complex networks. Phys. Rev. E **90**(1), 012811 (2014)
11. Tonne, I., Pihl, J.: Literacy education, reading engagement and library use in multilingual classes. In: Pihl, J., van der Kooij, K.S., Carlsten, T.C. (eds.) Teacher and Librarian Partnerships in Literacy Education in the 21st Century. NRNV, pp. 63–74. SensePublishers, Rotterdam (2017). https://doi.org/10.1007/978-94-6300-899-0_5

12. Walsh, A.: The potential for using gamification in academic libraries in order to increase student engagement and achievement. Nord. J. Inf. Literacy High. Educ. 6(1), 39–51 (2014)

13. Xin, L., Haihong, E., Junde, S.: Community detection based on readers' borrowing records. In: 2013 IEEE International Conference on Green Computing and Communications (Green-Com) and IEEE Internet of Things (iThings/CPSCom) and IEEE Cyber, Physical and Social Computing. pp. 1001–1005. IEEE (2013)

14. Xin, L., E, H., Song, J., Song, M., Tong, J.: Book recommendation based on community detection. In: Zu, Q., Vargas-Vera, M., Hu, B. (eds.) ICPCA/SWS 2013. LNCS, vol. 8351, pp. 364–373. Springer, Cham (2014). https://doi.org/10.1007/978-3-319-09265-2_37

15. Yan, F., Zhang, M., Tang, J., Sun, T., Deng, Z., Xiao, L.: Users' book-loan behaviors analysis and knowledge dependency mining. In: Chen, L., Tang, C., Yang, J., Gao, Y. (eds.) WAIM 2010. LNCS, vol. 6184, pp. 206–217. Springer, Heidelberg (2010). https://doi.org/10.1007/978-3-642-14246-8_22

Knowledge Extraction and Knowledge Graph Construction Based on Campus Security Logss

Songfei Cao, Xiaoqiang Di, Yue Gong, Weiwu Ren[✉], and Xingxu Zhang

School of Computer Science and Technology, Changchun University of Science and Technology, No. 7089 Weixing Road, Changchun 1300022, Jilin, China
renww@cust.edu.cn

Abstract. Campus security log is an important information and data source of protecting campus network security. The analysis and application for campus security log are not inadequate, and security administrator is puzzled by the massive and multi-source security logs. It is difficult to extract implicit knowledge from security logs and to visualize it. How to extract and visualize it has been an urgent problem to be solved in the application of security knowledge engineering. Therefore, a knowledge extraction model based on entity relation triples is proposed in this paper, which deals with structured or semi-structured campus security logs. The knowledge graph of campus security logs is built by the extraction model and visualized in the form of graph. In the experiment, the implicit attack sources, methods and paths of security logs are analyzed and discovered by knowledge graph of campuses security logs. The experimental results demonstrate that the proposed model not only can extract implicit knowledge, but also efficiently visualize knowledge as graph.

Keywords: Knowledge graph · Campus security log · Knowledge extraction · Visualization · Multi-source and massive

1 Introduction

Knowledge graph is a technical method that uses graph model to describe knowledge and model the relationship between everything in the world [14], which is composed of entities, relations and attributes. It is essentially a knowledge base of semantic network, which can also be easily understood as a multi-relation graph, consisting of nodes and edges. Knowledge graph has been widely used in many industries and has shown increasing value in many areas, such as Semantic Retrieval, Question Answering, Data Analysis and other fields show increasing value. In terms of semantic search, effective semantic search of knowledge graph requires a simple and efficient search paradigm, which allows users to query and browse data in an intuitive, transparent and easy-to-use manner [15]. For example, Wang [16] mentioned that representation learning can be used for natural language semantic retrieval, and semantic retrieval based on knowledge

This work is supported by Jilin Science and Technology Development Plan Project of China (20190302070GX).

© Springer Nature Singapore Pte Ltd. 2020
X. Sun et al. (Eds.): ICAIS 2020, CCIS 1253, pp. 354–364, 2020.
https://doi.org/10.1007/978-981-15-8086-4_33

graph can be applied in natural language. Lu [10] proposes a graph-based Chinese WSD method with multi-knowledge integration to solve word disambiguation in natural language processing. In the aspect of Question Answering, natural language dialogues help people to acquire knowledge from knowledge base.

At present, knowledge graph is widely used in natural language, and there are also applications in the security field. For example, Niu [1], by using knowledge embedding method (attribute, opinion, opinion word) as a word vector into the Knowledge Graph by TransG, which is the application of knowledge map in the field of natural language. The article of Michael [5] describes the ontology developed for network security knowledge graph, which is an innovative use of knowledge graph in the security field. In the article of Jia [6], a five-element model of network security knowledge base was proposed. This model firstly constructed ontology based on structured and unstructured data, and then established ontology network security knowledge base. However, knowledge graph is rarely applied in security engineering. This paper is a practical application of knowledge graph in security log field.

Log is an important data to record the behavior of the system and user, and a lot of valuable information can be obtained by analyzing logs. The log records the information of intrusion detection analysis, and through the log analysis, it can check whether the network or system has the intrusion behavior of illegal security policies and the signs of being attacked [19]. Previous log studies mainly included log feature analysis, log fault diagnosis, log enhancement, etc., aiming to effectively improve log quality [8]. The current log is generated by host, virtual machine, storage, network security and other types of equipment and applications, which is characterized by multi-sourced, massive and unstructured. Therefore, how to convert logs into structured or visual data is a big problem, knowledge graph provides the possibility for unstructured data to be transformed into semi-structured or structured data. Literature [13] proposes a visualization method of console logs, which shows the amount of information recorded by each log entity in the system and the relation between entities. It is an innovative use of log visualization technology. Han [18] introduced the structure and key technologies of the network security situation awareness system in his paper, which is also the development direction of knowledge graph in network security visualization. At present, there is little literature on the visualization of campus security log using knowledge graph technology.

The campus security log is multi-source and massive, which is generated by the security equipment of the campus information center, and brings many troubles to security personnel during processing. Progress can hardly be made with traditional methods. Knowledge graph can well deal with knowledge extraction of security log and visualization problem at the same time. In this paper, a new security log extraction model is proposed to extract structured and semi-structured data. Then the Neo4j graph database is used to construct the knowledge graph of security log by processing the data. Finally, the logical analysis of the knowledge graph of security log is carried out to discover hidden relations in the security log.

2   Basic Theory

Knowledge graph are usually used to express more standardized and high quality data. In recent years, descriptive data analysis [7] has attracted more and more attention.

Descriptive data analysis is a method that relies on semantic description of the data itself to realize data analysis. Different from computational data analysis, it is mainly based on the establishment of various data analysis models. Descriptive data analysis highlights the semantics of pre-extracted data, establishes logic between data, and realizes data analysis by relying on logical reasoning methods (such as DataLog) [12]. This paper, the logic between entities and relations is established through triples, then the knowledge graph of security log is constructed, and finally, the further mining of security log is realized according to the descriptive data analysis method.

Knowledge graph was proposed by Google in 2012 as a knowledge base to enhance its search engine capabilities. And the current knowledge graph has been used to refer to a wide variety of large-scale knowledge bases. Knowledge graph describe relation facts in the form of triples (entity 1- relation - entity 2) [9]. A triple is a general representation of knowledge graph, which corresponds to an edge in the knowledge base network and the two entities connected by the edge. This is a common representation. For example, the resource description framework (RDF) technical standard published by the world wide web consortium (W3C) [11] is based on triples. Entity is a basic element of knowledge graph, which can refer to specific names, places, countries, dates, etc. Relation is the semantic relation between two entities, and different relations exist between different entities [20]. Attributes and attribute values are used to describe the characteristics inside the entity. The easiest way to store knowledge graph in a relational database is to create a table with three columns in the relation database. The schema for this table is: Triple (subject, predicate, object), which stores each triple in the knowledge graph as a row of records in the triple table. In the article of wang [17], he mentioned that the visual analysis of abnormal detection of knowledge graph refers to the using of the visual means of knowledge graph to analyze and find out the patterns or abnormal states that do not meet the expectations. However, he did not point out the practical application of knowledge graph in the security field. In this paper, after the security log is structured, the open source Neo4j graph database is used to build the security log knowledge graph. Firstly, the original log text was obtained, where the source IP, url, purpose IP, types of the log text are used as entities of triples, and the operations between two different IPs are used as relations. The source IP is the external IP of the school, and the purpose IP is the public network IP corresponding to the internal server of the school. Each IP is treated as an entity, and then a series of operations between source IP and purpose IP are used to extract useful relations between them. Each entity has corresponding attributes, such as the source IP location, source IP port number, attack method, the purpose IP also has attributes, such as the purpose IP port number, etc. There are three main types of relationship extracted in this paper: visit relationship, corresponding relationship and belong relationship. The following sections describe how to extract the entities from the log text and how to construct these three relations.

3   Core Algorithm

The entity and relation extraction of the security log in this article is also an important part of the security log knowledge graph. The data used is derived from the log records generated by the security devices in the campus information center. Currently, a large amount of data exists in the form of unstructured data, such as news reports, scientific literature and government documents. Text data oriented knowledge extraction has been a widely concerned issue. Log is a kind of unstructured data, so how to extract effective data in log is also a big problem. This paper analyzes the log generated by intrusion detection system and the useful information generated by network firewall. The following main characteristics of information are analyzed: time, source IP, source port, url, purpose IP, purpose port, type, protocol, method, severity level, action, description, hazard description, a total of 13 characteristics. Time, source IP, source port, purpose IP, purpose port and url are extracted from the logs of intrusion detection system, and the other seven characteristics are extracted from the network firewall device by the time of intrusion detection system and the way of IP binding. Other features are presented in a structured way. The following sections describe in detail how to extract these six characteristics from unstructured logs.

As shown in Fig. 1, log text data is input first. After analysis, each log text has these entity characteristics, including time, source IP, source port, destination IP, destination port, url, and so on. Then the whole log text is segmented, and the next step is entity identification of the six characteristics. Starting from the first segment, if there are several entity characteristics in this segment, the content of the entity will be saved, and then the next segment will be traversed to do the same operation. If these entities do not exist, the next segment is also traversed, and then the entity identification is performed as above, until the loop traverses the entire text. This ends the traversal process of the first log text, and the next text feature extraction process is the same. The entity feature algorithm extracted from the security log device is shown in Algorithm 1:

Algorithm 1 Entity content Extraction

Input: feature Dj={time,source IP,source Port,url,purpose IP,purpose Port},a seg- ment t={$s_1,s_2,...,s_n$}

Output: entity content

Initialize:$i \leftarrow i + 1$

while $i \le n$ **do**
  for $j \in [0, 1, 2, 3, 4, 5]$ **do**
    if D_j in segment s_j **then**
      select entity content
      save entity content to Document
      $i \leftarrow i + 1$
    end if
  end for
  $i \leftarrow i + 1$
end while

Through the extracted effective entity features above, the next step is data processing. There are currently four entities and three relations defined. The four entities are respectively "source", "url", "purpose" and "types". The three relations are "visit", "corresponding" and "belong". The other nine characteristics are attributes of these four entities and three relations. The visit relation is the access operation of the source IP to the URL, the corresponding relation is the purpose IP corresponding to the URL, and the belongs relation is the type of operation of the source IP to the purpose IP.

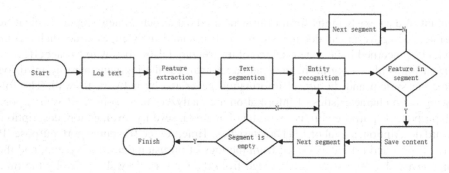

Fig. 1. Algorithm flow chart.

Then, triples are used to represent the relation between all the nodes, respectively: "source-visit-url", "url- corresponding-purpose" and "purpose-belong-types". Which this paper mainly defines 15 types of security: SQL injection, URL protection, WEB-SHELL upload, WEB login plaintext transmission detection, Weak password protection for web login, WEB whole site system vulnerability, XSS attacks, Method filtering, Buffer overflow detection, Directory traversal attacks, Website scanning, File download filtering, System command injection, Information leakage attack, Active defense. The constructed triples are shown in Table 1:

Table 1. Triple table of security log knowledge graph.

Entity 1	Relation	Entity 2
Source url purpose	Visit corresponding belong	url purpose types

Graph Database is a new type of non-relational database based on graph theory, which abstracts a graph into nodes, edges and other basic elements and stores them in a specific topological data structure. Each object in the graph database is a node, which can have multiple attributes, and the relationship between nodes is represented as edges [4]. Currently, knowledge graph is based on the data structure in the form of graph, and there are two main storage methods: RDF storage format and graph database [2]. Neo4j is a popular graph database that stores application data in the form of nodes, relationships, and attributes. Neo4j can easily represent the joined data and retrieve the joined data quickly. It can easily represent semi-structured data, and its query and construction language Cypher [3] is similar to SQL language. Cypher language is a special query language of Neo4j graph database. It has rich expressiveness, high query efficiency and can efficiently query and update graph database. With Neo4j, the hardware can be used more efficiently, thus reducing the cost. Therefore, this paper selects Neo4j graph database as a way to show the knowledge graph.

The entire process of building the security log knowledge graph is described below, as shown in Fig. 2:

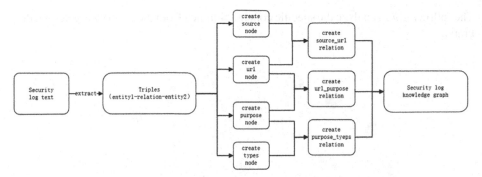

Fig. 2. Construction process of security log knowledge graph.

1. The security log is exported from the server equipment of the campus information center, and the features extracted by the algorithm 1 are preprocessed with the data. At the same time, effective entities are extracted according to the data filtered by firewall, there are mainly 4 kinds of entities and 3 kinds of relations.
2. The content we extracted in step 1 is constructed into triples (entity 1- relation - entity 2). There are three main relation types of triples, as shown in Table 1.
3. Use Neo4j graph database to create source node, url node, purpose node and types node.
4. Use Neo4j graph database to create source url relation, url purpose relation, and pupose types relation.

4 Experiments

The experiments in this paper are based on the Neo4j graph database introduced above. Firstly, the extracted entity and relation pairs are composed into three re- lation types: "source-visit-url", "url-corresponding-purpose" and "purpose-belong- types". Then the algorithm designed in this paper is used to insert the corresponding nodes and relations in Neo4j to construct the security log knowledge graph. Use the Cypher statement to present the contents of the knowledge graph. Enter the Cypher query statement: MATCH (n) RETURN (n) to present the nodes in the graph database. Because there are too many nodes in the knowledge graph, only part of the structure can be displayed.

As shown in Fig. 3, this is only a partial graph, showing a part of the security log knowledge graph. The whole security log knowledge graph has a total of 7260 nodes and 8989 kinds of relationships. Because IP involves campus private data, we use sourceIP, URL, purposeIP instead of a specific source IP, URL, and purpose IP, without showing the specific IP address and url. The name of the node is shown in the figure, and all four types of nodes are displayed in different colors. Although the same type of node has the same color, each node has different attributes and is unique. The outermost layer of light blue node represents the sourceIP, and the second layer of yellow node represents the url, the third layer of the red node represents the purposeIP, and the middle purple node represents the types. The security log knowledge graph composed of the above four kinds of nodes and three kinds of relations can clearly show the unique effect diagram.

The following will analyze the specific content obtained from the security log knowledge graph.

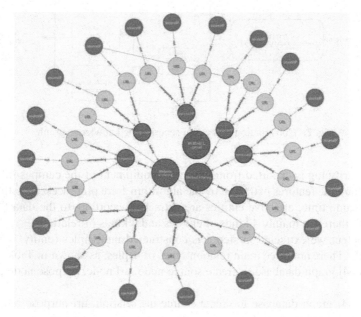

Fig. 3. Overview of the security log knowledge graph.

Figure 4 shows a simple chain of attacks, drawn from the sourceIP visiting url, then from the url to the corresponding purposeIP, and then from purposeIP to types. The attack chain diagram makes it clear to the user that this attack is a method filtering attack. As can be seen from Fig. 5, the attack chain diagram is a little more complex than that in Fig. 4, because the source IP visits multiple urls, while the destination IP corresponds to more than one url, and then it can be seen that the last attack type is a WEB upload vulnerability.

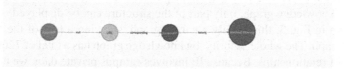

Fig. 4. Security log knowledge graph attack chain diagram-1.

The source IP attack chain expansion diagram are shown in Figs. 6 and 7. There is only one source IP (light blue node). In Fig. 6, two urls are visited by source IP, and in Fig. 7, multiple urls are visited by sourceIP, each of which corresponds to a different purposeIP, and each purposeIP belongs to a different type. It can be clearly seen from Fig. 7 that the source IP has carried out 6 different types of attacks. First, an attacker can

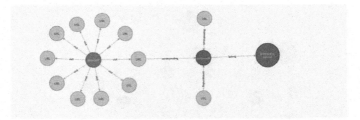

Fig. 5. Security log knowledge graph attack chain diagram-2.

find out the valid information of the website by visiting different urls, such as website container, script type, database type, website directory, etc. Then, finds out the IP address of the corresponding url to find the purpose port service and other related information. The related websites were found to have vulnerabilities, so malicious operations, such as promote privileges, WEBSHELL server upload and operation system command injection are carried out, and the source IP is marked as illegal, adding it to the blacklist. Finally, we can analyze that this is a type of malicious attack.

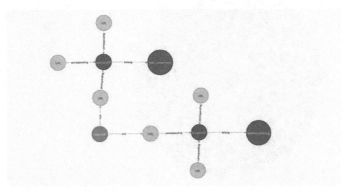

Fig. 6. Security log knowledge graph attack chain diagram-3.

Figures 8 and 9 present a type breakdown diagram and a type overview diagram, respectively. Figure 8 shows the purpose IP corresponding to SQL injection, from which we can find different kinds of url have the same type of SQL injection, which shows that these sites protection work can do it is not very well. There are some loopholes and protective measures should be strengthened.

As can be seen from Fig. 9, there are 15 attack types in total, each of which has a corresponding target IP. Some have relatively few purpose IPs, and some have quite many. As can be seen from the figure, the two largest areas are URL protection and website scanning, from which we can analyze that the source IP first did the website scanning of target site, then a firewall and other security equipment defined the operation as a web site scan type and URL protection. Next, attackers performed invasion on the url and purpose IP after acquiring useful information of the websites as well as their vulnerabilities. As can be seen from the figure, there are three parts: method of filtering,

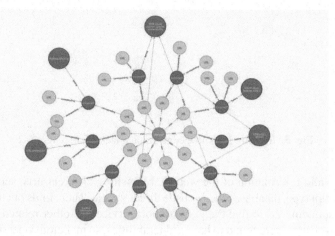

Fig. 7. Security log knowledge graph attack chain diagram-4.

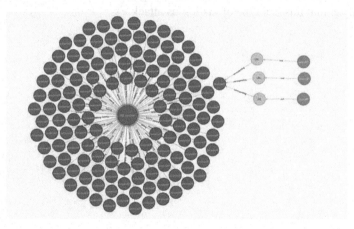

Fig. 8. A breakdown of the type of security log knowledge graph.

SQL injection and WEBSHELL upload. Then we can learn that the attackers do most of these three operations, so as to strengthen the security work on the website and server.

We can determine whether the attacker has attacked the campus website ac- cording to the display effect of the knowledge graph and the effective information mined inside. Firstly, it can be found that which attack type has the most number of IPs according to the knowledge graph, and it can be determined whether there is a vulnerability or whether there is sensitive information in the website. Next, attackers will filter methods on this website, trying to bypass the site protection settings, and further search the vulnerabilities of the website. Finally, it was found that WAF or firewall of the website could be bypassed, and then SQL injection or operation of lifting the privilege was carried out on the website, thereby obtaining campus database information and endangering the security of campus data. Through the above experiments, it can be seen from the above experiments that the visual practice effect of the security log in the knowledge map is obvious. At the same

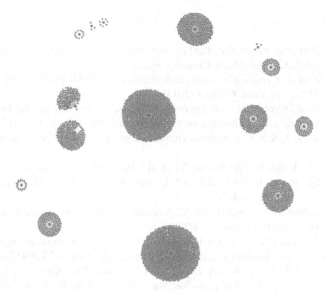

Fig. 9. Overview of the security log knowledge graph type.

time, useful information can be mined from the existing knowledge graph, which can restore the process of hacker attack on the website and further strengthen the campus network security.

5   Conclusions and Future Work

This paper applies knowledge graph technology to campus security log, which is an innovative practice of knowledge graph in the security field. Firstly, entities and relations are extracted from the security log, and the data is preprocessed. Then, the knowledge graph of the security log is constructed through the Neo4j graph database. Through the knowledge graph renderings constructed, descriptive data analysis method can be used to clearly show which of the purpose IPs are vulnerable to attack, whether the devices and servers corresponding to these IP store sensitive information. Simultaneously, through the analysis of an attacker's attack process, the information of the attacker's attack process can be mined, so as to strengthen the protection of the most attacked target website or server. In this way, the security of the campus network will be improved.

In the next step, we will specifically analyze the logs on a larger scale, not only in the aspect of security logs, but also in the logs of user behavior. Meanwhile, we will further mine the information in the logs. By applying the reinforcement learning method to the security log entity relation extraction, the knowledge graph technology can be more practical and automatic in the log extraction, and the knowledge graph can be further applied in the specific security field.

References

1. Bohan Niu, Y.H.: An improved method for web text affective cognition computing based on knowledge graph. Comput. Mater. Continua **59**(1), 1–14 (2019)
2. De Abreu, D., et al.: Choosing between graph databases and RDF engines for consuming and mining linked data. In: Cold. Citeseer (2013)
3. Francis, N., et al.: Cypher: an evolving query language for property graphs. In: Proceedings of the 2018 International Conference on Management of Data, pp. 1433–1445 (2018)
4. Huang, H., Yu, J., L.X.X.Y.: Review on knowledge graphs. Comput. Syst. Appl. **28**(6), 1–12 (2019)
5. Iannacone, M., Bohn, S., Nakamura, G., et al.: Developing an ontology for cyber security knowledge graphs. In: Proceedings of the 10th Annual Cyber and Information Security Research Conference, pp. 1–4 (2015)
6. Jia, Y., Qi, Y., Shang, H., Jiang, R., Li, A.: A practical approach to constructing a knowledge graph for cybersecurity. Engineering **4**(1), 53–60 (2018)
7. Kaminski, M., Grau, B.C., Kostylev, E.V., Motik, B., Horrocks, I.: Foundations of declarative data analysis using limit datalog programs. arXiv preprint arXiv:1705.06927 (2017)
8. Liao, X.K., Li, S.S., Dong, W., Jia, Z.Y., Liu, X.D., Zhou, S.L.: Survey on log research of large scale software system. Ruan Jian Xue Bao/J. Softw. **27**(8), 1934–1947 (2016)
9. Liu, Z., Sun, M., Liu, Z., Sun, M., Lin, Y., Xie, R.: Knowledge representation learning: a review. J. Comput. Res. Devel. **53**(2), 247–261 (2016)
10. Lu, W., et al.: Graph-based chinese word sense disambiguation with multi-knowledge integration. Comput. Mater. Continua **61**(1), 197–212 (2019)
11. Miller, E.: An introduction to the resource description framework. Bull. Am. Soc. Inf. Sci. Technol. **25**(1), 15–19 (1998)
12. Motik, B., Nenov, Y., Piro, R.E.F., Horrocks, I.: Incremental update of datalog materialisation: the backward/forward algorithm. In: Twenty-Ninth AAAI Conference on Artificial Intelligence (2015)
13. Rabkin, A., Xu, W., Wildani, A., Fox, A., Patterson, D.A., Katz, R.H.: A graphical representation for identifier structure in logs. In: SLAML (2010)
14. Singhal, A.: Introducing the knowledge graph: things, not strings. Official Google Blog **5**, 16 (2012)
15. Wang, H., Penin, T., Xu, K., et al.: Hermes: a travel through semantics on the data web. In: Proceedings of the 2009 ACM SIGMOD International Conference on Management of Data, pp. 1135–1138. ACM (2009)
16. Wang, R., Wang, M., Liu, J., Yao, S., Zheng, Q.: Graph embedding based query construction over knowledge graphs. In: 2018 IEEE International Conference on Big Knowledge (ICBK), pp. 1–8. IEEE (2018)
17. Wang, Y., Luo, S., Y.Y.Z.H.: A survey on knowledge graph visualization. J. Comput.-Aided Des. Comput. Graph. **31**(10) (2019)
18. Han, W., Tian, Z., Z.H.L.Z.Y.J.: System architecture and key technologies of network security situation awareness system YHSAS. Comput. Mater. Continua **59**(1), 167–180 (2019)
19. Weiwu, R., Bochen, Z., Xiaoqiang, D., Yinan, L.: Density clustering anomaly intrusion detection algorithm based on ABC-DBSCAN. J. Jilin Univ. (Sci. Edn.) **56**(1), 95–100 (2018)
20. Zenglin, X., Yongpan, S., Lirong, H., Yafang, W.: Review on knowledge graph techniques. J. Univ. Electron. Sci. Technol. Chin. (4), 589–606 (2016)

Research on the Influence of Different Network Topologies on Cache Performance for NDN

Min Feng[1], Huanqi Ma[2], Yong Hu[3], and Meiju Yu[1]([✉])

[1] College of Computer Science, Inner Mongolia University, Hohhot, China
1565295661@qq.com, csymj@imu.edu.cn
[2] 32153 Troops of the Chinese People's Liberation Army, Beijing, China
1336131432@qq.com
[3] North United Powerd Co., Ltd., Hohhot, China
nupc_nupc@126.com

Abstract. Named Data Network (NDN) is one of the most promising future Internet architectures and replaces the "thin waist" of TCP/IP hourglass model with the named data. Because all routers in the NDN network can cache contents passing by, users can obtain content from routers who cache the content without going to the remote server. Therefore, NDN greatly reduces network traffic and improves the speed of content distribution and retrieval. In this study, we focus on the impact of network topology on NDN cache performance. We utilize a dynamic popularity-based cache permission strategy for NDN which is called DPCP, take five different network topologies into account, and observe the influence on DPCP. The simulation experiments show that the DPCP strategy has the best cache performance in the nine-grid network topology with single-user and single-server and the 16-square grid network topology with single-user and single-server.

Keywords: Named data network · Network topology · NDN cache · DPCP cache policy

1 Introduction

At present, the core of the Internet is the TCP/IP protocol, which was originally designed for end-to-end host communication. However, with the rapid development of the Internet, the number of Internet users has exploded, and the content of network data has also expanded rapidly. Its own defects will lead to some problems such as low flexibility, congestion, and low scalability, so that it cannot cope with the increasing the growth of large-scale data content distribution [1]. The IDC report shows that by 2020, the global total data will exceed 40ZB (equivalent to 4 trillion GB) [2], the number of users and users' requirements for network service quality continue to improve, the existing TCP/IP-based Internet architecture shows more and more drawbacks, not only cannot meet the user's online experience, and the shortage of IP address resources has become a big problem. The NDN provides security mechanisms based on the data content itself

© Springer Nature Singapore Pte Ltd. 2020
X. Sun et al. (Eds.): ICAIS 2020, CCIS 1253, pp. 365–375, 2020.
https://doi.org/10.1007/978-981-15-8086-4_34

and a relatively flexible routing cache, which overcomes some problems such as network address translation and insufficient security. Therefore, NDN will be the typical representative of the most potential development in the future Internet architecture.

The biggest advantage of the NDN is that the content cached at the routing node can be requested by other routing nodes. This feature greatly realizes the reusability of network content resources and reduces the repeated transmission of the same content, thereby improving the utilization of network resources shortens the request response time [3]. In the NDN, the performance of the cache directly determines the performance of the network. Therefore, the research on the cache performance in the NDN is of great significance, and the factors affecting the performance of the cache strategy are the most important.

In this article, we focus on the study of one of the factors that affect cache performance, the network topology. We studied five different network topologies, based on the DPCP cache policy, simulated the experiment by setting the cache size and simulation time, and analyzed the results. Our goal is to verify the DPCP cache policy used in this experiment, and the performance of the caching performance is best under which network topology.

The rest of this paper is structured as follows. The second part introduces the existing work on the NDN caching strategy. The third section introduces the proposed research methods. The fourth section describes the simulation model used for the evaluation and the evaluation results. The fifth section is devoted to the conclusion.

2 Related Work

NDN, as a typical representative of the most potential Internet architecture in the future, is favored by many people, and people are constantly exploring the optimal cache strategy.

For the redundancy and inefficiency of most caching strategies in the NDN architecture, a cache placement strategy BEP based on node mediation and edge content popularity is proposed to place the most popular content on the most important nodes. To make efficient use of scarce cache resources [4]. In order to achieve efficient NDN cache replacement, a cache replacement strategy combining dynamic popularity with request cost is designed. Each node is caused to separately calculate the dynamic popularity of the cached content and the weighted (DPC) value of the request cost, and based on the value, the replacement of the cached content, retaining the content of high popularity and high request cost. On this basis, according to the DPC value of the content, it classifies the cache decision algorithm and selects the node placement cache [5].

Literature [6] studies the deterministic cache and probabilistic cache in NDN, and proposes a hybrid NDN cache strategy (HDP) combining deterministic cache and probabilistic cache. Based on the idea of regional partitioning, a deterministic caching strategy based on heat is adopted at the edge of the network, and a probabilistic caching strategy based on cache revenue and content heat is adopted in the network core, thereby combining the advantages of the two caching strategies to further improve the performance of the NDN cache. Literature [7] proposes a content caching strategy Path-LCE strategy, which combines the LCE caching strategy and the path coordination strategy in the traditional NDN network to cache the file content. Path coordination strategy is adopted in the core routing nodes to reduce content redundancy and improve cache space utilization. Use the LCE policy on the edge routing node to get the content hit as soon as possible.

Literature [8] proposed GFcache, a greedy fault cache considering the failure rate and failure frequency. When data is requested, temporary failure may occur. GFcache uses greedy opportunistic algorithm to cache damaged data, which is used to realize fault information sharing among users and reduce unnecessary data repeated cache. GFcache includes FARC capture and replacement algorithm. The algorithm adapts to data content damage failure by considering the occurrence rate and failure frequency of data failure. The cached data can be obtained quickly to meet the normal data access, so it has a good hit rate. Literature [9] proposes a research on improving memory cache management based on spark, which proposes RDDs caching and LRU optimization methods based on partition features. It will automatically monitor the cache usage on each node. When there is a content RDD that needs to be reused, it will cache based on previous experience. When the memory capacity is insufficient, LRU strategy is used to replace the cache. This strategy can effectively improve the memory utilization. Literature [10] considers four characteristics of RDD when RDD needs to be replaced due to insufficient memory, which makes the cache more valuable, and this method further improves the efficiency of job execution.

3   Method

3.1   Dynamic Popularity-Based Caching Permission (DPCP)

The cache mechanism of the Dynamic Popularity-Based Caching Permission (DPCP) [11] is: the use of the DPCP cache policy to cache data information on a node must meet the following two conditions: (1) DPCP enables all routers on the path to obtain popularity values of content carried by interest packets and data packets, and compare whether the value is averaged and the average popularity value on the node to determine whether to cache. If the value is greater than the average popularity value of the node, it may be cached, otherwise it will not be cached. (2) DPCP introduces the cache control flag CC, and determines whether to cache by determining the value. If the value of CC is 0, it will be cached, otherwise it will not be cached. By introducing CC, the redundancy of adjacent routers is effectively reduced and the utilization of cache resources is improved.

There are four tables in DPCP, which are CS table, FIB table, PIT table, and Content Popularity Table (CPT). The functions of the four tables are as follows:

The CS table (Content Store table), which mainly stores data. When the packet passing through the router satisfies the cache condition, the contents of the packet are cached in the CS table.

The FIB table (Forwarding Information Base) plays the role of information routing. When the interest packet sent by the user arrives at the router, if the router fails to find the matching content in the CS table, the next node is selected through the FIB table to forward the interest packet.

The PIT table (Pending Interest Table) is mainly for the interest packets that fail to meet the demand, and records the interface information of the interest packets entering the router. If the same request is entered from a different interface, there is no need to create a new PIT entry, and only the interface information of the incoming node needs to be added to the generated corresponding request entry. When the required content of the interest package matches successfully and returns to the node, the returned data packet only needs to be returned to the requester from the node that the interest packet recorded in the PIT table entries, and the corresponding PIT entry is deleted.

The CPT table (Content Popularity Table), which is a new table structure added by DPCP, mainly stores the state of the cache control flag CC. The router reads the state of the cache control flag CC through the table to determine whether to store the information of the data packet, thereby avoiding storing the same redundant copy in the neighboring router.

The DPCP cache policy is used to determine whether the router caches data information, which effectively reduces the redundancy of adjacent router data, improves the utilization of cache resources, increases the diversity of data in the network, and reduces the replacement frequency of content in the router.

3.2 Several Common Network Topologies

(1) **Topology 1:** The topology is shown in Fig. 1, which is a topology of a binary tree structure. In this topology, there are multiple users and one server, and users can only reach the server through one link.

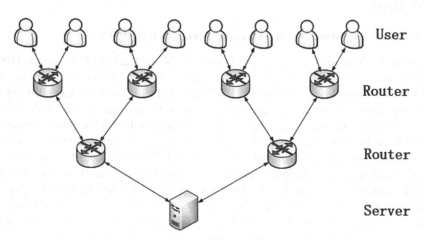

Fig. 1. Structure of topology 1.

(2) **Topology 2:** The topology is shown in Fig. 2, which is a topology of a nine-grid structure. In this topology, there is only one user and one server, and user can reach the server through multiple links.

(3) **Topology 3:** The topology is shown in Fig. 3. This topology is similar to the structure of topology 2. It is a topology of a sixteen-grid structure. The topology also has only one user and one server, but the user-to-server link in the topology is more than topology 2.

User

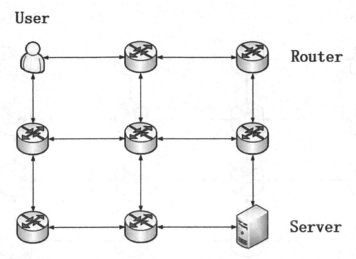

Fig. 2. Structure of topology 2.

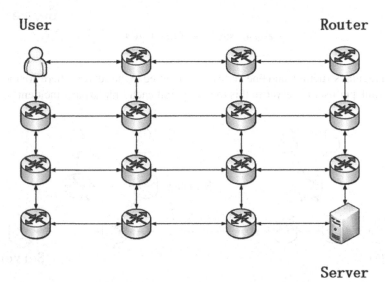

Fig. 3. Structure of topology 3.

(4) **Topology 4:** The topology is shown in Fig. 4. The topology is similar to the topology 3. The only difference is that there is only one user in topology 3, and there are four users in the topology. Compared to topology 3, the user-to-server link in this topology has a corresponding reduction.

(5) **Topology 5:** The topology is shown in Fig. 5. The topology is similar to the topology of a mesh structure, but it is different from the mesh topology. In the middle of the top of the topology is a quadrilateral structure. Each vertex of the quadrilateral has

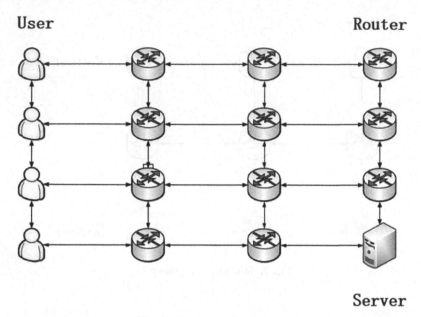

Fig. 4. Structure of topology 4.

a triangular structure, and one vertex is connected to the server. There are more than one link per user to server in this topology, but each link has a coincident segment.

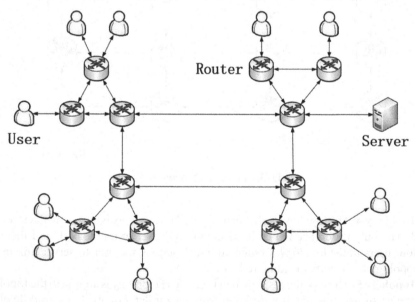

Fig. 5. Structure of topology 5.

3.3 Experimental Method

ndnSIM

ndnSIM is a well-known module of the NS-3 open source framework, which can be considered the most complete simulator because it can accurately represent all aspects of the NDN architecture. As a new network layer protocol model implementation, it can run on any available link layer protocol model, network layer protocol model and transport layer protocol model. This flexibility allows for the simulation of a wide variety of homogeneous and heterogeneous scenarios. The simulator is implemented in a modular form, using a separate set of C++ classes to model the behavior of each network layer entity in the NDN: Content Store (CS), Pending Interest Table (PIT) and Forwarding Information Base (FIB), network and applications program interface, interest table forwarding strategy, etc. In addition, the simulator provides a large number of interfaces and sets of helpers to perform tracking behavior of each component and NDN traffic flow [9].

The new version of the ndnSIM component based on the NS-3 Named Data Network (NDN) simulator has undergone extensive refactoring and rewriting. The key new features in the new version: the packet format is changed to the NDN packet format, and ndnSIM uses the implementation of the basic NDN primitive from the ndn-cxx library (NDN C++ library with eXperimental eXtensions).

Specific Method

In order to study the impact of different network topologies on cache performance, we decided to conduct a comparison test of different network topologies based on a caching strategy, and verify the cache structure to be more suitable for what kind of network structure. First, we chose to experiment on the ndnSIM simulator. Secondly, we choose DPCP cache policy, which is used to judge whether the router caches data information, effectively reduces the redundancy of adjacent router data, improves the utilization of cache resources, increases the diversity of data in the network, and reduces the replacement frequency of the content in the router. Again, we choose five representative network topologies. After the preparation is completed, we change the cache size of each network topology node based on the DPCP cache policy on the ndnSIM simulator, and set different simulation times for simulation experiments. After comparing and analyzing the simulation results, we come to the conclusion of this paper is that the DPCP cache policy is more suitable for the topology of topology 2 and topology 3.

4 Simulation

4.1 Simulation Parameter Settings

In this experiment, we selected five different network topologies. The simulation time of two groups of variables (simulation time and cache size) is 200, 400 and 600 respectively, and the cache size is 10, 50 and 100 respectively. The experimental parameters are set as shown in Table 1.

Table 1. Simulation parameter table

Parameter name	Font size and style
DPCP enable	1
CC enable	1
Cache limit	10, 50, 100
Simulation time	200, 400, 600
Number of contents	10000
S of Zipf	1.5
Q of Zipf	0
Frequency	25

4.2 Simulation Comparison Index

In this experiment, we compare the following three indicators to illustrate the impact of different network topologies on the cache situation:

(1) Cache hit rate: the ratio of the total number of packets cached by all nodes to the total number of interest packets requested by all users.
(2) Cache replacement rate: the ratio of the number of cache replacements for all routers to the number of routers.
(3) Cache diversity: the ratio of the number (type) of different data in the cache to all the cache capacity.

4.3 Simulation Results and Analysis

We completed the experiment through the above parameters and topology settings. Since the system is in the start up phase at the initial stage of the simulation phase, the performance is unstable and there is an error. Therefore, in the process of processing the experimental data, we calculate the average value of the experimental data obtained from three groups of simulation time, so as to make the experimental results more accurate.

Cache Hit Ratio

Figure 6 compares the cache hit rates of the five topologies at different cache sizes. According to the chart, we can visually see:

When the cache size is small, the impact of topology on cache hit rate is obvious. DPCP has the highest cache hit rate in topology 3, the second in topology 2, and the lowest in topology 4.

When the cache size is large, the effect of different topology on cache policy is not obvious. This is because when the cache setting is large, there will be more content cached by nodes, and most of the content requested by users will have cache copies in the router. Therefore, in this case, the cache hit rate tends to be saturated, so the figure

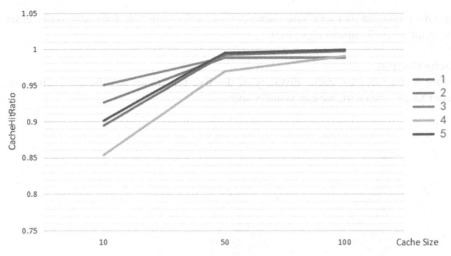

Fig. 6. Comparison of cache hit ratios under different caches.

shows that the cache hit rate in different topological environments has little difference, and the impact on the cache strategy is not obvious.

Cache Replacement Rate

Figure 7 compares the cache replacement rates for the five topologies at different cache sizes. According to the chart, we can visually see:

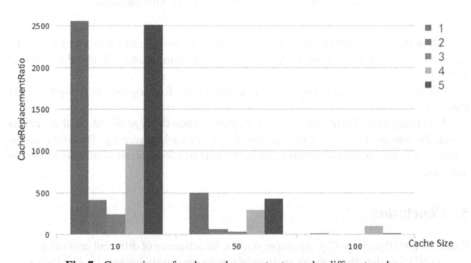

Fig. 7. Comparison of cache replacement rates under different caches.

When the cache size is small, DPCP has the lowest cache replacement rate in topology 3, the second lowest in topology 2, and the highest in topology 5.

When the cache size is large, the cache replacement rate in the five topologies tends to 0. This is because the cache is large and there are many cached contents. Most of the contents requested by users have cache copies in the router, so the cache replacement rate is quite small, almost close to 0.

Cache Diversity
Figure 8 compares the cache diversity of the five topologies at different cache sizes. According to the chart, we can visually see:

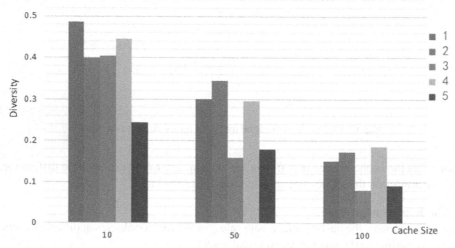

Fig. 8. Comparison of cache diversity under different caches.

When the cache size is small, the cache diversity is the highest in topology 1, the second in topology 4, the third in topology 3, the fourth in topology 2, and the lowest in topology 5.

When the cache size is large, the diversity of the five topologies is significantly reduced.

According to the definition of cache diversity, when the type of data in the cache is larger, the smaller the cache capacity, the higher the cache diversity. Therefore, as the cache size value increases, the diversity in various topological environments gradually decreases.

5   Conclusion

Based on DPCP cache policy, this paper studies the influence of different network topologies on NDN cache. Through the analysis of the above simulation results, it is found that different network topologies do have an impact on NDN cache, which mainly affects the following three aspects: cache hit rate, cache replacement rate and cache diversity. According to the above three aspects, DPCP has the best performance in topology 2 and topology 3.

Acknowledgment. This work is supported by the Inner Mongolia Natural Science Foundation of China under Grant No. 2018MS06024, the Research Project of Higher Education School of Inner Mongolia Autonomous Region under Grant NJZY18010, the National Natural Science Foundation of China under Grant No. 61862046 and the CERNET Innovation Project under Grant No. NGII20180626.

References

1. Fei, Y., Zhu, H., Li, X.: Modeling and verification of NLSR protocol using UPPAAL. In: 2018 International Symposium on Theoretical Aspects of Software Engineering (TASE) (2018)
2. He, Y.: Research on the reconstruction of the rational orbit of network public opinion in big data thinking. Fujian Theor. Stud. (5), 42–45 (2016)
3. Liu, W.: Research on cache strategy in named data network (2015)
4. Chen, J., Zheng, Q., Wang, S.: NDN caching strategy based on node median and edge popularity. Comput. Eng. (2019)
5. Guo, C., Zheng, Q., Ding, Y., Wang, S.: Cache strategy based on dynamic popularity and request cost in named data networking. Comput. Eng (2018)
6. Song, C., Li, C., Liu, X.: Hybrid NDN caching strategy based on region division. Appl. Res. Comput. (2019)
7. Song, Q., Wu, J., Ma, Y., Hu, Z.: Path-LCE: a NDN cache policy based on LCE and path coordination policy. J. Huazhong Univ. Technol. (Nat. Sci. Ed.) (S1) (2016)
8. Deng, M., Liu, F., Zhao, M., Chen, Z., Xiao, N.: GFCache: a greedy failure cache considering failure recency and failure frequency for an erasure-coded storage system. Comput. Mater. Continua 58(1), 153–167 (2019)
9. Wang, S., Zhang, Y., Zhang, L., Cao, N., Pang, C.: An improved memory cache management study based on spark. Comput. Mater. Continua 56(3), 415–431 (2018)
10. Wang, S., et al.: A dynamic memory allocation optimization mechanism based on spark. Comput. Mater. Continua 61(2), 739–757 (2019)
11. Yu, M., Li, R.: Dynamic popularity-based caching permission strategy for named data networking (2018)
12. Tortelli, M., Piro, G., Grieco, L.A., Boggia, G.: On simulating bloom filters in the ndnsim open source simulator. Simul. Model. Pract. Theory 52, 149–163 (2015)
13. Acs, G., Conti, M., Gasti, P., Ghali, C., Tsudik, G.: Cache privacy in named-data networking (2013)
14. Shailendra, S., Sengottuvelan, S., Rath, H.K., Panigrahi, B., Simha, A.: Performance evaluation of caching policies in NDN - an ICN architecture (2016)
15. Wang, G., Liu, J., Li, X., Yang, S., Li, G.: Modeling chunk-based content placement in information centric networking. J. China Univ. Posts Telecommun. (03), 48–54 (2017)
16. Rezazad, M., Tay, Y.C.: Ndn; mem: an architecture to alleviate the memory bottleneck for named data networking. In: Workshop on Student Workhop. ACM (2013)
17. Cui, X., Liu, J., Huang, T., Chen, J., Liu, Y.: A novel in-network caching scheme based on betweenness and replacement rate in content centric networking. J. Electron. Inf. Technol. 36(1), 1–7 (2014)

Research on Vehicle Network Routing Algorithm Based on Statistical Behavior

Hui Li[✉], Jun Feng, Yanli Gong, and Jialing Liu

School of Electronics and Automation, Inner Mongolia Electronic Information Vocational
Technical College, Hohhot 010070, Inner Mongolia, China
lihui_v@126.com

Abstract. With the development and popularization of mobile communication
terminals, a new wireless mobile delay tolerant network called the Vehicle interconnection is proposed. Routing algorithm is one of the hotspots and difficulties in
the vehicle networks. The vehicle networks with social attributes is widely used, so
it is of great significance to study the routing algorithm in the vehicle networks with
social attributes. Many routing algorithms based on static community have been
proposed. However, in the communication process of the vehicle networks, due to
the interference of selfish nodes, energy constraints, communication barriers and
other factors, the community in the network shows dynamic uncertainty. In order
to improve the success rate of information delivery and reduce the delivery delay
when multiple factors interfere with the vehicle network, this paper studies the
vehicle network routing algorithm based on the uncertain community. Based on
the existing research at home and abroad, this paper studies the interference factors
of communication in the vehicle networks, monitors, discovers and forecasts the
dynamic change trend of uncertain communities, constructs the community ratio-
nality intelligent evaluation system model, designs and implements the routing
algorithm of the vehicle networks based on uncertain communities, and verifies
the effectiveness of the algorithm.

Keywords: Vehicle networks · Stratified model of vehicle network · Community
division · Vehicle trajectory

1 Introduction

With the progress of communication technology and the development of Internet of
things, the vehicle networks has gradually become one of the research hotspots in the
field of computer and communication. The vehicle networks have broad application
prospects in road traffic safety, guidance, location and information sharing, and has
been widely valued in the world.

The original version of this chapter was revised: The affiliation information of
the authors has been changed. The correction to this chapter is available at
https://doi.org/10.1007/978-981-15-8086-4_66

However, at present, the vehicle networks have not been widely used. This is because the vehicle networks have obvious deficiencies in information transmission. In order to solve this problem, researchers put forward two solutions: to improve the ability of information transmission by improving the network structure of the vehicle networks, or to improve the communication utility of the vehicle networks by improving the routing algorithm of information transmission in the vehicle networks.

Due to the randomness of the vehicle's mobile behavior in the vehicle networks, the network structure composed of vehicles changes rapidly. However, the routing algorithm often forwards messages based on the topological structure in the network. In this case, the message routing must be quite different from the traditional wired network and wireless ad hoc network. At present, the improvement of the communication efficiency of the vehicle networks is mainly achieved by improving the efficiency of the routing algorithm of the vehicle networks. The research of routing algorithm is one of the hotspots in the vehicle networks. The existing routing algorithm of the vehicle networks is mainly based on the logical structure model of the network, that is, based on the statistical characteristics of the stability between vehicles in the network, the evolution process of the logical topology of the network is analyzed, and the routing algorithm is designed by combining the statistical characteristics and the evolution of the logical topology of the network. In urban road traffic, due to the stable statistical characteristics of the driver's movement behavior, the vehicle movement behavior has a certain statistical regularity because of the influence of the driver. Therefore, the vehicle movement behavior and the driver's statistical behavior have a certain connection.

2 Related Work

In recent years, with the development of mobile communication terminals, researchers have proposed a new type of wireless mobile ad hoc network for the vehicle network. In vehicle network, there is no end-to-end link between nodes, message transmission delay, low cost, suitable for easy network infrastructure in the Harsh environment communications [1–4].

Social relations exist in the social relationship of the vehicle network. At present, there have been a variety of vehicle networks routing algorithms [9–11], based on community division [5–8]. The existing partitioning algorithm is based on the steady-state topology; however, in vehicle network, the nodes with the selfishness of different types of news propagation, node topology and topology on different available, sensitive and unsteady state news shows, the partitioning algorithm of the method to be reused, it will consume a large amount of computing time the processor. By statistically modeling the vehicle's mobile behavior model in urban road traffic, the paper analyzes the stable statistical characteristics of vehicles, constructs a statistical model that reflects the stable logical structure and internal connection of the vehicle network, and analyzes the future of the vehicle based on the statistical characteristics of the vehicles in the network. Behavior, and design vehicle networking routing algorithms based on statistical characteristics and analysis of future behavior.

3 Proposed Approach

3.1 Tasks Need to Accomplish

The paper studies the vehicle movement behavior in urban road traffic, and finds its statistical and stable characteristics. Due to the influence of the driver's stable behavior, the vehicle's movement trajectory, destination, and encounter timing are presented as strong reproducibility of time and space. This reproducibility is between vehicles and roads, vehicles and locations, and between vehicles. The performance of stable statistical behavior. Therefore, through the statistics and analysis of the vehicle's movement behavior, the corresponding statistical model is established for the vehicle, and based on its statistical model, the vehicle behavior prediction is carried out. Based on the pre-judgment of vehicle behavior, the thesis designs a vehicle routing algorithm based on behavior statistics. And the main research content includes:

(1) Collecting data

Data collection is the first content to be studied in this paper, and data collection has certain difficulties. The paper intends to communicate and coordinate with the teachers in many colleges and universities in the university city, and launch as many volunteers as possible to participate in the experimental vehicle network to build a research-type car network with a certain number of vehicles.

(2) Analyze the statistical behavior of vehicles

In the process of road traffic, although there is no stable connection between the vehicles in the network, stable message routing cannot be performed, but because the driver is the teacher of the university city college, and because of the teachers, teachers and places There is significant spatiotemporal repeatability, and its movement behavior is frequent and stable. Vehicle behavior based on driver behavior expectations also has stable statistical characteristics. Stable connections between vehicles can be mapped to stable statistical models between vehicles and between vehicles and locations.

(3) Predicting the behavior model of the vehicle

The pre-judgment model of vehicle movement behavior is established by (1) constructing the research-type vehicle network used for data collection and the statistical model based on the frequent and stable connection of vehicles established by (2). The model can predict the movement trajectory of the vehicle and the timing of the encounter.

(4) Vehicle routing algorithm based on statistical behavior

First, analyze the characteristics of the message spread in the Internet of Vehicles.
Secondly, using the vehicle's stable behavioral statistical model to predict the vehicle's mobile behavior, and based on the pre-judgment results and vehicle activity analysis, it provides decision-making basis for message forwarding. Finally, the design of

the vehicle routing algorithm based on vehicle behavior statistics is completed, and the effectiveness of the routing algorithm proposed in this paper is verified by the verification in the experimental network. This is the key work to be completed in this paper.

3.2 Overall Design

The paper interconnects the vehicles of various institutions to form a network of vehicles with a certain number of vehicles. The car network is affected by the stable statistical characteristics of the driver (for example, the driver often has a colleague relationship, and may be in the same residential area in the urban area), and has a certain stable relationship. Through the data collection of the vehicle network composed of the volunteers provided by the colleges and universities, the vehicle explores the stable characteristics of the vehicle, and predicts the vehicle's mobile behavior based on the statistical model. The vehicle routing algorithm based on behavior statistics is designed and verified. Communication efficiency. Specific steps are as follows:

First, build a certain scale of experimental vehicle networking with stable characteristics for data collection.

Then, behavioral statistical modeling, through the analysis of the vehicle's mobile behavior, using the frequent pattern mining technology in data mining to study the stable statistical characteristics between vehicles, that is, the stable connection between vehicles caused by the stable connection of the driver, and finally Establish stable linkages and statistical models between vehicles.

Next, based on the behavioral statistical model between vehicles, predict the movement trajectory, speed, direction of the vehicle and the timing and position of the encounter between the vehicles, and complete the design of the vehicle routing algorithm based on the statistical model.

Finally, the verification and testing of the routing algorithm is completed. Based on the data, the paper analyzes the frequent and frequent connections in the data, studies the correlation between multiple scenes in the mobile model and the multiple scenes in the encounter model, and establishes a mathematical model representation of the stable relationship. Analyze changes in the behavior of the vehicle and predict the characteristics of the vehicle and space within a certain period of time. The vehicle routing algorithm based on behavior statistics is designed, and the data is transmitted in the volunteer test vehicle network. The data transmission efficiency is analyzed and the effectiveness of the routing algorithm is verified.

3.3 Stratified Model Algorithm

Stratified Model. The key of building a Statistical behavior model is to determine the sensitivity of mobile nodes to different types of messages, that is, the mobile nodes that are sensitive to the same type of messages are divided into the same layer. In the vehicle networks, under all specific scenarios, all nodes have been informed of the types of messages propagated in the network.

Algorithm 1:
Statistical behavior model
Input: the physical mobile node set J.
Output: the logical layer H_K .
{
   1.ENQUEUE(Q_2,S) //Messages in message set S are placed in queue Q_2 in turn
   2.While Q_2.h!=NULL //The Q_2 queue head element is not empty
   3. DEQUEUE(Q_2,M_K) //Take the Q_2 queue head element into the M_K
   4. ENQUEUE(Q_1, J) //Put the nodes in J into queue Q_1 in turn
   5. While Q_1.h!=NULL //The Q_1 queue head element is not empty
   6.   DEQUEUE(Q_1, N_i++) //Take the Q_1 queue head element into the N_i
   7.   Send M_K to N_i //Send message M_K to N_i
   8.   If Pop(Ni.Message_Memory_STACK==M_K)
     //If N_i can pass message M_K
   9. N_i->VK_i, add(H_K, VK_i) //Setting up VK_i for N_i on HK
   10. End While
   11. End While
}

Topology Model. In the vehicle network which is affected by human behavior, the movement and meeting of the nodes have social attributes. The analysis of social relations between the nodes is steady. According to the characteristics of the vehicle network, the following algorithm of social relation topology is established on the vehicle network layer.

Algorithm 2:
model of social relation topology.
Input: node set I_K.
Output: the social relationship topology model on H_K .
Map_to_graph()
{
   1.Set(min_rtime, min_mdis , min_mtime , min_mcont)
   2.While run_time>min_rtime //Network runtime longer than a given threshold
   3.   While i:1->n ; j:1->n
   5.   If Dis(V_{Ki}, V_{Kj}); <= min_mdis //Meeting of nodes
   4.   If Stay_T(V_{Ki}, V_{Kj}); >min_mtime //Meet effectively
   6.   num_cont$_{ij}$++; //Number of effective meeting times
   7.   End If
   8.   End If
   9.   If num_contij > min_mcont //Meeting times meet threshold
   10.   Connect(V_{Ki}, V_{Kj}); //Connect VKi and VKj
   11.   End If
   12.   End While
   13.End While
}

Algorithm map the mobile nodes to logical nodes, and Algorithm 2 establishes a steady social relation topological graph model on the nodes set up by Algorithm 1.

4 Simulation Results and Analysis

4.1 Analysis of Experimental Results

The algorithm is implemented in C language, and several groups of simulation experiments have been carried out on the computer. The hardware configuration used in the experiment is as follows: the processor is Inter(R) Core(TM) i5-2410 M 2.3 GHz CPU,The memory is 4 GB, and the operating system is Windows 7 ultimate.

After the simulation vehicle network runs 48 h, the nodes form a more stable social topological relationship.

As shown in Fig. 1, the multi-vehicle trajectory display function in the system compresses the trajectory data of different vehicles into groups, and performs the line segments of different colors.

Fig. 1. Multiple sets of vehicle tracks (Color figure online)

As shown in Fig. 2, it is a multi-vehicle multi-track annotation function in the system. All vehicles are marked with status points. The way of labeling is special point marking, which does not mark ordinary points, thus reducing the number of points required. The list on the left can select the number of the vehicle. Since the data set used in this article does not collect the license plate table corresponding to the vehicle ID, the ID is displayed, and the track can be hidden by clicking on the list on the left or the hidden button in the lower right corner.

As shown in Fig. 3, it is the bicycle track marking function in the system. In addition to the position of the data set, this paper also includes the violation type and real-time speed, and combines the real-time position with the characteristic attributes of the vehicle to achieve better.

Fig. 2. Vehicle track mark function

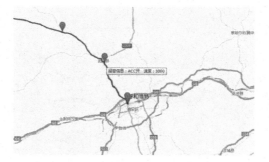

Fig. 3. Single vehicle trajectory map

5 Conclusions

The original intention of the development of the traffic data visualization platform is to facilitate the user to observe the spatiotemporal trajectory data and convert the abstract data into a specific image. The entire system is easy to get started, and you don't need extra learning and operations to get the data model you want. This platform currently implements bicycle track and multi-vehicle trajectory query, in which multi- vehicle trajectory and bicycle trajectory are different modes, multi-vehicle trajectory is suitable for observing traffic network conditions, and bicycle trajectory is suitable for observing the behavioral law of a vehicle's trajectory.

Acknowledgment. The authors wish to thank Inner Mongolia Higher Education Research Project under Grant NJZY17474.

References

1. Pelusi, L., Passarella, A., Conti, M.: Vehicle networksing: data forwarding in disconnected mobile ad hoc networks. IEEE Commun. Mag. **44**(11), 134–141 (2006)
2. Xiong, Y.P., Sun, L.M., Niu, J.W., Liu, Y.: Vehicle network. J. Softw. **20**(1), 124–137 (2009)

3. Niu, J.W., Zhou, X., Liu, Y., Sun, L.M., Ma, J.: A Message Transmission Scheme for Community-Based Vehicle networks. J. Comput. Res. Dev. **46**(12), 2068–2075 (2009)
4. Juang, P., Oki, H., Wang, Y., Martonosi, M., Peh, L.S., Rubenstein, D.: Energy-efficient computing for wildlife tracking:design tradeoffs and early experiences with ZebraNet. ACM SIGPLAN Not. **37**(10), 96–107 (2002)
5. Tara, S., Zygmunt, J.H.: The shared wireless infostation model: a new ad hoc networking paradigm(or where there is a whale, there is a way). In: Proceedings of the 4th ACM international symposium on Mobile ad hoc networking & computing, pp. 233–244, USA, New York (2003)
6. Kernighan, B.W., Lin, S.A.: Efficient heuristic procedure for partitioning graphs. Bell Syst. Tech. J. **49**(2), 291–307 (1970)
7. Palla, G., Derenyi, I., Farkas, I., Vicsek, T.: Uncovering the overlapping community structure of complex networks in nature and society. Nature **435**(7043), 814–818 (2005)
8. Girvan, M., Newman, M.E.J.: Community structure in social and biological networks. Proc. Nat. Acad. Sci. **99**(12), 7821–7826 (2002)
9. Newman, M.E.J.: Fast algorithm for detecting community structure in networks. Phys. Rev. E **69**(6), 066133 (2004)
10. Pan, H., Crowcroft, J., Yoneki, E.: Bubble rap:social-based forwarding in delay tolerant networks. IEEE Trans. Mobile Comput. **10**(11), 1576–1589 (2011)
11. Peng, J., Li, M.S., L, T., Li, L.F., Li, H.Y.: Nodal sociality-based data forwarding for vehicle network. J. Sichuan Univ. (Eng. Sci. Ed.) **45**(5), 57–63 (2013)
12. Qin, J., Zhu, H.Z., Zhu, Y.M., Liu, L., Xue, G.T., Li, M.L.: POST: exploiting dynamic sociality for mobile advertising in vehicular networks. In: 2014 IEEE Conference on Computer Communications, pp. 1761–1769, Toronto, Canada (2014)

Design of Automatic Fire Extinguishing Device for IoT Transformer Box

Ruihang Wang, Liangliang Li, Jianfu Chen, and Xiaorong Zhao(⊠)

College of Computer Engineering, Jiangsu University of Technology, Changzhou 213001,
People's Republic of China
zhaoxr432698@sina.com

Abstract. This paper introduces the causes and hazards of electrical fires, and analyzes the current status and deficiencies of electrical fire related applications. Based on technologies such as the Internet of Things, artificial intelligence and automatic control, a device for monitoring, fire detection and automatic fire extinguishing of electrical equipment has been developed. Through a large number of experiments, the device monitors the electrical equipment in real time and accurately, and recognizes the fire in the electrical place in a timely and reliable manner. The automatic fire extinguishing reaction is rapid and will not damage the equipment twice.

Keywords: Electric · Fire · IoT · Automatic fire extinguishing

1 Introduction

According to the statistics of the China Emergency Management Department, a total of 237,000 fires were reported nationwide in 2018, of which electrical fires accounted for 34.6% of the total. Electrical fires occur mostly in summer and winter, because the summer temperatures are high, which has a great impact on the heating of electrical equipment. Some electrical equipment will cause fire when the heating temperature rises during operation. In winter, the air is dry and it is easy to generate static electricity and cause fire. In terms of time, it often occurs in festivals, holidays or nights. Due to the fire, the scene is unattended, it is difficult to find it in time, and the spread is expanded into disaster [1]. Electrical fires are characterized by distribution, continuity and concealment. There is no obvious sign before the occurrence of electrical fires. In case of fire, it is difficult to extinguish the fire. It cannot be extinguished by conventional methods. Personnel cannot be close to each other and cannot save, causing huge losses to the safety of national life and property. Therefore, equipment monitoring, fire detection and automatic fire extinguishing in electrical places Technical research is very valuable.

Nowadays, the degree of social electrification and intelligence has reached a certain level [2]. Advanced technologies such as remote monitoring of electrical places, fire alarms, and network cameras are gradually being applied, but the automatic fire extinguishing technology of electrical fires is still in the initial stage of development. In the event of an electrical fire, if the fire-fighting measures are not taken in time, the

© Springer Nature Singapore Pte Ltd. 2020
X. Sun et al. (Eds.): ICAIS 2020, CCIS 1253, pp. 384–392, 2020.
https://doi.org/10.1007/978-981-15-8086-4_36

consequences are unimaginable and often result in greater loss of life and property. For this purpose, a set of automatic substation fire extinguishing device based on network communication is designed and implemented in this article. This device can realize remote monitoring and automatically detect the internal conditions of the substation. Once an abnormal situation occurs, it will judge and handle it accordingly This article has designed and implemented a set of automatic transformer box fire extinguishing device based on network communication. This device can realize remote monitoring and automatically detect the internal situation of the transformer box. Once an abnormal situation occurs, it will judge and deal with it accordingly [3].

At present, relevant fields attach great importance to the research on electrical fire detection and automatic fire extinguishing. Commonly used electrical fire detection methods include residual current method, temperature measurement method, smoke measurement method and fire tube automatic fire extinguishing method. The residual current is known as the leakage current. In fact, any electrical equipment, any one of the power lines has more or less residual current. The residual current is generally the normal leakage current of the live conductor to the ground, so it is also called leakage residual electricity. The temperature measurement method measures the line temperature. Due to short circuit, leakage, excessive load, etc., the current in the circuit will increase sharply and the temperature of the conductive line will increase. Since the current and temperature of the line satisfy a certain mathematical relationship, we can measure the current in the line by measuring the line temperature, and thus can indirectly discover the line faults and hidden dangers. The smoke concentration method is a method of detecting the concentration of smoke in the air to identify a fire. The fire probe device is composed of a pressure vessel containing a fire extinguishing agent, a container valve, and a fire probe and a release tube capable of releasing the fire extinguishing agent. Place the fire tube near the top where the fire source is most likely to occur, and at the same time, rely on a number of detection points (line types) along the fire tube for detection. Once in a fire, the fire tube is softened and blasted at the highest point of the heated temperature, releasing the extinguishing medium through the fire tube itself (direct system) or nozzle (indirect system) to the protected area.

Electrical fires are mostly used for gas fire extinguishing. They have the characteristics of rapid fire extinguishing and no damage to electrical equipment. The fire extinguishing mechanism of three commonly used gases: IG541 gas fire extinguishing system uses the mechanism of suffocation to extinguish fires, which is a physical fire extinguishing method. The fire extinguishing agent is a mixture of 52% nitrogen, 40% argon and 8% carbon dioxide. Typically, the protected area contains 21% oxygen and less than 1% carbon dioxide. When the oxygen in the protection zone drops below 15%, most of the combustibles will stop burning [4]. After the IG541 system fire extinguishing agent is released, it can reduce the oxygen in the protection zone to 12.5% to achieve the asphyxiating effect. Heptafluoropropane is mainly a chemical suppression mechanism for extinguishing fires. It is a colorless, odorless, non-corrosive, non-conductive gas with a density approximately six times that of air and a liquid at a certain pressure. After the extinguishing agent is released, the liquid state becomes a gaseous state and absorbs a large amount of heat, which can lower the temperature of the protection zone and the flame. The most important thing is that the heptafluoropropane fire extinguishing agent is composed of macromolecules. By inerting the active free radicals in the flame, active chain breaking is achieved. The hot aerosol fire extinguishing mechanism involves several fire extinguishing mechanisms such as cooling fire extinguishing and chemical suppression. The fire extinguishing agent is stored in a solid form under normal pressure. When the fire extinguishing device operates, the solid substance undergoes a redox exothermic reaction, thereby forming a large amount of hot aerosol smoke [5]. In aerosol smoke, the ratio of gas to solid product is about 6:4. The solid particles are mainly metal oxides, carbonates or hydrogencarbonates, carbon particles and a small amount of metal carbides; the gas products are mainly N_2, a small amount of CO_2 and CO. The metal salt particles undergo heat fusion and gasification at high temperature to absorb the heat in the protection zone and the flame. At the same time, the solid microparticles and the vaporized metal ions can adsorb and affinity react the active genes in the combustion to reduce the combustion free radicals [6].

Although the above methods have been widely used in electrical equipment rooms, there are still some shortcomings, especially in the accuracy of electrical fire monitoring, the timeliness and reliability of fire detection and automatic fire extinguishing. Therefore, based on the technologies of Internet of Things, artificial intelligence and automatic control, combined with relevant standards in the field, this paper develops a new scheme for equipment monitoring, fire detection and automatic fire extinguishing in electrical equipment rooms. It is suitable for various electrical places, with real-time monitoring and accurate identification. The characteristics of the fire to achieve the purpose of automatic fire extinguishing in a timely manner.

2   Fundamental

The device mainly combines equipment monitoring, fire detection and automatic fire extinguishing, and combines it with the Internet and server through the controller to realize the function of the Internet of Things. The controller is responsible for receiving the device information collected by the device monitoring module, transmitting it to the server for storage, detecting the device through an algorithm, for routine maintenance, abnormal maintenance of the device, and aging of the device in advance to help the administrator intelligently manage a large number of device. The equipment monitoring module can be customized according to different equipment, and can monitor the temperature, running power, operating status, circuit status and other information of the equipment. The fire detection module combines a variety of sensors to detect all aspects of the electrical environment. For important parts of the equipment, special sensor detection is used to make the fire detection result more comprehensive, stable and fast. The automatic fire extinguishing module can react quickly after the fire detector detects a fire and quickly extinguish the fire.

3   Circuit Design

The device uses a variety of techniques to comprehensively monitor electrical equipment and fire detection and automatic fire extinguishing [7]. Since the residual current method, smoke detection method and fire detector are relatively mature, they are not discussed in detail here. The working principle of the fire detection module, controller and server is described. The basic schematic diagram of the automatic fire extinguishing module is shown in Fig. 1. The entire system workflow is shown in Fig. 2. The entire working process of the system is as follows: 1. Initialize first; 2. Initialize the weight detection of the fire extinguishing agent; 3. Clear the abnormal flag; 4. Determine whether the weight detection timing is up; Calibration judgment and calibration; 5, check the weight of the fire extinguishing agent; 6, check whether the weight is abnormal, if yes, set the abnormal flag, if not, skip to calibration judgment and calibration; 7, RS485 communication judgment; If the time is up, collect the temperature of the knife room. If the time is not up, skip to setting the default value to judge; 9. Determine whether the 8-way temperature is less than the set value; 10, set the default value judgment, if yes, restore the default value, if no exception handling, and finally jump to clear the exception flag.

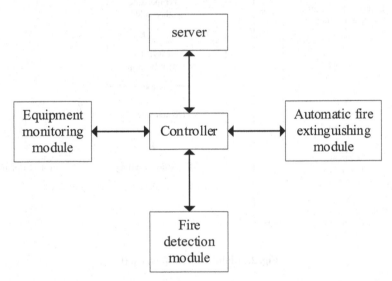

Fig. 1. Overall structure diagram of automatic fire extinguishing device for IoT transformer box.

3.1 Fire Detection Module Design

The fire detection module is directly in contact with the detected point through the PT100 thermocouple, and the temperature of the point is measured in real time. The resistance value of the PT100 thermocouple changes with the change of temperature, and the changed resistance value is converted into voltage by the circuit and amplified by 100. After multiple times, it is sent to the A/D conversion module of the controller. The controller converts the collected analog quantity into digital quantity through the A/D conversion module, and then updates the temperature value of the real-time temperature register after the actual temperature value is obtained by the algorithm. After the Modbus protocol on the RS485 bus polls the value of the real-time temperature register of the controller, the real-time change of the temperature is analyzed to determine whether the

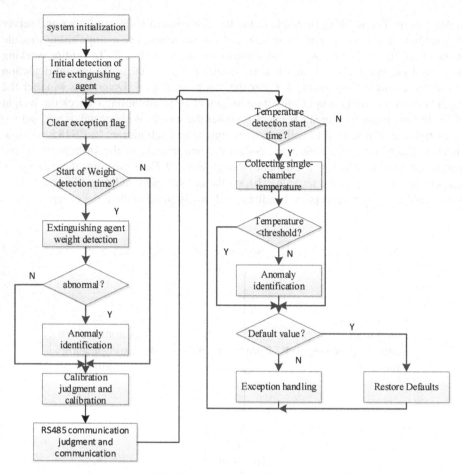

Fig. 2. Main program flow chart

device has a fire hazard. If the temperature is abnormal, the device has a safety hazard and the manager is notified to perform maintenance. Once the detected temperature rises abnormally, the system will be identified as a fire when the threshold is reached. The server will immediately issue a fire extinguishing command to the controller through the Modbus protocol of the RS485 bus and alert the management personnel to a fire. Once the controller receives the fire extinguishing command, it will immediately open the gas fire extinguisher to extinguish the fire. If the gas fire extinguisher is exhausted, the fire has not been completely extinguished, and then the fire hydrant is fired to prevent the fire extinguisher from completing the fire extinguishing operation. The fire extinguisher also has a self-checking function to monitor the quality and pressure of the fire extinguisher. The controller monitors the quality of the fire extinguisher and changes the pressure. If the fire extinguishing task has just been performed or the gas may leak, the server will remind the management personnel to supplement the gas and maintenance.

The contact resistance of the high-voltage distribution cabinet blade is the only cause of temperature rise. It is the best safety measure to detect the temperature of the knife chamber and introduce a reasonable control strategy. The guillotine chamber belongs to the high-voltage and high-power part, and the collection temperature must ensure the safety and reliability of the detection and control system. Figure 3 consists of a PT100 and resistors AR1~AR3 to form a temperature-collecting bridge. It is amplified by an amplifier circuit AIC2 with high input impedance and high common-mode rejection ratio, and then a linear isolation circuit consisting of AIC3 and AOP0. The isolation voltage is up to 2500 V, and finally the temperature signal is sent to the AD conversion circuit. The resistance of the AR4 determines the amplification factor of the temperature acquisition module and the measurement temperature range.

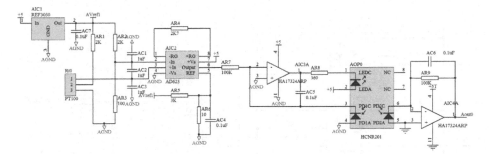

Fig. 3. Design of Anti-heating Circuit of Gate of High-voltage Distribution Cabinet

3.2 Controller Design

After the controller is powered on, the clock, timer, serial port, IO port, and A/D conversion module are initialized for 2 s, and the symmetric heavy module is initialized. After all initialization ends, the controller will start the interrupt, and then the system starts to work. Mode, the timer generates an interrupt every 1 ms, and the time variable of the weighing module starts to accumulate time. After each accumulated 3 s, the A/D value of the weighing chip is read once, and then the actual weight of the weighing is obtained by calculation. Update to the weighing value register. At the same time, the time variable of the temperature measurement will also start to accumulate time, and the AD conversion function will be called once every 1 s of the temperature measurement time variable. After the AD conversion function is called, the AD value of 8 PT100s is sequentially sequenced, and the AD value of each channel is collected 8 times for digital filtering. After obtaining the final accurate AD value, the actual temperature value collected by PT100 is calculated by the algorithm, and then 8 are updated respectively. Temperature register. The controller monitors the serial port interrupt while updating the temperature register and the weighing register. If the serial port generates an interrupt, the data received by the serial port is sequentially stored in the queue and the bus idle time is accumulated. If the bus is idle for more than 3.5 characters, it is considered One frame of data transfer is completed. After the data is received, the data is first moved to another buffer, and then the address, checksum, function code, register address, etc. contained in the data are checked. Perform the corresponding function after the check is completed. If the check, function code or register address is found to be incorrect, the corresponding error code is returned.

In order to prevent high voltage serialization of the RS485 data line, two levels of protection measures are used, as shown in Fig. 4. The first stage consists of fast optocoupler RIC2~RIC4, the isolation voltage is 2000 V, the switching speed can make RS485 communication rate reach 115200 bps; the second level consists of RD1~RD3 and PTC1~PCT2 self-recovery protection circuit, when RS485 bus From high voltage series, RD1~RD3 are turned on instantaneously, PTC1 and PTC2 pass large current, resistance heats up, resistance value increases, high voltage falls completely on PTC1 and PTC2, protects the communication function of MAX485.

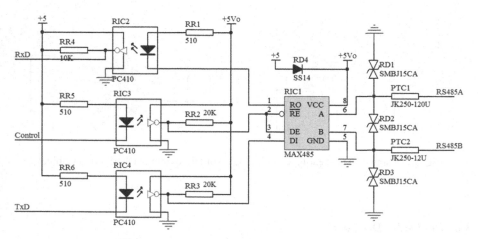

Fig. 4. RS485 high voltage isolation circuit design

3.3 Introduction to the Working Principle of the Server

After the server is turned on, the value of the temperature register and the weighing register is polled to the controller every 10 ms through the Modbus protocol on the RS485 bus, and then compared with the data obtained by the previous polling. Once the temperature rises abnormally, it will immediately correspond to the corresponding the controller issues a fire extinguishing command, and the screen prompts the management personnel to have a fire. During the course of the work, the server draws a real-time temperature profile based on the polled data. During use, if the fire extinguisher is leaking due to excessive storage time, it will leak slowly. After the server finds the problem through the analysis of the data, it will prompt the manager to maintain the corresponding fire extinguisher.

The controller software organizes the architecture using signal passing and time slice methods. The core code is as follows:

```
Init_Device();
 delay_ms(2000);
 Get_Maopi();
 EA = 1;
 while(1)
 {
  if(time_1 > = 3000)
  {
ERROR_FLAG = 0;
  time_1 = 0;
  EA = 0;
  Get_Weight();
  EA = 1;
 if(Final_Value[8] > Setup_Parameter[1])
    ERROR_FLAG = 1;
  }
  scanf();
  RX485_Driver();
  if(time > = 1000)
  {
  time = 0;
  AD_Handle();
  for(i = 0;i < 8;i ++)
    if(Final_Value[i] > Setup_Parameter[0])
     ERROR_FLAG = 1;
  }
 If (ERROR_FLAG == 1)
  {
   if(uK1 == 0 && uK2 == 0)
   {
    delay_ms(1000);
    if(uK1 == 0 && uK2 == 0)
    {
    Setup_Parameter[0] = 150;
    Setup_Parameter[1] = 1;
    delay_ms(10);
    }
    else
    Error_Handle();
   }
  }
}
```

4 Conclusion

Because the electrical site itself is prone to fire, and the management personnel can not manage on-site 24 h, in the event of a fire, managers often cannot immediately detect it. When it is discovered, the fire is already very obvious and often causes huge losses.

After analysis, the fire characteristics of electrical fires are mainly due to excessive temperature caused by various reasons, and light equipment failure, which will lead to fire. A monitoring module can be installed at key parts of the electrical equipment to not only monitor the operating status of the equipment, but also detect the occurrence of fire. The automatic fire-extinguishing module can automatically destroy the country in an unsupervised state, extinguish it in the event of a fire, prevent the fire from continuing to expand, and miss the best fire-fighting opportunity [8].

This application study combines electrical equipment monitoring, fire detection and automatic fire extinguishing to detect equipment fire safety hazards through intelligent algorithms, prevent problems before they occur, use multi-sensor technology to detect fires, make fire detection more rapid and accurate, and use advanced The gas fire extinguishing technology realizes the rapid extinguishing of the fire, and can completely extinguish the electric fire within the design range within 5 s to 10 s. After investigation, there are many places where electrical fires occur, the places are complex and changeable, and the equipment inside is also diverse. At present, the application research has not carried out experiments on more electrical places, and only experiments are carried out on some of the most common places. Experiment with more sites to expand the scope of application research.

Acknowledgments. This work was financially supported by Jiangsu Innovation and Entrepreneurship Project (No. 201911463008Z), Jiangsu Province Industry-University-Research Cooperation Project (No. BY2018191).

References

1. Hamid, Q., Barbarosou, M., Papageorgas, P., Prekas, K., Salame, C.T.: Automatic recognition of electric loads analyzing the characteristic parameters of the consumed electric power through a non-intrusive monitoring methodology. Energy Procedia **119**, 742–751 (2017)
2. Ruixiang, L., Yingying, L., Yaqiong, Q., Te, M., Bo, W., Xiangyang, L.: Street-level landmarks acquisition based on SVM classifiers. CMC-Comput. Mater. Continua **59**(2), 591–606 (2019)
3. Xiaorong, Z., et al.: A high gain noise cancelling 3.1-10.6 GHz CMOS LNA for UWB application. Comput. Mater. Continua **60**(1), 133–145 (2019)
4. Jun, Y.: Discussion on preventing fire from residual current. Electr. Energy Manag. Technol. **8**, 22–26 (2007)
5. Xin, L.: Fire tube technology research and its application. Sci. Technol. Inf. **27**, 49–50 (2012)
6. Hayashi, T.: Computerized integrated automatic control system for electric power networks. IFAC Energy Syst. Manag. **22**(17), 223–228 (1989)
7. Tao, C., Lizeng, Z., Xuecheng, F., Jianjun, X., Cheng, H.: Study on electrical initial fire automatic extinguishing technology based on superfine powder. China Saf. Sci. J. **25**(11), 53–57 (2015)
8. Chao, Z., Chunhe, Y., Shangwei, W., Xiaolong, Z., Wen, N.: A straightforward direct traction boundary integral method for two-dimensional crack problems simulation of linear elastic materials. Comput. Mater. Continua **58**(3), 761–775 (2019)

A Practical Quantum Private Query Protocol Based on Bell States and Single Photons

Dong-Mei Liu, Li-Li Yan$^{(\boxtimes)}$, Yan Chang, and Shi-Bing Zhang

School of Cybersecurity, Chengdu University of Information Technology,
Sichuan 610000, China
Yanlili@cuit.edu.cn.com

Abstract. As a kind of practical quantum key distribution protocol, quantum private queries have attracted extensive attention. In this paper, we use Bell states and single photons to transmit information. The user sends a certain quantum state to the database, and the database random measures it in the Z basis or B basis. Based on the measurement results, the database will declare two classic bits of information to distinguish different quantum states. Finally, the database will know all the key, and the user will have a 1/4 probability to get a key. We also analyze the security of the proposed protocol in terms of the inside attacks and outside attack. In addition, our protocol is a one-way quantum protocol, which can resist the joint-measurement attack and reduce the communication complexity.

Keywords: Quantum private query · Single photons · Bell state · One-way

1 Introduction

Classical cryptography consists of two parts: one is the design and research of encryption algorithms, the other is cryptanalysis, which is known as cryptographic deciphering. Classical cryptographic analysis also applies to quantum cryptography. Quantum cryptography is a subject based on the development of modern classical cryptography. It uses the basic principles of quantum physics to ensure the security of information. Theoretically, quantum cryptography can overcome the computational complexity of classical cryptography and make the existing cryptography insecure. At present, although quantum cryptography has made great progress in the protection of classical information, the study of quantum information cryptography protection cannot be ignored.

In recent years, many scholars have focused their research on Quantum Secret Sharing Protocol (QSS) [1], Quantum Walks Protocol (QW) [2], Quantum Key Agreement (QKA) [3], Quantum Dialogue (QD) [4], Quantum Signatures (QS) [5], Quantum Private Comparison (QPC) [6] or Quantum Private Query (QPQ) [7–26], Quantum Secure Direct Communication (QSDC) [27],Quantum Teleportation (QT) [28]. Among them, the environment of quantum private query protocol is theoretically unconditional security. The most important thing about the quantum private query protocol is to ensure that the information of users and databases is not leaked. In secure multi-party computation, quantum privacy query should not only meet the requirements of private information

© Springer Nature Singapore Pte Ltd. 2020
X. Sun et al. (Eds.): ICAIS 2020, CCIS 1253, pp. 393–402, 2020.
https://doi.org/10.1007/978-981-15-8086-4_37

retrieval (PIR) [7] to protect user privacy (that is, the user gets the desired item and the database does not know the user's retrieval address), but also satisfies the requirement of symmetric private information retrieval (SPIR) [8] of the protection of the database information (user cannot obtain besides has paid the entry of other database information).

In 2008, Giovannetti et al. [9] first proposed quantum private queries (GLM-protocol), which ensured that the information obtained by users was limited and fraudulent. GLM-protocol improves communication complexity and computational complexity, unfortunately, but does not tolerate loss. Jacobi et al. [10] proposed a practical private database queries based on a quantum-key-distribution protocol (J-protocol), which listed the detailed post-processing process and security analysis. J-protocol is easy to implement and has strong fault tolerance, and a detailed template is listed for follow-up work. Gao et al. [11] proposed flexible quantum private queries based on quantum key distribution, in addition to the need to prepare $|0\rangle$, $|1\rangle$.it also needs to include $|0\rangle' = \sin\theta|0\rangle + \cos\theta|1\rangle$ and $|1\rangle' = \sin\theta|0\rangle - \cos\theta|1\rangle$. To get better database security and user security by adjusting the value of the θ. Subsequently, Quantum Private Query (QPQ) based on Quantum Key Distribution (QKD) has become a research hot spot. The previous was used a single bit during post-processing. Wei et al. [12] proposed the practical quantum private query of blocks based on unbalanced state Bennett-Brassard-1984 quantum-key-distribution protocol, which allows users to query once get multiple bits without revealing user privacy. Yang et al. [13] put together the idea of semi-quantum key distribution to propose private database queries using one quantum state ($|+\rangle$), which saves quantum resources and guarantees user security and database security.

Liu et al. [14] proposed the QKD-based quantum private query without a failure probability, which has the advantage of being easy to implement and tolerating loss. This protocol is fraud-sensitive and can get the upper bound of database leak information through calculation. In the same year, Gao et al. [15] proposed post-processing of the oblivious key in quantum private query (*kN-N*, *N-N* and *rM-N*). The general security hole is that users can obtain additional information about the database through multiple queries. For the initial key, we need effective error correction to solve the various noise problems encountered. In 2016, Wei [16] proposed practical quantum private query with better performance in resisting joint measurement attack. Then Wei [17] proposed a generic construction of Quantum-Oblivious-Key Transfer-Based private query with ideal database security and zero failure in 2018, which is an improved cyclic differential phase shift protocol that compresses the finally obtained key bits. Gao-X et al. [18] proposed quantum private query based on Bell states and single photons to resist collective noise by using a non-de-coherent (DF) state.

At present, there are still many achievements in quantum private queries. Gao et al. [19] summarized the research results in recent years, gave the realization of some circuits, and proposed quantum private query: a new kind of practical quantum cryptographic protocols. In the same year, Yang [3] proposed a new quantum key agreement protocols based on Bell states. Chang et al. [21] proposed Quantum private Query protocol based on EPR pairs. Then she [20] proposed a practical two-way QKD-based quantum private query with better performance in user privacy. The user measures the information from the database and rearranges it, then the rearrange information resend to database to ensure that the user data was not leak. This protocol is fraud sensitive and resistant to Trojan horse attacks. Li N. et al. [24] proposed quantum private query with perfect performance universally applicable against collective-noise, by constructing four photons to resist collective noise. Pei et al. [5] proposed the practical quantum private query of blocks based on the two-dimensional QKD system in 2019, which has better practicability than the high-dimensional quantum system. The rearrangement - shift - add technique was adopted to solve the security problem in post-processing. Finally, Gao et al. [25] proposal quantum private query: a new kind of practical quantum cryptographic protocol. Wang [26] proposed a new protocol for quantum private query against joint-measurement attack according the procedure of 'receive → measure → re-prepare → resend'.

In this paper, we propose a one-way quantum private query protocol (QPQ), which uses Bell states and single photons to transmit information, and finally declares two classical bit information to distinguish the eight different state information. The work in this paper: one is to use eight state to convey information; the second is to announce the result with 2 bits of classical information. Every time a message is delivered, the database knows all the key information, and the user gets the key information with 1/4 probability. The structure of this paper is organized as follows. In Sect. 2, we present detailed protocol steps. In Sect. 3, we give a detailed security analysis. In Sect. 4, we detail the characteristics of the protocol. Finally, conclude the article.

2   QPQ Protocol Based on Bell States and Single Photons

This paper proposes a one-way quantum private query based on Bell states and single photons. There is a sequence of photon pair randomly in eight states $\{|00\rangle, |01\rangle, |10\rangle, |11\rangle, |\phi^+\rangle, |\phi^-\rangle, |\varphi^+\rangle, |\varphi^-\rangle\}$. In order to distinguish the eight kinds of quantum states, two classical bits are be announced. Here are four Bell states:

$$|\beta_{k_{2i}k_{2i+1}}\rangle = \frac{1}{\sqrt{2}}(|0k_{2i+1}\rangle + (-1)^{k_{2i}}|1\bar{k}_{2i+1}\rangle)$$

$$|\beta_{00}\rangle = |\phi^+\rangle = \frac{1}{\sqrt{2}}(|00\rangle + |11\rangle)$$
$$|\beta_{01}\rangle = |\varphi^+\rangle = \frac{1}{\sqrt{2}}(|01\rangle + |10\rangle)$$
$$|\beta_{00}\rangle = |\phi^-\rangle = \frac{1}{\sqrt{2}}(|00\rangle - |11\rangle)$$
$$|\beta_{00}\rangle = |\varphi^-\rangle = \frac{1}{\sqrt{2}}(|01\rangle - |10\rangle)$$

2.1   The Proposed Protocol

The protocol contains too many states to distinguish by 0/1. So I put forward by announcing two classical binary 00,01,10,11 to distinguish among them. The specific process is as follows:

Step 1 : Bob randomly generates quantum sequence of length $4N$, containing $2N$ pairs of particles, which are randomly in states $|00\rangle, |01\rangle, |10\rangle, |11\rangle, |\phi^+\rangle, |\phi^-\rangle, |\varphi^+\rangle, |\varphi^-\rangle$ and then Bob sends the sequence to Alice.

Step 2 : When Alice receives the particle from Bob, it first use half of the particle pairs for eavesdropping detection to find the attacker. Alice selects half of the pairs and notifies Bob to announce the initial state of the pairs. Then, Alice chooses the corresponding basis measurement according to the initial state of these particles. If the initial state is $|00\rangle/|01\rangle/|10\rangle/|11\rangle$, Z basis $\{|0\rangle, |1\rangle\}$ is adopted. If the initial state is $|\phi^+\rangle/|\phi^-\rangle/|\varphi^+\rangle/|\varphi^-\rangle$, the particle should be measured by Bell basis. If the result measured by Alice is different from the initial state published by Bob, the eavesdropper is proved to exist and the execution is suspended. After proving that there are no eavesdroppers, Alice and Bob drop all the pairs of particles used for eavesdropping detection and proceed to the next step.

Step 3 : After the eavesdropping detection is completed, the remaining particle sequence length of Alice and Bob is 2 N, including N pairs of particles. Alice randomly generates the binary number $a_N = \{0, 1\}^N$ as the initial key k^r for the database. If the ith position in a_N is 0, that is, $a_i = 0$, Alice measures the ith particle pair in the particle sequence with the Z basis. If $a_i = 1$, the Bell basis is used to measure the ith particle pair in the particle sequence.

Step 4 : For each pair, Alice announces two classical bits 00, 01, 10, 11 by measurement result. If the measurement result is $\{|00\rangle, |\phi^+\rangle\}$, Alice declares the classical bit '00'; if the measurement result is $\{|11\rangle, |\phi^-\rangle\}$, Alice declares the classical bit '10'; if the measurement result is $\{|01\rangle, |\varphi^+\rangle\}$, Alice declares the classical bit '01'; if the measurement result is $\{|10\rangle, |\varphi^-\rangle\}$, Alice declares the classical bit '11'.

Step 5 : According to Alice's announcement and Bob's initial state, Bob can be inferred the oblivious key correctly with the probability of $P = 1/4$. All the conjectures are shown as follows (Table 1):

For example, when Bob prepares $|\phi^+\rangle$, if Alice announces 10, Bob can infer that Alice is measured with Z basis, and the measurement result is $|11\rangle$, so Bob can infer that his oblivious key must be 0. The remaining Alice announced the result 00, Bob can't infer Alice is which type of measurement result $\{|00\rangle, |\phi^+\rangle\}$, so it can't be inferred.

Step 6 : through the above steps, Alice as the database has obtained the original key k^r of length N, while Bob will obtain the 1/4 key in the original key k^r. Both obtain the final key K through the traditional post-processing process [15], which can adopt the general method of quantum privacy query. Alice, the owner of the entire database, has a key length of k^r. After negotiation, Alice and Bob cut the original key k^r and grow it into k substrings with the length of n ($nk = N$). Then, both parties will bitwise XOR the k substrings, and finally get the key K of length n by compression. Bob only knows one of them (according to the classical post-processing method, it can finally reach that the user Bob only knows one of them). If Bob knows the jth bit of the key, K_j, and wants to get the ith bit of the database, X_i, Bob asks Alice to shift the whole key K to the left of the loop $s = j-i$ bit. After the move, the bit of key Bob knows is used to encrypt the contents of the database he wants. Finally, Alice encrypts the database bitwise with the final key K.

Table 1. The relationship between user Bob and database Alice

Bob's initial state	Alice measurement basis (raw key)	Alice measurement result	Alice announcement	Bob deduction(key)
$|\phi^+\rangle$	Z basis(0)	$|00\rangle$	00	?
	Z basis(0)	$|11\rangle$	10	10(0)
	B basis(1)	$|\phi^+\rangle$	00	?
$|\phi^-\rangle$	Z basis(0)	$|00\rangle$	00	00(0)
	Z basis(0)	$|11\rangle$	10	?
	B basis(1)	$|\phi^-\rangle$	10	?
$|\varphi^+\rangle$	Z basis(0)	$|01\rangle$	01	?
	Z basis(0)	$|10\rangle$	11	11(0)
	B basis(1)	$|\varphi^+\rangle$	01	?
$|\varphi^-\rangle$	Z basis(0)	$|01\rangle$	01	01(0)
	Z basis(0)	$|10\rangle$	11	?
	B basis(1)	$|\varphi^-\rangle$	11	?
$|00\rangle$	Z basis(0)	$|00\rangle$	00	?
	B basis(1)	$|\phi^+\rangle$	00	?
	B basis(1)	$|\phi^-\rangle$	10	10(1)
$|11\rangle$	Z basis(0)	$|11\rangle$	10	?
	B basis(1)	$|\phi^+\rangle$	00	00(1)
	B basis(1)	$|\phi^-\rangle$	10	?
$|01\rangle$	Z basis(0)	$|01\rangle$	01	?
	B basis(1)	$|\varphi^+\rangle$	01	?
	B basis(1)	$|\varphi^-\rangle$	11	11(1)
$|10\rangle$	Z basis(0)	$|10\rangle$	11	?
	B basis(1)	$|\varphi^+\rangle$	01	01(1)
	B basis(1)	$|\varphi^-\rangle$	11	?

3 Security Analysis

3.1 External Attack (Intercept and Resend Attack)

In this paper, if Eve knows the initial state of Bob's preparation and the measurement basis selected by Alice. It will be able to send fake photons to Alice successfully, and Eve can get the key without being discovered. But the truth is that Eve knows nothing, as detailed below:

Eve first intercepts the photons of Bob sent to Alice, and Eve sends photon to Alice after random measurements. In step 2 of the eavesdropping detection process, if Alice's measurement results are consistent with Bob's announced state, then Eve passes the eavesdropping detection and is not found. So Alice will only detect Eve's eavesdropping behavior with a certain probability.

For example, assuming that Bob's initial state is $|00\rangle$, it is intercepted by Eve before being sent to Alice. Since Eve does not know the photon state sent by Bob, it needs to measure with Z or B basis. The result of Eve is $|00\rangle$ to measure with Z basis, and the results for him are $\frac{1}{2}|\phi^+\rangle$, $\frac{1}{2}|\phi^-\rangle$ to measure with B basis. Alice randomly uses the measurement basis to measure: $|00\rangle$ using Z basis measurement results as $|00\rangle$, B basis measurement results as $\frac{1}{2}|\phi^+\rangle$ or $\frac{1}{2}|\phi^-\rangle$; $|\phi^+\rangle$ using Z basis measurement results as $\frac{1}{2}|00\rangle$ or $\frac{1}{2}|11\rangle$, B basis measurement results as $|\phi^+\rangle$; $|\phi^-\rangle$ using Z basis measurement results as $\frac{1}{2}|00\rangle$ or $\frac{1}{2}|11\rangle$, B basis measurement results as $|\phi^-\rangle$. So, Eve can pass the detection with the probability of $P_0 = \frac{3}{8}$ after Alice has measured it. If the message passed is n bits, the probability of being able to check Eve's eavesdropping behavior is $P_1 = 1 - (\frac{3}{8})^n$.

In the case where the number of transmitted messages is relatively large, the probability that Eve is detected is 1. Therefore, this protocol is sufficiently secure in the case of external attacks.

3.2 Internal Attacks

3.2.1 Database Privacy

A. *Joint-measurement attack*

Since this protocol is one-way, and it uses the initial state of Bell states and single photons, our protocol has its own advantages. This one-way protocol separates the two basic elements of the carrier state and the carrier state information that is useful to the last bit of the key. Even if Bob knows the state by himself, he can't get the final key from his own information. When Bob transports the message to Alice, Alice announces the message based on the measurement. Alice, who is the database, knows all the keys, but she can't determine the position of Bob's key just by the information she knows.

In the end, Bob can only know the key position with 1/4 probability through the results announced by Alice and his own preparation status. These two basic elements are located in Alice and Bob. Bob knows the state and cannot infer the results without notifying the messages. When Bob can derive a message based on the results announced by Alice, the photon is no longer in Bob and has been passed to Alice. So our protocol can overcome joint measurement attacks.

B. *Insert attack*

As a user, Bob wants to select some photons in the process of preparing the initial photons to eavesdrop by inserting the auxiliary system to obtain more database information. He could attach an auxiliary system to these photons. Bob deduces the original key bit by performing appropriate unitary operations on the auxiliary system and then measuring the result. We suppose Bob's attack on $|\phi^+\rangle$ and $|\phi^-\rangle$ as follows.

$$U_E \otimes |0\rangle \bullet |E\rangle = a|0\rangle|e\rangle + b|1\rangle|f\rangle$$
$$U_E \otimes |1\rangle \bullet |E\rangle = c|0\rangle|g\rangle + d|1\rangle|h\rangle$$

Insert the auxiliary photons into $|\phi^+\rangle$ and $|\phi^-\rangle$, then do the Unitary operation:

$$|\phi^+\rangle = U_E \otimes |\phi^+\rangle$$
$$= \frac{1}{\sqrt{2}}[(a|0e\rangle + b|1f\rangle) \otimes |0\rangle + (c|0g\rangle + d|1h\rangle) \otimes |1\rangle]$$
$$= \frac{1}{\sqrt{2}}[a|0e0\rangle + b|1f0\rangle + c|0g1\rangle + d|1h1\rangle]$$

$$|\phi^+\rangle = U_E \otimes |\phi^-\rangle$$
$$= \frac{1}{\sqrt{2}}[(a|0e\rangle + b|1f\rangle) \otimes |0\rangle - (c|0g\rangle + d|1h\rangle) \otimes |1\rangle]$$
$$= \frac{1}{\sqrt{2}}[a|0e0\rangle + b|1f0\rangle - c|0g1\rangle - d|1h1\rangle]$$

Bob wants to ensure that eavesdropping is not detected after inserting the auxiliary photons, $|\phi^+\rangle$ and $|\phi^-\rangle$ needs to meet the following conditions: $b|1f0\rangle + c|0g1\rangle = 0$, $b|1f0\rangle - c|0g1\rangle = 0$. So $b = c = 0$.

$$|\phi^+\rangle = \frac{1}{\sqrt{2}}(a|0e0\rangle + d|1h1\rangle)$$

$$|\phi^-\rangle = \frac{1}{\sqrt{2}}(a|0e0\rangle - d|1h1\rangle)$$

In the prepared insert photons, Bob did not detect the probability of eavesdropping being $P = \frac{a^2 + d^2}{2}$. When the number of photons used for eavesdrop detection is sufficient, it is sure to check for eavesdropping.

C. The Fake Signal Attack

After the malicious user Bob obtains the secret key, the quantum state may be prepared and measured in other ways, that is, a fake quantum state (fake signal attack) may be transmitted. But in our protocol, the original key is generated by Alice (the measurement basis chosen by Alice), that is, Bob cannot affect the original key by sending a forged state, and in addition, his malicious behavior will be detected in eavesdropping (in step 2). Bob sends forged photons, and once Alice discovers that her measurements are inconsistent with Bob's announcement, she has discovered eavesdropping.

Bob performs fake signal attack by preparing fake state $|K\rangle$:

$$|K\rangle = \frac{1}{\sqrt{2}}(|111\rangle + |000\rangle + |001\rangle + |010\rangle + |101\rangle + |110\rangle)$$
$$= |+\rangle \bullet |\phi^+\rangle + |-\rangle \bullet |\phi^-\rangle + |0\rangle \bullet |\varphi^+\rangle + |1\rangle \bullet |\varphi^-\rangle$$

Bob only keeps photon 1 and sends 2, 3 photons to Alice. He can know the state of the photons sent to Alice through the state of the 1 photon in his hand. When Alice receives four Bell states, it randomly uses Z basis or B basis to measure. Assume that the measurement result of Alice is $|\phi^+\rangle$, and Bob is required to publish the initial state in step 2. If Bob publishes $|\phi^+\rangle$, it is impossible to detect Bob's eavesdropping; Once Bob announces the result is $|\phi^-\rangle, |\varphi^+\rangle, |\varphi^-\rangle$, Bob must have the behavior of eavesdropping attack. That is to say, Bob must have prepared the fake photons. When there are more transmitted photons, eavesdropping detection in joint measurement attack can surely find Bob's eavesdropping behavior.

3.2.2   User Privacy

If the database is dishonest, user privacy may be stolen. Our one-way protocol can resist Trojan horse attack. In a fraud-sensitive environment, if dishonest Alice wants to get Bob's other information, it may be detected. Alice has only the ability to measure and announce, and the whole process has no chance of inserting photons. Announcements are determined by the measurement results, and the measurement results are determined by selection of basis. As described in the above table, all photons which are randomly measured with Z or B basis received by Alice and declared. The agreement in principle limits the capabilities of the database Alice, and her announcements and measurements are generally not error-prone. When Alice measures the result as $|00\rangle$, the user Bob cannot judge that the initial preparation state is $|00\rangle, |\phi^+\rangle, |\phi^-\rangle$ without declaring the classical bit. Once Alice announces 00 and can infer the key, Bob can conclude that the initial state must be $|\phi^-\rangle$. In the case where the initial state of Bob is $|00\rangle, |\phi^+\rangle$, Bob cannot infer the key.

Once the message is sent to Alice, it is separated from Bob. Alice, who does not know Bob's initial state, can only guess Bob's key with a 1/2 chance based on her message. So the probability of Alice's eavesdropping being detected is $1 - \frac{1}{2^n}$.

4   Features of the Protocol

The proposed protocol is one-way. The eight states $|00\rangle, |01\rangle, |10\rangle, |11\rangle, |\phi^+\rangle, |\phi^-\rangle, |\varphi^+\rangle, |\varphi^-\rangle$ are distributed, which reduces quantum resources and has the ability to resist noise. Quantum private query protocol based on Bell states and single photons can effectively implement the key distribution process and ensure the security of user and database. Because it is a one-way protocol, we focus on the protection of database privacy during security analysis. Because the user prepares the photons to the database, the database does not use 'Measure - Preparation - Resend', there is no chance for database to attack.

Bob wants to get the key and must uses the result announced by Alice. Most of the previous protocols were single photons. So the announced results were easily distinguished by the classic 0 or 1. In this protocol, we are able to distinguish these eight states only by declaring the classic two-bits binary (00, 01, 10 and 11). It due to the complexity of the initial photons preparation. Finally, Bob guesses the original key with 1/4 probability. After all quantum key distributions have been completed, the average number of bits $\bar{n} = Np^k$ known to Bob and the value required to restart the protocol $P = (1 - p^k)^N$ (without knowing certain bits) can be obtained by adjusting the parameter k (substrings number) or N (database size).

5   Conclusion

In this paper, we propose a QPQ protocol based on Bell states and single photons to transmit information, and finally the protocol announce two classical bit information to distinguish the different states. One of the more practical aspects of our article is to include all of eight state information. Second, the final key is obtained by announcing two classic bits. The database will know all of the 2-bit classic information, and each time the message is delivered, the user will get the key with 1/4 probability.

This protocol has the advantages of most one-way protocols, but needs to be improved to achieve large-scale, high-dimensional data transmission. Due to the use of Bell states and single photons, it has a certain ability to resist noise in the quantum transmission channel. A variety of photon states also reduce the difficulty of preparing quantum and save quantum resources.

Acknowledgments. This work is supported by NSFC (Grant Nos.61572086, 61402058), Sichuan Science and Technology Program (Grant Nos. 2017JY0168, 2018TJPT0012, 2018GZ0232, 2018CC0060, 2017GFW0119, 2017GZ0006, 2016GFW0127), the National Key Research and Development Program (No. 2017YFB0802302), Sichuan innovation team of quantum security communication (No.17TD0009), Sichuan academic and technical leaders training funding support projects (No. 2016120080102643).

References

1. Gao, X., Zhang, S., Chang, Y.: Cryptanalysis and improvement of the semi-quantum secret sharing protocol. Int. J. Theor. Phys. **56**(8), 2512–2520 (2017). https://doi.org/10.1007/s10773-017-3404-9
2. Yang, Y.-G., Han, X.-Y., Li, D., Zhou, Y.-H., Shi, W.-M.: Two quantum coins sharing a walker. Int. J. Theor. Phys. **58**(3), 700–712 (2018). https://doi.org/10.1007/s10773-018-3968-z
3. Yang, Y.-G., Li, B.-R., Li, D., Zhou, Y.-H., Shi, W.-M.: New quantum key agreement protocols based on bell states. Quantum Inf. Process. **18**(10), 1–11 (2019). https://doi.org/10.1007/s11128-019-2434-z
4. Yang, Y.-G., Gao, S., Zhou, Y.-H., Shi, W.-M.: New secure quantum dialogue protocols over collective noisy channels. Int. J. Theor. Phys. **58**(9), 2810–2822 (2019). https://doi.org/10.1007/s10773-019-04165-w
5. Cai, X.-Q., Wang, T.-Y., Wei, C.-Y., Gao, F.: Cryptanalysis of multiparty quantum digital signatures. Quantum Inf. Process. **18**(8), 1–12 (2019). https://doi.org/10.1007/s11128-019-2365-8
6. Gao, X., Zhang, S.-B., Chang, Y., Yang, F., Zhang, Y.: Cryptanalysis of the quantum private comparison protocol based on the entanglement swapping between three-particle w-class state and bell state. Int. J. Theor. Phys. **57**(6), 1716–1722 (2018). https://doi.org/10.1007/s10773-018-3697-3
7. Chor, B., Goldreich, O., Kushilevitz, E., Sudan, M.: Private information retrieval. In: Proceedings of the 36th Annual IEEE Symposium on Foundations of Computer Science (FOCS 1995), pp. 41–51 (1995)
8. Gertner, Y., Ishai, Y., Kushilevitz, E., Malkin, T.: Protecting data privacy in private information retrieval schemes. Sci. J. Comput. Syst. **60**, 592–629 (2000)

9. Giovannetti, V., Lloyd, S., Maccone, L.: Quantum private queries. Phys. Rev. Lett. **100**, 230502 (2008)
10. Jacobi, et al.: Practical private database queries based on a quantum-key-distribution protocol. Phys. Rev. A **83**(2) 022301(2011)
11. Gao, F., Liu, B., Wen, Q.Y., Chen, H.: Flexible quantum private queries based on quantum key distribution. Opt. Express **20**, 17411–17420 (2012)
12. Wei, C.Y., Gao, F., Wen, Q.Y., Wang, T.Y.: Practical quantum private query of blocks based on unbalanced state Bennett-Brassard-1984 quantum-key-distribution protocol. Sci. Rep. **4**, 7537 (2014)
13. Yang, Y.-G., Zhang, M.-O., Yang, R.: Private database queries using one quantum state. Quantum Inf. Process. **14**(3), 1017–1024 (2014). https://doi.org/10.1007/s11128-014-0902-z
14. Liu, B., Gao, F., Huang, W., Wen, Q.: QKD-based quantum private query without a failure probability. Sci. China Phys. Mech. Astron. **58**(10), 1–6 (2015). https://doi.org/10.1007/s11 433-015-5714-3
15. Gao, F., Liu, B., Huang, W., Wen, Q.Y.: Postprocessing of the oblivious key in quantum private query. IEEE. J. Sel. Top. Quantum **21**, 6600111 (2015)
16. Wei, C.Y., Wang, T.Y., Gao, F.: Practical quantum private query with better performance in resisting joint measurement attack. Phys. Rev. A **93**, 042318 (2016)
17. Wei, C.Y., Cai, X.Q., Liu, B., Wang, T.Y., Gao, F.: A generic construction of quantum-oblivious-key transfer-based private query with ideal database security and zero failure. IEEE Trans. Comput. **67**, 2–8 (2018)
18. Gao, X., Chang, Y., Zhang, S.-B., Yang, F., Zhang, Y.: Quantum private query based on bell state and single photons. Int. J. Theor. Phys. **57**(7), 1983–1989 (2018). https://doi.org/10.1007/s10773-018-3723-5
19. Gao, F., Qin, S.J., Huang, W., Wen, Q.Y.: Quantum private query: A new kind of practical quantum cryptographic protocols. Sci. China Phys. Mech. Astron. **62**, 070301 (2019)
20. Chang, Y., Zhang, S.-B., Wan, G.-g., Yan, L.-L., Zhang, Y., Li, X.-Y.: Practical two-way QKD-based quantum private query with better performance in user privacy. Int. J. Theor. Phys. **58**(7), 2069–2080 (2019). https://doi.org/10.1007/s10773-019-04062-2
21. Chang, Y., Xiong, J.X., Gao, X., Zhang, S.B.: Quantum private query protocol based on EPR Pairs. Chin. J. Electron. **27**, 256–262 (2018)
22. Zheng, T., Zhang, S.B., Gao, X., Chang, Y.: Practical quantum private query based on Bell state. Sci. Mod. Phys. Lett. A **34**, 24 (2019)
23. Liu, B., et al.: QKD-based quantum private query protocol in the single-photon interference communication system. IEEE Access **7**, 104749–104758 (2019)
24. Li, N., Li, J., Chen, X., Yang, Y.: Quantum private query with perfect performance universally applicable against collective-noise. IEEE Access **7**, 29313–29319 (2019)
25. Gao, F., Qin, S., Huang, W., Wen, Q.: Quantum private query: a new kind of practical quantum cryptographic protocol. Sci. China Phys. Mech. Astron. **62**(7), 1–12 (2019). https://doi.org/10.1007/s11433-018-9324-6
26. Wang, Y., Guo, F.Z., Liu, L., Huang, W., Wen, Q.Y.: A new protocol for quantum private query against joint-measurement attack. Sci. Int. J. Theor. Phys. **58**, 1828–1835 (2019)
27. Zhong, J.F., Liu, Z.H., Xu, J.: Analysis and improvement of an efficient controlled quantum secure direct communication and authentication protocol. Comput. Mater. Continua **57**(3), 621–633 (2018)
28. Tan, X.Q., Li, X.C., Yang, P.: Perfect quantum teleportation via bell states. Comput. Mater. Continua **57**(3), 495–503 (2018)

Improved Analytic Hierarchy Process Based on Fuzzy Synthesis Theory for User Behavior Evaluation

Yishan Gao[✉], Shibin Zhang, and Yuanyuan Huang

School of Cybersecurity, Chengdu University of Information Technology,
Chengdu 610225, China
498251651@qq.com

Abstract. The credibility assessment of network users' behavior is indispensable for the study of trusted networks. This paper proposes an evaluation model of users' behavior. Firstly, users' uncertain behavior is quantitatively shown based on the fuzzy comprehensive evaluation. Then, use the von Neumann entropy with weight to optimize the collected evidence; the weight value of each behavior attribute is calculated by the improved analytic hierarchy process in the form of clustering and merging; finally, the comprehensive evaluation value of the target layer is obtained by calculation, and whether the users' behavior is credible or not is decided according to the comprehensive credibility. The simulation experiment shows that the users' behavior evaluation model proposed in this paper has accurate judgment results for the behavior of network users.

Keywords: User' behavior · Fuzzy decision making · Von Neumann's entropy weight method · Improved analytic hierarchy process

1 Introduction

With the development of the Internet and its widespread use, the security of the network has become very prominent and important. However, the traditional network structure system is not enough to meet the needs of today's network security development. Therefore, solving the nature of network security issues has become an indispensable development, and trusted networks have proposed that network security issues can be solved from the inside. Article [1] refers to the basic concepts of trusted networks and some of the research currently in them.

Based on the previous studies, this paper proposes an improved analytic hierarchy model based on fuzzy synthesis, which can expand the feasibility of fuzzy sets and optimize the evidence by combining quantum information entropy weight method. A comprehensive evaluation of user behavior is accomplished through a complete set of computing system models. It is necessary to establish the security of the relevant system evaluation behavior for the user's behavior and behavioral results, achieve the purpose of maintaining network security, and realize the process from static security system to dynamic processing.

© Springer Nature Singapore Pte Ltd. 2020
X. Sun et al. (Eds.): ICAIS 2020, CCIS 1253, pp. 403–411, 2020.
https://doi.org/10.1007/978-981-15-8086-4_38

In 1996, M. Blaze et al. pioneered the concept of trust management [2]. On this basis, they also proposed a trust management system; Ma Ning [3] et al. Used fuzzy set theory to evaluate air quality and created an incomplete mathematical evaluation method, which has a highly effective and practical reference significance. It not only develops a trustworthy computing model based on vector mechanism in a universal environment, but also uses an improved evidence theory method to model this.

2 Fuzzy Decision Hierarchy Clustering Theory

2.1 Fuzzy Set Theory

In the classical set theory, whether an element belongs to a set, only true or false, but when a concept is ambiguous, for example, 20 people in a room are grouped according to "high". Everyone has a different definition of "high and low", which contains subjective awareness of height and is ambiguous. Therefore, another quantitative description mechanism is needed to reflect the ambiguity of the situation, and at the same time it is intuitive and concise.

L.A. Zaden proposed a fuzzy set in 1965, Definition: Let the domain be a non-empty set Z, z be an element in Z, and satisfy the following mapping for any $z \in Z$: $Z \to [0,1], z \mapsto \mu_A(z) \in [0,1]$.

Then the set $A = \{(z \mid \mu_A(z))\}, \forall z \in Z$ consisting of the z value and the corresponding membership function is called the fuzzy set on Z. Among them, weigh $\mu_{A(z)} = 1$ is the degree of membership of z to A. The value range is [0, 1].

2.2 Hierarchical Analysis Based on Clustering and Merging

In 1988, some people put forward the idea of applying clustering in the AHP method [4]. It is mainly used to calculate the order of the judgment matrix when the number of comparison objects is large, which leads to a large workload, so the clustering and merging algorithm can reduce the workload of this calculation. However, in this paper, it is mainly to solve the "uncommensurable object", that is, when the importance of the compared objects is too large, the construction error of the judgment matrix is avoided. The specific idea of the algorithm is: Assume that the objects that are compared by x are first divided into several classes according to the degree of importance, and the importance between the objects being compared in each class is not too different. In this case, you can use the 1–9 scale method taught by Saaty to find the weights of the compared objects in each class, and then use the merging algorithm to convert the weights of the compared objects of each class into the object at all.

2.3 Evidence Optimization Algorithm

Behavioral Evidence. User behavior evidence refers to the underlying values that can be used to assess user behavior. It can usually be obtained directly from hardware and software (including open source detection software such as crawlers). The evidence of behavior of network users is usually also ambiguous, so it will be represented by specific behavioral evidence.

Evidence normalization (also called standardization) is the basic work of data. In this paper, min-max standardization (discrimination normalization) is adopted, and the original evidence is linearly transformed so that the result values are mapped to [0–1], and the conversion function is as follows (1):

$$X^* = \frac{X - \min}{\max - \min} \tag{1}$$

Note: When new evidence is added, you need to redefine max and min.

The data obtained by repeating the above normalized pre-processing is periodically collected, which not only satisfies the long-term behavior of the user, but also eliminates the single chance. Let there be m kinds of behavioral evidence in the evidence set, and n is the number of collections. The data matrix $X = (x_{ij})_{m*n}$, x_{ij}, which constitutes the original behavioral evidence, represents the preprocessed data of the i-th behavior of the jth data acquisition.

Von Neumann Entropy Optimization Evidence with Weight. In information theory, entropy can measure uncertainty data [5]. Understanding the Application of Quantum Algorithms through the Literature of Zhao Dou [6] et al. On the contrary, the larger the entropy, the greater the uncertainty and the smaller the amount of information. According to the characteristics of entropy, the influence of a certain behavioral evidence on the degree of dispersion can be judged by calculating the entropy weight. If the degree of dispersion is greater, it means that the impact of the data on the evaluation is greater, that is, the importance ranking is higher, and the opposite is the later. Based on the understanding of weights, this paper uses the improved von algorithm [7], which will treat each evidence differently, so their influence on behavior evaluation is different, thus distinguishing the importance of behavioral evidence. Obvious.

1. Von Neumann entropy algorithm:
   Initialize behavioral data adjacency matrix $A = [a_{ij}]$ using Eq. (2):

$$\prod_{j \to i} = \frac{k_i}{\sum_l k_l} \tag{2}$$

Loop execution: traversing all the evidence to construct a layer 0 data set $l_0 = \{v_{01}, v_{02}, v_{03} \dots\}$.
Correct l_0 All nodes constructed in $\{v_{01}, v_{01}, v_{03} \dots\}$ Computational value $D = \sum_{j=1}^{M} d_{ij}^2$, Referred to as $f(D_{01}, D_{02}, D_{03} \dots)$, among them. $f(x) = x^\alpha, \alpha \in (0.2, 0.4, \dots, 2)$.
Using the formula (3), find the Lapucas matrix $K = |E|$:

$$L_G = \frac{1}{2K}(D - A) \tag{3}$$

Using the formula (4) to obtain the von Neumann entropy of the matrix h_A, among them λ_i Refers to the eigenvector value of the matrix.

$$h_A = -\sum \lambda_i \log_2 \lambda_i \tag{4}$$

delete l_0 All the data in the order $n \leftarrow 1$. And recalculating the Von Neumann, entropy of the matrix h_A, calculate the change value of von Neumann's entropy ΔA. Sort the data based on the change value.

2. Method for determining the weight coefficient (entropy method [7]) Find the forward and negative indicators according to Eqs. (5) and (6):

Positive indicator (the larger the positive indicator value, the better):

$$x_{ij} = [\frac{x_{ij} - \min(x_1, x_2, \ldots, x_{ij})}{\max(x_1, x_2, \ldots, x_{ij}) - \min(x_1, x_2, \ldots, x_{ij})}] \times 100 \qquad (5)$$

Reversal indicator (the smaller the value of the negative indicator, the better):

$$x_{ij} = [\frac{\max(x_1, x_2, \ldots, x_{ij})}{\max(x_1, x_2, \ldots, x_{ij}) - \min(x_1, x_2, \ldots, x_{ij})}] \times 100 \qquad (6)$$

among them x_{ij}. The data value of the i-th behavior for the jth data acquisition. Calculate the proportion of the i-th behavior under the jth time, and calculate the comprehensive score by the weighting formula (7):

$$P_{ij} = \frac{X_{ij}}{\sum\limits_{i=1}^{n} X_{ij}} \qquad (7)$$

Finally, the final optimization value of the evidence of an indicator can be obtained by formula (8):

$$X_m = \sum_{i=1}^{n} P_i \bullet X_{mi} \qquad (m = 1, 2, \ldots, m) \qquad (8)$$

3 User Behavior Assessment Model Based on Fuzzy Set Theory to Improve Analytic Hierarchy Process

In order to solve the limitation of the unreasonable weighting problem of the traditional hierarchical analysis algorithm construction judgment matrix, this paper proposes an improved hierarchical algorithm (clustering and merging algorithm) based on 1–9 fuzzy scale based on the 1–9 scale method of Professor Saaty. The algorithm is divided into two steps, clustering and merging. First, a 1–9 fuzzy scale evaluation table is given first, as shown in Table 1.

3.1 Clustering Method

Assumed data set $E = \{e_1, e_2, \ldots, e_i, \ldots, e_m\}$, e_i for the i-th data, there are a total of m data.

Table 1. 1–9 fuzzy scale evaluation table.

Behavioral importance evaluation	A_i is extremely unimportant compared to A_j	A_i is very unimportant compared to A_j	A_i is obviously not important compared with A_j	A_i is slightly less important than A_j	A_i is as important as A_j	A_i is slightly more important than A_j	A_i is significantly more important than A_j	A_i is very important compared to A_j	A_i is extremely important compared to A_j
Importance scale value	[0.1, 0.9]	[0.2, 0.8]	[0.3, 0.7]	[0.4, 0.6]	[0.5, 0.5]	[0.6, 0.25]	[0.7, 0.2]	[0.8, 0.15]	[0.9, 0.1]

Note: When the importance is between the two, take the middle value.

1. First select an object from m compared objects e_1'. As a benchmark for comparison, and let class $t(1) = e_1'$ (There is currently only one element in class $t(1)$ e_1', with other evidence e_1'. Compare if you think the object is better than e_1' important, and the ratio of the importance of the two is not greater than a certain scale value $f(k)_{max}$, the object is assigned to the class $t(1)$; if it is determined that the object is not e_1' important, but the importance of the two is not less than a certain scale $f(k)_{min}$, the object is divided into the class $t(-1)$; otherwise the object is divided into the class $l(1)$. When the class $l(1)$ is an empty set, the classification ends. At this time, two categories are divided into $t(1)$, $t(-1)$. Otherwise, go to step 2.

2. Select an object from $l(1)$ e_2' As a benchmark, and let class $t(2) = e_2'$, And then use other objects in $l(1)$ with e_2' for comparison, if it is judged that the object ratio e_2' important, but the ratio of the importance of the two is not greater than a certain scale value $f(k)_{max}$, the object is classified as class $t(2)$; if it is judged that the object is not e_2' important, but the ratio of the importance of the two is not less than $f(k)_{min}$, the object is classified as $t(-2)$; otherwise, the object is classified as $l(2)$. If $l(2)$ is an empty set, the classification ends. At this time, four categories are divided into $t(-2)$, $t(-1)$, $t(1)$, $t(2)$, otherwise go to step 3. At this time, there are four categories. Otherwise, $L(2)$ will continue to be classified in the same operation.

3. Suppose a total of x-step classification is performed, and $l(x)$ satisfies the empty set, then the classification ends. At this time, the total is divided into $2\times$ classes. The ratio of importance between objects in each class is not greater than a certain $f(k)_{max}$ or no less than a certain $f(k)_{min}$. Using its properties (when an object of $T(i)$ is larger than $T(j)$, satisfying $T(i) \gg T(j)$), the classes can be sorted by importance, and then In the 2X class, it can be obtained according to importance from small to large: $T(-1) \ll T(1) \ll T(-2) \ll T(2) \ll \ldots \ll T(-i) \ll T(i) \ll \ldots \ll T(-X) \ll T(X)$.

4. Use the ahp method to find the maximum weight and the minimum weight in each category (this is the unnormalized weight vector of each evidence by fuzzy analysis decision theory). For example: $W_{max}^{T(-1)}$, $W_{min}^{T(-1)}$; $W_{max}^{T(1)}$, $W_{min}^{T(1)}$.

3.2 Merging Method

The hypothesis is divided into two categories: $T(-1)$ and $T(1)$, there are d comparison objects in $T(-1)$ ($e_1^{T(-1)}, e_2^{T(-1)}, \ldots, e_d^{T(-1)}$); there are p comparison objects in $T(1)$.

1. Calculate the weight values of each type, and find the maximum weight value and the minimum weight value for each class.

2. The important proportional coefficient k between t(1) and t(−1) is determined by the object corresponding to the maximum and minimum weight values of Eq. (9) (the judge can be judged according to his own judgment):

$$K = \frac{A_{min}^{T(1)}}{A_{max}^{T(-1)}} \tag{9}$$

3. From Eq. (10), find the combined weight vector v′ of all objects in t(1) and t(−1) (get the ranking weight of all evidence under the same attribute layer):

$$\omega' = \frac{W_1^{T(-1)}}{W_{max}^{T(-1)}}, \frac{W_2^{T(-1)}}{W_{max}^{T(-1)}}, \ldots, \frac{W_p^{T(-1)}}{W_{max}^{T(-1)}}, \frac{W_1^{T(1)}}{W_{min}^{T(1)}} \times K, \frac{W_2^{T(1)}}{W_{min}^{T(1)}} \times K, \ldots, \frac{W_d^{T(1)}}{W_{min}^{T(1)}} \times K \tag{10}$$

Note: When there are more than two classes after clustering, repeat the above steps to merge.

3.3 Normalization

The sort weight vector is normalized by Eq. (11):

$$\omega_i = \frac{\omega_i'}{\sum\limits_{i=1}^{m} \omega i}, \quad (i = 1, 2, \ldots, m) \tag{11}$$

3.4 Fuzzy Comprehensive Evaluation

Finally, the evaluation value of an attribute layer can be obtained by formula (12): the superiority of the evidence and the corresponding index weights. The evaluation value and the target weight of each attribute layer are weighted and calculated, and finally the fuzzy comprehensive evaluation value of the user behavior is obtained:

$$G = \sum\limits_{i=1}^{m} \omega_i X_i \tag{12}$$

4 Simulation Experiments and Analysis

In this experiment, through the simulated network simulation platform (the platform interface is shown in Fig. 1), you can log in to the administrator to view relevant information in the background, and collect the user's behavior data: generally, the server-based log method can be used to obtain a large number of users for a long time. The behavior data is completed within the client; and the client collects user behavior data, that is, the web server automatically assigns an ID to the client and records it in the client's cookies. This experiment uses the server log to record the long-term operational behavior of a user on this platform and evaluate the user's behavioral safety factor based on the overall model.

Fig. 1. Platform interface

4.1 Behavioral Evidence Collection and Optimization

Collect evidence of user behavior and classify it into three categories based on attributes (integrity, security, stability). The obtained evidence is preprocessed according to formula (1); then the final optimization process is performed according to formulas (2)–(8). Table 2 shows the results:

4.2 Calculate the Fuzzy Weights of Indicators at All Levels

According to the idea of clustering and merging, the sorting weights are obtained by combining formulas (9)–(11). The normalization calculation is then performed by Eq. (11). Table 3 shows the results:

4.3 Fuzzy Comprehensive Evaluation

The evaluation value of each attribute and the comprehensive evaluation value of the target layer are calculated according to the formula (12). The obtained attribute evaluation value results are shown in Table 4 below:

According to the weight of the first-level index obtained in Table 3, the comprehensive evaluation value of the user behavior is calculated: 0.795.

Finally, the calculation results are evaluated by the expert's rating standard, and the final grade evaluation is obtained. From the results, it can be seen that the overall evaluation of the user is in the upper middle range.

5   Conclusion

Because the behavior of network users is uncertain and subjective, the comprehensive evaluation method using fuzzy decision is more accurate than other direct use of probability to analyze user behavior. The weighted von Neumann entropy optimizes the evidence, which is more accurate than the general entropy weight optimization evidence, and can provide a basis for subsequent control and management of user misconduct. Li Chunhua [8] Designed an effective data integrity auditing program, which can learn some methods to perform audit analysis on the completeness of data. The improved algorithm can avoid the traditional consistency error problem and make the weights more correct.

Table 2. Evidence processing

Evidence name (A_i, B_i, C_i)	Trust rule	Evidence pretreatment	After the evidence is optimized (X_m)
Average bandwidth occupied by users (A1)	Less than 300 Kbps is a full trust level	(0.9, 0.75, 0.8, 0.85, 0.9)	0.85
Average storage resources occupied by users (A2)	Below 1 MB is the full trust level	(0.85, 0.7, 0.8, 0.75, 0.8)	0.8
User name/password input error number (A3)	0 times belong to full trust	(0.9, 0.85, 0.9, 0.8, 0.85)	0.85
Access to sensitive services (B1)	0 times belong to full trust	(0.8, 0.85, 0.9, 0.75, 0.8)	0.8
Scan port number (B2)	0 times belong to full trust successively	(0.75, 0.7, 0.8, 0.75, 0.85)	0.75
Guess the number of passwords (B3)	0 times belong to full trust	(0.8, 0.85, 0.75, 0.9, 0.8)	0.8
Attempt to override the number of times (B4)	0 times belong to full trust	(0.75, 0.7, 0.8, 0.85, 0.8)	0.8
Number of file operations created (C1)	Full trust within 20 times	(0.85, 0.75, 0.8, 0.8, 0.9)	0.8
Number of times to modify file permissions (C2)	Within 5 times, it is within the safe range	(0.8, 0.7, 0.75, 0.8, 0.75)	0.75
Duration of access to the system (C3)	Below 20 ms is a safe range	(0.9, 0.8, 0.75, 0.8, 0.85)	0.8
Sensitive vocabulary query times (C4)	0 times is a complete security trust	(0.6, 0.75, 0.8, 0.75, 0.8)	0.75

Table 3. Index weights at all levels

User behavior evidence	Clustering operation	Consolidation operation	Consolidation operation	First-level indicator weight
A	0.825	(0.825, 0.9)	0.862	0.348
B	0.8	(0.8, 0.85)	0.825	0.333
C	0.775	(0.775, 0.8)	0.787	0.319

Table 4. Attribute evaluation value

Attribute layer	A	B	C
Evaluation value	0.87	0.782	0.733

Acknowledgments. The authors would like to thank the reviewers for their detailed reviews and constructive comments, which have helped improve the quality of this paper. This work was supported in part by the National Key Research and Development Project of China (No. 2017YFB0802302), the Science and Technology Support Project of Sichuan Province (No. 2016FZ0112, No. 2017GZ0314, No. 2018GZ0204), the Academic and Technical Leaders Training Funding Support Projects of Sichuan Province (No. 2016120080102643), the Application Foundation Project of Sichuan Province (No. 2017JY0168), the Science and Technology Project of Chengdu (No. 2017-RK00-00103-ZF, No. 2016-HM01-00217-SF).

References

1. Fan, T.: Research on basic concepts and basic attributes of trusted networks. J. Chifeng Coll. (Nat. Sci. Ed.) (5), 55–57 (2007)
2. Blaze, M., Feigenbaum, J., Lacy, J.: Decentralized trust management. In: IEEE Symposium on Security & Privacy (1996)
3. Ning, M., Guan, J., Liu, P., Zhang, Z., O'Hare, G.M.P.: GA-BP air quality evaluation method based on fuzzy theory. Comput. Mater. Continua **58**(1), 215–227 (2019)
4. Wu, J.: Decomposition in analytic hierarchy. J. Wuhan Inst. Urban Constr. (3), 47–52 (1996)
5. Song, L., Hu, Z., Yang, Y., et al.: Decision table reduction based on evidence entropy for uncertainty metrics. J. Nat. Univ. Defense Technol. **30**(5), 94–98 (2008)
6. Dou, Z., Xu, G., Chen, X., Yuan, K.: Rational non-hierarchical quantum state sharing protocol. Comput. Mater. Continua **58**(2), 335–347 (2019)
7. Yang, X.: Research on importance ranking of social network nodes based on von Neumann entropy. Guangxi University (2017)
8. Li, C., Wang, P., Sun, C., Zhou, K., Huang, P.: WiBPA: an efficient data integrity auditing scheme without bilinear pairings. Comput. Mater. Continua **58**(2), 319–333 (2019)

Location Privacy Protection Algorithm Based on the Division Method of Voronoi in the Internet of Vehicles

Peng-shou Xie, Xue-ming Han[(✉)], Tao Feng, Yan Yan, and Guo-qiang Ma

School of Computer and Communications, Lanzhou University of Technology, 287 Lan-gong-ping Road, Lanzhou 730050, Gansu, China
hxmhan@163.com

Abstract. Position fuzzy algorithm has certain security, but it doesn't fit well with the actual situation of the Internet of vehicles in road network. So, in order to reduce the deviation from the actual situation, divide the road network into Voronoi diagram, then choose the path that satisfies k-anonymity and l-diversity, and sort the weights of each road. Then add a section of the road near the road weight of the vehicle that needs to be anonymous to the anonymous set, and combining positional blurring based on this algorithm. Not only can it meet the K-anonymity of the vehicle, but it can also guarantee K-anonymity from the space area, in addition to satisfying the l-diversity of the road network. The way effectively avoids the characteristic attacks of the road network. And the algorithm has less time complexity and relative anonymity and a higher anonymity success rate. To some extent, the disadvantages are reduced that some anonymous protection algorithms being greatly deviated from the actual situation.

Keywords: Internet of Vehicles · Voronoi partition · L-Diversity · Location privacy · Anonymous protection algorithms

1 Introduction

The rapid development of the Internet of Things, Communication technology is rapidly improving, the arrival of 5G cellular network will accelerate the development of the Internet of Things [1]. The computing power of mobile devices is rapidly increasing. These mobile devices can also be carried on many devices. Location-based services are an integral part of people in modern society. For example, query nearby hotels and schools, how to find the nearest bus stop, etc. Internet of Vehicles is an emerging product, which developed from the foundation of the Internet of Things, that is, vehicular ad hoc networks (VANETs) [2–4]. Usually the physical layer/MAC layer uses the 802.11p protocol [5], and the networking technology selects the Ad-hoc method. To effectively reduce communication delay and ensure high-speed movement, and the network quality of the vehicle under frequent changes in the network topology. The Internet of Vehicles aims to provide vehicle-to-vehicle (V2V) communication and vehicle-to-infrastructure

© Springer Nature Singapore Pte Ltd. 2020
X. Sun et al. (Eds.): ICAIS 2020, CCIS 1253, pp. 412–422, 2020.
https://doi.org/10.1007/978-981-15-8086-4_39

(V2I) communication. The system mainly includes onboard unit (OBU) and application unit. (application unit, AU) and road side unit (RSU) [6].

GPS and location services are a double-edged sword [7], They greatly facilitated people's lives. But at the same time, personal privacy leaks have become a serious problem. Personal income, identity information, physical condition is extremely easy to leak. And may be illegally used, protecting location privacy is an urgent task [8]. The privacy of the Internet of vehicles is closely related to the privacy of the individual. So, protecting the privacy of the Internet of vehicles is also extremely important. A series of information such as the location, trajectory, and vehicle number of the vehicle are easily leaked. These leaks are easily exploited by attackers and have catastrophic consequences [9]. So how to protect location privacy is a problem that deserves in-depth study.

2 Research Background

Gruteser M first combined K anonymity, using P2P architecture, generalized the area containing K users into a rectangular area on the plane [10], and the request is sent to the LBS anonymous server through the area instead of the specific location, so the probability of the user being attacked becomes 1/K. This method utilizes the K anonymous [11] privacy protection model and has high security performance. In response to the lack of k anonymity, later scholars proposed l-diversity and t-close [12]. Many of the later privacy protection algorithms are based on this principle. Although the position blur has certain security, it also has certain weaknesses. And these methods are based on Euclidean space, they can't be better suited to the Internet of Vehicles network conditions and are vulnerable to be attacked.

In view of the shortcomings of location blurring methods, many privacy protection methods under road network conditions have been proposed. Such as location semantics [13], ring anonymity, etc. [14]. Dai Jiazhu [15] proposed a method for generating anonymous locations of sensitive locations in a road network environment. The method is based on spatial division, firstly generating a Voronoi diagram unit for the intersection of the road network according to the L-differential requirement of the road network, Then consider the sensitivity of the user's location and generate an anonymous area for the user's location. The proposed algorithm can better solve the problem that the anonymous region generated by the general k-anonymous algorithm is still in the sensitive range, thus better protecting the user's location privacy.

Li Weizhen [16] proposed a space-time association privacy protection scheme based on spatio-temporal correlation, including two algorithms, a map segmentation algorithm and a pseudo-content generation algorithm. It is very good to avoid the attacker guessing the real information of the user based on the correlation between time and space. Finally, the effectiveness and safety of the proposed scheme are proved by experiments. Liang Huichao [17] divided the entire road network into network Voronoi cells (NVC) which are independent and non-overlapping. Secondly, the Hilbert curve is used to traverse the road network space, and all the points of interest on the road network are sorted according to the Hilbert order. Overcome the shortcomings of traditional k-anonymity against inference attacks. Theoretical analysis and experimental results show that the proposed privacy protection scheme can effectively protect user location privacy. Zhou

Yihua and other scholars [18] are vulnerable to multiple query and reasoning attacks for spatial anonymity, which brings privacy exposure problems. A random k-hidden set is constructed to satisfy location k-anonymity and location l-diversity. It provides a service provider with a location-based service for users without knowing the exact results of the user.

We have studied these methods in depth, analyzed the advantages and disadvantages of these methods, and formed a location privacy protection algorithm based on Voronoi diagram. And the system architecture is based on the central server architecture. We firstly divide the Voronoi diagram of the road network, generate a road network with K-anonymity and l-diversity, and then sort the road weights on the road network, and select the right weight similar to the road segment where the anonymous vehicle is required. The value of the road segment is added to the anonymous set, and performing the location privacy protection algorithm process.

3   Privacy Protection Algorithm Related Process

3.1   Architecture of Privacy Protection

Figure 1 is an anonymous system architecture for the location privacy protection of the Internet of vehicles, based on the third-party central server architecture. When a vehicle in the Internet of Vehicles needs to be anonymous, it first sends the request to the central server. And it may have to go through the middle RSU, The RSU then forwards the request information to the central server. The central server locates the section of the vehicle that needs to be anonymous. Then perform an anonymous algorithm process, and form an anonymous set, then the third-party server sends the anonymous set to the LBS server for positioning. And return the result to a third-party server. The third-party server performs the necessary result refinement and returns the request to the vehicle network user. It may have to go through the middle RSU. After user of the Internet of vehicles make necessary calculation of the results. finally getting the result it needs, anonymous process ends. It is the working process of the privacy protection architecture. And the related description in the architecture is as follow:

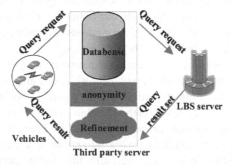

Fig. 1. Anonymous system architecture of location privacy protection in the Internet of Vehicles.

Anonymous demand: $Q : \{(x_i, y_i), K, L, S_{min}, S_{max}, t_q\}$, (x_i, y_i) represents the position coordinate of the i-th vehicle. K is anonymity. The size of K is proportional to the strength of the need for anonymous protection. L is the number of roads set. Adding the roads to the anonymous set can reduce the probability of edge attack. Combined with K, L, the probability of being attacked becomes $\frac{1}{k*l}$. S_{min} and S_{max} can dynamically control the size of the anonymous area. Trying to control the anonymous area in this area to prevent the anonymous box from being too large. Internet of vehicles is dynamic, the network topology at different times is completely different, and the vehicles are in different positions, so by setting a certain delay t_q to guarantee that the Internet of vehicles will not have much difference in a short period of time. The main purpose of anonymous protection is to reduce the resource consumption of the server while satisfying the privacy of the location. Thereby reducing the delay of server processing and improving the quality of service.

Regional control: Let the points that make up the graph of the anonymous area be:$\{(x_1, y_1), (x_2, y_2), (x_3, y_3) \ldots \ldots (x_n, y_n)\}$, and let the maximum distance of the area polygon $G(x_0, y_0)$ to the node constituting the polygon of the anonymous area be R, then:

$$R = \text{Max}\left\{\sqrt{(x_i - x_0)^2 + (y_i - y_0)^2}\right\}, \text{ Among them } i = 0, 1, 2 \cdots n$$

$$(x_0, y_0) = \left(\frac{\sum_{i=1}^{n} x_i}{n}, \frac{\sum_{i=1}^{n} y_i}{n}\right) \tag{1}$$

According to R, the size of the anonymous frame area S can be controlled.

3.2 Dividing the Road Network into Voronoi Units

Let the set of discrete points with n uniformly distributed in the plane area CS $=$ $\{CS_1, CS_2, CS_3 \cdots CS_n\}$. The Voronoi region $V(CS_i)$ formed by any point $CS_i \in CS$ is a set of all points in the U to the minimum point of the CS_i distance, which is called the V zone. As shown in Fig. 2 $V(CS_1) = \{A | \text{dist}(A, CS_1) \leq \text{dist}(A, CS_k)A \in U, k \neq 1\}$, dist(A,B) represents the Euclidean distance between points A and B, and CS_i is called Voronoi diagram generator. The entire city Voronoi diagram with CS_i as the generator can be expressed as $V(U) = \{V(CS_1), V(CS_2) \cdots V(CS_n)\}$. Obviously, adjacent V zones have common edges and do not overlap each other to cover the entire road network area.

This study abstracts the road network into an undirected graph with edge weights, denoted by G(V, E), the V represents the node set of the road network, and the v_i indicates the intersection of the road network. And E represents the collection of edges in the road network. Any e_{ij} indicates that the road network nodes v_i and v_j are directly connected. In order to meet the requirements of road segment diversity, dividing the road network into Voronoi units, A point of the node dimension degree$(P_i) \geq d_m$ is selected as a V map generation element. This ensures that the points in each V zone can reach d_m. Satisfying the diversity of roads. putting dm $\geq$ 3 (Fig. 3).

Vehicles are distributed on every road, and vehicles are distributed at different times, so the Internet of Vehicles is a dynamic network. Node information changes rapidly. However, in a very short period of time, the distribution of vehicles on the road network is approximately the same. It is possible to study it in a short time t. The privacy protection

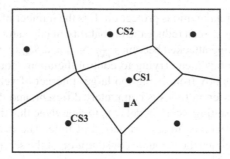

Fig. 2. CS generator.

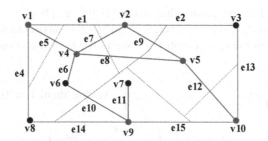

Fig. 3. Dividing the road network according to Voronoi diagram.

algorithm is combined with the Voronoi road network partitioning and is performed on the previously described architecture. This algorithm is also based on the classic K-anonymity and l-diversity algorithm. A vehicle wants to request a location service, so it sends the request $Q : \{(x_i, y_i), K, L, S_{min}, S_{max}, t_q\}$ to the central server or RSU. Then the central server determines the road according to the privacy protection algorithm and forms a set of hidden areas with the vehicles of the surrounding roads. Then initiate a request to the location server. And The location server receives the request and queries it. And the location server Send the relevant results after the query to the requester. Finally, the requester calculates his actual location based on his position. the entire anonymous process ends.

3.3 Algorithm Process Description

A vehicle wants to request a location service, so it sends the request to the location server. After receiving the location request, the central server can view the location of the requested vehicle and the network topology and network status of the node at this time. First the location server locates the road where the current vehicle is located. In particular, this road refers to the road in the Voronoi area where the vehicle is located. At this time, the location server counts the number of vehicles K_0 on the road where the vehicle is located. Counting the number of vehicles on other roads in the Voronoi area where the vehicle is located, expressed as $k_i, i = 1, 2, 3$. Anonymous server calculates the weight of each road $W_i, i = 0, 1, 2 \ldots$. The weights W are arranged in ascending order. Let the road diversity required is LC. The greedy algorithm is used to make the local mean of the weights closest to the mean of the road where the vehicle is used. Set the number of road users after sorting to $K_m \cdots K_{-3}, K_{-2}, K_{-1}, K_0, K_1, K_2, K_3 \cdots K_n$, there may be equal situations. At this time, we only need to juxtapose them. The corresponding weight is $W_m \cdots W_{-3}, W_{-2}, W_{-1}, W_0, W_1, W_2, W_3 \cdots W_n$. After adding l roads, then judge the number of vehicles on L roads. If the total number is greater than k, judge the polygonal area of anonymous vehicles. If $S_{min} \leq S_0 \leq S_{max}$ and $\Delta T < T_{max}$ (no timeout), So anonymous success. In this case, the anonymous server sends the anonymous result to the anonymous vehicle. Finally, Anonymous vehicles select their own location information from the results containing multiple location information according to their own location needs.

Input: undirected graph G; user set W, fuzzy position C of user C (x, y, r), r is the center of the fuzzy circle, Privacy needs KC, Road difference LC.

Output: participating anonymous user location set S.

Step 1: Locate the road section where the user is located, and count the road section number set in Voronoi area where the user is located, Set the road section number as L_i $i = 1, 2, 3 \cdots n$, where i is the i-th section. Set k_i $i = 1, 2, 3 \cdots n$, k_i is the number of vehicles on the i-th road.
Step 2: Calculate the weight of each road, that is, the proportion of the number of vehicles on a road in all vehicles.

$$W_i = \frac{k_i}{\sum_0^i k_i} i = 1, 2, 3 \cdots n \tag{2}$$

Step 3: Arrange the roads according to the weight W_i.
Step 4: Add the user's first road section L_0. if the number of road sections joined is L, then L = 1
Step 5: If $L \leq LC$, LC is the road section diversity value. Add a second section to s. Set the weight difference w between the user's road and other roads. Weight difference between section L_i and reference section L_0 is $W_{0i} = |W_0 - W_i|$. If $W_{0-1} \geq W_{0+1}$, (suppose -1 is the left side of the sorted segment's base segment and +1 is the right side of the sorted segment's base segment) then add the road section on the left of the sorted road section. Otherwise, join the right section. Now compare W_{0-2}, W_{0+1}. And add the road section with larger weight. Repeat the same process.
Step 6: If $L < LC$, return to step 5, otherwise proceed to the next step.
Step 7: Judge the number of vehicles K in all sections of S. If K < KC, return to Step 6, otherwise proceed to the next step.
Step 8: If $k \geq KC$, proceed to the next step.
Step 9: If t < T, proceed to the next step, otherwise anonymous failure. Wait for next anonymity.
Step 10: Calculate the polygon area S_0 of all vehicles participating in the anonymous process in S. if $S_{min} \leq S_0 \leq S_{max}$, Anonymous success, otherwise anonymous failure, waiting for the next anonymous. When the next time anonymous, if the cache has not expired, the information in the cache is imported to reduce the anonymous time.

Step 11: S contains the set of road segments and the corresponding vehicle collection, anonymous time and the size of the anonymous box.

The privacy protection algorithm as is showed in Table 1.

Table 1. The algorithm of privacy protection

| Input: | G: W:C(x, y, r): KC:LC |
| Output: | Location set S |

1: $l_i, i = 1,2,3 \cdots m$; k_j $j = 1,2,3 \cdots n$ // Count the number of road segments in the Voronoi area where the user is located l_i, the number of vehicles k_j

2: $W_i = \frac{k_j}{\sum_0^i k_j}$ $i = 1,2,3 \cdots m, \ j = 1,2,3 \cdots n$

3: sort W_i

4: $S \leftarrow (x_q, y_q), S \leftarrow L_0$

5: L=1, if L < LC, goto 7

6: else goto 7

7: If $W_{0-i} \geq W_{0+i}$, $S \leftarrow L_{0-i}$ $i = 1,2,3 \cdots$

8: else $S \leftarrow L_{0+i}$

9: if $\sum K < KC$, goto 9

10: else goto 7

11: if t<T , goto 11

12: else fail

13: $v_1 \leftrightarrow v_2, v_2 \leftrightarrow v_3 \cdots v_{n-1} \leftrightarrow v_n, v_n \leftrightarrow v_1$ // Connect the outermost vehicle in the Voronoi area for regional generalization

14: $S_0 = \frac{1}{2} \left\{ \begin{vmatrix} x_1 & y_1 \\ x_2 & y_2 \end{vmatrix} + \begin{vmatrix} x_2 & y_2 \\ x_3 & y_3 \end{vmatrix} + \cdots + \begin{vmatrix} x_n & x_n \\ x_1 & y_1 \end{vmatrix} \right\}$ // Calculate the area of the generalized area

15: if $S_{min} \leq S_0 \leq S_{max}$, success

16: Print S

4   Experiment and Result Analysis

MATALAB 2018b environment was used in the experiment. In Intel (R) core i7-7700HQ CPU @ 2.80 GHz processor, 16 GB memory. NVIDIA GTX 1060 graphic display, and Microsoft Windows 10 professional operating system. The location simulation data of mobile terminal is generated by Thomas Brinkhoff road network data generator, which uses the traffic map of Oldenburg city in Germany to generate 2000 nodes.

Risk of privacy disclosure as is showed in Eqs. 3.

$$R_d = \frac{1}{K - K_0} \tag{3}$$

In the equation, K is the degree of anonymity, and K_0 is the number of vehicles that an attacker can exclude in a certain anonymity. Under a certain degree of anonymity, this algorithm can reduce the probability of being attacked, and the degree of privacy disclosure is less than k-anonymity, as is showed in Fig. 4. This is due to the addition of l-diversity on the basis of k-anonymity.

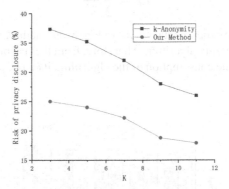

Fig. 4.   Risk of privacy disclosure.

For the success rate of anonymity, we can see from Fig. 5 that our method has a slightly lower success rate than the anonymous ring algorithm. This is because in order to reduce the consumption of time, this algorithm does not search for vehicles across the Voronoi area to form an anonymous set. However, the overall success rate still reaches more than 85%, so it is feasible.

The time consumption of the algorithm can be considered from the following aspects: Anonymous wait time T_w, anonymous processing time T_d, transmission delay T_t and query time T_q.

The algorithm consumption time is showed in Eqs. 4

$$T = T_w + T_d + T_t + T_q \tag{4}$$

Anonymous wait time and transfer time are usually ignored. Only consider anonymous processing time and query time. When considering the performance of the algorithm,

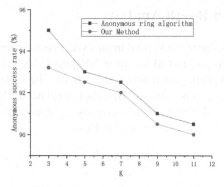

Fig. 5. Anonymous success rate.

only the anonymous processing time T_d is considered. The average anonymous time is generally used to measure the performance of the algorithm. As formula 5.

$$\overline{T_d} = \frac{\sum T_d}{\sum U_s} \tag{5}$$

As can be seen from the experimental results of Fig. 6, our method has less time consumption than the ring anonymity algorithm. Therefore, from the risk of privacy leakage, your success rate and the time consumption of the algorithm, it can be seen that the algorithm has better superiority.

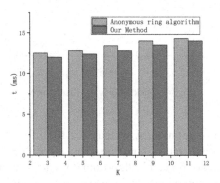

Fig. 6. Anonymous time consuming.

The algorithm uses fuzzy location, K-anonymity and l-diversity methods to make the location information more secure. In addition to this, the algorithm also by judging the size of the overall anonymous box to effectively control server resource consumption. To achieves a certain balance between location privacy protection and server resource consumption. At the same time, it avoids the situation where all vehicles are in a centralized position and high-density attacks occur. Dividing the Voronoi diagram allows the server and the vehicle to be in an effective communication range, so that the anonymous process has a higher communication quality. A certain area range is used to control the size of the anonymous area, then to control the server overhead, and avoiding the situation where all vehicles are concentrated in one extreme situation, in the time the probability of privacy leakage reaches 100%.

5 Conclusion

The privacy protection based on LBS location service has become a research hotspot. How to better hide the location of vehicles is a very important problem in privacy protection. We carefully study the shortcomings of fuzzy location method. And combined with the specific characteristics of the road network, using K-anonymity and l-diversity, arrange the road sections according to the weight, Add the road section near the weight of the road where the vehicle needs to be anonymous to the anonymous set, and put these anonymous vehicles into a fuzzy set in the location, the experimental results show that this method has a smaller risk of privacy disclosure, an acceptable anonymous success rate and a smaller time complexity, and it better meets the actual situation of the road network. However, this method also has a lot of shortcomings, which need to be further optimized in the future. And the actual road network is very complex, including not only roads, but also buildings and other things, and the current road is not only one layer, how to establish privacy protection algorithm in line with these actual road network needs further study. And the dynamic of the Internet of vehicles is also an important content to be studied.

Acknowledgement. This research is supported by the National Natural Science Foundations of China under Grants No.61862040 and No. 61762060 and 61762059, The authors gratefully acknowledge the anonymous reviewers for their helpful comments and suggestions.

References

1. Li, S., Xu, L.D., Zhao, S.: 5G Internet of Things: a survey. J. Ind. Inf. Integr. **10**, 1–9 (2018)
2. Sakiz, F., Sen, S.: A survey of attacks and detection mechanisms on intelligent transportation systems: VANETs and IoV. Ad Hoc Netw. **61**, 33–50 (2017)
3. Wang, X., Jiang, J., Zhao, S., Bai, L.: A fair blind signature scheme to revoke malicious vehicles in VANETs. Comput. Mater. Continua **58**(1), 249–262 (2019)
4. Duan, X., et al.: Adaptive handover decision inspired by biological mechanism in vehicle Ad-hoc networks. Comput. Mater. Continua **61**(3), 1117–1128 (2019)
5. Shah, A.F.M.S., Ilhan, H., Tureli, U.: Modeling and performance analysis of the IEEE 802.11P MAC for VANETs. In: 42nd International Conference on Telecommunications and Signal Processing, TSP 2019, pp. 393–396 (2019)
6. Kim, D.-Y., Kim, S.: A data download method from RSUs using fog computing in connected vehicles. Comput. Mater. Continua **59**(2), 375–387 (2019)
7. Zhao, H., Li, M.: Centroid-based KNN query in mobile service of LBS. In: IEEE/IFIP Network Operations and Management Symposium: Cognitive Management in a Cyber World, NOMS 2018, pp. 1–6 (2018)
8. Jagwani, P., Kaushik, S.: Privacy in location based services: protection strategies, attack models and open challenges. In: Kim, K., Joukov, N. (eds.) ICISA 2017. LNEE, vol. 424, pp. 12–21. Springer, Singapore (2017). https://doi.org/10.1007/978-981-10-4154-9_2

9. Asuquo, P., et al.: Security and privacy in location-based services for vehicular and mobile communications: an overview, challenges, and countermeasures. IEEE Internet Things J. **5**(6), 4778–4802 (2018)
10. Mingyan, X., Zhao, H., Xinsheng, J., Wei, S.: Mobile P2P fast location anonymity algorithm based on user distribution perception. J. Softw. **29**(7), 1852–1862 (2018)
11. Fei, F., Li, S., et al.: K-anonymity based schema for location privacy preservation. IEEE Trans. Sustain. Comput. **4**(2), 156–167 (2019)
12. Sei, Y., et al.: Anonymization of sensitive quasi-identifiers for l-diversity and t-closeness. IEEE Trans. Dependable Secure Comput. **16**(4), 580–593 (2019)
13. Ma, M.: Enhancing privacy using location semantics in location based services. In: 2018 IEEE 3rd International Conference on Big Data Analysis, ICBDA 2018, pp. 368–373 (2018)
14. Ni, W., Chen, X.: Study on privacy preference in privacy-friendly neighborhood Neighbor query of software **27**(7), 1805–1821 (2016)
15. Dai, J., Hua, L.: Method for generating anonymous location of sensitive locations in road network environment. Comput. Sci. **43**(3), 137–144 (2016)
16. Li, W., Ding, W., Meng, J., Hui, L.: Privacy protection scheme based on spatiotemporal association in location service. J. Commun. **39**(05), 134–142 (2018)
17. Liang, H., Wang, B., Cui, N., Yang, K., Yang, X.: Privacy protection method of interest point query in road network environment. J. Softw. **29**(3), 703–720 (2018)
18. Zhou, Y., Jianhang, D., et al.: Location privacy nearest neighbor query method based on Voronoi diagram. J. Beijing Univ. Technol. **44**(2), 225–233 (2018)

Safety Helmet Detection Method Based on Faster R-CNN

Shuqiang Guo, Dongxue Li, Zhiheng Wang, and Xinxin Zhou(✉)

Northeast Electric Power University, Jilin 132012, Jilin, China
zxx51@qq.com

Abstract. In order to reduce the probability of safety accidents caused by non-wearing helmet, we proposed an improved Safety helmet wearing detection method based on Faster R-CNN. We use Faster R-CNN as the basic algorithm for Safety helmet detection. This paper uses VGG16 feature extraction network to extract the characteristics of the helmet. Region Proposal Network is used to extract detection regions and to predict positions and categories. We use the video monitoring at the substation entrance and exit as the data set to determine the target frame parameters. Finally, We use euclidean distance to compare the relationship between the return position of the human head and the return position of the helmet. A method to determine whether the helmet is worn correctly by comparing the regression position of the head with the helmet. Experiments show that the improved algorithm not only satisfies the real-time detection task in helmet wear detection, but also has high detection accuracy.

Keywords: Faster R-CNN · Deep learning · Safety helmet detection · Euclidean distance

1 Introduction

With the continuous development of artificial intelligence, machine vision and other technologies, intelligent video monitoring technology has also been greatly improved. Intelligent video surveillance technology is based on computer vision and artificial intelligence research. It can locate, recognize and track the scene in video sequence, and analyze and judge the behavior of the target. In recent years, safety production has attracted the attention of enterprises. The enterprise believes that only by guaranteeing the safety of employees can the interests of the enterprise be guaranteed. However, unsafe behaviors often occur in the actual production process. The cause of most production safety incidents is caused by unsafe behavior of workers. Such as entering the workplace beyond permission, not wearing labor protection products correctly, or ignoring safety warnings, etc. Most of the workers died in accidents without helmet, so the behavior without helmet is the focus of enterprise monitoring and prevention. If some methods can automatically detect whether workers wear safety helmets in surveillance video, then the probability of security incidents can be greatly reduced.

© Springer Nature Singapore Pte Ltd. 2020
X. Sun et al. (Eds.): ICAIS 2020, CCIS 1253, pp. 423–434, 2020.
https://doi.org/10.1007/978-981-15-8086-4_40

Safety helmet wear detection is bound to become an indispensable technology in production safety. Many researchers have made in-depth research on the automatic identification technology of safety helmet. Hu Tian et al. [1] used YCbCr color model to detect skin color and locate human face through skin color. Next, they use wavelet transform for image preprocessing, and then build and train BP (Back Propagation) neural network for safety helmet recognition. Dalal et al. [2] proposed a helmet wearing state detection algorithm based on gradient direction histogram (HOG) feature. Then, they use Hu moments as feature vectors of images, and then use Support Vector Machine (SVM) to recognize the safety helmet. Liu Yunbo et al. [3] detect foreground targets by moving target detection algorithm. Then, they extract the upper part (1/3) of the foreground moving target. Finally, they judged whether the staff wore safety helmet or not according to the color characteristics. Feng Guochen et al. [4] proposed a method of machine vision, which uses Mixture Gauss Model to detect the foreground. Then, they process the connected regions (image expansion and edge detection) to identify the human body. Finally, they use the estimation method to locate the position of the safety helmet, and then select SIFT features and color statistical features to identify the safety helmet. However, these safety helmet wearing state detection algorithms have poor recognition stability and are vulnerable to external interference.

Traditional target detection methods have the problems of relatively complex calculation and very slow detection speed. In recent years, target detection methods based on deep learning have emerged. Deep learning [7] has powerful feature extraction ability, and a forward propagation can effectively extract all the characteristics of box information. Therefore, many scholars apply deep learning method to the task of target detection. Target detection methods [8] based on in-depth learning can be generally divided into two categories. Target detection methods based on in-depth learning can be generally divided into two categories. In general, target detection methods based on in-depth learning can be divided into two categories: candidate region-based detection methods and regression model-based detection methods. The task of target detection requires locating the position of the target in the image and determining the category of the target at the same time. The first step of deep learning method based on candidate regions is to extract candidate regions, that is, to find possible regions of interest. At the early stage of deep learning algorithm research, sliding window, selective search, rule block and other methods are adopted to extract candidate areas. These methods often waste a lot of computing time and can not achieve higher detection speed. But this kind of target detection algorithm has high accuracy and good effect on small target detection. The detection method based on regression model does not need the process of extracting candidate boxes. It directly regresses the location and possible categories of the target on the image. So it has obvious advantages in speed.

To sum up, the traditional target detection algorithm is used for many problems of helmet wear detection. Firstly, Faster R-CNN detection method based on candidate regions is used to improve the detection accuracy of the safety helmet detection algorithm. In the detection process, we are faced with the following problems: low pixel, large interference from the background, and unreasonable camera Angle for video stream collection. Therefore, the safety helmet part of human head in the image usually occupies a small area of the whole image and affects the detection accuracy. In this paper, the low-level feature and high-level semantic feature of convolution layer are combined to obtain the detailed feature information of small targets. At the same time, we use the position regression contrast method to detect whether the safety helmet is properly worn. This method reduces the wearing error detection rate.

2 Faster R-CNN

2.1 The Principle of Faster R-CNN

Faster R-CNN is composed of three modules: basic feature extraction network, region proposal network (RPN) which generates candidate regions and Fast R-CNN [5] target classification and detection. Firstly, we input the image into the basic feature extraction network, and use the multi-layer convolution layer of the network to extract the features of the image target to obtain the feature map of the input image. Then, the RPN module generates candidate regions and uses the "attention" mechanism to enable Fast R-CNN to detect targets directionally. RPN network generates a series of target candidate boxes of workers and safety helmet and other components in advance, and then Fast R-CNN detects and recognizes the target based on the extracted candidate boxes.

2.2 Region Proposal Network

RPN is used to extract detection regions. It can share the convolution feature of the whole image with the whole detection network and predict 300 candidate regions of high quality (2000 predicted by Selective Search). RPN uses d n × n sliding windows to process the feature map matrix of the last shared convolutional layer output. The feature map matrix is mapped to a d-dimensional feature vector. The vector passes through two fully connected layers of the border regression layer (reg) and the target classification layer (cls). The position of each sliding window predicts k suggested areas at the same time. Therefore, the regression layer of the frame has 4 k outputs (x, y, w and h are the center coordinates and width and height of the proposal box respectively) to determine the position of the target. The classification layer has 2 k score outputs to estimate the probability that each suggestion box belongs to foreground (without distinguishing specific categories) or background. k reference boxes are called anchors. Anchor parameterizes k suggestion boxes. Each anchor corresponds to a scale and a ratio. Each anchor takes the current sliding window center as a reference point. The convolution mapping of size $W \times H$ has a total of $W \times H \times k$ anchors. The structure of RPN network is shown in Fig. 1.

It examines the anchor of each image in the training set (each image contains a manually labeled GT box). If the overlap ratio of anchor and GT box is the largest, it is recorded as a positive sample. Alternatively, the overlap ratio of the GT box to the anchor greater than 0.7 is also recorded as a positive sample. If the overlap ratio of anchor to GT box is less than 0.3, it is recorded as a negative sample. The remaining anchors and anchors that cross the boundaries of the image are not used for final training. The calibration process is shown in Fig. 2.

Different anchors can be generated by different scales and aspect ratios. This is shown in anchor1, anchor2, and anchor3 in Fig. 4. Among them, anchor1 and GT box

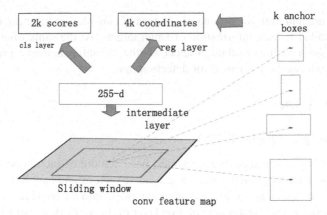

Fig. 1. Structure characteristics of RPN network

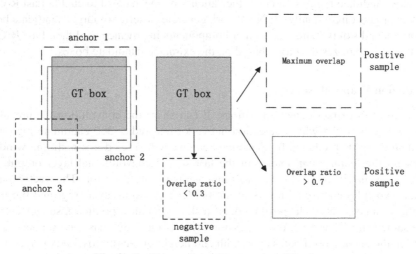

Fig. 2. Positive and negative sample calibration

have the largest overlap ratio, so they are recorded as positive samples. The overlap ratio of anchor2 to GT box is greater than 0.7, so it is also recorded as a positive sample. The overlap ratio of anchor3 to GT box is less than 0.3, so it is recorded as a negative sample. A judgment is made for each GT box area. We discard the rest of the anchor and the anchor that exceeds the bounds of the image.

The total loss function for RPN is defined as:

$$L(\{p_i\}, \{t_i\}) = \frac{1}{N_{cls}} \sum_i L_{cls}(p_i, p_i^*) + \lambda \frac{1}{N_{reg}} \sum_i p_i^* L_{reg}(t_i, t_i^*) \tag{1}$$

Where, i is the index of each anchor in the mini batch. p_i is the prediction probability of each anchor i belonging to the target. If anchor is marked as a positive sample, then the tag p_i^* of GT box takes 1. If anchor is marked as a negative sample, then the tag p_i^* of GT box takes 0. t_i is the vector that predicts the four parameterized coordinates of the bounding box. t_i^* is the vector corresponding to GT box. L_{cls} is the logarithmic loss of two types of targets (target and non-target). L_{reg} is the regression loss.

L_{reg} is defined as:

$$L_{reg}(t_i, t_i^*) = R(t_i - t_i^*) \qquad (2)$$

Where, R is a robust loss function:

$$Smooth_{L1}(x) = \begin{cases} 0.5x^2 & |x| \le 1 \\ |x| - 0.5 & \text{otherwise} \end{cases} \qquad (3)$$

$p_i \times L_{reg}$ means that only $p_i^* = 1$ has a regression loss, $p_i^* = 0$ has no regression loss. The output of layer cls and layer reg consists of (p_i) and (t_i) respectively. (p_i) and (t_i) are normalized by N_{cls} (generally 256), N_{reg} and (typically 2400) and λ (set to 10).

The four coordinates of the regression process are shown as follows:

$$t_x = (x - x_a)/w_a, \quad t_y = (y - y_a)/h_a \qquad (4)$$

$$t_w = \log(w/w_a), \quad t_h = \log(h/h_a) \qquad (5)$$

$$t_x^* = (x^* - x_a)/w_a, \quad t_y^* = (y^* - y_a)/h_a \qquad (6)$$

$$t_w^* = \log(w^*/w_a), \quad t_h^* = \log(h^*/h_a) \qquad (7)$$

Where, subscripts x and y are the central coordinates of the enveloping box. The subscripts w and h are respectively the width and height of the enveloping box. Three sets of parameters: The prediction box coordinate is $[x, y, w, h]$; Anchor is $[x_a, y_a, w_a, h_a]$; The coordinate of ground truth is $[x^*, y^*, w^*, h^*]$. $\{t\}$ is the offset of the prediction box relative to the anchor center position and the scale of the width and height. $\{t^*\}$ is the offset and scale of ground truth relative anchor.

During the training, 256 anchors randomly sampled in each image are used to calculate the loss. If all anchors participate in the training, too many negative samples will lead to the low prediction accuracy of the model for positive samples. Among them, the ratio of positive and negative samples in 256 anchors is 1:1. If the number of positive samples is less than 128, supplement them with negative samples.

2.3 Structure of Faster R-CNN Network

Faster R-CNN [6] combines the Region Proposal Network and Fast R-CNN into a single network model. The RPN network replaces the Selective Search method. Generate a suggestion box network and a target detection network shared convolution feature. Therefore, Faster R-CNN implements end-to-end detection. The structure of the Faster R-CNN network is shown in Fig. 3. The overall target detection framework is roughly as follows:

1. Input images of any size into CNN convolution layer for feature extraction.

2. Each image uses the RPN network to generate high quality suggestion boxes. Approximately 300 suggestion boxes are produced for each image.
3. The suggestion box is mapped to the convolution feature graph of the last layer of CNN.
4. The size of each suggestion box is fixed by the RoI pooling layer.
5. The classification layer and the border regression layer are used to make specific classification judgment and accurate border regression.

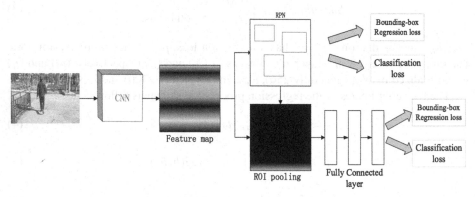

Fig. 3. The structure of Faster R-CNN network

3   Euclidean Distance Detection Algorithm

Our detection algorithm is to detect whether a worker wears a helmet. Most of the relevant research is to use the method of positioning to the worker first, and then judging whether to wear a helmet by edge and color detection. These methods are not only complicated in steps and algorithms, but also have accumulated errors. The problem of whether a worker wears a helmet is generally the following: a worker who wears a helmet properly;

Fig. 4. Hard hat and head target frame

a worker who does not wear a helmet on his hand; a worker who does not carry a helmet. The position of the worker holding the helmet in the hand is relatively far from the head position. We use Euclidean distance to compare the relationship between the regression position of human head and the regression position of helmet to judge whether to wear the helmet or not. Specific steps are as follows:

Step 1: Select the target box. We determine the position of the head relative to the helmet. Therefore, we should mark the two target boxes of helmet and head in the training set of target detection. There are two types of target boxes: helmet and head. As shown in Fig. 4. The number in the figure represents the location information of the target box.

Step 2: Regression of position coordinates. t^* was calculated by ground truth box and anchor box in RPN training. t^* represents the conversion relationship between the ground-truth box and the anchor box. We use t^* to train RPN. The RPN finally outputs a t representing the conversion relationship between the predicted box and the anchor box. The t and anchor box can calculate the true coordinates of the prediction box.

Step 3: Judge the wearing of helmet. Coordinate regression gives the coordinates of the helmet and head. We can set a threshold δ to distinguish whether or not to wear a helmet. d is the distance between the regression coordinates of the head target box and the regression coordinates of the head target box. $d < \delta$ indicates that the helmet is detected to be properly worn; $d > \delta$ indicates that the helmet was not properly worn. The specific process is shown in Fig. 5.

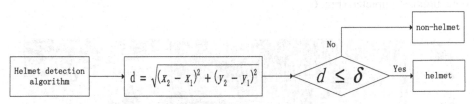

Fig. 5. Relative distance discrimination process

We choose reasonable thresholds through experimental training. The judgment is automatically made when the distance satisfies the threshold. The detailed operation flow is as follows:

1. The network obtains the target coordinates. The position coordinates of the helmet are $X_k = [x_1, y_1]^T$. The position coordinates of the head are $Z_k = [x_2, y_2]^T$. The Euclidean distance d between the two is $d = \sqrt{(x_2 - x_1)^2 + (y_2 - y_1)^2}$.
2. During the detection process, a threshold for distinguishing whether or not to wear the helmet is obtained according to the correct detection of wearing the helmet. The threshold is used to determine if the distance between the head and the helmet is satisfactory.

4   Experimental Results and Analysis

4.1   Experimental Data Set

Object detection based on deep learning requires a large number of data sets to train an excellent model. We don't have ready-made data sets to use. We need to make a set of hard hat data sets. The video surveillance data is mainly derived from the entrance monitoring equipment of the substation.

Our data is mainly video data. We need to use video editing software to process the video into frames. The image is normalized so that the resolution is consistent with the setting of real-time image acquisition module. Next, we label and format the data. We use Labelmmg (image annotation tool) to mark the video dataset image. Labellmg saves the annotation information of the image to an XML file. We use Lawelmg to draw the bounding box of the helmet. The helmet destination information is saved as an XML file. The xml file includes information such as the file name, path, size, target name, and bounding box of the image. We'll create a new folder named Annotations to add all the XML files.

We divide the filtered video dataset into three categories: training dataset (train), test dataset (test), and validation dataset (val). In the training set, the positive sample is the data of workers who enter the camera area and wear helmets. The negative sample is the data of the workers with the helmet in hand and those without the helmet. We will make the completed training set, verification set, test set and training verification set named train.txt, val.txt, test.txt, trainval.txt and save them as txt files. The data set for the helmet detection is completed (Fig. 6).

Fig. 6. Data set

4.2   Evaluation Method

We adopt some evaluation methods to evaluate the effectiveness of the detection algorithm of wearing helmet. The experiment uses precision, recall, real-time to measure the effectiveness of the detection algorithm. TP (True positive) is a positive sample predicted by the model to be positive. FP (False positive) represents the negative samples predicted by the model to be positive. FN (False negative) represents the positive sample predicted by the model to be negative. The evaluation method is as follows:

(1) Accuracy rate:

$$precision = \frac{TP}{TP + FP} \tag{8}$$

(2) Recall rate:

$$recall = \frac{TP}{TP + FN} \tag{9}$$

(3) Real-time: The real time is one of the most important evaluation indicators of an intelligent video surveillance system. In this study, the time complexity of our algorithm was defined as the ratio of the processing time of all frames and the actual playing time of the video.

The Precision-recall (PR) curve is obtained by changing the recognition threshold to change the Precision and Recall values. While the Recall value is increasing, the value of Precision is kept at a very high level, so the performance of this classifier is better. Therefore, the area under the (PR) curve is used to evaluate the performance of the detection algorithm.

4.3 Experimental Results Analysis

This experiment was conducted on GTX1080Ti graphics card and on Tensorflow target detection framework. We first tested the experimental results of Faster R-CNN using the original resnet-50 [9] characteristic network model. In addition, the experimental results of AlexNet [10], ZFNet [11] and VGG16 [12] are used for comparison. As shown in Table 1. In this paper, an experiment is carried out on a homemade hardhat data set to verify the performance of the algorithm in the task of hardhat detection. Experimental results show that when Faster R-CNN algorithm adopts VGG16 characteristic network model for detection tasks, the detection accuracy of Faster R-CNN algorithm is more optimized than other networks under the premise of ensuring a certain detection recall rate (Fig. 7).

In this paper, VGG16 characteristic network model based Faster R-CNN algorithm is adopted for helmet detection. The experimental results showed that the test accuracy of Faster R-CNN was improved by 7.1%, and the recall rate was increased by 6.5%. The detection effect of the algorithm on the actual picture is shown in Fig. 9. The green box shows the detected safety helmet. In order to compare the performance, we chose three classical target detection methods: HOG+SVM, YOLO [14], SSD [13] and Faster R-CNN for comparison (Fig. 8). The recall rate, accuracy and real-time performance of these four methods are shown in Table 2. Faster R-CNN algorithm not only improves the accuracy value, but also greatly improves the detection rate. Therefore, for real-time detection tasks, Faster R-CNN performs better.

Table 1. Network model results of different feature extraction

Method	Network model	Recall ratio	Precision ratio
Faster R-CNN	ZFNet	77.3%	74.9%
Faster R-CNN	AlexNet	84.6%	79.4%
Faster R-CNN	ResNet-50	87.6%	82.6%
Faster R-CNN	VGG16	94.7%	89.1%

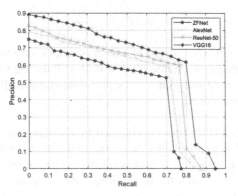

Fig. 7. Precision-recall curve of different feature extraction networks

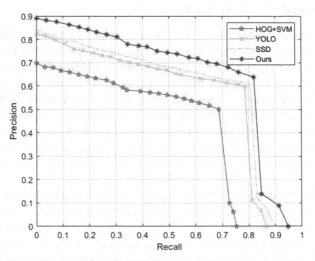

Fig. 8. Precision-recall curves of different detection methods

Fig. 9. The result of helmet detection algorithm. (Color figure online)

Table 2. Results of different detection methods

Method	Recall ratio	Precision ratio	Real-time
HOG+SVM	75.3%	69.9%	5.5
YOLO	86.6%	82.4%	4.3
SSD	89.8%	84.2%	4.1
Faster R-CNN	94.6%	89.3%	3.2

5 Conclusions

In this paper, we developed a helmet wear detection method based on the improved Faster R-CNN algorithm. We used video monitoring at the entrance of substation experiment center as the data set to carry out the safety helmet wearing test. RPN network makes use of border regression layer to carry out accurate border regression for the recommended area. Euclidean distance was used to compare the regression position of the head and the regression position of the helmet to determine whether to wear the helmet. Experiments show that the improvement of the Faster R-CNN network not only guarantees higher detection accuracy but also Faster detection speed. This method can meet the requirements of accuracy and real-time detection of helmet wearing in monitoring video.

Acknowledgement. This research is partially supported by:
1. Research Foundation of Education Bureau of Jilin Province (JJKN20190710KJ).
2. Science and Technology Innovation Development Plan Project of Jilin city (20190302202).

References

1. Tian, H.: A face detection method based on structural analysis and neural network. Comput. Eng. Des. **09**, 18–21 (2002)

2. Dalal, N., Triggs, B.: Histograms of oriented gradients for human detection. In: IEEE Computer Society Conference on Computer Vision and Pattern Recognition, vol. 1, pp. 886–893 (2005)
3. Yu, L., Zhong, Y., Xiaoyong, Y., Guangchi, L., Bo, H.: A novel multi-hop algorithm for wireless network with unevenly distributed nodes. Comput. Mater. Continua **58**(1), 79–100 (2019)
4. Yunbo, L.: Research on monitoring of workers' helmet wearing at the construction site. Electron. Sci. Technol. **28**(04), 69–72 (2015)
5. Guochen, F.: Research on automatic identification technology of the safety helmet based on machine vision. Mach. Des. Manuf. Eng. **44**(10), 39–42 (2015)
6. Girshick, R.: Fast R-CNN. In: IEEE International Conference on Computer Vision, pp. 1440–1448. IEEE (2015)
7. Ren, S., He, K., Girshick, R.S.: Faster R-CNN: towards real-time object detection with region proposal networks. In: International Conference on Neural Information Processing Systems, pp. 91–99. MIT Press (2015)
8. Lan, S., Chen, G., Xin, H., Yingjie, W., Yan, G.: Differentially private real-time streaming data publication based on sliding window under exponential decay. Comput. Mater. Continua **58**(1), 61–78 (2019)
9. Wu, H., Zhao, J.: Automated visual helmet identification based on deep convolutional neural networks. Comput. Aided Chem. Eng. **44**, 2299–2304 (2018)
10. Cai, L., Qian, J.: A method for detecting miners based on helmets detection in underground coal mine videos. Min. Sci. Technol. **21**, 553–556 (2011)
11. He, K., Zhang, X., Ren, S.: Deep residual learning for image recognition. In: IEEE Conference on Computer Vision and Pattern Recognition (CVPR). IEEE Computer Society (2016)
12. Krizhevsky, A.F., Sutskever, I.F., Hinton, G.S.: ImageNet classification with deep convolutional neural networks. In: NIPS. Curran Associates Inc. (2012)
13. Liu, W., et al.: SSD: single shot multibox detector. In: Leibe, B., Matas, J., Sebe, N., Welling, M. (eds.) ECCV 2016. LNCS, vol. 9905, pp. 21–37. Springer, Cham (2016). https://doi.org/10.1007/978-3-319-46448-0_2
14. Zhihua, X., Lihua, L., Tong, Q., Shim, H.J., Xianyi, C., Byeungwoo, J.: A privacy-preserving image retrieval based on AC-coefficients and color histograms in cloud environment. Comput. Mater. Continua **58**(1), 27–43 (2019)

Transmission Line Galloping Detection Based on SURF Feature and FLANN Matching Algorithm

Shuqiang Guo, Qianlong Bai, Baohai Yue, Xianjin Li, and Xinxin Zhou[✉]

NorthEast Electric Power University, Jilin 132012, China
zxx51@qq.com

Abstract. This paper first analyzes the causes of the formation of transmission line galloping, and then introduces the advantages and disadvantages of common online monitoring methods. Aiming at the problems of traditional image matching algorithms, such as fewer feature extraction points, high mismatch rate and slow matching speed, the solution is proposed. This paper uses the combination of SURF and FLANN matching algorithms to solve. The SUFR feature is quite ideal in terms of detail compared with the SIFT feature, and the calculation of the extremum using the Hessian matrix improves the speed of feature extraction, making it simple and efficient. FLANN algorithm adopts tree structure to realize storage and search, which can effectively solve the problem of slow matching of high-dimensional features. The experimental results show that the proposed method can meet the requirements of on-site real-time detection in the online dance monitoring of transmission lines, and has certain anti-interference ability for rotation and illumination changes.

Keywords: Transmission line galloping · SURF · FLANN

1 Introduction

When an overhead transmission line becomes a non-circular cross-section wire due to the presence of foreign matter, a lateral wind is simultaneously encountered, and a low-frequency vibration phenomenon occurs. When the torsional frequency is synchronized with the frequency of its vertical motion, a large self-excited oscillation occurs, which will lead to wire galloping [1]. The galloping of conductor can be attributed to nonlinear dynamics in nature. In 1932, Den Hartog first explained the mechanism of conductor galloping in theory and established the Den Hartog galloping model. In 1972, on the basis of wind tunnel experiments, Nigol proposed the famous Nigol torsion-induced dance mechanism [2, 3].

The conductor galloping is a great hazard to the transmission system. Wire dancing can cause the tension between the towers to increase, further causing damage to components such as insulators [4–6]. The current monitoring methods can be divided into two categories: manual monitoring and online monitoring. Manual monitoring is mainly to

© Springer Nature Singapore Pte Ltd. 2020
X. Sun et al. (Eds.): ICAIS 2020, CCIS 1253, pp. 435–443, 2020.
https://doi.org/10.1007/978-981-15-8086-4_41

set up a dedicated observation station in the severely affected area to record the galloping of the conductor. On-line monitoring technology mainly relies on accelerometers [7], fiber optic sensors [8], high-precision GPS installed on the transmission line to collect data, and further combines aerodynamics, mechanics, meteorology, etc. to establish a galloping model for wire galloping detection. The analysis of the mechanism of the dance based on the dynamic equation is too complicated, and the field environment changes rapidly, so the model is not easy to establish [9–11]. Sensor-based wire gallop detection is costly and difficult to maintain. At present, online monitoring technology based on digital image processing technology has great advantages [12]. This method captures the dancing video of the field conductors through a camera attached to the tower and transmits it back to the control center via the wireless network. In the latter stage, the image feature point matching method is used to detect the transmission line galloping, and the displacement variation and the offset angle of the transmission line are calculated.

2 SURF Feature Point Detection and Matching Principle

2.1 Introduction to SURF Features

Image matching refers to comparing the window correlation coefficients of the same size in the target area and the search area by the matching algorithm, and using the matching criterion to obtain the center point of the largest window of the correlation coefficient in the search area as the best matching point. The conventional wire gallop detection method is based on matching contour features to calculate the offset distance and offset angle of the wires in the image to be detected with respect to the transmission line in the original background image [13, 14]. This method has problems of less feature points extracted and high mismatch rate. The SURF feature (Speeded Up Robust Features) is an improvement to the SIFT feature. The Hessian matrix is used to approximate the differential calculation process of the image pyramid. Compared with the SIFT feature, the calculation speed is greatly improved. The main steps are:

(1) Construct the Hessian matrix. For any point $p(x, y)$ in the image, the Hessian matrix $H(x, \sigma)$ corresponding to the scale value σ is:

$$H(x, \sigma) = \begin{vmatrix} L_{xx}(x, \sigma) \; L_{xy}(x, \sigma) \\ L_{xy}(x, \sigma) \; L_{yy}(x, \sigma) \end{vmatrix} \tag{1}$$

Where $L_{xx}(x, \sigma)$, $L_{xy}(x, \sigma)$, and $L_{yy}(x, \sigma)$ are the second-order partial derivatives at point P, which are: $\frac{\partial^2 g(\sigma)}{\partial x^2}$, $\frac{\partial^2 g(\sigma)}{\partial x \partial y}$, $\frac{\partial^2 g(\sigma)}{\partial y^2}$, and the Gaussian function is defined as:

$$g(\sigma) = \frac{1}{2\pi\sigma^2} e^{-\frac{x^2+y^2}{2\sigma^2}} \tag{2}$$

The discriminant of the H matrix is: $Det(H) = L_{xx}L_{yy} - L_{xy}L_{xy}$. Essentially, the second-order partial derivative in the horizontal direction at point P is multiplied by the second-order partial derivative in the vertical direction and then subtracted from the square of the P-point horizontal and vertical second-order partial derivative. This value is used to discriminate the local feature points of the image. $L(x, y)$ in the Hession matrix discriminant is the Gaussian convolution of the original image. Since the Gaussian kernel obeys the positive distribution, the coefficient is getting smaller and smaller from the center point. In order to improve the operation speed, the SURF algorithm uses a box filter instead of the Gaussian filter L, so a weighting coefficient of 0.9 is multiplied on L_{xy}. In order to balance the error caused by the use of the box filter approximation, the H matrix discriminant can be expressed as:

$$Det(H) = L_{xx}L_{yy} - (0.9 * L_{xx})^2 \qquad (3)$$

(2) Generate feature vectors, perform feature point filtering, and perform precise positioning. Each pixel processed by the Hessian matrix is compared to its image domain (the same size image) and all adjacent points of the scale domain. When it is greater than all adjacent points, the point is the extreme point. The detection point in the middle should be compared with 8 pixels in the 3 * 3 neighborhood of the image in which it is located, and 18 pixels in the adjacent 3 * 3 neighborhoods of the adjacent two layers, for a total of 26 pixels.

(3) Calculate the main direction of the feature. The method adopted is to statistically character the Harr wavelet in the circular neighborhood of the feature point, that is, in the circular neighborhood of the feature point, the sum of the horizontal and vertical Harr wavelet features of all points in the 60° sector is counted, and then the sector is separated by 0.2 radians. The rotation is performed, and the Harr wavelet feature value in the region is again counted, and finally the direction of the sector with the largest value is taken as the main direction of the feature point.

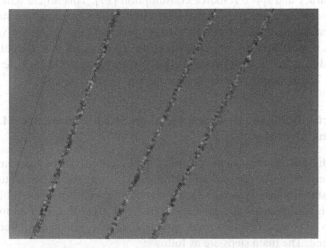

Fig. 1. Schematic diagram of SURF feature points

(4) Generate a feature descriptor. Take 4 * 4 rectangular block around the feature point, but the direction of the obtained rectangular area is required to be along the main

direction of the feature point, instead of rotating the angle θ every time like the SIFT algorithm. The Harr wavelet features of the horizontal and vertical directions of 25 pixels are then counted in each sub-area, where the horizontal and vertical directions are relative to the main direction. The Harr wavelet feature is the sum of the horizontal direction values, the sum of the vertical direction values, the sum of the absolute values of the horizontal direction values, and the absolute sum of the vertical directions. Therefore, a total of 4 * 4 * 4 dimensional vectors are used as descriptors of the SURF features.

SURF feature point detection is performed on the transmission line image. The sample images are as Fig. 1.

2.2 FLANN Matching Algorithm

Muja and Lowe proposed the FLANN algorithm [15, 16] in 2009, which solved the problem of slow calculation of nearest neighbors in high-dimensional data. The core of the algorithm is to find the nearest neighbor point to the instance point by using the Euclidean distance. The Euclidean distance is defined as:

$$D(\mathrm{x}, \mathrm{y}) = \|X, Y\| = \sqrt{\sum_{i=1}^{d} (X_i - Y_i)^2} \tag{4}$$

The FLANN matching algorithm is generally implemented based on a K-means tree or a KD-TREE search operation. Index types and retrieval parameters can be recommended based on the distribution characteristics of the data set, the requirements for mapping accuracy and space resource consumption [17]. This article will use a higher precision k-means tree to represent the search points as a tree structure storage. When searching, first compare the values of the target point and the split point with a certain dimension as a reference, determine whether the target point is in the left area or the right area, and then compare the loop with the corresponding node until the target search is successful. The principle is as shown in Fig. 2.

2.3 Conductor Galloping Detection Based on SURF Feature and FLANN Matching Algorithm

It is mainly divided into two steps: (1) using the video backed by the camera fixed on the tower, intercepting the corresponding frame, extracting the SURF feature with high illumination stability for rotation and scale transformation. (2) For the problem of slow matching of high-dimensional features, the FLANN algorithm is used to convert the feature points to be matched into a tree structure storage, which can effectively speed up the matching. The main steps are as follows:

(1) Perform filtering, denoising, graying and other preprocessing on the original image, and perform Hough transform line detection to detect the transmission line and perform fitting.

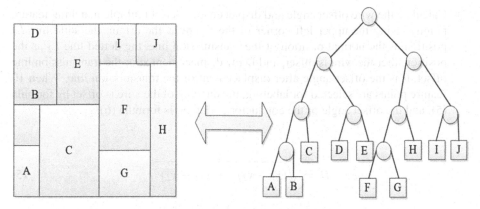

Fig. 2. Schematic diagram of FLANN feature search

(2) Select the ROI area. The characteristics of the transmission line image are relatively large, the transmission line is thin and long, and the width generally occupies 3-5 pixels wide, so the area we are interested in is relatively concentrated. The region of interest can be obtained by fitting the wire with a polygon.

(3) Create a template. In windless weather, images are captured using a camera attached to the tower. That is, the captured original image without dancing is used and the template is created based on the image segmentation.

(4) The ROI area is selected for the detected image, and then the template is matched. The schematic diagram of the conductor galloping is as Fig. 3.

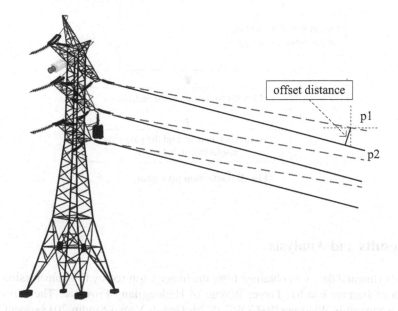

Fig. 3. Schematic diagram of wire galloping detection

(5) Calculate the wire offset angle and displacement. Select multiple matching feature points, taking the upper left corner of the figure as the origin, the solid line L_1 position as the normal position of the transmission line, the dotted line L_2 as the position after the wire is offset, and D the displacement after the transmission line offset. θ is the offset angle after displacement of the transmission line. When 10 feature points are selected for labeling, the dancing of the wire is offset by formula (5), and the offset angle of the conductor galloping is formula (6).

$$D = \sqrt{(x_1 - x_2)^2 + (y_1 - y_2)^2} \tag{5}$$

$$\theta = \arctan(\frac{x_1 - x_2}{y_1 - y_2}) \tag{6}$$

The complete inspection process is as Fig. 4:

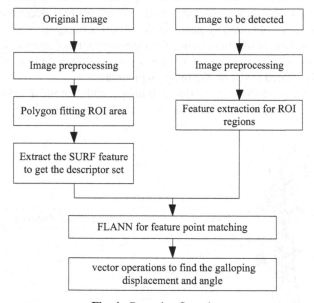

Fig. 4. Detection flow chart

3   Results and Analysis

The experimental data was obtained from the image captured by the transmission tower camera of Jiamusi Electric Power Bureau of Heilongjiang Province. The experimental environment is Windows10+CORE i5 7th Gen + Visual Studio 2013+openCV3.4. Compared with the traditional SIFT method, the method can find more feature points, and the distribution density of the key feature points of the two images obtained by the algorithm is higher than the distribution density of the key feature points obtained by the SIFT algorithm. This provides favorable conditions for the matching of the next feature. The FLANN-based matching method can improve the matching speed.

The experimental matching example results are as follows (Figs. 5 and 6):

Fig. 5. SURF feature point matching diagram

Fig. 6. SURF feature point matching diagram

The following is a comparison table of the number of features, the operation time, and the matching accuracy of the SITF feature and the SURT feature combined with the FLANN algorithm (Table 1):

Table 1. SIFT and SURF feature extraction comparison table

Algorithm	Number of features	Number of matches	Processing time(s)	Matching accuracy
Reference [18] Algorithm	245	161	2.3	0.65
SURF+FLANN	252	179	1.4	0.17

It can be seen from the table that the number of features extracted by the literature [18] and the number of SURF matches are slightly lower, but due to the complexity of the SIFT algorithm, it takes a long time in the process of feature point extraction.

Select 10 pairs of marked feature points from the matched features, and establish a coordinate system with the coordinate origin O(0,0) in the upper left corner. Perform the operation to approximate the displacement and offset angle. Matching with 10 matching points, calculate the average displacement and offset angle as shown in the following Table 2:

Table 2. Calculation of galloping distance and offset angle

Number	Displacement distance (pixels)	Offset angle (degrees)
1	46.840	16.113
2	59.439	12.633
3	38.327	15.124
4	62.817	13.815
5	44.643	15.529

4 Conclusion

Based on the analysis of the cause and monitoring method of conductor galloping, this paper uses SURF algorithm to extract feature points and combines FLANN calculation to match the feature points to calculate the angle and distance of conductor galloping. The experimental results show that SURF reduces the feature dimension, and the expression of feature details is also ideal. At the same time, it has good adaptability to the brightness and rotation of the image. Extracting the SURF features on the transmission line and combining the FLANN algorithm to quickly match the high-dimensional feature points can make the method well applied to real-time processing. However, there are individual outliers, which can eliminate the outliers after SURF feature extraction, thus improving the accuracy of matching.

Acknowledgement. This research is partially supported by:
1. Research Foundation of Education Bureau of Jilin Province (JJKN20190710KJ).
2. Science and Technology Innovation Development Plan Project of Jilin city (20190302202).

References

1. Li, L., Jiang, W., Cao, H.J.: Galloping of transmission tower-line system and anti-galloping research. Appl. Mech. Mater. **47**(44), 2666–2670 (2010)

2. Nigol, O., Buchan, P.G.: Conductor galloping part I - Den Hartog mechanism. IEEE Trans. Power Apparatus Syst. **100**(2), 699–707 (1981)
3. Nigol, O., Buchan, P.G.: Conductor galloping-part ii torsional mechanism. IEEE Trans. Power Apparatus Syst. **100**(2), 708–720 (1981)
4. Di, Y.X., Zhu, K.J., Liu, B., et al.: Analysis on galloping responses of transmission tower-line system. Appl. Mech. Mater. **602**(605), 3025–3028 (2014)
5. Zhang, L., Li, Q., Ji, K., Liu, B.: Research on the test of transmission line galloping. IOP Conf. Ser.: Earth Environ. Sci. **128**(1), 012123 (2018)
6. Guo-Ming, M., Ya-Bo, L., Nai-Qiang, M., et al.: A fiber Bragg grating-based dynamic tension detection system for overhead transmission line galloping. Sensors **18**(2), 365–372 (2018)
7. Gang, X., Yufan, Z., Lishan, D., Guozhao, W., Bojian, L., Kin-chuen, H.: Efficient construction of b-spline curves with minimal internal energy. Comput. Mater. Continua **58**(3), 879–892 (2019)
8. Kumar, P., Singh, A.K.: Optimal mechanical sag estimator for leveled span overhead transmission line conductor. Measurement **137**(2), 691–699 (2019)
9. Kim, H.S., Byun, G.S.: A study on the analysis of galloping for power transmission line Industrial Electronics. In: IEEE International Symposium on Proceedings. ISIE 2001. IEEE (2001)
10. Xiong, X., et al.: A calculation model for on-line monitoring of conductor galloping based on the length method. Adv. Mater. Res. **915**(916), 1242–1247 (2014)
11. Anitescu, C., Atroshchenko, E., Alajlan, N., Rabczuk, T.: Artificial neural network methods for the solution of second order boundary value problems. Comput. Mater. Continua **59**(1), 345–359 (2019)
12. Li, Z., Feng, S., Wang, S., et al.: Transmission line dancing monitoring based on digital image processing technology. Ind. Control Comput. **23**(06), 36–37 (2010)
13. Yang, W., et al.: Study on monitoring for power transmission line galloping based on monocular vision method. In: International Conference on Power System Technology, pp. 1571–1575. IEEE, Chengdu (2014)
14. Xionglve, L., Junhua, X., Zhiping, C., Tao, Y., Chak, F.C.: Analyzing the structure and connectivity of continent-level internet topology. Comput. Mater. Continua **59**(3), 955–964 (2019)
15. Jinlong, W., Zhifeng, Z.: Image matching algorithm based on SITF feature extraction and FLANN search. Comput. Meas. Control **26**(02), 175–178 (2018)
16. Feng, Y., Sun, Y.: Image matching algorithm based on SURF Feature extraction and FLANN search. J. Graph. **36**(04), 650–654 (2015)
17. Wang, Q., et al.: Power line feature extraction based on optimized SURF algorithm. In: International Conference on Applied Robotics for the Power Industry, pp. 172–175, Xian (2012)
18. Ni, F.: Sag Measurement and Galloping Monitoring of Power Transmission Line Based on Image Detection. North China Electric Power University (2013)

A Method to Improve Identification Performance of UHF RFID Systems

Jiang Xu[✉]

School of Computer and Software, Nanjing University of Information Science and Technology, Nanjing, China
12130398@qq.com

Abstract. Dynamic frame slotted ALOHA (DFSA) has been widely adopted to reduce tag collisions in a Ultra High Frequency (UHF) radio frequency identification (RFID) system . In the existing DFSA algorithms, the reader needs to accurately estimate tag backlog and set a new frame length which is equal to the backlog to close to the theoretical maximum throughput 36.8% of the framed ALOHA. To overcome throughput limitation and improve the identification efficiency, we propose an efficient slot-hopped algorithm based on ALOHA protocol. The slot-hopped mechanism was used in each frame to skip collision and idle slots. Accordingly, the scheme significantly reduces collision and idle slots. The performance analysis and simulation results show that the proposed algorithm outperforms other ALOHA-based protocols.

Keywords: RFID · Anti-collision · ALOHA · Slot-hopped

1 Introduction

Recently, there has been an increasing demand in the development of communications systems for the automatic identification of objects [1]. Radio frequency identification technology makes it possible and has attracted extensive attention. One of the major challenges of RFID system is the tag collision problem resulted from sharing the common wireless channel by all devices in the system [2]. Tag collision occurs when multiple tags simultaneously respond to the reader with their signals. This collision degrades the RFID system's identification performance. Hence, the primary goal of anti-collision protocols is to minimize the total identification time, i.e., the time required to identify all tags, or equivalently to maximize the system throughput.

Tag anti-collision protocols have been proposed to improve the identification efficiency in many applications mainly can be divided into two categories ALOHA-based [3–5] and tree-based protocols [6–8]. All these tree-based protocols based on the collision bit identification and tracking techniques. In the High or Low Frequency (HF/LF) RFID systems, the asynchronization is not present; the bit-tracking technique is easy to achieve. However, it is very difficult to achieve in Ultra High Frequency (UHF) RFID system, including EPCglobal C1 Gen2 [9] and ISO 18000-6B systems. The reason is that as defined in EPCglobal C1 Gen2 standard, modulation signals feature a different

© Springer Nature Singapore Pte Ltd. 2020
X. Sun et al. (Eds.): ICAIS 2020, CCIS 1253, pp. 444–454, 2020.
https://doi.org/10.1007/978-981-15-8086-4_42

symbol rate, which deviates up to $\pm 22\%$ between the single tags in a UHF RFID system [10]. And, the arrival times of tag responses also vary in a range as large as 24 microseconds (μs). That means that, we could not detect which bits are collided with others in the UHF RFID systems. Compared with the tree-based algorithms, the ALOHA-based anti-collision algorithms are more suitable for UHF RFID systems, because it does not identify a specific collision position. It is easy to implement in a real RFID system.

The DFSA is a popular version of ALOHA-based protocols widely applied in EPC-global C1 Gen2 standard. The performance of DFSA depends on both the accuracy of tag backlog estimation and the frame length setting [11–18]. To increase the accuracy of tag backlog estimation, most of the previous anti-collision protocols [3–5] require large computational load or large amount of memory. For ease of algorithm implementation, the author in [12] presents an anti-collision protocol which can be easily applied into a computation-limited reader and can achieve throughput close to the theoretical maximum (0.368).

To overcome the throughput limitation of DFSA, we propose an efficient tag identification protocol based on slot-hopped mechanism. Considering the disparity between slot durations, the slot-optimal algorithm may not be effective in terms of identification time. Thus, the time efficiency, identification speed, and other metrics have been taken into account in our scheme. Compared with conventional DFSA, our proposed scheme can achieve much higher time efficiency and faster identification speed.

The rest of this paper is organized as follows. The DFSA algorithm used in EPCglobal C1 Gen2 standard is briefly reviewed in Sect. 2. The proposed scheme is presented in Sect. 3. Simulation results and performance comparisons are given in Sect. 4. Finally, we draw conclusion in Sect. 5.

2 DFSA Description in EPCglobal C1 Gen2

The DFSA was applied in EPCglobal C1 Gen2 standard for solving the anti-collision problems. One of the primary features of DFSA is the dynamic adjustment of frame length. The performance of DFSA depends on whether frame length is accurately adjusted. To implement the DFSA, the EPCglobal C1 Gen2 standard provides interrogator with series of commands, including **Select**, **Query**, **QueryAdjust**, **QueryRep**, and **Ack**. Before tags are identified, an interrogator first uses the **Select** command to select a particular tag group for further inventory and access. Second, the interrogator begins an inventory round by transmitting a **Query** command with parameter Q which is in the range of 0 to 15 and represents the value of frame length of 2^Q. As the Query command is received, each tag generates a 16-bit random value **RN16** and extracts a Q-bit subset from the RN16 as the tag's slot counter. This counter is decreased by command **QueryRep**. Until the counter reaches zero, the tag responds the interrogator with its **RN16**. The Query command has three possible outcomes: single tag reply, collided reply, and no reply, as shown in Fig. 1 [9].

If only one tag replies, the interrogator acknowledges the tag by sending an **ACK** command. If multiple tags reply, a collision of **RN16s** will be detected and no tags can be identified. These collision tags will contend again in the next rounds. If no tags reply, the interrogator will end the slot after a short period of waiting time. Until all 2^Q time slots have been examined, the current inventory round finishes. The interrogator needs to start a new inventory round using the **Query** command to identify any collision tags. An example presented in Fig. 2 illustrates the anti-collision process with the DFSA scheme.

The reader starts first inventory round by using a **Query** command with the initial frame length of 4. Tag1 and tag 3 respond with their **RN16s** in time slot2. The collision of **RN16s** will be detected, and no tags can be identified. Tags 2 and 4 transmit their **RN16s** in slots 4 and 3, respectively, and thus can be successfully identified after the reader sends an **ACK** command. Since a collision occurs in time slot2 during the first inventory round, another round is required. Hence, the reader determines a new frame length 2, and broadcasts it by **Query** command. Finally, all tags were identified by the reader.

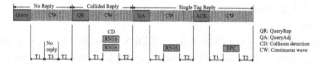

Fig. 1. Three outcomes for a given slot

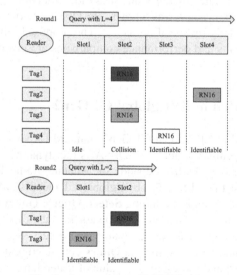

Fig. 2. An example with DFSA scheme

3 The Proposed Scheme

In this section, we present a novel protocol based on slot-hopped. We define the data format that tags respond to the **Query** command of a reader.

$$T_{resp}(i) = [RN11|sc = i] + [RN5|sc = i + 1] \qquad (1)$$

where $T_{resp}(i)$ is denoted as the tags' response data in **i**-th time slot within a frame, and **sc** is the current slot counter of tag. From Eq. (1), we know the data format can be divided into two parts. The first part is tag's **RN11** in current time slot **I**; the other part is the **5**-length random sequence generated by tags whose **sc** equals $i + 1$ after **RN11** time delay. The **RN5** part is used to predict the next slot state of a frame. When the reader receives the response data from tags in current slot **i**, there are four cases of **RN5** as follows.

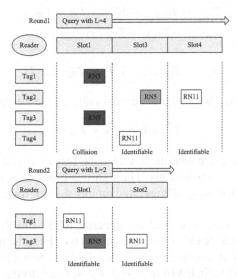

Fig. 3. An example with our proposed protocol

Case1: No tags generate the **RN5**. Accordingly, it demonstrates that the next slot $i + 1$ is idle which can be hopped by the reader. In the next slot, the reader will allow tags whose **sc** equal $i + 2$ to respond its request command.
Case2: The **RN5** is generated by one tag; hence the reader can identify a tag successfully in the next slot $i + 1$.
Case3: The **RN5s** are generated by more than one tag. That is to say, the next slot $i + 1$ is the collision slot, similar to case1, the next slot $i + 1$ can be hopped by the reader. In the next slot, the reader will allow tags whose sc equal $i + 2$ to respond its request command.
Case4: Multiple tags generate the same '**RN5**'. This will lead to '**RN5**' collision. In other words, the next slot is failed to be hopped. The collision will occur because multiple tags will transmit their **RN16s** to the reader simultaneously.

We apply the proposed algorithm to the same previous example, where four tags exist within the reader's range. The identification procedure is illustrated in Fig. 3. We can compare the required time for four tags identification between Fig. 2 and Fig. 3. The required time for the example with DFSA scheme described in the Fig. 2 can be expressed as

$$T^1 = T_{idle} + T_{col} + 4 \times T_{succ} \tag{2}$$

herein T_{idle}, T_{succ}, and T_{col} are the time durations for idle, successful, and collision slot can be written as:

$$T_{idle} = T_{QueryRep} + T_1 + T_3 \tag{3}$$

$$T_{succ} = T_{Query} + 2(T_1 + T_2) + T_{RN16} \\ + T_{ACK} + T_{PC+EPC+CRC} \tag{4}$$

$$T_{col} = T_{QueryRep} + T_1 + T_{RN16} + T_2 \tag{5}$$

According to the Fig. 3, the required time for all tags identification can be written as

$$T^2 = T_{col} + 4 \times T_{succ} \tag{6}$$

As time parameters specified in the EPCglobal C1 Gen2, T^1, and T^2 can be computed as 9100 μs and 8800 μs, respectively. Through this example, it may be seen that our proposed algorithm can identify all tags more rapidly than the traditional ALOHA-based algorithms.

Tag1 and tag3 select the same slot2, and generate **RN5**, (**10010**) and (**11011**), respectively. Subsequently, the 'RN5' collision occurs in the slot1; the reader can predict the slot2 is a collision slot. According to case3, the slot2 can be hopped by the reader.

Tag4 and tag2 send their **RN16** in slots 3 and 4, respectively, and thus can be successfully identified by the reader because the two slots are singly occupied. Since slot2 is collision slot, this implies there are at least two tags, which need to be identified. Hence, another inventory round is required. In the round2, the reader completes the identification of all tags because no collision occurs in this round. Compared with Fig. 2, we know the lower number of slots is required to identify all tags by using our proposed scheme. Consider n tags that need to be identified using frame length L.

Assumed that the length of random sequence **5**, which is used to predict a slot state. Let P_r denote the probability that r tags select the same slot, which can be written as

$$P_r = \binom{n}{r}\left(\frac{1}{L}\right)^r\left(1 - \frac{1}{L}\right)^{n-r} \tag{7}$$

Accordingly, we obtain the probabilities of successful and collision for the slot as

$$P_s = \binom{n}{1}\left(\frac{1}{L}\right)\left(1 - \frac{1}{L}\right)^{n-1} \tag{8}$$

$$P_c = 1 - \left(1 - \frac{1}{L}\right)^n - \binom{n}{1}\left(\frac{1}{L}\right)^1\left(1 - \frac{1}{L}\right)^{n-1} \tag{9}$$

$$P_{fail\text{-}hop} = \sum_{r=2}^{n} P_r \binom{2^5}{1} \left(\frac{1}{2^5}\right)^r$$

$$= \sum_{r=2}^{n} \binom{n}{r} \left(\frac{1}{L}\right)^r \left(1 - \frac{1}{L}\right)^{n-r} \binom{2^5}{1} \left(\frac{1}{2^5}\right)^r \tag{10}$$

Furthermore, we denote $P_{fail\text{-}hop}$ as the probability that the collision slot is failed to be hopped. $P_{fail\text{-}hop}$ corresponds to the probability that r tags generate the same 'RN5' in the same slot. Since the collision slot will not be hopped when two or more tags generate the same 'RN5'. We can have Eq. (10). In order to derive the maximum channel throughput, we assume that both collision slot and idle slot are stuck in the middle of successful slots which can be depicted in the Fig. 4.

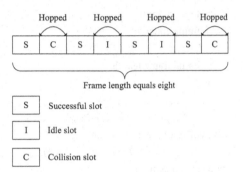

Fig. 4. An example of the proposed scheme

Let $P_{succ\text{-}hop}$ denote the probability that the collision slot is succeeded to be hopped. $P_{succ\text{-}hop}$ can be derived as

$$P_{succ\text{-}hop} = P_c - P_{fail\text{-}hop} = P_c - \sum_{r=2}^{n} P_r \binom{2^5}{1} \left(\frac{1}{2^5}\right)^r \tag{11}$$

Based on the analysis above, the ideal channel efficiency can be given by

$$U_{idea} = \frac{LP_s}{L - L \cdot P_{succ\text{-}hop} - L(1 - P_s - P_c)} \tag{12}$$

In the real RFID system, the situation depicted in Fig. 4 does not always occurs, the actual channel efficiency can be given by:

$$U = \frac{E(S)}{L - E(c) - E(e)} \tag{13}$$

where $E(S)$ is the number of tags successfully identified by the reader during an inventory cycle with frame length L. $E(c)$, and $E(e)$ are the number of collision slots hopped and the number of idle slots hopped during an identification process, respectively. They are measured by the reader during the identification process. Considering the disparity between slot duration, the guarantee of achieving the optimal time efficiency must be taken into consideration in the design of the anti-collision algorithm. We defined time efficiency $T_{efficiency}$ as follow.

$$T_{efficiency} = \frac{ST_{succ}}{ST_{succ} + ET_{idle} + CT_{coll}} \tag{14}$$

Here, S, E, and C are the successful slots, idle slots and collision slots provided by the reader. T_{succ}, T_{idle} and T_{coll} are the time duration of S, E and C, respectively. For feasible and efficient to implement an anti-collision algorithm, a simple method is required to reduce the computation complexity for estimating the tag backlog.

```
Slot-hopped ALOHA ()
{    cycle_counter=0;
     // frame counter
     L=L_ini;
     // initial frame length
     do {
             cycle_counter++;
             [E, S, C, C^l]=performReadCycle(L);
     // slots number of previous frame
             n_est=performTagEstimate(L, C^l);
     // estimate tag quantity n_est
             L=L_new;
             // set a new frame length
     } while (C^l!=0)
             // repeat read process if collision occurs
}
```

Fig. 5. The pseudo code of the slot-hopped ALOHA protocol

We adopt Schoute's estimate method in our proposed algorithm. Thus, the tag backlog can be written as [4]

$$n_{est} = S^1 + 2.39C^1 \tag{15}$$

where S^1 is the number of the single occupied slots and C^1 is the collision slots (including the collision slots successfully hopped by the reader).

As analyzed above, our slot-hopped ALOHA protocol is summarized in Fig. 5.

4   Numerical and Analytical Results

In this section, the identification performance of the proposed algorithm and the reference methods was examined by our extensive simulations based on the Monte Carlo technique.

We first compare the time efficiency of various anti-collision protocols including GDFSA [5], Q-algorithm [9], and FEIA [12–19]. To evaluate the specific time efficiency of our proposed algorithm, we need to calculate the time intervals of every step and command used in the anti-collision process. The primary time parameters used in the simulations are listed in Table 1. The parameters are set according to the EPCglobal C1 Gen2 standard.

Table 1. Primary time parameter for EPCglobal C1 Gen2

Parameters	Values	Parameters	Values
Data coding	Miller subcarrier modulation	Number of subcarrier cycles per symbol	4
R → T preamble	112.5 μs	PC + EPC + CRC16	800 μs
T → R preamble	112.5 μs	T_1	62.5 μs
Tari (reference time interval)	6.25 μs	T_2	62.5 μs
$RN5$	31.25 μs	DR (divide ratio)	8
T_{succ}	2012.5 μs	T_3	52.08 μs
T_{idle}	300 μs	T_4	15.625 μs
T_{coll}	750 μs	$RN11$	68.75 μs

The initial frame size is set to 64 when the number of tags increasing from 5 to 1500. Figure 6 shows the simulation results for normalized time efficiency according to Eq. (14). The results show that our proposed scheme can achieve higher time efficiency. It can be found that as the number of tags increase, the performance of our scheme converges to 0.8, which is more than FEIA's efficiency 0.7. Although FEIA's time efficiency could keep stable by adopting the in-frame adjustment mechanism to fast and efficiently adjust frame length, it does not break through the limitation of DFSA.

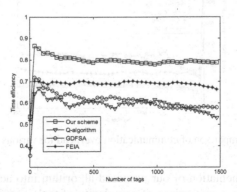

Fig. 6. Comparison of time efficiency for various algorithms

Figure 7 presents the simulation results for the total time required to identify all tags with initial frame size 64. To read 1300 tags, the proposed scheme spends about 3.30 s, i.e., the read speed is 400 tags per second. Meanwhile, the read speed of Q-algorithm, GDFSA, and FEIA are 278 tags/s, 286 tags/s, and 345 tags/s, respectively. In real RFID systems, a read speed is a key metric for multiple tags identification especially in logistics management. According to the simulation results, our algorithm could meet the speed requirement.

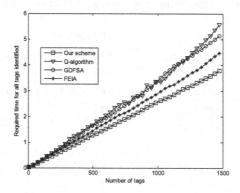

Fig. 7. Required time for all tag identified

Moreover, in Fig. 8 we compare the complexity of communication of our anti-collision algorithm with the other algorithms. It gives average number of bits for identifying one tag when $5 \leq n \leq 1500$. Similar to the results for the time efficiency, our proposed algorithm has less complexity than the other algorithms. The communication overhead of our scheme is 408 bits for identifying one tag. By contrast, FEIA, GDFSA, and Q-algorithm require 470 bits, 535 bits, and 550 bits for one tag identification.

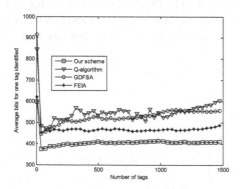

Fig. 8. Comparison of communication overhead for various algorithms

For better implementation of our proposed algorithm into actual UHF RFID systems, we also provide a comparison of complexity of tag's circuit, and computational complexity of algorithm. The results of the comparisons are shown in Table 2.

Table 2. Comparison of other metrics

Algorithms	Extra circuit requirement	Computational complexity
Our proposed scheme	$(11 + 4)$ RNG	$O(1)$
Q-algorithm	$(16 + 4)$ RNG	$O(1)$
GDFSA	$(16 + 4)$ RNG	$O(N - C_1 - 2C_k + 1)$
FEIA	$(16 + 4)$ RNG	$O(1)$

Where RNG is the random number generator, N is the maximum number of tags during the reader's coverage. C_1 and C_k are numbers of successful slots and collision slots computed by the reader in a frame, respectively. The number of RNG required for our proposed scheme is significantly less than the size involved in the Q-algorithm, GDFSA, and FEIA algorithms. From comparisons above, we can know our algorithm, which requires low complexity, can be easily implemented on UHF RFID systems [20–24].

5 Conclusion

In this paper, a feasible and efficient anti-collision algorithm has been proposed for EPCglobal C1 Gen2 systems. Our proposed algorithm is based on the mechanism of slot-hopped and a simple but sufficiently accurate estimator for tag backlog. Analytical and simulation results show that the proposed algorithm outperforms existing ALOHA-based protocols.

Acknowledgment. We would like to thank the anonymous reviewers for their valuable comments.

This job is also supported by Scientific Research Program Funded by Shaanxi Provincial Education Department (No. 2013JK1139, No. 2013JK0583), China Postdoctoral Science Foundation (No. 2013M542370), the Specialized Research Fund for the Doctoral Program of Higher Education of China (No. 20136118120010), the Specialized Research Fund for the Doctoral Program of Higher Education of China Grant (No. 20136118120010). And this project is also supported by NSFC Grant (Program No. 11301414 and No. 11226173).

References

1. Finkzeller, K.: RFID Handbook: Fundamentals and Applications in Contacts Smart Cards and Identification. Wiley, West Sussex (2004)
2. Wei, W., Yong, Q.: Information potential fields navigation in wireless Ad-Hoc sensor networks. Sensors 11(5), 4794–4807 (2011)
3. Dheeraj, K., Chin, K.W., Raad, R.: A survey and tutorial of RFID anti-collision protocols. IEEE Commun. Surv. Tutor. 12(3), 400–421 (2010)
4. Vogt, H.: Efficient object identification with passive RFID tags. In: Mattern, F., Naghshineh, M. (eds.) Pervasive 2002. LNCS, vol. 2414, pp. 98–113. Springer, Heidelberg (2002). https://doi.org/10.1007/3-540-45866-2_9
5. Wei, W., Xu, Q., Wang, L., et al.: GI/Geom/1 queue based on communication model for mesh networks. Int. J. Commun. Syst. 27(11), 3013–3029 (2014)

6. Chen, W.-T.: An accurate tag estimate method for improving the performance of an RFID anti-collision algorithm based on dynamic frame length ALOHA. IEEE Trans. Autom. Sci. Eng. **6**(1), 9–15 (2009)

7. Wei, W., Yang, X.L., Zhou, B., et al.: Combined energy minimization for image reconstruction from few views. Math. Probl. Eng. **16**(7), 2213–2223 (2012)

8. Pan, Y., Peng, Q., Zhou, Q., et al.: Reducing tag collision in radio frequency identification systems by using a grouped dynamic frame slotted ALOHA algorithm. Acta Phys. Sin. **62**(14), 148401-1–148401-2 (2013)

9. Wei, W., Yang, X.L., Shen, P.Y., et al.: Holes detection in anisotropic sensornets: topological methods. Int. J. Distrib. Sens. Netw. **21**(9), 3216–3229 (2012)

10. Wang, Y., Liu, Y., Leung, H., et al.: A multi-bit identification protocol for RFID tag reading. IEEE Sens. J. **13**(10), 3527–3536 (2013)

11. Liu, Z., Ji, J., et al.: An anti-collision. Acta Electron. Sin. **41**(11), 2156–2160 (2013)

12. Wei, W., Qiang, Y., Zhang, J.: A bijection between lattice-valued filters and lattice-valued congruences in residuated lattices. Math. Probl. Eng. **36**(8), 4218–4229 (2013)

13. Song, J., Guo, Y., et al.: An adjustive hybrid tree anti-collision algorithm for RFID multi-tag identification. Acta Electron. Sin. **42**(4), 685–689 (2014)

14. EPC Global: EPC radio-frequency identify protocols class-1 generation-2 UHF RFID protocol for communications at 860 MHz–960 MHz, ver. 1. 2. 0, October 2008

15. Angerer, C., Langwieser, R., Rupp, M.: RFID reader receivers for physical layer collision revocery. IEEE Trans. Commun. **58**(12), 3526–3537 (2010)

16. Wei, W., Srivastava, H.M., Zhang, Y., et al.: A local fractional integral inequality on fractal space analogous to Anderson's inequality. In: Abstract and Applied Analysis, vol. 46, no. 8, pp. 5218–5229. Hindawi Publishing Corporation (2014)

17. Chen, W.-T.: A feasible and easy-to-implement anticollision algorithm for the EPCglobal UHF class-1 generation-2 RFID protocol. IEEE Trans. Autom. Sci. Eng. **11**(2), 485–491 (2014)

18. Wei, W., Fan, X., Song, H., Fan, X., Yang, J.: Imperfect information dynamic Stackelberg game based resource allocation using hidden Markov for cloud computing. IEEE Trans. Serv. Comput. **11**(1), 78–89 (2016). https://doi.org/10.1109/tsc.2016.2528246

19. Su, W., Alchazidis, N.V., Ha, T.T.: Multiple RFID tags access algorithm. IEEE Trans. Mob. Comput. **3**(2), 174–187 (2010)

20. Su, J., Hong, D., Tang, J., Chen, H.: An efficient anti-collision algorithm based on improved collision detection scheme. IEICE Trans. Commun. (中科院4区) **E99-B**(2), 465–469 (2016)

21. Su, J., Zhao, X., Luo, Z., Chen, H.: Q-value fine-grained adjustment based RFID anti-collision algorithm. IEICE Trans. Commun. (中科院4区) **E99-B**(7), 1593–1598 (2016)

22. Su, J., Sheng, Z., Hong, D., Leung, V.C.M.: An efficient sub-frame based tag identification algorithm for UHF RFID systems. In: IEEE International Conference on Communications (ICC 2016), pp. 1–6 (2016)

23. Su, J., Wen, G., Hong, D.: A new RFID anti-collision algorithm based on the Q-ary search scheme. Chin. J. Electr. (电子学报英文版) **24**(4), 679–683 (2015)

24. Su, J., Sheng, Z., Xie, L.: A collision-tolerant-based anti-collision algorithm for large scale RFID system. IEEE Commun. Lett. (中科院3区) **21**(7), 1517–1520 (2017)

A New Multi-tree Search Algorithm for RFID Tag Identification

Jiang Xu$^{(\boxtimes)}$

School of Computer and Software, Nanjing University of Information Science and Technology,
Nanjing, China
12130398@qq.com

Abstract. In order to improve the efficiency of radio frequency identification in internet of things, we proposed a novel hybrid algorithm-Adaptive Multi-tree Time Slot (AMTS) anti-collision algorithm based on the ALOHA algorithm and Multi-tree search algorithm. In AMTS, tags are rapid assigned to slots of frame and if some tags collide in a slot, the collided tags in the slot will be identified by adaptive multi-tree search according to collision factor. Analysis of performance and the results of simulation show that the proposed algorithm significantly outperforms other existing hybrid schemes.

Keywords: RFID · Anti-collision · ALOHA · AMTS

1 Introduction

Radio frequency identification (RFID) has been considered an emerging technology for fast identification of massive tags which are attached to the objects. It is widely used in various application systems, and become one of the key technologies in the Internet of Things (IOT) [1]. When many RFID tags transmit their signals simultaneously to the reader, collision of tags will happen. Therefore, tag anti-collision algorithm is an important research area in RFID systems. Generally, tag anti-collision algorithms can be grouped into two broad categories: aloha-based algorithms [2–6], tree-based algorithms [7–9, 13].

The Aloha-based algorithm was first developed for random access in packet radio networks. To improve efficiency, the slotted ALOHA were proposed [2]. The advantage of the slotted ALOHA protocol is that it is simple. The disadvantage of the slotted ALOHA protocol is slow throughput under high traffic loads. Thus, the framed ALOHA was developed [3]. To further improve the system efficiency, the various dynamic frame slotted ALOHA schemes [4–6] are presented and widely adopted in some RFID standards. Aloha-based algorithms can largely reduced the collision probability, but they have the tag starvation problem that a particular tag may not be identified for a long time. Furthermore, in order to obtain the maximum efficiency, the number of tags needs to be estimated in aloha-based algorithms. Obviously, it will increase the computational cost. Tree-based algorithms can solve the tag starvation problem, but they have relatively long identification delay if there are too many tags in the range of reader. Therefore, many

© Springer Nature Singapore Pte Ltd. 2020
X. Sun et al. (Eds.): ICAIS 2020, CCIS 1253, pp. 455–463, 2020.
https://doi.org/10.1007/978-981-15-8086-4_43

researchers proposed hybrid algorithms [10, 11]. The authors in [10] proposed a hybrid query tree algorithm that combines a tree based query protocol with a slotted back off mechanism. The authors in [11] presented three tag anti-collision protocols based on binary tree slotted ALOHA (BTSA) algorithm, whose best performance can achieve 0.425.

In this paper, we combine the advantages of aloha-based and multi-tree search algorithm to propose a novel hybrid tag collision algorithm. The advantages of the proposed scheme are to propose an accurate and simple estimation method of the number of tags in collision slots, and its efficiency is not affected by the variance of the number of tags and the IDs distribution of tags.

2 System Model

The AMTS protocol initializes a frame and divides the frame into a number of slots. Each tag will randomly selects a slot and transmit its ID to the reader. If collision occurs, the reader records the current slot counter (SC) and pushes it into stack. At the end of a frame, the reader will realize all of the collision slots. Tags in a collision slot will be resolved by adaptive multi-tree search algorithm. When tags in all collision slots are successfully identified, the whole identification completes. Figure 1 shows an execution example of AMTS algorithm, where tags in the first slot and fifth slot in the frame with length L collide, and are resolved by 2-ary search and 4-2-ary search respectively.

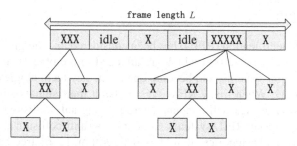

Fig. 1. An execution example of AMTS algorithm

3 AMTS Protocol

This section will propose two adaptive multi-tree time slot protocol, whose procedure involves dynamic frame length adjustment and adaptive M-ary search algorithm. The benefit of AMTSs is that, its adjustment procedure is very simple.

The keys of the AMTS are how to accurate estimate the number of tags in collision slots and the adjustment of m value of the M-ary search algorithm. In this paper, we proposed two methods to achieve it: CF-AMTS and MF-AMTS, respectively.

(1) CF-AMTS algorithm

We define the collision factor:

$$\mu = \frac{k}{n} \tag{1}$$

In which k is the collision bit numbers of current slot, n is the length of tags' IDs. It is assumed that there are m unidentified tags in current slot. The probability that any bit will not be collide denoted as $1/2^{m-1}$, we then have

$$\mu = \frac{n[1 - (1/2)^{m-1}]}{n} \tag{2}$$

Equation (2) indicates that collision factor is higher when m is larger. When the allocated total search depth is N, the probability that tag is identified in depth one is $P_1 = (1 - 1/N)^{m-1}$ and the probability that tag is identified in depth r is $P_r = P_1(1 - P_1)^{r-1}$. The expected value of search depth can be given by

$$E(r) = \sum_{r=1}^{\infty} rP_r = \sum_{r=1}^{\infty} rP_1(1 - P_1)^{r-1} = -P_1 \frac{d \sum_{r=1}^{\infty} [(1 - P_1)^r]}{d(P_1)}$$

$$= -P_1 \frac{d[\frac{1-P_1}{P_1}]}{d(P_1)} = -P_1 \left(\frac{-P_1 - (1 - P_1)}{P_1^2}\right) = \frac{1}{(1 - 1/N)^{m-1}} \tag{3}$$

Then, we can derive the average slots for identifying m tags

$$T_{N-ary} = NE(r) = \frac{N}{(1 - 1/N)^{m-1}} \tag{4}$$

From (4), we will have

$$\begin{cases} T_{2-ary} \geq T_{4-ary}, & m \geq 3 \\ T_{2-ary} < T_{4-ary}, & m < 3 \end{cases} \tag{5}$$

From (2) and (5), we know that it should adopt 4-ary search algorithm when $m \geq 3$ otherwise the 2-ary search algorithm. The collision factor largely reflects the information of the number of unidentified tags in collision slot, but it is not accurate due to the effect of ID's distribution of tags. Therefore, the estimation error degrades the efficiency performance if only use the collision factor. The custom command QueryRP was introduced for solve this problem. When $\mu \geq 0.75$, the reader send the command QueryRP which allows tags allocated into the slot to return the 4-bit data which includes upper 2-bit of collision bits. On receiving a QueryRP command, a tag shall performs AND operation between upper 4-bit of its UID and (1100), then transfers the upper 2-bit into decimal number x and returns the 4-bit data whose x-th bit is 1 others are 0. For example, there are two tags collided into one time slot. The IDs of tags are 11010001 and 11101010. The collision factor is 0.75. It will give rise to empty slots if reader performs the 4-ary search algorithm. Through the QueryRP command reader can detects the existing collision prefix. Thus, the empty slots will be avoided. Figure 2 illustrates the process of identification by using QueryRP command.

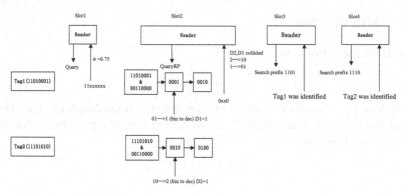

Fig. 2. Tags' identification example in 4-ary tree

(2) MF-AMTS algorithm

We propose MF-AMTS algorithm in this sub-section. The algorithm will estimate the number of tags in collision slots by using Mapping Function which can be described as follows [13].

Require: k-bit string $b = b_{k-1}b_{k-2}\ldots b_0$
(b_i: a binary value)
Ensure: K-bit string $p = p_{K-1}p_{K-2}\ldots p_0$
($K = 2^k$, p_i: a binary value)

1: Initialize an integer $I = 0$ and p such that $p_i = 0$ for all i
2: **for** j $= 0$ to k-1 **do**
3: $I = I + b_j * 2^j$
4: **end for**

Table 1. Mapping table

2 bits	4 bits
00	**0001**
01	**0010**
10	**0100**
11	**1000**

Table. 1 shows the mapping table for 2bits which is generated by Mapping Function. In MF-AMTS algorithm, when the tag receives a search command from the stack of the reader, and the search string is ε or matches the prefix of the tag ID, then it responses the 2bits from the MSB of the rest part of the tag ID except the prefix. At this time, these 2bits are mapped into 4bits by the mapping table. Let the number of 'x' to be t in the mapped 4bits, then the reader will adopt the 4-ary search if $t \geq 3$ otherwise the 2-ary search algorithm. As mentioned above, the IDs of tags are 11010001 and 11101010 in a collision slot whose slot number is stocked in the stack of the reader. The identification process is illustrated in Table. 2. In slot1 of Table. 2, two tags (1101 0001, 1110 1010) having the prefix of 11, respond with (01 → 0010) and (10 → 0100), respectively, which produce 0xx0. Thus, the next search command is 110 due to the number of x is $t = 2$.

Table 2. Identification process for example

Slot	Search command	Response	Identification
1	ε	0xx0	
2	110	0100	11010001
3	111	0010	11101010

Compared Table. 2 with Fig. 2, we can know that the required slots number of MF-AMTS is smaller than CF-AMTS because of no additional QueryRP command.

Figure 3 shows the flowchart of adaptive m-ary search algorithm and proposed AMTS, respectively.

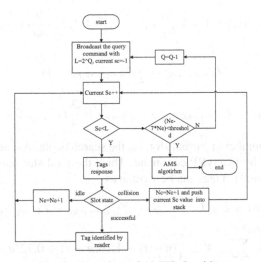

Fig. 3. Flowchart of AMTS algorithm

The difference of two AMTS algorithms is determined mechanism of AMS algorithm. The determined mechanism of CF-AMTS is depended on collision factor and QueryRP command. That of MF-AMTS is according to mapping table.

4 Performance Analysis

In this sub-section, we analyze the total slot number for identifying all tags in two AMTS, and then analyze the system efficiency. The total slot number is defined by a sum of the frame length L and required slot number in AMS block. We assume that there are M unidentified tags in AMS block. In the case that search depth is k along and the average three tags on every leaf-node. When search depth above k, the RFID system will adopt 2-ary search algorithm otherwise 4-ary search algorithm. The total slot number of AMTS is derived as:

$$T_{total} = T_{aloha} + T_{tree} = L + T_{4-ary-total} + T_{2-ary-total} \tag{6}$$

Where $T_{4\text{-ary-total}}$ is the total slot number in a full 4-ary tree, which can be written as

$$T_{4-ary-total} = \sum_{i=0}^{k} 4^i = \sum_{i=0}^{\lceil \log_4^{m/3} \rceil - 1} 4^i \tag{7}$$

From Fig. 2 we can know that the QueryRP command need to occupy a slot, the total slot number of QueryRP equal to the slot number of collision: $T_{QueryRP} = T_{4\text{-ary-coll}}$. According to the analysis of [12], we can compute the total slot number $T_{4\text{-ary-total}}$, the idle slot number $T_{4\text{-ary-idle}}$ and the collision slot number $T_{4\text{-ary-coll}}$ as follows:

$$T_{4-ary-total}(m) = 1 + 4 \sum_{j=0}^{\infty} 4^j [1 - (1 - 4^{-j})^m - \frac{m}{4^j}(1 - 4^{-j})^{m-1}] \tag{8}$$

$$T_{4-ary-coll} = \frac{1}{4}(T_{4-ary-total} - 1) \tag{9}$$

$$T_{4-ary-idle} = T_{4-ary-total} - T_{4-ary-coll} = \frac{3}{4}T_{4-ary-total} - m + \frac{1}{4} \tag{10}$$

Here m is the tags number in current slot, j is the search depth. As mentioned above, the idle slot is avoided by QueryRP command. Thus, the total slot number of CF-AMTS which is used to identify n tags can be written as

$$T_{CF-AMTS-total}(n) = L + T_{4-ary-total} + T_{2-ary-total} - T_{4-ary-idle} + T_{4-ary-coll}$$

$$\approx L + \sum_{j=0}^{\lceil \log_4^{n-s} \rceil - 1} 4^i + \frac{5}{3}(n - s) - 1.16(n - s) + 0.72(n - s) \tag{11}$$

The total slot number of MF-AMTS can be derived as

$$T_{MF-AMTS-total}(n) = L + T_{4-ary-total} + T_{2-ary-total} - T_{4-ary-idle}$$

$$\approx L + \sum_{j=0}^{\lceil \log_4^{n-s} \rceil - 1} 4^i + \frac{5}{3}(n - s) - 1.16(n - s) \tag{12}$$

Where n is the total number of tags, s is the successful slot number when the frame length is L. Let U denotes the system efficiency when ATMS identifies n tags. Then, the efficiency U can be given by

$$U = \frac{n}{T_{total}(n)} \tag{13}$$

5   Numerical and Analytical Result

The performance of the proposed AMTS is simulated. Figure 4 shows the average required slots for one tag identification when $5 \leq n \leq 500$ compared with Splitting BTSA [11]. Splitting BTSA takes 2.3 slots, whereas CF-AMTS and MF-AMTS take from 1.4 to 1.6 slots, 1.8 to 2 slots, respectively. Figure 5 presents the system efficiencies of Splitting BTSA, CF-AMTS and MF-AMTS.

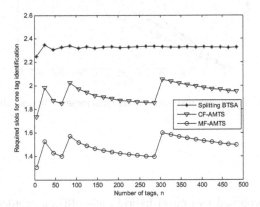

Fig. 4. Simulation results: Required slots of one tag identification

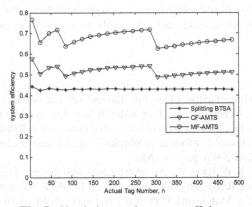

Fig. 5. Simulation results: system efficiency

Similar to the results for the one tag identification, AMTS can achieve higher system efficiency than Splitting BTSA. From Fig. 5, when the number of tags increases from 5 to 500, the efficiency curve of Splitting BTSA protocol is nearly horizontal at around 0.4. Our proposed schemes can achieve efficiency from 0.5 to 0.6 and 0.64 to 0.76. The system efficiency could be improved from 19% to 37% in CF-AMTS and 52% to 81% in MF-AMTS. In Fig. 6, we compare the read performance of Splitting BTSA with that of our proposed schemes, including CF-AMTS and MF-AMTS. We find from Fig. 6 that of the three algorithms, the MF-AMTS requires fewest slots to read a set of tags.

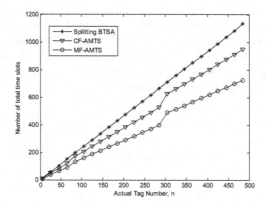

Fig. 6. Simulation results: the total slots required to read all tags

6 Conclusion

In this letter, we proposed two novel hybrid anti-collision protocols for identifying multiple RFID tags within the reader field. The proposed schemes not only have higher efficiency but also require no estimation of the number of tags, and hence can avoid the computational cost of the estimation. Through theoretical analysis and simulation results, we show that our schemes can achieve the better performance [14–18].

References

1. Finkenzeller, K.: RFID-Handbook Fundamentals and Applications in Contactless Smart Cards and Identification (Second Edition). John Wiley & Sons Ltd, New York (2003)
2. Liu, L., Lai, S.: ALOHA-Based anti-collision algorithms used in RFID system. In: Proceedings of 2006 International Conference on Wireless Communications, Networking and Mobile Computing (WiCOM 2006), pp. 1–4 (2006)
3. Klair, D.K., Chin, K.W, Raad, R.: An investigation into the energy efficiency of pure and slotted Aloha based RFID anti-collision protocols. In: IEEE International Symposium on a World of Wireless, Mobile and Multimedia Networks (IEEE WoWMoM 2007), pp. 1–4 (2007)

4. Lee, S.R., Joo, S.D., Lee, C.W.: An enhanced dynamic framed ALOHA algorithm for RFID tag identification.: In Proceedings International Conference Mobile and Ubiquitous Systems: Networking and Services, pp. 1–5. IEEE, USA (2005)
5. Li, B., Wang, J.Y.: Efficient anti-collision algorithm utilizing the capture effect for ISO 18000-6C RFID protocol. IEEE Commun. Lett. **15**(3), 352–354 (2011)
6. Chen, W.T.: An accurate tag estimate method for improving the performance of an RFID anticollision algorithm based on dynamic frame length ALOHA. IEEE Trans. Autom. Sci. Eng. **6**(1), 9–15 (2009)
7. Myung, J., Lee, W., Srivastava, J.: Adaptive binary splitting for efficient RFID tag anti-collision. IEEE Commun. Lett. **10**(3), 144–146 (2006)
8. Law, C., Lee, K., Siu, K.Y.: Efficient memoryless protocol for tag identification. In: Proceedings of the 4th International Workshop on Discrete Algorithms and Methods for Mobile Computing and Communications, pp. 75–84. ACM Press, New York, USA (2000)
9. Kim, Y., kim, S., et al.: Improved 4-ary query tree algorithm for anti-collsion in RFID system.: In International Conference on Advanced Information Networking and Applications, pp. 699–704 (2009)
10. Bonuccelli, M.A., Lonetti, F., Martelli, F.: Tree slotted Aloha: a new protocol for tag identification in RFID networks. In: International Symposium on World of Wireless, Mobile and Multimedia Networks, pp. 1–6 (2006)
11. Wu, H., Zeng, Y.: Efficient framed slotted ALOHA protocol for RFID tag anticollision. IEEE Trans. Autom. Sci. Eng. **8**(3), 581–588 (2011)
12. Hush, D.R., Wood, C.: Analysis of tree algorithms for RFID arbitration. In: Proceedings of IEEE Symposium on Information Theory, pp. 107–116 (1998)
13. Shin, J.M., Jeon, B.C., Yang, D.M.: Multiple RFID tags identificaion with M-ary query tree scheme. IEEE Commun. Lett. **17**(3), 604–607 (2013)
14. Su, J., Hong, D., Tang, J., Chen, H.: An efficient anti-collision algorithm based on improved collision detection scheme. IEICE Trans. Commun. (中科院4区) **E99-B**(2), 465–469 (2016)
15. Su, J., Zhao, X., Luo, Z., Chen, H.: Q-value fine-grained adjustment based RFID anti-collision algorithm. IEICE Trans. Commun. (中科院4区) **E99-B**(7), 1593–1598 (2016)
16. Su, J., Sheng, Z., Hong, D., Leung, V.C.M.: An efficient sub-frame based tag identification algorithm for UHF RFID systems. In: IEEE International Conference on Communications (ICC 2016), pp. 1–6 (2016)
17. Su, J., Wen, G., Hong, D.: A new RFID anti-collision algorithm based on the Q-ary search scheme. Chin. J. Electr. (电子学报英文版) **24**(4), 679–683 (2015)
18. Su, J., Sheng, Z., Xie, L.: A collision-tolerant-based anti-collision algorithm for large scale RFID system. IEEE Commun. Lett. (中科院3区) **21**(7), 1517–1520 (2017)

A Direct Self-adaptive Fuzzy Control System for a Single-Arm Manipulator

Xiaokan Wang[✉] and Qiong Wang

Henan Mechanical and Electrical Vocational College, Xinzheng 451191, China
wxkbbg@163.com

Abstract. In A manipulator system is a highly nonlinear and strongly coupled multi-input and multi-output complex system. This makes it difficult to obtain a precise mathematical model of the manipulator system. In addition, the external influence factors of load variation, random disturbance and model uncertainties greatly increase the difficulty of trajectory tracking control. Therefore, this paper studies manipulator trajectory tracking control and makes full use of the advantages of a simple design, does not require a precise object model, and presents an easily acceptable and understandable control mechanism and strategy via a traditional fuzzy control method. In order to compensate for low control accuracy, an adaptive fuzzy controller is proposed for single-arm manipulator control, and the stability of the controller is proved by the Lyapunov function. According to the deviation between the actual system performance and the ideal performance, the controller can directly adjust the parameters of the controller and then make the output of the system track the ideal output closely. The traditional PID controller and adaptive fuzzy controller are used to simulate and analyze the high precision trajectory tracking control of the manipulator by use of MATLAB/Simulink, and the simulation results are compared. The results show that the trajectory tracking control accuracy of the adaptive fuzzy controller is higher than that of the traditional PID controller, and the steady-state error is smaller. The robustness, anti-interference ability and response speed of the adaptive fuzzy controller are high. The validity of the algorithm is verified.

Keywords: Single arm manipulator · Nonlinearity · Adaptive fuzzy control · Trajectory tracking

1 Introduction

A manipulator control system is a multi-variable, nonlinear, coupled dynamic system. It is difficult to design an effective controller via mathematical models. In the artificial intelligence field, people have gradually applied the theory of fuzzy logic and neural networks to control systems. In the traditional methods, such as PID control and moment control, the compensation control of the part that cannot be accurately calculated is carried out using fuzzy methods and neural networks, and the control accuracy has been improved to a certain extent.

© Springer Nature Singapore Pte Ltd. 2020
X. Sun et al. (Eds.): ICAIS 2020, CCIS 1253, pp. 464–473, 2020.
https://doi.org/10.1007/978-981-15-8086-4_44

Kumar et al. [1] designed an interval type-2 fuzzy PID controller for a redundant robotic manipulator. Londhe et al. [2] proposed a robust single-input fuzzy controller for the trajectory control of an autonomous underwater vehicle control system. Abdelhamid et al. [3] presented an uncertain adaptive fuzzy control method to overcome the singularity problem in the indirect adaptive feedback linearization control of a two-link manipulator. Nguyen et al. [4] proposed proposed a finite-time adaptive fuzzy tracking control method to deal with the uncertainties and external disturbances of the control system of parallel robots by using the fuzzy theory. At the same time, the algorithm does not need to learn the relevant knowledge of robot dynamics. The simulation results show that the algorithm has good convergence and stability, and achieves the control purpose of the design. Navvabi et al. [5] presented an adaptive fuzzy sliding mode observer control method, which can effectively control the strong state dependence and complexity of the manipulator parameters, ensure the stability and robustness of the system, and is very effective for real-time industrial applications. Ji-Hwan et al. [6] proposed an advanced fuzzy sliding mode control method. The simulation of a nonlinear rigid manipulator with two connecting rods shows that the method can control the unknown system effectively. Dong et al. [7] presented a fuzzy robust control algorithm for under-actuated manipulator system. The cumulative performance and control cost of the system are used as performance indicators for optimal control design. Dong et al. [8] proposed a fuzzy method for optimal control design of uncertain flexible joint manipulators, and an adaptive robust controller is designed to ensure the deterministic performance and fuzziness of the system. Baigzadehnoe et al. [9] proposed an adaptive fuzzy backstepping position tracking control scheme for multi-robot manipulator system is proposed. The problem of position and force tracking control for a rigid-body cooperative robot system with unknown dynamics model and unknown external disturbance is solved. Chang et al. [10] proposed an adaptive fuzzy state feedback control method for a single-link robotic manipulator system.

With the improvement of tracking accuracy and speed of manipulator control systems, uncertainties such as friction and disturbances bring new challenges to manipulator control. By analyzing the theoretical knowledge of manipulator kinematics, the kinematics equation of the manipulator can be established by describing the rigid body posture and transforming the coordinates [11–13]. Then, a dynamic model of the manipulator is constructed via the Lagrange function. The uncertainty of the manipulator is approximated using a fuzzy system for a double-joint machine. For the manipulator system, the design of the robust fuzzy control system is completed and is independent of the precise mathematical model of the object. The performance of the designed controller is analyzed by simulation experiments. To address the problem of low control accuracy in the control system, a direct adaptive fuzzy control algorithm is proposed. A feedback controller and an adaptive control law for adjusting parameter vectors are designed to make the output of the system track the ideal output closely, so as to obtain more precise control of the manipulator. Through simulation, the trajectory tracking performance of the manipulator under the control of different control algorithms is considered, which demonstrates the effectiveness of the designed control algorithm.

With the rapid development of China's economy, the demand for coal is increasing. Therefore, there are still many coal enterprises. Due to the unbalanced development of coal mining enterprises, some of them are advanced in equipment, and some of them are relatively backward, which leads to the continuous occurrence of mine accidents. In the mine disaster, most of them are caused by gas explosion, which makes the coal mining face severe challenges.

2 Dynamics Analysis of a Single-Arm Manipulator

The control input function of the manipulator system can be expressed by a Lagrange function, which can be regarded as a relation expressed by the difference of the total kinetic energy E_k of the system minus the total potential energy E_p of the system [17, 18]:

$$L = E_k - E_p \tag{1}$$

Next, taking a two-degree-of-freedom manipulator as an example, the dynamic properties of the manipulator are analyzed. The structure is shown in Fig. 1.

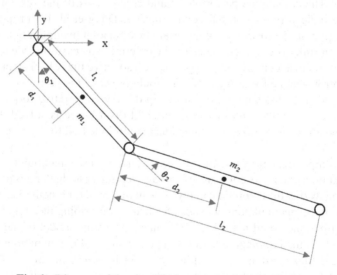

Fig. 1. Diagram of the simplified structure of the manipulator.

In which, O_1 is joint 1 and O_2 is joint 2; l_1 is the length of the connecting rod 1 and l_2 is the length of the connecting rod 2; m_1 is the centroid of the connecting rod 1 and m_2 is the centroid of the connecting rod 2; d_1 is the distance from the center of mass m_1 to the first joint O_1 and d_2 is the distance from the center of mass m_2 to the joint O_2; θ_1 is the rotation angle of the connecting rod 1 and θ_2 is the rotation angle of the connecting rod 2.

The coordinate system is established by taking the first joint O_1 as the origin [19–21].

$$L = E_k - E_p$$

$$= \frac{1}{2}m_1 d_1^2 \dot{\theta}_1^2 + \frac{1}{2}m_2 l_1^2 \dot{\theta}_1^2 + \frac{1}{2}m_2[d_2(\dot{\theta}_1 + \dot{\theta}_2)]^2 + m_2 l_1 \dot{\theta}_1 d_2(\dot{\theta}_1 + \dot{\theta}_2) \cos\theta_2$$

$$- m_1 g d_1 (1 - \cos\theta_1) - m_2 g l_1 (1 - \cos\theta_1) - m_2 g d_2 [1 - \cos(\theta_1 + \theta_2)] \qquad (2)$$

$$\frac{\partial L}{\partial \dot{\theta}_1} = m_1 d_1^2 \dot{\theta}_1 + m_2 l_1^2 \dot{\theta}_1 + m_2 d_2^2 (\dot{\theta}_1 + \dot{\theta}_2) + m_2 l_1 d_2 (2\dot{\theta}_1 + \dot{\theta}_2) \cos\theta_2$$

$$= (m_1 d_1^2 + m_2 l_1^2)\dot{\theta}_1 + m_2 l_1 d_2 (2\dot{\theta}_1 + \dot{\theta}_2) \cos\theta_2 + m_2 d_2^2 (\dot{\theta}_1 + \dot{\theta}_2) \qquad (3)$$

$$\frac{\partial L}{\partial \theta_1} = -m_1 g d_1 \sin\theta_1 - m_2 g l_1 \sin\theta_1 - m_2 g d_2 \sin(\theta_1 + \theta_2)$$

$$= -(m_1 g d_1 + m_2 g l_1) \sin\theta_1 - m_2 g d_2 \sin(\theta_1 + \theta_2) \qquad (4)$$

We can obtain the expression of the torque τ_1 and τ_2 on joint 1 and 2:

$$\tau_1 = \frac{d}{dt}\frac{\partial L}{\partial \dot{\theta}_1} - \frac{\partial L}{\partial \theta_1} = D_{11}\ddot{\theta}_1 + D_{12}\ddot{\theta}_2 + D_{112}\dot{\theta}_1\dot{\theta}_2 + D_{122}\dot{\theta}_2^2 + D_1 \qquad (5)$$

$$\tau_2 = D_{21}\ddot{\theta}_1 + D_{22}\ddot{\theta}_2 + D_{212}\dot{\theta}_1\dot{\theta}_2 + D_{211}\dot{\theta}_2^2 + D_2 \qquad (6)$$

In which,

$$\begin{cases} D_{11} = m_1 d_1^2 + m_2 l_1^2 + m_2 d_2^2 + 2m_2 l_1 d_2 \cos\theta_2 \\ D_{12} = m_2 d_2^2 + m_2 l_1 d_2 \cos\theta_2 \\ D_{112} = -2m_2 l_1 d_2 \sin\theta_2 \\ D_{122} = -m_2 l_1 d_2 \sin\theta_2 \\ D_1 = (m_1 d_1 + m_2 l_1)g \sin\theta_1 + m_2 g d_2 \sin(\theta_1 + \theta_2) \end{cases} \qquad (7)$$

The general expression of the moment of the manipulator can be obtained by combining formulas (6) and (7):

$$\tau = D(q)\ddot{q} + C(q, \dot{q})\dot{q} + G(q) \qquad (8)$$

3 System Hardware Design3. Design of a Direct Self-adaptive Fuzzy Control System

3.1 Design of the Direct Adaptive Fuzzy Controller

The adaptive fuzzy controller of the manipulator can be described in the formula (9):

$$u = u_D(x|\theta) \qquad (9)$$

In which, u_D is a fuzzy system, θ is a fuzzy set, and its parameters can be adjusted.

If x_1 is $A_1^{l_1}$ and .... and x_n is $A_n^{l_n}$, then u_D will be $S^{l_1\cdots l_n}$, $l = 1, 2, \ldots, m$; $i = 1, 2, \ldots, n$.

By using the product inference engine, single-valued ambiguity and central average defuzzifier [26], the fuzzy system can be expressed as follows:

$$u_D = (x|\theta) = \frac{\sum_{l_1=1}^{m_1} \cdots \sum_{l_n=1}^{m_n} y_u^{l_1\cdots l_n} \left(\prod_{i=1}^{n} \mu_{A_i}^{l_i}(x_i)\right)}{\sum_{l_1=1}^{m_1} \cdots \sum_{l_n=1}^{m_n} \left(\prod_{i=1}^{n} \mu_{A_i}^{l_i}(x_i)\right)} \tag{10}$$

Let a free parameter $\bar{y}_u^{l_1\cdots l_n}$ be included in a set, then the fuzzy controller is

$$u_D = (x|\theta) = \theta^T \xi(x) \tag{11}$$

In formula (19), $\xi(x)$ is a $\prod_{i=1}^{n} m_i$ dimension vector whose $l_1 \ldots l_n$ element is:

$$\xi(x) = \frac{\prod_{i=1}^{n} \mu_{A_i}^{l_i}(x_i)}{\sum_{l_1=1}^{m_1} \cdots \sum_{l_n=1}^{m_n} \prod_{i=1}^{n} \mu_{A_i}^{l_i}(x_i)} \tag{12}$$

We can input the initial parameters of the fuzzy control rules into the fuzzy controller.

3.2 Design of the Adaptive Control Law

Choosing an appropriate adaptive law:

$$\dot{\theta} = \gamma e^T p_n \xi(x) \tag{13}$$

The Lyapunov function is

$$V = \frac{1}{2} e^T P e + \frac{b}{2\gamma} (\theta^* - \theta)^T (\theta^* - \theta) \tag{14}$$

So we can choose

$$\dot{V} = -\frac{1}{2} e^T Q e - e^T p_n b w \tag{15}$$

For $Q > 0$, w articleis the most approximate error, we can design enough fuzzy systems $u_D(x|\theta)$, which make w sufficiently small and satisfy $\left| e^T p_n b w \right| < \frac{1}{2} e^T Q e$, and then $\dot{V} < 0$.

4 Analysis of Simulation Results

If the controlled object is a single-arm manipulator, the dynamic model of the manipulator control system can be obtained [28]:

$$\ddot{\theta} = -\frac{1}{I}(d\dot{\theta} + mgl \cos \theta) + \frac{1}{I}(\tau - \tau_d) \tag{16}$$

In which, τ_d represents the friction model. A friction model is a model that combines viscidity friction and coulomb friction.

$$\tau_d = \text{sgn}(\theta(t))(k_1|\dot{\theta}(t)| + k_2) \tag{17}$$

In which, k_1 and k_2 are both positive constants.

The position of the manipulator system is given by $x_d(t) = \sin(\pi t)$. The six membership functions of the system are: $\mu_{N3}(x) = 1/(1 + \exp(5(x + 2)))$, $\mu_{N2}(x) = \exp(-(x+1.5)^2)$, $\mu_{N1}(x) = \exp(-(x+0.5)^2)$, $\mu_{P1}(x) = \exp(-(x-0.5)^2)$, $\mu_{P2}(x) = \exp(-(x-1.5)^2)$, $\mu_{P3}(x) = 1/(1 + \exp(-5(x - 2)))$.

The initial condition of the designed system is $[1, 0]$, and the initial value of is 0. The control law is $Q = \begin{bmatrix} 50 & 0 \\ 0 & 50 \end{bmatrix}$, $k_1 = 1$, $k_1 = 10$, and the adaptive parameter is $\gamma = 50$.

It can be seen from Fig. 2 that with the passage of time the control algorithm proposed in this paper can make the control input signal more and more stable and gradually weaken the disturbance signal in the control system.

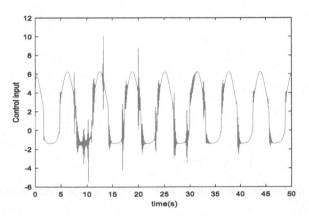

Fig. 2. Control input signal.

It can be seen from Fig. 3 that the position tracking curve (blue) obtained by the PID controller is quite different from the expected position tracking curve (green). The position tracking curve (red) obtained by the direct adaptive fuzzy control system is different to that of the manipulator. The desired curve for position tracking is almost identical. Through comparative analysis, it is found that the proposed algorithm is better than the traditional PID control method. The traditional PID controller fluctuates greatly from -0.5 to 0.5, and the error between the traditional PID control and the studied system fluctuates within the range of 0.01. Therefore, the proposed control method has better performance.

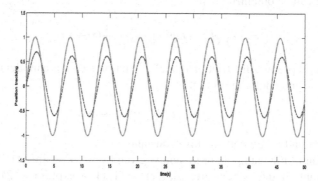

Fig. 3. Position tracking curve of the PID controller and the direct adaptive fuzzy control system ($k_p = 1$). (Color figure online)

It can be seen from Fig. 4 that under the same initial conditions the position tracking performance of the PID controller is still far from that of the direct adaptive fuzzy control system. The better position tracking error also fluctuates between -0.1 and 0.08. Therefore, we can demonstrate that the proposed direct adaptive fuzzy control system has better control performance than the traditional PID control system.

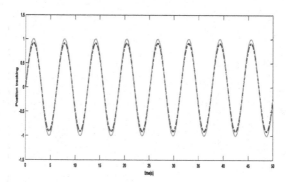

Fig. 4. Position tracking error curve of the PID controller and the direct adaptive fuzzy control system ($k_p = 10$).

5   GUI Design of the Manipulator Control System

MATLAB is a relatively advanced and new engineering technology. The numerical computation and visualization facilities make it more useful than many other programming languages. Compared with other software with the same functionality, MATLAB is more useful in scientific computing and visualization. In this study, the direct adaptive fuzzy control system includes a GUI utility, which enhances the usability. The interface is shown in Fig. 5 and 6.

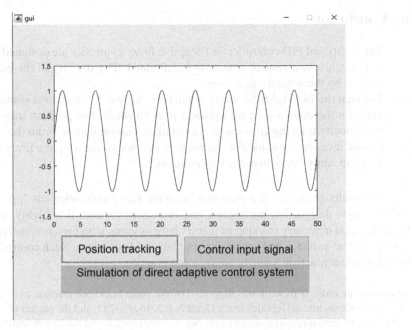

Fig. 5. GUI position tracking operation results.

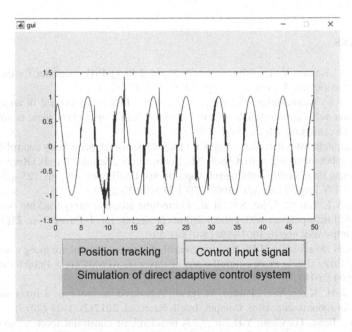

Fig. 6. GUI control input signal operation results.

6   Conclusion

(1) The traditional PID controller and adaptive fuzzy controller are designed. The control principle and control scheme are elaborated. The stability of the controller is verified by theoretical calculation.

(2) Through the MATLAB/Simulink simulation software, the control simulation diagram for the double-joint manipulator is established. The position tracking curve and velocity tracking error curve are obtained via simulation. From the simulation results, it can be seen that the control performance of the adaptive fuzzy controller is significantly better than the PID controller.

The results show that the proposed adaptive fuzzy controller has high precision with a simple design, few parameters and fast control speed. It is highly suitable for high precision trajectory tracking of manipulator systems with high nonlinearity, strong coupling, time-variance and uncertainty in real world situations. Such control problems have important practical value in engineering practice.

Acknowledgments. This work was supported by the youth backbone teachers training program of Henan colleges and universities under Grant No. 2016ggjs-287, and the project of science and technology of Henan province under Grant No. 172102210124, and the Key Scientific Research projects in Colleges and Universities in Henan Grant No. 18B460003.

References

1. Kumar, A., Kumar, V.: Evolving an interval type-2 fuzzy PID controller for the redundant robotic manipulator. Expert Syst. Appl. **73**(3), 161–177 (2017)
2. Londhe, P.S., Santhakumar, M., Patre, B.M., et al.: Task space control of an autonomous underwater vehicle manipulator system by robust single-input fuzzy logic control scheme. IEEE J. Oceanic Eng. **42**(1), 13–28 (2017)
3. Abdelhamid, B., Mouhamed, C., Najib, E.: Indirect robust adaptive fuzzy control of uncertain two link robot manipulator. In: Chadli, M., Bououden, S., Zelinka, I. (eds.) Recent Advances in Electrical Engineering and Control Applications. LNEE, vol. 411, pp. 125–139. Springer, Cham (2017). https://doi.org/10.1007/978-3-319-48929-2_10
4. Nguyen, V.T., Lin, C.Y., Su, S.F., et al.: Finite-time adaptive fuzzy tracking control design for parallel manipulators with unbounded uncertainties. Int. J. Fuzzy Syst. **21**(3), 545–555 (2018). https://doi.org/10.1007/s40815-018-0569-1
5. Navvabi, H., Markazi, A.H.D.: Position control of Stewart manipulator using a new extended adaptive fuzzy sliding mode controller and observer (E-AFSMCO). J. Franklin Inst. **355**(5), 2583–2609 (2018)
6. Hwang, J.-H., Kang, Y.-C., Park, J.-W., et al.: Advanced interval type-2 fuzzy sliding mode control for robot manipulator. Comput. Intell. Neurosci. **2017**(2), 1–11 (2017)
7. Dong, F., Jiang, H., Chen, Y.H., et al.: A novel robust constraint force servo control for under-actuated manipulator systems: fuzzy and optimal. Asian J. Control **1677**(1), 213–224 (2017)
8. Dong, F., Zhao, X., Jiang, H., et al.: Optimal fuzzy adaptive control for uncertain flexible joint manipulator based on D-operation. IET Control Theory Appl. **12**(9), 1286–1298 (2018)

9. Baigzadehnoe, B., Rahmani, Z., Khosravi, A., et al.: On position/force tracking control problem of cooperative robot manipulators using adaptive fuzzy backstepping approach. ISA Trans. **70**(8), 432–446 (2017)
10. Chang, W., Li, Y., Tong, S.: Adaptive fuzzy backstepping tracking control for flexible robotic manipulator. IEEE/CAA J. Autom. Sin. **35**(2), 1–9 (2018)
11. Yen, V.T., Nan, W.Y., Cuong, P.V.: Recurrent fuzzy wavelet neural networks based on robust adaptive sliding mode control for industrial robot manipulators. Neural Comput. Appl. **18**(5), 1–14 (2018). https://doi.org/10.1007/s00521-018-3520-3
12. Zhi, L., Wang, F., Yun, Z.: Adaptive visual tracking control for manipulator with actuator fuzzy dead-zone constraint and unmodeled dynamic. IEEE Trans. Syst. Man Cybern. Syst. **45**(10), 1301–1312 (2017)
13. Yen, V.T., Nan, W.Y., Cuong, P.V., et al.: Robust adaptive sliding mode control for industrial robot manipulator using fuzzy wavelet neural networks. Int. J. Control Autom. Syst. **15**(6), 2930–2941 (2017)
14. Wang, F., Chao, Z.Q., Huang, L.B., et al.: Trajectory tracking control of robot manipulator based on RBF neural network and fuzzy sliding mode. Comput. Simul. **34**(11), 353–359 (2017)
15. Guan, J.S., Lin, C.M., Ji, G.L., et al.: Robust adaptive tracking control for manipulators based on a TSK fuzzy cerebellar model articulation controller. IEEE Access **6**(6), 1670–1679 (2017)
16. Jiang, H., Chen, Y.H., Zhao, X., et al.: Optimal design for robust control of uncertain flexible joint manipulators: a fuzzy dynamical system approach. Int. J. Control **91**(1), 1–28 (2017)
17. Wang, F., Chao, Z.Q., Huang, L.B., et al.: Trajectory tracking control of robot manipulator based on RBF neural network and fuzzy sliding mode. Cluster Comput. **12**(4), 1–11 (2017). https://doi.org/10.1007/s10586-017-1538-4
18. Du, Z., Wei, W., Yan, Z., et al.: Variable admittance control based on fuzzy reinforcement learning for minimally invasive surgery manipulator. Sensors **17**(4), 844–849 (2017)
19. Fan, Y., Wang, W., Ying, L., et al.: Fuzzy adaptive switching control for an uncertain robot manipulators with time-varying output constraint. Complexity **2018**, 1–10 (2018)
20. Ye, D., Wang, D.: Research on tracking error of serial manipulator using improved fuzzy PID control. J. Jinggangshan Univ. (Nat. Sci. Ed.) (03), 72–75 (2019)
21. Xu, W.: Prediction algorithm of ship crane manipulator trajectory based on fuzzy control. Ship Sci. Technol. **40**(22), 208–210 (2018)
22. Liu, J., Cao, W., Xu, H., et al.: Adaptive fuzzy-PID control of accurate orientation for auto-detect seedling supply device. Trans. Chin. Soc. Agric. Eng. **33**(9), 37–44 (2017)
23. Strong, B., Zhou, X.: Research on control of improved fuzzy PID manipulator. Mach. Manuf. Autom. **47**(02), 160–163 (2018)
24. Min, W., Lingzhi, A.: Research on Simulation of control system of double-joint manipulator based on MATLAB. J. Plast. Eng. **24**(06), 136–142 (2017)
25. Run, M., Hongli, G., Xingguo, S.: RBF neural network manipulator control based on fuzzy compensation. J. Southwest Jiaotong Univ. **53**(03), 638–645 (2018)
26. Xie Bin, Ding Zhenjie, Jiang Wei. Design of adaptive fuzzy control system for multi-joint manipulator based on MIMO system. J. Qiqihar Univ. (Nat. Sci. Ed.) **32**(04), 20–24+48 (2016)
27. Niu, Y., Liu, Q.: Robot adaptive fuzzy sliding mode control based on MIMO system. China J. Agric. Mach. Chem. **36**(02), 265–268+256
28. Li, S., Deng, F., Zhao, X.: A new perspective on fuzzy control of the stochastic T-S fuzzy systems with sampled-data. Sci. China Inf. Sci. **62**(10), 203–209 (2019)

Research and Design of Intelligent Gas Concentration Monitoring and Alarming Instrument Based on PIC Single Chip Microcomputer

Xiaokan Wang[✉] and Qiong Wang

Henan Mechanical and Electrical Vocational College, Xinzheng 451191, China
wxkbbg@163.com

Abstract. In order to automatically monitor the gas concentration in the mine in real time, ensure the safety of coal mine production and protect the life safety of employees, an intelligent gas concentration monitoring and alarm instrument based on PIC single-chip microcomputer is designed. The equipment uses LXK-3 sensor to detect the gas concentration in the mine, and transmits the collected data to the single-chip microcomputer in the form of voltage; uses the single-chip microcomputer direct drive mode to dynamically display the gas concentration, when the gas concentration exceeds the limit, timely sends out the sound light alarm signal; realizes the wireless transmission of the communication data between the upper and lower computers by using nRF2401. The equipment has the characteristics of stable control, real-time communication and strong adaptability, which is of great significance for the real-time monitoring of gas concentration in the mine.

Keywords: Gas concentration · PIC microcontroller · Wireless transmission · Alarm

1 Introduction

With the rapid development of China's economy, the demand for coal is increasing. Therefore, there are still many coal enterprises. Due to the unbalanced development of coal mining enterprises, some of them are advanced in equipment, and some of them are relatively backward, which leads to the continuous occurrence of mine accidents. In the mine disaster, most of them are caused by gas explosion, which makes the coal mining face severe challenges.

In order to reduce the occurrence of gas explosion accidents, in addition to strengthening mine ventilation management, the concentration of gas in coal mines can also be monitored in real time. Blanco-Novoa Oscar et al. [1] proposed an economic and effective radon remote monitoring system of the Internet of things to solve the problem of radon exposure, which can obtain accurate concentration measurement values, trigger events to prevent dangerous situations and warn users, in addition, it can activate

© Springer Nature Singapore Pte Ltd. 2020
X. Sun et al. (Eds.): ICAIS 2020, CCIS 1253, pp. 474–483, 2020.
https://doi.org/10.1007/978-981-15-8086-4_45

mitigation devices (such as forced ventilation) to reduce radon concentration. Sabilla et al. [2] used MQ Series electronic nose to estimate the air concentration by artificial neural network, which achieves better performance. Zhao Q et al. [3] designed a concentration detection system based on acoustic relaxation attenuation, which can accurately measure the attenuation intensity and flight time of ultrasonic wave in real time, and detect the concentration of mixed gas safely and efficiently, so as to reduce the emission of pollutants. Therefore, it is necessary to design a new, easy to operate, economic and practical intelligent gas sensor alarm to reduce the incidence of mine accidents [4–8].

As one of the three major energy sources in China, coal supports the sustained and rapid development of national economy. Through the underground mining of coal resources, the gas (mainly methane CH4) and other gases produced have certain potential safety hazards to the operators. When the concentration is too high, it can cause major safety accidents such as mine explosion. For this reason, we have developed an intelligent gas concentration monitoring and alarming instrument based on PIC single chip microcomputer. The equipment can monitor and display the gas concentration in real time and dynamically. The collected data is sent to the control center through wireless transmission technology, and the automatic control is realized through nonlinear compensation and automatic adjustment. The system has the advantages of small size, high measurement accuracy, high test reliability and easy to carry.

2 Overall Design Scheme of the System

The intelligent gas concentration monitoring and alarm instrument based on PIC single-chip microcomputer is mainly composed of power module, data acquisition and processing module, communication module, display module and sound light alarm module. The working process is as follows: the lxk-3 thermal catalytic gas concentration sensor is used to monitor the CH4 gas concentration in the mine in real time, and the collected gas concentration information is amplified, filtered and shaped by the precise integrated amplification circuit. At this time, the gas concentration data is directly input into the Ra0 port of the single chip computer as the input signal of the whole monitoring control system; the input value and the internal SCM The preset values stored in advance are compared, and the judgment and control are made in time according to the actual comparison results, and the dynamic monitoring and display of gas concentration are carried out. If the set value is exceeded, the equipment can send out sound and light alarm signals timely and accurately, so that the technical operators can arrange evacuation and evacuate the operators in time. The data of the equipment can be transmitted wirelessly by using nRF2401 in combination with the upper and lower computers, which is more convenient to provide dynamic monitoring data for the technical personnel on the well. The principle block diagram of the intelligent gas monitoring and alarm instrument based on PIC single-chip microcomputer is shown in Fig. 1.

3 System Hardware Design

3.1 Selection of Single Chip Microcomputer

Single chip microcomputer is the core of system control, which determines the reliability and stability of the whole system. This design needs real-time monitoring and control of

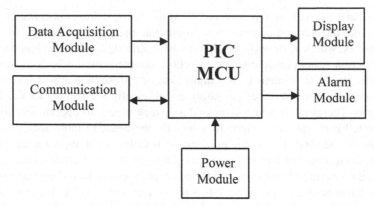

Fig. 1. Principle block diagram of intelligent gas monitor based on PIC single chip microcomputer

gas concentration data, upload through wireless transmission, and need dynamic display and alarm. After analyzing the expected function of the system and comparing the cost performance of various models of devices, it is decided to use PIC16F877 MCU developed by microchip company as the core device. The device has flash program memory function, can repeatedly burn programs, use simplified instruction set, simple development, high reliability and strong driving ability. At the same time, it has advantages of superior development environment, anti transient ability of pins, self-contained watchdog timer, low power consumption, strong confidentiality and so on. It is especially suitable for industrial control occasions with high reliability requirements.

3.2 Power Module

The power supply mainly provides different levels of voltage for each unit of the system, single-chip microcomputer and each integrated circuit. The voltage levels designed in this system are 12 V, 5 V and 3.3 V. The power frequency 220 V alternating current is reduced, rectified and filtered to obtain 12 V voltage; the three terminal integrated voltage regulator lm7805 is used to obtain 5 V voltage; the voltage linear voltage regulator tps7333 is used to obtain a stable and fixed output voltage of 3.3 V, which can meet the power demand of the system well, ensure the stability of the whole system, and have a high working efficiency. The circuit design of the power module is shown in Fig. 2.

3.3 Data Acquisition and Processing Module

The data signal acquisition module includes two parts: sensor selection and signal processing. The module realizes the detection of gas concentration in the real working environment, and provides the required data for the control system through linear processing of amplification circuit.

Selection of Gas Concentration Sensor
LXK-3 thermal catalytic gas sensor developed by 718 Research Institute of CSIC is suitable for the detection and alarm of natural gas, liquefied petroleum gas, city gas and